An Unprecedented Election

Media, Communication, and the Electorate in the 2016 Campaign

Benjamin R. Warner, Dianne G. Bystrom,
Mitchell S. McKinney, and Mary C. Banwart,
Editors

 PRAEGER™

An Imprint of ABC-CLIO, LLC
Santa Barbara, California • Denver, Colorado

Library of Congress Cataloging in Publication Control Number: 2017047088 (print)

ISBN: 978-1-4408-6065-2 (print)
      978-1-4408-6066-9 (ebook)

22 21 20 19 18   1 2 3 4 5

This book is also available as an eBook.

Praeger
An Imprint of ABC-CLIO, LLC

ABC-CLIO, LLC
130 Cremona Drive, P.O. Box 1911
Santa Barbara, California 93116-1911
www.abc-clio.com

This book is printed on acid-free paper (∞)

Manufactured in the United States of America

Contents

**Part Three   Communication Attitudes and Behaviors
of the Electorate**

Understanding the Unprecedented 2016 Campaign: Two Historical Candidacies Yield an Unexpected Result

Benjamin R. Warner and Dianne G. Bystrom

Four days after the 2016 presidential election, Sam Wang, a professor of neuroscience at Princeton University and publisher of the Princeton Election Consortium site, ate a bug on national television. On November 7, the day before the 2016 U.S. presidential election, *Wired* published a lengthy article in which they declared that Wang had replaced *FiveThirtyEight*'s Nate Silver as the true election data hero (Nesbit, 2016). How did Wang unseat the reigning king of political prognostication? It was the bold certainty with which he forecast the election—Wang declared Hillary Clinton the victor on October 18, more than three weeks before the 2016 election. As explained in the November 7 profile, "Wang has been the intrepid election data explorer furthest out this election cycle, never once wavering from his certainty of a Clinton win" (Nesbit, 2016, para. 9). When the dust settled on November 8 and Donald Trump was declared the 45th president of the United States, election forecasters were left shaking their heads (Cox & Katz, 2016; Jackson, 2017; Sabato, Kondik, & Skelley, 2016), political scientists found themselves questioning all assumptions (Gelman, 2016), and—to make good on a wager he lost when Trump won—Wang ate a cricket on CNN (Wang, 2016).

It is therefore quite clear that the results of the 2016 election surprised many. But does the unexpected outcome justify our claim that this election was unprecedented? After all, in 1948, Harry Truman famously beat the polls to defeat Thomas Dewey. In an article titled "Clinton-Trump probably won't be the next 'Dewey defeats Truman,'" Harry Enten (2016) makes the case that 2016 was in fact unique. As Enten explained, whereas the numbers used to predict Clinton's win were drawn from hundreds of polls conducted by dozens of pollsters, only four pollsters were infrequently tracking the race in 1948. Furthermore, pollsters in 1948 used considerably less sophisticated sampling methodologies. In addition, expectations in 1948 were not aided by statistical election forecast models. Wang's model projected a greater than 99% chance that Clinton would win (Wang, 2016). The *Huffington Post* model was only moderately less confident, assigning a 98% probability to a Clinton victory (Jackson, 2017). The most cautious, the model at *FiveThirtyEight*, gave Clinton a 71% chance of winning (Silver, 2016). Still, in 1948, as in 2016, many overly confident forecasters and pundits would have been wise to attend to the narrowing of the polls. *FiveThirtyEight*'s final election forecast had Clinton winning the popular vote by 3.6% (Silver, 2016), down from almost double that number in October (Enten, 2016). Clinton ended up winning the popular vote by 2.1%, making the polling miss five times lower than in 1948 and comparable to the polling miss in 2012 (Clement, 2017). So although the national polls were more accurate in 2016 when compared to 1948, the outcome was arguably more unexpected.

Ultimately, however, our claim that the 2016 election was unprecedented has far more to do with the two major-party candidates and their campaigns than with the surprise outcome. The case that Clinton was an unprecedented candidate is somewhat self-evident. She became the first woman to ever be nominated by a major political party to head its ticket. Her defeat ensured the continuation of the more-than-200-year monopoly men have held on the presidency—a streak rooted in numerous social and structural inequalities (Watson & Gordon, 2003). Furthermore, in her bid to become the first woman elected president, Clinton faced unprecedented challenges. Three of these challenges, in particular, are worthy of extended consideration: one, that her campaign was targeted by a hostile foreign rival in a bid to undermine confidence in U.S. democracy; two, that she was the focus of an FBI investigation that became unusually public; and three, that a scandal regarding her handling of e-mails dominated media coverage of her candidacy.

Russian interference in democratic elections is a growing element of their strategic foreign policy (Paul & Matthews, 2016). Russia has intervened in elections in Ukraine, Bulgaria, Estonia, Germany, France, Australia, and the United States (Dorell, 2017). To do this, they employ upwards of 1,000 people tasked with spreading and amplifying misinformation and conspiracies through various online platforms (Paul & Matthews, 2016). In the 2016 election, this army of online trolls was utilized to push false news stories and conspiracies about Clinton in key battleground states such as Michigan, Wisconsin, and Pennsylvania (Roberts, 2017). Independent researchers estimate that this strategy resulted in disinformation about Clinton being viewed more than 213 million times (Timberg, 2016). The efforts of this propaganda campaign were primarily directed at portraying Clinton as a criminal who was hiding a potentially fatal illness (Timberg, 2016). This misinformation campaign was only part of Russia's interference in the election. Russia was also responsible for hacking into e-mail accounts that granted them access to communications from the Democratic National Committee (DNC) and high-level Clinton staffers (Fisher, 2017). To emphasize how unprecedented Russia's interference was in the 2016 election, it is worth quoting former FBI director James Comey in his testimony before the U.S. Senate Intelligence Committee:

> We're talking about a foreign government that, using technical intrusion, lots of other methods, tried to shape the way we think, we vote, we act. That is a big deal. And people need to recognize it. It's not about Republicans or Democrats. They're coming after America, which I hope we all love equally. They want to undermine our credibility in the face of the world. They think that this great experiment of ours is a threat to them. So they're going to try to run it down and dirty it up as much as possible. (Comey, 2017, para. 452)

Although Comey's testimony illustrates the significance of Russia's intervention, he will likely be remembered for his role in another facet of the 2016 election. Clinton was under FBI investigation for the early part of the campaign to determine if her decision to use a private e-mail server resulted in unlawful handling of classified information. Although the investigation revealed that Clinton did not break any laws (see Comey, 2017, para. 586), the public nature of the FBI investigation created a truly unprecedented circumstance for the Democratic nominee.

It is traditional for any FBI investigation to be conducted without public comment and, if no charges are brought, for the FBI to never publicly confirm the existence of an investigation. Comey broke with this precedent on July 5, 2016, by holding a press conference to discuss the conclusion of the FBI investigation into Clinton's handling of classified information as it related to her use of a private e-mail account. In an op-ed in *The Washington Post*, Matthew Miller (2016), a former director of the Justice Department's public affairs office, expressed disagreement with Comey's decision to hold a public press conference on the closing of the investigation specifically because it broke with this precedent. Miller went on to critique the content of the press conference. In addition to announcing that there would be no criminal charges brought against Clinton, Comey harshly criticized her conduct. Miller wrote that, in doing so, Comey "violated time-honored Justice Department practices," "set a dangerous precedent," and "committed a gross abuse of his own power" (Miller, 2016, para. 1). He argued that the press conference violated rules designed to protect subjects of investigation; "[Comey] ignored those rules to editorialize" and "recklessly speculated" about things for which he had "no evidence" (Miller, 2016, para. 7).

Criticism of Comey grew when, on October 28, he sent a letter to Congress to inform them that the FBI was examining e-mails discovered on a computer linked to a long-time Clinton aide. Two former deputy attorneys general, one who served under former president Bill Clinton and one who served under former president George W. Bush, jointly authored an op-ed chastising Comey for his intervention into the election (Gorelick & Thompson, 2016). In the editorial, they explained that the FBI has a long-standing policy of not commenting on political matters in the 60 days prior to an election and, thus, that Comey's letter was literally unprecedented. Trump's Department of Justice appears to have agreed with this characterization. In a now infamous memo, Rod Rosenstein, the deputy attorney general under Trump, wrote that "almost everyone agrees that the Director made serious mistakes" (Norwood & Godfrey, 2017, para. 4). Rosenstein called Comey's handling of the e-mail investigation "a textbook example of what federal prosecutors and agents are taught not to do" (Norwood & Godfrey, 2017, para. 7).

If the actions of Russia and the FBI created historically unique challenges for Clinton, tensions between her and the media were a well-established feature of her nearly 40 years of public service. However, the extent to which Clinton's handling of her private e-mail server dominated coverage of her is noteworthy. A study conducted by Harvard University's Shorenstein Center on Media, Politics, and Public Policy found that, despite the seemingly endless litany of controversies surrounding Trump, Clinton's scandals received more media coverage (Patterson, 2016). Furthermore, whereas coverage of Trump's scandals changed as each new controversy emerged, coverage of Clinton's scandals focused almost exclusively on her e-mails. A study conducted by researchers at Gallup, Georgetown University, and the University of Michigan found that e-mails dominated what people reported having heard about Clinton "almost every week of the campaign" (Edwards-Levy, 2017, para. 3). Another study found that a full quarter of all mentions of Clinton on Fox News included a reference to her e-mails (Leetaru, 2017). Network nightly news broadcasts devoted nearly three times as much coverage to Clinton's e-mails as all policy issues combined (Boehlert, 2016). Comey's letter about Clinton's e-mails led media coverage six of seven days from October 29 to November 4, 2016 (Silver, 2017).

Furthermore, media coverage of Clinton's e-mail scandal was overwhelmingly negative. According to the Harvard study, the coverage was more than 95% negative in most outlets and, in the outlet with the friendliest treatment of the story (*The Washington Post*), coverage was 90% negative (Patterson, 2016). This study also found that the coverage was generally without substance. Rather than focus on the possible ethical and strategic consequences of Clinton's e-mails, "journalists wrote instead on how the email scandal was causing her to lose voter support" (Patterson, 2016, para 48).

We can debate about whether coverage of Clinton's e-mail was warranted by the significance of the scandal (Shafer, 2016) or was a farcical overreaction to a pedestrian controversy (Yglesias, 2016). What is beyond dispute, however, is that Clinton faced a truly unprecedented opponent. In 227 years, Trump is the only president to have never served a single year in either public office or military service (Crockett, 2017). The two presidents who make the closest comparisons are Woodrow Wilson, who served two years as governor of New Jersey before winning the presidency, and Grover Cleveland, who served two years as the mayor of Buffalo, New York, and two years as the governor of New York. Trump's candidacy was also unique, first, because he was historically unpopular both when he launched his campaign and when he won the presidency; second, because his campaign itself was unconventional by modern standards; and third, because of his ability to survive a series of controversies and gaffes.

In May 2015, roughly a month before he announced his candidacy for president, a *Washington Post-ABC News* poll found that 16% of respondents had a favorable view of Trump compared to 71% who viewed him unfavorably (Blake & Clement, 2015). The 58-point net negative rating was unprecedented for a presidential candidate. Former Speaker of the House Newt Gingrich was the only former presidential candidate to have had a net negative rating even close to Trump's at minus 32 points (Blake & Clement, 2015). Although his favorability improved over the course of the campaign, by Election Day Trump was still viewed unfavorably by 60% of voters compared to 38% who viewed him favorably, according to the national exit poll (Shepard, 2016). These numbers were even worse than his historically unpopular opponent, as Clinton was viewed unfavorably by 54% of voters (Shepard, 2016). A majority of voters (60%) also indicated that they did not think Trump was qualified to be president, although even among this group, 18% reported voting for him (Shepard, 2016). Trump entered the presidency with 40% approval, making him the most unpopular president on record to ever assume the office (Langer, 2017).

As might be expected from such an atypical candidate, Trump ran an unconventional campaign. According to his campaign staff, the Trump campaign viewed traditional expenditures on field offices, paid staff, advertising, and message testing as unnecessary investments (Golshan, 2016). The campaign outsourced its field organization in key swing states to the Republican National Committee (Murray & Killough, 2016), paid significantly fewer professional staff when compared to other modern campaigns, and did not engage in standard message-testing (Golshan, 2016). The campaign also aired far fewer television advertisements: 76,068 compared to 198,689 from Clinton (Fowler, Ridout, & Franz, 2016). When combined with all expenditures from outside groups, the imbalance was 262,400 ads on behalf of Clinton's campaign compared to 102,358 on behalf of Trump in the general election. This kind of ad imbalance is rare in presidential elections where campaigns often expend equal resources to offset the potential gains from their opponents (Sides & Vavreck, 2014). The Trump campaign's unusual strategy prompted numerous headlines in the summer of 2016 such as "There is no Trump campaign" (Graham, 2016), "Donald Trump does not have a campaign" (Sarlin, Tur, & Vitali, 2016), and "Trump doesn't have a national campaign" (Gold, 2016).

Trump's candidacy was also unusual in its resilience. On numerous occasions, Trump would do or say something that sparked a controversy, causing pundits to wonder if he had terminally undermined his hopes of winning the presidency. To illustrate this point, *Politico* generated a list of 37 events that would have "ended the campaign of any other politician" (Kruse & Gee, 2016, para. 1). Their list included his infamous insinuation that Mexican immigrants were rapists; his implication that former Republican presidential nominee and sitting U.S. Senator John McCain was not a war hero because he was a prisoner of war (Trump preferred people who had not been captured); his apparent belief that Megyn Kelly, then a Fox News host and presidential debate moderator, asked him difficult questions because she was menstruating; his insulting imitation of Serge Kovaleski, a reporter for *The New York Times* who has a congenital condition that affects his joints; his commitment to war crimes (torture and targeting civilian family members of terrorists); his argument that a federal judge could not be fair in a case about Trump University because of his ethnicity; his public feud with parents of a U.S. soldier who was killed while serving in Iraq; his Gerald Ford-esque misunderstanding of Russian aggression into Eastern Europe; his insinuation that somebody should assassinate Clinton should she be elected; and his claim that Obama founded the terrorist organization ISIS (Kruse & Gee, 2016). This noncomprehensive list of controversial statements and gaffes all occurred before an *Access Hollywood* tape recording surfaced in which Trump appeared to brag about committing sexual assault, a controversy that preceded 15 women coming forward to accuse him of the very actions he described in the recording (Nelson & Crockett, 2017).

As all of this illustrates, whatever else can be said of the 2016 presidential election, it was truly ùnprecedented. The first female nominee of a major political party was defeated by the first president to ever win election without serving in public office or the military. A hostile foreign government intervened to undermine the democratic process and possibly influence the outcome. One candidate was under FBI investigation that became unusually public; the other campaign is, at the time of this writing, under another FBI investigation for possible involvement in Russia's intervention. The media fixated on an e-mail scandal surrounding one of the candidates while breathlessly covering a seemingly endless list of controversies that emerged from her opponent. In the end, Trump's unconventional campaign secured a majority in the Electoral College, shocking pundits, defying prediction models, and upending numerous theories in political science and communication.

This book responds to the unprecedented 2016 election by presenting a series of studies conducted by leading scholars of political communication that examine some of the most important dynamics and events of the campaign, as well as the months that followed the surprising outcome. In examining the unprecedented nature of the 2016 campaign and election and its aftermath, the chapters that follow focus on the media, the candidates, and the electorate.

The book's first part—**Media Coverage**—features eight studies that examine the use, content, and effects of traditional and new media channels during the presidential campaign. In the first three chapters, the use of national survey samples at three distinct stages during the campaign reveal the effects of partisan media use, as well as major media events, on the political attitudes, participation, and voting intention of respondents. The next four chapters employ rhetorical analysis, an experimental design, and content analysis to examine how the media covered the candidates and their campaigns. Political satire played an increasingly important role in the 2016 campaign with a new cast of television comedians as well as old standbys such as *Saturday Night Live*, whose portrayal of Trump is the focus of Chapter 8.

The book begins with an examination of national survey data collected at the end of the primary election season to determine not only where people turned for news and information, but also with whom they discussed politics in the context of the election. In "Selective Exposure and Homophily During the 2016 Presidential Campaign," Natalie Jomini Stroud and Jessica R. Collier examine the media use of survey respondents by political party; ideology; and intent to vote for Clinton, Trump, or Democratic challenger Bernie Sanders. Besides examining the effects of partisan selective exposure on media use and homophily on voters' political discussion networks, their study extends previous research by analyzing how these two predictors are related to each other.

Chapter 2, "What Mobilizes Partisans? Exploring the Underlying Pathways Between Partisan Media and Political Participation," also reports the results of survey data to examine the relationship between partisan media use and political participation, political discussion, political information efficacy, and cynicism. Authors Heesook Choi, Benjamin R. Warner, and Freddie J. Jennings analyze the results of their national online survey of adults—conducted about a month after the national nominating conventions—within the framework of the O-S-R-O-R model of media effects. Their findings advance our theoretical understanding of the mobilizing power of partisan media and its effects on political participation.

In Chapter 3, "Media Event Influence in the 2016 Race: The Debates, Trump Groping Tape, and the Last-Minute FBI Announcement," Esther Thorson, Samuel M. Tham, Weiyue Chen, and Vamsi Kanuri report the results of a rolling cross-sectional survey conducted each day in the 49 days prior to the November 8, 2016, election to assess the effects of five significant "media events" on voting intention and attitudes toward candidates Clinton and Trump. Their use of rolling cross-sectional data and a stacked regressions analysis of the results provided a sensitive measurement of the effects of the three presidential debates as well as the release of the Trump groping video and news that the FBI was reopening the Clinton e-mail investigation.

After examining media effects on voters during the 2016 presidential campaign, we next turn to the content of coverage. Chapter 4, "The Rhetoric of Impossible Expectations: Media Coverage of Hillary Clinton's 2016 General Election Campaign," digs deep into how the media treated Clinton's historic campaign. Through a rhetorical analysis, Kristina Horn Sheeler examines more than 750 major news media reports during four key general election campaign moments—Clinton's nomination and acceptance speech at the Democratic National Convention in July, her bout with pneumonia in September, her performance in the first presidential debate, and Comey's surprise October announcement about the FBI reopening its investigation into her e-mails—to demonstrate the narrative of scandal that overshadowed her candidacy.

In Chapter 5, "Depends on Who Is Asking: An Endorsement Experiment During the 2016 Presidential Election," Kalyca Becktel and Kaye D. Sweetser report the results of an online experiment that considers the influence of endorsements on the assessments of first-time voters on the authenticity and characteristics of Libertarian Party presidential candidate, Gary Johnson. Participants read news stories in which the headline and one paragraph were manipulated to include an endorsement of Johnson by newspapers, celebrities, military leaders, or politicians to examine which were the most effective. Their study investigates the public relations impact of endorsements and provides practical advice for political campaigns.

Charges of incivility on the part of the presidential candidates and their supporters were a common complaint of the 2016 campaign. In Chapter 6, "Attributions of Incivility in Presidential Campaign News," Ashley Muddiman examines these charges through a content analysis of 633 newspaper articles published between Labor Day and Election Day. Articles were coded on whether they included a statement that either Clinton or Trump—or their supporters—were engaging in some form of incivility, such as name calling, attacking, or bullying; spreading misinformation and lies; displaying discrimination or bigotry; or being unfit to be president. Her findings contribute to the discussion about the role of news organizations in a rapidly changing environment.

In light of the criticisms about the media's coverage of the 2016 presidential campaign, Daniela V. Dimitrova and Kimberly Nelson investigate "Fact-Checking and the 2016 Presidential Election: News Media's Attempts to Correct Misleading Information from the Debates" in Chapter 7. Through a content analysis of articles from three national newspapers, they examined 231 fact-checking statements to determine how the news media performed their watchdog role according to established criteria after each of the three presidential debates. In addition to reporting the results of their study, the authors make suggestions on how journalists can improve their fact-checking function especially in today's polarized political environment.

Part One concludes with an analysis of the rhetorical functions of comedic political impersonation in Chapter 8, " 'I'm About to Be President; We're All Going to Die': Baldwin, Trump, and the Rhetorical Power of Comedic Presidential Impersonation." Authors Will Howell and Trevor Parry-Giles trace the developments in comedic presidential impersonation from 1928 to 2017—including the 2016 presidential campaign, election, and new administration, during which actor Alec Baldwin portrayed Trump in a record 15 of the 18 episodes of *Saturday Night Live* that ran in the final four weeks of the campaign through his first 100 days as president. Their analysis suggests a new function for comedic presidential impersonations.

Part Two—**Campaign Communication**—features eight studies that examine not only the communication strategies of Clinton and Trump but also Michelle Obama and female and male candidates running for the U.S. House of Representatives in 2016. Five of these chapters examine presidential candidate communication during the primary and presidential debates as well as in their campaign speeches, interviews, and tweets. One chapter analyzes former First Lady Obama's speeches at three Democratic National Conventions. Two chapters examine political television ads: one looking at their effects during late-night comedy television shows and the other focusing on their content in mixed-gender U.S. House races.

In Chapter 9, "Processing the Political: Presidential Primary Debate 'Live-Tweeting' as Information Processing," Josh C. Bramlett, Mitchell S. McKinney, and Benjamin R. Warner explore presidential primary debate social watching behaviors through a content analysis of college students' tweets and their responses to pre- and post-debate surveys. Their goal was to explore how viewers acquire issue knowledge from debates, as well as the relationship between political attitudes and social watching behaviors in a real-time setting. Their study provides an in-depth examination of tweet content to more fully explore message processing, including issue/image focus, positive/negative assessment, and agreement/disagreement with candidate issue positions.

In Chapter 10, "Donald Trump and the Rejection of the Norms of American Politics and Rhetoric," Robert C. Rowland argues that Trump's campaign is best understood within the rhetorical frameworks of "nationalistic populism" and the "strongman." In developing this argument, he describes the principal elements defining Trump's rhetorical practice—populist themes that tapped into economic uncertainty, nationalistic themes that tapped into fears that American society was undergoing fundamental change, and the desire for a strong leader who could fix problems based on the power of leadership—through an analysis of his July 21, 2016, speech at the Republican National Convention accepting the party's nomination for president.

In Chapter 11, we turn to the evolving rhetoric of former First Lady Obama through an analysis of her speeches at the Democratic National Convention in 2008, 2012, and 2016. In "'The Greatest Country on Earth': The Evolution of Michelle Obama's American Dream," Ryan Neville-Shepard and Meredith Neville-Shepard demonstrate through rhetorical analysis how Obama honed her message over time by outlining commitments to the traditional family structure, by promoting the materialistic myth of the American dream, and later by using her adopted voice of "republican mother" to frequently incorporate narratives about her children that served as metonyms for the protection of all vulnerable people in society.

Chapter 12 considers the role of religious rhetoric in the 2016 campaign. In "Loss of Faith: A Realignment of Religion on the Campaign Trail," Brian Kaylor explores the religious rhetoric of Clinton and Trump during the 2016 presidential campaign through an analysis of their major speeches, interviews, and three general election debates. His analysis shows how the most openly secular presidential nominee in decades won with record support of white evangelicals. The 2016 election demonstrated, once again, that the candidate who talks the most about God and faith—not necessarily the one who is the most personally religious—prevailed, creating a shift in rhetorical religious expectations and a more evangelical political milieu.

Television advertising also plays an important communication role in modern presidential campaigns, with Clinton much more likely to use this strategy than Trump in 2016. In Chapter 13, "Late Night with Donald Trump: An Exploration of the Combined Effects of Political Comedy and Political Advertising," Freddie J. Jennings, Calvin R. Coker, Josh C. Bramlett, Joel Lansing Reed, and Joshua P. Bolton report the results of an experiment that embedded pro-Clinton and anti-Trump political ads sponsored by the Clinton campaign and a Super PAC supporting her candidacy into the late-night talk show, *Late Night with Seth Meyers*. After watching the episode, 559 participants completed a survey that measured their feelings toward both candidates as well as their democratic trust and attributions of malevolence.

In Chapter 14, "Going on Defense: The Unprecedented Use of Defensive Appeals in 2016 U.S. Presidential Debates," Corey B. Davis applies the functional theory of political campaign discourse to examine the extent to which Clinton and Trump used acclaims, attacks, and defenses in their three 2016 general election debates in comparison to past presidential debates. His study also identifies a prominent accusation leveled at each candidate during the debates

(Clinton's use of a private server to store sensitive government e-mails and Trump's disparaging comments about women and his alleged sexual assault of them), provides an analysis of the strategies of apologia used by both candidates in response to those attacks, and considers their effectiveness.

With a woman running against a man for president for the first time in U.S. history, it is also important to assess the gender dynamics of down-ballot races in 2016. In Chapter 15, "Gender and Videostyle in 2016: Advertising in Mixed-Gender Races for the U.S. House," Kelly L. Winfrey and James M. Schnoebelen explore the communication strategies used by women and men competing in congressional districts across the country. Through a content analysis of 187 television ads, they examine the issues, images, persuasive strategies, and production techniques used by candidates in the 42 most competitive mixed-gender races for the U.S. House of Representatives to determine whether women and men used similar or different approaches to appeal to voters.

Part Two closes with Chapter 16, "From Interactivity to Incitement: Ubiquitous Communication and Elite Calls for Participation," which examines the potentially lasting implications of Trump's political discourse on American democracy. Joshua M. Scacco, Kevin Coe, and Delaney Harness begin their analysis by proposing a four-part typology that helps clarify the possible outcomes of elite calls for participatory action. They then offer three case studies from the 2016 campaign, the presidential transition, and the first week of Trump's presidency that highlight the most normatively concerning forms of discourse present in the typology. In the process, they situate Trump's discourse within relevant historical and political context.

This book's third and final part—**Communication Attitudes and Behaviors of the Electorate**—features seven chapters that explore how voters reacted to the presidential candidates and their campaigns during the primary phase, general election, and aftermath of the 2016 election. Five of these chapters examine the effects of candidate communication on the political knowledge, political cynicism, and political information efficacy of voters. Two chapters focus on the dynamics of race and gender in reactions to the presidential candidates as well as the results of the election.

Part Three opens with Chapter 17, "Corn Belt Controversy: Intraparty Divisions and Political Cynicism at the 2016 Iowa Caucuses," by Joel Lansing Reed, Sopheak Hoeun, Josh C. Bramlett, Molly Greenwood, and Grace Hase. They examine intraparty dynamics on the eve of the February 1, 2016, Iowa caucuses by surveying attendees at rallies of the four top-polling presidential candidates—Democrats Clinton and Sanders and Republicans Trump and Ted Cruz—on their levels of political interest, cynicism, external efficacy, and political information efficacy. Their study exposes the deep divisions between supporters of "insider" and "outsider" candidates in both major political parties and sheds light on the unique nature of rally-goers.

In Chapter 18, "Exploring and Explaining Communication, Knowledge, and Well-Being Sex Differences Related to the 2016 U.S. Presidential Primary

Season," R. Lance Holbert, Esul Park, and Nicholas W. Robinson surveyed 960 adults between July 13 and July 15, 2016, to examine differences between women and men in their political media use, knowledge about the U.S. presidential primaries, and an experiential well-being in their day-to-day activities. Their study explores the degree to which what at first glance appears to be a sex difference may actually be due to third variables, such as demographics, political individual differences, measures of political optimism, and campaign-specific attitudes and behaviors.

Chapter 19 also explores the role of gender in the 2016 presidential campaign and election. In "Gender and the Vote in the 2016 Presidential Election," Kate Kenski begins with an overview of the gender gap in American politics and describes significant events involving gender during the 2016 primaries and general election. She then examines entrance and exit polls to demonstrate how gender shaped citizen support for the candidates during the nomination and general election phases. Her analysis shows how gender interacted with race, marital status, and partisanship in important ways in determining support for an often sexist political newcomer versus an experienced woman—the first to be nominated for president by a major political party.

In Chapter 20, "#election#elección: Latino Twitter Users and Reactions to Presidential Political Gaffes," we turn to another important constituency in the 2016 presidential campaign. Samantha Hernandez begins by exploring the literature on Latino identity, political outreach, and the history and effects of political scandals and gaffes. She then analyzes tweets gathered for a 24-hour period immediately after the Clinton campaign reached out to Latino voters by comparing the candidate to an "abuela" (Spanish for grandmother) and Trump's reference to "bad hombres" during a presidential debate to determine whether or not they received the same amount of attention and, specifically, how Latinos reacted to the gaffes.

Chapter 21, "Analyzing Tweets About the 2016 U.S. Presidential 'Blunder' Election," also focuses on the increasing use of Twitter in presidential campaigns. Michael W. Kearney examines the statuses posted by 212 randomly selected followers of highly visible partisan and nonpartisan accounts to help make sense of the evolution of public opinion during the 2016 U.S. election. His study reports the frequency and sentiment (political versus nonpolitical) of content posted by partisan Republican, partisan Democrat, and nonpartisan moderate Twitter users in relation to major events of the 2016 election, such as the Iowa caucuses, WikiLeaks publishing e-mails stolen from the Democrat National Committee, and news regarding Trump's alleged ties to Russia and a new federal investigation into Clinton's e-mails.

Chapter 22 focuses on "Understanding the Authoritarian Voter in the 2016 Presidential Election." Through an analysis of survey data collected from more than 2,000 respondents, Sumana Chattopadhyay explores how voters' authoritarian predispositions acted as a moderator between favorability toward Trump and such variables as political information efficacy, trust, cynicism, political interest, conservatism, evangelism, age, gender, race, education, and party identification. Her study expands research on authoritarianism, which has mostly explored which third variable moderates the relationship between authoritarianism and dependent variables like conservatism and traditionalism, by examining how authoritarian predisposition itself can act as a moderator.

This book concludes with an examination of "Social Dominance, Sexism, and the Lasting Effects on Political Communication from the 2016 Election." In Chapter 23, Mary C. Banwart and Michael W. Kearney report the results of an online survey of 244 participants who responded to measures of sexism, social dominance orientation (SDO), partisanship, and their perceptions of the presidential candidates' images. The purpose of their study was to examine how two dominance-related ideologies—sexism and SDO—influenced how voters perceived Clinton and Trump in 2016, as well as to explore the relationship between sexism and candidate image, including character, intelligence, leadership, charm, benevolence, and homophily.

In total, these 23 chapters present original insights from leading scholars in political communication that span a diversity of expertise and methodology to help explain critical events related to the 2016 election. In so doing, this collection responds to an unusual campaign by indexing many of its most important features while also advancing our understanding of political communication so as to better prepare us for future election cycles. Never before has a woman been nominated to lead a major party in its bid to secure the U.S. presidency. Never before has such a true political outsider won the presidency. The interplay of these two historical candidacies combined with atypical contextual events to produce a campaign highlighted by foreign intervention, an unusually public FBI investigation, media coverage caught between fixation on a protracted scandal on one side and a seemingly endless stream of controversies on the other, and a one-of-a-kind campaign strategy deployed by the candidate who would ultimately declare victory on November 8. With this book, we hope to demonstrate that the campaign was as heuristically valuable as the outcome was surprising. On November 9, 2016, experts, pundits, scholars, and prognosticators were left questioning assumptions and scrambling to understand what happened. The pages that follow are our attempt to shed light on the events surrounding the often befuddling, truly unexpected, and eponymously unprecedented 2016 campaign.

References

Blake, A., & Clement, S. (2015, July 9). Donald Trump's severe unpopularity, visualized. *The Washington Post*. Retrieved from https://www.washingtonpost .com/news/the-fix/wp/2015/07/09/donald-trump-is-about-as-unpopular -as-vladimir-putin/?utm_term=.b4dd6178643e

Boehlert, E. (2016, November 2). How the media's email obsession obliterated Clinton policy coverage. *Media Matters.* Retrieved from https://www.media matters.org/blog/2016/11/02/how-media-s-email-obsession-obliterated -clinton-policy-coverage/214242

Clement, S. (2017, February 6). The 2016 national polls are looking less wrong after final election tallies. *The Washington Post.* Retrieved from https:// www.washingtonpost.com/news/the-fix/wp/2016/11/10/how-much -did-polls-miss-the-mark-on-trump-and-why/?utm_term=.53ef70cc f0da

Comey, J. (2017, June 8). Full text: James Comey testimony transcript on Trump and Russia. *Politico.* Retrieved from http://www.politico.com/story/2017/06 /08/full-text-james-comey-trump-russia-testimony-239295

Cox, A., & Katz, J. (2016, November 15). Presidential forecast post-mortem. *The New York Times.* Retrieved from https://www.nytimes.com/2016/11/16 /upshot/presidential-forecast-postmortem.html

Crockett, Z. (2017, January 23). Donald Trump is the only US president ever with no political or military experience. *Vox.* Retrieved from https://www.vox .com/policy-and-politics/2016/11/11/13587532/donald-trump-no -experience

Dorell, O. (2017, September 7). Alleged Russian political meddling documented in 27 countries since 2004. *USA Today.* Retrieved from https://www .usatoday.com/story/news/world/2017/09/07/alleged-russian-political -meddling-documented-27-countries-since-2004/619056001/

Edwards-Levy, A. (2017, May 21). Here's just how much Hillary Clinton's emails dominated the campaign. *Huffington Post.* Retrieved from http://www .huffingtonpost.com/entry/hillary-clinton-emails-poll_us_5921c7aae4b0 34684b0d1840

Enten, H. (2016, October 18). Clinton-Trump probably won't be the next 'Dewey Defeats Truman.' *FiveThirtyEight.* Retrieved from https://fivethirtyeight .com/features/clinton-trump-probably-wont-be-the-next-dewey-defeats -truman/

Fisher, M. (2017, January 8). Russian hackers find ready bullhorns in the media. *The New York Times.* Retrieved from https://www.nytimes.com/2017/01 /08/world/europe/russian-hackers-find-ready-bullhorns-in-the-media .html?rref=collection%2Fnewseventcollection%2Frussian-election-hack ing&_r=0

Fowler, E. F., Ridout, T. N., Franz, M. M. (2016). Political advertising in 2016: The presidential election as outlier? *The Forum, 14,* 445–469. doi: 10.1515 /for-2016-0040

Gelman, A. (2016, December 8). Nineteen lessons for political scientists from the 2016 election. *Slate.* Retrieved from http://www.slate.com/articles/news _and_politics/politics/2016/12/_19_lessons_for_political_scientists _from_the_2016_election.html

Gold, M. (2016, June 10). Trump doesn't have a national campaign. So the GOP is trying to run one for him. *The Washington Post.* Retrieved from https://www

.washingtonpost.com/politics/trump-doesnt-have-a-national-campaign-so
-the-gop-is-trying-to-run-one-for-him/2016/06/09/

Golshan, T. (2016, December 8). Trump's unconventional campaign hasn't convinced campaign managers to change their ways. *Vox.* Retrieved from
https://www.vox.com/policy-and-politics/2016/12/8/13846378/trump
-unconventional-campaign

Gorelick, J., & Thompson, L. (2016, October 29). James Comey is damaging our
democracy. *The Washington Post.* Retrieved from https://www.washing
tonpost.com/opinions/james-comey-is-damaging-our-democracy/2016
/10/29/894d0f5e-9e49-11e6-a0ed-ab0774c1eaa5_story.html?utm_term
=.8c7990617cbc

Graham, D. A. (2016, June 9). There is no Trump campaign. *The Atlantic.* Retrieved
from https://www.theatlantic.com/politics/archive/2016/06/there-is-no
-trump-campaign/486380/

Jackson, N. (2017, January 3). Why HuffPost's presidential forecast didn't see a
Donald Trump win coming: Here's how we blew it and what we're doing
to prevent a repeat. *Huffington Post.* Retrieved from http://www.huffington
post.com/entry/pollster-forecast-donald-trump-wrong_us_5823e1e5e
4b0e80b02ceca15

Kruse, M., & Gee, T. (2016, September 25). The 37 fatal gaffes that didn't kill
Donald Trump. *Politico.* Retrieved from http://www.politico.com/magazine
/story/2016/09/trump-biggest-fatal-gaffes-mistakes-offensive-214289

Langer, G. (2017, January 17). Trump to enter office as most unpopular president
in at least 40 years, poll finds. *ABC News.* Retrieved from http://abcnews
.go.com/Politics/trump-remains-unpopular-presidency-hand-poll/story
?id=44815005

Leetaru, K. (2017, February 1). How much coverage did CNN actually devote to
Clinton's emails? Here's the data. *The Washington Post.* Retrieved from
https://www.washingtonpost.com/news/monkey-cage/wp/2017/02/01
/how-much-coverage-did-cnn-actually-devote-to-clintons-emails-heres
-the-data/?utm_term=.9b0be91cfe11

Miller, M. (2016, July 6). James Comey's abuse of power. *The Washington Post.*
Retrieved from https://www.washingtonpost.com/opinions/james-comeys
-abuse-of-power/2016/07/06/7799d39e-4392-11e6-8856-f26de2537a
9d_story.html?utm_term=.eeff1c40747a

Murray, S., & Killough, A. (2016, June 10). Donald Trump's unconventional
approach to building a ground game. *CNN.* Retrieved from http://www
.cnn.com/2016 /06/09/politics/donald-trump-ground-game/index.html

Nelson, L., & Crockett, E. (2017, January 19). Sexual assault allegations against
Donald Trump: 15 women say he groped, kissed, or assaulted them. *Vox.*
Retrieved from https://www.vox.com/2016/10/12/13265206/trump-accu
sations-sexual-assault

Nesbit, J. (2016, November 7). 2016's election data hero isn't Nate Silver. It's Sam
Wang. *Wired.* Retrieved from https://www.wired.com/2016/11/2016s-elec
tion-data-hero-isnt-nate-silver-sam-wang/

Norwood, C., & Godfrey, E. (2017, May 10). Rosenstein's case against Comey, annotated. *The Atlantic*. Retrieved from https://www.theatlantic.com/poli tics/archive/2017/05/rosenstein-letter-annotated/526116/

Patterson, T. E. (2016, December 7). News coverage of the 2016 general election: How the press failed the voters. *Shorenstein Center on Media, Politics, and Public Policy*. Retrieved from https://shorensteincenter.org/news-coverage -2016-general-election/?platform=hootsuite

Paul, C., & Matthews, M. (2016). The Russian 'firehose of falsehood' propaganda model: Why it might work and options to counter it. *Rand*. Retrieved from http://www.rand.org/pubs/perspectives/PE198.html

Roberts, R. (2017, March 30). Russia hired 1000 people to create anti-Clinton "fake news" in key U.S. states during election, Trump-Russia hearings leader reveals. *Independent*. Retrieved from http://www.independent.co.uk/news /world/americas/us-politics/russian-trolls-hilary-clinton-fake-news-elec tion-democrat-mark-warner-intelligence-committee-a7657641.html

Sabato, L. J., Kondik, K., & Skelley, G. (2016, November 9). Mea culpa, mea culpa, mea maxima culpa. *Sabato's Crystal Ball*. Retrieved from http://www.cen terforpolitics.org /crystalball/articles/mea-culpa-mea-culpa-mea-maxima -culpa/

Sarlin, B., Tur, K., & Vitali, A. (2016, June 6). Donald Trump does not have a cam- paign. *MSNBC*. Retrieved from http://www.msnbc.com/msnbc/donald-trump -does-not-have-campaign

Shafer, J. (2016, September 28). The myth of disproportionate media coverage: Does disproportionate coverage of a news story even exist? Hell no. *Politico*. Retrieved from http://www.politico.com/magazine/story/2016/09/clinton -emails-media-coverage-proportion-overblown-214298

Shepard, S. (2016, November 9). 60 percent of voters view Trump unfavorably. *Politico*. Retrieved from http://www.politico.com/blogs/donald-trump -administration/2016/11/60-percent-of-voters-view-trump-unfavorably -231086

Sides, J. & Vavreck, L. (2014). *The Gamble*. Princeton, NJ: Princeton University Press.

Silver, N. (2016, November 8). Final election update: There's a wide range of outcomes, and most of them come up Clinton. *FiveThirtyEight*. Retrieved from http://fivethirtyeight.com/features/final-election-update-theres-a-wide -range-of-outcomes-and-most-of-them-come-up-clinton/

Silver, N. (2017, May 3). The Comey letter probably cost Clinton the election. *FiveThirtyEight*. Retrieved from https://fivethirtyeight.com/features/the -comey-letter-probably-cost-clinton-the-election/

Timberg, C. (2016, November 24). Russian propaganda effort helped spread 'fake news' during election, experts say. *The Washington Post*. Retrieved from https://www.washingtonpost.com/business/economy/russian-propaganda -effort-helped-spread-fake-news-during-election-experts-say/2016/11/2 4/793903b6-8a40-4ca9-b712-716af66098fe_story.html?utm_term=. da5cec230edf

Wang, S. (2016, November 18). Why I had to eat a bug on CNN. *The New York Times*. Retrieved from https://www.nytimes.com/2016/11/19/opinion/why-i-had -to-eat-a-bug-on-cnn.html?_r=0

Watson, R. P., & Gordon, A. (2003). *Anticipating Madam President*. Boulder, CO: Lynne Rienner.

Yglesias, M. (2016, November 4). The real Clinton email scandal is that a bullshit story has dominated the campaign. *Vox*. Retrieved from https://www.vox .com/policy-and-politics/2016/11/4/13500018/clinton-email-scandal -bullshit

PART 1

Media Coverage

CHAPTER ONE

Selective Exposure and Homophily During the 2016 Presidential Campaign

Natalie Jomini Stroud and Jessica R. Collier

Although all presidential elections are noteworthy, the 2016 election in the United States was particularly so. The mainstream media's virtual certainty that Hillary Clinton would be the next president met with the reality that Donald Trump was elected the 45th president of the United States. Even the primary elections were filled with surprises as Clinton faced a serious challenge from Bernie Sanders, a self-proclaimed democratic socialist, and Trump emerged as the Republican Party's nominee despite numerous attacks from his opponents. Throughout the race, the media chronicled the fortunes of the candidates, although how the candidates were portrayed varied depending on the media source. Partisan media outlets covered the candidates differently, not only in the general election, but also during the primaries. At the same time, electoral politics crept into everyday conversations throughout the country.

The purpose of this chapter is to look at where people turned for news and information and with whom they discussed politics in the context of the 2016 election. In particular, we analyze the partisan composition of the public's mediated and interpersonal contacts. The results show that partisan selective exposure and homophily exist and that using like-minded media and having like-minded discussion partners is more prevalent than hearing opposing viewpoints. Further, the two patterns are related to one another; however, the relationship is weak.

To reach these conclusions, we used data from the 2016 Texas Media and Society Survey from the Annette Strauss Institute for Civic Life at the University of Texas at Austin. The survey was fielded by the GfK Group (formerly Knowledge Networks) in both English and Spanish. GfK employs a probability-based sampling strategy to recruit panelists to participate in online surveys and provides Internet access to those lacking it. For this particular study, we analyzed data from 1,009 survey participants from the United States. Taking into account all phases of obtaining respondents, from the initial survey, to those agreeing to be part of the panel, to those participating in this particular survey, the response rate is 4.6%. Data collection took place between May 24 and June 14, 2016. Respondents had to be over the age of 18 to participate.

The timing of the survey is important to contextualize. By the time that the survey entered the field, Donald Trump was the presumptive Republican nominee, and although Clinton became the presumptive Democratic Party nominee during the survey field period by exceeding the number of necessary convention delegates, she had "maintained a commanding pledged delegate lead over Bernie Sanders since Super Tuesday (March 1)" (Montanaro, 2016). It is within this context that we examine the public's media diets and political discussion partners.

In the following sections, we first analyze the prevalence of using media matching one's political beliefs, a behavior known as partisan selective exposure. We next turn to an investigation of one's discussion network to find out whether people talked politics with like-minded others versus those holding different views. Third, we look at the two in concert to find out if homophily and partisan selective exposure are related to one another. We close by discussing the implications of this research.

Partisan Selective Exposure

Partisan selective exposure is the motivated preference for messages matching one's partisan identity relative to messages articulating the opposite viewpoint. The pattern was noted in early communication research (e.g., Berelson, Lazarsfeld, & McPhee, 1954), and a mechanism to understand this phenomenon was developed in psychology (Festinger, 1957). According to the theory, Republicans gravitate toward Republican-leaning over Democrat-leaning messages, and Democrats do the opposite. Although it is clear that the preference for like-minded information is not absolute—even steadfast partisans look at information contradicting their views from time to time (Garrett, 2009)—the tendency has been widely demonstrated (Hart et al., 2009; Iyengar & Hahn, 2009; Ryan & Brader, in press; Stroud, 2008, 2011).

In electoral contexts, partisans tend to use media sources consistent with their political leanings (Stroud, 2011). Conservatives and Republicans are more likely than those with different political viewpoints to read newspapers endorsing Republican presidential nominees, to listen to conservative talk radio programs, to watch Fox News, and to access conservative-leaning political Web sites. Liberals and Democrats are more apt to read newspapers endorsing Democratic presidential nominees, to listen to liberal talk radio programs, to watch MSNBC and CNN, and to access liberal-leaning political Web sites.

Although numerous reasons have been proposed for why partisans display a preference for like-minded information, one compelling explanation has to do with perceptions of information quality (Fischer, Schultz-Hardt, & Frey, 2008). When faced with many different sources of information from which to choose, people make rational choices about what to use based on their judgments of what information is higher quality. It just so happens that information quality judgments are connected to people's beliefs—information matching one's beliefs is judged to be more credible than is information that is contradictory (Metzger, Hartsell, & Flanagin, in press). Mainstream media can seem less credible than like-minded partisan sources; indeed, perceiving the mainstream media as biased against one's views correlates with looking for like-minded media (Borah, Thorson, & Hwang, 2015).

The behavior of partisan selective exposure yields mixed democratic consequences from a normative perspective. Research has connected the use of like-minded media with political polarization, misperceptions, political participation, and the adoption of distinct issue priorities (Dilliplane, 2011; Garrett et al., 2014; Meirick & Bessarabova, 2016; Stroud, 2011; Tsfati & Nir, 2017). Partisan selective exposure as the norm could be seen as disconcerting given the increased levels of polarization and misperceptions. Yet it has the desirable effect of boosting participation.

Examining the extent to which partisan selective exposure appeared during the 2016 campaign offers another instance in which to analyze the theory. Further, the circumstances in 2016 provide a strong rationale for renewed attention. The heated Republican primary race divided conservative media outlets, with popular media hosts expressing support for different candidates (Gass, 2016). *National Review*, a stalwart conservative magazine, featured an anti-Trump agenda. Popular conservative media personalities Michael Medved and Glenn Beck came out against his candidacy. Sean Hannity on Fox News, however, explicitly endorsed Trump. Although Clinton did not divide liberal-leaning media in the same way, several news sources noted a lack of excitement about her candidacy. Headlines on outlets such as the *Washington Post* and NBC News reported that Clinton faced an "enthusiasm gap." Further, Bernie Sanders' primary challenge did yield approval from some on the left, such as *Democracy Now!* host Amy Goodman (Simon, 2016).

To assess the prevalence of partisan selective exposure, we first looked at the frequency with which Democrats and Republicans reported having gotten news from each of 12 sources. In Table 1.1, we show percentages of media use by partisanship. For this comparison, the labels "Democrat" and "Republican" include strong identifiers, weak identifiers, and those who reported leaning toward each party (see Petrocik, 2009). We did not include independents because only 39 identified as such after including party leaners in the partisan categories. As shown in Table 1.1, there is not a single outlet used by a majority of either Democrats or Republicans. The largest percentage of Democrats reported getting news from CNN (28.0%), whereas the largest percentage of Republicans reported getting news from the Fox News cable channel (33.6%).

Further, there are significant differences in the percentages of Democrats and Republicans attending to nearly every outlet. Democrats were more likely than Republicans to say that they used CNN, National Public Radio (NPR), MSNBC, the *Huffington Post*, *The New York Times*, and *The NewsHour*. A higher

Table 1.1   Percentages of Democrats and Republicans Using News Outlets

	Partisanship	
News Outlet	**Democrat (%)** $n=530$	**Republican (%)** $n=422$
CNN*	28.0	16.3
NPR*	16.8	10.0
MSNBC*	17.1	6.8
*Huffington Post**	14.3	5.2
New York Times*	10.9	5.0
NewsHour on PBS*	8.4	3.9
Washington Post	8.4	5.0
USA Today	8.2	11.0
Wall Street Journal	5.0	7.3
*Drudge Report**	0.9	3.7
Rush Limbaugh*	0.5	9.2
Fox News*	13.4	33.6

Note: * $p<0.05$ using $\chi^2(1)$ statistic. Question wording for media use: "From which sources did you get news IN THE PAST 14 DAYS, that is from [INSERT DAY OF THE WEEK] two weeks ago through today. If you are unsure, please DO NOT select it." Partisanship assessed from 1 "strong Republican" to 7 "strong Democrat." Strong, weak, and leaning Democrats and Republicans are combined. Those identifying as independents without partisan leaning ($n=39$) are not shown.

percentage of Republicans than Democrats reported using the *Drudge Report*, Rush Limbaugh, and Fox News. There were no significant differences by party in use of the *Washington Post*, *USA Today*, or the *Wall Street Journal*.

To further explore partisan selective exposure, we computed a summary measure of the total number of left-leaning outlets and the total number of right-leaning outlets used by each individual. In order to categorize the media as left or right leaning, we first looked at perceptions of media bias for each outlet (see a related strategy used by Dilliplane, 2011). On the survey, participants were asked whether 12 different outlets had a liberal bias, a conservative bias, or neither type of bias. We analyzed how users of each source perceived its bias. As shown in Table 1.2, there was considerable variability. Across the sources, Rush Limbaugh, *Drudge Report*, and Fox News were rated as having a conservative bias by more than 50% of their users. *The Huffington Post*, *The New York Times*, MSNBC, and National Public Radio were reported as having a liberal bias by more than 50% of their users.

Media outlets where over 50% of users perceived a liberal or a conservative bias were assigned to one of two categories: left-leaning media or right-leaning media. Three sources were coded as right-leaning media (*Rush Limbaugh Show*,

Table 1.2   Perceptions of Bias by Users of Media Outlets

	n	Liberal (%)	Neither (%)	Conservative (%)
		Perceived Bias		
Rush Limbaugh	52	0.0	2.5	**95.0***
Drudge Report	23	5.3	15.8	**68.4***
Fox News	237	9.0	20.5	**54.8***
Wall Street Journal	67	15.5	34.5	32.8
NewsHour on PBS	78	37.9	47.0	6.1
New York Times	88	**58.5***	12.2	9.8
MSNBC	145	**60.5***	16.3	10.1
Huffington Post	115	**55.9***	21.6	3.9
NPR	160	**55.6***	29.6	10.4
Washington Post	79	37.7	23.2	18.8
CNN	247	37.0	36.1	11.9
USA Today	104	33.7	28.3	9.8

Note: * denotes more than 50% of users agreed on perception of liberal/conservative bias. Question wording for perceived bias: "[Rush Limbaugh Show (radio)] . . . please indicate whether you think it has a [liberal/conservative], or neither type of bias." "Slight liberal bias" and "strong liberal bias" coded as liberal. "Slight conservative bias" and "strong conservative bias" coded as conservative. Rows do not total to 100 due to "don't know" responses.

Drudge Report, and Fox News cable channel) and four sources were coded as left-leaning media (*The New York Times*, MSNBC, *Huffington Post*, and National Public Radio). This categorization is similar to that of other studies relying on content-based rationales (see Stroud, 2011). We note, however, that these outlets cannot be considered as equally partisan on the right and the left; this sort of analysis is beyond the scope of our chapter.

To assess partisan selective exposure, we looked at the relationship between partisanship and our summary measures of exposure to right- and left-leaning media. As shown in Table 1.3, fewer than 3 in 10 Democrats (28.6%) and Republicans (26.5%) reported using like-minded media and no cross-cutting media. Note that this does not mean that these individuals avoided media of the opposite leaning—the sources that we considered were limited, and we were not able to look at the particular content consumed within each source. When looking at the data for the outlets we did measure, however, Republicans were significantly more likely to consume left- *and* right-leaning outlets in comparison to Democrats, although the percentages are notably small regardless of partisanship.

To examine whether selective exposure exists for
sanship, we analyzed the partisan media measure b   ....ai ideology. A similar, and slightly more pronounced, pattern than th exhibited for partisanship can be seen for ideology. Thirty-six percent of libe. .ls and 27% of conservatives reported using only like-minded media (see Table 1.4). Further, liberals consumed left-leaning media at a greater frequency than they consumed right-leaning media, and the opposite was true for conservatives.

The same pattern of selective exposure holds for presidential primary vote choice, albeit with a few nuances. Because fewer than 100 respondents voted for any particular Republican candidate other than Trump, we combined those voting for other Republican candidates and compared them to Trump voters. As shown in Table 1.5, Clinton supporters were more likely to avoid both right- and left-leaning media outlets compared to both Sanders supporters and

Table 1.3   Exposure to Partisan Media by Partisanship

	Democrat	Republican
Neither	56.8% [a]	52.2% [a]
Right-leaning media	8.2% [a]	26.5% [b]
Left-leaning media	28.6% [a]	11.3% [b]
Both	6.4% [a]	10.0% [b]
N	530	422

$\chi^2(3)=84.46$, $p<.001$

Note: Columns with different subscripts differ significantly from each other using a Bonferroni correction.

Table 1.4   Exposure to Partisan Media by Political Ideology

	Liberal	Moderate	Conservative
Neither	50.8% $_a$	63.5% $_b$	51.4% $_a$
Right-leaning media	5.6% $_a$	12.9% $_b$	27.2% $_c$
Left-leaning media	36.3% $_a$	18.1% $_b$	10.2% $_c$
Both	7.3% $_{a,b}$	5.5% $_b$	11.2% $_a$
N	297	338	337

$\chi^2(6) = 113.78, p < .001$

Note: Question wording for ideology: "In general, do you think of yourself as . . ."; scale 1–7 with 1 being "extremely liberal" and 7 being "extremely conservative." Columns with different subscripts differ significantly from each other using a Bonferroni correction.

Table 1.5   Exposure to Partisan Media by Presidential Primary Vote Choice

	Clinton	Sanders	Trump	Other Republican
Neither	58.6% $_a$	38.9% $_b$	43.8% $_{a,b}$	37.0% $_b$
Right-leaning media	3.9% $_a$	5.3% $_a$	39.6% $_b$	30.4% $_b$
Left-leaning media	29.7% $_a$	51.6% $_b$	4.2% $_c$	20.7% $_a$
Both	7.8% $_a$	4.2% $_a$	12.5% $_a$	12.0% $_a$
N	132	101	111	114

$\chi^2(9) = 107.81, p < .001$

Note: Question wording for presidential candidate preference: "For whom did you vote?" Those indicating that they voted in the Democratic primary could choose Hillary Clinton, Bernie Sanders, or other. Those indicating that they voted in the Republican primary could choose Jeb Bush, Ben Carson, Ted Cruz, John Kasich, Marco Rubio, Donald J. Trump, or other. Columns with different subscripts differ significantly from each other using a Bonferroni correction.

those supporting non-Trump Republican candidates. Further, there were no differences by candidate preference in using both left- and right-leaning media; less than 13% of primary voters used both.

Interesting differences appeared when looking at the use of partisan media, however. Sanders voters were significantly more likely to use left-leaning media than all of the other voters, including Clinton voters. Trump voters were significantly less likely to do the same compared to those voting for other candidates, including those voting for other Republican candidates. Clinton and Sanders voters were significantly less likely to use right-leaning media compared to Trump and other Republican voters.

Homophily

People can encounter like-minded views not only from the media, but also during their day-to-day lives when interacting with other people. Scholars have known for many years that people's networks tend to be homophilous (McPherson, Smith-Lovin, & Cook, 2001). Early research in political communication noted that people most commonly discussed politics with others sharing their views (e.g., Berelson, et al., 1954) and later work confirmed the relationship. People talk about politics more frequently with those close to them, such as family members and close friends—precisely the people with whom a person is likely to agree politically (Mutz, 2006).

There are many reasons why people have homophilous networks. One explanation is based on availability. To the extent that people are geographically sorted and live among others sharing their political views, they may have little opportunity to encounter those espousing different perspectives. If those with another perspective are not nearby, it seems obvious that people would end up discussing politics with like-minded others not because they prefer it, but because these are the available discussion partners.

Yet there is compelling evidence that having like-minded discussion partners results from more than just availability. First, research suggests that geographic sorting has increased over time (Bishop, 2008). In 2016, *The New York Times* reported that the number of landslide counties had further increased in the 2016 election (Aisch, Pearce, & Yourish, 2016). As people have more mobility and money to decide where to live, Bishop argues, they sort into more like-minded communities. Bishop cautions that the sorting is not necessarily based on politics—people may select their residence based on its proximity to other cultural markers that are correlated with partisanship, such as churches or alternative movie theaters. The net effect, however, is increased sorting based on partisanship. Second, it is clear that people opt for like-minded others when they have the choice. When using online dating Web sites or evaluating resumes for a job, people are attracted to those sharing their political orientation (Gift & Gift, 2015; Huber & Malhotra, 2016). If homophily were incidental, we would not expect to see these patterns.

The partisan composition of one's interpersonal discussion partners has democratic implications. Discussing politics with those *not* sharing one's viewpoint, known as cross-cutting exposure, connects with lower levels of political participation and attitude polarization, but also heightened understandings of different political perspectives (Huckfeldt, Mendez, & Osborn, 2004; Mutz, 2006). Research assigning people to discussion groups confirms that encountering disagreement can prompt more robust argument repertoires (Price, Cappella, & Nir, 2002). Just as with the use of like-minded media, the consequences of discussing politics with diverse others are not wholly desirable or undesirable from a democratic standpoint. Although participation may be democratically desirable, the lack of understanding different views may not be.

Analyzing people's discussion networks is particularly appropriate in the contentious 2016 election season. Within both the Democratic and Republican parties, there was disagreement among elites about the best candidate. These disagreements could have spilled into public discourse, interrupting friendships and increasing disagreement in discussion networks. In the aftermath of the general election, the Pew Research Center reported that 23% had "changed their settings to see fewer posts from someone on social media because of something related to the 2016 presidential election" (Oliphant & Smith, 2016). And of all sources, *Cosmopolitan* magazine reported that ". . . readers say this election is hurting their relationships" (Thomson-DeVeaux, 2016). Because of the contentious election, we revisit questions of cross-cutting exposure and homophily within the context of the last days of the 2016 primaries.

For the purposes of this analysis, survey respondents were asked to name up to three discussion partners with whom they discuss politics. For each partner named, respondents were asked to identify the partisanship of that individual. To understand the composition of the respondents' discussion networks, we created a measure parallel to the one that we used for partisan selective exposure. We categorized people as having no partisan discussion partners, only left-leaning discussion partners, only right-leaning discussion partners, or discussion partners from both parties. If respondents reported a right-leaning and a left-leaning discussion partner, they were categorized as having both in their network. If respondents did not identify a party for their discussion partners or referred to their discussion partners as independent, they were categorized as having neither right- nor left-leaning discussion partners. Across the sample, 31% did not discuss politics with anyone they considered a Democrat or a Republican, 25% discussed politics only with discussion partners they identified as Republicans, 30% discussed politics only with Democrats, and 13% discussed politics with at least one Democrat and at least one Republican.

To understand homophily within these networks, we compared the partisan makeup of the discussion network to each individual's partisan identity. This comparison reveals that many discussion networks are entirely homogenous (see Table 1.6). Forty-seven percent of Democrats reported only left-leaning discussion partners, and 52% of Republicans reported only right-leaning discussion partners.

To identify whether this pattern persisted for measures beyond partisanship, we compared respondents' discussion network makeup across political ideology and presidential vote choice during the 2016 primaries. A similar pattern of homophily emerged for political ideology (see Table 1.7). Of self-reported liberals, 52.6% identified left-leaning discussion partners, whereas 47.3% of conservatives identified right-leaning discussion partners. Moderates

Table 1.6   Discussion Network Makeup by Partisanship

	Democrat	Republican
Neither	30.9% [a]	24.4% [b]
Right-leaning discussion partners	7.9% [a]	52.2% [b]
Left-leaning discussion partners	47.3% [a]	9.7% [b]
Both	13.9% [a]	13.6% [a]
N	530	422

$\chi^2(3)=276.21$, $p<.001$

Note: Question wording for discussion network partisanship: "Do you think that [discussant] normally favors: Democrats, Republicans, Different parties depending on the issue or election, or Neither Democrats nor Republicans?" Columns with different subscripts differ significantly from each other using a Bonferroni correction.

Table 1.7   Discussion Network Makeup by Political Ideology

	Liberal	Moderate	Conservative
Neither	25.2% [a]	38.2% [b]	24.6% [a]
Right-leaning discussion partners	9.6% [a]	19.8% [b]	47.3% [c]
Left-leaning discussion partners	52.6% [a]	26.4% [b]	16.0% [c]
Both	12.6% [a]	15.5% [a]	12.1% [a]
N	297	338	337

$\chi^2(6)=177.60$, $p<.001$

Note: Columns with different subscripts differ significantly from each other using a Bonferroni correction.

fell in the middle, although they had slightly more left-leaning discussion partners (26.4%) than right-leaning ones (19.8%).

The pattern also persisted for presidential primary vote choice (see Table 1.8). A majority of individuals preferred a presidential candidate matching the partisan makeup of their interpersonal discussions. For those voting for Clinton or Sanders, this equated to greater proportions of left-leaning discussion partners in their networks. For those voting for Trump or other Republicans, this equated to greater numbers of right-leaning discussion partners in their networks.

Like-Minded Media and Like-Minded Discussion Partners

Although the literatures on homophily and partisan selective exposure share much in common, there are also important differences. In terms of similarities,

Table 1.8   Discussion Network Makeup by Presidential Primary Vote Choice

	Clinton	Sanders	Trump	Other Republican
Neither	15.6% a	14.7% a	22.1% a	15.1% a
Right-leaning discussion partners	5.5% a	10.5% a	50.5% b	60.2% b
Left-leaning discussion partners	65.6% a	57.9% a	9.5% b	7.5% b
Both	13.3% a	16.8% a	17.9% a	17.2% a
N	132	101	111	114

$\chi^2(9) = 163.09, p < .001$

Note: Columns with different subscripts differ significantly from each other using a Bonferroni correction.

discussions with similar others and like-minded partisan media diets are connected to both political participation and polarization. Yet important differences distinguish the two. It is possible that media selections are more purposeful—many Americans have cable and Internet access that would allow them to choose any outlet or Web site they so desire. Interpersonal conversations, however, may involve less choice. One is not always able to choose with whom to discuss politics. And politics can arise in conversations even if someone would prefer that it did not. Further, people are free to disagree with what they see in the media without any fear of social repercussions, whereas interpersonal conversations are rife with possible pitfalls if one were to get into an argument about politics. For these reasons, it would be a mistake to assume that exposure to like-minded others and like-minded media follow the same patterns. Comparing interpersonal and media data, however, is notoriously difficult, as Chaffee and Mutz (1988) note. Finding that one is more prevalent or a stronger predictor than the other could be an artifact of differences in measurement rather than differences between interpersonal and mediated communication.

Despite this important caveat, many scholars have developed theories and conducted research aiming to connect interpersonal discussions and media exposure. The differential gains model, for instance, proposes an interaction between news use and interpersonal discussion in predicting political participation (Scheufele, 2002). Other analyses propose that news media use prompts political discussion, which, in turn, leads to civic participation (Shah, Cho, Eveland, & Kwak, 2005). These studies suggest that it is important to consider the roles of both media diets and interpersonal conversations when examining participation. They are mute, however, on the role of partisan media and partisan discussion networks in particular.

Only a few studies have compared partisan media diets and interpersonal networks directly. Mutz and Martin (2001) asked people to report their exposure to different political viewpoints in their interpersonal networks and media diets. Their data from 1996 showed that people believed they encountered far more disagreement via the media than they did among the top three people with whom they discussed politics. Echoing these findings, Gentzkow and Shapiro (2011) analyzed ideological segregation by medium and type of interaction, finding that "face-to-face interactions tend to be more segregated than news media" (p. 1816). To reach this conclusion, the authors analyzed both Internet browsing data and survey data on media use and face-to-face interactions. These studies suggest important differences between interpersonal discussion networks and media diets, but also pit the two against each other to see which yields more exposure to disagreement. In this chapter, instead of comparing the two, we will analyze the relationship between the two—how many people both consume like-minded partisan media and have a mainly like-minded discussion network?

More common than directly comparing partisan media use to the partisan composition of one's discussion network, research has proposed that the two predict political outcomes of interest. In an early investigation of this question, Beck, Dalton, Greene, and Huckfeldt (2002) found that survey respondents' perceptions of the partisanship of their discussion partners and their perceptions of media bias correlated with their vote choice in the 1992 presidential election. In a more contemporary example, Kim (2015) uncovered significant interactions between selective exposure and disagreement with discussion partners when predicting polarization. In the United States, high disagreement reduced the effect of selective exposure on polarization. Thus, disagreement in interpersonal networks may blunt the polarizing effects of partisan media exposure. These empirical demonstrations consider interpersonal and mediated partisan exposure both as distinct effects and as combined effects. Theoretically, Shah, McLeod, Rojas, Cho, Wagner, and Friedland (2017) propose that partisan media and partisan discussion networks motivate participation, different perceptions of reality, and distrust of those holding different political views. Adding to the literature thus far, we consider the relationships between the partisanship of the media people use and those with whom they discuss politics.

To analyze these relationships, we use the summary measures of partisan media use and the partisan makeup of one's interpersonal discussion network created earlier. In the analyses that follow, we explore the relationship between these two measures for Democrats and Republicans separately (see Tables 1.9 and 1.10, respectively). The percentages displayed in each table add to 100% across all rows and columns (with slight divergences due to rounding).

In Table 1.9, we see that self-reported Democrats were most likely to have left-leaning discussion partners and use neither left- nor right-leaning media

Table 1.9   **Partisan Media Consumption by Makeup of Interpersonal Discussion Networks**

	Democrats Only			
	Neither	**Right-leaning media**	**Left-leaning media**	**Both**
Neither	21.1%	3.4%	5.0%	1.4%
Right-leaning discussion partners	4.1%	0.7%	2.0%	0.9%
Left-leaning discussion partners	25.6%	3.4%	15.2%	3.0%
Both	6.1%	0.7%	6.3%	0.9%

$\chi^2(9)=30.31$, $p<.001$, $n=530$

(at least according to the limited operationalization we employ here). One quarter of Democrats fit in this cell. The next most common category for Democrats was to have no partisan discussion partners and to use no partisan media; 21.1% of Democrats did not engage in partisan selective exposure and did not have homophilous networks based on our measures. The third most common cell was Democrats who both used left-leaning media and had left-leaning discussion partners; 15.2% of Democrats followed this pattern. All other cells are populated by far fewer Democrats. Looking across the table, 45.8% of Democrats used left-leaning media or had left-leaning discussion partners and reported no right-leaning exposure (5.0%+25.6%+15.2%). Nearly a third reported at least some exposure to right-leaning views. The remaining 21.1% reported no partisan media use or discussion. These results provide support for the idea that discussion networks and media diets have similar partisan compositions, but the relationship is far from strong.

Although the ideal within the literature suggests that it is beneficial to have cross-cutting networks and consume media across the political spectrum, Table 1.9 reflects that this occurs for only a small percentage of Democrat respondents (0.9%). Democrats are unlikely to consume partisan media from both sides and have discussion partners in their interpersonal networks from both parties. Rather, selective exposure to media and homophilous interpersonal discussions of politics appear to co-occur.

Next, we turn to the analysis for Republicans. In Table 1.10, we see that for Republicans the pattern of consuming like-minded media and having like-minded discussion partners is similar. The most common cell among Republicans is exactly the same as the one for Democrats—24.1% of Republicans did not use partisan media but had like-minded discussion partners. For Republicans, the next most common category was to have right-leaning

Table 1.10   Partisan Media Consumption by Makeup of Interpersonal
              Discussion Networks

	Republicans Only			
	Neither	**Right-leaning media**	**Left-leaning media**	**Both**
Neither	15.5%	4.5%	3.4%	1.0%
Right-leaning discussion partners	24.1%	17.6%	4.7%	5.8%
Left-leaning discussion partners	6.0%	1.0%	1.8%	0.8%
Both	6.8%	3.4%	1.3%	2.1%

$\chi^2(9)=22.55, p<.001, n=422$

discussion partners and use right-leaning media (17.6%). The third category was to have no Democrats or Republicans among one's top three political discussion partners and to use none of the partisan media outlets we identified; 15.5% of Republicans fell into this cell. Again, looking across the table, 46.2% of Republicans used right-leaning media or had right-leaning discussion partners and reported no left-leaning exposure (4.5% + 24.1% + 17.6%). Thirty-eight percent reported at least some exposure to left-leaning views. The remaining 15.5% reported no partisan media use or discussion. As with Democrats, there is a relationship between using like-minded media and having a like-minded discussion network, but it is weak in magnitude.

Also echoing the findings for Democrats, only a very small percentage of Republicans reported having a bipartisan media diet as well as a cross-cutting interpersonal network (2.1%). These data further show that selective exposure to media and homophily within one's social circles are not confined to one partisan identification or another. The two do, however, appear to be related to each other.

Discussion

In the context of the contentious 2016 election, this chapter examines partisan selective exposure and homophily, finding evidence for both at the end of the primary campaign. We note that we are looking at self-reported media diets and interpersonal discussion networks. The former has been critiqued along methodological grounds—namely that people cannot accurately report their exposure (see Prior, 2009). There are legitimate questions about whether self-reported media exposure correlates with actual behavior (Dvir-Gvirsman, Tsfati, & Menchen-Trevino, 2016). Yet there is some support for the program list technique we use in this chapter (Dilliplane, Goldman, & Mutz, 2013; see also Prior, 2013 and Goldman, Mutz, & Dilliplane, 2013). Further, people are better able to report on the partisanship of their discussion partners accurately than they are to weigh in on the partisanship of the media they consume (see Mutz & Martin, 2001). We therefore rely on their self-reports of the partisanship for their discussion partners, but use summary measures of partisan bias to decide which outlets would be coded as left and right leaning.

Three separate measures of personal beliefs were used to measure selective exposure: partisanship, ideology, and primary election vote choice. Few systematic differences appeared across the partisanship and ideology measures. In general, a higher percentage of liberals reported using left-leaning media (36.3%) and conversing with Democrats (52.6%) than did Democrats (28.6% and 47.3%, respectively). This likely is because the ideology measure separates moderates. Republicans and conservatives used right-leaning media and discussed politics with right-leaning others at similar rates. The primary election vote choice data, however, add nuance to our understanding. Although Democratic voters and Republican voters had similar discussion networks, regardless of the candidate for whom they voted, differences appeared in their media diets. Clinton voters and those voting for other Republican candidates used left-leaning media at similar rates. Those voting for Sanders and Trump, however, are quite different. Sanders voters were far more likely to use left-leaning media, and Trump voters far less so. This demonstrates the utility of using different measures of beliefs to understand exposure to partisan communication. It also highlights the need for future research to examine the causal direction of the relationships that are only analyzed cross-sectionally in this chapter. Did media exposure affect vote choice, or vice versa? Previous research suggests that these relationships may be bidirectional (e.g., Dilliplane, 2014; Stroud, 2008).

The most important contribution of this chapter, however, is to analyze the relationship between homophily and partisan selective exposure. Past literature has looked at the two as distinct predictors (Beck et al., 2002) or in combination using an interaction (Kim, 2015) when predicting outcome variables like political polarization. When looking at descriptive statistics, scholars have compared exposure to like-minded others and media to see which yields more diverse views (Gentzkow & Shapiro, 2011; Mutz & Martin, 2001). Analyzing the extent to which the two are correlated has received less attention. This chapter demonstrates that there are significant relationships between the two, although they are not very strong in magnitude.

The lack of a strong relationship may speak to the mechanism behind the two phenomena. Whereas news media use is self-selected and purposeful in many circumstances, the same may not always be the case when thinking about conversations. People may end up discussing politics with people they wouldn't otherwise choose and more frequently than they might desire. More research is needed to understand whether this accounts for the observed relationships.

The results of this chapter demonstrate that partisan selective exposure and like-minded discussions were in evidence at the close of the 2016 primary elections. The measures we used here cannot tell us how common the behaviors were—we do not have complete data about all the media outlets used nor about all discussion partners. For those outlets and discussion partners that we analyzed, however, like-minded exposure was more common than cross-cutting exposure. In an election extraordinary for many reasons, it is noteworthy that at least in this way, 2016 was rather ordinary.

References

Aisch, G., Pearce, A., & Yourish, K. (2016, November 10). The divide between red and blue America grew even deeper in 2016. *The New York Times*. Retrieved from https://www.nytimes.com/interactive/2016/11/10/us/politics/red-blue-divide-grew-stronger-in-2016.html?_r=0

Beck, P. A., Dalton, R. J., Greene, S., & Huckfeldt, R. (2002). The social calculus of voting: Interpersonal, media, and organization influences on presidential choices. *American Political Science Review, 96*(1), 57–73. doi: 10.1017/S0003055402004239

Berelson, B. R., Lazarsfeld, P. F., & McPhee, W. N. (1954). *Voting: A study of opinion formation in a presidential campaign*. Chicago, IL: University of Chicago Press.

Bishop, B., with Cushing, R. G. (2008). *The big sort: Why the clustering of like-minded America is tearing us apart*. Boston, MA: Houghton Mifflin Company.

Borah, P., Thorson, K., & Hwang, H. (2015). Causes and consequences of selective exposure among political blog readers: The role of hostile media perception in motivated media use and expressive participation. *Journal of Information Technology & Politics, 12*(2), 186–199. doi: 10.1080/19331681.2015.1008608

Chaffee, S. H., & Mutz, D. C. (1988). Comparing mediated and interpersonal communication data. In R. P. Hawkins et al. (Eds.), *Advancing communication science: Merging mass and interpersonal processes* (pp. 19–43). Newbury Park, CA: Sage.

Dilliplane, S. (2011). All the news you want to hear: The impact of partisan news exposure on political participation. *Public Opinion Quarterly, 75*(2), 287–316. doi: 10.1093/poq/nfr006

Dilliplane, S. (2014). Activation, conversion, or reinforcement? The impact of partisan news exposure on vote choice. *American Journal of Political Science, 58*(1), 79–94. doi: 10.1111/ajps.12046

Dilliplane, S., Goldman, S. K., & Mutz, D. C. (2013). Televised exposure to politics: New measures for a fragmented media environment. *American Journal of Political Science, 57*(1), 236–248. doi: 10.1111/j.1540-5907.2012.00600.x

Dvir-Gvirsman, S., Y. Tsfati, and E. Menchen-Trevino. (2016). The extent and nature of ideological selective exposure online: Combining survey responses with actual web log data from the 2013 Israeli elections. *New Media & Society, 18*(5), 857–877. doi: 10.1177/1461444814549041

Festinger, L. (1957). *A theory of cognitive dissonance.* Redwood City, CA: Stanford University Press.

Fischer, P., Schulz-Hardt, S., & Frey, D. (2008). Selective exposure and information quantity: How different information quantities moderate decision maker's preference for consistent and inconsistent information. *Journal of Personality and Social Psychology, 94*(2), 231–244. doi: 10.1037/0022-3514 .94.2.94.2.231

Garrett, R. K. (2009). Politically motivated reinforcement seeking: Reframing the selective exposure debate. *Journal of Communication, 59*(4), 676–699. doi: 10.1111/j.1460-2466.2009.01452.x

Garrett, R. K., Gvirsman, S. D., Johnson, B. K., Tsfati, Y., Neo, R., & Dal, A. (2014). Implications of pro- and counterattitudinal information exposure for affective polarization. *Human Communication Research, 40*(3), 309–332. doi:10.1111/hcre.12028

Gass, N. (2016, April 20). Cruz blasts talking heads 'in the tank for Trump.' *Politico.* Retrieved from http://www.politico.com/blogs/2016-gop-primary -live-updates-and-results/2016/04/ted-cruz-sean-hannity-clash-trump -222195

Gentzkow, M., & Shapiro, J. M. (2011). Ideological segregation online and offline. *The Quarterly Journal of Economics, 126*(4), 1799–1839. doi: 10.1093/qje /qjr044

Gift, K., & Gift, T. (2015). Does politics influence hiring? Evidence form a randomized experiment. *Political Behavior, 37*(3), 653–675. doi: 10.1007/s11109 -014-9286-0

Goldman, S. K., Mutz, D. C., & Dilliplane, S. (2013). All virtue is relative: A response to Prior. *Political Communication, 30*(4), 635–653. doi: 10.1080 /10584609.2013.819540

Hart, W., Albarracín, D., Eagly, A. H., Brechan, I., Lindberg, M. J., & Merrill, L. (2009). Feeling validated versus being correct: a meta-analysis of selective exposure to information. *Psychological Bulletin, 135*(4), 555–588. doi: 10.1037/a0015701

Huber, G. A., & Malhotra, N. (2016). Political homophily in social relationships: Evidence from online dating behavior. *Journal of Politics, 79*(1), 269–283. doi: 10.1086/687533

Huckfeldt, R., Mendez, J. M., & Osborn, T. (2004). Disagreement, ambivalence, and engagement: The political consequences of heterogeneous networks. *Political Psychology, 25*(1), 65–95, doi: 10.1111/j.1467-9221 .2004.00357.x

Iyengar, S., & Hahn, K. S. (2009). Red media, blue media: Evidence of ideological selectivity in media use. *Journal of Communication, 59*(1), 19–39. doi: 10.1111/j.1460-2466.2008.01402.x

Kim, Y. (2015). Does disagreement mitigate polarization? How selective exposure and disagreement affect political polarization. *Journalism & Mass Communication Quarterly, 92*(4), 915–937. doi: 10.1177/1077699015596328

McPherson, M., Smith-Lovin, L., & Cook, J. M. (2001). Birds of a feather: Homophily in social networks. *Annual Review of Sociology, 27*, 415–444. doi: 10.1146/annurev.soc.27.1.415

Meirick, P. C., & Bessarabova, E. (2016). Epistemic factors in selective exposure and political misperceptions on the right and left. *Analyses of Social Issues and Public Policy, 16*(1), 36–68. doi: 10.1111/asap.12101

Metzger, M. J., Hartsell, E. H., & Flanagin, A. J. (in press). Cognitive dissonance or credibility?: A comparison of two theoretical explanations for selective exposure to partisan news. *Communication Research.* doi: 10.1177/00936 50215613136

Montanaro, D. (2016, June 6). Clinton has enough delegates to claim Democratic Nomination. All Things Considered. *National Public Radio.* Retrieved from http://www.npr.org/2016/06/06/481020591/why-hillary-clinton-will-be -called-the-presumptive-nominee

Mutz, D. C. (2006). *Hearing the other side: Deliberative versus participatory democracy.* New York, NY: Cambridge University Press.

Mutz, D. C., & Martin, P. S. (2001). Facilitating communication across lines of political difference: The role of mass media. *American Political Science Review, 95*(1), 97–114.

Oliphant, B., & Smith, S. (2016). How Americans are talking about Trump's election in 6 charts. *Pew Research Center.* Retrieved from http://www.pew research.org/fact-tank/2016/12/22/how-americans-are-talking-about -trumps-election-in-6-charts/

Petrocik, J. R. (2009). Measuring party support: Leaners are not independents. *Electoral Studies, 28*, 562–572. doi: 10.1016/j.electstud.2009.05.022

Price, V., Cappella, J. N., & Nir, L. (2002). Does disagreement contribute to more deliberative opinion? *Political Communication, 19*(1), 95–112. doi: 10.1080 /105846002317246506

Prior, M. (2009). The immensely inflated news audience: Assessing bias in self-reported news exposure. *Public Opinion Quarterly, 73*(1), 130–143. doi: 10.1093/poq/nfp002

Prior, M. (2013). The challenge of measuring media exposure: Reply to Dilliplane, Goldman, and Mutz. *Political Communication, 30*(4), 620–634. doi: 10.1080 /10584609.2013.819539

Ryan, T. J., & Brader, T. (in press). Gaffe appeal: A field experiment on partisan selective exposure to election messages. *Political Science Research and Methods.* doi:10.1017/psrm.2015.62

Scheufele, D. A. (2002). Examining differential gains from mass media and their implications for participatory behavior. *Communication Research, 29*(1), 46–65. doi: 10.1177/009365020202900103

Shah, D. V., Cho, J., Eveland, W. P., & Kwak, N. (2005). Information and expression in a digital age: Modeling Internet effects on civic participation. *Communication Research, 32*(5), 531–565. doi: 10.1177/0093650205279209

Shah, D. V., McLeod, D. M., Rojas, H., Cho, J., Wagner, M. W., & Friedland, L. A. (2017). Revising the communication mediation model for a new political communication ecology. *Human Communication Research, 43*(4), 491–504. doi: 10.1111/hcre.12115

Simon, S. (2016). By staying in race, Bernie may drive movements, but not media. Weekend Edition Saturday. *National Public Radio.* Retrieved from http://www.npr.org/2016/05/21/478962839/by-staying-in-race-bernie-may-drive-movements-but-not-media

Stroud, N. J. (2008). Media use and political predispositions: Revisiting the concept of selective exposure. *Political Behavior, 30*(3), 341–366. doi: 10.1007/s11109-007-9050-9

Stroud, N. J. (2011). *Niche news: The politics of news choice.* New York, NY: Oxford University Press.

Thomson-DeVeaux, A. (2016, October 17). Cosmopolitan.com readers say this election is hurting their relationships. *Cosmopolitan.* Retrieved from http://www.cosmopolitan.com/politics/a6439626/trump-clinton-election-ending-friendships/

Tsfati, Y., & Nir, L. (2017). Frames and reasoning: Two pathways from selective exposure to affective polarization. *International Journal of Communication, 11*, 301–322.

CHAPTER TWO

What Mobilizes Partisans? Exploring the Underlying Pathways Between Partisan Media and Political Participation

Heesook Choi, Benjamin R. Warner, and Freddie J. Jennings

Partisan media are hardly a new feature of the U.S. political landscape. In the 19th century, newspapers were explicitly loyal to political parties (Schudson, 1992). Perhaps because of an emphasis on advocacy and political organizing, the rise of the partisan press was associated with a previously unprecedented level of political participation (Schudson, 1992). Though much of the news media landscape in the second half of the 20th century was dominated by the three major broadcasting networks, fragmentation resulting from cable news and digital media technologies has coincided with a re-emergence of partisan media (Dilliplane, 2011). The polarizing consequences of these emergent partisan media are well documented (Dvir Gvirsman, 2014; Garrett, Dvir Gvirsman, Johnson, Tsfati, Neo, & Dal, 2014; Feldman, Myers, Hmielowski, & Leiserowitz, 2014; Levendusky, 2013; Stroud 2010; Warner, 2010, 2017).

However, there is relatively less research about the potentially mobilizing effects of these ideological outlets (Chan & Lee, 2014; Dilliplane, 2011; Moehler & Conroy-Krutz, 2016; Wojcieszak, Bimber, Feldman, & Stroud, 2016). In particular, the mechanisms that underlie partisan media effects on participation have been largely neglected.

This study utilizes the 2016 presidential election to examine the link between partisan media use and political participation. Based on the O-S-R-O-R framework (background Orientation-Stimulus-Reasoning-outcome Orientation-Response), we propose structural relationships between audience motivation (i.e., partisanship), partisan media use, political talk, cognitive outcomes (i.e., political information efficacy, external efficacy, and cynicism), and political participation. Our findings lend support to the O-S-R-O-R model of indirect media effects on participation through political talk and these cognitive outcomes. (The existing literature simply uses the acronym this way: O-S-R-O-R [Orientation-Stimulus-Reasoning-Orientation-Response]).

Mobilizing Effect of Partisan Media

People who consume friendly media are more likely to participate in a variety of political activities (Chan & Lee, 2014; Dilliplane, 2011; Moehler & Conroy-Krutz, 2016; Stroud, 2011). Survey research shows that exposure to pro-attitudinal information can promote enthusiasm, accelerating political participation (Brundidge, Garrett, Rojas, & Gil de Zuniga, 2014; Dilliplane, 2011; Stroud, 2011). Experiments also link attitude-consistent information with participation (Wojcieszak et al., 2016; Knobloch-Westerwick & Johnson, 2014). Hence, it is reasonable to suspect an effect of partisan media on political participation. However, media effects are often indirect through communication processes (Eveland, 2001; Eveland, Shah, & Kwak, 2003; McLeod et al., 2001; Shah, Cho, Eveland, & Kwak, 2005; Shah et al., 2007; Sotirovic & McLeod, 2001). Despite the theoretical basis to assume mediation, formal tests are generally restricted to direct effects models. However, a few scholars have started to examine the mechanisms that underlie the relationship between partisan media use and political engagement. For example, Wojcieszak et al. (2016) found that issue understanding, emotional reactions (i.e., positive emotions), and attitude strength mediated the relationship between partisan media use and political participation. Similarly, Knobloch-Westerwick and Johnson (2014) demonstrated that attitude-consistent information increased intent to participate in politics.

Our study extends analysis of possible mediators that link partisan media use with participation by drawing on the O-S-R-O-R framework. In what follows, we develop a theoretical model for the mediated effects of partisan media on political participation and test the model through an online panel survey conducted in the run-up to the 2016 election.

O-S-R-O-R Model of Communication Effects

Early media effects research adopted a simple S–R (Stimulus–Response) framework. These studies suggested that the media had either a powerful or limited effect on opinions, attitudes, and behaviors (Gerbner, Gross, Morgan, & Signorielli, 1994; Larzarsfeld, Berelson, & Gaudet, 1948; Sparks, 2012). This direct effects approach has been criticized on the grounds that it fails to consider individual differences in motivations for and patterns of media use (Rubin, 1984) and cognitive processes underlying media effects (Markus & Zajonc, 1985). The O-S-O-R framework was established to illustrate the dynamic relationships underlying media effects (Markus & Zajonc, 1985; McLeod, Kosicki, & McLeod, 1994). Information and entertainment motives are central to media selection (Rubin, 1984). These motivations influence media consumption (Krcmar & Strizhakova, 2009) as well as audience behaviors (Papacharissi & Rubin 2000) and information processing (Eveland et al., 2003). Hence, these initial orientations (O) precede media use (S), which results in changes in attitudes (O), and thus behaviors (R).

The communication mediation model (McLeod et al., 2001; Shah et al., 2005; Sotirovic & McLeod, 2001) and the cognitive mediation model (Eveland, 2001) are extensions of the original O-S-O-R framework that situate a new mediating step, "reasoning," between stimulus and outcome orientations (hence, O-S-R-O-R). This model theorizes that interpersonal and intrapersonal communication are reasoning processes that function as mediators between news use and cognitive and behavioral political outcomes (Cho, Shah, McLeod, McLeod, Schroll, & Gotlieb, 2009; Shah et al., 2007).

Theoretical Model

By integrating existing research on partisan media and political participation with the O-S-R-O-R framework of media effects, we advance an overarching conceptual model in which partisan media use influences political participation through political communication. This theoretical model allows us to systematically examine the participatory effects of partisan media use by proposing structural relationships in which partisanship serves as background orientation, partisan media use (i.e., liberal media and conservative media) as stimuli, political talk as reasoning, political information and external efficacy and political cynicism as outcome orientations, and political participation as response.

The First Orientation: Partisanship

In this study, we situate party affiliation as the first "O," expecting that partisanship will guide an individual's partisan media exposure. In the high-choice media environment, people tend to seek news consistent with their political predispositions (Feldman et al., 2014; Iyengar & Hahn, 2009; Lazarsfeld et al., 1948)—though they do not necessarily avoid discrepant information (Garrett & Stroud, 2014). This type of partisan selective exposure is motivated by a desire to receive attitude-affirming information (Lazarsfeld et al., 1948; Stroud, 2011). Individuals are more likely to seek information from their preferred candidate or party (Iyengar & Hahn, 2009; Lazarsfeld et al., 1948) and news outlets that affirm their viewpoints on particular issues such as climate change (Feldman et al., 2014). Therefore, we propose the following hypotheses:

H1a: Democrats will be more likely to consume liberal media.

H1b: Republicans will be more likely to consume conservative media.

Stimuli: Partisan Media

In general, informational use of media is closely related to cognitive and behavioral outcomes (Prior, 2007). Those who consume news are more likely to have greater political knowledge, efficacy, and participation (Delli Carpini & Keeter, 1996; Eveland et al., 2003; Park, 2015). Media use also influences political cynicism, such that negative media coverage of political issues leads to greater cynicism in politics (Cappella & Jamieson, 1997).

Unlike traditional media, which strive for balance and objectivity, partisan media report the news with perspectives tailored to specific political orientations (Dilliplane, 2011; Stroud, 2011; Wojcieszak et al., 2016). For example, partisan media give more prominent coverage to issues and events that favor pro-attitudinal ideologies, while minimizing coverage of issues and events that challenge them (Baum & Groeling, 2008). Research has shown growing evidence of systematic partisan differences in news consumption, and pro-attitudinal news tends to encourage political participation (Dilliplane, 2011; Iyengar & Hahn, 2009; Knobloch-Westerwick & Johnson, 2014; Stroud, 2011). Therefore, we propose the following hypothesis:

H2a: Partisan media use will be positively associated with political participation.

Interpersonal and intrapersonal communication mediate the effects of media consumption on political participation (Cho et al., 2009; Eveland, 2001; Eveland et al., 2003; McLeod, Daily, Guo, Eveland, Bayer, Yang, & Wang, 1996; Shah et al., 2005, 2007; Sotirovic & McLeod, 2001). McLeod and his colleagues (2001) argue that the effects of media on political outcomes are strong but largely through their effects on individual communication behaviors (e.g., information seeking, interpersonal communication) (Shah et al.,

2005, 2007). By incorporating mass and interpersonal communication into the processes that lead to participatory behaviors, they highlighted political conversation among citizens as a key variable in the study of media effects on civic and political engagement (Shah et al., 2005). In the context of a political campaign, a communication mediation model theorizes that political talk is an antecedent to outcome variables such as political knowledge and efficacy, serving as both "a source of information and a site of deliberation" (Shah et al., 2007, p. 698). Therefore, we propose the following hypothesis:

H2b: Partisan media use will be positively associated with political talk.

The effects of political communication on participation should primarily manifest through their influence on key political attitudes. Political information efficacy, or a person's belief that she has sufficient information to participate meaningfully in politics, is a critical outcome of exposure to political information (Kaid, McKinney, & Tedesco, 2007). Conversely, external political efficacy, or the belief that the governing body is responsive to the will of the people, is a vital antecedent to political engagement (Craig, Niemi, & Silver, 1990). Nonpartisan news consumption influences cognitive outcomes such as political knowledge and efficacy (Eveland, 2001; Eveland et al., 2003; Jung, Kim, & Gil de Zuniga, 2011). Wojcieszak et al. (2016) linked partisan media use to more strongly held attitudes—a potential sign of a link between partisan media and information efficacy. Furthermore, Warner (2017) found that pro-partisan media use was associated with higher political information efficacy. Finally, Knobloch-Westerwick and Johnson (2014) found that partisan media influenced participation intent, which may suggest more confidence that political institutions are responsive to an active citizenry. Therefore,

H2c: Partisan media use will be positively associated with political information efficacy.
H2d: Partisan media use will be positively associated with external political efficacy.

Though these cognitive outcomes should generally increase political participation, partisan media may also foster some attitudes that undermine an engaged citizenry. Negative coverage of politics (common in partisan media) engenders public distrust in government and politics (Cappella & Jamieson, 1997; Fu, Mou, Miller, & Jalette, 2011). Therefore,

H2e: Partisan media use will be positively associated with political cynicism.

Reasoning: Political Talk

The two-step flow model (Katz & Lazarsfeld, 1955) highlighted the role of interpersonal communication to argue for minimal direct effects of media. Contemporary communication scholars, however, pay close attention to political discussion as a key mediator in the effects of media on civic and political participation (McLeod et al., 2001; Shah et al., 2005, 2007). Political discussion has been linked to increased cognitive political outcomes, such as political knowledge and efficacy, which result in increased political participation (Hardy & Scheufele, 2005; Moeller, De Vreese, Esser, & Kunz, 2014; McLeod et al., 2001; Sotirovic & McLeod, 2001). In short, the information people encounter in partisan media will provide fodder for interpersonal conversations—which should serve to enhance the direct effects of partisan media. Therefore:

H3a: Political talk will be positively associated with political information efficacy.

H3b: Political talk will be positively associated with political external efficacy.

H3c: Political talk will be positively associated with political cynicism.

Because political expression, online and offline, has a direct effect on political engagement (Chan, 2016; Jung et al., 2011), we propose the following hypothesis:

H3d: Political talk will be positively associated with political participation

The Second Orientations: Political Efficacy and Cynicism

The second set of orientations consists of political information efficacy, external efficacy, and political cynicism. Political efficacy is defined as "the feeling that political and social change is possible, and that the individual citizen can play a part in bringing about this change" (Campbell, Gurin, & Miller, 1954, p. 187). This cognitive construct has two components: internal and external efficacy (Balch, 1974). Internal efficacy relates to self-perception that a person is capable of understanding and influencing politics, and external efficacy relates to the feeling that government institutions and officials are responsive to the needs and demands of individuals (Hoffman & Thomson, 2009; Niemi, Craig, & Mattei, 1991). Political information efficacy is a variant of internal efficacy tailored to communication effects and focused on the informational component of internal efficacy (Kaid et al., 2007). Media use has been linked to greater internal and external political efficacy (Hansen & Pedersen, 2014), which predicts political participation (Pollock, 1983). Therefore, we expect that political information efficacy and external political efficacy will positively influence political participation.

H4a: Political information efficacy will be positively associated with political participation.

H4b: External political efficacy will be positively associated with political participation.

Political cynicism is defined as "the degree of negative affect toward the government and is a statement of the belief that the government is not functioning and producing outputs in accord with individual expectations" (Miller, 1974, p. 952). The sense of frustration in the government can be also defined as "mistrust generalized from particular leaders or political groups to the political process as a whole—a process perceived to corrupt the persons who participate in it and that draws corrupt persons as participants" (Cappella & Jamieson, 1997, p. 166). This lack of trust and negativity toward government and politics discourages voters from engaging in meaningful political activities (Cappella & Jamieson, 1997; Erber & Lau, 1990). Therefore, we expect that political cynicism negatively influences political engagement.

H4c: Political cynicism will be negatively associated with political participation.

Response: Political Participation

Political participation is commonly defined as activities by which citizens attempt to influence governmental decision-making processes (Cohen, Vigoda, & Samorly, 2001). Verba and Nie (1972) define it as "those activities by private citizens that are more or less directly aimed at influencing the selection of governmental personnel and/or the actions they take" (p. 2). Verba, Nie, and Kim (1978) further narrow the activities to "legal" activities, excluding protests and violence. More recently, Verba, Schlozman, and Brady (1995) refer to political participation as "activity that has the intent or effect of influencing government action—either directly by affecting the making or implementation of public policy or indirectly by influencing the selection of people who make those policies" (p. 38). Following Verba et al.'s (1995) definition, the present study defines political participation as legal activities to influence the government.

Modeling Mediated Relationships Between Partisan Media Use and Political Participation

Most of the earlier hypotheses imply both direct and indirect effects of partisan media on political participation (see Figure 2.1). Partisan media use, political talk, political efficacy, and cynicism are expected to have direct effects on political engagement. In addition, the O-S-R-O-R model hypothesizes indirect effects in which the intermediate variables influence political behaviors. Therefore, we propose the following hypotheses:

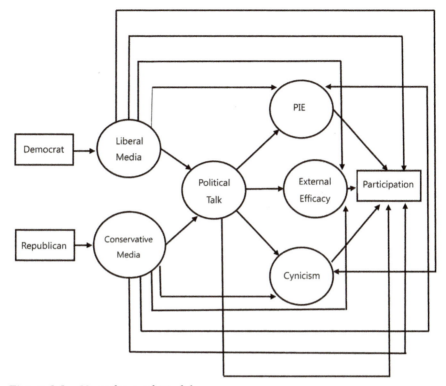

Figure 2.1 Hypothesized Model

H5a: Those who use more partisan media will engage in more political discussion and, through the association between political talk and political information efficacy, participate more in the political process.

H5b: Those who use more partisan media will engage in more political discussion and, through the association between political talk and political external efficacy, participate more in the political process.

H5c: Those who use more partisan media will engage in more political discussion and, through the association between political talk and cynicism, participate less in the political process.

Method

Procedure

An online survey was distributed by Qualtrics before the 2016 presidential election between August 26, 2016, and September 1, 2016. Qualtrics maintains partnerships with numerous actively managed market research companies to provide access to online panels with large and diverse samples of participants. The sample for this study was quota-stratified on age, race, and gender to match the most recent census data. The data collection procedure was approved by the institutional review board at the host university.

Participants

A total of 2,014 adults participated in this survey. Respondents ranged in age from 19 to 87 ($M=47.59$, $SD=16.26$). A slight majority identified as female ($n=1029$, 51%), and most were white ($n=1392$, 69%) compared to African American ($n=242$, 12%), Hispanic/Latinx ($n=262$, 13%), or Asian ($n=78$, 4%). Many reported having completed a bachelor's degree ($n=542$, 27%) or a postgraduate degree ($n=441$, 22%). Consistent with the national trend, respondents were more likely to identify as Democrat or Democratic leaning ($n=1055$, 52%) than Republican or Republican leaning ($n=617$, 31%) or independent ($n=342$, 17%).

Measures

We divide partisan media into two distinct types: liberal and conservative. Research has shown that Republicans prefer news from conservative media outlets, including Fox News, whereas Democrats prefer liberal sources such as MSNBC and avoid Fox News (Iyengar & Hahn, 2009; Levendusky, 2013). In addition, those who watch liberal cable news (e.g., MSNBC) are more likely to watch political comedy (Hmielowski, Holbert, & Lee, 2011). Therefore, we operationalize liberal media use as watching MSNBC news and political satire and reading liberal political blogs or Web sites; we operationalize conservative media use as watching Fox News, listening to conservative talk radio, and reading conservative political blogs and Web sites.

Liberal Media Use

Participants were asked how many days in the typical week (0–7) they 1) watched MSNBC news; 2) read liberal political blogs or Web sites; and 3) watched political comedy ($M=1.21$, $SD=1.51$, $\alpha=.71$).

Conservative Media Use

Participants were asked how many days in the typical week (0–7) that they 1) watched Fox News; 2) read conservative talk radio; and 3) read conservative political blogs and Web sites ($M=1.18$, $SD=1.59$, $\alpha=.74$).

Political Talk

Participants were asked to respond to the following three items on a 5-point scale (0=never, 4=a great deal): "How much have you talked about Donald

Trump or Hillary Clinton?" "How often do you tend to talk about politics?" and "How much have you talked about the 2016 election?" ($M=2.48$, $SD=.99$, $\alpha=.91$).

Political Information Efficacy

Participants responded to four items on a 1 to 5 agreement scale from Kaid and colleagues (2007): "I consider myself well qualified to participate in politics," "I feel that I have a pretty good understanding of the important political issues facing our country," "I think that I am better informed about politics and government than most people," and "If a friend asked me about the presidential election, I feel I would have enough information to help my friend figure out who to vote for" ($M=3.68$, $SD=.85$, $\alpha=.86$).

External Efficacy

Participants responded to four items on a 1 to 5 agreement scale (see Craig et al., 1990; Kushin & Yamamoto, 2010; Pinkleton & Austin, 2001): "My vote makes a difference," "I have a real say in what the government does," "I can make a difference if I participate in the election process," and "Voting gives people an effective way to influence what the government does" ($M=3.46$, $SD=1.01$, $\alpha=.91$).

Political Cynicism

Participants responded to eight items on a 1 to 5 agreement scale adapted from the American National Election Survey (ANES) survey (Craig et al., 1990): "Politicians cannot be trusted," "Politicians are corrupt," "Politicians are dishonest," "Politicians are more interested in power than what people think," "Politicians make promises that are never kept," "Politicians are too greedy," "Politicians always tell the public what they want to hear instead of what they actually plan to do," and "Politicians are more concerned about power than advocating for citizens" ($M=3.82$, $SD=.77$, $\alpha=.94$).

Political Participation

This variable was measured by asking participants: "Have you talked to anyone to try to convince them why they should vote for or against a particular candidate?" "Have you worked for any political party or candidate during this campaign?" "Have you attended any meetings or election rallies for a candidate or political party?" "Have you put up a yard sign or bumper sticker or have you worn a campaign button for any candidate or political party?" and "Have you given any money to a political party or candidate?" Responses were summed to create an overall participation score ($M=.83$, $SD=1.17$).

Results

The hypotheses were tested in structural equation modeling (SEM) using lavaan (Rosseel, 2012) for the R ecosystem. A two-step procedure recommended by Kline (2016) was adopted in which a measurement model was fit to confirm the factor structure of the variables. The measurement model achieved adequate fit, $\chi2(118)=621.302$, $p<.001$, RMSEA$=.046$ (.042-050), CFI$=.977$, NNFI/TLI$=.970$, SRMR$=.029$. A structural model was then fit to evaluate the hypothesized paths. In addition to the latent variables, dummy variables were included to indicate the party with which the participant was affiliated. Political participation was included as an observed (not latent) variable because it was measured as an index. Each variable was also regressed on control variables for age, gender, race, and educational attainment. The structural model fit was adequate, $\chi2(206)=1926.704$, $p<.001$, RMSEA$=.064$ (.062-.067), CFI$=.928$, NNFI/TLI$=.900$, SRMR$=.078$. The final path model is presented in Figure 2.2.

To test the theoretical model, a series of nested model comparisons were conducted in which each hypothesized path was constrained to equal zero

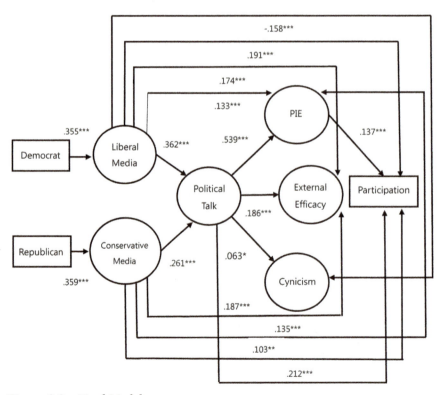

Figure 2.2   Final Model

(i.e., the null hypothesis) and the resulting change in chi-square was evaluated to assess whether the constraint was tenable (e.g., whether enforcing the null hypothesis reduced model fit by a statistically significant margin; see Kline, 2016). Direct effects are presented in Table 2.1. All mediated hypotheses were tested by examining the confidence interval of the product of the direct

Table 2.1   Latent Regression Paths for Final SEM Model

	LM	CM	PT	PIE	EE	Cyn	PP
Path	B (S.E.)	B (S.E.)	B (S.E.)	B (S.E.)	B (S.E.)	B (S.E.)	B (S.E.)
Covariates							
Age	−.012***	−.003*	.006**	.012***	.011***	−.004**	−.001
	(.002)	(.002)	(.002)	(.002)	(.002)	(.002)	(.002)
Female	−.276***	−.247***	.044	−.359***	.035	−.119*	−.049
	(.057)	(.054)	(.052)	(.057)	(.051)	(.048)	(.049)
Edu	.357***	.143**	.009	.236***	.003	−.099*	.016
	(.057)	(.053)	(.052)	(.056)	(.051)	(.048)	(.048)
Non-White	.075	.251***	−.220***	−.054	.278***	−.059	−.128*
	(.064)	(.061)	(.058)	(.063)	(.057)	(.054)	(.054)
Independent Variables							
Dem	.794***	.063	.420***	.105	.574***	−.369***	.088
	(.080)	(.074)	(.075)	(.082)	(.075)	(.070)	(.071)
Rep	.106	.836***	.413***	.150	.297***	−.068	.052
	(.085)	(.083)	(.081)	(.089)	(.081)	(.076)	(.076)
LM			.372***	.169***	.178***	−.147***	.197***
			(.036)	(.041)	(.039)	(.036)	(.036)
CM			.278***	.178***	.199***	−.003	.111**
			(.033)	(.037)	(.034)	(.032)	(.032)
PT				.668***	.185***	.057*	.214***
				(.037)	(.028)	(.026)	(.032)
PIE							.111***
							(.028)
EE							−.031
							(.027)
Cyn							−.018
							(.025)

Note: Results were generated using Maximum Likelihood estimation in Lavaan For R. Education was created as an indicator variable by coding 1 if the respondent has a college degree or beyond and 0 if not. *$p < .05$; **$p < .01$; ***$p < .001$. Final model fit: $\chi^2(206) = 1926.704$, $p < .001$, RMSEA = .064 (.062–.067), CFI = .928, NNFI/TLI = .900, SRMR = .078. LM (Liberal Media), CM (Conservative Media), PT (Political Talk), PIE (Political Information Efficacy), EE (External Efficacy), Cyn (Cynicism).

Table 2.2   Indirect Effects of Partisan Media

Path	5,000 Bootstraps Resamples		
	B (SE)	LLCI	ULCI
Theoretical Model			
D>LM>PT>PIE>PP	.022 (.006)	.011	.034*
D>LM>PT>EE>PP	−.002 (.001)	−.005	.001
D>LM>PT>Cyn>PP	.000 (.001)	−.002	.001
R>CM>PT>PIE>PP	.017 (.005)	.008	.028*
R>CM>PT>EE>PP	−.001 (.001)	−.004	.001
R>CM>PT>Cyn>PP	.000 (.000)	−.001	.001

Note: All estimates generated from 5,000 bootstrapped resamples. Unstandardized coefficients, standard errors, and 95% confidence intervals are presented. *Indicates that the confidence interval does not contain zero. LM (Liberal Media), CM (Conservative Media), PT (Political Talk), PIE (Political Information Efficacy), EE (External Efficacy), Cyn (Cynicism).

paths to determine whether it crossed zero (Preacher & Hays, 2008). All indirect effects are presented in Table 2.2.

H1 predicted that partisanship would be associated with partisan media use. As illustrated in Figure 2.2 and recorded in Table 2.1, the results are consistent with the hypotheses. Democrats were more likely to use liberal media, and Republicans were more likely to use conservative media. After accounting for selective approach, there was no evidence of selective avoidance—Democrats were not less likely to use conservative media, nor were Republicans less likely to use liberal media.

H2 predicted that partisan media use would be associated with greater political participation, greater political talk, greater political efficacy, and more cynicism. The results presented in Table 2.1 are generally consistent with these hypotheses. For liberal media use, every one-unit increase was associated with a corresponding .197-point increase in political participation, .372-point increase in political discussion, .169-point increase in political information efficacy, and .178-point increase in external efficacy. However, contrary to the hypothesis, liberal media use was associated with a .147-point decrease in cynicism. For conservative media use, every one-unit increase was related to a corresponding .111-point increase in participation, .278-point increase in political talk, .178-point increase in political information efficacy, and .199-point increase in external efficacy. Conservative media use was not significantly associated with cynicism.

H3 predicted that political talk would be associated with greater political information efficacy, external efficacy, and more political cynicism. It also predicted that political talk would have a direct effect on political participation. The results presented in Table 2.1 are consistent with these hypotheses. Every one-unit increase in political talk was associated with a .668-point increase in political information efficacy, .185-point increase in external efficacy, and .214-point increase in participation. Consistent with the hypothesis, each one-unit increase in political talk was associated with a .057-point increase in cynicism.

H4 predicted that greater political information efficacy and external efficacy would be associated with greater political engagement, whereas greater political cynicism would be associated with less political participation. As presented in Table 2.1, the results were partially consistent with these hypotheses. Every one-unit increase in political information efficacy was associated with a corresponding .111-point increase in political participation. However, external political efficacy and cynicism were not significantly associated with political participation.

H5 predicted that partisan media use would increase political discussion and, as a result, engender political information efficacy, external efficacy, and participation, while also increasing political cynicism, which dampens political engagement. As illustrated in Figure 2.2 and recorded in Table 2.2, these hypotheses were partially supported. As documented in Table 2.2, there was a significant indirect association between partisan media use and political information efficacy through political talk and an indirect association between partisan media use and political participation through this process. There were significant indirect associations between partisan media use and external political efficacy and political cynicism through political discussion, but there was no indirect association between partisan media use and political participation through this process.

Discussion

This study tested the mobilizing effects of partisan media use by accounting for the various mechanisms that mediate the influence of partisan media consumption on participation. Unlike the existing research, which mostly accounts for the direct relationship between partisan media exposure and participatory behaviors (Brundidge et al., 2014; Dilliplane, 2011; Stroud, 2011), this study employed the O-S-R-O-R model to explore possible mediating processes between partisan media use and participation. Based on this model, we proposed structural relationships in which 1) partisanship serves as a background orientation, 2) partisan media as stimuli, 3) political talk as a reasoning process, 4) political efficacy and cynicism as outcome orientations, and 5) political participation as the response. Our results were consistent with most of these expectations—though political information efficacy was much more important than cynicism or external efficacy in influencing participation. Findings are discussed next, as are limitations and directions for future research.

Consistent with research on partisan selective approach (Iyengar & Hahn, 2009; Stroud, 2011), Democrats were more likely to consume MSNBC news, liberal political blogs and Web sites, and political comedy, whereas Republicans were more likely to consume Fox News, conservative talk radio, and conservative political blogs and Web sites. What is noticeable here, however, is that although these partisans exposed themselves to consonant information, they seemed to do so without systematically avoiding challenging information. There was no negative association between partisan identification and cross-partisan media. This finding adds support to the argument that people prefer opinion-reinforcing information but do not also avoid opinion-challenging information (Garrett, 2009a, 2009b; Garrett & Stroud, 2014).

Partisan media directly and indirectly influenced political participation. The indirect association was such that those who used partisan media more frequently were more likely to talk about politics and thus likely to express greater political information efficacy. This is consistent with the communication mediation approach advanced by the O-S-R-O-R framework (McLeod et al., 2001; Shah et al., 2005, 2007; Sotirovic & McLeod, 2001)—though political information efficacy was the only outcome orientation to influence participation. External efficacy and cynicism were not mediators of this process. It seems that pro-attitudinal partisan media use encouraged interpersonal communication about politics, which translated into greater confidence in understanding politics and thus greater political participation. These findings advance the model of communication effects on political participation by identifying political information efficacy as a vital psychological path that connects communication behaviors and political participation.

It is worth noting that there does not appear to be a direct link between partisanship and political participation. It seems that exposure to pro-attitudinal information is an integral part of the process of translating partisanship into mobilization. This not only supports existing research on the participatory effect of partisan media (Stroud, 2011), but also adds support to the argument against limited media effects in the fragmented digital age (Holbert, Garrett, & Gleason, 2010).

Although our data generally support our proposed model, there were some interesting discrepancies between our results and our hypotheses. First, political information efficacy only partially mediated the relationship between political talk and participation. This suggests that other mechanisms may contribute to the effects of media consumption on participation. Political knowledge (Jung et al., 2011) and issue understanding, emotion, and attitude strength (Wojcieszak et al., 2016) are likely candidates. Second, research has shown that political cynicism is a personal-psychological construct that tends to dampen political participation (Cappella & Jamieson, 1997; Erber & Lau, 1990). We did not, however, find evidence of a demobilizing effect of cynicism. Future research should continue to test the effects of cynicism. If more evidence is not marshaled in defense of the claims that cynicism undermines positive democratic outcomes, we may conclude that conventional wisdom is unduly critical of this attitude. Finally, research has shown that online activities are distinct from offline activities not only in media consumption and interpersonal communication, but also in political behavior (Jung et al., 2011; Katz & Rice, 2002; Shah et al., 2005). Future studies should distinguish between partisan media effects on online and offline participation in the O-S-R-O-R framework.

As with any study, ours has important limitations. First, our analyses are based on cross-sectional survey data. Although we hypothesized causal relationships in our model, our data cannot verify the causal direction. Future research should use longitudinal or experimental data to test the various causal paths hypothesized here. Second, this study only investigated partisan media. Research suggests that the high-choice media environment encourages people to seek information from a wide variety of sources (Garrett 2009a, 2009b; Holbert, Hmielowski, & Weeks, 2012; Webster, 2007). Including other types of media in future analyses will expand our findings to a more comprehensive picture of people's media consumption.

Conclusion

In this study we explored possible underlying mechanisms and pathways between partisan selective exposure and political participation in the context of the 2016 presidential election. Based on the O-S-R-O-R framework of media effects, we proposed and tested structural relationships between audience motivation (i.e., partisanship), partisan media use, political talk, personal-psychological outcomes (i.e., political information efficacy, external political efficacy, and political cynicism), and political participation. We found that partisanship is a significant predictor of partisan media use. Consistent with existing research on participatory media effects, we also found that political talk and political information efficacy are important mediators of the effect of partisan media on participation. These findings advance our theoretical understanding of the mobilizing power of partisan media and provide some good news to augment the often-grim accountings of the partisan media environment. Partisan media facilitates political talk, through which people become more confident in their ability to understand government and politics, which, as a result, increases political participation.

References

Balch, G. I. (1974). Multiple indicators in survey research: The concept "sense of political efficacy." *Political Methodology, 1*(2), 1–43. Retrieved from http://www.jstor.org/stable/25791375

Baum, M. A., & Groeling, T. (2008). New media and the polarization of American political discourse. *Political Communication, 25,* 345–365. doi: 10.1080/105 84600802426965

Brundidge, J., Garrett, R. K., Rojas, H., & Gil de Zuniga, H. (2014). Political participation and ideological news online: "Differential gains" and "differential losses" in a presidential election cycle. *Mass Communication and Society, 17,* 464–486. doi: 10.1080/15205436.2013.821492

Campbell, A., Gurin, G., Miller, W. E. (1954). *The voter decides.* Evanston, IL: Row, Peterson and Company.

Cappella, J. N., & Jamieson, K. H. (1997). *Spiral of cynicism: The press and the public good.* New York: Oxford University Press.

Chan, M. (2016). Social network sites and political engagement: Exploring the impact of Facebook connections and uses on political protest and participation. *Mass Communication and Society, 19*(4), 430–451. doi: 10.1080/1520 5436.2016.1161803

Chan, M., & Lee, F. L. F. (2014). Selective exposure and agenda setting: Exploring the impact of partisan media exposure on agenda diversity and political participation. *Asian Journal of Communication, 24*(4), 301–314. doi: 10.1080 /01292986.2014.903424

Cho, J., Shah, D. V., McLeod, J. M., McLeod, D. M., Schroll, R. M., & Gotlieb, M. R. (2009). Campaigns, reflection, and deliberation: Advancing an O-S-R-O-R model of communication effects. *Communication Theory, 19,* 66–88. doi:10 .1111/j.1468-2885.2008.01333.x

Cohen, A., Vigoda, E., & Samorly, A. (2001). Analysis of the mediating effect of personal-psychological variables on the relationship between socioeconomic status and political participation: A structural equations framework. *Political Psychology, 22*(4), 727–757. doi: 10.1111/0162-895X.00260

Craig, S. C., Niemi, R. G., & Silver, G. E. (1990). Political efficacy and trust: A report on the NES pilot study items. *Political Behavior, 12,* 289–314. doi: 10.1007/BF00992337

Delli Carpini, M. X., & Keeter, S. (1996). *What Americans know about politics and why it matters.* New Haven, CT: Yale University Press.

Dilliplane, S. (2011). All the news you want to hear: The impact of partisan news exposure on political participation. *Public Opinion Quarterly, 75*(2), 287–316. doi: 10.1093/poq/nfr006

Dvir Gvirsman, S. (2014). It's not that we don't know, it's that we don't care: Explaining why selective exposure polarizes attitudes. *Mass Communication and Society, 17,* 74–97. doi: 10.1080/15205436.2013.816738

Erber, R., & Lau, R. R. (1990). Political cynicism revisited: An information-processing reconciliation of policy-based and incumbency-based interpretations of changes in trust in government. *American Journal of Political Science, 34*(1), 236–153. Retrieved from http://www.jstor.org/stable/211 1517

Eveland, W. P. (2001). The cognitive mediation model of learning from the news: Evidence from nonelection, off-year election, and presidential election contexts. *Communication Research, 28*(5), 571–601. doi: 10.1177/009365001 028005001

Eveland, W. P., Shah, D. V., & Kwak, N. (2003). Assessing causality in the cognitive mediation model: A panel study of motivations, information processing, and learning during campaign 2000. *Communication Research, 30*(4), 359–386. doi: 10.1177/0093650203253369

Feldman, L., Myers, T. A., Hmielowski, J. D., & Leiserowitz, A. (2014). The mutual reinforcement of media selectivity and effects: Testing the reinforcing spirals framework in context of global warming. *Journal of Communication, 64,* 590–611. doi:10.1111/jcom.12108

Fu, H., Mou, Y, Miller, M. J., & Jalette, G. (2011). Reconsidering political cynicism and political involvement: A test of antecedents. *American Communication Journal, 13*(2), 44–61. Retrieved from http://ac-journal.org/journal/pubs /2011/summer/Cynicism_Proof.pdf

Garrett, R. K. (2009a). Politically motivated reinforcement seeking: Reframing the selective exposure debate. *Journal of Communication, 59,* 676–699. doi:10 .1111/j.1460-2466.2009.01452.x

Garrett, R. K. (2009b). Echo chambers online?: Politically motivated selective exposure among Internet news users. *Journal of Computer-Mediated Communication, 14,* 265–285. doi:10.1111/j.1083-6101.2009.01440.x

Garrett, R. K., Dvir Gvirsman, S., Johnson, B. K., Tsfati, Y., Neo, R., & Dal, A. (2014). Implications of pro- and counterattitudinal information exposure for affective polarization. *Human Communication Research, 40,* 309–332. doi: 10.1111/hcre.12028

Garrett, R. K. & Stroud, N. J. (2014). Partisan paths to exposure diversity: Differences in pro- and counterattitudinal news consumption. *Journal of Communication, 64,* 680–701. doi:10.1111/jcom.12105

Gerbner, G., Gross, L., Morgan, M., & Signorielli, N. (1994). Growing up with television: The cultivation perspective. In J. Bryant, & D. Zillmann (Eds.), *Media effects: Advances in theory and research* (pp. 17–41). Hillsdale, NJ: Erlbaum.

Hansen, K. M., & Pedersen, R. T. (2014). Campaigns matter: How voters become knowledgeable and efficacious during election campaigns. *Political Communication, 31,* 303–324. doi: 10.1080/10584609.2013.815296

Hardy, B. W., & Scheufele, D. A. (2005). Examining differential gains from Internet use: Comparing the moderating role of talk and online interactions. *Journal of Communication, 55*(1), 71–84. doi: 10.1111/j.1460-2466.2005.tb02659.x

Hmielowski, J. D., Holbert, R. L., & Lee, J. (2011). Predicting the consumption of political TV satire: Affinity for political humor, The Daily Show, and The Colbert Report. *Communication Monographs, 78*(1), 96–114. doi: 10.1080 /03637751.2010.542579

Hoffman, L. H., & Thomson, T. L. (2009). The effect of television viewing on adolescents' civic participation: Political efficacy as a mediating mechanism. *Journal of Broadcasting & Electronic Media, 53*(1), 3–21. doi: 10.1080 /08838150802643415

Holbert, R. L., Garrett, R. K., & Gleason, L. S. (2010). A new era of minimal effects? A response to Bennett and Iyengar. *Journal of Communication, 60,* 15–34. doi:10.1111/j.1460-2466.2009.01470.x

Holbert, R. L., Hmielowski, J. D., & Weeks, B. (2012). Clarifying relationships between ideology and ideologically oriented cable TV news use: A case of suppression. *Communication Research, 39*(2), 194–216. doi:10.1177/0093650211405650

Iyengar, S. & Hahn, K. S. (2009). Red media, blue media: Evidence of ideological selectivity in media use. *Journal of Communication, 59,* 19–39. doi:10.1111/j.1460-2466.2008.01402.x

Jung, N., Kim, Y., & Gil de Zuniga, H. (2011). The mediating role of knowledge and efficacy in the effects of communication on political participation. *Mass Communication and Society, 14*(4), 407–430. doi: 10.1080/15205436.2010.496135

Kaid, L. L., McKinney, M. S., & Tedesco, J. C. (2007). Political information efficacy and young voters. *American Behavioral Scientist, 50*(9), 1093–1111. doi: 10.1177/0002764211398089

Katz, J. E., & Rice, R. E. (2002). Project syntopia: Social consequences of Internet use. *IT & Society, 1*(1), 166–179. Retrieved from https://pdfs.semanticscholar.org/3797/b339d056f6dcdb3d8b9a7698d9f28c2102b3.pdf

Katz, E., & Lazarsfeld, P. F. (1955). *Personal influence: The part played by people in the flow of mass communications.* Glencoe, IL: Free Press.

Kline, R. (2016). *Principles and practice of structural equation modeling.* New York: Guilford.

Knobloch-Westerwick, S., & Johnson, B. K. (2014). Selective exposure for better or worse: Its mediating role for online news' impact on political participation. *Journal of Computer-Mediated Communication. 19,* 184–196. doi:10.1111/jcc4.12036

Krcmar, M., & Strizhakova, Y. (2009). Uses and gratifications as media choice. In T. Hartmann (Ed.), *Media choice: A theoretical and empirical overview* (pp. 53–69). New York: Routledge.

Kushin, M. J., and Yamamoto, M. (2010). Did social media really matter? College students' use of online media and political decision making in the 2008 election. *Mass Communication & Society, 13,* 608–630. doi:10.1080/15205436.2010.516863

Lazarsfeld, P. F., Berelson, B., & Gaudet, H. (1948). *The people's choice: How the voter makes up his mind in a presidential campaign.* New York: Columbia University Press.

Levendusky, M. (2013). Partisan media exposure and attitudes toward the opposition. *Political Communication, 30,* 565–581. doi: 10.1080/10584609.2012.737435

Markus, H., & Zajonc, R. B. (1985). The cognitive perspective in social psychology. In G. Lindzey, & E. Aronson (Eds.), *The handbook of social psychology* (pp. 137–230). New York: Random House.

McLeod, J. M., Daily, K., Guo, Z., Eveland, W. P., Bayer, J., Yang, S., & Wang, H. (1996). Community integration, local media use, and democratic processes. *Communication Research, 23*(2), 179–209. doi: 10.1177/00936509 6023002002

McLeod, J. M., Kosicki, G. M., & McLeod, D. M. (1994). The expanding boundaries of political communication effects. In J. Bryant, & D. Zillmann (Eds.), *Media effects: Advances in theory and research* (pp. 123–162). Hillsdale, NJ: Erlbaum.

McLeod, J. M., Zubric, J., Keum, H., Deshpande, S., Cho, J., Stein, S., & Heather, M. (2001, August). Reflecting and connecting: Testing a communication mediation model of civic participation. Paper presented at the annual meeting of the Association for Education in Journalism and Mass Communication, Washington, D.C.

Miller, A. H. (1974). Political issues and trust in government: 1964–1970. *The American Political Science Review, 68*(3), 951–972. doi: 10.2307/1959140

Moehler, D. C., & Conroy-Krutz, J. (2016). Partisan media and engagement: A field experiment in a newly liberalized system. *Political Communication, 33*(3), 414–432, doi: 10.1080/10584609.2015.1069768

Moeller, J., De Vreese, C., Esser, F., & Kunz, R. (2014). Pathway to political participation: The influence of online and offline news media on internal efficacy and turnout of first-time voters. *American Behavioral Scientist, 58*(5), 689–700. doi: 10.1177/0002764213515220

Niemi, R. G., Craig, S. C., & Mattei, F. (1991). Measuring internal political efficacy in the 1988 national election study. *The American Political Science Review, 85*(4), 1407–1413. doi: 10.2307/1963953

Papacharissi, Z., & Rubin, A. M. (2000). Predictors of Internet use. *Journal of Broadcasting and Electronic Media, 44*(2), 175–196. doi: 10.1207/s15506878 jobem4402_2

Park, C. S. (2015). Pathways to expressive and collective participation: Usage patterns, political efficacy, and political participation in social networking sites. *Journal of Broadcasting & Electronic Media, 59*(4), 698–716. doi: 10.1080/08838151.2015.1093480

Pinkleton, B. E., & Austin, E. W. (2001). Individual motivations, perceived media importance, and political disaffection. *Political Communication, 18*(3), 321–334. doi:10.1080/10584600152400365

Pollock, P. H. (1983). The participatory consequences of internal and external political efficacy: A research note. *The Western Political Quarterly, 36*(3), 400–409. doi: 10.2307/448398

Preacher, K. J., & Hayes, A. F. (2008). Asymptotic and resampling strategies for assessing and comparing indirect effects in multiple mediator models. *Behavior Research Methods, 40,* 879–891. doi:10.3758/BRM.40.3.879

Prior, M. (2007). *Post-broadcast democracy: How media choice increases inequality in political involvement and polarizes election.* New York: Cambridge University Press.

Rosseel, Y. (2012). Lavaan: An R package for structural equation modeling. *Journal of Statistical Software, 48,* 1–36. Retrieved from http://www.jstatsoft.org/v48/i02/

Rubin, A. M. (1984). Ritualized and instrumental television viewing. *Journal of Communication, 34*(3), 67–77. doi: 10.1111/j.1460-2466.1984.tb02174.x

Schudson, M. (1992). Was there ever a public sphere? If so, when? Reflections on the American case. In C. Calhoun (Ed.) *Habermas and the public sphere* (pp. 143–163). Cambridge, MA: The MIT Press.

Shah, D. V., Cho, J., Eveland, W. P., & Kwak, N. (2005). Information and expression in a digital age: Modeling Internet effects on civic participation. *Communication Research, 32*(5), 531–565. doi: 10.1177/0093650205279209

Shah, D. V., Cho, J., Nah, S., Gotlieb, M. R., Hwang, H., Lee, N. J., . . . & McLeod, D. M. (2007). Campaign ads, online messaging, and participation: Extending the communication mediation model. *Journal of Communication, 57,* 676–703. doi:10.1111/j.1460-2466.2007.00363.x

Sotirovic, M., & McLeod, J. M. (2001). Values, communication behavior, and political participation. *Political Communication, 18*(3), 273–300. doi: 10.1080/10584600152400347

Sparks, G. G. (2012). *Media effects research: A basic overview.* Boston: Wadsworth/Cengage Learning.

Stroud, N. J. (2010). Polarization and partisan selective exposure. *Journal of Communication, 60,* 556–576. doi:10.1111/j.1460-2466.2010.01497.x

Stroud, N. J. (2011). *Niche news: The politics of news choice.* New York: Oxford University Press.

Verba, S. & Nie, N. H. (1972). *Participation in America: Political democracy and social equality.* New York: Harper and Row.

Verba, S., Nie, N. H., & Kim J. (1978). *Participation and political equality: A seven-nation comparison.* Chicago: The University of Chicago Press.

Verba, S., Schlozman, K. L. & Brady, H. E. (1995). *Voice and equality: Civic voluntarism in American politics.* Cambridge, MA: Harvard University Press.

Warner, B. R. (2010). Segmenting the electorate: The effects of exposure to political extremism online. *Communication Studies, 61,* 430–444. doi: 10.1080/10510974.2010.497069

Warner, B. R. (2017). Modeling partisan media effects in the 2014 U.S. midterm elections. *Journalism & Mass Communication Quarterly.* Advanced online publication.

Webster, J. G. (2007). Diversity of exposure. In P. Napoli (Ed.), *Media diversity and localism: Meaning and metrics* (pp. 309–326). Mahwah, NJ: Erlbaum.

Wojcieszak, M., Bimber, B., Feldman, L., & Stroud, N. J. (2016). Partisan news and political participation: Exploring mediated relationships. *Political Communication, 33,* 241–260. doi: 10.1080/10584609.2015.1051608

Media Event Influence in the 2016 Race: The Debates, Trump Groping Tape, and the Last-Minute FBI Announcement

Esther Thorson, Samuel M. Tham, Weiyue Chen, and Vamsi Kanuri

In this chapter, we ask what impact demographic variables, partisanship, political knowledge, interest in hard news and political campaigns, and candidate advertising awareness had on attitudes toward the presidential candidates and intent to vote for them. Controlling for these variables provides the opportunity to ask whether there were measurable effects of five significant "media events": the three presidential debates and two scandalous revelations, the tape of Trump talking about groping women, and FBI director James Comey's announcement of the reopening of the e-mail case against Democratic presidential candidate Hillary Clinton. There has been extensive media discussion of whether the latter two events influenced the election outcome (Apruzzo Schmidt, Goldman, & Lichtblau, 2017; "With These Hands," 2016;

Silver, 2016a). Our study provides scientific evidence for an answer, at least in terms of the impact of these events on voting intention and attitudes toward the candidates.

The Rolling Cross-Sectional Methodology

To evaluate the effects of so many variables and events wielding their impact dynamically over time, we employed a rolling cross-sectional (RCS) survey methodology. RCS was first used in presidential elections in 1984 (Bartels, 1988; Brady & Johnston, 1987) and used ever since in the National Annenberg Election Survey (Romer, Kenski, Winneg, Adasiewicz, & Jamieson, 2006). RCS methodology involves initial identification of a large sample of respondents. Then, every day, a random subsample is drawn, and the people in the subsample are contacted by e-mail and asked to respond to the survey until a daily target number of respondents is reached. Thus, not only are the participants randomly selected, but the day they are interviewed is also randomly selected. In this study, we sampled 100 respondents every day from September 20 to November 7, the day before the 2016 election, for a total of 49 days.

RCSs have been analyzed in a number of ways, for example, by graphing an n-day prior moving average in a measure of interest (e.g., political knowledge) and then identifying major political events to see if they correlate with changes in the slope of that variable (Campbell & Stanley, 1971). RCS data also have been aggregated over some portion of the sample (e.g., a week) and then regressions run for each sample (Hardy & Scheufele, 2005).

Here, however, we introduce an analysis strategy that provides a stronger tool for testing the impact of variables suspected to influence attitudes about candidates and voting intention, and one that provides a replacement for the interruption analysis (e.g., see Hardy & Scheufele, 2005, Figure 2) to demonstrate effects of single events. The interruption analysis is vulnerable to its highly inferential nature—that is, how much change there must be between before and after the event—and the analysis does not control for variables other than the occurrence of the event. Thus, replacing it with the analysis here is a significant methodological improvement.

Much of the social scientific study of presidential elections has relied on cross-sectional surveys, which although informative, fail to capture changes occurring over time. Panel studies are less common and do provide tests of change over time (Anderson, 2005), but are plagued with problems like differential loss of respondents and the sensitization of respondents who persist. Rolling cross-sections, in contrast, provide dynamic information without the undesirable sensitization of respondents. At each point in time, rolling cross-sections survey different but equivalent random subsamples of respondents, each subsample drawn randomly from the same overall sample. For that reason, each day's sample is roughly equivalent to all others, except that the respondents in each group represent experiences in different points in time. This makes the method ideal for demonstrating the effect of events isolated in time, while simultaneously providing extensive control over the effect of other variables.

This study employs a "stacked regression" analysis. We stacked individual data from each day and subjected it to linear regressions to determine whether the effects of the independent variables are significant. In stacked regressions, the error terms are calculated for each day, allowing all independent variables to be evaluated in terms of clustered individual error terms (Bertrand, Duflo, & Mullainathan, 2004). This is similar to using cross-sectional survey data each day to evaluate the significance of the independent variables, but has two advantages. First, the stacked cross-sectional data improve the power of the analysis, as there are more observations. This means we can have more confidence in the statistical significance of the estimates. Second, an increase in the number of observations and clustering data on the day of the observations makes it possible to obtain consistent and unbiased estimates with smaller standard errors—an important condition when one is interested in testing the directionality (as opposed to the magnitude) of the estimates. It should be noted that neither aggregating all data over time and performing regressions on it nor multiple regressions done each day or cluster of days yields the same results as the stacked regressions (e.g., compare with the analyses of Hardy & Scheufele, 2005).

Not only do stacked regressions provide a tool for testing the relationships between determinants of voting intention and attitudes toward the presidential candidates, but events can be coded in terms of the day they occurred (in our case with a one-day lag because people need time to become aware of the events) and then the impact of those events, given the control of all the other independent variables, can be tested. So, for example, on October 7, 2016 (day 20), the groping video of Republican presidential candidate Donald Trump was released; so from the subsequent day on, the impact of that event is considered to have been operating. However, before looking at event effects, we must control as many other variables as possible.

Major Determinants of Attitudes and Intention to Vote for the 2016 Presidential Candidates

The 2016 presidential election was historic in many ways. Trump had never run for public office, mostly eschewed traditional political advertising, and instead received massive news coverage for his prolific tweets. He also extensively employed social media-based advertising. Clinton was the first woman to be nominated by a major political party to run for president of the United States, and she used television advertising far more heavily than Trump did. From September 5 to Election Day, Clinton showed 198,689 ads at an estimated cost of $119.9 million. Trump showed 76,068 ads at an estimated cost of $66.3 million (Fowler, Ridout, & Franz, 2016). Clinton's advertising was much less focused on policy than most previous presidential advertising (Fowler et al., 2016). Only 30% of Clinton's television ads involved self-promotion, and only these ads focused on policy. Fully half of Clinton's ads attacked Trump, and 90% of these focused on Trump's character and fitness for office, with only 10% of the ads focused on policy. In contrast, 70% of Trump's ads were about policy and were "contrast" spots where he critiqued Clinton but also talked about his own policies (Fowler et al., 2016).

Another sea change from previous presidential campaigns was the hugely increased use of digital advertising, which includes both Web-based ads and social media ads. In 2016, it is estimated that $1 billion was spent on digital advertising. Although television advertising remained the 900-pound gorilla with $6 billion spent, the use of digital advertising grew 5000% from 2000 to 2016 (Fowler et al., 2016). The 2016 election, therefore, was the first where the second greatest expenditure was for digital advertising (Gebelhof, 2016; Kafka, 2016). The digital revolution not only influenced advertising expenditures, but for the first time, the same percentage of Americans used social media to obtain news about the presidential race as the percentage who used local TV, and more than the percentage who used network nightly news on TV (Mitchell, Gottfried, Barthel, & Shearer 2016). One third of 18- to 29-year-olds reported social media were most helpful to them for learning about the presidential race.

Given these extraordinary changes, it is important to revisit the impact of classic political variables on determining candidate attitudes and intent to vote for them. As in all studies of political processes, the fundamental impact of demographics must be controlled. A second critical variable is partisanship, always important, but likely of even greater impact in the 2016 race (Jessee, 2010). A third important variable is interest in the campaign and, closely related, interest in hard news about politics. We look at the role of knowledge, here measured in terms of three specific types of knowledge, and at the effects of political advertising awareness, critical because of the large difference between the two campaigns in the use of advertising. We test the effects of debates on attitudes about candidates and voting intention. Finally, we ask about the effects of the Trump groping event and the FBI announcement about reopening the e-mail case against Clinton.

Demographics

Demographics played a large role in 2016 voting, and this study includes demographics as controls for examining the role of theoretical variables. According to Edison Research exit poll data (Tyson & Maniam, 2016), white non-Hispanics voted for Trump (58%) over Clinton (37%). Blacks preferred

Clinton (88% to 8%). Women voted for Clinton (54% to 42%), and men preferred Trump (53% to 41%). College graduates preferred Clinton (52% to 43%). Those without a college education preferred Trump (52% to 44%). Those age 18 to 29 voted for Clinton (55% to 37%), whereas those 65 and older voted more strongly for Trump (57% to 45%). Statistician Nate Silver, the founder and editor of *FiveThirtyEight*, reported that education was the critical determinant of the presidential vote, not income (Silver, 2016b). High-education, medium-income counties voted for Clinton. High-income, medium-education counties preferred Trump. We expected, given our sample was representative of U.S. demographics, that the variables age, gender, education, income, and race would reflect these same general patterns.

Partisanship Effects

Partisanship and its influence on voters' attitudes and behavior have long been studied by scholars. Bartels (2000) showed increases in partisan-driven voting from 1972 to 1996. In fact, partisan voting in 1996 was 77% larger than that of 1972. Bartels (2002) further showed that partisan bias shapes and reinforces the public's perceptions of campaign events and political figures. Similarly, in their study of the 2000 U.S. election, Hillygus and Jackman (2003) concluded that partisanship played an important role in affecting voters' preferences toward candidates. Those studying political polarization argue that ordinary Americans are not as polarized as are a narrow political class of politicians, activists, pundits, and other assorted political enthusiasts (e.g., Fiorina, Abrams, & Pope, 2008).

However, other significant studies demonstrate that polarization is also marked in ordinary Americans who differentiate along party lines over many political issues and candidate preferences (Abramowitz & Saunders, 2008; Jacobson, 2012; Sunstein, 2009). Further, the more involved Americans are politically, the more polarized their attitudes and beliefs are (Abramowitz & Saunders, 2008). Finally, partisanship has been shown to be strongest for voters with low policy information, and it is strong even for voters with sophisticated policy information (Jessee, 2010), again demonstrating how important a variable partisanship is. Given the support for the dominant role of partisanship in voting and attitudes toward candidates, we predicted that:

H1: Partisanship will be highly predictive of candidate attitudes and voting intention, even when many strict controls for other variables are applied.

Political Interest in General and Interest in Political Campaigns

Strömbäck and Shehata (2010) point out that political interest is one of the most important predictors of voting (McLeod, Scheufele, & Moy, 1999), together with political knowledge (Delli Carpini & Keeter, 1997; Eveland & Scheufele, 2000), and civic and community participation (McLeod et al., 1999; Oskarson, 2007; Verba, Burns, & Schlozman, 1997). They quote Van Deth and Elff (2004, p. 478) as saying, "Without a minimum level of curiosity about politics, citizens would not even be aware of the political process or of opportunities to defend their well-being or contribute to collective decisions." Interest in the 2016 presidential election was unusually high. The Pew Research Center (2016) reported during the summer of 2016 that 74% of voters said it really mattered who won the election, higher than in any previous election. 85% of voters said they were following the news about the election very closely, higher than in 2012 (71%) and 2008 (81%). Republicans (77%) and Democrats (76%) both reported the same high level of interest. Based on this pattern of impact, we expect:

H2: After control for partisanship, political interest will positively predict voting intention for both Clinton and Trump.

Similarly, we expect that:

H3: After control for partisanship, higher political interest will predict greater liking for both Clinton and Trump.

Interest in Hard News

Those with interest in hard news are typically politically knowledgeable and are motivated to vote. But the impact of heavy news consumption depends on news content. The 2016 election was marked by extremely high candidate news negativity (Patterson, 2016). An extensive content analysis of coverage of the election from the second week of August 2016 through November 7, the day before the election—including all three networks, the three cable networks, *The New York Times*, *The Washington Post*, *Wall Street Journal*, *USA Today*, and the *Los Angeles Times*—showed that Clinton's campaign coverage was far more negative (64%) than positive (36%). Trump's coverage was even more negative (77%). Stories about the "fitness" for office for both candidates were 87% negative. The study also showed that since 1988 tone in presidential news coverage has been more negative than positive, with 2016 the second most negative election. Not only was a huge negativity bias operating in news coverage, but only 10% of the stories were about policy; 42% were horse-race framed, 17% were about controversies, and 24% were about "other" (Patterson, 2016).

Given the predominant negative tone about the candidates and the focus on the horse race and controversies, both of which are known to directly influence attitudes about candidates (Althaus & Kim, 2006), we expected that the more people consumed the news media, the more negative they would feel about both candidates and that this negativity would motivate them against voting for either of the two candidates:

H4: Greater interest in hard news about the campaign will have negative effects on attitudes toward Clinton and Trump, and on intention to vote for either of them.

Impact of Political Knowledge

Political knowledge is another important variable in that it provides an index of political sophistication (e.g., Delli Carpini & Keeter, 1997; Luskin, 1987; Neuman, 1986) as well as political awareness (Zaller, 1992). Delli Carpini and Keeter (1993) identified three kinds of political knowledge, including knowledge about candidate stances on issues, knowledge about how government and politics work in general (e.g., how many judges are there on the U.S. Supreme Court?, or in other words, "what government is and does"), and knowledge about news events that occur during an election. Examining the role of these types of content questions in the National Election Surveys (NES) led Delli Carpini and Keeter to conclude that these three types of knowledge were so highly intercorrelated that they could be appropriately combined. However, Thorson and Kim (2012) showed that there are different predictors of the three kinds of knowledge. Race and political interest predict government knowledge, race and gender predict issue stance knowledge, and gender and political interest predict knowledge of political news. This finding suggests that it may be important to look at the three types of political knowledge independently.

Other studies of political knowledge provide evidence that it affects attitudes toward candidates and that voters have less information about the candidate that they are not voting for (Gramberg & Holmberg, 1990). The "impression-driven model" of candidate evaluation (Lodge, McGraw, & Stroh, 1989; Lodge, Steenbergen, & Brau, 1995) suggests that the information and knowledge voters have are critical to their attitude toward candidates. As for political knowledge and voting intention, Kenski (2002) found that respondents with higher knowledge of candidates' issue positions and policy proposals showed a higher tendency to adhere firmly to a vote choice. Jessee (2010) suggested that the more political information and knowledge voters have, the less likely partisanship would influence their votes. However, he also noted that even among the most knowledgeable voters, partisanship remains influential. Given the variation in how different kinds of knowledge influence voting and candidate attitudes, we posited a research question:

R1: How will the three types of knowledge influence attitudes toward Clinton and Trump and voting intention for each of them?

The Influence of Advertising Awareness

Goldstein and Ridout (2004) suggested that little is known about how advertising influences attitudes toward candidates or voting for them, primarily because of the problem of measuring exposure to advertising (i.e., advertising awareness). The first challenge for measuring advertising awareness is the fact that people are poor at recalling specific information about media content they have viewed (e.g., Niemi, Katz, & Newman, 1980). Second, voting and paying attention to political messages are highly intercorrelated (e.g., Goldstein & Ridout, 2004). This correlation makes it difficult to distinguish whether intention to vote causes attention to political advertising or vice versa.

Although this study does not solve the problem of measuring advertising message exposure, it does bring some improved measurement features to it. First, instead of asking about exposure to a specific ad and the details of people's memory for it, we simply asked people "in the past week, how often have you seen any advertisements for any of the presidential candidates?" This more simplified question seems likely to make the task more feasible in spite of human memory limitations. Further, in a previous study of this data set (Thorson, Tham, Chen, & Kanuri, in press), we showed that the percentage of people in a geographic region (state) who indicated they had seen ads for Clinton or Trump in the previous week was significantly correlated with two objective indices of opportunities to have done so, that is, the number of ads that had been run in that state and the amount of money spent for political ads in that state. Although identifying ad numbers and expenditures by state and the self-report of advertising awareness by state are both subject to noise, their high correlation lends external validity to the measure of political advertising awareness employed here.

As noted earlier in this chapter, Clinton aired approximately three times more ads than Trump (Fowler et al., 2016). This creates a media landscape where the majority of the ads seen were likely for Clinton. Most of these ads focused on character judgment attacks as opposed to addressing policy (Fowler et al., 2016). In an environment with a great amount of negativity and similar themes of ads repeated, we anticipate that Clinton's ads would have different effects for those with different political stances. We believe that with the persistence of attack ads over time, there would be an increase in positive attitudes for Clinton supporters, whereas there would be a negative effect on attitudes toward Trump and intention to vote for him.

H5: Exposure to advertising, most likely to have been Clinton's, will have a positive effect on attitudes toward Clinton and an increase in voting intention for Clinton.

H6: Exposure to advertising, most likely to have been Clinton's, will have a negative effect on attitudes toward Trump and a decrease in voting intention for Trump.

The Effect of Debates

A main focus in the present study is to ask, when all relevant demographics and most of the usual culprits for determining attitudes toward candidates and intention to vote for them are controlled, are there measurable influences of major news events on the two dependent variables? Probably the kind of political event whose influence has been most commonly posited and tested are debates, which are "media events" that include the media hype before the debates and all the analyses of who won and why after them (e.g., Dayan & Katz, 1995; Tsfati, 2003). Although the research has focused on debate impact on political knowledge and interest (e.g., Holbrook, 1999) and on perceived salience of campaign issues (Swanson & Swanson, 1978), some of it focused on audiences' voting intentions and political attitudes (e.g., Pfau, 1987), as well as on perceptions of the candidates (e.g., Pfau & Kang, 1991). Although findings differ, there is little evidence that debate watching influences voting preference (Benoit, McKinney, & Holbert, 2001; Carlin & McKinney, 1994; McKinney & Carlin, 2004), except for the most unknowledgeable, uninterested citizens (e.g., Carlin & McKinney, 1994; Chaffee & Choe, 1980; McKinney & Carlin, 2004).

In asking whether there were debate effects on attitudes toward Clinton and Trump, and voting intentions for them, it is important to consider the specifics of these debates and the size of their audiences. The three presidential debates occurred on September 26, October 9, and October 19, 2016. The first and third debates had record-sized audiences (84 million viewers for debate one and 71.6 million viewers for debate three, compared to 59.2 million for the third debate in 2012). The second debate had a respectable 66.5 million viewers. Polls taken after the first debate showed a close tie between Clinton and Trump, with some polls (ABC/*The Washington Post*) saying Clinton won (46% to 41%) and others calling public opinion tied (CBS/*The New York Times* (42% to 42%). The same general pattern of public opinion held for the second debate. In the third debate, the polls showed stronger opinion for Clinton, winning by 13 points in a CNN/ORC poll (Agiesta, 2016). Given that in this study we are only looking at those who indicated they would vote for one of the two major-party candidates and not at independents or undecideds, we posed only one research question:

RQ2: Do debates affect attitudes toward Clinton and Trump and intent to vote for them?

Scandals

The 2016 election also involved two controversial and scandalous news stories, which were often argued by the popular press to have influenced the outcome of the election (Edkins, 2016). On October 7, the news broke of a 2005 *Access Hollywood* tape of Trump bragging about kissing, groping, and trying to have sex with women and saying "when you're a star, they let you do it" (Fahrenthold, 2016). On October 28, FBI director Comey announced a reopening of the Clinton e-mail case (Jacobs, Siddiqui, & Ackerman, 2016). Both of these events received inordinate news coverage, and many argued that either story might have destroyed the chances of the involved candidate (Edkins, 2016). Because of their extraordinarily high salience in the news media, this analysis examined their impact on attitudes toward the candidates and voting intention.

RQ3: What were the effects of the Trump groping video and FBI announcement about Clinton's e-mails on attitudes toward the candidates and intention to vote for them?

Method

A rolling cross-sectional data set was collected from a national Qualtrics panel. The survey focused on political behaviors and attitudes as well as advertising awareness over 49 days during the fall 2016 election (September 20 through November 7). Each day, approximately 100 respondents were randomly selected from a large Qualtrics sample and surveyed. The total number of respondents included 4,782 adults.

Measures

Self-reported advertising awareness was measured as a general question and by medium. The general question was a single item that asked "In the past week, how often did you see advertisements for Clinton or Trump?" This was measured on a 5-point scale: 1=never, 2=rarely, 3=occasionally, 4=fairly often, and 5=very often. If respondents indicated they had seen any advertising, they were then asked to indicate "Where did you see any advertisements?" Respondents were asked to check all the media in which they thought they had seen any political ads, including television, web sites, print news, Facebook, Twitter, and radio. Only television advertising awareness was used in this analysis because that measure had been supported by correlations with the number of ads and total advertising expenditures per state (Thorson et al., in press).

Partisanship affiliation was measured by the following item: "Which of the following best describes your party affiliation?" In the survey, this was measured with a 7-point scale: 1=strong Democrat, 2=Democrat, 3=Independent-leaning Democrat, 4=Independent, 5=Independent-leaning Republican, 6=Republican, and 7=strong Republican.

Interest in hard news ($r=.66$, $p<.01$) was measured by the following two items: "In general, how interested are you in politics and national government?" and "In general, how interested are you in news and current events?" This was measured with a 5-point scale: 1=not at all interested, 2=not very interested, 3=somewhat interested, 4=moderately interested, and 5=extremely interested.

Interest in political campaigns was measured with a single item: "In general, how interested are you in political campaigns and issues?" This was measured with a 5-point scale: 1=not at all interested, 2=not very interested, 3=somewhat interested, 4=moderately interested, and 5=extremely interested.

Political knowledge/civic was measured with an index of three multiple choice questions: "The practice in the Senate of debating a bill indefinitely to prevent it from being passed is known as . . ." "Whose responsibility is it to determine if a law is constitutional or not?" and "How much of a majority is required for the U.S. Senate and House to override a presidential veto?"

Political knowledge/candidate was measured with an index of three multiple choice questions. They were "Which candidate favors increasing the federal minimum wage?" "Donald Trump has stated that the United States should limit the entry of which group into the country?" and "Which of these jobs has Hillary Clinton held?"

Political knowledge/current events was measured by an index of four multiple choice questions. Eight sets of questions were asked over the course of the 49 days. Each set featured a question about Trump, Clinton, a national event, and an international event. The questions were changed every six days in order to equalize the relative recency of the questions.

Attitude/Clinton was measured by an index of four items. The questions were "Hillary Clinton: In the past week, how often has each of these people or groups or ideas made you feel?" For each question, an adjective was used at the end to describe the individual, and the four adjectives used were "inspired," "enthusiastic," "worried" (reverse coded), and "angry" (reverse coded). These were measured on a scale of 1=never, 2=rarely, 3=occasionally, 4=fairly often, and 5=very often.

Attitude/Trump was measured by an index of four items. The questions were "Donald Trump: In the past week, how often has each of these people or groups or ideas made you feel?" For each question, an adjective was used at the end to describe the individual, and the four adjectives used were "inspired," "enthusiastic," "worried" (reverse coded), and "angry" (reverse coded). These were measured on a scale of 1=never, 2=rarely, 3=occasionally, 4=fairly often, and 5=very often.

Respondents also answered demographic questions. Age ranged from 18 to 89. Gender was coded 1 for females and 0 for males; 68.3% of the respondents were female. The categories for race were white (74.0%), black, (11.4%), Asian (2.8%), Hispanic (9.8%), and other (2.0%). The distribution for education was high school or less (38.0%), some college (20.0%), an associate's degree

(8.2%), a college degree (20.9%), and a masters' degree and above (12.9%). The distribution of income was less than $25,000 (17.8%), from $25,000 to $49,999 (22.1%), from $50,000 to $74,999 (18.6%), from $75,000 to $99,999 (18.6%), and more than $100,000 (22.8%).

Results

Table 3.1 shows the stacked regression results in a binomial logistic analysis (0=Clinton, 1=Trump). Event represents the three debates and two scandal events identified in the columns. The regressions in Table 3.1 were also run with the addition of Attitude/Trump and Attitude/Clinton to test whether candidate attitudes would mediate any of the other independent variables. Due to space constraints, that table is not shown. Note that all independents and those voting for a third-party candidate are excluded from the analysis. Tables 3.2 and 3.3 show stacked regression analyses predicting attitudes toward Clinton and Trump.

As can be seen, there are significant effects of demographics, and they are all consistent with reported voting outcomes. In Table 3.1, older people, less educated people, males, and none of the minorities (black, Hispanic, and Asians) voted for Trump. After Attitude/Trump and Attitude/Clinton were added, the effects of gender, being Asian, and being Hispanic disappeared, suggesting they were mediated by attitudes toward the two candidates.

Table 3.2 (Attitude/Clinton) shows that being older; more educated; and black, Asian, and Hispanic all predicted more positive attitudes toward Clinton.

Table 3.3 (Attitude/Trump) shows that being younger, less educated, being male, and not black or Hispanic predicted a more positive attitude toward Trump.

H1 predicted the major impact of partisanship on attitudes and intent to vote even after controls were included. Partisanship is strongly significant in Table 3.1, with Republicans intending to vote for Trump. This effect remains significant when Attitude/Trump and Attitude/Clinton are added, consistent with the hypothesis.

H2 suggested that higher campaign interest would positively predict voting intention for both Clinton and Trump. This was incorrect, in that campaign interest inclined people to vote for Trump. As expected, being Republican predicted a more negative attitude toward Clinton and a more positive attitude toward Trump.

H3 suggested that higher campaign interest would predict greater liking for Clinton and Trump. Inconsistent with the hypothesis, campaign interest increased liking for Clinton and reduced liking for Trump.

H4 suggested that greater interest in hard news about the campaign would have negative effects on attitudes toward and intention to vote for both Clinton and Trump. Hard news interest predicted not voting for Trump (see Table 3.1), and therefore the hypothesis was only partially supported. However, hard news interest had negative effects on both Attitude/Trump and Attitude/Clinton. This finding strongly supports Patterson's (2016) claim that the extraordinary negativity of news coverage of the two candidates seriously damaged attitudes toward them, even though people nonetheless go ahead and vote consistent with their partisanship. More will be said about this effect in the discussion.

RQ1 asked how the three types of knowledge would influence attitudes toward Clinton and Trump and voting intention for each of them. All three types of knowledge predicted not voting for Trump. The only instance where the variable failed to be significant was in the Trump groping regression, where civic knowledge was no longer significant. When Attitude/Trump and Attitude/Clinton were added to the regressions, only candidate knowledge remained significant, and it predicted not voting for Trump. It is likely that civic knowledge and current events knowledge were mediated by their effects on Attitude/Trump and Attitude/Clinton. Interestingly, civic knowledge made attitudes toward Clinton more negative, but both candidate knowledge and current events knowledge made attitudes toward Clinton more positive. Even more interesting, all three types of knowledge had negative effects on attitudes toward Trump. The differential effects of the three types of knowledge support the value of disaggregating them from a unidimensional measure of knowledge.

H5 suggested that advertising awareness would have a positive effect on attitudes toward Clinton and increase voting intention for her. H6 suggested that exposure to advertising would have a negative effect on attitudes toward Trump and decrease voting intention for him. Contrary to the hypothesis, advertising awareness was not a significant predictor of voting for Trump or Clinton in either the main regressions or where Attitude/Trump and Attitude/Clinton were added.

RQ2 asked whether the debates would affect attitudes toward Clinton and Trump and intent to vote for them. As can be seen in Table 3.1, none of the debates had a significant effect on voting intention. This was also true in the equations where Attitude/Trump and Attitude/Clinton were added. The pattern is much different, however, for attitude effects. Debate 2 had a negative effect on attitudes toward Clinton, whereas the other two had no effect. Debates 1 and 2 had a negative effect on attitudes toward Trump, whereas Debate 3 was not significant.

RQ3 asked whether the Trump groping video and the FBI announcement about Clinton's e-mails would affect attitudes toward Clinton and Trump and intent to vote for them. Neither of the events predicted voting intention, regardless if Attitude/Trump and Attitude/Clinton were added. As might be expected, the Trump groping effect had no effect on attitudes toward Clinton but a large negative on attitudes toward Trump. Analogously, the FBI announcement had a large negative effect on attitudes toward Clinton, but no effect on attitudes toward Trump.

Table 3.1 Predictors of Voting Preference for Each of the Debates and Scandal Events

Predictors	Debate #1	Trump Groping	Debate #2	Debate #3	FBI Announcement
Event	−0.16	−0.04	0.02	0.02	0.10
	(0.11)	(0.09)	(0.09)	(0.09)	(0.10)
Age	0.02***	0.02***	0.02***	0.02***	0.02***
	(0.00)	(0.00)	(0.00)	(0.00)	(0.00)
Education	−0.21***	−0.21***	−0.20***	−0.21***	−0.20***
	(0.04)	(0.04)	(0.04)	(0.04)	(0.04)
Income	0.01	0.01	0.01	0.01	0.01
	(0.06)	(0.06)	(0.06)	(0.06)	(0.06)
Female	−0.25**	−0.25**	−0.25**	−0.25**	−0.25**
	(0.10)	(0.10)	(0.10)	(0.10)	(0.10)
Black	−1.69***	−1.69***	−1.68***	−1.68***	−1.68***
	(0.23)	(0.23)	(0.23)	(0.23)	(0.23)
Asian	−0.97***	−0.98***	−0.98***	−0.98***	−0.98***
	(0.30)	(0.30)	(0.30)	(0.30)	(0.30)
Hispanic	−0.63***	−0.62***	−0.62***	−0.62***	−0.62***
	(0.18)	(0.18)	(0.18)	(0.18)	(0.18)

	Model 1	Model 2	Model 3	Model 4
Hard News Interest	-0.18*	-0.18*	-0.18*	-0.18*
	(0.09)	(0.09)	(0.09)	(0.09)
Campaign Interest	0.23***	0.23***	0.23***	0.23***
	(0.07)	(0.07)	(0.07)	(0.07)
Partisanship	1.35***	1.35***	1.35***	1.35***
	(0.04)	(0.04)	(0.04)	(0.04)
Civic Knowledge	-0.11*	-0.11	-0.11*	-0.12*
	(0.06)	(0.07)	(0.07)	(0.07)
Candidate Knowledge	-0.62***	-0.62***	-0.63***	-0.63***
	(0.08)	(0.08)	(0.08)	(0.08)
Current Events Knowledge	-0.10**	-0.10**	-0.09**	-0.08
	(0.05)	(0.05)	(0.05)	(0.05)
Advertising Awareness	0.05	0.05	0.05	0.05
	(0.05)	(0.05)	(0.05)	(0.05)
Observations	3972	3972	3972	3972
Wald chi^2 (15)	1174.76	1174.76	1174.76	1174.76
Pseudo R^2	0.56	0.56	0.56	0.56
Log pseudo-Likelihood	-1160.56	-1160.56	-1160.56	-1160.56

$*p<.10, **p<.05, ***p<.01$

75

Table 3.2 Predictors of Attitude Toward Clinton for Each of the Debates and Scandal Events

Predictors	Debate #1	Trump Groping	Debate #2	Debate #3	FBI Announcement
Event	0.00	−0.04	−0.05*	−0.01	−0.06*
	(0.04)	(0.03)	(0.03)	(0.03)	(0.03)
Age	0.00***	0.00***	0.00***	0.00***	0.00***
	(0.00)	(0.00)	(0.00)	(0.00)	(0.00)
Education	0.04***	0.04***	0.04***	0.04***	0.04***
	(0.01)	(0.01)	(0.01)	(0.01)	(0.01)
Income	−0.01	−0.01	−0.01	−0.01	−0.01
	(0.01)	(0.01)	(0.01)	(0.01)	(0.01)
Female	−0.02	−0.02	−0.02	−0.02	−0.02
	(0.03)	(0.03)	(0.03)	(0.03)	(0.03)
Black	0.33***	0.33***	0.33***	0.33***	0.33***
	(0.04)	(0.04)	(0.04)	(0.04)	(0.04)
Asian	0.17**	0.17**	0.17**	0.17**	0.17**
	(0.08)	(0.08)	(0.08)	(0.08)	(0.08)
Hispanic	0.11**	0.11**	0.11**	0.11**	0.11**
	(0.05)	(0.05)	(0.05)	(0.05)	(0.05)

Hard News Interest	-0.05**	-0.05**	-0.05**	-0.05**	-0.05**
	(0.02)	(0.02)	(0.02)	(0.02)	(0.02)
Campaign Interest	0.10***	0.10***	0.10***	0.10***	0.10***
	(0.02)	(0.02)	(0.02)	(0.02)	(0.02)
Partisanship	-0.43***	-0.43***	-0.43***	-0.43***	-0.43***
	(0.01)	(0.01)	(0.01)	(0.01)	(0.01)
Civic Knowledge	-0.12***	-0.12***	-0.12***	-0.12***	-0.11***
	(0.02)	(0.02)	(0.02)	(0.02)	(0.02)
Candidate Knowledge	0.10***	0.10***	0.10***	0.10***	0.10***
	(0.02)	(0.02)	(0.02)	(0.02)	(0.02)
Current Events Knowledge	0.03***	0.03***	0.03***	0.03***	0.03***
	(0.01)	(0.01)	(0.01)	(0.01)	(0.01)
Advertising Awareness	0.02	0.02*	0.02*	0.02	0.02*
	(0.01)	(0.01)	(0.01)	(0.01)	(0.01)
Observations	4782	4782	4782	4782	4782
Wald chi^2 (15)	8536.79	8501.52	8489.25	8721.65	8304.74
Log pseudo-Likelihood	-6103.26	-6102.22	-6101.55	-6102.22	-6101.79

$*p<.10, **p<.05, ***p<.01$

Table 3.3 Predictors of Attitude toward Trump for Each of the Allegations or Presidential Debate

Predictors	Debate #1	Trump Groping	Debate #2	Debate #3	FBI Announcement
Event	−0.11*	−0.11***	−0.08**	0.00	0.05
	(0.04)	(0.04)	(0.04)	(0.04)	(0.04)
Age	0.01***	0.01***	0.01***	0.01***	0.01***
	(0.00)	(0.00)	(0.00)	(0.00)	(0.00)
Education	−0.05***	−0.05***	−0.05***	−0.05***	−0.05***
	(0.01)	(0.01)	(0.01)	(0.01)	(0.01)
Income	0.01	0.01	0.01	0.01	0.01
	(0.01)	(0.01)	(0.01)	(0.01)	(0.01)
Female	−0.25***	−0.26***	−0.26***	−0.25***	−0.25***
	(0.03)	(0.03)	(0.03)	(0.03)	(0.03)
Black	−0.12***	−0.12***	−0.12***	−0.12***	−0.12***
	(0.04)	(0.04)	(0.04)	(0.04)	(0.04)
Asian	0.04	0.03	0.03	0.04	0.04
	(0.10)	(0.09)	(0.09)	(0.10)	(0.10)
Hispanic	−0.13***	−0.13***	−0.13***	−0.13***	−0.13***
	(0.05)	(0.05)	(0.05)	(0.05)	(0.05)

Hard News Interest	-0.05**	-0.05**	-0.05**	-0.05**	-0.05**
	(0.02)	(0.02)	(0.02)	(0.02)	(0.02)
Campaign Interest	0.19***	0.19***	0.19***	0.19***	0.19***
	(0.02)	(0.02)	(0.02)	(0.02)	(0.02)
Partisanship	0.36***	0.36***	0.36***	0.36***	0.36***
	(0.01)	(0.01)	(0.01)	(0.01)	(0.01)
Civic Knowledge	-0.15***	-0.15***	-0.15***	-0.15***	-0.16***
	(0.02)	(0.02)	(0.02)	(0.02)	(0.02)
Candidate Knowledge	-0.16***	-0.16***	-0.16***	-0.16***	-0.17***
	(0.02)	(0.02)	(0.02)	(0.02)	(0.02)
Current Events Knowledge	-0.06***	-0.07***	-0.07***	-0.06***	-0.05***
	(0.02)	(0.02)	(0.02)	(0.02)	(0.02)
Advertising Awareness	0.00	0.00	0.00	0.00	0.00
	(0.01)	(0.01)	(0.01)	(0.01)	(0.01)
Observations	4782	4782	4782	4782	4782
Wald chi² (15)	5753.68	5262.51	5359.79	5420.26	5416.15
Log pseudo-Likelihood	-6539.38	-6536.31	-6539.49	-6543.09	-6542.12

*p<.10, **p<.05, ***p<.01

Discussion

The study shows some surprising outcomes. First, for those who claim that Comey lost the election for Clinton, there is mixed evidence. The FBI announcement did have a significant negative effect on attitudes toward Clinton, and although Clinton attitude was a significant predictor of voting for her and not voting for Trump, there was not a direct negative effect of reducing Clinton voting intent. Although this study did not include a technical analysis of the mediation effects of candidate attitude, it seems likely that the effect of the announcement was mediated onto voting intention by the reduced positive attitude toward Clinton. When interpreting this result, it must be kept in mind that the analysis did not include independents or those who intended to vote for third-party candidates. Once this group is analyzed, it may be that the real damage to intention to vote for Clinton occurred for them. For those who intended to vote for her and for those who intended to vote for Trump, there was no direct effect.

The same general pattern can be seen for the Trump groping video. There was a highly significant negative effect on attitudes toward Trump, and that negativity was mediated through indirect effects on intent to vote, but there was no direct negative effect on voting intent.

The debate effects also showed this pattern. Debate 2 had a negative effect on attitudes toward Clinton, but as we saw, the popular press generally reported that both Debates 1 and 2 were not dominated by either candidate. Only Debate 3 was generally thought to have been "won" by Clinton. Nevertheless, Debates 1 and 2 both had significant negative effects on attitudes toward Trump, with no effect of Debate 3. Again, none of the debates had a direct effect on voting intent. It should be kept in mind that attitudes toward Clinton and Trump involved respondents of both major political parties. This could mean, then, that Democrats who saw Trump in the debates were quite negatively affected, but that Republicans were not thus affected.

The same could be true of the differential effects on all events on Republicans being exposed to them. If a Democrat likes Trump less after a debate or after the groping tape, this will make no difference to voting intent because that Democrat is not intending to vote for Trump anyway. Still, there was a lot of talk about Republicans voting for Clinton simply because they found Trump unacceptable, but the actuality of this having happened with any frequency is considered unlikely (Feldman & Herrmann, 2016), with exit polls reporting that 87% of Republicans voted for Trump.

What is most interesting about the event-based results is that the Trump groping tape and the FBI announcement had just as large an effect as any of the three debates. As controversial and sometimes scandalous news almost instantaneously reverberates through the news echo chamber, it will be increasingly important to establish just how big the impact is on voting. For example, it was suggested (Keating, 2017) in the third week of April 2017 that the French election outcome was significantly influenced by the terrorist bombing on the Champs-Élysées just a few days before the election. Rolling cross-sectional data analyzed as here, analyzed with stacked regressions can help answer that question. And the answer is particularly compelling, given that so many other potentially confounding variables are controlled out when the event's effects are measured.

The bottom line is that the debates, the groping tape, and the FBI announcement did have effects on candidate attitudes, and their effects on voting intent were likely mediated through candidate attitude effects. Further analyses will determine what the impact was on independents.

Nearly as interesting as the results about news event effects is the finding that interest in hard news had consistent negative effects on attitudes toward both candidates and on intention to vote for either of them. This is exactly the kind of demobilizing and alienating effect that Patterson (2016) has long argued to be the net result of the increasing negativity of news story tone about politics, candidates, and elections. Indeed, the degree of negativity in news about both candidates, although part of an ongoing trend, was of significant magnitude to lead to a major critique of news performance (Patterson, 2016). Our results demonstrate clearly the damage to both candidate attitudes and voting intention. Again, it will be important to examine the effect of attention to hard news on independents.

Third, the past 20 years have seen consensus that "political knowledge" is appropriately measured as unidimensional even though knowledge questions vary in terms of what kind of political information they index. Here, civic knowledge, candidate knowledge, and current events knowledge produced important and distinct impacts on attitudes toward candidates and intent to vote. This suggests the unidimensionality of political knowledge should be revisited and challenged.

In 2016 the effectiveness of political television advertising was challenged by those arguing for more use of social media and digitally based advertising, as well as by Trump's win in spite of using drastically less television advertising than Clinton (see Thorson et al., in press). Advertising awareness did show significant positive impact on attitudes toward Clinton, but no effects on attitudes toward Trump, which is surprising given how 70% of Clinton's ads attacked Trump. There were no direct effects of advertising awareness on voting intent for either candidate. Again, advertising may have its major effect on the independents and undecideds, which remains to be tested, but given how much money Clinton invested in television, its effects were quite muted in the present results.

The use of rolling cross-sectional data and the stacked regressions analysis applied to the results are promising. Not only did the method allow identification of the operation of variables known to be important to candidate attitude and intent to vote, but it also allowed sensitive measurement of the effects of events. Interestingly, the events showed a small and occasional effect on the impact of other variables, suggesting interactions that are beyond the scope of the present study to analyze further. For example, both the impact of civic knowledge and current events knowledge changed as a function of which event was entered into the regressions (see Table 3.1). The interaction of event effects with characteristics of individuals (i.e., demographics, partisanships, knowledge, etc.) has not been possible to identify without the longitudinal measurement involved in rolling cross-sections.

As with all studies, there are caveats. First, the impacts on independents and those intending to vote for third-party candidates were not included, and the results may look very different for them. Second, exploration of mediating effects, which are suggested but not specifically demonstrated, was beyond the scope of this chapter. The mediational relationships will be important to explore.

References

Abramowitz, A. I., & Saunders, K. L. (2008). Is polarization a myth? *The Journal of Politics, 70*(2), 542–555. Retrieved from www.jstor.org/stable/10.1017/s0022381608080493

Agiesta, J. (2016). Hillary Clinton wins third presidential debate, according to CNN/ORC poll. CNN. Retrieved from http://www.cnn.com/2016/10/19/politics/hillary-clinton-wins-third-presidential-debate-according-to-cnn-orc-poll/index.html

Althaus, S. L., & Kim, Y. M. (2006). Priming effects in complex information environments: Reassessing the impact of news discourse on presidential approval. *Journal of Politics, 68*(4), 960–976. doi: 10.1111/j.1468-2508.2006.00481

Anderson, B. (2005). The value of mixed-method longitudinal panel studies in ICT research: Transitions in and out of "ICT poverty" as a case in point. *Information, Community & Society, 8*(3), 343–367. doi: 10.1080/13691180500259160

Appuzo, M., Schmidt, M., Goldman, A., & Lichtlaw, E. (2017, April 22). Comey tried to shield the FBI from politics. Then he shaped an election. *The New York Times.* Retrieved from https://www.nytimes.com/2017/04/22/us/politics/james-comey-election.html?_r=0

Bartels, L. M. (1988). *Presidential primaries and the dynamics of public choice.* Princeton, NJ: Princeton University Press.

Bartels, L. M. (2000). Partisanship and voting behavior, 1952–1996. *American Journal of Political Science, 44*(1), 35–50.

Bartels, L. M. (2002). Beyond the running tally: Partisan bias in political perceptions. *Political Behavior, 24*(2), 117–150. Retrieved from https://www.jstor.org/stable/2669291

Benoit, W. L., McKinney, M. S., & Lance Holbert, R. (2001). Beyond learning and persona: Extending the scope of presidential debate effects. *Communication Monographs, 68*(3), 259–273. doi: 10.1080/03637750128060

Bertrand, M., Duflo, E., & Mullainathan, S. (2004). How much should we trust differences-in-differences estimates? *The Quarterly Journal of Economics, 119*(1): 249–275. doi: 10.3386/w8841

Brady, H. E., & Johnston, R. (1987). What's the primary message: Horse race or issue journalism? In G. R. Orren & N. W. Polsby (Eds.), *Media and momentum: The New Hampshire Primary and nomination politics* (pp. 127–86). Chatham, NJ: Chatham House.

Campbell, D. T., & Stanley, J. C. (1971). *Experimental and quasi-experimental designs for research* (vol. 4). Skokie, IL: Rand McNally.

Carlin, D. B., & McKinney, M. S. (1994). *The 1992 presidential debates in focus.* Westport, CT: Praeger Publishers.

Chaffee, S. H., & Choe, S. Y. (1980). Time of decision and media use during the Ford-Carter campaign. *Public Opinion Quarterly, 44*(1), 53–69. doi: 10.1086/268566

Dayan, D., & Katz, E. (1995). Political ceremony and instant history. In A. Smith (Ed.), *Television: An international history* (pp. 169–88). Oxford, UK: Oxford University Press.

Delli Carpini, M. X., & Keeter, S. (1993). Measuring political knowledge: Putting first things first. *American Journal of Political Science,* 1179–1206. Retrieved from https://www.jstor.org/stable/2111549

Delli Carpini, M. X., & Keeter, S. (1997). *What Americans know about politics and why it matters.* New Haven, CT: Yale University Press.

Delli Carpini, M. X., & Keeter, S. (2000). What should be learned through service learning? *Political Science & Politics, 33*(3), 635–638.

Eveland, W. P., Jr., & Scheufele, D. A. (2000). Connecting news media use with gaps in knowledge and participation. *Political Communication, 17*(3), 215–237. doi: 10.1080/105846000414250

Edkins, B. (2016, December 13). Study: Trump benefited from overwhelmingly negative tone of election news coverage. *Forbes.* Retrieved from https://www.forbes.com/sites/brettedkins/2016/12/13/trump-benefited-from-overwhelmingly-negative-tone-of-election-news-coverage-study-finds/#33a73e9f3202.

Fahrenthold, D. (2016, October 8). Trump recorded having extremely lewd conversation about women in 2005. *The Washington Post.* Retrieved from https://www.washingtonpost.com/politics/trump-recorded-having-extremely-lewd-conversation-about-women-in-2005/2016/10/07/3b9ce776-8cb4-11e6-bf8a-3d26847eeed4_story.html?utm_term=.fa950a0cf116.

Feldman, S., & Herrmann, M. (2016, November 9). CBS News exit polls: How Donald Trump won the U.S. presidency. *CBS News.* Retrieved from http://www.cbsnews.com/news/cbs-news-exit-polls-how-donald-trump-won-the-us-presidency.

Fiorina, M. P., Abrams, S. A., & Pope, J. C. (2008). Polarization in the American public: Misconceptions and misreadings. *The Journal of Politics, 70*(2), 556–560. Retrieved from www.jstor.org/stable/10.1017/s00223816080 8050x

Fowler, E. F., Ridout, T. N., & Franz, M. M. (2016). Political advertising in 2016: The presidential election as an outlier? *The Forum, 14*(4), 445–469. doi: 10.1515/for-2016-0040

Gebelhoff, R. (2016, August 8). How will the Internet change political advertising? *The Washington Post.* Retrieved from https://www.washingtonpost.com /news/in-theory/wp/2016/08/08/how-will-the-internet-change-political -advertising/?utm_term=.1c6f4db11948.

Goldstein, K., & Ridout, T. N. (2004). Measuring the effects of televised political advertising in the United States. *Annual Review of Political Science, 7*, 205–226. doi: 10.1146/annurev.polisci.7.012003.104820

Gramberg, D., & Holmberg, S. (1990). The Berrelson paradox reconsidered: Intention-behavior changes in U.S. and Swedish election campaigns. *Public Opinion Quarterly, 54*(4), 530–550. doi: 10.1086/269226

Hardy, B. W., & Scheufele, D. A. (2005). Examining differential gains from Internet use: Comparing the moderating role of talk and online interactions. *Journal of Communication, 55*(1), 71–84. doi: 10.1111/j.1460-2466.2005.tb02659.x

Hillygus, D. S., & Jackman, S. (2003). Voter decision making in election 2000: Campaign effects, partisan activation, and the Clinton legacy. *American Journal of Political Science, 47*(4), 583–596. doi: 10.1111/1540-5907.00041

Holbrook, T. M., & DeSart, J. A. (1999). Using state polls to forecast presidential election outcomes in the American states. *International Journal of Forecasting, 15*(2), 137-142. doi: 10.1016/S0169-2070(98)00060-0

Jacobs, B., Siddiqui, S., & Ackerman, S. (2016, October 28). Newly discovered emails relating to Hillary Clinton case under review by FBI. *The Guardian.* Retrieved from https://www.theguardian.com/us-news/2016/oct/28 /fbi-reopens-hillary-clinton-emails-investigation

Jacobson, G. C. (2012). The electoral origins of polarized politics: Evidence from the 2010 cooperative congressional election study. *American Behavioral Scientist, 56*(12), 1612–1630. doi: 10.1177/0002764212463352

Jessee, S. A. (2010). Partisan bias, political information and spatial voting in the 2008 presidential election. *The Journal of Politics, 72*(2), 327–340. doi: 10.1017/S0022381609990764

Kafka, P. (2016, April 7). 2016: The year election ads finally come to the Internet. *Recode.* Retrieved from https://www.recode.net/2016/4/7/11585922/face book-google-political-campaign-ads.

Keating, J. (2017, April 21). Do terrorist attacks actually impact election results? *Slate.* Retrieved from http://www.slate.com/blogs/the_slatest/2017/04/21 /do_terrorist_attacks_actually_impact_election_results.html.

Kenski, K. M. (2002, August). *Gender, knowledge, and time of voting decision: An examination of decision certainty during the 2000 presidential campaign.* Paper presented at the annual meeting of the American Political Science Association, Boston, MA.

Lodge, M., McGraw, K. M., & Stroh, P. (1989). An impression-driven model of candidate evaluation. *American Political Science Review, 83*(02), 399–419. Retrieved from https://www.jstor.org/stable/1962397

Lodge, M., Steenbergen, M. R., & Brau, S. (1995). The responsive voter: Campaign information and the dynamics of candidate evaluation. *American Political Science Review, 89*(02), 309–326. Retrieved from https://www.jstor.org/stable/2082427

Luskin, R. C. (1987). Measuring political sophistication. *American Journal of Political Science, 31*(4), 856–899. Retrieved from www.jstor.org/stable/2111227

McKinney, M. S., & Carlin, D. B. (2004). Political campaign debates. In L. L. Kaid (Ed.), *Handbook of political communication research* (pp. 203–234). Mahwah, NJ: Lawrence Erlbaum.

McLeod, J. M., Scheufele, D. A., & Moy, P. (1999). Community, communication, and participation: The role of mass media and interpersonal discussion in local political participation. *Political Communication, 16*(3), 315–336. doi: 10.1080/105846099198659

Mitchell, A., Gottfried, J., Barthel, M., & Shearer, E. (2016, July 7). The modern news consumer. *Pew Research Center.* Retrieved from http://www.journalism.org/2016/07/07/the-modern-news-consumer.

Neuman, W. R. (1986). *The paradox of mass politics: Knowledge and opinion in the American electorate.* Cambridge, MA: Harvard University Press.

Niemi, R. G., Katz, R. S., & Newman, D. (1980). Reconstructing past partisanship: The failure of the party identification recall questions. *American Journal of Political Science, 24*(4), 633–651. Retrieved from https://www.jstor.org/stable/2110951

Oskarson, M. (2007). Social risk, policy dissatisfaction, and political alienation. In S. Svallfors (Ed.), *The political sociology of the welfare state: Institutions, social cleavages, and orientations* (pp. 117–148). Redwood City, CA: Stanford University Press.

Patterson, T. (2016, December 7). News coverage of the 2016 general election: How the press failed the voters. *Shorenstein Center on Media, Politics, and Public Policy.* Retrieved from https://shorensteincenter.org/news-coverage-2016-general-election/?platform=hootsuite#Trumps_Coverage.

Pew Research Center. (2016, July 17). Campaign engagement and interest. Retrieved from http://www.people-press.org/2016/07/07/1-campaign-engagement-and-interest.

Pfau, M. (1987). The influence of intraparty political debates on candidate preference. *Communication Research, 14*(6), 687–697. doi: 10.1177/009365087014006004

Pfau, M., & Rang, J. G. (1991). The impact of relational messages on candidate influence in televised political debates. *Communication Studies, 42*(2), 114–128. doi:10.1080/10510979109368327

Romer, D., Kenski, K., Winneg, K., Adasiewicz, C., & Jamieson, K. H. (2006). *Capturing campaign dynamics, 2000 and 2004: The National Annenberg Election Survey.* Philadelphia: University of Pennsylvania Press.

Silver, N. (2016a, November 6). How much did Comey hurt Clinton's chances? *FiveThirtyEight.* Retrieved from https://fivethirtyeight.com/features/how-much-did-comey-hurt-clintons-chances

Silver, N. (2016b, November 22). Education, not income, predicted who would vote for Trump. *FiveThirtyEight.* Retrieved from http://fivethirtyeight.com/features/education-not-income-predicted-who-would-vote-for-trump

Strömbäck, J., & Shehata, A. (2010). Media malaise or a virtuous circle? Exploring the causal relationships between news media exposure, political news attention and political interest. *European Journal of Political Research, 49*(5), 575–597. doi: 10.1111/j.1475-6765.2009.01913

Sunstein, C. R. (2009). *Going to extremes: How like minds unite and divide.* Oxford, UK: Oxford University Press.

Swanson, L. L., & Swanson, D. L. (1978). The agenda setting function of the first Ford-Carter debate. *Communication Monographs, 45*(4): 347–353. doi: 10.1080/03637757809375979

Thorson, E., & Kim, S. (2012, May). *Measurement of political knowledge in American adolescents.* Paper presented at the annual meeting of the International Communication Association, Phoenix, AZ.

Thorson, E., Tham, S. M., Chen, W., & Kanuri, V. (in press). Awareness of presidential candidate advertising during 56 days of the 2016 presidential race. *The Journal of Current Issues and Research in Advertising.*

Tsfati, Y. (2003). Does audience skepticism of the media matter in agenda setting? *Journal of Broadcasting & Electronic Media, 47*(2), 157–176. doi: 10.1207/s15506878jobem4702_1

Tyson, A., & Maniam, S. (2016, November 9). Behind Trump's victory: Divisions by race, gender, education. *Pew Research Center.* Retrieved from http://www.pewresearch.org/fact-tank/2016/11/09/behind-trumps-victory-divisions-by-race-gender-education.

Van Deth, J. W., & Elff, M. (2004). Politicization, economic development and political interest in Europe. *European Journal of Political Research, 43*(3), 477–508. doi: 10.1111/j.1475-6765.2004.00162

Verba, S., Burns, N., & Schlozman, K. L. (1997). Knowing and caring about politics: Gender and political engagement. *The Journal of Politics, 59*(4), 1051–1072. Retrieved from https://www.jstor.org/stable/2998592

With these hands. (2016, October 13). *The Economist.* Retrieved from http://www.economist.com/news/briefing/21708704-republican-nominee-has-violated-his-party-and-america-these-hands

Zaller, J. 1992. *The nature and origins of mass public opinion.* New York: Cambridge University Press.

CHAPTER FOUR

The Rhetoric of Impossible Expectations: Media Coverage of Hillary Clinton's 2016 General Election Campaign

Kristina Horn Sheeler

On Tuesday, July 26, 2016, Hillary Clinton became the first woman nominated by a major political party for the office of president of the United States. On Wednesday, July 27, newspapers around the country hailed this "first" with headlines championing the milestone alongside a compelling series of visuals that included former President Bill Clinton, primary challenger Bernie Sanders, and exuberant Clinton supporters. Missing in the imagery were pictures of Clinton herself. Compound this with narratives that questioned everything from Clinton's trustworthiness to her overabundance of policy knowledge during a campaign when such knowledge was not valued, and we have evidence of an even stronger prohibition against female presidentiality than some argued existed in 2008. This chapter will assess the dominant media frames that evolved over the course of Clinton's general election campaign in 2016, noting the pernicious backlash that still exists against women's political authority.

Talk about politics and political campaigns matters (Hart, 2000). The prevailing storylines through which political candidates are presented in the news are well documented; everything from sporting events to battles and even romance guide our understanding of how to view, understand, and partici-pate in political campaigns (Entman, 1993; Hahn, 2003; Patterson, 1993). Whereas framing the campaign as a game or battle with winners and losers positions voters as spectators, the romance frame aligns the candidate as the masculine suitor who "woos" the citizenry (Hahn, 2003; Jamieson, 1992). When female candidates enter the campaign, post-feminist narratives convey that women are capable of running for president, and failures are the result of mistakes on the campaign trail rather than any lingering remnant of sex-ism (Dow, 1996; Sheeler & Anderson, 2013; Vavrus, 2002).

Alongside post-feminism, anti-feminism tells us that women are tempera-mentally unfit for presidential office (Sheeler & Anderson, 2013). Often called out for its overt sexism, anti-feminism was a potent force fueling opposition against Clinton in 2016. These perspectives blind us to the debilitating ways by which we evaluate women who seek presidential power, often positioning the woman, regardless of her credentials, as untrustworthy, unsettling, and outside of the norm of what Trevor Parry-Giles and Shawn J. Parry-Giles (2002) define as "presidentiality."

The 2016 campaign was no exception. The general election campaign will be remembered as one of the nastiest on record, with name calling and ques-tionable "facts" as key campaign strategies. Clinton, the former secretary of state for the outgoing Democratic president, Barack Obama, not only had to communicate carefully in a political landscape replete with double binds (Jamieson, 1995), but also had to do so at a time when her Republican oppo-nent, Donald Trump, was gaining ground because of his anti-Washington, pro–working-class message that resonated with a large segment of the popu-lation who saw themselves as forgotten by Washington and the Democratic Party.

The dominant media frames worked against Clinton in 2016. This chapter does not argue that the media caused Clinton's defeat; the factors are far too complicated to make that assessment here. The media frames through which her general election campaign was presented to the public reinforced the nar-rative that Clinton was unrelatable, untrustworthy, and ill suited for the office of the president, despite her years of experience and knowledge of pol-icy, well above that of her challenger. One could argue that the media framed candidate Trump as similarly unfit, but that narrative also included Trump's toughness and virility (aligning him with masculine norms of the presidency), Trump's version of the facts without qualification (regardless of the veracity of the claim), and his emotional connections with working-class voters. More-over the media did not have experience covering such an unconventional candidate, whereas 30 years of history exists with candidate Clinton and a dominant frame to fall back on (Parry-Giles, 2014). Simply quoting Trump's version of the facts without fact-checking or noting the occasions when he "looked presidential" normalized his campaign, whereas Clinton's coverage often framed her negatively, at the same time calling her too smart or part of the establishment.

Thus, Clinton faced impossible expectations. This chapter analyzes more than 750 major news media reports during four key general election moments accessed primarily via www.lexisnexis.com. Assessment of Clinton's nomination and acceptance speech at the Democratic National Convention (DNC), her bout with pneumonia, the first debate, and finally the October e-mail surprise demonstrate the negative framing with which Clinton had to contend, culminating in the narrative of scandal that overshadowed her candidacy.

Who Won the Nomination?

Newspaper coverage of Clinton's historic nomination for the U.S. presidency reminds us that a woman is an anomaly when it comes to presidential authority. On July 27, 2016, *The New York Times* front page published the headline "Democrats make Clinton historic nominee" with a picture of exuberant Clinton supporters holding signs reading "Girl Power" and the familiar blue H logo. To the right of the picture was the subheading "Bill Clinton stirs convention hall after Sanders appeals for unity" (Healy & Martin, 2016). Below the fold, articles told of Clinton's need for "Others [to] speak for her character" (Chozick, 2016a) and the "concern [if Clinton wins,] occupying the first spouse" (Healy, 2016a) with a picture of Bill Clinton addressing the DNC the night before. One could reasonably ask "Which Clinton won the nomination?" and, importantly, "Where was Hillary?" on this historic occasion.

The New York Times was not the exception. Newspapers around the country depicted the historic nomination using images of Bill Clinton, Sanders, and Hillary Clinton supporters and not the woman who actually made history. One can peruse www.newseum.org on July 27, 2016, to see evidence of this claim. Of the 10 daily newspapers with the highest circulation (Cision, 2016), *am New York* was the only one to devote the front page completely to Hillary Clinton with a full-page image of a smiling Clinton pulled from the archives of an earlier campaign. The headline read: "The first lady: Clinton makes history with presidential nomination," with "first" in yellow and larger font, although Clinton's first name was missing from the accolades.

Three of the top 10 dailies eventually chose images of Clinton on the jumbotron from the convention the night before, but the coverage was far from glowing. *The Wall Street Journal*, which had an image of Bill Clinton in its first edition, published a later edition with Hillary Clinton on the jumbotron. The accompanying headlines read "Clinton wins historic nomination," "After tough battle, a landmark moment" (Nicholas & Tau, 2016), and "For some women, gender isn't enough" (Nelson & Adamy, 2016). The headline "Hillary Clinton's trade opportunism" directed readers to the opinion page. *USA Today* paired the photo with the headlines "First woman" and "A moment in U.S. history" and a quotation by U.S. Senator Barbara Mikulski. Clinton supporters appeared below the fold with a story and headline: "12 years later, Obama has similar defining speech to give" (Korte, 2016). *Newsday* used the headline "The first: Clinton makes history as only woman to win major-party nomination" and a picture of Bill Clinton with the caption " 'Best darn changemaker I ever met': Ex-president states case for Hillary." Reminding voters of the difficult campaign, President Obama's and former President Clinton's voices are represented with the suggestion that Hillary Clinton's gender is what got her this far, but it may not be enough to win the presidency.

Others newspapers chose different imagery entirely. A photo of police officers reviving a man on the street next to the headline "For Clinton, star power burns bright: Her family, Obamas, Sanders and others lend experience and popularity to her fight against Trump" (Memoli, 2016) headlined the *Los Angeles Times*. The *Chicago Tribune* featured Bill Clinton under the headline "Clinton claims nomination" and a second reading "Bill Clinton says nominee 'best darn change-maker I've met' " (Barabak & Megerian, 2016). Clinton's first name appeared in *The Washington Post*, "Historic nomination for Hillary Clinton," with a photo of Bill Clinton and another of Sanders with the story, "Only the Clintons: Bill delivers the speech no one else could" (Maraniss, 2016). Interesting, the right-hand column ran a story titled "First woman to top a major ticket: Second day is devoted to revamping her image" (Rucker & Tumulty, 2016) and below that "A milestone that some already take for granted" (Tumulty & Phillip, 2016). Neither the *New York Daily News* nor the *New York Post* made mention of the historic win on the front page.

Overshadowing Clinton's historic victory, the convention coverage undermined her credibility and agency. She was, at best, contained on the jumbotron, at worst invisible, flawed, and relatively voiceless, with headlines indicating Bill Clinton's and Sanders' vocal role in the convention and Hillary Clinton's need to have others "speak for her." Importantly, *The New York Times* concern, if Clinton wins, is keeping her husband busy. *The Wall Street Journal* tells us that Clinton's gender won't be enough, and *The Washington Post* proclaims Clinton needs to revamp her image. The *Los Angeles Times* suggests that Clinton is not the star; she needs help from others to boost her popularity.

The negative media accounts continued the morning after Clinton officially accepted the nomination, falling back on a theme from 2008 that she is dangerous and cannot be trusted (Sheeler & Anderson, 2013). *The Washington Post* reminded readers of a challenge facing Clinton: how to "transcend [voters'] doubts about her character" (Rucker & Gearan, 2016a). *The New York Times* followed suit, "asking the public to set doubts aside" and proclaiming: "The trust of the American electorate remains out of her reach. Its affections still elude her" (Barbaro, 2016).

Not only did Clinton face a trust deficit coming out of the convention, but also a policy deficit. Clinton knows policy; that she received very little policy coverage during the convention season sparks concern. According to an analysis of convention news coverage by Thomas Patterson (2016), Clinton's "policy and issue positions received only a third of the coverage afforded Trump's—a mere 4 percent versus his 13 percent." Stunningly, Trump was more likely to be quoted about Clinton's policies than Clinton herself (Patterson, 2016). Moreover, 10% of the coverage Clinton received during the convention "revolved around allegations of wrongdoing" (Patterson, 2016). Patterson found that Clinton received some positive press, but on balance, during the convention week, the tone was "roughly as much negative as positive" and was devoid of one of Clinton's strengths: her knowledge of policy.

Clinton entered the 2016 general election campaign a different sort of candidate. Not only was she not seen or heard effectively in the media narrative during the convention, reminiscent of the prohibition against women speaking in public that Karlyn Kohrs Campbell (1989) writes about in *Man Cannot Speak for Her*, but voters were reminded that her nomination was different, historic even, even as she was painted as flawed and untrustworthy. Falling back on old narratives uncomfortable with a woman wielding political power, the nomination coverage set the stage for the scandal frame that dominated the Clinton campaign.

"A Deplorable Gaffe and a Hot Wobble"

According to *The Guardian*'s Richard Wolffe (2016), "Hillary Clinton had a terrible weekend . . . Just as she looked like she was heading for a landslide, the combination of a deplorable gaffe and a hot wobble has thrown the campaign into disarray." When news broke of Clinton's collapse after the 9/11 memorial service, speculation mounted regarding her health, fitness, and stamina, fueling the Trump campaign's gendered allegation that she was unfit for office. The criticism compares to opposition the early suffragists faced that women are "more delicate and excitable, [with] nerves [that] could not withstand the pressures of public debate or the marketplace" (Campbell, 1989, p. 11). Moreover, any woman who ventured outside the home, as Campbell argues, lost her "alleged moral superiority" and became "tainted" (p. 10). Remnants of this anti-feminist perception fueled the fitness narrative to the extent that Clinton's efforts to explain her pneumonia diagnosis as "no big deal" and something to "power through" could not gain traction. What the Clinton campaign framed as a strength and indication of her tireless efforts for the American public became a further example of her secrecy. The implication was: Can she really be trusted? Her campaign was not strong, but vulnerable.

Post-feminist discourses bolstered the anti-feminist claim. Clinton's decision to keep her illness a "secret" was her fault, her mistake, and not indicative of a larger cultural assumption of which any woman must be wary: being perceived as not tough enough. Moreover, we are led to believe that Clinton *gave* Trump the edge by not disclosing her illness. Even David Axelod, a former advisor to President Obama, suggested as much with his tweet on September 12, 2016: "Antibiotics can take care of pneumonia. What's the cure for an unhealthy penchant for privacy that repeatedly creates unnecessary problems?" The comment led to a twitter back-and-forth between Jennifer Palmieri, Clinton's communication director, and Kellyanne Conway, Trump's campaign manager, laying the blame at Clinton's feet. *The Washington Post* (Rucker & Gearan, 2016b), *The New York Times* (Dominus, 2016), and *The Guardian* (Freedland, 2016a) concurred. Axelrod concluded with the tweet: "When the exact same problems crop up in separate campaigns, with different staff, at what point do the principals say, 'Hey, maybe it's US?'" The problem *is* us, except not the "us" to whom Axelrod refers; the problem is our cultural anxiety around powerful women.

Political analysts gave credibility to the frame, underscoring the bigger question of Clinton's transparency, honesty, and even mental health as legitimate campaign issues. *The Washington Post*'s Chris Cillizza (2016a) signaled as much: "Hillary Clinton's health just became a real issue in the presidential campaign." *Politico* reported "Clinton scare shakes up the race: Physical weakness caught on camera turns health conspiracy into a legitimate campaign concern" (Thrush, Vogel, & Karni, 2016). Nicole Wallace and Steve Kornacki on the *Today Show* noted the problematic way the campaign handles crises; it takes too long "to get to the truth" (Nash, 2016). Clinton should have garnered sympathy, but the decision reinforced "a pattern" of lacking transparency. Numerous outlets echoed this theme, including ABC's *Good Morning America* (Corn, 2016), CNN *New Day* (Murphy, 2016a), *The New York Times* (Chozick & Healy, 2016), *The Washington Post* (Rucker & Gearan, 2016b), and even *The Guardian* (Roberts & Siddiqui, 2016) and the *London Times* (Blakely, 2016). *USA Today* went so far as to engage readers in a #tellusatoday poll, asking "Is Clinton OK to lead?" with the subhead "Mental health is far more critical than physical" ("Is Clinton OK," 2016).

Not only did the media narrative blame Clinton and call into question her trustworthiness and fitness, but Trump was praised in comparison for his restraint: "Trump restraint demonstrates new discipline" (Raasch, 2016; see also Burns & Haberman, 2016; Chozick, 2016b; Flegenheimer, 2016). What should have been an advantage as Clinton attempted to "power through" turned, instead, into a mistake and a Trump gain as the news media reported on his disciplined, even sympathetic response.

Two days prior to Clinton's 9/11 stumble, she famously declared: "you could put half of Trump's supporters into . . . the basket of deplorables." She described them as "racist, sexist, homophobic, xenophobic, Islamaphobic—you name it"

(Reilly, 2016). Trump didn't wait to seize on the comment, saying it demonstrated Clinton's elitism and hatred of hard-working Americans. Clinton tried to refocus on Trump, but it was too late. The comment fueled claims that Clinton was out of touch with, even disrespectful of voters themselves. Although the comment could be read as trying to energize her base, Trump and his surrogates underscored the message that Clinton lacked concern for hard-working Americans. Clinton, normally so measured with her words, slipped again.

Missing was the fuller context for what Clinton admitted was a gross generalization. She spoke at an LGBT gathering about her promise to pass the Equality Act, comprehensive affordable healthcare, "take on homelessness," "end the cruel and dangerous practice of conversion therapy," and work "toward an AIDS-free generation" (Reilly, 2016). The comment was meant to urge her audience to keep fighting, "don't get complacent," and assume that Trump could never win the election. "We are living in a volatile political environment. You know, to just be grossly generalistic, you could put half of Trump's supporters into what I call a basket of deplorables, right?" She also goes on to urge understanding and empathy.

The next day brought statements from both campaigns, but the message that resonated was not Clinton's—except that she had done something else for which she expressed regret. Clinton said she "regret[ted] saying 'half,'" but doubled-down on the deplorable comment, vowing that she will not "stop calling out bigotry and racist rhetoric" when she hears it. She tried to emphasize her message of empathy "and the very real challenges we face as a country where so many people have been left out and left behind (Merica & Tatum, 2016). What we heard was Clinton did something wrong and the Trump-Pence campaign's charge against her fitness for office. As Trump tweeted, "Wow, Hillary Clinton was so insulting to my supporters, millions of amazing, hard working people. I think it will cost her at the polls." Mike Pence (2016), at a Values Voter conference also retorted: "The truth of the matter is that the men and women who support Donald Trump's campaign are hard-working Americans . . . They are not a basket of anything. They are Americans and they deserve your respect . . . No one with that low of an opinion of the American people should ever be elected to the highest office in the land." Republican National Committee chair Reince Priebus tweeted: "The truly deplorable thing in this race is the shameful level of condescension and disrespect @HillaryClinton's showing to her fellow citizens." Trump confirmed: "How can she be president of our country when she has such contempt and disdain for so many great Americans? Hillary Clinton should be ashamed of herself, and this proves beyond a doubt that she is unfit and incapable to serve as president of the United States" (Lopez & Mason, 2016).

Early September was not kind to Clinton's campaign. A generalization meant to call out the negative rhetoric of the Trump campaign became a rallying cry for his supporters and evidence of Clinton's disdain for those she hoped to serve. Coupled with the decision to maintain privacy about her pneumonia diagnosis, a situation in which Clinton should have claimed sympathy, turned into a referendum on her fitness and trustworthiness. Anti-feminist and post-feminist discourses played a role in the coverage. Instead of providing context for Clinton's remarks or calling out what Clinton believed to be divisive rhetoric on the part of the Trump campaign, the media legitimized the argument against her fitness. Instead of exploring why a female candidate feels the need to "power through," the frame tells us she has erred. Falling back on powerful stereotypes prohibiting women's political power, the developing storyline surrounding Clinton's candidacy reinforced the impossible expectations she faced, a theme that is perhaps best demonstrated during the first debate.

"Note to Hillary Clinton: You Can Be Whip-Smart . . . Yet Still Blow It Spectacularly"

The New York Times ran this headline on the day of the first presidential debate (Healy, 2016b). Expectations are important. Normally campaigns do everything possible to lower expectations, praising their opponent's debate prowess in an effort to lower the bar. In Clinton's case, the narrative reminded us that she is smart, knows policy, yet could still "blow it," primarily because expectations are so incredibly low for Trump. Moreover, Clinton has to be mindful of gender stereotypes; she cannot come across as "pushy" and must wait to interject, being careful not to talk over candidate Trump, whereas the same strategy would not undermine candidate Trump's credibility (Healy, Chozick, & Haberman, 2016).

According to Jonathan Freedland (2016b), writing for the September 23, 2016, *The Guardian*:

> So low are expectations for his performance on Monday—where it is assumed that his opponent, a seasoned debater, will wipe the floor with him—that if Trump manages to speak in vaguely coherent sentences and not deliver a misogynist insult to Clinton's face, his advocates will declare that he looked "presidential" and anoint him the winner . . .

> And for all her experience, Clinton heads toward this first, and therefore most important, debate facing some serious obstacles. She's been advised that she mustn't interrupt too much or talk over Trump: apparently voters react badly to seeing a woman act that way. According to a *New York Times* report well sourced from inside Hillary's debate preparation team, "she does not want to be seen as pushy and play into gender stereotypes." This was not something Barack Obama, or husband Bill, ever had to worry about.

Political analysts confirmed the impossible expectations. On CNN, Scott Adams noted: "Clinton has to be perfect and then maybe a little extra" (CNN

Newsroom, 2016). Clinton has more experience, which means Trump has "an opportunity," according to Bob Cusack (Tabacoff, 2016). John Phillips explained the low bar for Trump: "I think he's going to shock people and show them that there's a lot more to him than that description. Hillary, of course, is billed as the wonk who's just someone who spent all of her life in politics" (CNN *Tonight*, 2016). Charles Krauthammer suggested "that if he [Trump] just shows up not foaming at the mouth, if he looks normal, relaxed, and sort of reasonable, he wins automatically" (Lowell, 2016). Even Andrea Mitchell noted that Trump "could go 90 minutes, misstating facts, let's say, but looking smooth, being the performer, and she [Clinton] is the studious schoolmarm constantly saying you're wrong about that, that's a lie. It's not an appealing persona" (*Meet the Press Daily*, 2016). Trump is "graded on a curve" according to *MSNBC*'s Joe Scarborough (Korson, 2016). Democratic consultant Hank Sheinkopf claimed "'All Trump has to do is smile, behave and not be crazy and hope Hillary makes a mistake. The bar is so low for him and high for her. He may well redefine how debates are judged'" (Campanile, Schultz, & Golding, 2016).

Clinton was at fault for lowering the bar for Trump going into the debate, similar to earlier stories blaming Clinton for giving Trump the edge during her bout with pneumonia. She often touted Trump's lack of fitness—"A man you can bait with a tweet is not a man we can trust with nuclear weapons," a line she first tweeted on July 29, 2016. In other words, post-feminism suggests the blame belongs to Clinton for effectively lowering the bar such that Trump only had to "look presidential" for a few moments to come out on top. The narrative did not dig deeper to interrogate, instead, the impossible expectations Clinton faced or why the frame legitimized such a perspective in Trump's favor.

Post-debate coverage recounted Clinton's faults, even though she won. The *Washington Post*'s Cillizza (2016b) concluded: "This was a clear win for [Clinton] on virtually every front." However, before reaching that conclusion, we learn that Clinton "wasn't perfect," was "overly rehearsed and robotic," and "showed too much head and not enough heart." Given that readers look for headlines and rarely read an article to the end (Dockterman, 2014), stories like this undermine Clinton's performance. The *Los Angeles Times*, in reporting international opinion after the debate, concluded that Clinton won, but she needed to do better. Quoting a former Mexican diplomat, "'Hillary wins by points when she needed a knockout'" (McDonnell & Sanchez, 2016).

The second and third debates were a series of nasty, personal exchanges (Halper, Schultz, & Fears, 2016; "Second presidential debate," 2016; Slack & Jackson, 2016). Trump supporters likely were buoyed by his performance during the second debate. *USA Today* declared: "Trump fights back" (Przybyla, 2016). According to NBC News, Trump "rallied" his supporters and "showed up to the second debate against Hillary Clinton looking more focused, more relaxed, and more vicious'" (Sarlin & Seitz-Wald, 2016). *CBS News* reported Trump "sort of" won the second debate: "He kept Hillary Clinton on the defensive, didn't have a meltdown, and even had a couple of decent zingers . . . he gets points for not imploding" (Rahn, 2016). Sources noted Trump's "calm" and collected start to the third debate (Chozick & Barbaro, 2016; Friedman, 2016; Joseph, 2016). However, true to form, the final debate quickly turned into a "bitter and deeply personal confrontation" (Pace & Lerer, 2016) that concluded with Trump interrupting Clinton, calling her "such a nasty woman."

As Kathleen Hall Jamieson explained in a *New York Times* interview, insulting powerful women such as Clinton is a way to cut "them down to size and [plays] into discomfort with women in power" (Miller, 2016). Jamieson observes that insults are rarely as overt as those Trump flung during this campaign season. Yet some journalists noted Clinton's assertiveness in the third debate, aligning with the #nastywoman theme on Twitter. For example, Chozick and Barbaro (2016) wrote that "Clinton turns the tormentor." She "mansplained," "interrupted," "mocked," and "outmaneuvered Mr. Trump with a surprising new approach: his. Flipping the script, she turned herself into his relentless tormentor, condescending to him repeatedly and deploying some of his own trademark tactics against him."

The trajectory of media coverage during the debates moved from "Clinton wasn't good enough" to "Trump imploded." She appeared to have the advantage going into the last two weeks of the election. However, the debates and corresponding media coverage during the 2016 election cycle differed from previous elections regarding policy discussion. Writing in *The New York Times*, Alan Rappeport (2016) laments: "Lost in the bluster and bombast has been the kind of detailed policy talk that traditionally consumes candidates this time of year. While onstage stalking and shimmying kept body-language experts busy, many who care about tax policy, immigration, health care and climate change were left with little to chew on." Moriah Balingit (2016) in *The Washington Post* had a similar observation. The journalist wrote about a social studies teacher who asked his students to watch the debates and write about what they learned about each candidate's position on four policy issues. "Several students found they couldn't complete the assignment . . . [T]here wasn't much national policy to analyze" (Balingit, 2016). Given Clinton's policy strength, it is not clear that voters heard a message that would compel them to vote *for* Clinton rather than simply *against* her opponent. As a result, the edge that Clinton may have had coming out of the debates was not likely based on an understanding of what she would do if elected. And then the e-mails surfaced . . . again.

"The Biggest Political Scandal Since Watergate"

Trump rallied his supporters at a campaign event in Golden, Colorado, on October 30, 2016, declaring the latest revelation about Clinton's e-mails "the biggest political scandal since Watergate" (Pace & Thomas, 2016; Siddiqui & Gambino, 2016; Wagner, Sullivan, & Gearan, 2016). The line was followed by cheers of "lock her up" from the crowd. Eleven days prior to the November 2016 election, FBI director James Comey announced that e-mails had been discovered that appeared "to be pertinent" to the previously closed investigation into Clinton's use of a private e-mail server while secretary of state. Although it was not clear whether the e-mails were new or contained anything of significance, this latest controversy revived the narrative that Clinton had acted in an "extremely careless" manner and solidified the scandal frame that had been building throughout the general election campaign. The revelation also energized the Trump campaign. As *The Guardian* reported, "Donald Trump, who has pledged to jail Clinton if elected, claimed vindication" (Ackerman, 2016).

Clinton and her surrogates focused on Comey and his overzealous handling of the e-mail information so close to the election, demanding that he release "the full and complete facts immediately." Regardless of whether the story was about Comey or Clinton, voters heard scandal, often from the mouths of Trump and his supporters, repeated in print and television news. Clinton was secretive and could not be trusted, which by now was a familiar refrain in election coverage. Moreover, the reporting brought back two references damaging to Clinton: Anthony Weiner and his inappropriate behavior, associating impropriety with the Clinton campaign; and Kenneth Starr, a reference to Monica Lewinsky and the investigation during Bill Clinton's presidency. Language such as controversy, uncertainty, bombshell, and especially scandal accentuated Clinton's vulnerability and associated her, once again, with wrongdoing.

The Clinton e-mail story garnered twice the coverage in major newspapers across the country as any headline about Trump the week prior to the election (Savillo, 2016). Similarly, broadcast evening news had significantly more minutes devoted to the Clinton e-mail controversy than policy issues (Boehlert, 2016). According to Patterson (2016), "What appeared to be missing from this negative coverage, however, was context . . . [A]lthough Clinton's email issue was clearly deemed important by the media, relatively few stories provided background to help news consumers make sense of the issue." The focus of the press, instead, was on "polls, projections, and scandal."

On November 6, the Sunday prior to the election, Comey announced the e-mail probe did not change the prior conclusion that Clinton did not engage in criminal activity, clearing her name once again. As the *New York Daily News* reported, "too bad millions already voted" (Silverstein & Greene, 2016). Trump continued to cast doubt on the investigation and on Clinton, and several sources reported Comey's decision by quoting Trump. For example, "'You can't review 650,000 new emails in eight days . . . You can't do it folks. Hillary Clinton is guilty. She knows it'" (Fahrenthold, Helderman, & Johnson, 2016; Finnegan, 2016; "Trump, Clinton sprint across U.S.," 2016). CNN ran a clip of Trump's rally as part of its coverage of Comey's decision (Murphy,

2016b). Moreover, CNN left open the possibility of further scandal: "The probe is considered over with regard to Clinton. Though with not all the deleted emails recovered and not all the devices in the FBI's possession, it is always possible something else could turn up that would require more review" (Bradner, Brown, & Perez, 2016).

The final stretch of the general election campaign was dominated by news of scandal. Given that each segment of general election coverage chose to report Clinton negatively, questioning her fitness and trustworthiness with a corresponding absence of policy and issue discussion, it is not surprising that Clinton was unable to break through the clutter with an alternative frame emphasizing her experience, policy knowledge, and lifetime of public service. Such an assessment conforms to what Parry-Giles (2014) finds in her extensive analysis of media coverage of Clinton from 1992 through the 2008 election cycle: "Whenever Clinton consequently stepped into the electoral or political arena, the frames of negativity were pronounced; once she stepped out, the surveillance typically dissipated along with the rhetorical vitriol" (p. 187). Hillary Clinton faced impossible expectations; she had to be nearly perfect, as some noted prior to the first presidential debate. Her experience wasn't enough, especially when that wasn't what voters were seeing and hearing. Instead, her campaign became synonymous with scandal.

At the end of the 2008 primaries, Clinton was asked about the sexism she experienced during that campaign season. She responded: "I believe this campaign has been a groundbreaker in a lot of ways. But it certainly has been challenging given some of the attitudes in the press, and I regret that, because I think it's been really not worthy of the seriousness of the campaign . . . It does seem as though the press at least is not as bothered by the incredible vitriol that has been engendered by the comments by people who are nothing but misogynists" (Romano, 2008). Unfortunately, this applies equally to 2016. Antifeminist sentiments ran strong in the campaign, fomenting stereotypes and fueling the backlash against Clinton's fitness for office. Moreover, post-feminism proved unmovable, as we experienced a campaign season that demonstrated our cultural anxiety over women's political achievements. Importantly, Clinton's political experience was all but erased during election coverage. Policy was a very small component of the story. Instead, the evolving narrative was about discrediting Clinton, the more qualified candidate. During the 2016 election cycle, political experience was not valued when the woman candidate had it.

A record number of women hope to challenge that conclusion in 2018. EMILY's List and VoteRunLead have both experienced an increased demand for their candidate training programs following the inauguration (Landsbaum, 2017), and both credit the 2016 election as the motivating factor. According to Stephanie Schriock, EMILY's List president, we've "heard from more than 11,000 women in all 50 states" (O'Keefe & DeBonis, 2017). According to one participant, a "key reason she's running is to dismantle the stereotypes Clinton faced. 'People aren't born thinking women are too hormonal to do something—that's a cultural thing . . . A lot of women are fed up with that'" (Landsbaum, 2017).

The frames through which Clinton was presented to the public during the 2016 presidential campaign suggest these women with new political aspirations will not have an easy road ahead. As coverage of Clinton during the general election cycle demonstrates, she went from being invisible, untrustworthy, and secretive to nasty, and finally, scandalous, illustrating the lack of ingenuity when it comes to media coverage of powerful political women. Instead of policy or qualifications, we heard unproven allegations associating Clinton with wrongdoing, not only from the press, but as reported forcefully from Trump and his supporters. Hopefully, the women who have declared their candidacies since January 2017 will be able to break such a debilitating narrative, compelling a different story no longer about our fear of powerful women, but one that captures women's agency and power in U.S. political culture.

References

Ackerman, S. (2016, October 30). Democrats pile pressure on FBI's Comey over eleventh-hour Clinton email letter. *The Guardian*. Retrieved from www.lexisnexis.com

Balingit, M. (2016, October 19). Keeping election talk G-rated. *The Washington Post*. Retrieved from www.lexisnexis.com

Barabak, M. Z., & Megerian, C. (2016, July 27). Bill Clinton says nominee "best darn change-maker I've ever met." *Chicago Tribune*. Retrieved from newseum.org

Barbaro, M. (2016, July 29). Asking the public to set doubts aside and put faith in competence. *The New York Times*. Retrieved from www.lexisnexis.com

Blakely, R. (2016, September 13). Less than half of U.S. voters believe Clinton's claims about her health: It's secrecy not symptoms that will do the real damage. *The Times* (London). Retrieved from www.lexisnexis.com

Boehlert, E. (2016, November 7). The media's final email flop, a fitting end to journalism's troubled campaign season. *Mediamatters.org*. Retrieved from https://mediamatters.org/blog/2016/11/07/media-s-final-email-flop-fitting-end-journalism-s-troubled-campaign-season/214357

Bradner, E., Brown, P., & Perez, E. (2016, November 7). FBI clears Clinton—again. *CNN Politics*. Retrieved from http://www.cnn.com/2016/11/06/politics/comey-tells-congress-fbi-has-not-changed-conclusions/

Burns, A., & Haberman, M. (2016, September 13). Trump seizes rival's absence to press case. *The New York Times*. Retrieved from www.lexisnexis.com

Campanile, C., Schultz, M., & Golding, B. (2016, September 26). Election 2016: It's a clash of the tighten [sic]. *The New York Post*. Retrieved from www.lexisnexis.com

Campbell, K. K. (1989). *Man cannot speak for her.* (2 vols.). Westport, CT: Praeger.

Chozick, A. (2016a, July 27). A show's star lets others speak for her character. *The New York Times.* Retrieved from www.lexisnexis.com

Chozick, A. (2016b, September 16). Recovering Clinton returns to the campaign trail, vowing new approach. *The New York Times.* Retrieved from www.lexisnexis.com

Chozick, A., & Barbaro, B. (2016, October 20). Interrupting, mocking and taunting, Clinton turns the tormentor. *The New York Times.* Retrieved from www.lexisnexis.com

Chozick, A., & Healy, P. (2016, September 13). Clinton set back by call to keep illness a secret. *The New York Times.* Retrieved from www.lexisnexis.com

Cillizza, C. (2016a, September 11). Hillary Clinton's health just became a real issue in the presidential campaign. *The Washington Post.* Retrieved from www.lexisnexis.com

Cillizza, C. (2016b, September 27). Winners and losers from the 1st presidential debate. *The Washington Post.* Retrieved from www.lexisnexis.com

Cision. (2016, May 11). Top 10 U.S. daily newspapers. Retrieved from http://www.cision.com/us/2014/06/top-10-us-daily-newspapers/

CNN Newsroom with Brooke Baldwin (Television broadcast). (2016, September 14). Atlanta: Turner Broadcasting System.

CNN Tonight (Television broadcast). (2016, September 8). Atlanta: Turner Broadcasting System.

Corn, M. (Executive Producer). (2016, September 12). *Good Morning America* (Television broadcast). New York: American Broadcasting Company.

Dockterman, E. (2014, February 14). People aren't actually reading the stories they tweet. *Time.com.* Retrieved from http://techland.time.com/2014/02/14/people-dont-read-stories-they-tweet/

Dominus, S. (2016, September 13). Resilient figure stumbles, and her fans wince in turn. *The New York Times.* Retrieved from www.lexisnexis.com

Dow, B. J. (1996). *Prime-time feminism: Television, media culture, and the women's movement since 1970.* New York: Times Books.

Entman, R. M. (1993). Framing: Toward a clarification of a fractured paradigm. *Journal of Communication, 43,* 51–58.

Fahrenthold, D. A., Helderman, R. S., & Johnson, J. (2016, November 7). FBI won't pursue charges against Clinton. *The Washington Post.* Retrieved from www.lexisnexis.com

Finnegan, M. (2016, November 6). Trump says FBI knows Clinton is guilty of crimes. *Los Angeles Times.* Retrieved from http://www.latimes.com/nation/politics/trailguide/la-na-trailguide-updates-trump-says-the-fbi-know-clinton-is-1478484190-htmlstory.html

Flegenheimer, M. (2016, September 14). An absence for Clinton at an inopportune time. *The New York Times.* Retrieved from www.lexisnexis.com

Freedland, J. (2016a, September 12). Hillary Clinton has allowed Trump to claim vindication. *The Guardian.* Retrieved from www.lexisnexis.com

Freedland, J. (2016b, September 23). President Trump? There's only one way to stop it happening. *The Guardian.* Retrieved from www.lexisnexis.com

Friedman, V. (2016, October 23). Final debate takes a more somber tone. *The New York Times*. Retrieved from www.lexisnexis.com

Hahn, D. F. (2003). *Political communication: Rhetoric, government, and citizens*. State College, PA: Strata.

Halper, D., Schultz, M., & Fears, D. (2016, October 9). Nasty exchanges, personal attacks dominate second debate. *The New York Post*. Retrieved from http://nypost.com/2016/10/09/nasty-exchanges-personal-attacks-dominate-second-debate/

Hart, R. P. (2000). *Campaign talk: Why elections are good for us*. Princeton, NJ: Princeton University Press.

Healy, P. (2016a, July 27). If Clinton wins, a concern: Occupying the first spouse. *The New York Times*. Retrieved from www.lexisnexis.com

Healy, P. (2016b, September 26). Debacle: What first debate of the 2000 race can teach Clinton. *The New York Times*. Retrieved from www.lexisnexis.com

Healy, P., Chozick, A., & Haberman, M. (2016, September 23). Debate prep? Hillary Clinton and Donald Trump differ on that, too. *The New York Times*. Retrieved from www.lexisnexis.com

Healy, P., & Martin, J. (2016, July 27). Bill Clinton stirs convention hall after Sanders appeals for unity. *The New York Times*. Retrieved from www.lexisnexis.com

Is Clinton OK to lead? #tellusatoday. (2016, September 12). *USA Today*. Retrieved from https://www.usatoday.com/story/opinion/2016/09/12/clinton-ok-lead-tellusatoday/90278914/

Jamieson, K. H. (1992). *Dirty politics: Deception, distraction and democracy*. New York: Oxford University Press.

Jamieson, K. H. (1995). *Beyond the double bind: Women and leadership*. New York: Oxford University Press.

Joseph, C. (2016, October 20). Denail [sic] of democracy: Paranoid Trump won't commit to elex results. *Daily News* (New York). Retrieved from www.lexisnexis.com

Korson, A. (Executive Producer). (2016, September 21). *Morning Joe* (Television broadcast). New York: National Broadcasting Company.

Korte, G. (2016, July 27). 12 years later, Obama has similar defining speech to give. *USA Today*. Retrieved from newseum.org

Landsbaum, C. (2017, February 9). First they marched, now more than 13,000 women are planning to run for office. *New York Magazine*. Retrieved from http://nymag.com/thecut/2017/02/an-unprecedented-number-of-women-plan-to-run-for-office.html

Lopez, L., & Mason, J. (2016, September 10). Clinton regrets calling "half" of Trump supporters "deplorable." *Reuters.com*. Retrieved from http://www.reuters.com/article/us-usa-election-clinton-idUSKCN11G063

Lowell, T. (Executive Producer). (2016, September 9). *The Kelly File* (Television broadcast). New York: Fox News Network.

Maraniss, D. (2016, July 27). Only the Clintons: Bill delivers the speech no one else could. *The Washington Post*. Retrieved from newseum.org

McDonnell, P. J., & Sanchez, C. (2016, September 28). Back story: World viewers weigh in on the U.S. debate. *Los Angeles Times*. Retrieved from www.lexis nexis.com

Meet the Press Daily (Television broadcast). (2016, September 21). *MSNBC*. New York: National Broadcasting Network.

Memoli, M. A. (2016, July 27). For Clinton, star power burns bright: Her family, Obamas, Sanders and others lend experience and popularity to her fight against Trump. *Los Angeles Times*. Retrieved from Newseum.org

Merica, D., & Tatum, S. (2016, September 12). Clinton expresses regret for saying "half" of Trump supporters are "deplorables." *CNN.com*. Retrieved from http://www.cnn.com/2016/09/09/politics/hillary-clinton-donald-trump -basket-of-deplorables/

Miller, C. C. (2016, October 22). The powerful woman: A prime target for jabs. *The New York Times*. Retrieved from www.lexisnexis.com

Murphy, J. (Senior Executive Producer). (2016a, September 12). *CNN New Day* [Television broadcast]. Atlanta: Turner Broadcasting System.

Murphy, J. (Senior Executive Producer). (2016b, November 7). Trump, Clinton is guilty and she knows it. *CNN New Day* [Television broadcast]. Atlanta: Turner Broadcasting System.

Nash, D. (Executive Producer). (2016, September 13). *Today* [Television broadcast]. New York: National Broadcasting Company.

Nelson, C. M., & Adamy, J. (2016, July 27). For some women, gender isn't enough. *Wall Street Journal*. Retrieved from newseum.org

Newseum. (2016, July 27). Wednesday, July 27, 2016. *Newseum.org*. Retrieved from http://www.newseum.org/todaysfrontpages/?tfp_display=archive-date &tfp_archive_id=072716

Nicholas, P., & Tau, B. (2016, July 27). After tough battle, a landmark moment. *Wall Street Journal*. Retrieved from newseum.org

O'Keefe, E., & DeBonis, M. (2017, April 21). Democrats partner with political newcomers aiming to create anti-Trump wave in 2018 midterms. *The Washington Post*. Retrieved from https://www.washingtonpost.com/politics /democrats-partner-with-political-newcomers-hoping-to-create-anti-trump -wave-in-2018-midterms/2017/04/21/91514ec8-2502-11e7-bb9d-8cd611 8e1409_story.html?tid=ss_tw&utm_term=.618e6423d963

Pace, J., & Lerer, L. (2016, October 20). Final showdown: Clinton and Trump meet for last debate. *St. Louis Post-Dispatch*. Retrieved from www.lexisnexis.com

Pace, J., & Thomas, K. (2016, October 30). Trump emboldened by Clinton email woes as she pushes back. *St. Louis Post-Dispatch*. Retrieved from www.lexis nexis.com

Parry-Giles, S. J. (2014). *Hillary Clinton in the news: Gender and authenticity in American politics*. Urbana: University of Illinois Press.

Parry-Giles, T., & Parry-Giles, S. J. (2002). *The West Wing*'s prime-time presidentiality: Mimesis and catharsis in a postmodern romance. *Quarterly Journal of Speech, 88*, 209–227. http://dx.doi.org/10.1080/00335630209384371

Patterson, T. E. (1993). *Out of order*. New York: Knopf.

Patterson, T. E. (2016, September 21). New coverage of the 2016 national conventions: Negative news, lacking context. Retrieved from https://shorenstein center.org/news-coverage-2016-national-conventions/

Pence, M. (2016, September 10). Remarks at Values Voter conference, Washington, DC. Retrieved from http://www.cnn.com/TRANSCRIPTS/1609/10/cnr .03.html

Przybyla, H. M. (2016, October 10). Trump fights back out of gate. *USA Today*. Retrieved from www.lexisnexis.com

Raasch, C. (2016, September 13). Quiet for once: Trump restraint demonstrates new discipline. *St. Louis Post-Dispatch*. Retrieved from www.lexisnexis.com

Rahn, W. (2016, October 10). Commentary: Who won the second presidential debate? *CBSNews.com*. Retrieved from http://www.cbsnews.com/news/com mentary-who-won-the-second-presidential-debate-donald-trump-hillary -clinton/

Rappaport, A. (2016, October 21). The debate that wasn't: So many words, so few about policy. *The New York Times*. Retrieved from www.lexisnexis.com

Reilly, K. (2016, September 10). Read Hillary Clinton's "basket of deplorables" remarks about Donald Trump supporters. *Time.com*. Retrieved from http:// time.com/4486502/hillary-clinton-basket-of-deplorables-transcript/

Roberts, D., & Siddiqui, S. (2016, September 13). Hillary Clinton campaign admits "we could have done better" handling pneumonia news. *The Guardian*. Retrieved from www.lexisnexis.com

Romano, L. (2008, May 20). Clinton puts up a new fight: The candidate confronts sexism on the trail and vows to battle on. *The Washington Post*. Retrieved from www.lexisnexis.com

Rucker, P., & Gearan, A. (2016a, July 29). *The Washington Post*. Retrieved from www.lexisnexis.com

Rucker, P., & Gearan, A. (2016b, September 13). Clinton wanted to "power through." *The Washington Post*. Retrieved from www.lexisnexis.com

Rucker, P., & Tumulty, K. (2016, July 27). First woman to top a major ticket: Second day is devoted to revamping her image. *The Washington Post*. Retrieved from newseum.org

Sarlin, B., & Seitz-Wald, A. (2016, October 10). 2016 presidential debate analysis: Donald Trump rallies faithful in 2nd showdown. *NBCNews.com*. Retrieved from http://www.nbcnews.com/storyline/2016-presidential-debates/pre sidential-debate-analysis-donald-trump-rallies-faithful-2nd-showdown -n663441

Savillo, R. (2016, November 4). Study: Top newspapers give Clinton email story more coverage than all other Trump stories. *Mediamatters.org*. Retrieved from https://mediamatters.org/research/2016/11/04/study-top -newspapers-give-clinton-email-story-more-coverage-all-other-trump -stories/214309

Second presidential debate turns nasty. (2016, October 10). *Hardball with Chris Matthews* (Television broadcast). *MSNBC*. New York: National Broadcasting Company.

Sheeler, K. H., & Anderson, K. V. (2013). *Woman president: Confronting postfeminist political culture*. College Station: Texas A&M University Press.

Siddiqui, S., & Gambino, L. (2016, October 29). Hillary Clinton demands FBI explain review of new batch of emails. *The Guardian*. Retrieved from www.lexisnexis.com

Silverstein, J., & Greene, L. (2016, November 7). Um, never mind about emails, and Comey says probe's over—too bad millions already voted. *Daily News* (New York). Retrieved from www.lexisnexis.com

Slack, D., & Jackson, D. (2016, October 9). Nastiest debate ever? Catch up on what you missed. *USA Today*. Retrieved from https://www.usatoday.com /story/news/politics/onpolitics/2016/10/09/live-blog-clinton-trump -debate-st-louis/91824188/

Tabacoff, D. (Executive Producer). (2016, September 7). *The O'Reilly Factor* (Television broadcast). New York: Fox News Network.

Thrush, G., Vogel, K. P., & Karni, A. (2016, September 11). Clinton scare shakes up the race. *Politico*. Retrieved from http://www.politico.com/story/2016 /09/hillary-clinton-health-trump-228008

Trump, Clinton sprint across U.S. as campaigns react to dramatic development in email case. (2016, November 7). *St. Louis Post-Dispatch*. Retrieved from www.lexisnexis.com

Tumulty, K., & Phillip, A. D. (2016, July 27). A milestone that some already take for granted. *The Washington Post*. Retrieved from newseum.org

Vavrus, M. D. (2002). *Postfeminist news: Political women in media culture*. Albany: State University of New York Press.

Wagner, J., Sullivan, S., & Gearan, A. (2016, October 30). Clinton: "It's unprecedented, and it's deeply troubling." *The Washington Post*. Retrieved from www .lexisnexis.com

Wolffe, R. (2016, September 12). Hillary Clinton had a terrible weekend. The alternative is far, far worse. *The Guardian*. Retrieved from www.lexisnexis.com

Depends on Who Is Asking: An Endorsement Experiment During the 2016 Presidential Election

Kalyca Becktel and Kaye D. Sweetser

Marketing to young people today increasingly relies on the use of influencers. Whether Hollywood celebrities or Internet-made sensations, advertisers and public relations professionals are increasingly turning to so-called influencers. By using the influencer's social capital and opinion leader status, it is hoped that the influencer can transfer product support directly to the general public through the endorsement. These tactics are not new. In fact, the use of opinion leaders has long been used in political public relations.

Taking a fresh focus on the resurgence of the old-fashioned opinion leader, now going by the moniker of influencer, this study seeks to understand how their endorsements might, if at all, affect young voters. Polling data historically show lower levels of youth vote participation in national elections, and some scholars have hypothesized that one of the cognitive blocks keeping these voters from casting a ballot is their lack of confidence in the information they have (Kaid, McKinney, & Tedesco, 2004, 2007). Our experiment focuses on the first-time young voter and manipulates the type of influencer endorsement to determine if a particular influencer is more successful in directing young voters' feelings toward a particular candidate.

Theoretical Foundation and Rationale

This research is guided by political information efficacy theory, first suggested by Kaid et al. (2004, 2007). Although the majority of political communication scholarship suggests that media consumption affects likelihood to vote (Drew & Weaver, 2006), Opdycke, Segura, and Vasquez (2013) found that it did not have an effect on voter participation. Instead, Opdycke et al. (2013) reported a significant relationship between information efficacy and the likelihood to vote. They found that political information efficacy and cynicism predicted vote likelihood. As such, this study will examine the changes in political information efficacy in an experimental setting where media content about the election is manipulated.

Political Information Efficacy

Previous research on voter turnout has looked for linkages between voter confidence and voting behavior. For example, Tan (1980) noted that well-informed citizens are most likely to vote. Building on work by Delli Carpini (2000) suggesting that young voters do not turn out at the polls because they fear they don't have enough information to vote, Kaid et al. (2004, 2007) developed a theory of political information efficacy. As noted by Sweetser and Kaid (2008), political information efficacy focuses only on the "voter's confidence in his/her own political knowledge and its sufficiency to engage the political process (to vote)" (p. 71). As such, the theory of political information efficacy operationalized the concept through measures to determine how confident—or not—young voters in particular were about their level of political knowledge. Kaid et al. (2007) found that young voters rated their confidence in political knowledge lower than did older adults.

In an experimental study, Tedesco (2011) found exposing participants to Internet messages can significantly increase political information efficacy. This experiment also revealed a gender gap, where women lagged behind men in their confidence about their political information. Looking at political party ideology, Democrats (who were predicted prior to the election to win) also reported higher levels of political information efficacy. Most interesting, however, is that exposure to a negative political message did not diminish participants' political information efficacy (Tedesco, 2011).

Since these initial studies, the political information efficacy theory has been used in research on nearly every presidential election. However, most recent studies pair political information efficacy with other theories, treating it as a concept as opposed to a theory and an independent variable used to predict a different theoretical concept. For example, Sweetser and Tedesco (2014) paired political information efficacy with organization–public relationship theory as a means to predict a relationship. This empirical investigation applies political information efficacy as the driving theoretical concept.

Authenticity

The search for an authentic candidate is undoubtedly exhausting during a time when politics are mediated by an increase of outside influences as Election Day draws near. Ironically, these outside influences include endorsements of candidates to increase their authenticity, which is thought to later translate into votes. The concept of authenticity is grounded in the candidates' morality, truth, individualism, and culture (Taylor, 1992). Voters' search for a candidate who is authentic is a hunt for a political figure who is perceived as reliable and genuine (Gilpin, Palazzolo, & Brody, 2010). In an article for *The Spectator* about the 2008 U.S. presidential campaign, Forsyth observed that the four winners—Democrats Barack Obama and Hillary Clinton and Republicans Mike Huckabee and John McCain—of the Iowa caucus and New Hampshire primary had appeared the most authentic in the crucial 72 hours of the campaign before those early contests (Forsyth, 2008).

The 2016 presidential election was muddied with more than 25 individuals announcing their candidacy more than 18 months before Election Day. To be heard against the cacophony of other candidates, presidential hopefuls brought an arsenal of endorsement tactics to be used as their voice of authenticity. *Rolling Stone* magazine online endorsed Democratic Party presidential candidate Clinton's authenticity when they wrote "Hillary Clinton gives another kind of authenticity when she speaks honestly about what change really requires" (Wenner, 2016). Willie Robertson, star of the reality TV show *Duck Dynasty*, explained that he liked Republican presidential candidate Donald Trump's authenticity during an October 27, 2015, interview on *Fox and Friends* (Robertson, 2015).

Sweetser (2017) surveyed first-time voters during the 2016 election and noted that respondents rated both candidates with neutral scores for authenticity. Even so, both Republicans and Democrats rated candidate Trump as having slightly greater authenticity than the more politically experienced candidate Clinton.

Characteristics

It is assumed that constituents vote based on a candidate's position on policy. However, the number of votes cast can also be associated with the human qualities of candidates and other attributes that appeal to personal attraction (Enelow & Hinich, 1982). Characteristics such as strength, sophistication, and honesty affect voter evaluations of candidates (Kaid, 1995). Therefore, the combination of policy positions and candidate characteristics affect voter decisions.

A candidate's characteristics are seen throughout numerous events during campaigning. Research on primary debates has concluded that they can affect viewer evaluations of the candidates, including their characteristics. For instance, Lanoue and Schrott (1989) found that primary debates during the 1988 presidential election had a profound effect on viewers' assessments of the candidates. In the 2000 election, Benoit, McKinney, and Stephenson (2002) discovered that primary debate viewers felt more confident about their voting decisions; formed judgments about lesser-known politicians; changed judgments about better-known politicians; and, in some circumstances, changed their voting intention. Other research lends additional support to the notion that primary debates can potentially change viewers' voting intentions and judgments of debaters (McKinney, Kaid, & Robertson, 2001; Pfau, 1987; Wall, Golden, & James, 1988; Yawn, Ellsworth, Beatty, & Kahn, 1998).

Candidate characteristics are also assessed during their rotation on the television entertainment circuit. During the 1960 presidential campaign, Richard Nixon sought to "humanize" himself by playing piano on *The Tonight Show* (Rosenberg, 2000). Decades later, Bill Clinton attempted to relate to young voters by playing the saxophone on the *Arsenio Hall Show* in 1992 (Rosenberg, 2000). Most recently, Hillary Clinton played a bartender opposite Kate McKinnon, who played Clinton, on *Saturday Night Live* during the 2016 election. By participating in entertainment television, political candidates try to demonstrate their authenticity for the world to see while simultaneously inviting the audience to judge whether they are being real or just faking it (Liebes, 2001).

Party Strength

One's own political party strength of affiliation has been found to play a role in precursors to voting behavior. Sweetser (2017) found that regardless of one's political party affiliation, support for one's own party candidate is predicted by strength of affiliation to one's party, the respondent's perceived credibility of the party, and opposition to the other party's candidate.

Method

Employing an online post-test–only experimental design ($N=879$), this study sought to investigate the impact of endorsement type on perceived level of authenticity and candidate assessment. Our study was designed to answer these research questions:

RQ1: Is there a difference in first-time voters' perception of candidate authenticity based on influencer type?

RQ2: Is there a difference in first-time voters' perception of candidate characteristics based on influencer type?

RQ3: Can political information efficacy predict first-time voters' perception of a candidate's authenticity?

RQ4: Can political information efficacy predict first-time voters' perception of a candidate's characteristics?

Sample

The participants in this sample represented a national pool of first-time voters, including those in several key battleground and election-deciding states during the 2016 presidential election. The independent variable in this study is the endorsement type. The dependent variables are participant's perception of the candidate with regard to authenticity and characteristics. The driving theoretical force in this study is political information efficacy.

Design

Participants were randomly assigned to one of four manipulation cells or control group in this experiment, which began on October 11, 2016, and concluded on November 4, 2016, just days before the November 8 election. For all manipulation cells, the stimulus was held constant with the exception of the independent variable of endorsement. Endorsement was operationalized in this study through the manipulation of a headline and one paragraph regarding an endorsement as a part of a larger news story about third-party candidate, Libertarian Gary Johnson. A third-party candidate was selected as this stimulus because, especially in the context of the 2016 election, the main party candidates were well known and endorsements may not have played a role in the shaping of voter perception. Cells included mention of the candidate being endorsed by these influencer types: newspapers, celebrities, military leaders (generals and admirals), or politicians. The control group did not receive an article and proceeded straight to the post-test.

Instrument

The post-test questionnaire in this study explored three main variables: authenticity, perception of the candidate, and political information efficacy.

Additional demographic questions about political involvement and disposition were asked.

Authenticity was measured using 10 items from Louden and McCauliff (2004). This authenticity scale had been previously used in political public relations research assessing political candidates (Sweetser, 2017; Sweetser & Tedesco, 2014). The authenticity items were summed into a single index (alpha=.87). Characteristics were measured using Kaid's (1995) 12-item semantic differential scale. Then characteristics were summed into a single index (alpha=.81).

Political information efficacy was measured using three items on a 5-point Likert-type scale, initially developed by Kaid et al. (2004, 2007). Scholars characterize these items as a measurement of internal efficacy. Items included measurement of how much one considered one's self qualified to participate in politics, the feeling that one was better informed about politics and government than most, or having a good understanding of the issues facing the nation. As traditionally done with the political information efficacy scale, the items were summed as a unidimensional index (alpha=.90).

Results

This post-test–only experiment manipulated the type of endorsement a political candidate received through media coverage. Endorsement manipulation included endorsement by celebrity ($n=165$), newspaper ($n=180$), military leader ($n=179$), and politician ($n=168$); the control group ($n=187$) was not exposed to a stimulus. A manipulation check revealed that participants understood and could correctly identify the stimulus to which they were exposed, x^2 (16, $N=855$)=2051.39, $p\leq.001$.

The participants in this study were primarily first-time voters. More than half ($n=460$; 52.3%) had never voted previously in the United States, and about one-third had voted in the most recent primary election ($n=272$; 31.4%). Only 6.3% ($n=55$) reported having voted in 2014. This voting behavior appears to be in line with representing the first-time voter, especially considering the average age of the participant was 21.06 ($SD=4.79$). A majority of the participants were registered to vote ($n=725$; 82.5%). Considering that even those who are not registered to vote are affected by presidential policy making, all participants were retained in this study.

The participants in this study showed diverse party affiliation, with 39.1% being Democrat ($n=344$), 29.4% being Republican ($n=258$), 17.1% being independent/no party ($n=150$), and 6% being Libertarian ($n=53$). Not all participants indicated party affiliation, with 6.8% ($n=60$) indicating "other." Not all participants offered their political party affiliation ($n=14$).

The rank party affiliation matched actual candidate support. That is, Clinton was the candidate most participants said they would vote for (43.8%,

$n=385$), followed by Donald Trump ($n=208$; 23.7%), Johnson ($n=78$; 8.9%), and Jill Stein ($n=18$; 2%).

Authenticity

An analysis of variance (ANOVA) examined whether there was a difference in the summative means index score for authenticity based on the experimental cell to which the participant was exposed. The ANOVA resulted in main effects, $F(4, 843)=4.407$, $p \leq .002$.

A Tukey post hoc analysis revealed that nearly every endorsement created a higher-level positive evaluation of authenticity of the candidate from participants than the control group. Specifically, politician endorsements ($M_{diff}=.23$, $p=.001$), newspaper endorsements ($M_{diff}=.17$, $p=.002$), and celebrity endorsements ($M_{diff}=17$, $p=.039$) resulted in higher perceived authenticity when compared to the control group. The only experimental cell that was not statistically significantly different from the control group was the military endorsement cell. Endorsements themselves did not produce interaction effects, meaning there was no change in perceived authenticity based on the type of endorsement. In answering RQ1, this means that endorsements, with the exception of military leadership endorsements, are generally a good political public relations tactic. The specific type of endorsement is not as important as the endorsement itself.

Characteristics

To answer RQ2, an ANOVA was conducted to examine if there was a difference in the summative index score for characteristics based on the experiment cell. The ANOVA resulted in main effects, $F(4, 857)=3.85$, $p \leq .004$.

A Tukey post hoc analysis revealed that, again, nearly every endorsement created a higher level of positive evaluations of candidate characteristics from the participants than the control group. Specifically, celebrity endorsements ($M=.19$, $p=.003$), military endorsements ($M=.15$, $p=.03$), and newspaper endorsements ($M=.15$, $p=.03$) resulted in higher evaluations of perceived candidate characteristics. The experimental cell that did not result in a statistically significant difference was the politician endorsement cell. As such, the answer to RQ2 finds evidence that perception of positive candidate characteristics are indeed influenced by endorsements for most types.

Additional Analysis

Following the analysis of variance, a Pearson correlation test was run to see if there was a relationship between authenticity and characteristics. Indeed, the two variables positively correlated at a moderate level ($r=.622$).

Political Information Efficacy as Predictor of Perceptions of Authenticity and Candidate Characteristics

In answering RQ3 and RQ4, separate linear regressions were run with political information efficacy as the independent variable. In predicting first-time voters' perceived authenticity of the candidate for RQ3, political information efficacy did significantly predict authenticity ($\beta = .095$, $p \leq .001$) but at a very low level (adjusted $R^2 = .035$, $p \leq .001$). As such, the answer to RQ3 is that it is difficult to say that political information efficacy had a tangible role in predicting authenticity. The results for RQ4 in testing the ability of political information efficacy as a predictor of candidate characteristics were not statistically significant.

Discussion

This study sought to determine whether endorsements from influencers, as one of the several tactics deployed by political public relations professionals and political advertisers, had an impact on voter perceptions of political candidates. The data here show that, indeed, the use of endorsements does shape a voter's perception of a candidate's authenticity and characteristics. This experiment demonstrates empirical support for the use of endorsements in the political arena when communicating with young and first-time voters.

Although this study did not intend to create a link between voting behavior as a result of endorsements, it initiates important early work on how endorsements might affect voter perceptions. In turn, voter perceptions and how they translate to votes cast need further investigation. Especially in the context of the 2016 election, it is not realistic to believe that reading an article about a third-party candidate may sway a voter to change his or her vote. However, this study provides a start in investigating the public relations impact of endorsements in shaping perceptions of political candidates.

When deciding on what tactics to deploy throughout a campaign, political public relations practitioners now know that the use of a politician, newspaper, or celebrity endorsement can result in increased perceived authenticity of their candidate client. Furthermore, political public relations practitioners can choose to use endorsements—specifically by celebrities, military leaders, and newspapers—as a way to bring the positive characteristics of the candidate to the forefront of the minds of voters.

Today's influencers do have an impact on young voters and the perceptions they have of presidential candidates. Because the findings in this study were so significant, it is important to push forward with scholarship to test what other components of a candidate's campaign are affected by endorsements and what among the various types of endorsements create the desired outcomes.

References

Benoit, W. L., McKinney, M. S., & Stephenson, M. T. (2002). Effects of watching primary debates in the 2000 U.S. presidential campaign. *Journal of Communication, 52*(2), 316–331. doi: 10.1111/j.1460-2466.2002.tb02547.x

Delli Carpini, M. X. (2000). Gen.com: Youth, civic engagement, and the new information environment. *Political Communication, 17*(4), 341–349. doi: 10.1080/10584600050178942

Drew, D., & Weaver, D. (2006). Voter learning in the 2004 presidential election: Did the media matter? *Journalism & Mass Communication Quarterly, 83*, 25–42. doi: 10.1177/107769900608300103

Enelow, J., & Hinich, M. (1982). Nonspatial candidate characteristics and electoral competition. *The Journal of Politics, 44*(1), 115–130. doi: 10.2307/2130286

Forsyth, J. (2008, January 16). British politicians should learn from the American primaries: Authenticity wins votes. *The Spectator*. Retrieved from https://www.spectator.co.uk/2008/01/british-politicians-should-learn-from-the-american-primaries-authenticity-wins-votes/

Gilpin, D., Palazzolo, E., & Brody, N. (2010). Socially mediated authenticity. *Journal of Communication Management, 14*(3), 258–278. doi: 10.1108/13632541011064526

Kaid, L. L. (1995). Measuring candidate images with semantic differentials. In K. Hacker (Ed.), *Candidate images in presidential election campaigns* (pp. 131–134). New York: Praeger.

Kaid, L. L., McKinney, M. S., & Tedesco, J. C. (2004, November). *Political information efficacy and young voters.* Paper presented at the annual meeting of the National Communication Association, Chicago.

Kaid, L. L., McKinney, M., & Tedesco, J. C. (2007). Political information efficacy and young voters. *American Behavioral Scientist, 50*(9), 1093–1111.

Lanoue, D. J., & Schrott, P. R. (1989). The effects of primary season debates on public opinion. *Political Behavior, 11*(3), 289–306. doi: 0.1007/BF00992301

Liebes, T. (2001). "Look me straight in the eye": The political discourse of authenticity, spontaneity, and sincerity. *Communication Review, 4*(4), 499–510. doi: 10.1080/10714420109359482

Louden, A., & McCauliff, M. (2004). The "authentic candidate": Extending candidate image assessments. In K. L. Hacker (Ed.), *Presidential candidate image* (pp. 85–102). Lanham, MD: Rowman & Littlefield.

McKinney, M. S., Kaid, L. L., & Robertson, T. A., (2001). The front-runner, contenders, and also-rans: Effects of watching a 2000 republican primary debate. *American Behavioral Scientist, 44*(12), 2232–2254. doi: 10.1177/00027640121958294

Opdycke, K., Segura, P., & Vasquez, A. M. (2013). The effects of political cynicism, political information efficacy and media consumption on intended voter participation. *Colloquy, 9*, 75–97.

Pfau, M. (1987). The influence of intraparty debates on candidate preference. *Communication Research, 14*, 687–697. doi: 10.1177/009365087014006004

Robertson, W. (2015, October 15). *Duck Dynasty* star Willie Robertson says Trump is "authentic." (S. Doocy, interviewer). [Audio file]. Retrieved from http://insider.foxnews.com/2015/10/27/duck-dynastys-willie-robertson-says-trump-authentic

Rosenberg, H. (2000, September 15). Candidates on talk-show circuit: If you don't schmooze, you lose. *Los Angeles Times,* section F.

Sweetser, K. D. (2017). Lesser of two evils?: Political organization-public relationship in the 2016 election. *American Behavioral Scientist, 61*(3), 345–356. doi: 10.1177/0002764217701216

Sweetser, K. D., & Kaid, L. L. (2008). Stealth soapboxes: Political information efficacy, cynicism, and uses of celebrity weblogs among readers. *New Media & Society, 10*(1), 73–98. doi: 10.1177/1461444807085322

Sweetser, K. D., & Tedesco, J. C. (2014). Effects of exposure and messaging on political organization-public relationships exemplified in the candidate-constituent relationship. *American Behavioral Scientist, 58*(6), 776–793. doi:10.1177/0002764213515221

Tan, A. S. (1980). Mass media use, issue knowledge and political involvement. *The Public Opinion Quarterly, 44*(2), 241–248. doi: 10.1086/268588

Taylor, C. (1992). *The Ethics of Authenticity.* Cambridge, MA: Harvard University Press.

Tedesco, J. C. (2011). Political information efficacy and Internet effects in the 2008 U.S. presidential election. *American Behavioral Scientist, 55*(6), 703–705. doi: 10.1177/0002764211398089

Wall, V., Golden, J., & James, H. (1988). Perceptions of the 1984 presidential debates and a select 1988 presidential primary debate. *Presidential Studies Quarterly, 18*, 541–563.

Wenner, J. (2016, March 23). Hillary Clinton for president. *Rolling Stone.* Retrieved from http://www.rollingstone.com/politics/news/hillary-clinton-for-president-20160323

Yawn, M., Ellsworth, K., Beatty, B., & Kahn, K. F. (1998). How a presidential primary debate changed attitudes of audience members. *Political Behavior, 20*(2), 155–181.

CHAPTER SIX

Attributions of Incivility in Presidential Campaign News

Ashley Muddiman

"You could put half of Trump's supporters into what I call the basket of deplorables."
—Hillary Clinton, September 9, 2016

"You can do anything . . . Grab them by the pussy. You can do anything."
—Donald Trump, October 7, 2016

By Election Day 2016, many people in the United States just wanted the election to be over. Nearly 60% of Americans were "worn out by so much election coverage" by June 2016—*before* the general election campaign even began—and approximately 50% of people perceived social media discussions of the election as disrespectful and uncivil (Duggan & Smith, 2016; Gottfried, 2016). Major news outlets described the election as "Evil Queen v. Evil Clown" (Kass, 2016), "nasty" (Samuelson, 2016), and "a scorched earth campaign" (Keneally & Liddy, 2016). Clearly, election 2016 was contentious, and media coverage of the campaign was extensive. But to what extent was the campaign uncivil, and who was to blame for the incivility?

Americans studied after the election certainly thought incivility was rampant. According to a post-election survey conducted by Weber Shandwick (2017), 69% of Americans across the political spectrum reported that the United States has a major civility problem and 75% believed that "incivility has risen to crisis levels." However, Donald Trump and Hillary Clinton voters disagreed on the extent to which each candidate behaved inappropriately, with 77% of Trump voters believing that Clinton acted uncivilly during the campaign and 89% of Clinton voters believing that Trump acted uncivilly during the campaign (Weber Shandwick, 2017). The quotations listed at the beginning of this chapter seem to support the thesis that a lack of respect for individuals was a recurring theme (Variety Staff, 2016); yet, anecdotally, not everyone agreed that the candidates were out of line when they made these statements. Clinton supporters, for instance, claimed that her "deplorables" comment was "inartful honesty" about Trump's base of supporters (Karni, 2016), and Trump supporters brushed off his comments by simply stating that "men at times talk like that" (Bradner, 2016). Although there is agreement that campaign 2016 was uncivil, there is no consensus as to the amount of incivility or who behaved uncivilly during the campaign.

This chapter investigates incivility in the 2016 campaign by studying news media reports that *attribute* uncivil behaviors to the candidates. I examine news articles for instances where journalists, commentators, or political figures alleged that the candidates behaved uncivilly. Theoretically, the news values and professional norms that guide journalists' coverage choices both predict that accusations of incivility will appear in the news—for instance, the journalistic value of conflict—and suggest that journalists may avoid printing such accusations—for instance, the journalistic value of appearing objective and fair (Schudson, 2001; Shoemaker & Reese, 1996). Studying journalists' portrayal of candidates as uncivil can offer suggestions about which news values win out during campaigns. Further, understanding when journalists do and do not print accusations of incivility provides a practical perspective on a recent journalistic controversy: whether to use the word "lie" and "liar" in connection with political statements. Some news organizations, like *The New York Times* (Berry, 2017), have publically stated that they use the word "lie" when appropriate, whereas others, like the *Wall Street Journal* (Sheppard, 2017), have taken the opposite view. In this chapter I examine a similar tension: whether journalists working for news outlets attributed incivility to one or both of the candidates or whether they described candidate behaviors without directly making judgments about incivility. In other words, I investigate whether news outlets encouraged their audiences to view the candidates through a lens of incivility or whether they encouraged audiences to make their own decisions about the appropriateness of the candidates' behaviors.

Attributions of Incivility and News Values

Incivility, fundamentally, is a violation of social norms (Ben-Porath, 2010; Jamieson & Hardy, 2012; Mutz, 2015). *What* violated social norms count as incivility varies across research studies. Within the realm of politics, these violated social norms have included a range of unacceptable behaviors, such as interpersonal impoliteness (Mutz, 2015), outrageous news language (Sobieraj & Berry, 2011), poor argumentation and spreading misinformation (Jamieson & Hardy, 2012; Muddiman, 2017), bigotry and threats to democracy (Papacharissi, 2004), and extremism and disordered political processes (Entman, 2011; Uslaner, 1996). In the case of the current study, all of these types of political incivility are taken into account.

Recently, scholars have begun acknowledging that whether something is "uncivil" can shift across individuals and contexts. Situating incivility within cultural norms encourages researchers to recognize that those norms may change depending on the people involved, the context, and the culture. For instance, a congressman yelling "you lie" at President Barack Obama during a joint address to the U.S. Congress in 2009 was an unprecedented and norm-violating act (Gerhart, 2009), whereas British members of parliament have created a culture in which insulting another MP is, largely, considered normal and acceptable (Taylor, 2016). Scholars have begun to test shifting perceptions of incivility, finding that perceptions of incivility are affected by individual differences, partisan group identity, and psychological traits (e.g., Kenski, Coe, & Rains, forthcoming; Muddiman, 2017; Mutz, 2015). Further, politicians use incivility strategically, deciding to call for civility or to label their opponents as "uncivil" when it suits their needs (Herbst, 2010). Thus, rather than approaching incivility as a list of behaviors that are—or are not—acceptable in a political campaign, this chapter understands incivility as a malleable concept.

Due to this malleability, coverage of political campaigns and political incivility deserve attention. Journalists may play a role in molding the concept of political incivility for audiences by discussing political candidates as norm violating or not. The vast majority of voters are not able to hear presidential candidates speak in person, and even fewer voters get to know the candidates personally (Hart, 1999). Media coverage of candidates thus constructs candidate images that voters use as they decide on their vote choice. Additionally, news coverage, from a framing perspective, can emphasize and deemphasize moral evaluations of newsworthy events (Entman, 1993). Describing candidates' actions as impolite, racist, undemocratic, and the like could signal to readers that they should consider candidates' behaviors as uncivil and unacceptable.

Whether journalists actually frame candidate behavior as beyond the norms of typical campaigns, however, is not a given. Journalists, through their professional training, organizational culture, and news routines, have developed their own norms that guide them in deciding what makes it into the news and what gets left out (Shoemaker & Reese, 2006). These news values may make journalists more or less likely to describe—or quote others who describe—a candidate as acting outside the bounds of civility.

On one hand journalists' adherence to the news value of conflict could increase the likelihood that charges of incivility enter news coverage during campaigns (Shoemaker & Reese, 1996). Clash between two people or groups provides interest to news narratives (Price, Tewksbury, & Powers, 1997), and conflict coverage tends to dominate news (Semetko & Valkenburg, 2000). During campaigns, news coverage often pits two candidates against each other as though they are two sports teams strategically vying to win the election. Pointing out the clash between two candidates or their campaigns would strongly align with the news value of conflict, even when that clash includes attributing ad hominem attacks, discriminatory behavior, threatening the stability of the U.S. government, or other uncivil acts to one or more candidates.

On the other hand, journalists may want to stay above the fray of the campaign, particularly in an effort to adhere to the professional norm of objectivity. This norm encourages journalists to fairly and impartially cover multiple perspectives without allowing their own biases to creep into the final articles (Schudson, 2001). Journalists, in attempting to appear unbiased, may avoid calling out candidate behaviors as inappropriate and uncivil, much like *The Wall Street Journal* avoids directly calling politicians' misstatements "lies." Even if journalists do allow an incivility attribution into the coverage, they may attempt to cover opposing candidates like Clinton and Trump in similar ways to avoid charges of partisan bias.

Drawing from incivility and news values research, this chapter tackles the questions: Did news coverage attribute incivility to the campaigns of Clinton and Trump? And, if so, how did this coverage vary across candidate, across news source and news type, and across the progression of a campaign?

Finding Attributions of Incivility in Campaign News

A content analysis of news articles published during the 2016 presidential campaign answers these questions. The content analysis included 633 articles published during the general election campaign in either *The New York Times* (NYT) or *The Wall Street Journal* (WSJ). The NYT and WSJ were ideal for this study for a number of reasons. First, both the NYT and the WSJ are prominent national newspapers, with circulations of 1.6 million (Ember, 2017) and 1.4 million (Media Kit, 2017), respectively, meaning that the coverage in these papers likely reached a wide audience. Next, as nationally prominent newspapers, other media sources likely follow their lead when it comes to news coverage, which in turn amplifies the effects of their content choices (Golan, 2006). Finally these two newspapers, as mentioned earlier in this chapter, have taken contrasting stances toward directly calling out politicians for lying. Examining both sources allows me to determine whether coverage in the WSJ and the NYT that called out politicians for their bad behavior aligned with the public stances of the newspapers.

I collected news articles using two databases: LexisNexis Academic, which archives articles published by the NYT, and ProQuest, which archives articles published by the WSJ. Within both databases I searched for all articles that included "Clinton" or "Trump" (or both) in the article headline and that were published between September 5, 2016 (Labor Day and the traditional start of the general election) through November 8, 2016 (Election Day). My search encompassed news articles and opinion articles published in both newspapers.* Duplicate articles, as well as letters to the editor and Web publications, were removed from the data set.

The articles were then coded for whether they included a statement claiming that either Clinton or Trump—or their respective supporters—were engaging in some form of incivility. The actual term "uncivil" was used in very few articles. Thus, news articles that attributed one of a variety of types of incivility to one of the two presidential candidates or their supporters were coded as "Present" for an incivility attribution. Drawing from previous content analyses that identified the presence or absence of incivility in news and online settings (e.g., Coe, Kenski, & Rains, 2014; Papacharissi, 2004; Sobieraj & Berry, 2011; Stroud, Scacco, Muddiman, & Curry, 2015), as well as theoretical approaches to incivility (Muddiman, 2017; Mutz, 2015), the articles were coded as including an incivility attribution if any *one* of the following activities was linked to either Clinton and her supporters or Trump and his supporters:

- Name calling, attacking, or bullying (e.g., "he's a bully")
- Generally being rude or impolite (e.g., "he's an indecent human being")
- Radicalism or extremism (e.g., Trump is "helping a radical fringe take over")
- Spreading misinformation and lies (e.g., Clinton is "incapable of telling the truth")
- Discrimination or bigotry (e.g., Clinton is a "bigot")
- Being a threat to democracy and the country (e.g., "He is a dangerous demagogue")
- Being unfit for the presidency (e.g., "The disdain that Hillary Clinton expressed . . . disqualifies her from public service")

Notably, some of these attributions of uncivil, unacceptable behavior could themselves be considered uncivil—for instance, labeling someone a liar, a bigot, and/or a bully are examples of impolite name calling—yet they also

---

*In the NYT, the news articles were labeled "National" or "Politics," and the opinion articles were labeled "Op-Ed." In the WSJ, the news articles were labeled "News" or "Feature," and the opinion articles were labeled "Commentary" or "Editorial."

reflect judgment calls about the actions of the individual candidates. Trump, for instance, was accused of committing "verbal treason" when he called for Russia to hack more of Clinton's e-mails (Martin & Chozick, 2016), and Clinton, according to one political commentator, "has been lying and has been doing everything to keep [her emails] from becoming public since she was caught [using a private email server]" (McGurn, 2016).

Thus, for the purposes of this study, the coders were not searching for uncivil actions themselves, but instead were looking for explicit claims from others (be they quotations from political figures or from the journalists themselves) that Clinton, Trump, or their supporters were engaging in behaviors that made the candidates unsuited for office. Take, for instance, a prominent example during the campaign: Trump's infamous *Access Hollywood* tape in which he bragged about aggressive sexual behaviors. A simple description of this recording was not coded as an incivility attribution even though the recorded discussion may be considered uncivil by many. However, if Clinton was quoted in a news article saying that, as demonstrated by the tape Trump is a sexist who demeans women, then the article was coded "Present" for an incivility attribution.

Two coders conducted a reliability analysis of 110 articles, making up approximately 17% of the sample. They determined whether two separate codes were present or absent in each article: (1) attributing incivility to Trump or his supporters (Krippendorff's $\alpha = .68$) and (2) attributing incivility to Clinton or her supporters (Krippendorff's $\alpha = .78$). The reliability was acceptable, though not particularly strong, by Krippendorff's (2004) standards, especially when coding for the presence of attributing incivility to Trump. Previous work concerning incivility has also noted the difficulty of earning high levels of reliability for a topic that is so influenced by individual perceptions, and thus other published work has argued that .67 is an acceptable threshold for incivility reliability (see, for instance, Coe et al., 2014). Using these two codes, an "incivility attributions" variable was created with four mutually exclusive levels: an article contained *no incivility attributions*, contained incivility attributions directed *only at Trump*, contained incivility attributions directed *only at Clinton*, or contained incivility attributions directed at *both candidates*.

The following sections overview the findings of this content analysis. Two data analysis points are important to note. First, because all articles that were available through the databases and that met the criteria detailed earlier were analyzed, no inferential statistics are necessary for this study. Descriptive statistics of the content analysis are used to overview the news coverage. Second, the results are discussed as percentages of coverage rather than as raw numbers because there were more articles published by the NYT in this time period than in the WSJ. Using percentages allows for a more even comparison between the two news sources.

Attributing Incivility to Hillary Clinton and Donald Trump

The answer to this chapter's first question—whether attributions of incivility made it into news coverage of the 2016 presidential campaign—is a clear "yes." Only 43% of the articles in the NYT and WSJ did *not* attribute any type of incivility to either of the candidates, meaning that more than half of the articles *did* include some type of incivility claim (see Figure 6.1).

At first glance it appears that the news value of conflict encouraged journalists to include attributions of incivility in their coverage of the campaign. Clinton, in the pages of the newspapers, was accused of corruption due to her use of a private e-mail server during her time as secretary of state (Tau & Nelson, 2016) and of having "bullied, attacked, shamed, and intimidated" the victims of her husband's sexual liaisons (Burns, Haberman, & Martin, 2016). Trump was pronounced a "bully" who engaged in "demeaning, degrading, insulting and assaulting [behavior toward] women" (Ballhaus, Hook, & Lee, 2016). Both candidates were described repeatedly as personally attacking their political opponents, spreading lies, and being dangerously unfit to hold the office of the presidency.

Notably, some evidence of the news value of objectivity appears as well. Fifteen percent of the articles included incivility attributions directed at both candidates. When combined with the 43% of articles that included no attributions of incivility whatsoever, it appears that journalists attempted to portray the candidates as equally civil or equally uncivil in 58% of the articles.

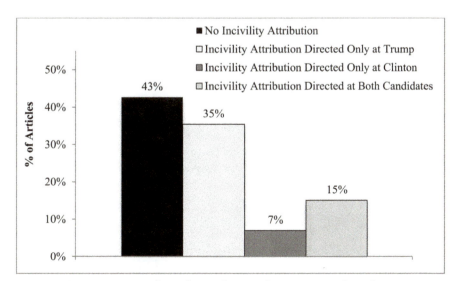

Figure 6.1   Percentage of Articles with or without an Incivility Claim

However, journalists did not print incivility attributions equally at all times. Articles that labeled only one candidate as uncivil tended to do so when describing Trump. Thirty-five percent of the articles analyzed described Trump alone in a way that implied he behaved in an unacceptable, uncivil manner (see Figure 6.1). Alternatively, only 7% of articles attributed uncivil behavior to Clinton alone.

Incivility Attributions Across Source and Article Type

The presence of incivility claims in news articles signaled that newspapers—even mainstream, relatively centrist papers—were willing to print attributions of incivility in their pages during the 2016 campaign. *Where* these attributions appeared also is a meaningful question. Incivility research suggests that individuals are likely to perceive their outgroup political party as behaving more uncivilly than the ingroup political party, even when partisans engage in the exact same behaviors (Muddiman, 2017; Mutz, 2015). Perhaps newspaper coverage of elections follows a similar pattern, with a newspaper that leans conservative being more likely to label Clinton as uncivil and a newspaper that leans liberal being more likely to label Trump as uncivil. The newspapers studied here largely offer mainstream news perspectives, but, relative to each other and based on audience perceptions and editorial content, the NYT tends to lean toward the left and the WSJ tends to lean toward the right (see, for details, Mitchell, Gottfried, Kiley, & Matsa, 2014; Stroud, Muddiman, & Lee, 2014; Wagner & Collins, 2014). Did the NYT include incivility attributions that favored Clinton, and did the WSJ include incivility attributions that favored Trump?

Some evidence of partisan news coverage appeared in the data (see Figure 6.2). The NYT, as expected, included a larger percentage of articles that attributed incivility only to Trump (44% compared to 25% for the WSJ), whereas the WSJ included a higher percentage of articles that attributed incivility only to Clinton (10% to 4%). Interestingly, a larger percentage of the WSJ's coverage (51%) compared to NYT coverage (36%) did not include any incivility attributions at all, meaning that a lack of Trump-only incivility attributions was not balanced out by a similarly sized increase in Clinton-only incivility attributions. Instead, the WSJ more often than not simply didn't attribute incivility to either of the candidates or their supporters.

Whether this partisan coverage appears in the news sections or the admittedly opinionated editorial sections is an important next step to test. Objectivity is not expected in editorial sections—in fact, the expectation is quite the opposite. Writers are supposed to offer their opinions, suggesting that editorial articles may be more likely to directly attribute incivility to one or both candidates.

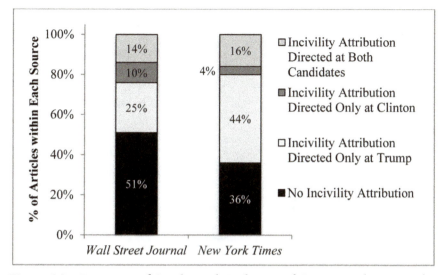

Figure 6.2   Percentage of Articles with Each Type of Content in the *New York Times* and *Wall Street Journal*

Yet in the news content overall there were few differences between the news coverage and the opinion coverage (see Figure 6.3a). In general, similar percentages of news and opinion articles claimed that only Trump was uncivil (35% and 36%, respectively) or that both candidates were uncivil (15% and 16%, respectively). Slightly larger differences appeared for the two other variables. There was a lower percentage of opinion articles (37%) that did not make a claim about incivility compared to news articles (45%). Additionally, there was a larger percentage of opinion articles (11%) that attributed incivility only to Clinton compared to news articles (5%). However, these differences were not substantial.

The results become more intriguing when examining news versus opinion coverage across the two news sources. The news articles for both sources followed a similar pattern: the highest percentage of news articles attribute incivility to only Trump, followed by articles attributing incivility to both candidates, and trailed by articles attributing incivility to only Clinton (see Figures 6.3b and 6.3c). The opinion articles, however, tell a different story. The NYT opinion articles were substantially more likely to call out Trump alone for behaving uncivilly, with more than half of the opinion articles doing so, whereas only 20% of WSJ opinion articles did the same. The difference is just as dramatic when comparing the papers' opinion section coverage of Clinton. The WSJ's opinion articles attributed incivility to Clinton alone 18% of the time and to both Clinton and Trump 20% of the time, for a total of 38%

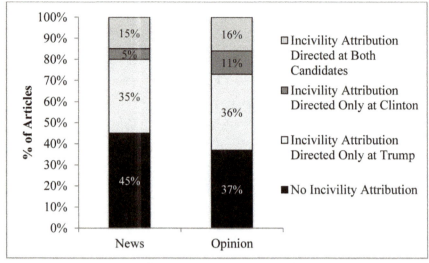

Figure 6.3a Percentage of Articles with Each Type of Content in News and Opinion Content Overall

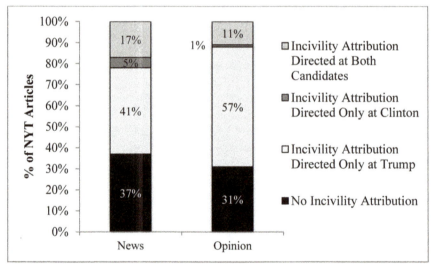

Figure 6.3b Percentage of Articles with Each Type of Content in News and Opinion Content in NYT

of articles making some incivility attribution to Clinton. In contrast the NYT only attributed incivility to Clinton alone in 1% of the opinion articles and to Clinton and Trump together in 11% of the articles, for a total of only 12% of the opinion articles attributing incivility to Clinton. Overall, news articles

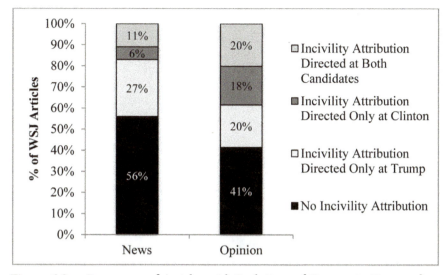

Figure 6.3c   Percentage of Articles with Each Type of Content in News and Opinion Content in WSJ

printed by the two papers were relatively consistent (though the WSJ made fewer incivility attributions overall than the NYT), but the opinion pages of the papers told two vastly different stories about the presidential candidates and their supporters. The WSJ portrayed both candidates as uncivil, whereas the NYT opinion writers largely agreed that Trump was the uncivil candidate.

Incivility Attributions Across Time

To this point the data suggest that newspapers print attributions of incivility toward presidential candidates and that the news source and type of article appear to influence to *whom* incivility is attributed. What remains unexplored, however, is *why*. What might prompt news coverage to include relatively direct accusations that a political candidate has acted out of line and beyond the scope of typically accepted political behavior? Beginning with the week of September 5 through November 1, 2016, I examined the weekly percentage of news articles that included attributions of incivility throughout the course of the campaign. Investigating these attributions over time allows for a comparison between news content and major campaign events to determine whether the events seem to drive incivility attributions or whether the claims remain relatively consistent across the campaign.

The influence of context and campaign events is most notable in relation to incivility attributions about Trump (see Figure 6.4). Throughout the entire campaign Trump-only attributions of incivility appeared more often than

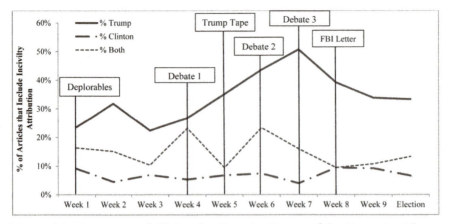

Figure 6.4   Percentage of All Articles Over the Course of the Campaign That Included Incivility Claims for Trump, Clinton, or Both Candidates (*Note:* Each week labeled in the figures represents a seven-day period beginning on a Monday and ending on a Sunday. For example, Week 1 includes Monday, September 5, through Sunday, September 11. The week labeled "Election" includes only Monday, November 7, and Tuesday, November 8. Debate 2 is listed as taking place in Week 6, even though it took place on Sunday of Week 5, because the news articles did not come out until the next day.)

other incivility attributions. This may be, in part, due to the Clinton campaign's strategy to repeatedly argue that Trump did not have the temperament to serve as president of the United States. During her nomination acceptance speech, for example, which took place a few weeks prior to the beginning of this data set, Clinton forcefully questioned Trump's fitness to serve as president of the United States. And it seems that news articles picked up and printed her attacks. As one WSJ article summarized, "Her speech . . . repeatedly slammed Republican nominee Donald Trump as unfit and someone who 'loses his cool at the slightest provocation'" (Meckler & Hughes, 2016). During the middle of the general election the percentage of articles that attributed incivility to only Trump increased substantially, particularly between Weeks 5 and 7. Notably, the *Access Hollywood* tape was released during Week 5. Trump was described as both "crude" and "sexist" due to this revelation. These incivility attributions kept linking Trump to inappropriate behavior, especially through the third debate. Overall, Trump was generally accused of incivility at higher levels than Clinton throughout the campaign, and the *Access Hollywood* recording seemed to buoy the high percentage of Trump-only incivility attributions.

Shifting focus to Clinton, the percentage of news articles published each week that only claimed Clinton behaved uncivilly remained relatively consistent throughout the campaign and never topped 9% of all articles. The consistency may have been due to a trickle of e-mails found on campaign staffers' computers and leaked to the public through WikiLeaks throughout the campaign. There were, however, two times in which her solo incivility attributions spiked. First, in the first week of data analyzed, Clinton made her "deplorables" remarks (see the beginning of the chapter for the exact quote) targeted at Trump supporters. In the news coverage following the statement, Clinton was described as "attacking" and "demeaning" Trump voters, a behavior that was largely deemed out of line with respectable political behavior. Second, toward the very end of the campaign a major announcement was made that the FBI was reopening its investigation regarding Clinton's use of a private e-mail server while she served as secretary of state. News articles, particularly when describing Clinton opponents' reactions to the reopened case, included references to Clinton's corruption "on a scale we have never seen before" (Chozick & Healy, 2016). In general, the attributions of Clinton-only incivility were infrequent but largely consistent across the campaign, although the two campaign events described earlier did align with spikes in Clinton-only incivility attributions.

Notably, there were a few moments during the election that aligned with a spike in articles that depicted *both* Clinton and Trump as uncivil candidates: 1) immediately after Clinton made the "deplorables" remarks, 2) after the first two official presidential debates, and 3) as Election Day approached. On one hand, as described earlier, Clinton's description of Trump supporters as a "basket of deplorables" might be demeaning and insulting to those supporters. On the other hand, every time her quotation was restated in a news story, it linked Trump with "racist, sexist, homophobic, xenophobic, [and] Islamaphobic" individuals, emphasizing that he is out of line with acceptable political behavior as well (Nelson & Trottman, 2016). Thus, many articles that mentioned Clinton's statement attributed incivility both to her *and* to Trump and his supporters. Similarly, after the debates, *both* campaigns were described as personally attacking the other side, and, as Election Day approached, news articles were able to draw from attributions of incivility linked to the candidates throughout the campaign. These events and the coverage that followed them further signaled that *both* candidates were unacceptable and uncivil alternatives for president of the United States.

Overall, there was not a one-to-one relationship between campaign events and attributions of incivility in news coverage, but there were moments in which salient campaign events allowed journalists to emphasize the professional norm of conflict in their stories. Scandals, as well as direct quotations from the candidates themselves, seemed to provide the most leeway in allowing journalists to make judgments about the morality of the candidates.

Conclusion

News coverage in the NYT and WSJ reflected what Americans reported feeling during and after the election: media coverage was exhausting and the campaign was uncivil. In fact, attributions of incivility appeared in a slight *majority* of articles printed during the election, demonstrating that journalists were not opposed to printing judgments about the morality of the two major-party presidential candidates. Although coverage in both sources indicated that Trump was most deserving of an incivility label, the WSJ was more likely than the NYT to attribute incivility to Clinton, and the NYT was more likely than the WSJ to attribute incivility to Trump—especially in the opinion sections of the papers. This finding suggests a slight partisan lean in use of incivility attributions across the news outlets. Finally, it appears that attributions of incivility are, at times, tied to concrete campaign events, rather than being used haphazardly throughout the campaign.

There are three study limitations to note. First, the article content analyzed here was published in only two print news sources and focused only on the presidential race. In the future, it will be important to expand studies of incivility attributions to regional and local news sources and elections to determine if these conclusions only apply on the national level. Second, coders only looked for the presence of an incivility attribution; they did not determine *who* made that claim. Although the data suggest that journalists who included incivility attributions in their articles were responding to conflict-heavy events in the campaign rather than any internal biases, it will be important in the future to determine whether the incivility attributions originated from the journalists themselves or from sources quoted in the news stories. Finally, this chapter focuses on mapping media content related to the 2016 election, but does not investigate the effects of the coverage overviewed here. Future studies also should test the effects of this type of coverage. Based on the findings of this study, it is important to ask: To what extent are individuals' perceptions of incivility, based on *attributions* made in the news media, constructed by journalists and political figures? Do these attributions change voters' conceptualizations of political incivility? Can attributions such as these change voters' opinions about candidates even more than the behaviors alone? All of these questions are ripe for future study.

Despite the limitations, this exploration of attributions of incivility in the news has a number of implications, both for theory and practice. First, the findings suggest that incivility is malleable. The *Access Hollywood* tape of Trump was at times described as "lewd language" and at other times described as "sexism." Clinton's statement calling Trump supporters a "basket of deplorables" led at times to descriptions of Clinton as a "bully" and at other times to accusations that her condescension should disqualify her from the presidency. At still other times neither of these actions were attributed as uncivil at all. Further, the same campaign activities were covered differently across the NYT and WST opinion pages. Context and partisanship matter in the decision to label an action as a violation of political norms, a finding that adds to recent indications that individual differences predict variation in perceptions of political incivility (e.g., Kenski et al., forthcoming; Mutz, 2015).

If incivility is a flexible concept, it should also come as no surprise that the values journalists use in deciding whether to include attributions of incivility in their news articles—particularly conflict and objectivity (Schudson, 2001; Shoemaker & Reese, 2006)—are flexible as well. On one hand, the value of fairness often won out. Most articles either did not include attributions of incivility about either candidate or they linked both Clinton *and* Trump with some type of uncivil act, suggesting that journalists did attempt to present the different parties evenly in many instances. This was especially true for the WSJ, where slightly more than half of the articles published did not include attributions of incivility at all.

Clearly, however, there was a clash between fairness and conflict. In many articles Trump alone was labeled uncivil. On one hand, this may be a positive development in journalism. Objectivity has been critiqued for promoting "he said-she said" news coverage in an effort to be even-handed even in instances where balance is not reflective of reality (Kovach & Rosenstiel, 2014). As this analysis, which spans the course of the full election cycle, suggests, journalists did seem to be reacting to events on the ground rather than relying on individual partisan biases; thus, perhaps a decrease in news balance is not all bad.

On the other hand, the decrease in objectivity also meant that there were differences in coverage between news outlets, which is troubling. Partisan selective exposure literature suggests that people are attracted to information that aligns with their political predispositions (Stroud, 2011). During the 2016 election, if conservative voters followed the WSJ opinion pages and conservative news outlets with similar content, they were likely to see a larger percentage of articles that linked Clinton with various types of incivility than liberal voters who followed the NYT opinion pages and liberal outlets with similar content. The opposite could be true for voters and news coverage about Trump.

The findings summarized in this chapter add to a discussion that is already occurring among news organizations as they try to determine their role in a rapidly changing news environment. Should journalists print attributions about behaviors—like bullying, lying, and corruption—that they believe are outside of the bounds of acceptable behavior? Or should they stick to the news value of fairness and objectivity by avoiding such claims altogether, leaving the morality judgments up to others? Although the current project cannot demonstrate whether one way of covering politics is better than the other, it does demonstrate that journalists *did* make judgments about candidate morality during the 2016 election and that these judgments differed in and across partisan spaces. Essentially, if it is true that liberals and conservatives live in different media worlds, the news outlets that people view may not only approach issues differently but also may have vastly different perspectives on who is an acceptable candidate for president and who is a criminal unfit for the office.

Acknowledgment

The author would like to thank Emma O'Neill for her assistance in analyzing news content for this project.

References

Ballhaus, R., Hook, J., & Lee, C. E. (2016, November 2). Tighter race brings a shift in tactics—Clinton, Trump focus ad spending on new states and home in closing arguments. *The Wall Street Journal,* A1.

Ben-Porath, E. N. (2010). Interview effects: Theory and evidence for the impact of televised political interviews on viewer attitudes. *Communication Theory, 20,* 323–347. doi: 10.1111/j.1468-2885.2010.01365.x

Berry, D. (2017, January 25). In a swirl of "untruths" and "falsehoods," calling a lie a lie. *The New York Times.* Retrieved from https://www.nytimes.com /2017/01/25/business/media/donald-trump-lie-media.html

Bradner, E. (2016, October 9). Giuliani on Trump tape: "Men at times talk like that." *CNN.* Retrieved from http://www.cnn.com/2016/10/09/politics/rudy -giuliani-donald-trump-state-of-the-union-debate

Burns, A., Haberman, M., & Martin, J. (2016, October 8). Tape reveals Trump boast about groping women. *The New York Times,* A1.

Chozick, A., & Healy, P. (2016, October 29). With 11 days to go, Trump says revelation "changes everything." *The New York Times,* A1.

Coe, K., Kenski, K., & Rains, S. A. (2014). Patterns and determinants of incivility in newspaper website comments. *Journal of Communication, 64,* 658–679. doi: 10.1111/jcom.12104

Duggan, M., & Smith, A. (2016, October 25). The political environment on social media. *The Pew Research Center: Internet, Science & Tech.* Retrieved from http://www.pewinternet.org/2016/10/25/the-political-environment-on -social-media/?utm_source=adaptivemailer&utm_medium=email&utm _campaign=10/25/2016%20social%20tone%20of%20politics&org=982 &lvl=100&ite=455&lea=77506&ctr=0&par=1&trk=

Ember, S. (2017, February 2). New York Times Co.'s decline in print advertising tempered by digital gains. *The New York Times.* Retrieved from https://www .nytimes.com/2017/02/02/business/media/new-york-times-q4-earnings .html

Entman, R. M. (1993). Framing: Toward clarification of a fractured paradigm. *Journal of Communication, 43,* 51–58. doi: 10.1111/j.1460-2466.1993.tb01304.x

Entman, R. M. (2011). Incivility and asymmetrical partisan warfare. *In the Name of Democracy: Political Communication Research and Practice in a Polarized Media Environment.* Retrieved from www.lsu.edu/reillycenter

Gerhart, A. (2009, October 12). Uncivil political discourse is a part of history. *Seattle Times.* Retrieved from: http://www.seattletimes.com/seattle-news /politics/uncivil-political-discourse-is-a-part-of-history

Golan, G. (2006). Inter-Media Agenda Setting and Global News Coverage. *Journalism Studies, 7*, 323–333. doi: 10.1080/14616700500533643

Gottfried, J. (2016, July 14). Most Americans already feel election coverage fatigue. *Pew Research Center.* Retrieved from http://www.pewresearch.org/fact-tank /2016/07/14/most-americans-already-feel-election-coverage-fatigue

Hart, R. P. (1999). *Seducing America: How television charms the modern voter.* Thousand Oaks, CA: Sage Publications, Inc.

Herbst, S. (2010). *Rude democracy.* Philadelphia: Temple University Press.

Jamieson, K. H., & Hardy, B. W. (2012). What is civil engaged argument and why does aspiring to it matter? *Political Science & Politics, 45*, 412–415. doi: 10.1017/S1049096512000479

Karni, A. (2016, September 10). Why Clinton isn't sweating "deplorables." *Politico.* Retrieved from http://www.politico.com/story/2016/09/hillary-clinton -deplorables-debate-227996

Kass, J. (2016, October 14). Presidential campaign: Evil queen vs. evil clown. *Chicago Tribune.* Retrieved from: http://www.chicagotribune.com/news/columnists /kass/ct-presidential-election-kass-1016-20161014-column.html

Keneally, M., & Liddy, T. (2016, October 13). A look at Trump's scorched earth campaign in the home stretch of the election. *ABC News.* Retrieved from: http://abcnews.go.com/Politics/trumps-scorched-earth-campaign-home -stretch-election/story?id=42775050

Kenski, K., Coe, K., & Rains, S. A. (forthcoming). Perceptions of uncivil discourse online: An examination of types and predictors. *Communication Research.* doi: 10.1177/0093650217699933

Kovach, B., & Rosenstiel, T. (2014). *The elements of journalism: What newspeople should know and the public should expect.* New York: Three Rivers Press.

Krippendorff, K. (2004). *Content analysis: An introduction to its methodology* (2nd ed.). Thousand Oaks, CA: Sage.

Martin, J., & Chozick, A. (2016, September 9). Vexing his allies, Trump keeps up praise of Putin. *The New York Times*, A1.

McGurn, W. (2016, November 1). Main street: Call Hillary Clinton's bluff. *The Wall Street Journal*, A11.

Meckler, L., & Hughes, S. (2016, July 29). Clinton makers her pitch—Candidate underlines contrasts to rival. *The Wall Street Journal*, A1.

Media Kit. (2017). *The Wall Street Journal.* Retrieved from: http://www.wsjmediakit .com/products/newspaper

Mitchell, A., Gottfried, J., Kiley, J., & Matsa, K. E. (2014, October 21). Political polarization and media habits. *Pew Research Center: Journalism & Media.* Retrieved from http://www.journalism.org/2014/10/21/political-polariza tion-media-habits

Muddiman, A. (2017). Personal and public levels of political incivility. *International Journal of Communication. 11*, 3182–3202. Retrieved from http://ijoc.org /index.php/ijoc/article/view/6137/2106

Mutz, D. C. (2015). *In-your-face politics: The consequences of uncivil media.* Princeton, NJ: Princeton University Press.

Nelson, C. M., & Trottman, M. (2016, September 12). Election 2016: Clinton backs off on "deplorables." *The Wall Street Journal,* A5.

Papacharissi, Z. (2004). Democracy online: Civility, politeness, and the democratic potential of online political discussion groups. *New Media & Society, 6,* 259–283. doi: 10.1177/1461444804041444

Price, V., Tewksbury, D., & Powers, E. (1997). Switching trains of thought: The impact of news frames on readers' cognitive responses. *Communication Research, 24,* 481–506. doi: 10.1177/009365097024005002

Samuelson, R. J. (2016, October 30). Why this campaign is so nasty. *The Washington Post.* Retrieved from: https://www.washingtonpost.com/opinions/how-a-ho-hum-economy-fueled-a-vicious-campaign-cycle/2016/10/30/bc3f96e2-9d2d-11e6-9980-50913d68eacb_story.html?utm_term=.1a75c51e9853

Schudson, M. (2001). The objectivity norm in American journalism. *Journalism, 2,* 149–170. doi: 10.1177/146488490100200201

Semetko, H. A., & Valkenburg, P. M. (2000). Framing European politics: A content analysis of press and television news. *Journal of Communication, 50,* 93–109. doi: 10.1111/j.1460-2466.2000.tb02843.x

Sheppard, K. (2017, January 1). Wall Street Journal editor says his newspaper won't call Donald Trump's lies "lies." *The Huffington Post.* Retrieved from http://www.huffingtonpost.com/entry/wall-street-journal-lies-donald-trump_us_586934b8e4b0eb586489df43

Shoemaker, P. J., & Reese, S. D. (1996). *Mediating the message: Theories of influences on mass media content* (2nd ed.). White Plains, NY: Longman Publishers USA.

Sobieraj, S., & Berry, J. M. (2011). From incivility to outrage: Political discourse in blogs, talk radio, and cable news. *Political Communication, 28,* 19–41. doi: 10.1080/10584609.2010.542360

Stroud, N. J. (2011). *Niche news: The politics of news choice.* New York: Oxford University Press.

Stroud, N. J., Muddiman, A., & Lee, J. K. (2014). Seeing media as group members: An evaluation of partisan bias perceptions. *Journal of Communication, 64,* 874–894. doi: 10.1111/jcom.12110

Stroud, N. J., Scacco, J. M., Muddiman, A., & Curry, A. L. (2015). Changing deliberative norms on news organizations' Facebook sites. *Journal of Computer-Mediated Communication, 20,* 188–203. doi: 10.1111/jcc4.12104

Tau, B., & Nelson, C. M. (2016, October 13). Election 2016: Emails show Clinton party links. *The Wall Street Journal,* A6.

Taylor, A. (2016, February 25). The petty, mean and deliciously rude ways British politicians insult one another. *The Washington Post.* Retrieved from: https://www.washingtonpost.com/news/worldviews/wp/2016/02/25/the-petty-mean-and-deliciously-rude-ways-british-politicians-insult-one-another/?utm_term=.40f35f54f4b7

Uslaner, E. M. (1996). *The decline of comity in Congress.* Ann Arbor: The University of Michigan Press.

Variety Staff. (2016, November 8). Remembering some of the most memorable quotes from the 2016 election. *Variety*. Retrieved from http://variety.com /2016/biz/news/election-2016-most-memorable-quotes-donald-trump -hillary-clinton-1201911983

Wagner, M. W., & Collins, T. P. (2014). Does ownership matter? The case of Rupert Murdoch's purchase of the Wall Street Journal. *Journalism Practice*, 8, 1–14. doi: /10.1080/17512786.2014.882063

Weber Shandwick. (2017, January 23). Poll finds Americans united in seeing uncivil nation; Divided about causes and civility of presidential candidates. *PR Newswire*. Retrieved from http://www.prnewswire.com/news -releases/poll-finds-americans-united-in-seeing-an-uncivil-nation-divided -about-causes-and-civility-of-presidential-candidates-300394885.html

Fact-Checking and the 2016 Presidential Election: News Media's Attempts to Correct Misleading Information from the Debates

Daniela V. Dimitrova and Kimberly Nelson

The 2016 presidential race was unprecedented in many ways and brought to the center of public discussion the role the news media must play in correcting information provided by political figures. Unfortunately, the campaign season made Americans too familiar with slanted campaign statements, false claims made by both presidential candidates, and the rise of fake news (Patterson, 2016). The slew of misleading information has highlighted the importance of a specific type of journalism meant to weed out the truth—namely, fact-checking. Looking back at the 2016 presidential campaign, some media critics have questioned how well the media performed, and some even blamed the media for the election outcome (Benton, 2016). In light of these criticisms, the goal of our study is to take a systematic look at the media's attempt to fact-check the presidential candidates during the final stretch of the 2016 race for the Oval Office. We examine how the news media performed their watchdog role by looking at several established criteria for fact-checking in the aftermath of the three presidential debates.

Rationale and Theoretical Foundations

The 2016 presidential campaign was long, heated, and often unmatched in negativity (Patterson, 2016). Both major political party candidates—Republican Donald Trump and Democrat Hillary Clinton—were found to be dodging the truth, slightly changing the truth, or even telling flat out lies (Bendery, 2016; "Comparing Hillary," 2016). The media's response to both candidates' misleading statements was to make sure the public was given a chance to learn the truth in order to make informed decisions when presented with a ballot on Election Day. Fact-checking journalism has been used in such media outlets as PolitiFact and FactCheck.org since the early 2000s, but a major spike in the amount of fact-checking sources occurred during the 2012 presidential election cycle (Graves, Nyhan, & Reifler, 2015). Besides media outlets that are dedicated sources of fact-checking, many mainstream media organizations also have adopted the new wave of political fact-checking, including *The New York Times*, *The Washington Post*, *USA Today*, the Associated Press, NPR, CNN, Fox, and MSNBC (Graves et al., 2015).

According to the results of a 2016 Pew Research Center survey, consumers of news also are interested in fact-checking. About 59% of respondents surveyed preferred to read facts presented "as is," instead of having journalists interpret the facts (Barthel & Gottfried, 2016). An interesting result reveals that roughly 80% percent of respondents who identified as either Clinton or Trump supporters "not only disagree over plans and policies, but also disagree on basic facts," showing that despite the rise in fact-checking journalism, there is still a dispute over what information is considered a solid fact (Barthel & Gottfried, 2016, para. 3).

A number of reasons could explain this survey outcome. For example, the Pew survey does not mention how many respondents read fact-checking articles on a regular basis. We are also unsure where respondents are receiving their news. Also, the dispute over misinformation could come from media organizations presenting the facts differently. Marietta, Barker, and Bowser (2015) conducted a mixed-methods study that looked into how consistent media outlets' fact-checking articles were with each other when covering the same event. Their findings suggested that the media disagreed about what information should be examined, and the researchers were left with mixed results on how media outlets answer questionable claims (Marietta et al., 2015). In other words, the journalists were asking different questions based on their own biases, which caused the disagreements in fact-checking the same event.

The finding of the lack of consistency among media organizations in the way they approach fact-checking is worth exploring further. It might not be so surprising that different media organizations would focus on different attributes of a selected speech, debate, campaign ad, or claim, as gatekeeping theory, discussed later, would suggest. The important question to ask refers to the idea of a "gold standard" of presenting fact-checking information to the public (Marietta et al., 2015). In other words, before considering the consistency of fact-checking coverage between media organizations, it might be important to examine how the news media apply best practices of covering misinformation. One of the goals of this study is to examine whether traditional media organizations are applying suggested approaches for correcting misinformation to their fact-checking coverage.

Gatekeeping Theory

To better understand how a media organization chooses what information makes it to their audiences and how that information is processed, we must acknowledge the basic concepts laid out in gatekeeping theory. In essence, the information that is selected to be turned into a story by a media organization goes through a selection process within that organization (Shoemaker, Vos, & Reese, 2009). The underlying "winnowing down" process is similar among different media organizations, but each organization carries its own characteristics that determine what information makes it through the gate and how that information is shaped and packaged for the public (Shoemaker & Vos, 2008).

Kurt Lewin's gatekeeping model (as cited in Shoemaker & Vos, 2008) is often referenced when explaining the process of news making. Information first makes its way to media organizations, often called channels in Lewin's model. These channels push the information through to different sections, where information is either abandoned or chosen to move forward to the next gate, where another section with gatekeepers—the decision makers who come in the form of a reporter or editor—will decide if the information makes it to the next gate. Another important attribute of Lewin's model are forces, which can aid or work against a piece of information moving through the channels. All forces do not carry the same weight of power to positively or negatively affect the information during selection processes (Shoemaker & Vos, 2008). For instance, if claims about the sexual assault allegations against Trump were being processed through a tabloid channel, "scandal" would be considered a positive force that would assist claims through the next gates.

The gatekeeping process becomes even more intricate with the hierarchy of influences proposed by Shoemaker and Reese (1991). There are five levels that interact with one another in different ways, including suppressing the influence that one level can have over the other on an object becoming news. The five levels are individual, routine, organizational, social institutions or extra-media, and societal influences. Each level in Shoemaker and Reese's (1991) hierarchy is important and can affect one another without having to follow the order of the hierarchy, where individuals (e.g., journalists) are at the micro level and societal institutions are at the opposite macro level.

According to Preston and Metykova (2009), almost all media work in institutionalized organizations. Thus, the organizational level has the power to overrun the individual and routine levels, taking away some of the autonomy from the micro levels of the hierarchy. Therefore, it is important to understand how media organizations influence the selection and the formation of fact-checking topics. Analyzing the process of how information is selected or discarded, how the importance of a news story is ranked against others, and how it is published reveals much about the ideologies and values of an organization (Preston & Metykova, 2009; Shoemaker & Reese, 1991). Which stories become news, and exactly what part of the information is highlighted, ultimately affect the political knowledge of the American public.

The Rise of Fact-Checking Journalism

Throughout the history of journalism, different phases have waxed and waned for decades. Objective journalism found its roots within the 1920s, creating a path for more journalistic trends over the next century (Graves et al., 2015). The goal of journalists, while remaining constant throughout the 20th and 21st centuries, has been part of the American media model for decades: to provide fair and objective reporting to their audience void of "personal and cultural biases" that could mar an accurate journalistic report (Kovach & Rosenstiel, 2014, p. 101). The recent trends of fact-checking, to some extent, seem to be a response to the public's declining trust of media organizations (Riffkin, 2015).

The practices of the news media since the 1950s have created an image far unlike the one they were striving for only a few decades earlier (Graves et al., 2015). At the beginning of the millennium, straight-news reports, published on the front page of newspapers and with no interpretation of the events being reported, decreased 85% from the 1950s (Graves et al., 2015). Interpretive reporting was taking over. The majority of the public does not seem to like this type of reporting. A recent Pew Research Center survey indicated that most Republicans disliked the interpretation of facts within media coverage, whereas Democrats were equally split—half did not mind it, and half disliked it (Barthel & Gottfried, 2016). It is possible that the fact-checking trend is an answer to the public's opinion of journalism. Graves et al. (2015) argue that fact-checking is a new genre of reporting that beckons back to the values and code of ethics established more than a century ago. They also describe fact-checking journalism as "truth-seeking" and a new form of being a "political watchdog" (Graves et al., 2015, p. 3).

Fact-checking journalism gained popularity in the early 2000s and dramatically increased during consequent election cycles (Graves et al., 2015).

Dedicated fact-checking sources were created at the turn of the 21st century, such as FactCheck.org, followed by PolitiFact, and *The Washington Post*'s Fact-checker only four years later (Fridkin, Kenney, & Wintersieck, 2015). Whereas traditional fact-checkers examined internal news reporting to verify information, today's fact-checkers focus on external political claims by public figures (Graves, 2016). In 2015, the number of fact-checking sources reached a total of 29 dedicated outlets—24 of which were in place by 2010 (Graves et al., 2015).

The rise in fact-checking should come as little surprise because roughly 80% of Americans who identify as either Democrat or Republican highly favor the use of fact-checking by media organizations (Kurtzleben, 2016). Both sides of the political spectrum appreciate the media's watchdog approach during election cycles, and the importance of fact-checking journalism seems more critical than ever in the aftermath of the 2016 presidential election. It is important for the American public to know what information presented by politicians is true and what is false. Those corrections need to happen swiftly and authoritatively. Nyhan and Reifler (2012) use social science evidence to create best practices for journalists to apply to their fact-checking coverage to be more successful in minimizing misperceptions. Their suggestions include the following: do not repeat false claims, just correct them; make the corrections to a claim as soon as possible; rely on credible sources; reduce partisan cues; and minimize the number of sources for a story that have political affiliations (Nyhan & Reifler, 2012). It is also important to understand if media organizations are choosing to avoid reporting information that does not align with their political ideology.

There is also a perceived danger if traditional news media engage in fact-checking too frequently. As Graves (2016) points out, fact-checkers are in a "tenuous" position and are often accused of being combative rather than "neutral arbiters" of fact. This raises the question: Is journalistic neutrality the same as objectivity? Both of these concepts are based on the news value of reporting factual information, which is the basis of fact-checking.

Fact-Checking in the 2016 Presidential Election

Considering the need for the news media to provide accurate information to the public, especially during political campaigns, this study sets out to investigate how leading media outlets performed this role in the lead-up to the 2016 presidential election. In particular, we focus on fact-checking of the three presidential debates, which drew unprecedented audience numbers ("First presidential," 2016) and were key in voter decision making (Katz, 2016). Specifically, we pose the following research questions:

RQ 1: What are the characteristics of fact-checking statements used by U.S. print media after each 2016 presidential debate?

RQ 2: How closely did U.S. print media follow established guidelines for correcting misinformation in their fact-checking coverage of the 2016 presidential debates?

Method

This study is based on a quantitative content analysis of U.S. print media. The objective of the analysis is to determine whether and how the national news media followed established guidelines for correcting misinformation in their fact-checking coverage of the 2016 presidential debates. The three debates present an ideal opportunity for the news media to fact-check the claims made by both candidates. The 2016 debates reached the largest audience in 36 years with 84 million viewers watching the first presidential debate on September 26, 2016 ("Third presidential," 2016). The second and third debates reached 66.5 million and 71.6 million viewers, respectively ("Second presidential," 2016). Additionally, research has shown that voters find the presidential debates to be helpful in learning about the candidates and contribute to their decision-making process (Heimlich, 2012; Holbrook, 1999).

Sample

The sample for this content analysis comes from the three leading national newspapers: *The New York Times*, *The Washington Post*, and *USA Today*. Because the analysis focuses on the fact-checking of the presidential debates, a purposive research design would be most appropriate. We focused on fact-checking coverage of each presidential debate in the three selected newspapers. The dates and locations for each of the three debates are as follows: September 26, 2016, Hofstra University; October 9, 2016, Washington University in St. Louis; and October 19, 2016, University of Nevada-Las Vegas. We used the online versions of each newspaper to retrieve the articles and searched each online newspaper's archive using the following keyword phrases: "presidential debate fact-check" or "presidential debate fact-check 2016" or "fact-check presidential debates." Using manual screening, articles that did not contain actual fact-checking analyses of the targeted debates or that were, for example, links to videos or outside reports were excluded.

Variables

Before moving onto the specific variables of our study, we first introduce the suggestions for "best practices" in fact-checking provided by Nyhan and Reifler (2012). Their guidelines are used in the variable conceptualization, which is explained in more detail next. According to Nyhan and Reifler (2012), media organizations should consider 10 suggestions when creating fact-checking content, as follows: (a) get the story right the first time, (b) early corrections are better, (c) beware making the problem worse, (d) avoid negations, (e) minimize repetition of false claims, (f) reduce partisan and ideological cues, (g) use credible sources, (h) don't give credence to the fringe, (i) use graphics where appropriate, (j) beware of selective exposure.

Using Nyhan and Reifler's (2012) guidelines, we created a number of coding variables. First, we determined the topic of the fact-check and the candidate being fact-checked (Clinton, Trump, or both candidates). Next, we coded for correction: that is, is the fact-checking statement correct (article states candidate statement is accurate); incorrect (article states candidate statement is inaccurate); partially correct (article states candidate statement is somewhat, but not completely, accurate; e.g., candidate exaggerated facts or cherry-picked content); or inconclusive (no explicit correction of claim is provided; statement cannot be determined as either accurate or inaccurate).

Coders noted if the fact-checking section repeated the false claim directly more than once. They also captured what kind of information was included to support the fact-check, including URL links, video, or tweets. Another variable captured the specific source mentioned to support or dispute the candidate claim. Sources could include individuals, government agencies such as the FBI, media organizations such as CNN, politicians, academics, scientists, nongovernmental organizations (NGOs), or fact-checking Web sites such as FactCheck.org or PolitiFact.com.

In addition to outside sources, the candidate's own previous statements can provide one of the best data points for fact-checking. Therefore, we coded for the use of a direct quote from a candidate or having a video of the candidate to support or dispute the claim. Finally, we coded if the fact-check mentioned the candidate as saying "I was joking" when making the original claim and whether the article as a whole used the words "fib," "flub," or any other descriptors of the candidates' claims.

Coding Process

Two graduate students served as coders. They were trained on the code sheet using fact-checking examples from the desired time period and performed test coding with the lead researcher to determine that variable definitions were clear and straightforward. A few variables were eliminated or collapsed after the initial coding phase.

An online code sheet using Qualtrics survey software was set up and used for coding, which allowed us to download the data directly into SPSS. A total of 32 fact-checks (14%) were selected to check coder agreement. Intercoder reliability was established at 91%, with percentage agreement ranging between 75% and 100%. A total of 231 fact-checking statements were analyzed.

Results

The first research question asked: What are the characteristics of fact-checking statements used by U.S. print media after each 2016 presidential debate? We looked at several variables to answer this question. But first, we noted a few interesting differences in style between the three newspapers under examination. *USA Today* used a bulleted list of fact-checking items at the top of the article and then broke down each item into a fact-checking paragraph, often relying on Twitter screenshots to dispute or support the claim. *The Washington Post* had longer fact-checking sections, often beginning the article with a video from the debate right up front. *The New York Times*'s fact-checking statements within the article were shorter—about a paragraph—and were all attributed to different contributors.

Beyond some of these stylistic differences, the topics of the fact-checks were similar. The topics ranged from NAFTA and ISIS to Clinton's e-mail scandal and Trump's leaked "Access Hollywood" videotape. Climate change, taxes, abortion, gun control, and healthcare were among the most common domestic issues in the fact-checking coverage. As for international issues, China, Iraq, Syria, the Iran deal, outsourcing jobs, and the trade deficit were frequently addressed.

In terms of which candidate was fact-checked more often after each presidential debate, the data show that Clinton was fact-checked in 25.1% of the cases, whereas Trump was fact-checked in 69.3% of the cases. The rest of the cases focused on fact-checking both candidates.

Not surprisingly, the majority of the fact-checks appeared immediately following each presidential debate: 75 items were fact-checked on September 26, 2016 (the day of the first debate) and September 27, 2016 (the day after); similarly, 93 fact-checks were published on October 9, 2016 (the day of the second debate) and on October 10, 2016 (the day after); and 63 fact-checks appeared on October 19, 2016 (the day of the last debate) and on October 20, 2016 (the day after). This would suggest that each of the three newspapers had a dedicated team of reporters ready to fact-check the debates at the same time as they were going on.

Perhaps the most interesting finding comes from the data on fact-checking correction. Out of 225 statements included here, 41 (18.2%) explicitly stated that the candidate's statement was correct, whereas 96 (42.7%) stated that candidate's statement was clearly inaccurate. A fair amount of the fact-checking sections found candidate statements to be somewhat or partially correct—57, or 25.3%, of the fact-checks we examined. Rather than stating that a candidate statement was clearly wrong, some articles explained that the statement was exaggerated or taken out of context. In other cases, the presidential candidate was described as "cherry picking" examples to criticize previous administrations. For example, *USA Today* reported that Trump had been "cherry picking" facts when he stated that Obamacare premiums would increase over the next year, citing the highest increased rate (Gore et al., 2016). It is not considered an entirely wrong claim, but it does have its issues, according to the fact-checkers. Terms such as "overstated" and "mostly misleading" also fit under this category.

Interestingly, there were a number of cases where the candidate's statement could not be or was not explicitly corrected and was labeled inconclusive by the coders; this was the case in 31, or 13.8%, of the fact-checks. A few articles stated that there was no evidence to back up candidate claims. This was the case, for example, with Trump claiming that he opposed the Iraq War. Comparing the three newspapers in terms of correction statements shows no statistically significant differences (see Table 7.1).

There were a couple of cases where the candidate was "technically correct" on the timeline of the events within the topic, but failed to mention accurate details laying out the whole picture. Several candidate statements were described as not specific enough to be able to be fact-checked; this was the case, for example, with Clinton's claim that her policies will not "add a penny to the national debt" (Kessler & Lee, 2016). The fact-checking analysis states that the claim does not have enough contextual support to state whether it is correct; however, it does use a graph to show how both Trump's and Clinton's plans are projected to affect the national debt over a 10-year period (Kessler & Lee, 2016).

Another important variable of interest captured whether the fact-checking section repeated the false claim directly more than once. A good example here is a repeat of Clinton's economic plans as they related to taxes in *USA Today* after the first presidential debate. Table 7.2 shows the results for each of the three newspapers. The low cell count for several cells did not allow us to test for statistical significance, but the cross-tabulations suggest some possible differences in the way false claim repeats were handled, with *USA Today* being most likely to do so.

We also captured what kind of information was included to support the fact-check: URL links, video, or tweets. Videos were not commonly used within the fact-checking section in all three newspapers. *USA Today* was the only

Table 7.1   Fact-Checking Statements Across Newspapers

Fact-Checking Statement	New York Times	USA Today	Washington Post
Correct	17 (21.8%)	11 (14.1%)	13 (18.8%)
Incorrect	32 (41%)	36 (46.2%)	28 (40.6%)
Partially correct	17 (21.8%)	23 (29.5%)	17 (24.6%)
Inconclusive	12 (15.4%)	8 (10.3%)	11 (15.9%)

Table 7.2   False Claim Repeated in Fact-Check Stories

False Claim Repeated More Than Once	New York Times	USA Today	Washington Post
Yes	4 (5.6%)	22 (29.3%)	4 (7.1%)
No	67 (94.4%)	53 (70.7%)	52 (92.9%)

Table 7.3   Use of URL Links in Fact-Check Stories

Active URL Links in Fact-Check	New York Times	USA Today	Washington Post
Yes	15 (19%)*	67 (81.7%)	58 (82.9%)
No	64 (81%)*	15 (18.3%)	12 (17.1%)

$p < .001$

newspaper that included tweets within their fact-checking. In terms of taking advantage of the World Wide Web by including active links in the aftermath of the debates, some interesting differences emerged (see Table 7.3). The differences between the three newspapers were statistically significant $x^2(2, N=231)=87.13$, $p<.001$). The results show that *The New York Times* was less likely to embed direct URL links in their fact-checking segments compared with *USA Today* and *The Washington Post*. This does not mean, however, that the so-called newspaper of record did not incorporate external links in other sections of their debate coverage.

Sources are critical components of news reporting and serve to establish journalistic credibility (Kovach & Rosenstiel, 2014). In the case of fact-checking, as noted by Nyhan and Reifler (2012), sources mentioned to support or dispute claims made by politicians become even more critical. We did not quantify the different types of sources used, but noted which specific individuals or organizations were cited in the fact-check. One general trend that we observed was relying on in-house reporting or referring to other media organizations such as CNN. *The Washington Post* seemed to rely more heavily on outside experts such as academics or scientists. All three newspapers were likely to incorporate NGO data or nonpartisan organizations in their fact-checking, which indicates an effort to keep objectivity and balance in their reporting. In an example from a *USA Today* article covering the final debate, journalists sourced reports from the Pew Charitable Trusts, the Brennan Center for Justice, and the U.S. Election Assistance Commission and cited Rutgers University professor Lorraine Minnite's book, *The Myth of Voter Fraud*, to fact-check Trump's statement about voter fraud in the United States (Gore et al., 2016). Fact-checking Web sites such as FactCheck.org or PolitiFact.com were also frequently incorporated in the coverage. An interesting fact-check after the second presidential debate included a link to Clinton campaign chairman John Podesta's e-mails from WikiLeaks.

In addition to outside sources, the candidate's own previous statements can provide one of the most convincing pieces of evidence in fact-checking. Therefore, we coded for use of a direct quote from the candidate or having a video of the candidate to support or dispute a claim. The data show that using a direct quote from the candidate being fact-checked is a common technique. Interestingly, *The New York Times* coverage utilized this technique much less frequently than did *USA Today* or *The Washington Post*, although the low count in one cell does not meet the minimum expected count (see Table 7.4). For example, a fact-check on Clinton regarding the Trans-Pacific Partnership (TPP) used an earlier quote of the former secretary of state from 2012 to supplement the analysis in *The Washington Post* and show she was wrong. Some direct quotes demonstrated the candidate was right, as was the case of Trump on immigration regarding deportation numbers that appeared in *USA Today*.

Finally, it is interesting to note that 17 items, or 7.4% of the coverage, used the words "fib" or "flub" to depict candidate statements, which appears to downplay the seriousness of the issue. However, only two of the fact-checks mentioned candidates as saying "I was joking" when making the original claim.

The second research question asked how closely U.S. print media followed established guidelines for correcting misinformation in their fact-checking coverage of the 2016 presidential debates. We offer point-by-point observations next, following Nyhan and Reifler's recommendations (2012).

Make corrections quickly. Looking at the dates of the fact-checking articles, it appears all three newspapers made a concerted effort to provide correct information immediately following each of the three debates. Specifically, all fact-checking articles we collected appeared the day of and the day after each presidential debate. Each newspaper likely had a team of journalists ready to conduct fact-checks quickly and share that information with the public in a timely manner. The false or misleading information provided by the candidates was corrected quickly with relevant and well-sourced data. The timeliness of the fact-checks appears to fall within recommended guidelines.

Do not repeat the misinformation. Nyhan and Reifler (2012) suggest that repeating misinformation only fuels more misinformation. However, this is

Table 7.4 Use of Direct Quote of Candidate in Fact-Check Stories

Direct Quote or Video of Candidate Statement	New York Times	USA Today	Washington Post
Yes	32 (40.5%)	66 (81.5%)	66 (95.7%)
No	47 (59.5%)	15 (18.5%)	3 (4.3%)

hard to avoid because you need to reference the false statement first. Although there weren't always direct quotes of the false claim, its core message was often reiterated in the process of disproving it. In general, journalists perhaps should be more aware to not directly repeat incorrect information and try to focus on reporting the correct information only.

Do not use sources perceived as biased. This is a general rule of thumb in journalism, but it seems even more vital in the case of fact-checking. If there is misinformation circulating that supports a Democratic candidate, using a Democrat-affiliated source will not alleviate the notion that a statement might not be true. If President Barack Obama, a Democrat, reinforces the notion that Clinton will *not* take away gun rights, to a pro-gun audience, then the audience will more than likely dismiss Obama's attempt to correct the false claim that Clinton plans to ban all gun sales in the United States. It is much better to use sources that are considered fair, an expert in the topic area, and nonpartisan (Nyhan & Reifler, 2012).

Looking at the use of sources when fact-checking the debates, the news media made a concerted effort to rely on nonpartisan organizations and NGOs. Data from organizations such as the Centers for Disease Control, the federal government, or New York State crime statistics, for example, were incorporated in the fact-checks. The three newspapers also tried to balance the sources used, for example, Fox News and MSNBC, within the same fact-check. Naturally, there were a number of cases where the candidates themselves were included in videos or direct quotes from previous statements. It was also interesting to see that self-referential coverage of each individual newspaper in the form of "as we have shown in a previous fact-check" was pretty common. Overall, the fact-checks seemed to rely on reputable and nonpartisan sources, as recommended (Kovach & Rosenstiel, 2014; Nyhan & Reifler, 2012; Poynter, 2017).

Use visuals to accompany the correction of misinformation. Using charts, graphs, infographics, and other types of visuals helps aid in fixing misinformation because it is less likely to be dismissed by readers, especially online, by giving them a quick snippet of correct facts. Overall, the three newspapers utilized photos and videos to accompany the article as a whole, but did not insert those into the individual fact-checks. Some good examples here include using a map to show North Atlantic Treaty Organization (NATO) member countries and using a graph to show how many gun deaths are classified as homicides.

Discussion and Recommendations

Political fact-checking as a genre has emerged as an important vehicle to fight misrepresentation of facts or misleading information by political figures (Graves, 2016). The goal of this study was to evaluate how leading national newspapers tried to correct information provided by the two presidential contenders during the 2016 presidential debates. The results show that journalists engaged in consistent practices to correct false claims, but there is also room for improvement in how they perform this fact-checking function.

As Nyhan and Reifler (2012) recommend, speculation and assumptions should be avoided by journalists at all costs. The content analysis reported earlier shows that U.S. print media avoided speculations or offering unsupported claims in their fact-checking coverage. The reporting, for the most part, relied on reputable sources and referenced solid data to either support or dispute candidate claims. However, there is still room for improvement when it comes to how the news media establish whether politicians' statements are true.

Fact-checking, by definition, is an "evidence-based" technique applied by journalists to objects, events, or topics of a questionable nature (Coddington, Molyneux, & Lawrence, 2014). At the same time, it is challenging to determine latent meaning or implicit political intention behind politicians' words. Without having to make an assumption about intention, journalists can still be more clear and straightforward in their fact-checking statements. It should be easier for the average reader to determine if something a politician said is correct, false, or only partially correct. Our analysis shows a number of cases where the "verdict" whether something that either Trump or Clinton claimed was actually supported by the facts was not explicit. This sort of inconclusive fact-checking is not helping voters make informed decisions.

Even using a phrase that negates the misinformation can be problematic (Nyhan & Reifler, 2012). Instead, using positive language, such as stating "Hillary Clinton is cleared of charges," seems to work better than stating "Hillary Clinton will not be indicted." Fact-checkers should try to employ more positive language whenever possible.

Another recommendation for the news media is to avoid repeating false claims. Although it is difficult to refute a claim without stating it first, it is good to try to minimize any unnecessary repetition of false information. It is important also to make the fact-checking statement as clear as possible for the typical busy reader and multitasking user.

It is simplistic, of course, to assume that fact-checking journalism will always accomplish its goal of correcting and, by extension, eradicating misleading information in the public sphere (Nyhan & Reifler, 2012). But in today's political environment, it is perhaps more important than ever to try to correct misinformation presented by political leaders quickly and decisively. It is the news media's responsibility as the Fourth Estate to keep political figures accountable and offer the most accurate information to the American public.

Ideally, solid reporting will create a consensus that all parties—whether political or ideological—agree to the facts presented within the fact-checking coverage. Another democratic ideal is that the public will make rational decisions after taking all facts and relevant information into consideration. The reality, however, is that voters often make subjective decisions through their own political and ideological prisms. Even when confronted with clearly false statements by political candidates, it is hard to measure whether or not the public will take such statements as something more than a political stunt to persuade people to favor one group's ideology over another.

This highlights another issue summarized well by Graves (2016, p. 192) in his book on the rise of political fact-checking: "Fact-checkers do celebrate the 'Internet revolution' for greatly easing access to original data and research. But these reporters openly lament the decline of journalism's 'gatekeeper' status, which media and political reformers so often paint as [a] positive development." In other words, the power of traditional media as *the* gatekeeper of information has greatly diminished with the advent of the Internet. Therefore, the influence of any fact-checking reporting they do depends on, first, whether traditional media will be sought out as information sources by the public, and second, on how much trust would the public place on their fact-checks versus other information floating on the Internet by the candidates themselves, by third parties, or by fake news Web sites.

With the proliferation of misleading information flowing through different mediums, such as tabloids, social media sites, and fake news sites during the last election, fact-checking journalism has appointed itself as the judge of whether or not a claim made by an elite figure, such as a political leader, an organization, or party, coincides with what has been presented as historically true about what is being examined. Fact-checking at its core is simply an in-depth look at whether or not something is true, based on current and previous trusted information. How much fact-checking matters in how the public makes voting decisions, especially in today's polarized political environment, deserves further investigation.

Limitations and Future Research

This analysis focused only on three leading national newspapers—namely *The New York Times*, *The Washington Post*, and *USA Today*. Future studies should incorporate a wider range of media organizations and consider adding traditional fact-checking news sites to the sample. Another limitation of the study is that it included coverage of the three presidential debates only. Expanding the analysis to encompass the entire campaign and candidate statements that appeared in the news media would be good to consider.

Because the study utilizes content analysis methodology, it cannot provide information about the effectiveness of fact-checking or how readers make sense of any new factual information they uncover. Future studies should employ experimental research designs to capture any causal effects of fact-checking coverage on potential voters. This type of study will allow journalists to better tailor their reporting to their audience.

Finally, it may be important to examine how fact-checkers themselves see their role in the current media landscape. Conducting interviews or focus groups with those reporters will provide a better understanding of how they make their own gatekeeper decisions and why they choose certain topics, issues, or sources versus others. Newsroom observations of daily journalistic practices and routines can also complement this body of research.

References

Barthel, M., & Gottfried, J. (2016, November 18). Majority of U.S. adults think news media should not add interpretation to the facts. *Pew Research Center*. Retrieved from http://www.pewresearch.org/fact-tank/2016/11/18 /news- media-interpretation- vs-facts/

Bendery, J. (2016, October 9). Here's a live tally of all the times presidential candidates lie during the debate. *Huffington Post*. Retrieved from http://www .huffingtonpost.com/entry/presidential-debate-lies-trump-clinton_us _57fae517e4b068ecb5df72a2

Benton, J. (2016, November 9). The forces that drove this election's media failure are likely to get worse. *Nieman Lab*. Retrieved from http://www.niemanlab .org/2016/11/the-forces-that-drove-this-elections-media-failure-are-likely -to-get-worse/

Coddington, M., Molyneux, L., & Lawrence, R. G. (2014). Fact-checking the campaign: How political reporters use Twitter to set the record straight (or not). *The International Journal of Press/Politics*, *19*(4), 391–409. doi:10.1177/1940 161214540942

Comparing Hillary Clinton, Donald Trump on the truth-o-meter. (2016). *Politi-Fact*. Retrieved from http://www.politifact.com/truth-o- meter/lists/people /comparing-hillary-clinton-donald-trump-truth-o-met/

First presidential debate of 2016 draws 84 million viewers. (2016, September 27). *The Nielsen Company*. Retrieved from http://www.nielsen.com/us/en/in sights/news/2016/first-presidential-debate-of-2016-draws-84-million -viewers.html

Fridkin, K., Kenney, P. J., & Wintersieck, A. (2015) Liar, liar, pants on fire: How fact-checking influences citizens' reactions to negative advertising. *Political Communication*, *32*(1), 127–151, doi: 10.1080/10584609.2014 .914613

Gore, D., Kiely, E., Jackson, B., Robertson, L., Farley, R., & Schipani, V. (2016, October 20). Fact-check: The fiery final debate between Trump and Clinton. *USA Today*. Retrieved from https://www.usatoday.com/story/news /politics/elections/2016/10/20/fact-check-trump-clinton-debate-las-vegas /92437230/

Graves, L. (2016). *Deciding what's true: The rise of political fact-checking in American journalism*. New York: Columbia University Press.

Graves, L., Nyhan, B., & Reifler, J. (2015, April 22). The diffusion of fact-checking: Understanding the growth of a journalistic innovation. *The American Press*

Institute. Retrieved from http://www.americanpressinstitute.org/wp-con
tent/uploads/2015/04/The-Growth-of-Fact-Checking.pdf

Heimlich, R. (2012, September 11). Most say presidential debates influence their
vote. *Pew Research Center*. Retrieved from http://www.pewresearch.org/fact
-tank/2012/09/11/most-say-presidential-debates-influence-their-vote/

Holbrook, T. M. (1999). Political learning from presidential debates. *Political Behavior, 21*(1), 67–89. Retrieved from http://www.jstor.org/stable/586586

Katz, A. (2016, October 22). Presidential debates set ratings records in 2016, but
does the format need to change? *Adweek*. Retrieved from http://www
.adweek.com/tv-video/presidential-debates-set-ratings-records-2016-does
-format-need-change-174205/

Kessler, G., & Lee, M. Y. H. (2016, October 20). Fact-checking the third Clinton-
Trump presidential debate. *The Washington Post*. Retrieved from https://
www.washingtonpost.com/news/fact-checker/wp/2016/10/20/fact
-checking-the-third-clinton-trump-presidential-debate/?utm_term=.28f64
deef8c5

Kovach, B., & Rosenstiel T. (2014). *The elements of journalism*. New York: Three
Rivers Press.

Kurtzleben, D. (2016, September 27). Do fact-checks matter? *NPR*. Retrieved from
http://www.npr.org/2016/09/27/495233627/do-fact- checks-matter

Marietta, M., Barker, D. C., & Bowser, T. (2015). Fact-checking polarized politics:
Does the fact-check industry provide consistent guidance on disputed realities? *The Forum, 13*(4), 577–596. doi:10.1515/for-2015- 0040

Nyhan, B., & Reifler, J. (2012). Misinformation and fact-checking: Research findings from social science. *New America Foundation*. Retrieved from http://
www.dartmouth.edu/~nyhan/Misinformation_and_Fact-checking.pdf

Patterson, T. E. (2016, December 7). News coverage of the 2016 general election:
How the press failed the voters. *Shorenstein Center on Media, Politics and
Public Policy*. Retrieved from https://shorensteincenter.org/news-coverage
-2016-general-election/

Preston, P., & Metykova, M. (2009). From news nets to house rules: Organisational
contexts. In P. Preston (Ed.), *Making the news: Journalism and news cultures
in Europe* (pp. 72–91). New York: Routledge.

Poynter. (2017). International Fact-Checking Network fact-checkers' code of
principles.
Retrieved from https://www.poynter.org/international-fact-checking-network
-factcheckers-code-principles

Riffkin, R. (2015). Americans' trust in media remains at historical low. Gallup.
Retrieved from http://www.gallup.com/poll/185927/americans-trust-media
-remains-historical-low.aspx

Second presidential debate of 2016 draws 66.5 million viewers. (2016, October 10). *The Nielsen Company*. Retrieved from http://www.nielsen.com/us
/en/insights/news/2016/second-presidential-debate-of-2016-draws-66-5
-million-viewers.html

Shoemaker, P. J., & Reese S. D. (1991). *Mediating the message: Theories of influences
on mass media content*. White Plains, NY: Longman Publishing Group.

Shoemaker, P. J., & Vos, T. P. (2008). Media gatekeeping. In D. W. Stacks & M. B. Salwen (Eds.), *An integrated approach to communication theory and research* (2nd ed.). (pp. 75–89). New York: Routledge.

Shoemaker, P. J., Vos, T. P., & Reese, S. D. (2009). Journalists as gatekeepers. In K. Wahl-Jorgensen, & T. Hanitzsch (Eds.), *The handbook of journalism studies* (pp. 73–87). New York: Taylor & Francis.

Third presidential debate of 2016 draws 71.6 million viewers. (2016, October 20). *The Nielsen Company.* Retrieved from http://www.nielsen.com/us/en/insights/news/2016/third-presidential-debate-of-2016-draws-71-6-million-viewers.html

"I'm About to Be President; We're All Going to Die": Baldwin, Trump, and the Rhetorical Power of Comedic Presidential Impersonation

Will Howell and Trevor Parry-Giles

Comedic political impersonations play a crucial role within contemporary American politics. Originally discouraged, then accepted as amusement, political impersonations now circulate widely to varied audiences to elicit laughter and generate new meaning. These new meanings are particularly important and valuable in specific political contexts, such as the transitions of power between presidents. As a hard-fought campaign gives way to the transition, and then during the president's first 100 days, citizens must reconcile their new leader's all-too-human shortcomings with the presidency's considerable power. In close, bitter elections, this reconciliation is even more vital, and parody (via impersonations) provides a symbolic vehicle for such reconciliation. Given the 2016 campaign's tenor and Donald Trump's unexpected election, citizens needed a particularly adept impersonation of the new president.

Although Alec Baldwin impersonated Donald Trump to widespread acclaim, we suggest his impersonation did not fulfill the crucial political function of candidate/president reconciliation. As if recognizing the need for comedic relief, *Saturday Night Live* (*SNL*) featured Baldwin more than any previous transition-period presidential impersonator. But throughout these sketches—and without any change between candidate Trump and President Trump—Baldwin impersonated Trump as a completely irredeemable character. Baldwin's Trump was physically unpleasant, malicious, and unintelligent; he possessed no traits that might help Trump's opponents see Trump as human, nor cause Trump's supporters to recognize his personal shortcomings. This impersonation was, furthermore, distant from the expectations of the presidency and could only lead to the conclusion that Trump was unfit for that office. We conclude that such an impersonation may represent a new rhetorical role for presidential impersonations in an era of polarized politics.

Baldwin's impersonation of Trump is only understood within the context of the rhetorical functions of comedic political impersonation. We historicize these functions, demonstrating a recurring tension between amusement and critique. This has manifested poignantly in the 20th century as mass media and political power grew in tandem. Focusing on this period, we trace developments in comedic presidential impersonation leading to the 2016 election. We argue that Baldwin's Trump impersonation failed to fulfill the rhetorical functions of prior comedic impersonations and offer some conclusions about this failure.

Rhetorical Functions of Comedic Presidential Impersonation

Presidential impersonations must, first and foremost, simulate an actual president. In saying this, we invoke Baudrillard's (1994) notion that simulation "substitut[es] the signs of the real for the real . . . and short-circuits all its vicissitudes" for an audience (p. 2). Baudrillard contrasts *simulation* with *pretending*: someone *pretending* to be ill might simply lie in bed, whereas someone *simulating* an illness actually manifests symptoms of the illness. Translating this example, a *simulated* political leader—a political impersonator—manifests characteristics of some actual politician to open new ways of understanding those characteristics. Distinct from fictional presidents (e.g., presidential characters in fictional films) or news coverage of actual presidents, political impersonations mean someone other than the actual politician depicts or portrays that leader. The impersonator relies on the real politician even as he or she distorts and denies reality's power; he or she asks an audience to believe that an actual president is represented by their portrayal. The impersonation's meaning, then, lies in the circumscribed gap between "reality" and the believable, plausible simulation.

This gap between reality and simulation contains fodder for audiences to revise their understanding of the institutional presidency. As Aristotle noted, humans have a "natural instinct for representation" and typically learn "by representing things" (Aristotle, 1932). Citizens have long learned from the impersonations of their politicians, which activate rhetoric's aesthetic and entertaining capacities (Farrell, 1986). As Smith (2009) noted, "All nations and all peoples tell stories about leaders; from Gilgamesh, Fu Xi, and Agamemnon to King David, King Arthur, and King Lear" (p. 3) In the Elizabethan era, for example, British culture produced history and king plays retelling the island's monarchical history. Sharpe (2009) proposed that these plays responded to anxieties about Elizabeth I's reign by impersonating past kings and queens. Amidst the "mounting tension between images of power and the realities of late sixteenth-century politics," these plays explored the role and scope of monarchy (p. 460). In contemporary American politics, comedic presidential impersonations have become so popular that Robinson (2010) argued they "[have] been conflated in Americans' minds" with presidential identity (p. 13). Impersonations' formal characteristics have, consistent with Burke's (1968) vision of rhetorical form, created an appetite in the mind of an audience—an appetite that the real political leaders must satiate.

An impersonation's rhetorical form informs both the political meanings emanating from the impersonation and the audience's experience—particularly if that form is comedic. Contrast, for example, Dennis Quaid's Bill Clinton impersonation with Darrell Hammond's Clinton impersonation. Hammond's humorous impersonation from *SNL* utilizes comic framing that, according to Burke, "maximize[s] consciousness" for audience members while positioning them to transcend and combat "[human] foibles" (1984, p. 171). Quaid's impersonation, from the HBO docudrama *The Special Relationship*, conversely serves a very different purpose: to illuminate an historical moment and that moment's actors. By applying Norton's (2004) maxim—"The form in which something is expressed determines its meaning"—to these examples, comedic impersonations become a valuable tool for audiences seeking to reconcile the human foibles of their political leaders (p. 102).

Such humanizing is an important rhetorical function of presidential impersonations. Smith (2009) correctly notes that most Americans will never meet a president, meaning their "knowledge of presidents is inevitably mediated through stories and pictures" (p. 4). This mediation has gradually transformed the president into "a master signifier, a locus for projections and desires that constitute our identity," Rubenstein argued (2008, p. 17). An impersonation, then, serves "as a site for an existential or experiential form of knowledge" about the president—thus making him accessible to citizens with that basic knowledge (Rubenstein, 2008, p. 6).

Comedic presidential impersonations thus fulfill several rhetorical functions. They simulate real presidents to develop an audience's understanding of both those individuals and the institution of the presidency. They humanize presidents for diverse and disconnected audiences; they also provide a roadmap for those audiences to make their peace with presidents' human foibles. Best of all, they complete these other functions while amusing and entertaining audiences.

1928–1963: Accepting Presidential Impersonation for Amusement

Despite their important civic functions, American comedians shunned presidential impersonations until the 1960s. When Will Rogers first impersonated presidents in 1928 and 1933, he did so to amuse his audience and humanize leaders whom he respected. But without proper context, Rogers's simulation might be identifiable as such and thus might confuse audiences—a particularly dangerous problem in precarious political situations such as war and the Great Depression. But as society acculturated mass media and the domestic political situation stabilized, people grew more comfortable with amusing mimicry of the president.

On January 4, 1928, Rogers imitated President Calvin Coolidge's voice "uttering nonsense" and expected his radio listeners to evaluate the content and discern that the voice was an impression (Robinson, 2010, p. 74). Because Rogers broadcast from his home, there was no firsthand audience to discern the difference between real and simulation and provide at-home listeners with laughter cues. Listeners believed Rogers "had shown bad taste," and Rogers wrote the Coolidges to apologize for "wound[ing] the feelings of two people who I most admire" (Rogers, 2005, p. 549; Robinson, 2010, p. 74). Rogers (2005) mimicked Coolidge, moreover, because he and his audience "love jokes about those we like" (p. 171). President Coolidge shrugged off the impersonation as "of rather small consequence," especially because Rogers's intention was "some harmless amusement" (Robinson, 2010, pp. 75–76). When Rogers again impersonated a president—Franklin Roosevelt (FDR), on November 19, 1933—a studio audience audibly laughed their approval (Rogers, 2005, pp. 441–445). Nonetheless, he feared FDR's disapproval and asked Roosevelt's press secretary to "ask the boss to excuse me, won't you?" "The boss" replied that "[he] liked it a lot" (Robinson, 2010, pp. 94–95).

In these first impersonations, Rogers fulfilled the rhetorical functions of comedic presidential impersonations. Rogers humanized Coolidge by parodying his individual characteristics—his well-known reservedness, for example ("Prohibition is going about as well as usual") (Robinson, 2010, p. 73). Rogers furthered his audience's understanding of the presidency when he parodied the earnest President Roosevelt's America-boosterism ("We're in a slump now, but we're coming out, and someday we'll make Russia proud that she ever recognized us") (Rogers, 2005, p. 444).

Despite overtly approving Rogers's comedy, Roosevelt took a stand that would hinder comedic impersonators for nearly 30 years. Ragland (1962) argued that because Roosevelt "used his voice and personality to extend the authority of the Executive Office" via radio, he also made the presidency vulnerable to vocal impersonations (p. 374). Roosevelt's press secretary, Steve Early, established a new policy in 1934 on behalf of the White House "that no imitations of the President will be carried over the airwaves" (Cull, 1997, p. 388). Movies were fine, but Early was concerned that "radio audience[s], especially late listeners" might be unable to discern between the real and the simulated Roosevelt (Ragland, 1962, p. 375). Networks dutifully fell in line, expressly forbidding entertainers from simulating the president's voice (Ragland, 1962; Schwartz, 2015). As peacetime gave way to World War II and Korea, White House aides began justifying the policy on public safety grounds: citizens needed to know if they were hearing or seeing the president and trust that sight/speech. A letter from George L. Morris to Bob Hope, following his 1949 radio impersonation of President Harry S. Truman, demonstrates the concern: "You must know that ridicule is the surest and quickest way to weaken and destroy our respect for the highest office in our country and with it will go representative government. We are thinking only of the office and not the man" (Morris, 1949).

The next time a president tried to control an impersonation, he was less successful. In November 1962, a nightclub comedian named Vaughn Meader impersonated President John F. Kennedy (JFK) "with great affection and respect" on a first-of-its-kind comedy album titled *The First Family*. Meader and his peers cast the White House as "a typical American home," and Meader impersonated Kennedy in humanizing, ordinary situations (Cull, 1997, p. 384; *The First Family*, 1962). The album sold 6.5 million copies in six weeks, making it the best-selling comedy album to date and igniting a JFK impersonation craze. Kennedy aide Arthur Schlesinger advised the president that presidential comedy was important, "and no sensible president ought to be in a position of being disturbed by it" (Cull, 1997, pp. 386–387). Kennedy heeded this advice; behind the scenes, though, White House aides fought those who did not identify an impersonation as such and who used impersonations in advertisements. Externally, they directly engaged businesses or stations while internally debating whether to involve the Federal Communication Commission. Neither action undercut the impersonation craze, and by April 1963, the White House had mostly conceded the issue (Cull, 1997, pp. 392–393).

1963–2017: *SNL* Unlocks the Rhetorical Potential of Presidential Impersonations

Between 1963 and the mid-1970s, three rhetorical shifts changed the tenor of comedic presidential impersonations and deepened their rhetorical functions. First, the presidency's credibility diminished during the Vietnam War. Beginning with Lyndon Johnson, then Richard Nixon, presidents interacted dishonestly with the public against a backdrop of small gains and significant casualties. A cornerstone of comedy, presidential incongruity was less humorous and undercut the office's credibility. These injuries redoubled during

Watergate, which revealed that the presidency might be filled by a criminal (Robinson, 2010, p. 184). Finally, in the face of Watergate, President Gerald Ford thwarted retribution by pardoning Nixon. Americans needed a mechanism to resolve discrepancies between their presidents and the ideal presidency. With the office's reputation in such tatters, comedic impersonations could be one such mechanism (Robinson, 2010, p. 187).

Against this new rhetorical backdrop, *SNL*'s impersonation of Ford underscored the discrepancy between the institutional presidency and Ford. In the show's fourth episode, Chevy Chase impersonated an unnamed president defined by his clumsiness: he bumbled a prepared speech, spilled his papers, and repeatedly banged his head on the podium. As if acknowledging Schlesinger's earlier concerns, the screen text established the gap between simulation and reality. "This is not the President of the United States," it read, and the podium featured "The Unofficial Seal" (Wilson, 1975a). But two episodes later, the screen warned that Chase's impersonation was "not a good impression of Gerald Ford"; and indeed, Chase made no effort to simulate Ford's voice, appearance, or personality. He merely assumed Ford's name and performed a bumbling out-of-touch character who, for example, answered a glass of water instead of a phone and blew his nose into his tie (Wilson, 1975b). But slapstick aside, Chase highlighted the incongruence between Ford and "the presidency." In one scene, Egyptian President Anwar Sadat called Ford mid-address:

> As president, I will change my mind wherever I want . . . [Answers ringing phone] Hello. Hotline. Anwar, uh . . . just a second . . . I'm on the air right now, I'll get you Kissinger, alright? [Picks up second phone, dials Henry Kissinger] Hank? Can you call to talk to Sadat for a minute? Thank you. [Holds the two phones to one another, then places them on the desk.] The point is: Do I really know what the issue is? Relevant? Irrelevant? Fault? Default? These are just hard words. (Wilson, 1975b)

Chase-as-Ford goes on to tell viewers that he is stalling critical legislation to improve his standing "with those conservative Republicans who might otherwise support Ronald Reagan" (Wilson, 1975b). Such attacks on the intelligence, character, and judgment of the president—first Johnson, then Nixon, then Ford—had been commonplace among Vietnam-era comedians, but not voiced through a presidential simulation.

Chase's Ford was also the first mass media comedic impersonation that recurred across a presidency, deepening its rhetorical functions. Prior comedic impersonations had been distinct (e.g., Hope impersonating Truman), or reoccurring but disconnected (e.g., Jack Riley impersonating Johnson on *Rowan and Martin's Laugh-In* or Rich Little impersonating Nixon on *All in the Family*). *SNL* relied on topical material and post-Vietnam audiences who wanted political humor—in part for some comic revenge against Ford. *SNL's* writers responded: of the 30 episodes between *SNL's* launch and Ford's 1976 loss, Chase impersonated Ford 11 times.

SNL revolutionized presidential impersonations in a third aspect: it traced the transition from candidate to president through comedic impersonation. Over its 42 seasons, *SNL* has shadowed seven presidential transitions with similar arcs: debate sketches in October before the election, a couple of president-elect sketches in November to January, and then several sketches during the president's first 100 days. Often these latter impersonations are "A Message from the President" in which newly inaugurated presidents speak directly to the camera. Transition sketches range from harmless humanizing humor (Clinton munching voters' food at McDonalds, for example) to more biting political observations (George H. W. Bush spending the last of his campaign money after winning on "one last, beautifully produced, negative ad") (Miller, 1988; Wilson, 1992).

In their comedic variety, *SNL's* transition sketches have brought about comedic presidential impersonations that fulfill the rhetorical functions discussed earlier. Between Coolidge and Ford (and continuing to today), the presidency expanded its powers over citizens' lives. The president will always be a human, and thus imperfect in his or her judgment, character, and intelligence. *SNL's* recurring impressions explore the changing institution while laughing about the individual, human foibles that distinguish everyone. H. W. Bush, for example, struggled to step from Reagan's shadow, and *SNL* engaged this the day after Bush's inauguration. In the sketch, Bush impersonator Dana Carvey calls to congratulate someone—only to be interrupted by Reagan impersonator Phil Hartman asserting his presidential prerogative to make the call first (Miller, 1989). Through parody like this, *SNL's* impersonations have helped citizens recognize that humans occupy the presidency, despite their deficiencies.

"Built from the DNA of Intolerance and Suspicion": Alec Baldwin's Donald Trump

Citizens particularly needed *SNL* to help process the Trump transition. The 2016 campaign left Americans polarized and angry. Trump's behavior raised serious questions among opponents about his character, intelligence, and judgment; and then he won despite losing the popular vote. As president-elect and president, Trump continued polarizing citizens through appointments, policies, and speeches. While Trump's opponents obsessed about his flaws, his supporters idealized him. His opponents needed assistance reconciling Trump and the presidency; his supporters needed assistance accepting the incongruities between Trump and the presidency.

And *SNL* responded: viewers saw Baldwin impersonate Trump nearly every week during the transition, more than any prior transition impersonator.

Baldwin appeared as the candidate, then president-elect, and then President Trump in 15 of the 18 episodes that ran in the transition period, which we define as the final four weeks of the campaign through the first 100 days of the new administration. This compares with 9 Obama sketches (Fred Armisen), 13 George W. Bush sketches (Will Ferrell), 8 Clinton sketches (Phil Hartman), 6 George H. W. Bush sketches (Dana Carvey), 4 Reagan sketches (Charles Rocket), and 10 Carter sketches (Dan Aykroyd). Unlike *SNL* impersonators prior to Ferrell (W. Bush), Baldwin's impersonation could be watched and shared online—and some sketches now have more than 20 million views (Jones, 2017). Audience demand is further reflected in *SNL*'s ratings, which are at a 23-year high as of May 2017 (Melas, 2017; Rose, 2017).

But we argue that *SNL* and Baldwin were ill suited to help citizens process Trump's transition because they impersonated Trump to be so completely terrible. Unlike Chase's Ford impersonation, which balanced individualized slapstick against critique about the presidency—the former a spoonful of sugar helping the latter medicine go down—Baldwin impersonated Trump without merit. Baldwin's Trump was, according to *The Atlantic*'s Jones (2017), "boiled clean of any remnant that could be mistaken for competence or redemption." The impersonation was remarkably consistent between candidate Trump, president-elect Trump, and finally President Trump. Baldwin left no pathway for Trump opponents to accept his claim to the presidency, dwelling on his myriad shortcomings and juxtaposing those with the presidency. In the process, he withheld the good-natured comedy that would help Trump supporters consider criticisms of their leader. We conclude that Baldwin's impersonation might—like Rogers's, Meader's, and Chase's—represent a new phase of comedic presidential impersonation for this era's polarized politics, geared toward galvanizing Trump's opponents to take political action.

Baldwin's Trump was, first and foremost, a visually unappealing simulation. The simulation was, however, accurate enough that a Dominican Republic newspaper mistakenly published a picture of Baldwin-as-Trump in lieu of Trump (Jones, 2017). To become Trump, Baldwin's "face spasms almost uncontrollably," squinting his eyes and jutting his lip outward (Jones, 2017). Baldwin-as-Trump entered the first sketch caked with bronze make-up. This is one of the few sketches that draws attention to Baldwin-as-Trump's "completely orange" skin and his mouth that "looks like a tiny little butthole" when he "stops talking" (King, 2016a). In future sketches, Baldwin simply reprised this grotesque appearance—but Baldwin-as-Trump's ugliness is a constant throughout the 15 transition sketches. When Baldwin-as-Trump says that 50% of Americans are "turned on by [him]," the audience laughs wildly (King, 2016a).

This physical ugliness was a counterpart to Baldwin-as-Trump's racist and sexist behavior. Baldwin described Trump as a person "made from hate," and that lineage is apparent in Baldwin's impersonation (Lytton, 2017). The Mexican president is "Señor Guacamole," and his wife and children are "taquito" and "chips and salsa" ("Tom Hanks/Lady Gaga," 2016). And when reminded that he called a Latina "Ms. Housekeeping," Baldwin's Trump says, "That's pretty funny" (King, 2016a). He addresses black people by the names of African American cultural figures ("Coltrane," "Denzel") (King, 2016a); nominalizes their skin color ("She's committed so many crimes she's basically a black") (King, 2016a); admits to using the n-word (King & Briganti, 2016a); and colludes with the Ku Klux Klan (King & Briganti, 2016b).

In Baldwin-as-Trump, women are derided at every turn: business executive Carly Fiorina is a "four," female judges are "lady judges" or "flight attendants," and Sexual Assault Awareness Month is "a subject near and dear to my hand" (King, 2016a; King & Briganti, 2017a; "Louis C.K./The Chainsmokers," 2017). Combining both racism and sexism, Baldwin-as-Trump labels black women "aliens" and proposes investigating them (King & Briganti, 2017d). On numerous occasions, Baldwin's impersonation garners a laugh by repeating something Trump actually said—"nasty woman," for example, or "Nobody has more respect for women than I do" ("Tom Hanks/Lady Gaga," 2016). A full 12 of the 15 transition sketches feature some indication that Trump is a racist and a sexist—leading Baldwin to confess, as he breaks character, "I just feel gross all the time" (King & Briganti, 2016a).

And there are plenty of times when Baldwin-as-Trump is vulgar without being racist or sexist. He promises that audiences "are going to cream [their] jeans" with his preparedness (King, 2016a). In an interview, he readily says the word "pussy" when a network anchor is uncomfortable uttering it (King, 2016a) and speaks about "ripping babies out of vaginas" in a debate sketch ("Tom Hanks/Lady Gaga," 2016). He commits several Freudian slips using variations on the word "pee" in connection to real-life allegations of a sex tape featuring Trump and urinating prostitutes (King & McCary, 2017). After acknowledging Holocaust Remembrance Day, he uses the number of Jews killed to talk about his inaugural crowd size (King & Briganti, 2017c). And when asked by a news anchor if he is "modeling appropriate and positive behavior for today's youth," he quickly answers, "No. Next?" (Briganti, 2016).

Such impersonated vulgarity, racism, and sexism create two gaps between real and simulation that obstruct the impersonation's rhetorical function. First, the narrow gap between the real and impersonated implies that the real Trump is as horrible as his impersonation. Chase's Ford was far clumsier than the real president, creating a wider gap between real and simulation. This allowed audiences leeway to consider whether Chase's critiques were apt or, like his clumsiness, out of character with the real Ford—a deliberate exaggeration rather than an imitation of Ford's actual disposition. But often, Baldwin-as-Trump repeats things the real Trump said verbatim—such as calling African Americans "the blacks" or talking about grabbing women "by the pussy." When Baldwin exaggerates something akin to these real-life statements—such as confirming that Trump used the n-word—audiences have reason to accept its truth and determine that the real Trump's human foibles are irredeemable.

In contrast to the *similarities* between real and impersonated Trump, the *differences* between impersonated Trump and the presidency challenge audiences to reconcile a "President Trump." When Rogers impersonated an overly sincere FDR, he impersonated a president so smitten with his country that he would go to comical lengths to prove its valor. Likewise, Meader's JFK brought the thoroughness and openness of presidential press briefings to discussions of household chores. These impersonations, in short, simulated the men occupying the office while also reflecting on the office's ideal. That office is not supposed to be held by a vulgar bigot like Baldwin's Trump—or the real Trump, potentially. Thus, when Baldwin-as-Trump says "I've got a very presidential answer for this" or "I was being super presidential," audiences laugh at the incongruity, and in so doing, they ratify the idea that Trump is incapable of being the president.

One way in which Trump is characterized as irredeemably unpresidential is through his lack of temperament. During the campaign season, this characterization came in outlandish statements in debates; sometimes offensive, sometimes confessional: "I was really spinning out of control there"; "I was trying to look cool" (King, 2016a; "Tom Hanks/Lady Gaga," 2016) and sometimes arrogant: "I'm the one who's got all the heavy hitters supporting me" ("Tom Hanks/Lady Gaga," 2016). Baldwin's Trump believes that Twitter is private (King & Briganti, 2016a), thinks Election Day is November 35 (Briganti, 2016), and knows more about Bill O'Reilly "than, say, healthcare" ("Louis C.K./The Chainsmokers," 2017).

As Trump became president-elect, *SNL* put Baldwin-as-Trump in scenarios that juxtaposed the temperament needed for the presidency with Trump's temperament. In the week after his inauguration, Trump places calls to foreign leaders after admitting, "I haven't been briefed," and proceeds to commit a series of diplomatic blunders: "America first, Australia sucks, your reef is failing, prepare to go to war" (King & Briganti, 2017c). Again and again, auxiliary characters underscore Trump's unpresidential temperament. In one sketch, Baldwin's Trump takes the judges who overturned his travel ban to *The People's Court* TV show to seek justice. When called upon to explain his position, he cannot: "These judges have been very disrespectful. I'm right. They're wrong"; and the judges are characterized as articulate, thoughtful, and pointed in their critique of Trump's legal reasoning (King & Briganti, 2017a). Another sketch features Baldwin's Trump returning to coal country for a rally with the people who elected him. Person after person poses a serious issue to Trump ("My premiums have gone up and I have to drive 90 minutes to see a doctor") only to be met with an inappropriate answer ("You like that I bombed Syria?") ("Louis C.K./The Chainsmokers," 2017). In these and many other moments, Baldwin creates a chasm between his simulation of Trump and the real expectations for the president of the United States.

The president is also not expected to be preeminently concerned with entertaining—yet Baldwin's Trump is. He asks audience members, "Are you not entertained?" in a debate and reminds them of his appearance in *Home Alone II* (King, 2016a; King & Briganti, 2016a). His final debate pitch—when Baldwin and *SNL* producers assumed Trump would lose the election—was a plea to "check out Trump TV" on the day after the election ("Tom Hanks/Lady Gaga," 2016). During the transition period, Baldwin's Trump obsessed about the entertainers performing at his inaugural, ratings of *The Apprentice*, and looking "super presidential" while shirking important transition duties (King & Briganti, 2016b; King & McCary, 2017; "Louis C.K./The Chainsmokers," 2017). Then, in office, he "pose[s] for pictures" and goes out of his way to spend time "with my people"—the people who fed off the entertaining qualities of his rallies ("Louis C.K./The Chainsmokers," 2017). Baldwin's impersonation prompts the question—should the president be preoccupied with entertaining?—but also offers a clear answer—no. The conclusion follows that Trump is incompatible with his office.

Finally, Baldwin's Trump harkens back to a Watergate-era lesson about the presidency: whoever occupies that office should not be conspiring and corrupt. This characteristic was dormant in pre-election sketches, but asserted itself once Trump was elected president. In a pre-election sketch, Trump colludes with the Ku Klux Klan, the FBI, and Russian President Vladimir Putin in order to win (King & Briganti, 2016a). One advisor (Kellyanne Conway) "spout[s] lies," while another (Steve Bannon) is represented by an evil skeleton in a black cloak (King & Briganti, 2017b; King & Briganti, 2017c; King & McCary, 2017). Once elected, Trump's corruption stems in part from his desire for personal enrichment. Even in an alien invasion scenario, Trump's defense of the aliens prompts a bystander to ask, "Does he have business ties on [their planet]?" (King & Briganti, 2017b).

But the chief source of Trump's corruption, according to Baldwin and *SNL*, is his collusion with Russia. Some reference to Russian collusion is made in 6 of the 15 transition sketches (King & Briganti, 2016a, 2016b, 2017c; King & McCary, 2017). Putin is referred to as "Trump's long-time crush" and testifies to his character for *The People's Court* (King & Briganti, 2017a). He poses as Santa Claus to give Trump a spy-camera doll (King & Briganti, 2016b) and as *CNN*'s Wolf Blitzer to blackmail Trump at a news conference (King & McCary, 2017). Most deviously, though, he dismissively brushes Trump aside to discuss oil drilling and territory with Secretary of State Rex Tillerson—after referring to Trump as "The Manchurian Candidate" (King & Briganti, 2016b).

In sum, Baldwin impersonates Trump to be personally deplorable and irreconcilable with the expectation of his elected office. Baldwin's Trump is corrupt and conspiring on multiple fronts, which are qualities foreign to the presidency. He misprioritizes entertaining citizens rather than leading as a president should. He also lacks presidential temperament by remaining ignorant and arrogant. His humanity is deficient, too. He is racist, sexist, vulgar, dishonest, and mean. Snide one-liners reiterate that he is unpopular with anyone other than his most ardent supporters.

"Remind People Again About Their Role": A Function of Presidential Impersonations?

Baldwin's irredeemable impersonation of Trump represented a definite, and perhaps calculated, break with previous comedic presidential impersonations. Contemporary comedic presidential impersonations had evolved to serve several rhetorical functions: humanizing the president, reconciling citizens to the president's foibles, and understanding both the individual and the office. Such impersonations fulfill the truly enlightened sense of comedy that, as Burke (1984) reveals, pictures people "not as vicious, but as mistaken" (p. 41). We might, therefore, expect that Baldwin's impersonation would critique Trump's performance of the presidency—but also provide rhetorical fodder for citizens to accept Trump in that office. Baldwin's close simulation of Trump, though, conveys the idea that he is irredeemable—and both the simulated and real Trumps are a far cry from proper simulations of the president. Baldwin himself acknowledged a desire to "dial it up as much as we can" to avoid humanizing Trump (Dibdin, 2016). What rhetorical function might such an impersonation fill?

Baldwin's comments about the 2016 election also reveal cynicism, but not apathy, about American politics. "These are very strange times in this country," Baldwin said in a post-election video for *Vanity Fair* (Busis, 2017). Baldwin spoke for both himself and (he believed) others when he asked hypothetically: "When have we ever had less faith in government than we do now?" (Yates, 2016). Perhaps, Baldwin reasoned, Trump was "the guy we need to see ourselves clearly"—a necessary shock "to the system to remind people again about their role in the process" (Jones, 2017).

Baldwin hoped his impersonation might help citizens play a greater role in American governance. As Trump's transition gave way to his inauguration, Baldwin made a plea via Twitter: "Let's stop for a moment to take a full account of where we are" (Baldwin, 2017). He saw his audience increasingly worried about "the maliciousness of this White House" (Melas, 2017). Given that he was "quoting Trump almost verbatim," Baldwin prophesied that people would not "be in the mood to laugh about it come September" 2017. He acknowledged that this was, in large part, because he created a "caricature of a more malicious Trump" (Press Association, 2017). He maintained, however, that his

Trump was "100 percent effective" at "remind[ing] people again about their role in the process" (Press Association, 2017).

Yet it seems doubtful that Baldwin meant *all* citizens. Out of character, Baldwin tweeted that the election had "changed forever . . . the meaning of the word 'Christian' as it applies to politics" (Baldwin, 2016). Then, in April, *SNL* produced an entire sketch about "Trump's people." The premise was that Baldwin-as-Trump had stopped in a mining town to commune with his supporters: "You people stand by me no matter what. It's like you found a finger in your chili but you still eat the chili because you told everyone how much you love chili. It's tremendous" ("Louis C.K./The Chainsmokers," 2017). Elsewhere, Baldwin-as-Trump mocked Trump voters who thought "[he was] going to bring every single job back to [their] town[s]" (King, Briganti, & Rodriguez, 2016). These and other sketches led Trump supporters to attack Baldwin and *SNL* on social media. They accused *SNL* of being, as one person put it, "nothing more than a political smear" and "heading down the road to continually divide the American people" (Barnish, 2017).

The divisiveness of Baldwin's impersonation might represent a new function for comedic presidential impersonations: motivating political action. Such comedy personalized and humanized leaders but now—in the form of Baldwin's Trump—it *dehumanizes* the leader. Baldwin's Trump is not bumbling but civil (as Chase's Ford), nor mildly lecherous but competent (as Hammond's Clinton), nor even dense but still principled (as Ferrell's George W. Bush). Instead, viewers see a simulation so horrible they could only embrace it if they already believed it to be true. Baldwin's impersonation calls into question Americans' collective political judgment—but only for Trump opponents. These are the people Baldwin hopes to remind "about their role in the process." We sincerely hope they find themselves galvanized to act. If they do not, *SNL* and Baldwin will have presented an impersonation that provides no room, no space, for electoral or political validation. Such an impersonation might amuse, even as it can ultimately only be civically harmful.

References

Aristotle. (1932). *Aristotle in 23 Volumes* (vol. 23). (W. H. Fyfe, Trans.). Cambridge, MA: Harvard University Press.

Baldwin, A. [ABFalecbaldwin]. (2016, November 9). One thing that is changed forever in this country is the meaning of the word "Christian" as it applies to politics. [Tweet]. Retrieved from https://twitter.com/ABFalecbaldwin /status/796225586549129217.

Baldwin, A. [ABFalecbaldwin]. (2017, January 20). All of the jokes/parody/comedy aside, let's stop for a moment to take a full account of where we are. This country is lost. It's in trouble. [Tweet]. Retrieved from https://twitter.com /abfalecbaldwin/status/822510836212269057?lang=en.

Barnish, T. (2017, April 9). "I actually see a lot of myself in you . . . ," Facebook (Saturday Night Live). Retrieved from https://www.facebook.com/snl /videos/10155123135371303/?comment_id=10155123834121303.

Baudrillard, J. (1994). *Simulacra and simulation.* (S. F. Glaser, Trans.). Ann Arbor: University of Michigan Press.

Briganti, P. (Director). (2016, October 15). Emily Blunt/Bruno Mars. *Saturday Night Live.* New York: NBC.

Burke, K. (1968). *Counter-Statement.* Berkeley, University of California Press.

Burke, K. (1984). *Attitudes Toward History.* Berkeley: University of California Press.

Busis, H. (2017, March 28). Alec Baldwin explains the real reason he decided to play Trump on S.N.L. *Vanity Fair.* Retrieved from https://www.vanityfair .com/hollywood/2017/03/alec-baldwin-donald-trump-impression-satur day-night-live-video.

Cull, N. (1997). No laughing matter: Vaughn Meader, the Kennedy administration, and presidential impersonations on radio. *Historical Journal of Film, Radio and Television, 17,* 383–399.

Dibdin, E. (2016, December 21). Alec Baldwin knows "SNL" runs the risk of humanizing Donald Trump. *Esquire.* Retrieved from http://www.esquire .com/entertainment/tv/news/a51723/alec-baldwin-snl-trump/.

Farrell, T. B. (1986). Rhetorical resemblance: Paradoxes of a practical art. *Quarterly Journal of Speech, 72,* 1–19.

The First Family, Volume One. (1962). [Audio CD]. New York: Cadence Records.

Jones, C. (2017, May). Alec Baldwin gets under Trump's skin. *The Atlantic.* Retrieved from https://www.theatlantic.com/magazine/archive/2017/05/alec-baldwin -gets-under-trumps-skin/521433.

King, D. R. (Director). (2016, October 1). Margot Robbie/The Weekend. *Saturday Night Live.* New York: NBC.

King, D. R., & Briganti, P. (Directors). (2016a, November 5). Benedict Cumberbatch/Solange. *Saturday Night Live.* New York: NBC.

King, D. R., & Briganti, P. (Directors). (2016b, December 17). Casey Affleck/ Chance the Rapper. *Saturday Night Live.* New York: NBC.

King, D. R., & Briganti, P. (Directors). (2017a, February 11). Alec Baldwin/Ed Sheeran. *Saturday Night Live.* New York: NBC.

King, D. R., & Briganti, P. (Directors). (2017b, April 15). Jimmy Fallon/Harry Styles. *Saturday Night Live.* New York: NBC.

King, D. R., & Briganti, P. (Directors). (2017c, February 4). Kristen Stewart/Alessia Cara. *Saturday Night Live.* New York: NBC.

King, D. R., & Briganti, P. (Directors). (2017d, March 11). Scarlett Johansson/ Lorde. *Saturday Night Live.* New York: NBC.

King, D. R., Briganti, P., & Rodriguez, R. (Directors). (2016, November 19). Kristen Wiig/The XX. *Saturday Night Live.* New York: NBC.

King, D. R., & McCary, D. (Directors). (2017, January 14). Felicity Jones/Sturgill Simpson. *Saturday Night Live.* New York: NBC.

Louis C. K./The Chainsmokers. *Saturday Night Live.* New York: NBC.

Lytton, C. (2017, June 8). Alec Baldwin: "Trump is the first presidential candidate made of hate." *The Telegraph*. Retrieved from http://www.telegraph.co
.uk/men/the-filter/alec-baldwin-trump-is-the-first-presidential-candidate
-made-of-h.

Melas, C. (2017, March 8). Alec Baldwin says he might give up his Trump impression on "SNL." *CNN Entertainment*. Retrieved from http://www.cnn.com
/2017/03/07/celebrities/alec-baldwin-trump-impression-snl/index.html

Miller, P. (Director). (1988, November 12). Demi Moore/Johnny Clegg & Savuka.
Saturday Night Live. New York: NBC.

Miller, P. (Director). (1989, January 21). John Malkovich/Anita Baker. *Saturday
Night Live*. New York: NBC.

Morris, G. L. (1949, October 26). *Letter to Bob Hope*. Motion Picture, Broadcasting
and Recorded Sound Division, Bob Hope Collection. Library of Congress.

Norton, A. (2004). *95 theses on politics, culture, & method*. New Haven, CT: Yale
University Press.

Press Association. (2017, March 30). Alec Baldwin says he may retire "satire-
resistant" Donald Trump impersonation. *The Guardian*. Retrieved from
https://www.theguardian.com/tv-and-radio/2017/mar/31/alec-baldwin
-satire-resistant-donald-trump-snl.

Ragland, J. (1962). Merchandisers of the First Amendment: Freedom and responsibility of the press in the age of Roosevelt, 1933–1940. *The Georgia Review,
16*, 366–391.

Robinson, P. M. (2010). *The dance of the comedians: The people, the president, and
the performance of political standup comedy in America*. Amherst: University
of Massachusetts Press.

Rogers, W. (2005). *The papers of Will Rogers: From the Broadway stage to the national
stage, September 1915-July 1928*. Norman: University of Oklahoma Press.

Rose, L. (2017, May 15). SNL's yuuuge year: 20 insiders reveal Alec Baldwin's
future as Trump, "Spicey" secrets and Lorne Michaels' election pep talk.
The Hollywood Reporter. Retrieved from http://www.hollywoodreporter
.com/features/snl-trump-ratings-bump-you-almost-feel-like-a-war
-profiteer-1003540

Rubenstein, D. (2008). *This is not a president: Sense, nonsense, and the American
political Imaginary*. New York: New York University Press.

Schwartz, B. (2015, May 6). The infamous "War of the Worlds" radio broadcast was
a magnificent fluke. *Smithsonian*. Retrieved from http://www.smithsonia
nmag.com/history/infamous-war-worlds-radio-broadcast-was-magni
ficent-fluke-180955180/.

Sharpe, K. (2009). *Selling the Tudor monarchy: Authority and image in sixteenth-
century England*. New Haven, CT: Yale University Press.

Smith, J. (2009). *The presidents we imagine: Two centuries of White House fictions on
the page, on the stage, onscreen, and online*. Madison: University of Wisconsin
Press.

Tom Hanks/Lady Gaga. (2016, October 22). *Saturday Night Live*. New York: NBC.

Wilson, D. (Director). (1975a, November 8). Candice Bergen/Esther Phillips. *Saturday Night Live*. New York: NBC.

Wilson, D. (Director). (1975b, November 22). Lily Tomlin. *Saturday Night Live*. New York: NBC.

Wilson, D. (Director). (1992, December 5). Tom Arnold/Neil Young. *Saturday Night Live*. New York: NBC.

Yates, E. (2016, September 8). Alec Baldwin: Trump could have won—Here's why he won't. *Business Insider*. Retrieved from http://www.businessinsider.com /alec-baldwin-explains-donald-trump-hillary-clinton-2016-9.

PART 2

Campaign Communication

Processing the Political: Presidential Primary Debate "Live-Tweeting" as Information Processing

Josh C. Bramlett, Mitchell S. McKinney,
and Benjamin R. Warner

The influence of televised campaign debates on political attitudes and behaviors has been a topic of great interest since John F. Kennedy and Richard Nixon met in the first televised general-election presidential debates in 1960. Presidential debates have been shown to increase citizen interest in the campaign (Chaffee, 1978), generate greater confidence and willingness to discuss politics with others (McKinney & Warner, 2013), increase knowledge about politics (Holbrook, 1999), and strengthen one's prior commitments to a candidate (Benoit, McKinney, & Holbert, 2001). Exposure to campaign debates has also been found to affect evaluations of candidate image (Best & Hubbard, 1999; Warner, Carlin, Winfrey, Schnoebelen, & Trosanovski, 2011). With televised debates lasting usually 60 to 90 minutes (and some primary debates lasting even two or more hours), these candidate exchanges provide an information-rich source of campaign communication that features a more sustained discussion of campaign issues than typically found in other forms of campaign communication.

Recent scholarly analysis has focused greater attention on debate learning effects, especially in relation to the increasing tendency for viewers to engage televised debates in a "second screen" environment. McKinney, Houston, and Hawthorne (2014) document the increasing number of debate viewers who participated in debate social watching during the 2012 presidential campaign, whereby viewers engage and process a televised debate message while interacting online with others who are part of their social media network (see also Thorson, Hawthorne, Swasy, & McKinney, 2015). A number of social watching studies have found that greater tweeting activity during presidential debates increases issue knowledge, specifically more accurate recall of candidate issue positions taken during the debate (Houston, McKinney, Hawthorne, & Spialek, 2013b; Jennings, Coker, McKinney, & Warner, 2017; McKinney et al., 2014; Thorson et al., 2015). Such processing of campaign issue information may occur because one is inclined to attune more closely to the debate message and issue content in order to formulate opinions that are expressed with one's social network via tweets and other social media posts. Other presidential debate scholars, however, have found that greater "debate viewing-social media multi-tasking" has a negative influence on debate issue learning (Gottfried, Hardy, Holbert, Winneg, & Jamieson, 2017). Here, results suggest that engaging in greater social media activity while debate watching actually hinders knowledge acquisition. Many questions remain unresolved and warrant further attention regarding the influence of social watching activity on debate viewers' political attitudes, candidate evaluations, and learning from debates.

The current study explores presidential primary debate social watching behaviors and involves two analytic components that examine the nature of information processing while viewing presidential debates. First, a content analysis of debate viewers' tweets captures the extent to which debate viewers focus their attention on candidate image and campaign issues, debate viewers' positive and negative assessments of the candidates, and the extent to which viewers agree or disagree with candidate issue statements. Second, viewers' pre- and post-debate survey responses are paired with features of their tweets to explore issue knowledge acquisition from debate viewing and the relationship between normative political attitudes and social watching behaviors. This study responds to Kim and Garrett's (2012) call to create more innovative ways to measure real-time information processing of political messages by utilizing live-tweeting as a proxy for information processing. In doing so, our analysis reveals that tweeting is related to post-debate knowledge acquisition, that a relationship exists between the confidence that debate viewers have in their political knowledge and the focus or content of their debate tweets, and that a relationship exists between debate viewers' confidence in their political knowledge and their willingness to engage in debate social watching messaging activity that features an argumentative posture.

Literature Review

Research spanning several decades has demonstrated rather convincingly that "campaign debates do indeed matter" (McKinney & Warner, 2013, p. 256); and, in fact, a number of these studies have concluded that primary debates have far greater effects than do general election debates. Specifically, primary debates generate greater shifts in vote preference (Benoit, Hansen, & Verser, 2003; McKinney & Warner, 2013), result in greater issue learning (Benoit et al., 2003), and significantly influence perceptions of candidate image (Lanoue & Schrott, 1989; Wall, Golden, & James, 1988).

Presidential primary debates preceded general-election televised debates, with the very first primary debate broadcast consisting of a 1944 radio debate between Republican presidential candidates Thomas Dewey and Harold Stassen. The very first televised primary debate occurred in 1956 between Democratic candidates Adlai Stevenson and Estes Kefauver (Jamieson & Birdsell, 1988). Despite the significance of primary debates, especially given their larger effects when compared to general election debates, there is considerably less scholarly research about primary debates relative to general election debates. This is surprising in light of the fact that a presidential election cycle features many more primary than general election debates. In the 2016 campaign cycle, for example, there were 21 primary debates, with the Republican primary candidates debating 12 times and the Democratic primary candidates debating 9 times, compared to only 3 general election debates between Democratic presidential candidate Hillary Clinton and Republican candidate Donald Trump.

Primary Debate Processing, Social Media, and Normative Democratic Outcomes

Exposure to televised campaign debates has been found to produce beneficial effects on attitudes of political engagement and normative democratic outcomes, such as producing a more informed electorate. McKinney and Warner's (2013) assessment of a decade of presidential debate effects studies, including both primary and general-election debates, found that debate exposure decreases political cynicism and increases political information efficacy (PIE), an individual's confidence in their political knowledge and ability to talk about politics with others. Additionally, exposure to campaign debates increases voters' general knowledge about politics, as those who watch debates are more likely to attune to and seek out additional political information following their debate viewing; and those who view televised debates also achieve greater knowledge from the issues discussed during the debates (Holbrook, 1999).

Presidential debate scholars have most recently turned their attention to citizens' "second screen" debate viewing, exploring both the content and effects of debate viewers' social watching behaviors. A number of studies from the 2012 presidential primary and general election debates explored how "live-tweeting" influenced viewers' engagement with presidential debates (e.g., Houston, Hawthorne, Spialek, Greenwood, & McKinney, 2013a; Houston et al., 2013b; McKinney, Houston, & Hawthorne, 2014; Thorson et al., 2015). Houston et al. (2013b) found that those who tweeted more frequently while debate watching achieved a greater sense of political engagement and heightened campaign interest. They also found that those who tweeted more frequently during the debate learned more as compared to those who tweeted less. In another study, Houston et al. (2013a) compared debate viewers who tweeted to those who watched a debate without engaging social media on a second screen. They found that those who tweeted while watching a debate paid closer attention to the debate and perceived the debates to be more important. McKinney et al. (2014) found that those debate viewers with higher pre-debate PIE tweeted more frequently during their debate viewing. Therefore, those who are more confident in their political knowledge and are willing to talk politics with others appear to engage in more frequent live-tweeting during their debate viewing as a form of political discussion. The increased confidence that one has in their political knowledge may also provide greater impetus to express one's political views with others in their social network. Thus, based on past findings relating to debate viewers' social watching behaviors, we predict:

H1: Participants with greater pre-debate PIE will tweet more frequently while watching a debate.

Because those with greater PIE tweeted more frequently during their debate viewing (McKinney et al., 2014), and given that those who tweeted more frequently during debate exposure learned more from the debate compared to individuals who tweeted less (Houston et al., 2013b), we also predict:

H2: Participants with greater pre-debate PIE will achieve greater debate learning (score higher on post-debate knowledge questions).

Next, we seek to further develop our understanding of the relationship between debate viewers' social watching behaviors and debate learning. In their analysis of primary debate viewers' social watching activity, Jennings et al. (2017) found that it was actually greater issue-based tweeting that increased debate viewers' knowledge acquisition. The Jennings et al. (2017) study, as we do in the present analysis, examined the content of debate viewers' tweets, whether comments focused on candidate image or campaign issue, and found that greater learning from debate exposure occurred among those whose tweeting activity during the debate was more issue versus image focused.

Tweeting about the issue content present in a campaign debate can be thought of as central-route information processing, and as Eveland (2004) found, this form of political discussion results in greater learning. Again, building on previous debate social watching findings we predict:

H3: Participants who tweet more about issues (versus candidate image) during the debate will achieve greater debate learning (score higher on post-debate knowledge questions).

As we continue to develop our understanding of the form of message processing that occurs with debate viewers' social watching activity, it seems likely that those who have greater confidence in their political knowledge and who are more willing to discuss politics with others may possess a more developed framework of political knowledge and greater motivation to engage in politics—and the debate message—at a central processing route of issue discussion. This dynamic suggests that:

H4: Participants with higher pre-debate PIE will tweet more about issues (versus candidate image) during the debate.

Certainly, the constructs of issue and image content are central elements of political messages. "Image" typically refers to a candidate's persona and character traits, whereas "issue" refers to policy matters (Kaid & Johnston, 1991). In campaign debate research, issue and image are particularly important topics of analysis. Audience perceptions of candidate image are greatly affected by debate exposure (McKinney, Rill, & Watson, 2011; McKinney & Warner, 2013), which is particularly true in primary debates, where candidates seek to build their image as the desired party leader and eventual nominee, and as these early campaign contests—as opposed to general-election debates—affect greater change in candidate preference (Benoit et al., 2003; McKinney & Warner, 2013). Also, as a rich source of issue information, debates produce more knowledgeable voters (Holbrook, 1999; McKinney & Warner, 2013). A very limited body of presidential debate research (e.g., McKinney, 2005; McKinney, Dudash, & Hodgkinson, 2003) has conducted comparative analysis that explores the relative issue/image learning from debates and finds that debate viewers attend more to image rather than issue features of the debate message. Although we previously predicted that certain debate viewers, namely those with higher PIE, will focus greater attention on issues, we know that not all viewers will have heightened confidence in their political knowledge and may therefore avoid discussion of political issues, instead focusing their attention on candidate image. Thus, we posit a general question regarding debate viewers' relative issue/image focus and question how issue/image tweeting may differ according to party debate:

RQ1: Will participants who live-tweet a presidential primary debate tweet more often about candidate image or campaign issues?

    RQ1a: Will Democrat and Republican debate viewers' tweets reflect differences in image or issue emphasis?

Much has been made of the public's cynicism toward politics in general, and toward political leaders specifically; and some have even argued that the nature of social media and online discussion of politics may contribute to even greater cynicism and negativity (Stachelski, 2016). Despite widespread political cynicism, and with millennials supposedly among our most politically cynical citizens (Miller, 2014), we must be careful to take into account the context of a primary debate and its chief audience as we consider how debate viewers may respond to this political message. The main audience for a presidential primary campaign, and primary debate, are those voters who identify with a particular party. Unlike a general-election debate where we often see disagreement or negative expression directed toward the opposition party candidate, there are no opposition party candidates in a primary debate. Hence, viewers may find more to agree than disagree with and thus perhaps respond more positively. If this is the case, it should be evident in the tone (positive/ negative) of tweets. We pose two questions relating to the tone or valence of debate viewers' comments, first asking about the overall tone of debates viewers' comments and then questioning the tone of debate watchers' comments directed toward each of the candidates within both parties' debates:

RQ2: What is the overall valence or tone (positive or negative) of debate viewers' Twitter comments?

    RQ2a: What is the relative tone (positive or negative) of debate viewers' tweets directed toward the candidates in both the Democrat and Republican primary debates?

Finally, in this study we are interested in the argumentative stance communicated by participant tweets. Though it may be difficult to formulate a sophisticated argument in the 140-character limit imposed on a single tweet, these truncated expressions can contain the kernel of an argument. To identify debate viewers' argumentative stance, we analyze issue tweets that express agreement or disagreement with candidates' issue positions. Here, we find the development of argumentative stance indicative of one who is actively engaged in evaluating and processing information, or updating an "online tally" (McGraw, Lodge, & Stroh, 1990). Politically sophisticated individuals are more likely to actively update their online tally in an "efficient" manner, whereas those who are less politically sophisticated will rely on prior memory of candidates (McGraw et al., 1990). Building from this line of research, Kim and Garrett (2012) proposed a hybrid model between the online and memory tallies and found that, although both can be utilized, the context of debates lends itself to online processing. The concept of argumentative stance—the expression of agreement or disagreement with candidates' issue positions—functions much like Kim and Garrett's (2012) online tally processing in which viewers respond to "attitude-consistent" and "attitude-discrepant information" (p. 365). An argumentative stance is evident when a debate viewer utilizes a tweet to express agreement or disagreement when encountering candidate claims.

We seek to first analyze the extent to which all viewers actively engage debate information in an argumentative fashion. Then, building on our previous prediction that those who are more confident in their political knowledge (higher PIE) will focus greater attention on issue tweeting, we extend this contention to predict a relationship between PIE and argumentative stance:

RQ3: To what extent will debate viewers' issue tweets take an argumentative stance—express agreement or disagreement—with each of the primary debate candidates' issue positions?

H5: Participants with higher pre-debate PIE will generate more tweets during the debate that take an argumentative stance—express agreement or disagreement—with candidates' issue positions.

Method

Participants and Procedure

A convenience sample of college students who received extra credit for their participation in this study viewed a taped and edited version of a presidential primary debate. The experiment featured two conditions: a Democratic primary debate held on March 9, 2016, that included two candidates (Hillary Clinton and Bernie Sanders) and a Republican primary debate held on March 10, 2016, that included four candidates (Ted Cruz, John Kasich, Marco Rubio, and Donald Trump). Both debates were downloaded from the Internet in their full form and edited to 40-minute versions for the experimental viewing sessions that took place in mid-March 2016. Prior to entering a classroom to watch their assigned debate, individuals were asked to indicate the major political party with which they identified or leaned most toward, with Republican Party affiliates and leaners assigned to watch the Republican primary debate and Democratic Party affiliates and leaners assigned to the Democratic primary debate condition. A total of 187 participants viewed the two debates: 50.3% ($n=94$) watched the Democratic debate and 49.7% ($n=93$) watched the Republican debate.

Participants completed a survey prior to viewing the debate. Upon completion of the online survey (hosted by Qualtrics), participants were read a prompt by study supervisors instructing them to tweet throughout the debate about anything they deemed "important." Participants tweeted during the debate using designated hashtags for each of the experimental conditions, and the program DataSift was utilized to capture every tweet posted that used these hashtags during the period of the debate experiment. Unique hashtags were generated and prescreened to ensure they were not utilized outside of the study. After viewing the debate, participants completed an online survey. Each participant identified their Twitter handle in their pre- and post-debate surveys, allowing their responses to be paired with their tweets.

A content analysis was conducted using all tweets collected from the experiment. A total of 506 tweets were collected and saved into a Microsoft Excel file. Following extensive coder training, two independent coders—graduate students in journalism and communication—were each given 50% of the sample for coding with an additional 38 tweets (7.5%) from the other coder's half of the sample to create an overlap of 15% for intercoder reliability. To assess intercoder reliability, Krippendorf's alpha was calculated using Hayes' K-Alpha macro with 1,000 bootstraps (Hayes, n.d.; Krippendorf, 2013).

Tweet Content Coding Categories

To examine whether or not tweets would focus more on candidate image or political issues (RQ1), an *image/issue focus* ($\alpha = .78$) variable was created, and coders were instructed to code each tweet for whether it focused on candidate image, campaign issue, a combination of campaign issue and candidate image, or neither.

Each tweet was also coded for its overall tone—positive and/or negative—and a *tweet valence* variable was developed (RQ2). Tweet valence assessed each Twitter comment as positive, negative, or neutral in tone and directed toward a specific candidate. Tone categories were mutually exclusive at the within-candidate level, but a tweet could be positive for one candidate and negative toward another. Acceptable reliability was achieved for tone of tweet as directed toward each candidate, including Hillary Clinton ($\alpha = .88$), Bernie Sanders ($\alpha = .94$), Donald Trump ($\alpha = .92$), Ted Cruz ($\alpha = 1.0$), Marco Rubio ($\alpha = .94$), and John Kasich ($\alpha = .90$).

A *candidate focus* variable was developed to determine the frequency of candidate mentions throughout the corpus of the Twitter content (RQ2a and RQ3). Here, a single tweet could focus on one or multiple candidates, or the tweet could focus on no candidates (or the tweet could also be coded as "cannot determine" candidate focus). Intercoder reliability for candidate mentions included Hillary Clinton ($\alpha = .96$), Bernie Sanders ($\alpha = .96$), Donald Trump ($\alpha = 1.0$), Ted Cruz ($\alpha = 1.0$), Marco Rubio ($\alpha = 1.0$), John Kasich ($\alpha = 1.0$), no candidates mentioned ($\alpha = .75$), and can't determine ($\alpha = -.01$). When the coding decisions for "no candidates" and "can't determine" were merged, a high intercoder reliability ($\alpha = .90$) was achieved.

Finally, to assess whether or not issue tweets expressed agreement or disagreement with candidates' issue positions, a coding category of *issue agree or disagree* was formulated (RQ3). For this category, if a tweet had first been identified as an issue or combination issue and image tweet, coders assessed whether the tweet expressed agreement or disagreement with a candidates' issue position or whether the tweet "takes no position" on the issue (and "can't determine" was also an available coding option). Agree/disagree was mutually exclusive at the within-candidate level, as a single tweet could not be coded as both agreeing and disagreeing with a candidate. A tweet could be coded as agreeing with one candidate and disagreeing with another. Intercoder reliability for the agree/disagree variable for each candidate included Clinton (α=1.0), Sanders (α=.81), Trump (α=.65), Cruz (α=1.0), Rubio (α=.74), Kasich (α=1.0), Takes No Position (α=.75), and Can't Determine (α=-.03). When the coding decisions for "takes no position" and "can't determine" were merged, the collapsed coding category achieved acceptable reliability (α=.80).

A few examples are provided to illustrate coding categories and decisions. First, the tweet "Bernie is right, money needs to go toward education instead of incarceration" is an example of a tweet that is issue focused and expressing agreement and positive tone toward Sanders. "Monroe Doctrine still lives" is an example of an issue-focused tweet with no candidate focus. The tweet "I am not sure if I can trust Hillary after Benghazi" is an example of a combination issue and image tweet, as it notes disagreement over the Benghazi issue along with the character facet of trust relating to Clinton. Another combination issue and image tweet is "Marco Rubio, very poised speaker when compared to Trump on foreign affairs." This tweet focuses on Rubio's persona or image as a poised speaker, along with his credibility on the issue of foreign affairs. This tweet is also an example of focusing on two different candidates, Rubio and Trump, with differing tone and stance toward each candidate (a positive tone of agreement toward Rubio yet negative tone of disagreement toward Trump).

Survey Measures

Political information efficacy. PIE, an attitudinal construct that measures the level of confidence one has in the political knowledge they possess (Kaid, McKinney, & Tedesco, 2007), was assessed before and after debate viewing. Participants indicated the extent to which they agreed with the following statements (from 1=*strongly disagree* to 5=*strongly agree*): I consider myself well qualified to participate in politics; I feel that I have a pretty good understanding of the important political issues facing our country; I think that I am better informed about politics and government than most people; and, If a friend asked me about the presidential election, I feel I would have enough information to help my friend figure out who to vote for. The items were averaged to create a composite variable, which was reliable before (α=.89) and after the debate (α=.86).

Debate knowledge. Debate knowledge was assessed in both the Republican and Democratic debates with five distinct multiple choice questions constructed based on candidate statements made during the debates. Correct responses were dummy-coded as 1=correct and 0=correct. A sum of correct responses was used to measure debate knowledge acquisition. The full list of post-debate knowledge questions is provided in the appendix.

Tweeting variables. Finally, to incorporate the content analysis of participants' tweets in conjunction with their survey responses, several categories were computed from the Twitter content coding. The total number of tweets sent by each username was tallied and associated with each participant's survey responses, as were their total number of issue, image, and combination tweets and their total number of issue agree/disagree tweets. To assess the extent to which individuals engaged in evaluative processing of issues relative to other types of tweeting, the variable "argumentative stance" was created by combining an individual's total number of agree and disagree tweets and dividing by their total number of tweets.

Results

Content Analysis

The tweets collected from the two primary debate viewing sessions consisted of a combined 506 tweets, with 50.4% of the tweets (n=255) posted by the Democratic debate participants and 49.6% of the tweets (n=251) posted by Republican debate viewers. Descriptive statistics were calculated to answer RQ1. In the overall sample, 39.1% of tweets (n=198) were issue focused, 31.2% (n=158) were image focused, 9.7% (n=49) consisted of issue-image combination tweets, and 19.9% (n=101) were neither image nor issue tweets. Thus, when processing the debate message as reflected in their Twitter comments, viewers focused more on issues discussed by the candidates than on candidate image.

RQ1a explored possible differences in viewers' issue/image focus between the Republican and Democratic debates. Here, significant results were found, χ^2=9.923 (3, 506), p<.05, V=.14, pointing to differences in how viewers of the Democratic and Republican debates processed the two debate messages as reflected in their tweets. The Democratic debate featured a higher percentage of issue tweets (43.5%, n=113, ASR=2) than the Republican debate (34.7%, n=87, ASR=-2). The Republican debate, on the other hand, featured more image tweets (35.1%, n=88, ASR=1.7) than the Democratic debate (27.8%, n=71, ASR=-1.7).

RQ2 and RQ2a explored positive and negative valence of social media comments and valence of comments directed toward specific candidates. A plurality of all tweets were positive in tone (36.9%, $n=178$), followed by negative tweets (32.2%, $n=155$), and then neutral tweets (30.9%, $n=149$). It is with specific candidates that greater differences are apparent. Of all candidates, Trump received the greatest number of negative tweets (again, from those debate viewers who identified as Republicans or leaning Republican), and Trump also had the greatest disparity in his negative-to-positive tweet ratio. In total, Trump was the subject of more negative tweets (49.1%, $n=58$) than positive tweets (20.3%, $n=24$). Clinton was also the subject of more negative (45.1%, $n=46$) than positive tweets (26.5%, $n=27$). Sanders was the focus of more positive tweets (52.3%, $n=67$) as compared to only 14.8% ($n=19$) of tweets that were negative. Cruz experienced more positive tweets (45.7%, $n=32$) than negative (25.7%, $n=18$). A majority of tweets about both Rubio and Kasich were positive in tone (see Table 9.1).

RQ3 explored issue agreement or disagreement with candidates as expressed in all issue and issue-image combination tweets. Of the 247 issue/issue-image combo tweets, half of these comments (50%, $n=123$) expressed clear agreement or disagreement with candidates' issue positions, and the remaining half (50%, $n=124$) of these tweets were coded as "takes no position or can't determine." The full results of issue tweets that agree and disagree with each candidate are presented in Table 9.2. Although the Democratic debate featured only two candidates, Clinton and Sanders, Sanders had far more agreement tweets (79%, $n=37$) than tweets agreeing with Clinton's issue positions (65%, $n=13$). In fact, of the tweets posted during the Democratic debate, Sanders

Table 9.1   Tweet Tone Toward Candidates

Candidate	Positive	Negative	Neutral	Total Tweets
Clinton	27	46	29	102
Sanders	67	19	42	128
Trump	24	58	36	118
Cruz	32	18	20	70
Rubio	18	6	6	30
Kasich	9	1	8	18
Democrats	0	0	1	1
Republicans	1	3	4	8
Obama	0	4	3	7
Total	178	155	149	482

Table 9.2   Issue Agreement and Disagreement with Candidates

Candidate	Agree	Disagree	Total
Clinton	13	7	20
Sanders	37	10	47
Trump	7	12	19
Cruz	16	3	19
Rubio	13	2	15
Kasich	3	0	3
Neutral or unclear	0	0	124
Total	89	34	247

was the focus of more than twice the number of issue-based tweets ($n=47$) than Clinton's issue-focused tweets ($n=20$). Other candidates also received far more issue agreement tweets than disagreements, as Cruz had 84% agreement (16 of 19 tweets) and Rubio had 87% issue agreement tweets (13 of 15), and although Kasich was the focus of only 3 issue tweets, all 3 (or 100%) were in agreement with his issue positions. The only candidate from both debates, Republican and Democrats, whose issue-focused tweets expressed more disagreement than agreement with their positions was Trump (37%, $n=7$ agreement; 63%, $n=12$ disagreement).

Survey Results

Our first hypothesis, based on previous findings by McKinney et al. (2014), predicted that those with higher PIE would tweet more during the debate. In the current study, H1 was not supported, as those with higher pre-debate PIE did not tweet more frequently than those with lower PIE. However, support was found for H2. Results of a linear regression were significant, $F(1,181)=10.792$, $p=.001$, $r^2=.056$, indicating that higher pre-debate PIE was an important predictor of post-debate knowledge, ($\beta=.24$, $p=.001$). In addition, H3 was supported. Significant results were observed, $F(1,181)=4.12$, $p<.05$, $r^2=.022$, indicating that issue tweeting was a positive predictor of knowledge outcomes ($\beta=.149$, $p<.05$). However, these results no longer reach significance when controlling for pre-debate PIE ($\beta=.128$, $p=.076$). Image tweeting and total frequency of tweeting were not significantly related to knowledge outcomes, and contrary to H4, there was no significant direct relationship between PIE and issue tweeting ($p=.21$). Still, taken together, these results do suggest that issue tweeting may predict post-debate knowledge gains. Finally, results were consistent with H5, $F(1,181)=6.5$, $p<.05$, $r^2=.035$, individuals higher in pre-debate PIE engaged in more argument stance-taking (agreeing and disagreeing with candidates' issue positions) as they processed debate messages ($\beta = .186$, $p < .05$).

Discussion

The current study sought to further our understanding of how individuals process political information as presented in debates, and particularly one's engagement with a televised debate message in a "second screen" environment. Through a content analysis of tweets posted during both a Democratic and Republican primary debate, paired with responses to pre- and post-debate surveys, our findings contribute to an understanding of political information processing in several important ways. First, in the combined pool of tweets from both debates, participants focused more attention on campaign issues than candidate images. When prompted to tweet about the most important aspects of the debates they were viewing, participants more frequently commented about issues. This finding is at odds with previous presidential debate research (e.g., McKinney, 2005; McKinney et al., 2003), which finds that viewers attend more to image versus issue features of the debate message. The McKinney et al. (2003) study asked debate viewers to recall what they had learned about the candidates and/or issues after viewing a 90-minute debate, and these memory-based assessments contained far more instances of candidate image than issue learning. Yet in the present study, when viewers engaged in live-tweeting of the debates, a proxy for online processing, it appears that they more frequently find issue content as the most important feature of the debate message.

There were also important differences in the content analytic results between the two debates' tweet focus. Republican debate viewers produced comments that suggest something of an image-issue parity, as just one additional image ($n=88$) than issue tweet ($n=87$) was posted during the Republican primary debate. In comparing viewer responses to the two party's debates, approximately 35% of tweets posted during the Republican debate were issue focused, whereas 44% of tweets in the Democratic debate were issue focused. It is likely that these dissimilarities are not due to systematic differences in how partisans process information, but rather a reflection of the content of the two debates. The Republican debate featured four candidates instead of two, and thus more opportunity to comment on the various candidates' personas and performances. An inspection of the two debate transcripts, supported by post-debate media commentary, suggests that the Republican debate focused more on candidate personality and image characteristics and less on policy discussion than did the Democratic debate. Still, in both debates, a substantive amount of issue-focused tweeting occurred.

The content analysis also revealed differences in the patterns of viewers' agreement and disagreement with candidates. As Table 9.1 shows, Sanders was the recipient of the most Twitter mentions within either party, and he enjoyed the greatest number of positive tweets across all candidates. As Table 9.2 shows, Sanders was the focus of more issue agreement tweets than all other candidates. Conversely, Trump, second only to Sanders in number of tweets, experienced the highest number of negative comments and also had the largest number of issue disagreement tweets (again, the only candidate in either debate with more issue disagreement than agreement tweets). Indeed, the reactions of our small sample of college students demonstrate the groundswell of support from young citizens that fueled Sanders' momentum during the primary process. Trump, too, struggled to attract young voters (Agiesta, 2016). Our participants' processing of these primary debates as demonstrated in the content of their Twitter messages adds insight to the dynamics of public opinion and candidate support reflective of millennial voters nationwide during the primary season.

Finally, results from our combined survey and Twitter content analysis furthers our understanding of how viewers engage with information in presidential debates. First, it is interesting that support for H1 was not found in the current study, as individuals with higher PIE—greater confidence in their political knowledge—did not engage in more frequent tweeting. This finding may be due to the nature of our experiment, with participants instructed to tweet about aspects of the debate they found important, and thus our participants may have been just as likely to comment during the debate no matter their confidence in their political knowledge. It may also be the case that, unlike the previous social watching studies conducted during the 2012 presidential campaign (e.g., McKinney et al., 2014; Thorson et al., 2015), a period in which Twitter was establishing itself as an important source of campaign communication, in 2016 those individuals who felt more secure in their political knowledge would be more willing to post their political comments and opinions. Now that Twitter is a more ubiquitous social media, particularly among millennials, posting one's thoughts and opinions may not require as much confidence in one's political knowledge. As social media evolve, continued exploration is needed to illuminate how citizens engage and process political messages via digital technologies.

It was the case, however, that individuals higher in PIE engaged in more political argumentation—their tweets expressed greater agreement and disagreement with candidates' issue positions. This behavior suggests a more active form of political information processing and engagement with the debate message. This finding may also demonstrate that those with greater confidence in their political knowledge possess a more complex cognitive political structure and are thus better able to assess the political information presented in the debate, as well as a stronger basis on which to accept or reject candidate claims. Such processing points toward the use of the "online tally" of information (McGraw et al., 1990), indicating that individuals with preconceived notions are able to actively assess how information they have just encountered measures up to their existing knowledge of a candidate or political issue.

In addition, although it was not observed that more frequent tweeting led to greater knowledge acquisition, we did find that tweeting more about issues resulted in greater—or more accurate—knowledge from the debate. Importantly, this finding is compared to the null result of image tweeting leading to greater knowledge outcomes. Combined, these results suggest that it is actually the type of tweeting and debate message processing, rather than frequency of tweeting, that may result in greater debate learning. Those engaged in more frequent issue-based tweeting, viewed as a more central form of information processing, achieve greater learning. As individuals with higher PIE learned more from the debate and tweeted more argumentative issue stances, these findings reinforce our original contention that individuals who tweet more about issues will learn more from the debate.

Limitations

As with any research project, there are several limitations with the present study. First, though we realize convenience samples of college student participants have their limitations, the use of young citizens to measure social watching debate behaviors seems appropriate for our study goals. In fact, meta-analytic analyses of debate viewing (Benoit et al., 2003) found no differences between studies that used student subjects and nonstudent "adult" subject pools. Although a sample of tweets from the general population may have provided greater insight into public assessment of the 2016 Republican and Democratic primary candidates, our focus in this study was on participants' social watching behaviors to more carefully explore the processing of a political message, a process that may function similarly with all debate viewers. In addition, a larger sample would have provided greater statistical power for more complex analyses. Finally, the experimental context of debate viewing and the inducement of extra credit may have altered our participants' debate watching behaviors.

Conclusion

This study adds to our understanding of "second screen" political communication engagement, a phenomenon that has been called "social watching" to describe viewers' engagement with a televised political message such as a candidate debate while interacting online with others who are part of one's social media network (McKinney et al., 2014; Thorson et al., 2015). The growing body of social watching literature (e.g., Houston et al., 2013a, 2013b; Jennings et al., 2017; McKinney et al., 2014; Thorson et al., 2015) has found that live-tweeting during a televised presidential debate results in different effects than simply watching a debate without simultaneous social media engagement and also produces a number of normative democratic outcomes, including enhanced learning from the debate message (see especially Houston et al., 2013a; Jennings et al., 2017). As Houston et al. (2013a) concluded in one of the earliest assessments of presidential debate viewers' social watching behaviors, "live-tweeting debates is an activity driven by engagement with and thoughtful processing of debate content" (p. 301). Viewers' processing of the debate message was the principle focus of the current study, and participants' live-tweeting during a Republican and Democratic primary debate provides a useful proxy of their information processing. Though many of the previous social watching debate studies have utilized more cursory-level content indicators of social watching activity, such as frequency of tweeting or candidate mentions, the analysis presented in this chapter provides a more in-depth examination of tweet content to more fully explore message processing, including issue/image focus, attitude valance (positive/negative assessment), and argumentative stance (agreement or disagreement with candidates' issue positions).

Our results indicate that increased issue tweeting is related to greater post-debate knowledge acquisition. This finding builds upon previous social media–debate learning results, which also found that individuals who tweeted more frequently during debate exposure learned more from the debate compared to individuals who tweeted less (Houston et al., 2013b) and results that showed greater issue-based tweeting during debate viewing increased knowledge acquisition (Jennings et al., 2017). Although others have argued that "debate viewing-social media multi-tasking" distracts viewers from learning (Gottfried et al., 2017), our results continue to support the contention that engagement with a televised debate message through online commenting, particularly if one's social media messaging is focused on issues, may produce more knowledgeable citizens. Our findings also reveal that debate viewers who are more confident in their political knowledge, those who are higher in PIE, are also more likely to process the debate message with responses that take an argumentative stance.

References

Agiesta, J. (2016, April 25). Poll: Trump's support among young voters historically low. *CNN.* Retrieved from http://www.cnn.com/2016/04/25/politics /donald-trump-young-voters/

Benoit, W. L., Hansen, G. J., & Verser, R. M. (2003). A meta-analysis of the effects of viewing U.S. presidential debates. *Communication Monographs, 70*(4), 335–350. doi:10.1080/0363775032000179133

Benoit, W. L., McKinney, M. S., & Holbert, R. L. (2001). Beyond learning and persona: Extending the scope of presidential debate effects. *Communication Monographs, 68*(3), 259–273. doi: 10.1080/03637750128060

Best, S. J., & Hubbard, C. (1999). Maximizing "minimal effects": The impact of early primary season debates on voter preferences. *American Politics Research, 27*(4), 450–467. doi:10.1177/1532673X99027004004

Chaffee, S. H. (1978). Presidential debates: Are they helpful to voters? *Communication Monographs, 45*, 330–346. doi:10.1080/03637757809375978

Eveland, W. P., Jr. (2004). The effect of political discussion in producing informed citizens: The roles of information, motivation, and elaboration. *Political Communication, 21*(2), 177–193. doi: 10.1080/10584600490443877

Gottfried, J., Hardy, B., Holbert, L., Winneg, K., & Jamieson, K. (2017). The changing nature of political debate consumption: Social media, multi-tasking, and knowledge acquisition. *Political Communication, 34*(2), 172–199. doi:10.1080/10584609.2016.1154120

Hayes, A. F. (n.d.). My macros and codes for SPSS and SAS. Retrieved from http://afhayes.com/spss-sas-and-mplus-macros-and-code.html

Holbrook, T. M. (1999). Political learning from presidential debates. *Political Behavior, 21*(1), 67–89. doi: 10.1023/A:1023348513570

Houston, J. B., Hawthorne, J., Spialek, M. L., Greenwood, M., & McKinney, M. S. (2013a). Tweeting during presidential debates: Effect on candidate evaluations and debate attitudes. *Argumentation and Advocacy, 49*, 301–311. doi: 10.1080/00028533.2013.11821804

Houston, J. B., McKinney, M. S., Hawthorne, J., & Spialek, M. L. (2013b). Frequency of tweeting during presidential debates: Effect on debate attitudes and knowledge. *Communication Studies, 64*(5), 548–560. doi:10.1080/10510974.2013.832693

Jamieson, K. H., & Birdsell, D. S. (1988). *Presidential debates: The challenges of creating an informed electorate.* New York: Oxford University Press.

Jennings, F. J., Coker, C. R., McKinney, M. S., & Warner, B. R. (2017). Tweeting presidential primary debates: Debate processing through motivated Twitter instruction. *American Behavioral Scientist, 61*(4), 455-474. doi:10.1177/0002764217704867

Kaid, L. L., & Johnston, A. (1991). Negative versus positive television advertising in U.S. presidential campaigns, 1960–1988. *Journal of Communication, 41*(3), 53–64. doi: 10.1111/j.1460-2466.1991.tb02323.x

Kaid, L. L., McKinney, M. S., & Tedesco, J. C. (2007). Political information efficacy and young voters. *American Behavioral Scientist, 50*, 1093–1111. doi:10.1177/0002764207300040

Kim, Y. M., & Garrett, K. (2012). Online and memory based: Revisiting the relationship between candidate evaluation processing models. *Political Behavior, 34*, 345–368. doi: 10.1007/s11109-011-9158-9

Krippendorf, K. (2013). *Content analysis: An introduction to its methodology* (3rd ed.). London: SAGE Publications.

Lanoue, D. J., & Schrott, P. R. (1989). The effects of primary season debates on public opinion. *Political Behavior, 11*(3), 289–306. doi: 10.1007/BF00992301

McGraw, K., Lodge, M., & Stroh, P. (1990). Online processing and candidate evaluation: The effects of issue order, issue importance and sophistication. *Political Behavior, 12*(1), 41–58. doi: 10.1007/BF00992331

McKinney, M. S. (2005). Engaging citizens through presidential debates: Does the format matter? In L. L. Kaid, D. G. Bystrom, & D. B. Carlin (Eds.), *Communicating politics: Engaging the public in democratic life* (pp. 209–221). New York: Peter Lang Publishing.

McKinney, M. S., & Carlin, D. B. (2004). Political campaign debates. In L. L. Kaid (Ed.), *Handbook of political communication research* (pp. 203–234). Mahwah, NJ: Lawrence Erlbaum Publishers.

McKinney, M. S., Dudash, E. A., & Hodgkinson, G. (2003). Viewer reactions to the 2000 presidential debates. In L. L. Kaid, J. C. Tedesco, D. G. Bystrom, & M. S. McKinney (Eds.), *The millennium election: Communication in the 2000 campaign* (pp. 43–58). Landham, MD: Rowman and Littlefield Publishers.

McKinney, M. S., Houston, J. B., & Hawthorne, J. (2014). Social watching a 2012 Republican presidential primary debate. *American Behavioral Scientist, 58,* 556–573. doi:10.1177/0002764213506211

McKinney, M. S., Rill, L. A., & Watson, R. G. (2011). Who framed Sarah Palin? Viewer reactions to the 2008 vice presidential debate. *American Behavioral Scientist, 55*(3), 212–231. doi:10.1177/0002764210392158

McKinney, M. S., & Warner, B. R. (2013). Do presidential debates matter? Examining a decade of campaign debate effects. *Argumentation and Advocacy, 49*(Spring), 238–258. doi: 10.1080/00028533.2013.11821800

Miller, J. (2014, April 29). "Millennials" cynical about politics: Harvard poll finds low interest in midterm elections. *Boston Globe.* Retrieved from https://www.bostonglobe.com/metro/2014/04/29/millenials-cynical-about-politics-new-harvard-poll-year-olds-finds/7f6e3tRFBS2GioZvkf71XL/story.html

Stachelski, D. (2016, August 4). Is the Internet making you cynical? *Huffington Post.* Retrieved from http://www.huffingtonpost.com/deborah-stachelski/is-the-internet-making-yo_b_11327734.html

Thorson, E., Hawthorne, J., Swasy, A., & McKinney, M. S. (2015). Co-viewing, tweeting, and Facebooking the 2012 presidential debates. *Electronic News, 9,* 195–214. doi:10.1177/1931243115593320

Wall, V., Golden, J. L., & James, H. (1988). Perceptions of the 1984 presidential debates and a select 1988 presidential primary debate. *Presidential Studies Quarterly, 18*(3), 541–563. Retrieved from http://www.jstor.org/stable/40574498

Warner, B. R., Carlin, D. B., Winfrey, K., Schnoebelen, J., & Trosanovski, M. (2011). Will the "real" candidates for president and vice president please stand up? 2008 pre- and post-debate viewer perceptions of candidate image. *American Behavioral Scientist, 53*(3), 232–252. doi:10.1177/0002764210392160

Appendix: Post-Debate Knowledge Questions

Democratic Primary Debate Knowledge Questions

*Denotes correct answer

1. In the debate you just watched, which candidate or candidates indicated they will not take money from the fossil fuel industry?
    *   Hillary Clinton
    *   Bernie Sanders*
    *   Both candidates said this

2. In the debate you just watched, which candidate or candidates argued that the cost of attending public colleges should be free for everyone?
    *   Hillary Clinton
    *   Bernie Sanders*
    *   None of the candidates argued that public college should be free for everyone

3. In the debate you just watched, which candidate or candidates said that we need a positive agenda for manufacturing?
    *   Hillary Clinton*
    *   Bernie Sanders
    *   Neither candidate mentioned a positive agenda for manufacturing

4. In the debate you just watched, which candidate or candidates claimed that the Monroe Doctrine allowed the United States the right to do whatever it wanted in Latin America?
    *   Hillary Clinton
    *   Bernie Sanders*
    *   Neither candidate mentioned the Monroe Doctrine

5. In the debate you just watched, which candidate claimed that no bank is too big to fail?
    *   Hillary Clinton*
    *   Bernie Sanders
    *   Neither of the candidates made this claim

Republican Primary Debate Knowledge Questions

1. In the debate you just watched, which candidate claimed that countries like China and Japan are devaluing their currency?
    *   Donald Trump*
    *   Ted Cruz
    *   Marco Rubio
    *   John Kasich

2. In the debate you just watched, which candidate claimed that Barack Obama is going to leave the United States with the smallest military since WWII?
    *   Donald Trump
    *   Ted Cruz
    *   Marco Rubio*
    *   John Kasich

3. In the debate you just watched, which candidate indicated that the country could have a strong environmental policy and, at the same time, have strong economic growth?
    *   Donald Trump
    *   Ted Cruz
    *   Marco Rubio
    *   John Kasich*

4. In the debate you just watched, which candidate discussed what they called the "Washington Cartel?"
    *   Donald Trump
    *   Ted Cruz*
    *   Marco Rubio
    *   John Kasich

5. In the debate you just watched, which candidate advocating abolishing the Internal Revenue Service (the IRS)?
    *   Donald Trump
    *   Ted Cruz*
    *   Marco Rubio
    *   John Kasich

CHAPTER TEN

Donald Trump and the Rejection of the Norms of American Politics and Rhetoric

Robert C. Rowland

Donald Trump's successful campaign for the presidency was unprecedented. By the middle of the primary season, it already was clear that Trump was "disrupting American politics," especially "the established rules of communicating with voters" (Giridharadas, 2016). This process would continue and even accelerate throughout the remainder of the campaign. Writing before the first debate, former Obama communication advisor David Axelrod (2016, p. SR7) provided a partial list of gaffes by candidate Trump during the general election campaign (and there were additional gaffes in the primaries) that normally would have been disqualifying for any other candidate:

> [H]is refusal to release his tax returns; his proposal (subsequently tweaked) that Muslims be barred from entering the United States; his racist smear of a Mexican-American judge; his attack on the Khan family, whose son died as an American soldier in Iraq; his assertion that President Obama founded the Islamic State; his invitation to the Russians to hack Clinton's emails. It's a litany too long to be excused (also see Rolfe, 2016).

Other gaffes would occur in the remainder of the campaign, including the release of a tape in which Trump seemed to brag about committing sexual assault.

After this incident, Michael Gerson, a leading conservative pundit, concluded that "Trump is sickeningly cruel, boorish, bonkers, subversive, conspiratorial, obsessive, authoritarian and reckless with the reputation of American democracy" (2016, October 17). Pundits believed that Trump could not win because he "violated every norm," but "it turned out many people didn't notice or didn't care" (Brooks, 2017, p. A25).

One would have expected Trump's rhetorical practice, which according to Inglehart and Norris (2016), "peddles a mélange of xenophobic fear tactics (against Mexicans and Muslims), deep-seated misogyny, paranoid conspiracy theories about his rivals, and isolationist 'America First' policies" by itself to be disqualifying. Moreover, the debates were a disaster for Trump. Commentary from two well-known conservative pundits illustrates the consensus on this point. Kathleen Parker criticized Trump for "utter incoherence," "inane responses or nonresponses," and "childish running commentary" (Parker, 2016), and Gerson (September 27, 2016) concluded that "the points scored against Trump were damaging. But the points he ceded would disqualify any normal politician." Gerson (September 27, 2016) added that Trump "was horribly out of his depth, incapable of stringing together a coherent three sentence case." Given Trump's many departures from the norms of American politics, any observer schooled in those norms would have expected him to lose decisively. It seems eminently clear, as Pippa Norris (2016) observed, that "commentators have had trouble understanding the rise of Donald Trump," a point echoed by David Neiwert (2016), who noted that "the normal rules simply do not apply with Trump," making 2016 a "curveball election" (Walsh, 2016).

The place to look for an explanation for how Donald Trump won despite a host of gaffes is in his rhetoric. Trump hardly had a campaign organization, bought few advertisements, and relied almost exclusively on his rhetoric and celebrity. It was his tweets and rallies that made him the Republican nominee and ultimately put him in the White House. What was it about his rhetoric that made him so effective? The most common explanation is that he used a populist approach to tap into public anxiety about the state of the economy and the speed of social change. Richard Linnett (2016) reflected this view when he claimed that populism was "what propelled Donald Trump to the White House," a conclusion supported by Taub (2016), who argued that Trump tapped into "the dramatic rise of a new kind of white populism" (also see Chotiner, 2017).

However, although there is little doubt that Trump's message contained elements of populism and that it resonated strongly with a working-class white audience, this explanation is insufficient. One difficulty is that although Trump's message had some populist elements, in other ways it was dissimilar from populist discourse. In order to make this point, it is important to consider the defining characteristics of populism.

Populism has been widely studied in rhetorical studies (Burkholder, 1989; Duffy, 2015; Erlich, 1977; Maddux, 2013; Rohler, 1999; Serazio, 2016; Woodward, 1983). This research indicates that although "populism is a recurring vocabulary," it can be expressed in many different ways, making it a "chameleonic and contradictory" form of political talk (Lee, 2006, pp. 357–358) that "has been largely stripped of its ideology" (Woodward, 1983, p. 57). Similarly, Kazin called "populism" an "elastic" and "flexible mode of persuasion" (1998, p. 3), and Rolfe concluded that populism is "a slippery term with no fixed meaning or ideology" (2016, p. 24).

At the same time, certain rhetorical markers are commonly found in populist rhetoric. In an important study, Lee identified "four interrelated and mutually reinforcing themes" that are found in populist discourse: a portrayal of the people "as heroic defenders of 'traditional' values," a description of the enemies of the people who are "tangibly different in race, class, or geographical location" and who threaten "the destruction of traditional values," a description of a system of economics and government that threatens the people, and a call for "apocalyptic confrontation" in service of "revolutionary change" (2006, pp. 358–362; also see Woodward, 1983). Notably, Lee demonstrated the applicability of this set of themes to populist discourse from the Progressive era through George Wallace, making a powerful argument that "[p]opulism is an argumentative frame" (2006, p. 363).

Trump's campaign clearly reflected elements of the populist frame, especially the depiction of the people as under assault and his focus on the dangers posed by those who are "tangibly different," but in other ways his approach was also dissimilar from populism. Notably, Trump did not argue that an apocalyptic confrontation was needed. And although he labeled the system as corrupt, he proposed many policies that would have further comforted the already quite comfortable. Moreover, he did not argue for the importance of revolutionary change. The change that was needed to "Make America Great Again" was simply to elect Trump. Additionally, Trump's persona was fundamentally in conflict with the norm in populist discourse. Kazin noted that typical villains in populist discourse include the "haughty financier" and the "stout industrialist—top hat on his fleshy head and diamond stickpin gleaming from his silk tie" (1998, p. 1). Lee made a similar observation, commenting that contemporary populists critiqued "power brokers making money hand over fist in between golf outings" (2006, p 373). In contrast, Trump built his reputation as one of those power brokers, bragged shamelessly about his wealth and the access it bought him, and even owned the golf course on which the outings occurred. Trump was a populist, but also a billionaire who bragged about how he had been able to make vast sums while paying his workers as little as possible. Charles Postel noted that based on "historical legacy," "Bernie Sanders looks very much like a populist for the 'Second Gilded Age,'" whereas "Donald Trump, with his gold-plated jets and mansions, looks very much like the type of plutocrat the populists held responsible for the injustices and inequities of their time" (Postel, 2015). Finally, the extraordinarily negative vision of Trump stands in contrast to other populist movements, since as Kazin (1998, p. 2) noted, "Populism is . . . a grand form of rhetorical optimism" about what "ordinary Americans" can accomplish. Thus, Trump's populism was fundamentally different from progressive populist movements from the Progressive era to the contemporary movement led by U.S. Senator Bernie Sanders.

In what follows, I argue that Trump's campaign is best understood as "nationalistic populism" and the "strongman." The key to explaining Trump's appeal is to recognize that his rhetorical approach contained three elements: populist themes that tapped into economic uncertainty, nationalistic themes that tapped fear that American society was undergoing fundamental change, and the desire for a strong leader who could fix problems simply based on the power of leadership. In order to develop this argument, I first describe the three primary elements defining Trump's rhetorical practice and then show how all three components were reflected in the most important speech expressing the essence of his campaign, his acceptance address at the 2016 Republican National Convention (RNC). Finally, I draw implications for understanding American politics.

Nationalistic Populism and the Strongman

Although Trump's presidential campaign violated several of the norms identified in Lee's (2006) study of the populist frame, it strongly enacted one crucial populist theme: the claim that ordinary Americans had not prospered because of elite domination. This theme is omnipresent in populist discourse of the left and right, leading Kazin to argue that "populism is not an ideology. It's an impulse, it's a form of expression, it's rhetoric" in which "speakers conceive of ordinary people as the noble assemblage . . . [and] view their elite opponents as self-serving and undemocratic, and seek to mobilize the former against the latter" (quoted in Chotiner, 2017; also see Kazin, 1998, p. 1). Influential scholar Cas Mudde (2004) defines "populism" as an *"ideology that considers society to be ultimately separated into two homogenous and antagonistic groups, 'the pure people' versus 'the corrupt elite.'"* Trump clearly enacted what Greven (2016) identified as "[p]opulism's central and permanent narrative," focusing on the "juxtaposition of a (corrupt) political class, elite, or establishment and the people as whose sole authentic voice the populist party [in this case the billionaire candidate] bills itself."

One reason this theme resonated was the "relative hardship experienced by many Trump supporters," especially "in the industrial Midwest," where Trump drew strong support in counties suffering from a variety of social problems, including obesity, diabetes, drug and alcohol abuse, and suicide (Edsall, 2017). F. Wilkinson (2017) cited the shocking finding that "the higher the death rate from overdose and suicide in Rust Belt areas, the more Trump tended to outperform Romney" and then concluded that "an increasing sense of material precariousness" helps explain "why low-density white America turned out to support a populist leader with disturbingly illiberal tendencies." Trump's "arguments played to white working-class voter identity" (Taub, 2017, p. A10) so effectively because his approach tapped the anger they felt about loss of economic and political power. The difficult economic situation facing many working-class supporters created a large population where Trump's "voice of the Everyman" (Parker, 2017) effectively appealed to "the 'common man'" with "tough talk against malevolent elites" (Postel, 2015).

One key factor was that as "blue-collar jobs have disappeared," a sense of "identity has been lost" producing a "majoritarian backlash" (Taub, 2016). Jan-Werner Mueller of Princeton noted that figures like Trump who tap into this backlash inevitably label "all other political contenders . . . as part of a self-serving, corrupt elite" and frame their disagreement with mainstream candidates as "never just a matter of disagreeing about policy," but as "personal" (quoted in F. Wilkinson, 2017). Mudde's (2004) comment that "[p]opulism is moralistic rather than programmatic" helps explain the angry tone of the Trump campaign, which typified the approach of populists who use "confrontation and conflict" to "prove that their supporters are indeed the 'real people,' the authentic majority, opposed only by a majority that betrays the homeland" (Mueller, quoted in F. Wilkinson, 2017).

The second element in Trump's rhetorical practice was a strident nationalism aimed at creating fear and anger. This nationalistic element distinguishes Trump's campaign from other populist movements. I noted earlier that the argumentative frame described by Lee (2006) is broad enough to include both liberal and conservative variants. However, nationalistic populism is clearly different from populist reform movements. In this regard, Postel (2015) notes that "more than half a century of historical scholarship has confirmed" that the "great majority" of populist leaders were committed to "social justice." Clearly, the nationalistic populism of Trump had little in common with progressive populism, including contemporary reformers such as Sanders. Rolfe noted that a populist leader "may variously imply the people to be all the citizens of a country; or to be those people sharing the same ethnic background as well as territory" (2016, p. 27), thereby distinguishing between themes found in the progressive and the nationalist variants. Greven (2016) added that nativist elements are common in "right-wing populism" which "defines the people as culturally homogenous" and "juxtaposes its identity and common interests . . . with the identity and interests of others, usually minorities such as migrants."

Clearly, perceived threats to identity played a major role in Trump's campaign, as did fear that alien "others" threatened this nation. Lilliana Mason noted "Older voters who scored high on racial resentment were much more likely to switch from Obama to Trump" based on "white male identity politics" (quoted in Taub, 2017, p. A10). Kazin identified the precedent for this form of identity-based populism, observing that Trump's "nativist appeals to white working-and middle-class Americans is not the populism of the People's Party but rather that of the Know-Nothing Party of the 1850s, which similarly argued that immigrants were taking Americans' jobs and breaking the nation's laws" (2016, p. 13). In embracing nativist rhetoric, Trump drew on a tradition of "ugly scapegoating of marginalized groups" (Postel, 2015), thereby tapping into the "anger" felt by white Americans (Kazin, 1998, p. 225). David Neiwert (2016) described Trump's nationalist populism as a "narrative which pits ordinary White working people against both liberals—who are cast as an oppressive class of elites—and the poor and immigrants, who are denigrated as parasites." Berezin (2016) added that Trump "exploited the fears, feelings of neglect, and fantasies of his voters" as well as "'anti-intellectualism' in American life." Underlying much of Trump's appeal was "a cultural backlash . . . against long-term, ongoing social change," especially "gay marriage, sexual equality, and tolerance of social diversity, all lumped under the phrase 'political correctness,'" a backlash fed by the fact that "[l]ess educated and older citizens fear becoming marginalized and left behind" (Norris, 2016). Another key factor was "the collapse of white identity," for a "majority group that has traditionally enjoyed the privilege of being considered 'us' rather than 'them'" (Taub, 2016).

Fear was one driving force behind the nationalistic element in Trump's rhetorical practice. Taub (2016) noted based on interviews with "dozens of social scientists" that key factors in the rise of what she labeled white populism included "fear of social change; fear of terrorist attacks and other physical threats," fears that were exacerbated by "the crisis of identity that many whites are experiencing as they struggle to maintain their position." Trump's "pitch to voters both created the sense of threat and promised a defense: a winning, political strategy for the age of identity politics" (Taub, 2017, p. A10). That groups demonized by Trump (undocumented immigrants and Islamic terrorists) in fact posed little threat to the safety of Trump's core supporters mattered not at all. Research indicates that many "supporters of Donald J. Trump . . . are terrified they are losing their country," and overall the country experienced "a climate of frustration and fright not seen since the 1960s, or even the 1850s" (Barbaro, Parker, & Gabriel, 2016). Berlet (2015) noted that Trump used "demonization" and "scapegoating" in creating a persona as "a right-wing populist bully" that was perfectly adapted to the feelings of his core supporters. This persona helped Trump send the message that people should "be afraid. Very, very afraid" (Roller, 2016), a strategy that clearly worked. Fear activated "a growing base of angry and frustrated White middle and working class people" (Berlet, 2015).

The third element in Trump's nationalist populism can be summarized as the rhetoric of the strongman in the age of reality TV. He tapped into a desire for a strong leader who could solve problems based on force of will. A number of scholars and pundits have noted Trump's use of what Emory political scientist Alan Abramowitz labeled "strongman rhetoric" (Roller, 2016). Leman (2016) put it succinctly, "Trump has spent this year running for strongman rather than president . . . and this has struck a chord." Trump's style of speaking offended millions of Americans, but it also tapped into "The Tea Partiers' dream of ending political correctness" and desire for "a strongman who would 'tell it like it is'" (Raban, 2017). For this group, "Trump's vernacular may be an unholy tangle of lies, misapprehensions, disinformation and personal insults," but his "locker-room trash talk" was consistent with his strongman persona and "exposed" Clinton's "rhetoric as stilted and artificial" (Raban, 2017). Raban (2017) added that "Trump has great gifts in the art of vengeance and humiliation," something that is quite evident in the rhetoric discussed later. Trump relied on "the appeal of forceful strong-man leadership, attack-dog politics, and racial and anti-Muslim animus" to activate his core supporters (Inglehart & Norris, 2016). The strongman (and the literature suggests a strongly gendered component) derives "authority not from the rules-based system that governs consolidated democracies, but from raw popular support" (Fisher & Taub, 2017, p. A8). In that regard, Berezin (2016) notes that a number of commentators have compared Trump's "physical appearance, personal style, and authoritarian ways" to Benito Mussolini.

Trump's "fear-stoking" (Roller, 2016) played a key role in this effort, a point supported by right-leaning columnist Jennifer Rubin (2016), who concluded that Trump won the Republican nomination "by appealing to, and fanning the flames of fear and resentment." The combination of fear-inducing strategies and claims that Trump alone could resolve the crisis threatening the nation was particularly well adapted to appeal to voters who "are especially sensitive to social change," and can be classified as "'authoritarian voters': people who have a strong desire to maintain order and hierarchies, along with a powerful fear of outsiders" (Taub, 2016). Social science research indicates that when members of this group "are scared, they seek out strongman leaders and support harsh, punitive policies against immigrants and other outsiders" (Taub, 2016).

It is important to recognize that Trump's brand of strongman populism was well adapted to the contemporary cult of the celebrity, a cultural development especially prominent in the unreal medium of reality TV. In this climate, Trump's persona as a successful businessman played a key role. His claim that "his personal wealth would make him . . . immune to the demands of the wealthy and other special interests" formed "the foundation of his populist appeal" (Neiwert, 2016). In that way, Trump is representative of the form of populism that is led by a "counter-elite" who can act as "a remarkable leader" to solve problems with "common sense" (Mudde, 2004). Part of his appeal, as Kazin (2016, p. 13) notes, is that he created a persona that "is a brilliant specimen of performance art," a conclusion echoed by Berlet (2015), who stated that "Trump is a political performance artist" who "unleashes the fearful and angry feelings" of his core supporters. Trump drew on "a celebrity culture that valorizes street smarts" and his persona as "the uber-successful billionaire and alpha male who lived in a golden tower" (Berezin, 2016). As the celebrity strongman, the "solution is not a particular set of policies, or any policies—it is *him*" (Rubin, 2016). In this cultural context, Trump's "crude, coarse, uninhibited language" constituted a "low" style that "helped him authenticate his claims to understand and connect to 'the people' . . . despite his vast private wealth and flamboyant celebrity lifestyle" (Moffitt & Ostiguy, 2016).

In retrospect, it is quite clear that the "energy" in the campaign emanated from the populist left and right. Bernie Sanders was a traditional progressive populist who called for action to limit economic elites and thereby empower ordinary people, a message that perfectly fit the "argumentative frame" described by Lee (2006). Trump's approach was different. While he attacked elites, the key enemies in his rhetoric were "others," especially undocumented immigrants and Islamic refugees. He demonized these groups in order to generate first fear and then anger and promised a better future to his core audience not based in a clear policy agenda, but based in a claim that a celebrity strongman could "Make America Great Again" simply through the force of his leadership.

In the next section, I show how Trump enacted the three elements of nationalistic populism in the most important speech of the campaign, his acceptance address at the Republican National Convention.

Nationalistic Populism and the Strongman at the RNC

It is striking how closely Trump's convention speech (July 22, 2016) matches the three-part model of nationalistic populism. Of course, there are elements that might be found in any acceptance address, including bragging about the primaries, attacks on his opponent, promises to serve the country, and praise for his supporters, including a statement "My pledge reads: I'm With You—the American People" (para. 206).

At the same time, the differences from the norm in convention speeches are striking. Notably, there was almost no defense of conservative ideology and no mention of Lincoln, Reagan, Teddy Roosevelt, Eisenhower, or other Republican heroes. Nor did he defend small government policies or support a Reaganesque commitment to peace through strength. In fact, there was almost no focus on public policy, although he made many grandiose claims without explanation of how he would achieve tremendous results. For example, he said, "We are going to lift the restrictions on the production of American energy. This will produce more than $20 trillion in job-creating economic activity over the next four decades" (paras. 167–168). The absence of explanation and evidence for this claim is obvious. There were also patently false claims, such as the statement that Hillary Clinton "wants to essentially abolish the Second Amendment" (para. 183). Although misleading statements are common in presidential campaigns, Trump's unexplained policy claims and outright falsehoods went well beyond the norm (Kessler & Lee, 2016). Moreover, Trump's "dark imagery and an almost angry tone" was "a sharp departure from the optimistic talk about American possibility that has characterized Republican presidential candidates since Ronald Reagan" (Healy & Martin, 2016, p. A1).

Although the speech failed to contain many of the elements common in convention addresses, it presented a coherent narrative containing the three elements identified earlier. In this narrative, the ordinary hard-working people of the nation face a national crisis of crime, terrorism, economic weakness, and foreign threat. This situation has been brought on by a corrupt political order that has allowed dangerous "others" (illegal immigrants, terrorists, and criminals) to create "a crisis for our nation" (para. 5). The solution is simply to elect Trump, who by the force of his personality will save the nation and thereby "make America great again" (para. 214).

The first element in Trump's nationalist populism was a description of the country as under siege. Trump described the nation in dystopian terms, stating early in the address that the "convention occurs at a moment of crisis for our nation. The attacks on our police, and the terrorism in our cities, threaten our very way of life" (para. 5). He added that "[a]ny politician who does not grasp this danger is not fit to lead our country" (para. 5), a statement that essentially labeled Secretary Clinton as un-American.

In Trump's dystopian vision, crime is a growing crisis with homicides up "17 percent in America's largest cities" and "[t]he number of police officers killed in the line of duty" up "almost 50 percent" (paras. 17, 21). The crime was driven by the "[n]early 180,000 illegal immigrants with criminal records, ordered deported from our country, [who] are . . . roaming free to threaten peaceful citizens" (para. 22). It was these illegal immigrants who took the life of "Sarah Root," "Kate Steinle," and "other Americans who have been so brutally murdered" (paras. 23, 125, 127). In Trump's vision of the nation, "laid-off factory workers" and whole "communities" have been "crushed by our horrible and unfair trade deals" (para. 73). Our cities are defined by poverty and crime with "58 percent of African American youth" not employed (para. 27). Overall, the economy is in tatters with "[h]ousehold incomes . . . down more than $4,000 since the year 2000" and "14 million people have left the work force entirely" (paras. 29, 30).

And in foreign affairs, in our dealings with Iran, Syria, Libya, and others, we have suffered "one international humiliation after another" (paras. 36–40). As a consequence of our weakness "the world is far less stable," ISIS and other terrorists threaten us, and we face "death, destruction, terrorism and weakness" (paras. 41, 44, 53).

The second element in Trump's nationalistic populism was the dangerous "other" who was responsible for the crisis. Early in the address, he attacked "corporate spin, the carefully crafted lies, and the media myths" (para. 13). The primary function of this attack on elites, however, was to set up his own claim to leadership as the strongman who knew how the system worked. The real villains in Trump's narrative were dangerous "others" who threatened "the forgotten men and women of our country, people who work hard but no longer have a voice" (paras. 74, 75). One enemy included the illegal immigrants who "are being released by the tens of thousands into our communities" (para. 22). He called for "a great border wall to stop illegal immigration, to stop the gangs and the violence, and to stop the drugs from pouring into our communities" (para. 131). Refugees from nations "compromised by terrorism" (para. 113) comprised another dangerous "other" who threatened Americans with "the violence and oppression of a hateful foreign ideology" (para. 105). Trump also focused on crime in the nation's "50 largest cities," shootings of police officers "in Georgia, Missouri, Wisconsin, Kansas, Michigan and Tennessee" and concluded that "[a]n attack on law enforcement is an attack on all Americans" (paras. 17, 92, 95). He added "I am the law and order candidate" (para. 98). Here, Trump used "coded language" "appealing to whites' racial anxieties about crime" (Associated Press, 2016). The ultimate villains were all those "politicians who will not put America first," because they "have rigged our political and economic system for their exclusive benefit" (paras. 58, 66). Hillary Clinton was merely "their puppet, and they pull the strings" (para. 69).

The third element in the address was Trump's persona as the heroic strongman who knew how the system works and could bring immediate change. He explained that he "joined the political arena so that the powerful can no longer beat up on people who cannot defend themselves" (para. 83). Through the power of his leadership, Trump, the epitome of the "strong man," will simply and quickly solve the nation's problem. He "will put America first" and ensure "safe neighborhoods, secure borders, and protection from terrorism," as well as "add millions of new jobs and trillions in new wealth" (paras. 58, 63, 64). Trump can immediately produce this change because "[n]obody knows the system better than me, which is why I alone can fix it" (para. 84). As the strongman who knows how the system works, Trump alone can bring change. He referenced his almost magical power to produce change again and again. For example, he stated, "When I take the oath of office near year, I will restore law and order to our country" and "ensure that all of our kids are treated equally" and "make our country rich again" (paras. 96, 101, 144). The results will be astonishing. He claimed, "I am going to bring back our jobs" and "I am not going to let companies move to other countries" and "[m]iddle-income Americans and businesses will experience profound relief, and taxes will be greatly simplified for everyone," kids will be rescued "from failing schools," and "trillions of dollars will start flowing into our country" (paras. 149, 163, 170, 173). His leadership would produce immediate change, "On

January 20, 2017, the day I take the oath of office, Americans will finally wake up in a country where the laws of the United States are enforced" (para. 136). In this vision, the strongman metaphorically can wave the magic wand of his strength and produce immediate and fundamental change. His vision was neither ideological nor pragmatic, but based in his persona as the strongman who would save the country by carrying out the popular will. For all the "forgotten men and women," "I am your voice" (paras. 74, 75, 207).

The three elements in Trump's message are clearly present in the convention address. The first element, the description of how the ordinary people have been harmed by uncaring elites, was evident in Trump's dystopian vision of a nation humiliated abroad, threatened by terrorism and crime at home, and facing economic collapse. Of course, Trump's dystopia bore little resemblance to the actual state of the nation (Kessler & Lee, 2016), but his vision was well designed to appeal to the white working class who felt threatened by economic and political change. The second element was a depiction of those who had produced the dystopia, including corrupt political elites, notably Hillary Clinton, but also "others"—illegal immigrants, terrorists, and criminals in central cities (coded language that drew on white fear of African Americans and Hispanics)—who threatened the political and cultural dominance of Trump's core constituency of working-class and lower middle-class white Americans. Trump's rhetoric was designed to create first fear and then anger. It is disquieting that his strategy was so successful.

The third element was to offer himself as the "strongman" who could solve the problems of the nation through the power of his personality. Unlike more conventional nominees, Trump did not lay out a policy agenda and back it up with explanation and evidence. In fact, only in a few cases did he provide any explanation of how his proposals would work. Rather, he simply said that his leadership would create vast wealth, huge numbers of jobs, end the threat of crime and terrorism, and so forth. His approach to leadership is best understood as a form of magical thinking. Perhaps the most important phrase in the speech was his statement that "I alone can fix it" (para. 84). The utter grandiosity of the claim, especially in the absence of clearly developed proposals with evidence supporting them, indicates both that the public desperately wanted change and that they saw a celebrity businessman without any experience in public office as an appropriate vehicle to bring about that change. Of course, after becoming president, it rapidly became clear that "he alone" could not bring change in the manner he had claimed. Only in a time when many felt utterly alienated from their government could such overblown claims have been found credible.

Conclusion

The resonance of the message in Trump's convention speech is both obvious and deeply unsettling. As I've demonstrated, it enacted the three components that defined his nationalistic populism and strongman persona. Perhaps the speech is so shocking because Trump rarely presented all aspects of his message in a coherent fashion. He often used tweets, interviews, and remarks at rallies to emphasize one or more of his dominant themes, but rarely tied them together in a coherent fashion. In fact, the word coherent is almost never applied to his rhetoric, but in Cleveland the entire package was presented.

When presented together, the magical thinking that functioned as a key component in his strongman persona was particularly evident. Jennifer Rubin wrote that the speech reflected "the talk of 1930's fascists, tin pot dictators and snake oil salesman" and added that his "language reeks of authoritarian loves and authoritarians." She concluded that it was a thoroughly "un-Republican and un-democratic" repudiation of great Republican leaders from Teddy Roosevelt to Ronald Reagan, "Forget the Shining City on the Hill. Now it's the Heart of Darkness" (Rubin, 2016). Ultimately, the absence of clear ideology or policy proposals in his campaign, a point that was demonstrated again in the debates, was not a decisive factor in voter decisions, a finding that emphasizes the alienation, fear, and anger felt by Trump supporters.

One reason that the lack of a clear policy agenda did not doom his campaign is that Trump drew on "anti-intellectualism, hostility toward 'elites' who claim that opinions should be based on careful study and thought" (Krugman, February 13, 2017, p. A21). The anti-intellectualism, along with "the blunt pugnacity" of his style, tapped into the nation's "long love affair with vernacular heroes" (Raban, 2017, p. SR7). The perceived authenticity that this "blunt pugnacity" produced played a key role in "Trump picking up support among working-class white voters who have voted Democratic in the past" (Raban, 2017; W. Wilkinson, 2017).

Another reason that Trump's message retained power despite the outlandish and mean-spirited nature of many of his claims is that he was able to "fit any criticism or attack into their [his supporters'] world view of being marginalized vis-à-vis a corrupt political establishment" (Greven, 2016). In addition, Mueller noted that "the extreme partisanship of the Republicans in the last quarter century . . . played an important role in making Trump possible" (quoted in F. Wilkinson, 2017). It is disquieting that another important factor was growing support for authoritarian leadership. Inglehart and Norris (2016) cite data from the 2011 World Value Survey indicating "almost half— 44 percent—of U.S. non-college graduates approved of having a strong leader unchecked by elections and Congress." This group provided strong support for Trump's election.

The combination of the strongman themes in Trump's rhetoric and his support from far-right groups points to the risk of a turn toward authoritarianism in American politics. Pippa Norris (2016) noted that Trump "fits the wave of authoritarian populists whose support has swelled in many Western democracies." On this topic, Susan Glasser (2017) made the alarming observation that "Mr. Trump's rhetoric and actions as president bear more than a passing resemblance to those of Mr. Putin during his first years consolidating power." Chip Berlet's (2015) comment in December 2015 that "[t]he examples of Trump's fascist-sounding rhetoric are numerous" is still more chilling. Paul Krugman (December 19, 2016, p. A21) added, "It takes willful blindness not to see the parallels between the rise of fascism and our current political nightmare." Clearly, sounding like an authoritarian to many commentators was not viewed as disqualifying by key constituencies that had enough power to elect Trump president.

Populist nationalism carries with it significant dangers for a democratic society. Max Fisher and Amanda Taub cited the erosion of democracy in Venezuela to support the broader point that "initial populist steps . . . can take on a momentum of their own, until the list of populist enemies has grown to include pillars of basic democracy" (2017 p. A8). That momentum can be curtailed by "strong democratic checks," but Fisher and Taub (2017, p. A8) added that "it is rarely obvious at the time which path [toward authoritarianism or back to democratic norms] a country is taking."

One irony is that although Trump's campaign depended upon his appeal to working-class whites, his administration's declared "economic policy would be an unambiguous transfer of income and power in the opposite direction: from the public to the rich" (Thompson, 2017). This result should not have been surprising because as Kazin (1983, p. 288) has noted, "Populism . . . too often allows the malicious to overshadow the hopeful." Another factor is that Trump's appeal to resentment was "rooted in emotional attachments, not policy goals" (Taub, 2017, p. A10). Waldman (2017) observed, "[F]or all of Trump's rhetoric about taking on the 'elite,' when it comes to making policy he's just as interested in enhancing corporate power at the expense of citizens as is Paul Ryan or Mitch McConnell."

Another implication that can be drawn from the rhetorical pattern that Trump used to win the presidency relates to the way campaigns are conducted. Trump's election indicates that norms for how a campaign should be conducted and how a presidential nominee should talk have changed. Richard Fausset observed, "At presidential altitude, the gold standard for political rhetoric used to be something like Lincoln's first inaugural address, with its carefully calibrated prose-poetry. Now the very notion of 'presidential' language and behavior has come in for a make-over" (2017, p. A10). Mark Danner argued that because of Trump, "the norms are gone, perhaps never to be fully restored" (2017, p. 4). Jeremy Peters added "that in today's political culture . . . each day seems to bring a fresh lowering of the bar for decency and civility" (2017, p. A10). Notably, according to Bill Adair, who created PolitiFact, "No one has come close to Trump in the high percentage of falsehoods" (quoted in Barstow, 2017, p. A17). In previous campaigns, obvious falsehoods or outlandish statements would have led to a failed candidacy. Trump, however, excelled at the politics of "spectacle." Tim Wu noted that Trump often could "win *by* losing. For what really matters are the contests themselves—the creation of an absorbing spectacle that dominates headlines, grabs audiences and creates a world in which every conversation resolves around Mr. Trump" (2017, p. SR6). It was not just the falsehoods, but the personal attacks and indictment of entire groups of people that threatened democratic norms. Conservative columnist Charles Krauthammer noted that "[s]uch incendiary talk is an affront to elementary democratic decency and a breach of the boundaries of American political discourse" (2016, p. A29), a point echoed by Bowersock, who concluded that the election was "the most grotesque indictment of American democracy since the landslide election" of Harding (2016, p. 6).

Clearly, the normal give and take of public debate did not work to expose either the extremist nature of many of Trump's proposals or the lack of warrant for those proposals. David Cole (2017, p. 35) noted:

> Following the election of Donald Trump, whose campaign benefited from demagogic appeals to racism, populism, the empty adulation of celebrity, fake news, and outright lies, it is easy to lament the state of the American marketplace of ideas. Trump proclaimed and tweeted one untruth after another; parts of the media dutifully fact-checked his assertions and reported that they were false. Yet this seems to have had little effect on a large enough proportion of the electorate to win him the presidency.

At the same time, it is important not to overstate the dangers posed by Trump's message. After all, he is president because "razor-thin layers of non-college-educated voters living in rural Michigan, Wisconsin and Pennsylvania . . . tipped the outcome of the election" (Berezin, 2016). It remains to be seen whether Trump's election has permanently changed the norms of American politics.

References

Associated Press. (2016, July 22). Critics: Trump convention speech signals shift to coded race language. *Chicago Tribune*. Retrieved from http://www.chicagotribune.com/news/nationworld/politics/ct-trump-coded-race-language-20160722-story.html

Axelrod, D. (2016, September 25). How Hillary Clinton could win. *The New York Times*, pp. SR 1, SR7.

Barbaro, M., Parker, A., & Gabriel T. (2016, March 13). Donald Trump's heated words were destined to stir violence, opponents say. *The New York Times*, p. A22.

Barstow, D. (2017, January 29). "Up is down": Unreality show echoes the past. *The New York Times*, pp. A1, A17.

Berezin, M. (2016, December 20). Donald Trump is a uniquely American populist. *New Republic.* Retrieved from https://newrepublic.com/article/139434
/donald-trump-uniquely-ameri.

Berlet, C. (2015, December 12). Trumping' democracy: Right-wing populism, fascism, and the case for action. *Political Research Associates.* Retrieved from
http://www.politicalresearch.org/2015/12/12/trumping-democracy-rig.

Bowersock, G. W. (2016, November 10). On the election—I. *New York Review of
Books,* 6.

Brooks, D. (2017, April 21). The crisis of western civilization. *The New York Times,*
p. A25.

Burkholder, T. R. (1989). Kansas populism, woman suffrage and the agrarian
myth: A case study in the limits of mythic transcendence. *Communication
Studies, 40,* 292–307. doi.org/10.1080/10510978909368282

Chotiner, I. (2017, February 24). Is Donald Trump a populist? *Slate.* Retrieved
from http://www.slate.com/articles/news_and_politicsl/interrogation
/2016/02

Cole, D. (2017, March 23). Why free speech is not enough. *New York Review of
Books,* pp. 34–35.

Danner, M. (2017, March 23). What he could do. *New York Review of Books,* pp. 4–5.

Duffy, C. (2015). States' rights vs. women's rights: The use of the populist argumentative frame in anti-abortion rhetoric. *International Journal of Communication, 9,* 3494–3501.

Edsall, T. B. (2017, February 2). The peculiar populism of Donald Trump. *The
New York Times.* Retrieved from https://www.nytimes.com/2017/02/02
/opinion/the-peculiar-populism-of-donald-trump.html

Erlich, H. S. (1977). Populist rhetoric reassessed: A paradox. *Quarterly Journal of
Speech, 63,* 140–151. doi.org/10.1080/00335637709383375

Fausset, R. (2017, January 25). Hall of mirrors. *The New York Times,* p. A10.

Fisher, M., & Taub, A. (2017, April 2). How does democracy erode? Venezuela is
a case in point. *The New York Times,* p. A8.

Gerson, M. (2016, September 27). Out of his depth, Donald Trump clings to
deception. *The Washington Post.* Retrieved from https://www.washington
post.com/opinions/out-of-his-depth-donald-trump-clings-to-deception
/2016/09/27/070feda6-84ca-11e6-a3ef-f35afb41797f_story.html?utm_term
=.f257517bb6cb

Gerson, M. (2016, October 17). Trump spirals into ideological psychosis. *The
Washington Post.* Retrieved from https://www.washingtonpost.com/opin
ions/trump-spirals-into-ideologgi

Giridharadas, A. (2016, March 14). Donald Trump breaks with tradition, and it's
paying off. *The New York Times.* Retrieved from https://nyti.ms/22g2byz

Glasser, S. (2017, February 19). Our Putin. *The New York Times,* p. SR1.

Greven, T. (2016, May). The rise of right-wing populism in Europe and the United
States: A comparative perspective. *Friedrich Ebert Stiftung.* Retrieved from
http://www.fesdc.org/fileadmin/user_upload/publications/Rightwing
Populism.pdf

Healy, P., & Martin, J. (2016, July 22). His tone dark, Donald Trump takes G.O.P. mantle. *The New York Times*, p. A1.

Inglehart, R. F., & Norris, P. (2016, August). Trump, Brexit, and the rise of populism: Economic have-nots and cultural backlash. *Harvard Kennedy School RWP 16-026.*

Kazin, M. (1998). *The populist persuasion: An American history* (rev. ed.). Ithaca, NY: Cornell University Press.

Kazin, M. (2016, March 22). How can Donald Trump and Bernie Sanders both be "populists"? *New York Times Magazine,* p. 13.

Kessler, G., & Lee, M. Y. H. (2016, July 22). Fact-checking Donald Trump's acceptance speech at the 2016 RNC. *The Washington Post.* Retrieved from https://www.washingtonpost.come/news/fact-checker/wp/2016/07/22/fa

Krauthammer, C. (2016, October 16). It's not the "locker room" talk; it's the "lock her up" talk. *Kansas City Star*, p. 29A.

Krugman, P. (2016, December 19). How republics end. *The New York Times*, p. A21.

Krugman, P. (2017, February 13). Ignorance is strength. *The New York Times*, p. A21.

Lee, M. J. (2006). The populist chameleon: The People's Party, Huey Long, George Wallace, and the populist argumentative frame. *Quarterly Journal of Speech*, *92*, 355–378. doi.org/10.1080/00335630601080385.

Leman, N. (2016, November 10). On the election—III. *New York Review of Books*, pp. 34–35.

Linnett, R. (2016, December 31). What the "godfather of populism" thinks of Donald Trump. *Politico.* Retrieved from http://www.politico.com/magazine/story/2016/12/populist-trump-fred

Maddux, K. (2013). Fundamentalist fool or populist paragon? William Jennings Bryan and the campaign against evolutionary theory. *Rhetoric & Public Affairs, 16,* 489–520.

Moffitt, B., & Ostiguy, P. (2016, October 20). Of course Donald Trump goes low. That's the populists' winning style. *The Washington Post.* Retrieved from https://www.washingtonpost.com/news/monkey-cage/wp/2016/10/20

Mudde, C. (2004). The populist zeitgeist. *Government and Opposition, 39,* 541–563. doi: 10.1111/j.1477-7053.2004.00135.x

Neiwert, D. (2016, June 21). Trump and right-wing populism: A long time coming. *Political Research Associates.* Retrieved from http://www.politicalresearch.org/2016/06/21/trump-and-right-wing-po

Norris, P. (2016, March 11). It's not just Trump. Authoritarian populism is rising across the West. Here's why. *The Washington Post.* Retrieved from https://www.washingtonpost.com/news/monkey-cage/wp/2016/03/11/1

Parker, K. (2016, September 27). Trump's night of sniffles and screw ups. *The Washington Post.* Retrieved from https://www.washingtonpost.com/opinions/trumps-night-ofsniffles-a

Parker, K. (2017, March 28). Republicans would rather have a king than a president. *The Washington Post.* Retrieved from https://www.washingtonpost.come/opinions/republicans-would-rather.

Peters, J. W. (2017, February 22). Downfall of a provocateur shakes the core of conservatism. *The New York Times*, p. A10.

Postel, C. (2015, February). If Trump and Sanders are both populists, what does populist mean. *American Historian*. Retrieved from http://tah.oah.org /february-2016/if-trump=and-sanders-are-both-populi

Raban, J. (2017, January 8). Telling it like it is, and winning. *The New York Times*, p. SR7.

Rohler, L. (1999). Conservative appeals to the people: George Wallace's populist rhetoric. *Southern Communication Journal, 64*, 316–322. doi.org/10.1080 /10417949909373146

Rolfe, M. (2016). *The reinvention of populist rhetoric in the digital age: Insiders & outsiders in democratic politics*. London: Palgrave Macmillan.

Roller, E. (2016, June 14). Donald Trump's fear factor. *The New York Times*. Retrieved from https://www.nytimes.com/2016/06/14/opinion/campaign-stop/donald

Rubin, J. (2016, July 21). Trump doubles down: Fear justifies a strongman. *The Washington Post*. Retrieved from https://www.washingtonpost.com/blogs /right-turn/wp/2016/07/21/tru

Serazio, M. (2016). Encoding the paranoid style in American politics: "Anti-establishment" discourse and power in contemporary spin. *Critical Studies in Media Communication, 33*, 181–194. doi.org/10.1080/15295036.2016 .1174338

Taub, A. (2016, November 9). Trump's victory and the rise of white populism. *The New York Times*. Retrieved from https://www.nytimes.com/2016/11/10 /world/americas/trump-white-po

Taub, A. (2017, April 13). Partisanship as a tribal identity: Voting against one's economic interests. *The New York Times*, p. A10.

Thompson, D. (2017, January 20). Trump's populism is a fiction. *The Atlantic*. Retrieved from https://www.theatlantic.com/business/archive/2017/01 /trumps-populis

Trump, D. J. (2016, July 22). Transcript of Donald J. Trump's remarks at the Republican national convention. *The New York Times*. Retrieved from https://www .nytimes.come/2016/07/22/us/politics/trump-transcript/rnc-address.html

Waldman, P. (2017, February 6). Donald Trump, a 'populist'? What a joke. *The Washington Post*. Retrieved from https://www.washingtonpost.com/blogs /plum-line/wp/2017/02/06/don

Walsh, D. (2016, September 13). Fearful and flummoxed: Watching the presidential race from abroad. *The New York Times*. Retrieved from https:/www .nytimes.com/2016/09/14/world/Americas/Hillary-clinton

Wilkinson, F. (2017, February 16). Why Donald Trump really is a populist. *Bloomberg View*. Retrieved from https://www.bloomberg.com/view/articles/2017 -02-16/why-donald-t

Wilkinson, W. (2017, January 9). A tale of two moralities, part one: Regional inequality and moral polarization. *Niskanen Center*. Retrieved from https:// niskanencenter.org/blog/tale-two-moralities-part-one-regional-i

Woodward, G. C. (1983). Reagan as Roosevelt: The elasticity of the pseudo-populist appeals. *Central States Speech Journal, 34*, 44–58. doi.org/10 .1080/10510978309368113

Wu, T. (2017, March 5). How Trump wins by losing. *The New York Times*, p. SR6.

CHAPTER ELEVEN

"The Greatest Country on Earth": The Evolution of Michelle Obama's American Dream

Ryan Neville-Shepard and Meredith Neville-Shepard

First Lady Michelle Obama delivered an address at the 2016 Democratic National Convention (DNC) that was widely praised as the "speech of a lifetime" (Tomasky, 2016). Like her husband's 2004 DNC speech, her oration "led many political pundits to ponder the possibility of her future presidential run" (Garcia, 2016, para. 1). Nelson (2016) claimed the address was "an elegant reclamation of family values and the American mainstream" (para. 5), in which she insisted that the "real America—or at least the America that the nation aspires to be" (para. 4), hinges on the values of "community and togetherness" (para. 5). Her description of America as "the greatest country on earth" was a departure from her declaration eight years earlier that she was proud of her country for the first time in her adult life, a moment that led critics to question her patriotism. Back then, she was characterized as a "reluctant political spouse" with a "raw authenticity" that often led to backlash (Thompson, 2016, p. C01). Thus, the aims of her 2008 convention address were vastly different than in 2016. Back then, her speechwriters attempted to assuage white anxiety and frame her as an acceptable candidate's spouse (Merida, 2008), adopting a strategy of avoiding mention of her own professional prowess and instead portraying her as a doting mother, loving wife, and hard-working daughter.

The transformation of Obama from a candidate spouse, who simply hoped to shake racist stereotypes, to a first lady comfortable enough to point out that the White House was built by slaves can best be explained by the creative license that her increasing popularity granted her over time. Her star status blossomed throughout President Barack Obama's first term, and, by her convention speech in 2012, she was "one of the most popular political figures in the country" (Thompson, 2012, p. A04). Therefore, she no longer had to "sell herself, as she did [in 2008]" (p. A04). Indeed, as Obama grew comfortable in her role, she became a more talented spokesperson for the Democratic Party and its ideology. Following her 2012 DNC speech, Tumulty and O'Keefe (2012) noted the increased potency of Obama's delivery and remarked that four years spent mastering the art of rhetoric allowed her to achieve "something close to intimacy with a crowd of 15,000" (p. A12).

Many journalists have noted that at the core of Obama's metamorphosis, especially as it played out in her convention addresses, was a message about the American Dream. In her first convention appearance in 2008 Obama was portraying herself as "American Dream in the flesh" ("Michelle's Triumph," 2008, p. 38). Some claimed she impressively managed to "[combine] tradition with progress in an appealing way" (Campbell, 2008, para. 21), while later describing, in unison with her husband, America in Reagan-esque terms, "a striving city under constant construction" (Fournier, 2016, para. 12). Yet some claimed that Obama's metamorphosis fell short and that her appeal to tradition undermined her ability to address social justice issues. For those critics, Obama's adoption of the "Mom-in-Chief" persona indicated she accepted a limited role in social change. Cottle (2013) argued the persona "wasn't merely a political strategy but also a personal choice," a decision to forgo "straight talk about abortion rights or Obamacare" (para. 7). Joining feminists who felt "a level of discomfort seeing Michelle Obama embrace a Norman Rockwell-esque vision of American motherhood" (Edgar, 2013, para. 7), Keli Goff of *Root* magazine complained that it was a "national shame" that the "most influential black [woman] on the planet . . . [is] not putting the weight of her office behind" key social issues (quoted in Cottle, 2013, para. 15). This criticism of Obama highlights a tension in her rhetoric: How could someone successfully lobby for progress by adopting such a traditional and limiting role?

In this chapter, we suggest that understanding Obama's political transformation requires a close analysis of her convention addresses in 2008, 2012, and 2016. When examined as a set, we argue that these speeches highlight Obama's use of measured rhetoric to transcend the duality inherent in the American Dream myth. We contend that Obama successfully synthesized the materialistic myth and the moralistic myth of the American Dream by interlinking the value of individualism with the value of collective responsibility.

We illustrate how she honed this message over time by outlining commitments to traditional family structure and promoting the dominant, materialistic myth of the American Dream, and later by using her adopted voice of "republican mother" to frequently incorporate narratives about her children that served as metonyms for the protection of all vulnerable people in society.

Our chapter develops over several sections. First, we outline the dualistic nature of the American Dream and review ways to transcend these differences. Second, we situate Obama's activism in the history of political advocacy by first ladies, describe her unique challenges as the first African American first lady, and summarize how scholars have criticized Obama's adoption of traditional roles as a failed opportunity to force conversations about social justice. In so doing, we suggest that such scholarship overlooks the complexity of Obama's "mothering" rhetoric, which we argue evolved greatly from 2008 to 2016 as she developed her persuasive strategy for straddling the American Dream duality—taking on a traditional role while espousing progressive values, telling an individualistic narrative while advocating for collective justice, and supporting her spouse while rising as an independent activist. We then analyze Obama's three convention speeches to show how she made such a shift. Finally, we close with a discussion of the implications of this chapter.

The Duality of the American Dream Myth

The American Dream has long been imagined in dualistic terms. Fisher (1973) described one strain of the American Dream as being grounded in the materialistic myth of "the puritan work ethic" and relating to values of "effort, persistence . . . initiative, self-reliance, achievement, and success" (p. 161). Those who ascribe to the materialistic myth value policies consistent with free enterprise and limited government. Moreover, its promise is that "if one employs one's energies and talents to the fullest, one will reap the rewards of status, wealth, and power" (p. 161). Alternatively, the moralistic myth is rooted in protecting the rights of individuals and promotes the values of "tolerance, charity, compassion, and true regard for the dignity and worth of each and every individual" (p. 161). Because the moralistic myth aims to create a just and equitable society, it often influences "cooperative efforts to benefit those who are less fortunate than others" (p. 162). Rowland and Jones (2007) summarized that "conservatives tend to emphasize narratives in which enactment of personal values ensures fulfillment of the American Dream," whereas liberals "focus on societal values (and policies flowing from them) as the key to achievement" (p. 432).

Although the two strains of the American Dream tend to be embodied by opposing parties, American political rhetoric has recently been dominated by the materialistic myth, meaning that certain constraints have compelled liberals to speak in the conservative vernacular. Conservatives have achieved a narrative victory, Rowland and Jones (2007) argued, because the "version of the American Dream privileging individual over communal responsibility has dominated political discourse" (p. 427). This was not always the case. "For much of the last century," Rowland and Jones maintained, "the focus of this narrative was on a balance between individual and communal responsibilities" (p. 427). The current dominance of the materialistic myth can be traced back to Ronald Reagan. Thus, the American Dream's dominant meaning is now linked to the moral of individual agency above all else, emphasizing the principle of hard work and promoting the notion that government intervention is antithetical to the interests of the American people. Adopting such a myth puts Democrats in a rhetorical quagmire. The dominance of the materialistic myth undercuts support for important social programs that help society's most vulnerable people, undermines advocacy for advancing the rights of marginalized citizens, and preserves the hegemony that perpetuates inequality.

Rather than submit to the symbolic dominance of the materialistic myth, rhetors can employ carefully crafted strategies to achieve "value re-orientation" (Rushing & Frentz, 1978, p. 70). Rushing and Frentz (1978) argued that this can be accomplished through dialectical transformation or dialectical synthesis. Dialectical transformation "entails an inversion from one prevailing set of values to another," in this case triggering a transformation from materialism to moralism (p. 70). Such a strategy is "the simplest because it does not necessitate the creation of a new value structure, but only the shift from one dominant set of values to another" (p. 70). Alternatively, dialectical synthesis merges one value system with another and thus "renews a sense of independence and community among those involved" (p. 71). Rather than giving way to a mythic tension that "can produce a cultural schizophrenia," Solomon (1983) maintained, valuing both materialism and moralism together can provide a necessary "complexity to our national life" (p. 275), ultimately reaffirming "the American Dream in all its contradictory richness" (p. 277).

The emergence of Barack Obama in 2004 not only came with a widely praised effort to chisel away at the dominance of the materialistic myth of the American Dream, but also to break down the binary between materialism and moralism. Rowland and Jones (2007) contended that "Obama attempted subtly to re-define the American Dream to move the pendulum away from a near-exclusive focus on individual responsibility and instead toward a larger focus on societal responsibility for achieving progress toward key goals" (p. 434). Thus, we know how Barack Obama attempted to reclaim the mythic force behind the American Dream, but we know less about the rhetorical journey of his partner, who went from claiming she just discovered pride in her country in 2008 to declaring that America was the "greatest country on Earth" in 2016. In the next section, we contend that Michelle Obama's reclamation of the American Dream was far subtler than her husband's. In order to meet the expectations of a political spouse, she began by adopting the role of the republican mother but subsequently evolved over the next eight years, using her personal narrative and experience as a parent to argue that collective effort is needed to protect the country's most vulnerable inhabitants.

The Republican Mother and the American Dream

A long history of candidate spouses and first ladies addressing party conventions preceded Obama's appearances at the Democratic National Convention. First ladies had been attending the conventions since at least Nellie Taft in 1912 and had been addressing the convention since Eleanor Roosevelt in 1940. Speeches by first ladies at national conventions have followed a basic rule, as Kathleen Hall Jamieson explained: "[Y]ou hear a role that walks in between the traditional spouse role and the role of a person who might speak in her own right" (quoted in Obaro, 2012, p. C01). In order to understand how Obama struck a balance and used the ethos of the "republican mother" persona to transform the dominant notion of the American Dream, this section describes the constraints first ladies face as political spokeswomen, reviews what previous scholars have characterized as shortcomings in Obama's advocacy rhetoric, and defines the concept of republican motherhood to demonstrate her evolution from 2008 to 2016.

The Constraints of First Lady Advocacy

First ladies have been expected to reflect the ideals of traditional womanhood, putting husband and children above all else. Whereas they initially went public only to speak on their husband's behalf (Blair, 2001), the role of the first lady grew in the 20th century, morphing from "social hostesses and ceremonial presences" to "emerging spokeswomen" and, eventually, to "political surrogates and independent advocates" (Gutin, 2000, p. 564). However, first ladies in the mid-20th century were limited in their ability to adopt the role of independent advocate, often encountering criticism suggesting they stick to "behind-the-scenes" activities (Blair, 2001, p. 212). Even contemporary first ladies are often restricted to issues reflective of traditional feminine norms, limiting activities to "volunteerism, moral citizenship, beautification, health, and education" (Parry-Giles & Blair, 2002, p. 575).

Modern first ladies are more likely to push "their own political agenda in much more public ways than their nineteenth-century counterparts" (Parry-Giles & Blair, 2002, p. 576), but doing so comes with various challenges. First ladies taking on the role of independent advocates are likely to be criticized as too ambitious (Blair, 2001). They are still bound in a "domestic role to the feminine ideals of wife and mother" (Dubriwny, 2005, p. 87), and, as such, they are expected to make "prudential decisions regarding performance options"

(Erickson & Thomson, 2012, p. 242). Moreover, contemporary first ladies are limited by institutional prescriptions. To be successful, they must set their agendas under the constraints of the roles adopted by former first ladies. They set their own precedents for first ladies yet to come, but, given the initial constraints that informed their choices, these precedents are likely to maintain at least some of the earlier, more traditional norms (Parry-Giles & Blair, 2002, p. 567). Thus, as activist first ladies like "Roosevelt and Johnson tempered their political activities with vocal commitments to motherhood and home," they "reified the 'caretaking' role for women" who would follow (pp. 577–578).

As the nation's first black presidential spouse, Obama faced additional constraints, which were especially apparent after expressing a newfound pride for her country in February 2008. The comment triggered a flood of negative criticism. Consequently, Meyers and Goman (2017) explained, Obama was given a makeover and forced into a "new, more acceptable narrative of who she was," leading to a series of media appearances that let the world see the "real" Michelle (p. 21). The makeover was a necessary response to the culture of post-identity politics, which represents the notion that "racialized and gendered identities . . . are somehow magically granted equal status and are therefore given the mandate to set aside historic, structural, interpersonal, and institutional discrimination" (Joseph, 2011, p. 58). Therefore, Joseph summarized, as the first black first lady and a descendent of slaves, Obama faced an "incredibly restrictive landscape in which [she was] . . . allowed to speak," forcing her to "couch her words as she carefully [fought] her verbal attacks" (p. 59). Any attempt to directly acknowledge racial discrimination, at least in Obama's early days as a political spouse, was met with immediate contempt.

Michelle Obama and the American Dream

Given the constraints of the institution of the first ladyship and cultural constraints of post-identity politics, Obama was restricted in the way she could lobby for social justice and shift American allegiance away from a pure commitment to the materialistic American Dream. Scholars have given her mixed reviews, specifically for the ways she talks about race, gender, and class. Those who praised Obama's handling of social justice issues applauded her for undertaking a careful effort to slip the topics into her speeches. Kahl (2009) stated that Obama mentioned race "only sporadically" in her 2008 DNC address, but that her comments were "the very core of her rhetorical orientation" (p. 318). Ultimately, Kahl summarized, the comments helped Obama use "her family's presence in the White House as a springboard for statements supporting racial inclusiveness" (p. 318). Lauret (2011) argued that Obama's claim in 2008 that she was "not supposed to be here" actually "signaled her awareness of all the obstacles in the way of African American ambition and achievement" (p. 108).

Most recently, Meyers and Goman (2017) took a more critical perspective of Obama's personal narrative. By relying too much on "anecdotes about her family and personal struggles," they contended, Obama's narrative "reflects a neoliberal ideology that advocates for individual responsibility and initiative" (p. 22). The central messages of this neoliberal rhetoric are that "racism and poverty are seen as obstacles to be overcome, but they are not insurmountable if the individual makes the right choices" and that "gender inequities are viewed through the lens of motherhood and the need to balance family and career, rather than within a broader gendered context that addresses sexual harassment, violence, and discrimination" (p. 22). Meyers and Goman suggested her message boils down to how "hard work and resolve will inevitably lead to a successful, happy life" (p. 26). Furthermore, they argued, "her recognition of gender bias is limited to the difficulties of raising children as a working mother" (p. 32). In short, the critique is that Obama's attention to inequity is minimal and that she repeatedly "creates a narrative that fails to concede the intractability of the structural inequalities of class, race, and gender within a capitalist system in which the middle-class is shrinking" (p. 32).

In contrast to Meyers and Goman (2017), Joseph (2011) wrote that the key to understanding Obama's rhetoric about the American Dream—specifically as it pertains to social justice issues—is to pay attention to her "reframes, redefinitions, and coded language" (p. 60). Instead of evaluating Obama "in the old binaristic framework of either 'selling out' . . . or 'being real,'" Joseph suggested that Obama should be appreciated for the ways she resists "the postidentity ideology" by "[deploying] elements of postidentity culture" (p. 63). Obama has frequently called for collectivism over individualism, but one needs to carefully read her rhetoric to pick up on this thread. In short, Joseph contended, Obama's use of "postidentity tropes is necessary for her voice to be heard by the mainstream of the country" (p. 69). We echo this point and suggest the key to her coded language is her motherly persona.

Republican Motherhood and the Coded Critique

Rather than seeing Obama's discussion of her rags-to-riches narrative as perpetuating neoliberal or materialistic ideology and instead of viewing her adoption of traditional femininity as a betrayal to feminism, more can be gained by tracing how she used her family stories and mothering language as stand-ins for meaningful, yet coded, social critiques. As someone who constantly referred to herself as "Mom-in-Chief," Obama located rhetorical power in the traditionally limiting identity of first lady as "first mother." Conventionally, the republican mother persona required first ladies to root their public role in domesticity and to model the behavior of good motherhood in ways that connected to civic life, including looking out for "the health and morality of the nation's children" (Parry-Giles & Blair, 2002, p. 567). Although they advocated more publicly, even activist first ladies from the second half of the

20th century were restricted to "motherly" issues. This tactic has raised critical concerns, because it highlighted the gendered nature of the first ladyship, "[emphasizing] her place within the home and her difference as *woman*" (Dubriwny, 2005, p. 90). Nevertheless, the republican mother persona also presents first ladies an opportunity to push for socially progressive policy in the name of strengthening families (p. 92).

Obama's adoption of mothering rhetoric is more complex than some have suggested, as it both reaffirms and resists stereotypes of nonwhite families. While mirroring the norms of white motherhood, particularly the concept of "intensive mothering [that] assumes a femininity that is both White and middle to upper class," Obama's enactment is simultaneously a mode of resistance against racial tropes of black women as bad mothers who lack control over their families (Hayden, 2017, p. 17). As Hayden summarized, Obama's prioritization "of Black daughters in a racist, sexist society stands firmly in line with women's suffrage, civil rights, marriage equality, and other social justice efforts" (p. 19). Obama also embraced the part of the "other-mother," Hayden contended, taking on the role of various African American women who have assumed responsibility not just for their own children but for the "welfare of the community as a whole" (p. 19).

Building off these previous studies, we agree that Obama's role as "Mom-in-Chief" has served to help "demystify her racial heritage" and has provided her a "nuanced rhetorical platform that is nonthreatening, wholesome, and comprehensible" (Kahl, 2009, p. 317). We extend these arguments, though, and describe how Obama's mothering rhetoric uses her family and children as a metonym, or a substitute, to talk about all those who are vulnerable in society. As Lauret (2011) suggested, and as we develop further, "For Michelle Obama . . . 'family' means extended family, whether by choice or necessity" (p. 105). It is a point that hides more deeply in her 2008 speech at the Democratic National Convention, but one that grows clearer as she returns to the DNC stage twice. Although striving to help her husband (and, later, Hillary Clinton) get elected, Obama's DNC speeches go beyond the domain of supporting act and enter the realm of advocating policy reform. Her reclamation of the American Dream is about acknowledging vulnerability, protecting those who need assistance, and, by the time she speaks in 2016, recognizing that challenges in the family are often the result of defects in public policy.

An American Dream Evolved: Michelle Obama at the Democratic National Conventions

In her DNC speeches, Obama embraced the traditional role of republican mother, a role that allowed her to subtly achieve dialectical synthesis, bridging the divide between the competing myths of the American Dream. We begin by showing that, on the surface, her rhetoric promotes traditional family values, individualism, and the materialistic myth. Then we provide evidence to support our assertion that deeper messages of social justice are embedded in her stories. In particular, we reveal how she makes the moralistic myth more palatable to audiences by employing a metonymic argument, using narratives about her family, especially her daughters, as a way to imply that Americans have a duty to protect vulnerable populations.

Obama grounded her DNC speeches in the values of a traditional family structure. The identity from which she speaks is that of wife and mother. When Obama (2008) introduced herself to America, she stated, "I come here as a wife who loves my husband . . . I come here as a mom whose girls are the heart of my heart and the center of my world" (paras. 7–8). In 2012, she again emphasized that her love for her husband and her children were the most important parts of her life: "Our life before moving to Washington was filled with simple joys . . . Saturdays at soccer games, Sundays at grandma's house . . . and a date night for Barack and me was either dinner or a movie, because as an exhausted mom, I couldn't stay awake for both" (Obama, 2012, para. 13). A key value within Obama's role as a mother is that of protection. Obama (2012) thanked supporters for "the incredible kindness and warmth that people have shown to [her] and [her] family, especially [their] girls" (para. 4). Building on this theme, Obama recounted that her biggest fears concerning her husband's presidency revolved around how to raise good kids in the spotlight. She had unwavering confidence in her husband's ability to lead the nation, but, as she put it, "Like any mother, I was worried about what it would mean for our girls if he got that chance. How would we keep them grounded under the glare of the national spotlight?" (Obama, 2012, paras. 10–11). In 2016, Obama still characterized the girls as essential to her identity, repeating "they are the heart of our hearts, the center of our world" (Obama, 2016, para. 2).

Beyond discussing her role as a mother, Obama further illustrated her commitment to traditional family values by recounting stories about her own parents. Obama (2008) characterized her father as "our provider, our champion, our hero" and described how he continued to work hard to support the family after he was diagnosed with multiple sclerosis (para. 10). Her use of this family narrative perfectly embodied materialism. She noted that, thanks to the "faith and hard work" of her parents, which both served as clear evidence to her and her brother that they were "loved" and allowed them to attend college, she knew "firsthand . . . that the American Dream endures" (para. 11). Obama (2008) also employed her husband's family story as exemplification of the materialistic myth of the American Dream. Similar to her family, Barack Obama grew up in a working-class environment, raised by his grandparents and "a single mother who struggled to pay the bills" (para. 12). Thus, she explained that she and her husband shared that same core principle "that you work hard for what you want in life" (Obama, 2008, para. 12). In 2012, Obama reiterated this point when she described how both of their families had worked tirelessly to provide them a better life. The similarity of their upbringings was an essential aspect of their courtship, helping her to recognize him as her "kindred spirit" (Obama, 2012, para. 17).

The family narratives recounted by Obama in her DNC speeches epitomize American individualism. Particularly, she relied on her father as an embodiment of the notion that all Americans can pull themselves up by their bootstraps if they just exert enough effort. Obama (2012) painted her father as a neoliberal hero, a man "determined" to provide for his family, who, despite debilitating obstacles, "hardly ever missed a day of work" (para. 23). Moreover, throughout all of his struggles, "he never stopped smiling and laughing—even when struggling to button his shirt . . . He just woke up a little earlier and worked a little harder" (Obama, 2008, para. 10). Such statements reify the conservative conceptualization of the American Dream. From the examples set by their parents, the Obamas learned not only the ethic of working hard, but also the value of doing so gracefully. Their parents "didn't begrudge anyone else's success . . . in fact, they admired it" (Obama, 2012, para. 37). Instead, she explained, "They simply believed in that fundamental American promise that, even if you don't start out with much, if you work hard and do what you're supposed to do, then you should be able to build a decent life for yourself and an even better life for your kids and grandkids" (paras. 38–39). With phrases like "do what you're supposed to do," Obama appealed to the republican idea of the American Dream in which individuals are responsible for their success and, thus implicitly, their failure. Expanding this narrative beyond her family unit, Obama (2008) praised Americans who lived out the same principles as her father, such as "people who work the day shift, kiss their kids goodnight, and head out for the night shift—without disappointment, without regret" and "military families who say grace each night with an empty seat at the table" (paras. 20–21).

In addition to describing the fulfillment of the American Dream by others, Obama explained how she and her husband were embodiments of the Dream narrative. Obama (2008) defined the country as a place "where a girl from the South Side of Chicago can go to college and law school, and the son of a single mother from Hawaii can go all the way to the White House" (para. 40). By identifying herself and her husband as living representations of the bootstrap myth, as well as praising those who raised them for passing down the principle of hard work, Obama openly affirmed the conservative faith in individualism. Furthermore, she clearly argued that this value should be passed on to future generations when she stated, "we want our children—and all children in this nation—to know that the only limit to the height of your achievements is the reach of your dreams and your willingness to work for them" (Obama, 2008, para. 13). However, the value of individualism only represents part of Obama's American Dream rhetoric. Lurking beneath the surface lies an encoded appeal to the collectivistic version of this narrative.

Due to its subtlety, Obama's advocacy for moralism can be easily overlooked. Similar to her use of family narratives to exemplify the materialistic strain of the American Dream, she appeals to traditional family structure in order to highlight the moralistic call to watch out for others. As Obama (2008) said of her brother, Craig Robinson, "At 6-foot-6, I've often felt like Craig was looking down on me too . . . literally. But the truth is, both when we were kids and today, he wasn't looking down on me. He was watching over me" (para. 3). She reiterated this theme a few lines later when she defined her brother as her "mentor" and "protector" (para. 6). In addition to her role as sister, Obama called upon her role as mother, discussing the matriarchal instinct and imperative to watch over those who are most vulnerable, especially children. Obama (2008) linked her personal role as protector of her own children to the societal need to care for all children, explaining "[my kids are] the first thing I think about when I wake up in the morning, and the last thing I think about when I go to bed at night. Their future—and all our children's future—is my stake in this election" (para. 8). Perhaps the most important words in this quotation are "my" and "ours." Rather than speaking in impersonal terms, she took on a mantle of direct responsibility in ensuring the fortification of the futures of all children and suggested that she expects her listeners to do the same.

In 2008, Obama expressed concern over how life in the presidential spotlight might affect her children, and in 2012, she connected those "worries four years ago about whether [they] were doing [what was] best for [their] girls" to an obligation to provide "a better world" for "all our sons and daughters" (Obama, 2012, paras. 96–97). Here, she appealed to the need for collective action. In order to "give them that sense of limitless possibility—that belief that here in America, there is always something better out there if you're willing to work for it," she argued that we must provide "all our children a foundation for their dreams and opportunities worthy of their promise" (para. 97). Rather than using individualistic language, Obama employed the collective language of "all" and "our."

In addition to emphasizing her role as protective mother, Obama connected her husband's role as a protective father to his care for all vulnerable people in society. The "man, who, when our girls were first born, would anxiously check their cribs every few minutes to ensure they were still breathing," she described, was the same man who spent his nights "hunched over his desk, poring over the letters people [had] sent him" (Obama, 2012, paras. 71–73). Not only do the Obamas believe that parents should work hard to protect their own children, but they also believe that these protective instincts should be applied more broadly—to "the father struggling to pay his bills," to "the woman dying of cancer whose insurance company won't cover her care," and to "the young person with so much promise but so few opportunities" (para. 74). By interlinking the duty of family protector to a charge of responsibility to care for people in general, Obama achieved dialectical synthesis to merge the values of the materialistic and moralistic myth of the American Dream. Rather than suggest that one can either watch out for themselves or attend to the needs of others, Obama showed how the first principle should inform the second.

Interestingly, Obama's metonym of motherhood became clearer in her later speeches; by 2016 it was apparent that her children served as stand-ins for vulnerable populations in need of government assistance. Obama (2016) again reflected on the initial decision to run for the White House, a decision that brought their young daughters into the public eye. Upon the first time seeing her 7- and 10-year-old in "those black SUVs with all those big men with guns," she wondered, "What have we done?" (para. 3). She explained her realization that this environment in which her daughters would be raised "would form the foundation for who they would become" (para. 3). Given their extraordinary circumstances, she knew they would have to work "every day" to "guide and protect" them (para. 4). Thus, Obama personalized the notion that, because it is grounded within one's environment, success is situational. Obama used her children as stand-ins for the notion that, in certain trying circumstances, people may need protection from others to make their way through life. Obama guided her children, who were made vulnerable targets due to their father's position, by teaching them that "the hateful language they hear from public figures on TV does not represent the true spirit of this country" (Obama, 2016, para. 4).

Later in her 2016 speech, Obama more explicitly used the mother–child relationship as a connection point for how people should treat others. Hillary Clinton, Obama (2016) explained, would make a great president because not only had she raised her own daughter "to perfection," but she had also devoted her life to "our nation's children" (para. 7). Using collectivistic language, Obama re-emphasized the notion that all people in society, not just politicians like Clinton and her husband, are responsible for the success of children. Although the moralistic myth is more encoded in her earlier speeches, in her 2016 speech, freed from her role as candidate spouse, she identified the specific protections she believed should be extended to all. Obama portrayed Clinton as an embodiment of the moralistic vision of the American Dream when she described her as a "champion" for children, a woman who helped "[k]ids who take the long way to school to avoid the gangs. Kids who wonder how they'll ever afford college. Kids whose parents don't speak a word of English but dream of a better life" (para. 7). She advocated for specific policy issues, stating, "Hillary has spent decades doing the relentless, thankless work to actually make a difference in their lives—advocating for kids with disabilities as a young lawyer. Fighting for children's health care as First Lady and for quality child care in the Senate" and "once again as Secretary of State, traveling the globe to keep our kids safe" (Obama, 2016, para. 8).

Her description of Clinton's dedication to protecting children, especially those with special needs, served as a marker of Obama's support for the values of social justice more broadly. Simultaneously, Obama wove in the ethics of hard work and determination, traditionally associated with the materialistic myth. "And when she didn't win the nomination eight years ago," Obama explained, "Hillary did not pack up and go home. Because as a true public servant, Hillary knows that this is so much bigger than her own desires and disappointments" (Obama, 2016, para. 8). Unlike the materialistic strain, however, Obama asserted that Clinton's hard work was not about advancement for herself or even her family. Rather, she worked tirelessly for the advancement of others. Here, Obama has appropriated a traditionally conservative principle in the service of promoting a progressive politician and collectivist agenda.

Furthermore, Obama's narrative of family evolved from 2008 when she primarily presented her family history as a representative anecdote of the materialistic strain of the American Dream. By 2012, Obama had woven the moralistic myth into her story. Even though her family worked hard, they were still disadvantaged and needed government help to ultimately achieve success. For example, she and her brother relied on "student loans and grants" to get through college. Even her father, whom she often portrayed as epitomizing neoliberal values, had to take "out loans when he fell short" on the "tiny portion" of tuition that he "had to pay" (Obama, 2012, paras. 24–26). Similarly, Obama used the story of her husband's grandmother to illustrate how oftentimes, no matter how hard one works, prejudice can still hold a person back. His grandmother worked her way up the ladder at a "community bank," Obama explained, "but like so many women, she hit a glass ceiling" (para. 32). Although she kept her nose to the grindstone, "waking up at dawn to catch the bus . . . arriving at work before anyone else . . . giving her best without complaint or regret," she was continually passed up for promotion by "men no more qualified than she was—men she had actually trained," men who would go on to outearn her, "while Barack's family continued to scrape by" (Obama, 2012, paras. 33–34).

Thus, Obama illustrated that both the value of individual hard work *and* the practice of government intervention (such as policies to reduce inequality) were required for disadvantaged Americans to succeed. As she explicitly pointed out later in the same speech, working hard and looking out for others should be simultaneous, not opposing, endeavors: "We learned about dignity and decency—that how hard you work matters more than how much you make . . . that helping others means more than just getting ahead yourself" (Obama, 2012, para. 40). Building on this, Obama co-opted the conservative strain of the American Dream in order to explain her husband's commitment to progressive policy. It was his familiarity with the endless hard work (yet constant struggle) of "folks like [her] dad and like his grandmother" that informed his signing of the Lilly Ledbetter Fair Pay Act and his decision to "cut taxes for working families and small businesses" (paras. 51–54).

Similarly, it was their personal familiarity with student loan bills that were "higher than [their] mortgage," that inspired his fight "to increase student aid and keep interest rates down" (Obama, 2012, paras. 61–63).

In 2016, Obama more clearly defined what it means to look out for others. For her, it meant guaranteeing certain rights for every child and every American. Obama (2016) explained, "I want a President who will teach our children that everyone in this country matters" and a president who believes that "when crisis hits, we don't turn away from each other . . . We lean on each other. Because we are always stronger together" (para. 12). In her first convention address, Obama (2008) had more subtly encoded this value within her rhetoric by describing her husband's work as a community organizer: "Instead of heading to Wall Street, Barack had gone to work in neighborhoods devastated when steel plants shut down and jobs dried up. And he'd been invited back to speak to people from those neighborhoods about how to rebuild their community" (para. 14). Although these people were living out the individualistic principle of hard work, many still "couldn't support their families after their jobs disappeared" (Obama, 2008, para. 15). Thus, simultaneously, Obama lauded hard work while also undermining the notion that those who are struggling are not trying hard enough.

In the pinnacle of her 2016 speech, Obama addressed the issues of gender and racial equality. Obama (2016) praised Clinton for putting "cracks in that highest and hardest glass ceiling" and for continuing on this path "until she finally breaks through, lifting all of us along with her" (para. 15). She described how African Americans "kept on striving and hoping" despite "the lash of bondage, the shame of servitude, [and] the sting of segregation" (para. 16). The most memorable moment of the speech came next when she pointed out that it was due to this fortitude that she and her children "wake up every morning in a house that was built by slaves" (para. 16). Here again, Obama joined the conventionally dualistic strands of the American Dream myth. On the one hand, she celebrated and reiterated her commitment to the value of hard work at all costs, and, on the other, she reminded Americans that some face greater obstacles and greater injustices than others. Clearly, she implied, it is the duty of citizens to rectify these injustices in order to level the playing field for all. By using Clinton as an embodiment of gender equality and herself as an embodiment of racial equality, Obama conveyed that this version of America is achievable—and in the process of being achieved—and that such progress is what makes America, "right now, the greatest country on earth" (2016, para. 17).

Conclusion

This chapter describes Michelle Obama's rhetorical evolution by analyzing her convention speeches for the ways she lobbies for moralism in a society dominated by materialism. In particular, we sought to explain how she reconciled the constraints she faced as the first African American first lady, which often compelled her to speak in the voice of republican mother, with her progressive values. Ultimately, we analyzed her three DNC speeches to illuminate how Obama achieved dialectical synthesis through a metonymy of motherhood, a strategy that not only addressed the constraints of the first ladyship, but also represented a coded way of arguing for a collective responsibility for others.

Our analysis has several implications. First, as we have illustrated, to fully understand Obama's rhetoric, it is important to examine its evolution over time. Because the constraints she faced changed throughout her time in the White House, Obama's ability to speak more directly about certain issues, such as gender and race, grew. Second, we have shown that appeals to motherhood are not inherently anti-feminist or wholly conservative. Instead, Obama used motherhood to her advantage, employing it as a rhetorical tool to covertly advocate for communal values. Third, we have built upon the nonbinary theory of the American Dream suggested by Rowland and Jones (2007). In analyzing the development of Obama's rhetoric, we have provided further support for the argument that the American Dream need not be imagined as a duality but as a myth that can bridge ideologies.

References

Blair, D. M. (2001). No ordinary time: Eleanor Roosevelt's address to the 1940 Democratic National Convention. *Rhetoric & Public Affairs, 4*, 203–222. doi: 10.1353/rap.2001.0021

Campbell, L. (2008, September 1). Campbell: Michelle Obama combines traditional values with progressive ones [Opinion]. *The Salt Lake Tribune*. Retrieved from http://archive.sltrib.com

Cottle, M. (2013, November 21). Leaning out: How Michelle Obama became a feminist nightmare. *Politico*. Retrieved from http://www.politico.com

Dubriwny, T. N. (2005). First ladies and feminism: Laura Bush as advocate for women's and children's rights. *Women's Studies in Communication, 28*, 84–114. doi: 10.1080/07491409.2005.10162485

Edgar, C. (2013, December 5). Michelle Obama: The one woman in America who actually has it all. *Salon*. Retrieved from http://www.salon.com

Erickson, K. V., & Thomson, S. (2012). First lady international diplomacy: Performing gendered roles on the world stage. *Southern Communication Journal, 77*, 239–262. doi: 10.1080/1041794X.2011.647502

Fisher, W. R. (1973). Reaffirmation and subversion of the American dream. *Quarterly Journal of Speech, 59*, 160–167. doi: 10.1080/00335637309383164

Fournier, R. (2016, July 28). Obama's new American exceptionalism. *The Atlantic*. Retrieved from https://www.theatlantic.com

Garcia, P. (2016, July 26). Speech at the DNC will go down in history. *Vogue*. Retrieved from http://www.vogue.com

Gutin, M. (2000). Using all available means of persuasion: The twentieth century first lady as public communicator. *Social Science Journal, 37*, 563–575.

Hayden, S. (2017). Michelle Obama, Mom-in-Chief: The racialized rhetorical contexts of maternity. *Women's Studies in Communication, 40*, 11–28. doi: 10 .1080/07491409.2016.1182095

Joseph, R. L. (2011). "Hope is finally making a comeback": First lady reframed. *Communication, Culture & Critique, 4*, 56–77. doi: 10.1111/j.1753-9137 .2010.01093.x

Kahl, M. L. (2009). First lady Michelle Obama: Advocate for strong families. *Communication and Critical/Cultural Studies, 6*, 316–320. doi: 10.1080/1479142 0903063794

Lauret, M. (2011). How to read Michelle Obama. *Patterns of Prejudice, 45*, 95–117. doi: 10.1080/0031322X.2011.563149

Merida, K. (2008, August 26). A defining moment; in Denver, Michelle Obama takes a deep breath and steps up to the podium and her supporting role. *The Washington Post*, p. A19.

Meyers, M., & Goman, C. (2017). Michelle Obama: Exploring the narrative. *Howard Journal of Communications, 28*, 20–35. doi: 10.1080/10646175.2016.1235520

Michelle's triumph [Editorial]. (2008, August 27). *Daily News*, p. 38.

Nelson, L. (2016, July 28). Democrats have stolen the GOP's best rhetoric—and the Republicans have noticed. *Vox*. Retrieved from http://www.vox.com

Obama, M. (2008, August 25). *Michelle Obama's convention speech.* [Transcript]. Retrieved from http://www.npr.org/templates/story/story.php?storyId =93963863

Obama, M. (2012, September 4). *Michelle Obama's convention speech.* [Transcript]. Retrieved from http://www.npr.org/2012/09/04/160578836/transcript -michelle-obamas-convention-speech

Obama, M. (2016, July 26). *Michelle Obama's speech at 2016 Democratic National Convention.* Retrieved from http://www.npr.org/2016/07/26/487431756 /michelle-obamas-prepared-remarks-for-democratic-national-convention

Obaro, T. (2012, September 4). The humanizers. *The Washington Post*, p. C01.

Parry-Giles, S. J., & Blair, D. M. (2002). The rise of the rhetorical first lady: Politics, gender ideology, and women's voice, 1789–2002. *Rhetoric & Public Affairs, 5*, 565–599. doi: 10.1353/rap.2003.0011

Rowland, R. C., & Jones, J. A. (2007). Recasting the American Dream and American politics: Barack Obama's keynote address to the 2004 Democratic National Convention. *Quarterly Journal of Speech, 93*, 425–448. doi: 10.1080 /00335630701593675

Rushing, J. H., & Frentz, T. S. (1978). The rhetoric of "Rocky": A social value model of criticism. *Western Journal of Speech Communication, 42*, 63–72. doi: 10 .1080/10570317809373925

Solomon, M. (1983). Villainless quest: Myth, metaphor, and dream in "Chariots of Fire." *Communication Quarterly, 31*, 274–281. doi: 10.1080/0146337830 9369516

Thompson, K. (2012, September 4). A political speech that can't seem too partisan. *The Washington Post*, p. A04.

Thompson, K. (2016, July 25). At the DNC opener, a prime slot for a first lady once uneasy with partisan politics. *The Washington Post*, p. C01.

Tomasky, M. (2016, July 26). DNC 2016: Michelle Obama's speech of a lifetime turns convention around for Hillary Clinton. *The Daily Beast*. Retrieved from http://www.thedailybeast.com

Tumulty, K., & O'Keefe, E. (2012, September 6). Michelle's milestone moment. *The Washington Post*, p. A12.

CHAPTER TWELVE

Loss of Faith: A Realignment of Religion on the Campaign Trail

Brian Kaylor

As Donald J. Trump placed his hand on a stack of two closed Bibles on January 20, 2017, it marked the culmination of a unique 18 months in American politics—particularly the role religion plays in contemporary campaigns. The thrice-married casino magnate who bragged about sexually assaulting women, cursed during campaign rallies, and claimed he did not need to ask God for forgiveness, not only won the election, but did so with a record percentage of white evangelicals. The most openly secular nominee in decades squeaked into the Oval Office with that record support. Had the number dipped down only a few percentage points to what more religious candidates like John McCain or Mitt Romney garnered, it likely would have moved just enough votes to flip the Electoral College. Adding to the unusual election, Hillary Clinton jettisoned her previously outspoken religiosity from her 2008 campaign and ignored the winning religious rhetorical strategy employed by Barack Obama, Bill Clinton, and Jimmy Carter. Adopting a religious rhetoric even more muted than John Kerry, she often sounded more secular than Trump, even as her past demonstrated much more authentic religiosity than he offered.

As politicians in recent decades brought God along on the campaign bus in hopes of winning the White House, scholars have explored the role religious rhetoric played in presidential campaigns. The election of the first Catholic president, John F. Kennedy, in 1960 garnered a lot of attention even as Kennedy himself largely shied away from faith discussions (e.g., Boller, 1979; Hart, 1977). With the election of born-again Sunday school teacher Carter in 1976, a new wave of scholarship emerged (Boase, 1989; Erickson, 1980; Hahn, 1980). Other recent candidates also gained attention for their God talk, especially Ronald Reagan (e.g., Boase, 1989; Domke & Coe, 2008; Porter, 1990), Bill Clinton (e.g., Lee, 2002; Ofulue, 2002), George W. Bush (e.g., Domke & Coe, 2008; Medhurst, 2002), and Obama (Crick, 2012; Johnson, 2012; Murphy, 2011). Ultimately, Carter's election did not just attract new scholarly attention, but also helped usher in a new era of religious-political rhetoric. In each of the 10 presidential elections from 1976 to 2012, the most religiously outspoken general election candidate prevailed (Kaylor, 2011, 2014). Winning candidates—as well as many other contenders—used a form of "confessional politics" with religious rhetoric characterized as testimonial, partisan, sectarian, and liturgical (Kaylor, 2011). This shift in rhetorical religious expectations—that is, the candidate who talks about God and faith the most wins, not necessarily the one who is the most religious personally—has created a more evangelical political milieu. Thus, whereas only 4 of the first 38 presidents could be classified as evangelical (Boller, 1979), 5 of the next 6 could be (Kaylor, 2011) with only George H. W. Bush not fitting that religious tradition in the age from Carter to Obama.

This chapter explores the religious rhetoric during the 2016 presidential campaign. Major campaign speeches and interviews were collected—88 for Clinton and 74 for Trump—along with the three general election debates. These texts were analyzed to identify religious references, like those to religious communities or leaders (e.g., church, Islam, individual clergy members); religious concepts or texts (e.g., prayer, Bible, faith); or personal religious commitment or theology (e.g., religious background or position). After considering how the two candidates invoked God, faith, and scriptures, important conclusions are discussed.

Mostly Muted Meditations

An analysis of major campaign speeches and interviews by Clinton noted little God talk from the lifelong Methodist. Compared to the campaign rhetoric of the man she hoped to follow in office, her husband, and even her own earlier unsuccessful run, her 2016 speeches included little religious references, especially in opening up about her personal faith beliefs. A large chunk of her religious references came in the repetitive use of two fairly innocuous statements. First, Clinton often employed—though not as consistently as most presidential nominees over the past three decades—the use of the civil religious "God bless" statements at the end of speeches. Additionally, she often phrased her policy goals as designed to help people reach their "God-given potential," another phrase not uncommon in political speech, even though Clinton appeared to use this more consistently than other recent presidential nominees. Neither statement indicates much personal faith, rising to little more than expected rhetorical garnish.

Many other faith-based statements by Clinton also slid by without much depth. On a couple occasions, she lumped the "faith community" into a list of groups like the business community, academic institutions, and civic groups when talking about her support or plans for bringing communities together. In one speech, she hit the idea more explicitly as she talked about those who volunteer in their community as part of a school, church, or synagogue. She added she served "through faith-based opportunities" as a teenager and her running mate Tim Kaine served with Jesuits in Honduras because "service is part of our faith" (Clinton, 2016c). Additionally, in a few speeches, she expressed her prayers for those affected by a tragedy in the news, such as for the family of Freddie Gray (a man killed in police custody in Baltimore), those affected by flooding in Houston, and those injured or killed in a train crash in New Jersey.

In terms of policy rhetoric, international affairs evoked the most religious references from Clinton, especially as she talked about refugees and immigrants. Talking about the refugee crisis, she noted during an interview that she wanted the United States to "emphasize" admitting those "who are most vulnerable, a lot of the persecuted religious minorities, including Christians, and some who have been brutalized, like the Yazidi women" (Clinton, 2015a). Just after Christmas, she alluded to her Christian faith when talking about caring for refugees and others:

> You know, we are still in the midst of the holiday season, and for those of us who celebrate Christmas, it's good to remember that we are called upon to care for the homeless and the stranger and the prisoner, the refugee. (Clinton, 2015c)

However, when asked on another occasion about prioritizing Christian refugees as some Republican presidential hopefuls explicitly proposed, Clinton responded, "I just don't think we should have religious tests about who we bring as refugees into our country" (Clinton, 2015b). She added in the next sentence that she recognizes that faith-based organizations often sponsor refugees. Clinton also used other several other occasions to criticize her Republican opponents for pushing a religious test—and for turning away orphans and other refugees. In several of those speeches, she connected proposed religious tests on refugees and proposed bans on Muslims as contrary to the United States' heritage of religious freedom. In a speech on the eve of the election, she also cited the "Golden Rule" as a teaching found in all major religions. She also refused calls—even when directly asked—to blame Islam for terrorism.

With just a few exceptions, Clinton's remarks about her personal faith were limited to one-sentence references to her childhood in a Methodist church or a lesson she learned as a Methodist. During her acceptance remarks at the Democratic National Convention, Clinton noted she learned from her "Methodist faith" as she talked about the importance of people helping each other: "Do all the good you can for all the people you can in all the ways you can as long as ever you can" (Clinton, 2016b). Commonly attributed to John Wesley, the founder of Methodism, these words popped into several more Clinton campaign speeches after the convention, and she at times called it a personal "creed." In a couple of other speeches, she noted that through her Methodist church as a young girl she met Mexican farmworkers and babysat for their kids, thus expanding her worldview. These references noted her past as a faithful Methodist, but offered little into her current religious practices.

The few occasions where Clinton offered a more detailed look into her personal religious beliefs came either when she spoke in a church or when a clergy member posed a question at a town hall. For instance, when a rabbi asked her at a town hall about balancing ego and humility, Clinton's answer included a couple of personal thoughts on faith:

> I feel very fortunate that I am a person of faith, that I was raised in my church and that I have had to deal and struggle with a lot of these issues about ambition and humility, about service and self-gratification, all of the human questions that all of us deal with . . . And it will be something that I continue to talk about with a—you know, with a group of faith advisers who are close to me. I get a scripture lesson every morning from a minister that I have a really close personal relationship with. And, you know, it just gets me grounded. (Clinton, 2016a)

She added that she gets the notes from the minister at 5:00 a.m. and that some "friends who are rabbis" also sometimes send her things to read. In her answer, she also referred to a teaching by Jesuit writer Henri Nouwen and his interpretation of a parable by Jesus.

Clinton also occasionally spoke in a church, generally a black church, and, therefore, a congregation strongly embedded in the Democratic base. During her 2008 campaign, she spoke in more churches and even ventured into events at conservative white congregations. In her 2016 speeches at churches, Clinton offered the most personal looks at her own religious beliefs and practices. For instance, in a speech at a black church in North Carolina, Clinton nearly assumed the role of a preacher kicking off worship as she quoted scripture to start her speech: "This is the day the Lord has made. Let us rejoice and be glad in it!" (Clinton, 2016d). Showing awareness of scriptures, she wove other biblical texts into her remarks, praising the church as one "founded in a house on a rock and that rock has been sturdy and steady" (Clinton, 2016d). Later in the speech, she cited and quoted a verse in the biblical book of Proverbs. She used the verse as a lead-in to her standard "God-given potential" line, thus baptizing that line with a more explicitly religious context than usual. She ended the speech with some theologizing:

> You know, God loves us all, right? We are called to care for and cherish each other. It's not easy, it is not. But that is our mission and that is what we are called to do, not only as Christians but as Americans, as human beings to understand and respect each other. . . . You've been doing this since Adam and Eve came here. But it is righteous work. Protecting all of God's children is America's calling. Remember what scripture also tells us: "Let us not become weary in doing good, for at the proper time we will reap a harvest if we do not give up." We will not grow weary and we will not lose heart. We will get up every single day, have faith in one another and in our future, and work for that better day for all of God's people. (Clinton, 2016d)

With a religious audience gathered in the pews of a church, Clinton finally allowed her religiosity to show.

Seeking Salvation

During his unusual path to the Oval Office, Trump offered unusual religious rhetoric that helped him successfully find political salvation from white evangelicals—and perhaps, he argued, even literal salvation. When addressing a religious-political gathering, Trump actually called winning the White House and removing a tax regulation affecting churches "the only way I'm getting to heaven" (Trump, 2016f). Whether Trump gets to heaven remains beyond the purview of this chapter, but that remark captures—big league— the unusual dynamic as a man with little biblical literacy or moral behavior became the savior of the politically powerful white evangelical voting bloc. After all, a more common reference to "heaven" in Trump's campaign rhetoric came as he told a story of a snake—an anti-immigrant parable he liked to use in speeches—invoking the name of "heaven" in vain and including other profane words usually frowned upon by Trump's evangelical supporters.

Trump's past behavior and untrusted conservatism initially led evangelicals to support other candidates during the primaries, especially those who attended church more frequently and those who lived outside the Deep South. Trump clumsily courted their support, such as when he trekked to Jerry Falwell's Liberty University and quoted "Two Corinthians" instead of the normal evangelical parlance of "Second Corinthians." Trump later blamed the incident on a religious-political activist—Tony Perkins—who gave Trump the verse with the word "liberty" in it, but did not coach Trump on saying it. Trump also released a campaign ad just before the Iowa caucuses where he held up his mother's Bible, a prop he took to the campaign trail as well.

Once Trump secured the nomination, however, traditional Republican voters in the pews quickly fell in line. On Election Day, Trump took 81% of white evangelical votes, a mark even passing the best levels achieved by G. W. Bush and Reagan (both at 78% for their re-elections). Trump also easily won Protestants overall and Catholics, though he lost among Christians of color and those of other or no faith.

Like Clinton, one of Trump's most common religious references came with his use of the civil religious "God bless" statements to end speeches. Whereas Clinton talked about helping people reach their "God-given potential," Trump frequently bragged he "will be the greatest jobs president that God ever created" (Trump, 2016b). Whereas Clinton a couple of times recited the "one nation under God" line from the Pledge of Allegiance (along with other lines), Trump frequently used a saying inspired by that: "one people, under one God, saluting one American flag." A couple of times, he even added "beautiful" before "American flag." These "God" statements followed in recent presidential campaign traditions, offering virtually no real insights into Trump's religiosity.

Trump also acted like Clinton by saying in several speeches that he offered his prayers for people in the news, though not quite as frequently as Clinton. His expressions of prayers included those for victims of flooding in Louisiana, the family of a religious-political activist who died (Phyllis Schlafly), and the families of two police officers killed in Iowa. Although Trump invoked prayer less often, he did something Clinton did not—he politicized his calls for prayers. While Trump criticized Clinton for "pay-for-play," he singled out the Clinton Foundation's work in Haiti, adding, "Let me stop here for a second and say how much we love and appreciate the Haitian-American community in Florida and across our country. We send our prayers to the many still suffering in Haiti from the earthquake" (Trump, 2016e). The prayer reference, tacked in as an afterthought during pandering to voters, functions more as part of a partisan attack than an expression of spiritual concern. On another occasion, Trump started with a call to prayer about a terrorist attack and then pivoted to a policy topic and partisan attack on Obama and Clinton:

> I'd like to take this moment to send our thoughts and prayers to everyone at the American University in Kabul, Afghanistan. They are going through a lot. We must defeat radical Islamic terrorism! Anyone who will not name our enemy is not fit to lead our country. (Trump, 2016c)

That "prayer" moment connected with Trump's most common religious reference—his frequent attacks on Islam and Muslims. With this rhetoric,

Trump offered the opposing position to Clinton's references about Islam and Muslims. He particularly framed Islam as a radical faith sparking terrorism and attempted to paint Muslims as natural enemies of Christians and Jews. He clearly framed the United States' fight against terrorism in religious terms and criticized Obama and Clinton for not doing so as well. Many of his references to Christians and Jews came as he talked about "radical Islam" and attacks in Middle Eastern nations. Trump even justified his support of waterboarding and other forms of torture by noting ISIS beheading Christians.

On a few other occasions, Trump also briefly mentioned religion for nonmilitary policy or political matters. He justified school choice in several speeches by noting it would help parents send kids to various schools, including religious ones. As he criticized Obama's moves to shift U.S. relations with Cuba, Trump promised to put new "demands" on "the Castro Regime," including "religious and political freedom for the Cuban people" (Trump, 2016g). In other speeches, he referenced leaked Democratic National Committee (DNC) e-mails showing controversial remarks, including a staffer criticizing conservative Christians. He claimed in one speech, "These e-mails are just the latest evidence of the hatred that the Clinton campaign has for everyday faithful Americans" (Trump, 2016h). In numerous speeches toward the end of the campaign, Trump also listed "defend religious liberty" in a quick laundry list of promises—even promising this more than Clinton despite her noting his "Muslim ban" would actually violate religious liberty.

Other than brief references to "radical Islam," "religious liberty," or "God bless," Trump usually saved his religious rhetoric for the discussion of one topic: eliminating the so-called "Johnson Amendment." A 1954 IRS tax code change—initially proposed by then-Senator Lyndon B. Johnson but passed by a bipartisan congressional vote and signed by President Dwight D. Eisenhower— the regulation prevents 501(c)(3) tax-exempt organizations from engaging in partisan campaigns to support or oppose a candidate. Although most houses of worship fall into that nonprofit status, the legislation was not designed to target them and does not treat them differently from other nonprofit 501(c)(3) groups. Yet conservative religious-political activists have targeted the regulation for years (Kaylor, 2015), seeing such a change as a way of allowing greater political activism by their congregations. Trump became the first presidential nominee to adopt the cause, quickly demonstrating the zealotry of a new convert. It was the elimination of the "Johnson Amendment" as president that Trump suggested would be his own way to get into heaven. He also pushed the repeal during his acceptance remarks at the Republican National Convention (RNC) and brought up getting rid of the "Johnson Amendment" as he discussed the leaked DNC e-mails showing a staffer criticizing some Christians.

Trump appeared a bit fuzzy on the details, often implying Johnson created the new regulation as president and suggesting it was designed to target just evangelicals (even though they were not a powerful political voting bloc until decades later) and apparently not realizing it only prevents partisan involvement. He argued:

> We call it the Johnson Amendment, where you are just absolutely shunned if you're evangelical, if you want to talk religion, you lose your tax-exempt status. We put into the platform, we're going to get rid of that horrible Johnson Amendment. And we're going to let evangelicals, we're going to let Christians and Jews and people of religion talk without being afraid to talk. (Trump, 2016a)

Trump claimed the regulation made religious leaders "timid" and afraid to speak out politically. Interestingly, he interrupted himself claiming it silenced evangelicals to brag about his support from evangelicals during the primaries. He added that once he removed the regulation, "religion can again have a voice" (Trump, 2016a). Speaking at the event where he saw this as his path to heaven, Trump explained how he first came to understand this issue and why "we're going to get rid of it so fast" (Trump, 2016f). He recounted holding a meeting with hundreds of Christian pastors after securing the nomination and asking for their support. When they told him that would be breaking the law and threaten their tax-exempt status, he asked why. He then decided to support repeal of the "Johnson Amendment" to make sure religious leaders are "able to freely express their thoughts and feelings on religious matters" (Trump, 2016f). As he recounted learning about the regulation and suggesting his motivation was so he could gain support of churches, Trump again mingled the facts inaccurately, claiming Johnson "single-handedly" created the rule because "there was a church in Houston that was giving him a hard time" (Trump, 2016f). Despite these alternative facts, Trump seemed convinced this issue proved his religious sincerity.

The closest Trump came to revealing any personal religious experiences or beliefs came in a couple of speeches at churches or meetings of religious-political groups. Speaking at a black church in Detroit, Trump praised black churches as "the conscience of our country," "the soul of our nation," "one of God's greatest gifts to America," and a key force in the Civil Rights Movement (Trump, 2016d). He praised those at the church for their work to "raise children in the light of God" and pledged to "defend your right to worship, so important" (Trump, 2016d). Toward the end of his remarks, he turned slightly toward theology, saying, "We're all brothers and sisters and we're all created by the same God" (Trump, 2016d). He also referred to "our Christian heritage" before concluding with a biblical quotation:

> I'd like to conclude with a passage from 1 John, Chapter 4. You know it? See, most groups I speak to don't know that. But we know it. If you want, we can

say it together: "No one has ever seen God, but if we love one another, God lives in us and his love is made complete in us." And that is so true. (Trump, 2016d)

In his remarks to the annual religious-political convention of the Family Research Council that often serves as a pilgrimage site for Republican politicians, Trump again aligned himself with a church-going crowd as he spoke of "our Christian heritage," adding, "It will be our faith in God and his teachings, in each other, that will lead us back to unity" (Trump, 2016f). Speaking to that religious crowd in Washington, D.C., Trump moved toward the theological, saying, "We are all equal, and we all come from the same Creator" (Trump, 2016f). He then returned to the same biblical passage to read:

There's a biblical verse that I have often read, and I want to repeat it again because I think it is so important to what we're trying to achieve right now for our country. It's from 1 John, Chapter 4: "No one has ever seen God; but if we love one another, God lives in us, and His love is made complete in us." So true. So true. (Trump, 2016f)

These moments at religious events offered the most theological and biblical comments from Trump, though he still offered little about his personal beliefs. He did, however, successfully refer to "First John" instead of "One John."

Conclusions

Few contemporary presidential campaigns offered as little God talk as the 2016 contest. Since 1976, only 1988 would even compare. Both 1988 and 2016 brought non-evangelicals into the White House (though both winning candidates won about 8 in 10 white evangelicals). Both campaigns featured a mainline Protestant—H. W. Bush in 1988 and Clinton in 2016—who, although practicing Christians, remained relatively quiet about their faith on the campaign trail. Both campaigns featured a virtually secular candidate—Michael Dukakis in 1988 and Trump in 2016. Dukakis, a Greek Orthodox by tradition, occasionally attended church and rarely spoke about it. Trump may be even less religious in practice, besting Dukakis as more secular and more profane. Yet Trump lost voters who claim no religion while easily winning Christians— the opposite of the showing for Dukakis. Important implications can be drawn from this unique campaign rhetoric.

First, the 2016 campaign again showed the importance of religious rhetoric instead of actual religiosity. Although the latter remains harder to analyze, multiple recent elections featured candidates who talked more about faith while beating candidates who actually attended church more (like Reagan over Carter in 1980, Kerry over G. W. Bush in 2004, and Trump over Clinton in

2016). The power of campaign rhetoric to win over voters seeking religious assurances apparently can cover a multitude of sins. Voters in the past overlooked Reagan's divorce and poor churchmanship as he proved he could talk the talk. Trump's obstacles included twice as many divorces, sexual scandals, casino businesses, and biblical illiteracy. Yet Trump still found the role of the most religiously outspoken candidate in the general election—and then placed his hand on two Bibles to take the oath of office.

Second, Trump's record support among white evangelicals—and strong support among Christians overall—shows the power of partisan affiliation over religiosity in voting decisions. When evangelicals voted for non-evangelical Republicans like McCain in 2008, they at least backed someone within their general religious worldview. Romney, a Mormon, moved that line for evangelicals in 2012, and Trump eliminated it. In terms of religion, Clinton stood closer, but political priorities trumped.

Third, Clinton's move toward quieter religiosity on the campaign trail placed her in company with Kerry, Dukakis, and other Democratic nominees who sat as spectators on Inauguration Day. Eight years earlier, Clinton touted her religious side, as did her primary competitors, Obama and John Edwards. In 2016, she faced another candidate who rarely talked about private religious beliefs, although for a secular Jew like U.S. Senator Bernie Sanders that proved authentic. Clinton also assisted Trump's outreach to white evangelicals and Catholics—a demographic that actually swings between the parties—by moving the Democratic Party further to the left on abortion. Her rhetoric on abortion and changes in the party's platform helped conservative activists rally the faithful behind Trump, despite his shallow anti-abortion credentials and helped keep the glass ceiling intact. A key question for the Democratic Party as it considers the various reasons for the loss remains: Did Clinton's campaign represent a departure from the religious rhetorical efforts of Obama and Bill Clinton, or will the party abandon outreach efforts toward the important slice of white evangelical and Catholic voters who could deliver political redemption?

Finally, what will the impact of Trump's success have long term on the current evangelical dominance on presidential politics? Does his victory prove their continuing influence, thus further solidifying rhetorical expectations for 2020 hopefuls? Or will a Trump scandal taint his strongest supporters and usher in a new political age just as the evangelical era of confessional politics started in part in the aftermath of the fall of Richard Nixon?

References

Boase, P. H. (1989). Moving the mercy seat into the White House: An exegesis of the Carter/Reagan religious rhetoric. *Journal of Communication and Religion*, 12(2), 1–9.

Boller, P. F., Jr. (1979). Religion and the U.S. presidency. *Journal of Church and State, 21,* 5–21.

Clinton, H. (2015a, September 20). Interview with John Dickerson of CBS News. *Face the nation.* In G. Peters & J. T. Woolley (Eds.), *The American Presidency Project.* Retrieved from http://www.presidency.ucsb.edu/ws/?pid=111423

Clinton, H. (2015b, November 19). Remarks and a question and answer session at the Council on Foreign Relations in New York City. In G. Peters & J. T. Woolley (Eds.), *The American Presidency Project.* Retrieved from http://www.presidency.ucsb.edu/ws/?pid=111416

Clinton, H. (2015c, December 29). Remarks at a town hall meeting in Portsmouth, NH. In G. Peters & J. T. Woolley (Eds.), *The American Presidency Project.* Retrieved from http://www.presidency.ucsb.edu/ws/?pid=111415

Clinton, H. (2016a, February 3). Remarks at the CNN Democratic Town Hall in Derry, NH. In G. Peters & J. T. Woolley (Eds.), *The American Presidency Project.* Retrieved from http://www.presidency.ucsb.edu/ws/?pid=111596

Clinton, H. (2016b, July 28). Address accepting the presidential nomination at the Democratic National Convention in Philadelphia, PA. In G. Peters & J. T. Woolley (Eds.), *The American Presidency Project.* Retrieved from http://www.presidency.ucsb.edu/ws/?pid=118051

Clinton, H. (2016c, September 30). Remarks at Sunrise Theatre in Fort Pierce, FL. In G. Peters & J. T. Woolley (Eds.), *The American Presidency Project.* Retrieved from http://www.presidency.ucsb.edu/ws/?pid=119151

Clinton, H. (2016d, October 2). Remarks at Little Rock AME Zion Church in Charlotte, NC. In G. Peters & J. T. Woolley (Eds.), *The American Presidency Project.* Retrieved from http://www.presidency.ucsb.edu/ws/?pid=119152

Crick, N. (2012). Barack Obama and the rhetoric of religious experience. *Journal of Communication and Religion, 35,* 35–49.

Domke, D., & Coe, K. (2008). *The god strategy: How religion became a political weapon in America.* Oxford, UK: Oxford University Press.

Erickson, K. V. (1980). Jimmy Carter: The rhetoric of private and civic piety. *Western Journal of Speech Communication, 44,* 221–235. doi.org/10.1080/10570318009374008

Hahn, D. F. (1980). One's reborn every minute: Carter's religious appeal in 1976. *Communication Quarterly, 28,* 56–62. doi.org/10.1080/01463378009369375

Hart, R. P. (1977). *The political pulpit.* West Lafayette, IN: Purdue University Press.

Johnson, A. E. (2012). Avoiding phony religiosity: The rhetorical theology of Obama's 2012 National Prayer Breakfast Address. *Journal of Contemporary Rhetoric, 2,* 44–53.

Kaylor, B. T. (2011). *Presidential campaign rhetoric in an age of confessional politics.* Lanham, MD: Lexington Books.

Kaylor, B. (2014). Altar calls: Religious segmentation in campaign appeals. In D. Bystrom, M. Banwart, & M. McKinney (Eds.), *alieNATION: The divide and conquer election of 2012* (pp. 277–295). New York: Peter Lang Publishing, Inc.

Kaylor, B. (2015). *Sacramental politics: Religious worship as political action.* New York: Peter Lang Publishing, Inc.

Lee, R. (2002). The force of religion in the public square. *Journal of Communication and Religion, 25*, 6–20.

Medhurst, M. J. (2002). Forging a civil-religious construct for the 21st century: Should Hart's "contract" be renewed? *Journal of Communication and Religion, 25*, 86–101.

Murphy, J. M. (2011). Barack Obama, the Exodus tradition, and the Joshua generation. *Quarterly Journal of Speech, 97*, 387–410. doi.org/10.1080/00335630.2011.608706

Ofulue, N. I. (2002). President Clinton and the White House prayer breakfast. *Journal of Communication and Religion, 25*, 49–63.

Porter, L. W. (1990). Religion and politics: Protestant beliefs in the presidential campaign of 1980. *Journal of Communication and Religion, 13*(2), 24–39.

Trump, D. J. (2016a, July 16). Remarks introducing Governor Mike Pence as the 2016 Republican vice presidential nominee in New York City. In G. Peters & J. T. Woolley (Eds.), *The American Presidency Project*. Retrieved from http://www.presidency.ucsb.edu/ws/?pid=117791

Trump, D. J. (2016b, August 15). Remarks at Youngstown State University in Youngstown, OH. In G. Peters & J. T. Woolley (Eds.), *The American Presidency Project*. Retrieved from http://www.presidency.ucsb.edu/ws/?pid=119503

Trump, D. J. (2016c, August 24). Remarks at the Mississippi Coliseum in Jackson, MS. In G. Peters & J. T. Woolley (Eds.), *The American Presidency Project*. Retrieved from http://www.presidency.ucsb.edu/ws/?pid=123198

Trump, D. J. (2016d, September 3). Remarks at Great Faith International Ministries in Detroit, MI. In G. Peters & J. T. Woolley (Eds.), *The American Presidency Project*. Retrieved from http://www.presidency.ucsb.edu/ws/?pid=119199

Trump, D. J. (2016e, September 6). Remarks at a rally at the Greenville Convention Center in Greenville, NC. In G. Peters & J. T. Woolley (Eds.), *The American Presidency Project*. Retrieved from http://www.presidency.ucsb.edu/ws/?pid=119197

Trump, D. J. (2016f, September 9). Remarks to the 11th annual Values Voter Summit in Washington, D.C. In G. Peters & J. T. Woolley (Eds.), *The American Presidency Project*. Retrieved from http://www.presidency.ucsb.edu/ws/?pid=119194

Trump, D. J. (2016g, September 16). Remarks at a rally at the James L. Knight Center in Miami, FL. In G. Peters & J. T. Woolley (Eds.), *The American Presidency Project*. Retrieved from http://www.presidency.ucsb.edu/ws/?pid=119208

Trump, D. J. (2016h, October 12). Remarks at the Southeastern Livestock Pavilion in Ocala, FL. In G. Peters & J. T. Woolley (Eds.), *The American Presidency Project*. Retrieved from http://www.presidency.ucsb.edu/ws/?pid=123517

Late Night with Donald Trump: An Exploration of the Combined Effects of Political Comedy and Political Advertising

Freddie J. Jennings, Calvin R. Coker, Josh C. Bramlett, Joel Lansing Reed, and Joshua P. Bolton

Over the course of the 2016 campaign, it became fashionable to decry the deeply depraved state of American political discourse. In a speech in Springfield, Illinois, on February 10, 2016, President Obama declared that American democracy was "threatened by a poisonous political climate that pushes people away from participating in public life. It turns folks off. It discourages them and makes them cynical" (Nakamura & Jaffe, 2016, para. 2). In a rare display of agreement with then-president Obama, Speaker of the House Paul Ryan (R-WI) lamented in a speech on March 23, 2016, that "our political discourse— both the kind we see on TV and the kind we experience among each other— did not use to be this bad and it does not have to be this way" (Ryan, 2016, para. 4). This common complaint about the state of democratic discourse is not limited to politicians. Georgetown philosophy professor Karen Stohr (2017, para. 2) wrote in an editorial for *The New York Times*, "Gone are the days when contempt for political rivals and their supporters was mostly communicated behind closed doors, in low tones not meant to be overheard." These sentiments are just a small sampling of the growing belief among political and media elites that American democracy is in trouble, in large part because of the types of political messages being circulated.

It would be easy to think of this collective rhetorical panic as hyperbolic, a feature of editorial pages that occurs on cue once every four years when a particularly nasty exchange occurs between candidates. But this concern may be more of a reality than an exaggeration in light of the wealth of communication research concerning the role of negativity and cynicism in American politics (see, for example, Ansolabehere & Iyengar, 1995 and Schenck-Hamlin, Procter, & Rumsey, 2000). Scholars of political communication suggest that two likely culprits for the cursing of democratic culture are political ads and the proliferation of political comedy. Political ads have become increasingly negative in tone (e.g., Benoit, 2014). Similarly, political comedy may foster a form of nihilism and cynicism in viewers that is antithetical to democracy (Hart & Hartelius, 2007). Existing empirical evidence concerning political ads and political comedy does not, however, support the prevailing public narrative concerning the threat negative discourse poses to democracy.

As such, we propose that empirical support for normatively negative democratic effects may be overstated. To substantiate this claim, we have designed an experiment with specific consideration for how ads and comedy are consumed in a more naturalistic environment. The design of our stimuli afforded us significant control without a corresponding sacrifice of ecological validity, thus empowering a conclusion rebutting, in part, the widespread panic over the state of political discourse. Our limited results, when set against the broader landscape of effects research on political ads and political comedy, imply claims of the extreme negative consequences of political ads and satire may warrant reconsideration.

In the following chapter, we suggest that there are, at most, modest normative effects for political ads and political comedy when those messages are presented in an information-rich environment designed to simulate real-life media consumption. We make the case that both political ads and political comedy may foster the normatively positive outcome of *ingroup skepticism* (Muirhead, 2014). Ultimately, we conclude with cautious optimism about the influence of political ads and comedy in a highly saturated political environment.

The chapter proceeds in three parts. First, the theoretical groundwork of the study is developed with specific focus on the normatively undesirable effects of political ads and political comedy. Second, the methodological choices of the experiment will be explained and results reported. Finally, the results will be discussed alongside arguments calling for temperance in the interpretation of political messaging.

Normative Effects of Political Ads

It is nearly impossible to avoid political ads, as ads are seen by television viewers regardless of their candidate preferences or partisan affiliation (Kaid, Fernandes, & Painter, 2011). Indeed, political ads are the primary way that political candidates communicate with the electorate, and they are designed to persuade voters and win elections (Goldstein & Ridout, 2004). As such, numerous empirical studies and meta-analyses have highlighted the persuasive effects of political ads (e.g., Ansolabehere & Iyengar, 1995; Atkin & Heald, 1976; Benoit, Leshner, & Chattopadhyay, 2007; Lau, Sigelman, & Rovner, 2007). However, political ads have effects that extend beyond one candidate or one election. They play an important role in shaping the political opinions of the American electorate and have normatively positive democratic outcomes, such as increasing voter turnout (Panagopoulos & Green, 2011) and influencing political knowledge (Benoit et al., 2007). These normative outcomes can influence the political temperament of a nation by changing the way citizens view the government, politicians, and even each other. Though normatively positive outcomes have been documented, there exists the possibility that the tone, frequency, and content of political ads could deter turnout or voter engagement (see, for a summary of this argument, Lau et al., 2007). As such, some have cautioned against the possible nefarious influence of political ads in the American political process (e.g., McGinnis, 1969; West, 1997).

Despite some normatively positive democratic outcomes, limited evidence suggests that ads create a less trusting and more cynical electorate (Schenck-Hamlin et al., 2000). In two experiments, Schenck-Hamlin and colleagues (2000) found that individuals respond more cynically about the government after watching negative political ads. Candidate-themed ads in particular eroded political trust among viewers and fostered a more cynical political climate (Schenck-Hamlin et al., 2000). This may be a result of the tendency for political ads to employ a tragic frame when discussing the political opposition (Kaylor, 2008). The language of the tragic frame, based on Kenneth Burke's (1984) work in *Attitudes Toward History,* is characteristic of appeals where an individual envisions an opposing actor as a "villain," irredeemable and intrinsically wrong (p. iii). As a tragic frame precludes the possibility of understanding and embracing the target of criticism, tragic frames in ads could foster a decreased tolerance of the political other and a generally negative attitude towards those with opposed political views.

There is some evidence that political ads increase polarization between members of the two political parties (Ansolabehere & Iyengar, 1995; Atkin & Heald, 1976). It is insufficient, Iyengar, Sood, and Lelkes (2012) argue, to think of polarization as simply an elite phenomenon or as the crystallization of distinct ideological platforms. Rather, polarization includes negative feelings towards the political outgroup, a construct commonly referred to as affect polarization. Affect polarization is not only significant, but growing (Haidt & Hetherington 2012; Iyengar et al., 2012). This animosity is not trivial or inconsequential; Iyengar and Westwood (2015) demonstrate that partisan individuals engage in "discrimination against the outgroup . . . based more on outgroup animus than ingroup favoritism" (p. 691). This discrimination may be exacerbated by a proliferation of negative political messages, specifically in the form of political ads (Benoit, 2014). We therefore make the following hypothesis:

H1: Exposure to negative political ads will a) foster affect polarization, b) diminish democratic trust, and c) increase attribution of malevolence.

Normative Effects of Political Comedy

Political ads exist alongside myriad political messages during a campaign, a landscape that now features a number of programs offering a comedic take on contemporary political issues. Though not new, political comedy programs—featuring individuals like Jon Stewart and Stephen Colbert and, more recently, Samantha Bee, John Oliver, Seth Meyers, and Trevor Noah—have entered the media mainstream over the past couple of decades (Jones, 2010). These programs can influence the political beliefs of their viewers regarding candidate evaluation and policy preferences (e.g., Kim & Vishak, 2008; Polk, Young, & Holbert, 2009). Though political comedy may have a positive political influence, it can have undesirable consequences as well. In perhaps the seminal work on the link between political comedy and cynicism, Baumgartner and Morris (2006) found that viewing *The Daily Show* increased cynicism by exposing people to the political "absurd." Additionally, political humor has the capacity to increase viewer cynicism by casting excessive political skepticism as clever and "hip" (Hart, 2013, p. 365). Hart and Hartelius (2007) suggest that political humor can fail to achieve normatively desirable democratic outcomes, with popular thought leaders like Jon Stewart introducing negativity and unreasonable expectations into the polity through their widely viewed television programs.

This cynicism towards political institutions is further complicated by the aforementioned discussion of affective polarization. If the political realm is constructed around a salient us–them dichotomy, political cynicism may be transported from institutions onto the political other. Because partisan affiliations function as social identities for many Americans (Iyengar et al., 2012), we should expect partisans to transfer negative attitudes onto members of the outgroup. Social identities, Tajfel and Turner (1986) explain, are important to an individual's self-concept and self-esteem. If political affiliations are conceived of as social identities, counterattitudinal political messages should threaten an individual's partisan social identification. Threats to an individual's social identity can result in increased identification with and salience in that identity (Branscombe, Ellemers, Spears, & Doosje, 1999), which leads to an increase in ingroup favoritism and outgroup denigration (Tajfel & Turner, 1986). In light of this possible link between political comedy and increased affect, we propose the following hypothesis:

H2: Exposure to political comedy will a) foster affect polarization, b) diminish democratic trust, and c) increase attribution of malevolence.

Multiplicative Effects of Ads and Comedy

Campaigns polarize the electorate as citizens develop stronger preferences for political candidates and parties (Sides & Vavreck, 2013). The amount of political communication, especially in battleground states, increases as an election nears (Goldstein & Ridout, 2004). Neither political ads nor political comedy are viewed in an information vacuum. Instead, they are part of the communicative tapestry in a political information–rich environment. Sides and Vavreck (2013) argue that the influence of any one form of political communication cannot be completely isolated. In other words, political ads help establish the context in which individuals view political comedy, and political comedy helps create the context in which political ads are processed. However, most published studies attempt to isolate the effects of political ads and comedy. Goldstein and Ridout (2004) bemoan the lack of ecological validity found in most studies of political ads and call for a more realistic viewing experience in experimental design. A rare exception, a study conducted by Ansolabehere and Iyengar (1994), embedded political ads into a news program. Similarly, to increase ecological validity, the current study embeds negative political ads into a political comedy segment. Based on the evidence summarized earlier concerning the contextual relationship between different types of political messages, we hypothesize:

H3: Exposure to negative ads embedded in political comedy will a) foster affect polarization, b) diminish democratic trust, and c) increase attribution of malevolence.

Additionally, the influence of negative ads and political comedy may not be uniform across political parties. The influence of party may be twofold: First, there are fundamental differences between the way Republicans and Democrats view the world and process information (Hibbing, Smith, & Alford, 2014; Shook & Fazio, 2009); and, second, individuals process like-minded messages differently than they do ideologically incongruent information (Lodge & Taber, 2000, 2013). As such, individuals are quick to dismiss or develop counterarguments for information that runs opposite their predispositions. On the other hand, like-minded information is accepted with less scrutiny. Because the stimuli (described later) feature both negative ads and political comedy that criticize the Republican presidential candidate, Donald Trump, we expect the effect will be conditional on party. More specifically, individuals who agree with the partisan message (Democrats) will process the information differently than those who find the message counterattitudinal (Republicans).

RQ1: How will the influence of negative ads and political comedy be conditioned by party affiliation?

Method

To investigate the impact of political ads, television commercials sponsored by Hillary Clinton's campaign and Priorities USA, a Super PAC supporting her candidacy, were embedded in the late night talk show *Late Night with Seth Meyers*. Campaign Media Analysis Group 2012 Senate data from the Wesleyan Media Project revealed that talk shows, behind local news programming, were the second most heavily advertised type of televised program. Furthermore, late night talk shows are popular among young adults (Hollander, 2005; Kissel, 2016)—a feature that accommodates our sample. *Late Night with Seth Meyers* was chosen as it leads its time slot among 18- to 49-year-olds for network television (Welch, 2016) and because Meyers is known for his politically oriented "A Closer Look" segments (Sims, 2016). Attack ads were utilized because political ads are most often negative (Devlin, 1993; Kaid, 1994). Finally, anti-Trump and pro-Clinton ads were utilized to create a one-sided information flow to represent not only Democrats' ad advantage in late night talk shows (Ridout, Franz, Goldstein, & Feltus, 2012), but also the Clinton campaign's dramatic outspending on ads over the Trump campaign (Murray, 2016).

Four conditions were created. Each condition featured a constructed episode of *Late Night with Seth Meyers* with three 2-minute commercial breaks. The first condition (*N*=147) contained a generic monologue and a political "Closer Look" segment that included political ads during each commercial break. The second condition (*N*=136) featured a traditional *Late Night* segment with no political content, but each commercial break still included the political ads. A third condition (*N*=143) showed the political *Late Night* segment, but featured only nonpolitical commercial ads. A control condition (*N*=133) featured a late night segment and commercials with no political content. These conditions were constructed using segments from multiple episodes of *Late Night with Seth Meyers*. Other than the political/nonpolitical substitutions described earlier, the experimental conditions contained identical content. Each condition was roughly 26 minutes in length.

Sample and Procedure

A total of 559 participants were recruited from three major universities, two in the Midwest and one in the South. The sample was predominantly female

(*N*=384, 68.8%) and had a mean age of 19.38 (*SD*=1.3). When prompted, 279 (49.9%) said they would support Clinton, 147 (26.3%) supported Trump, 62 (11.1%) would vote for a third-party candidate [Gary Johnson (39), Jill Stein (5), Evan McMullin (4), other (14)]; and 71 (12.7%) would not vote for any candidate. There were 46 (8.2%) strong Democrats; 92 (16.5%) Democrats; 117 (21%) that leaned Democrat; 88 (15.8%) with no partisan preference; 106 (19%) that leaned Republican; 80 (14.3%) Republicans; and 30 (5.4%) strong Republicans. Most participants identified as white, non-Hispanic (*N*=435, 77.8%); other participants identified as black (*N*=43, 7.7%), Asian (*N*=39, 7%), Hispanic (*N*=18, 3.2%), Native American (*N*=1, .2%), or Pacific Islander (*N*=1, .2%); and 22 (3.9%) identified as a race/ethnicity not listed.

Participants were randomly assigned to view one of four manufactured episodes of *Late Night with Seth Meyers*: 1) nonpolitical comedy, nonpolitical ads (control); 2) nonpolitical comedy, political ads; 3) political comedy, nonpolitical ads; and 4) political comedy, political ads. After watching the episode, participants were asked to complete a post-test using Qualtrics online survey software. First, basic demographic data such as age, gender, and party affiliation were collected. After providing demographic data, participants were presented with 101-point feeling thermometers gauging feelings toward both candidates. Additional scales measuring democratic trust and attribution of malevolence were presented.

Measures

Affect Political Polarization

Affect polarization was measured with feeling thermometer scales for Clinton and Trump. Participants were asked to rate a candidate on a scale of 0 to 100 with 0 representing the coolest, least favorable feeling, and 100 representing the warmest, most favorable feeling. The absolute value of the difference between the two candidates created a polarization score (*M*=41.22; *SD*=29.39).

Attribution of Malevolence

A tragic perception of a political candidate indicates that an individual views that politician as ill intentioned and malevolent. Attribution of malevolence measures the degree that an individual believes a candidate is purposely harming the country. Considering the target of the negative ads and political comedy—Republican presidential candidate Trump—participants were asked to respond from 1 (strongly disagree) to 5 (strongly agree) on a Likert scale to five items adapted from Warner and Banwart's (2016) measure of candidate benevolence: "I worry that Donald Trump is deliberately trying to hurt America"; "Donald Trump is knowingly sabotaging the country"; "Donald Trump doesn't care about America"; "I believe Donald Trump genuinely wants what is best for America" (reverse coded); and "I trust Donald Trump to do what he thinks is best for America" (reverse coded). The scale had good reliability ($\alpha=.906$; $M=2.98$; $SD=1.07$).

Democratic Trust

To measure an individual's level of trust of the government, five items, on a 5-point Likert scale, were utilized: "I feel very critical of our political system" (reverse coded); "Whatever its faults may be, the American form of government is still the best for us"; "There is not much about our form of government to be proud of" (reverse coded); "It may be necessary to make some major changes in our form of government in order to solve the problems facing our country" (reverse coded); and "I would rather live under our form of government that any other I can think of" ($\alpha=.667$; $M=2.71$; $SD=.64$).

Results

The hypothesized structural relationships and the moderating role of party were tested utilizing lavaan on the *R* ecosystem (Rosseel, 2012), which allows for both factor and path analysis. The confirmatory factor analysis revealed that the data fit the model well: $\chi^2(32)=86.85$, $p<.001$, CFI$=.977$, TLI$=.967$, RMSEA$=.055$ (.042 -.07), SRMR$=.041$. Three outcome variables (affect polarization, democratic trust, and attribution of malevolence to Trump) were regressed on the three dummy-coded experimental conditions: 1) Clinton- or pro-Clinton PAC–sponsored political ads attacking Republican presidential candidate Trump (political ads); 2) Seth Meyers' comedy episode featuring the political segment, "A Closer Look" (political comedy); and 3) political ads embedded in a political comedy episode featuring Meyers (political ads combined with political comedy). Partisanship was included in the model as a moderator of the effects of the experimental conditions and as an antecedent to the dependent variables. Partisanship was associated with trust in government and attribution of malevolence, but not polarization. In other words, both Republicans and Democrats were similarly polarized. Democrats attributed greater malevolence to Trump and were slightly more distrustful of the government. Partisanship also moderated the effect of the experimental stimuli on the outcome variables; the stimuli affected Democrats differently than Republicans. These conditional effects are discussed alongside the direct effects of each condition. Results are shown in Table 13.1.

The first hypothesis predicted political ads would increase polarization and attribution of malevolence while reducing democratic trust. Tests suggested exposure to anti-Trump ads did not have a noticeable effect on normative outcomes. Therefore, the first hypothesis was not supported. However, when testing for the interaction between party and exposure to negative political

Table 13.1 The Influence of Party, Condition, and the Interaction of Party and Condition on Affect Polarization, Democratic Trust, and Attribution of Malevolence

	Affect Polarization		Democratic Trust		Attribution of Malevolence to Trump	
	B(SE)	β	B(SE)	β	B(SE)	β
Party	-1.2 (1.54)	-.068	-.26 (.07)	-.411***	-.63 (.06)	-.806***
Condition						
Ads	11.63 (8.74)	.173	-.3 (.36)	-.127	-.6 (.33)	-.2
Comedy	18.87 (8.6)	.276*	-.53 (.36)	-.218	-.51 (.32)	-.165
Comedy+Ads	5.99 (8.45)	.09	-.12 (.35)	-.05	-.36 (.31)	-.119
Interaction of Condition and Party						
Ads*Party	-2.91 (2.17)	-.183	.1 (.09)	.184	.19 (.08)	.272*
Comedy*Party	-4.41 (2.1)	-.286*	.18 (.09)	.335*	.2 (.08)	.292**
Combination*Party	-.13 (2.04)	-.009	.07 (.09)	.14	.11 (.08)	.169

Note: * $p<.05$; ** $p<.01$; *** $p<.001$. Positive coefficients for party or interactions with party indicate a stronger effect for Republicans than for Democrats. Conversely, a negative coefficient indicates a stronger effect for Democrats than for Republicans.

ads, results indicate a moderating influence of party on attribution of malevolence to Trump. After watching political ads attacking Trump, Republicans
attributed greater malevolence to the Republican candidate. The effect, however, was isolated to Republicans (see Figure 13.1). In response to the research
question, party did moderate the influence of ads on attribution of malevolence, but not for polarization or democratic trust.

The second hypothesis projected that political comedy would foster polarization, lower trust in the government, and increase attribution of malevolence to Trump. The political comedy program did increase polarization
among the viewers ($\Delta\chi^2(1)=4.73$; LLCI$=.713$; ULCI$=36.023$), but did not
influence democratic trust or attribution of malevolence. The second hypothesis, thus, was partially supported. Additionally, partisanship significantly
interacted with the effects of exposure to political comedy on affect polarization, trust, and attribution of malevolence. Figure 13.2 illustrates the polarizing effect that political comedy had on partisans on both sides of the political
aisle; however, the affect polarization among independents was not influenced.
Political comedy that featured an anti-Trump message decreased trust in the
government significantly among Republicans (see Figure 13.3). Figure 13.4
illustrates an increase in attribution of malevolence to the Republican presidential candidate among Republican viewers but not among Democrats or
independents. For all three outcome variables, party significantly moderated
the influence of political comedy.

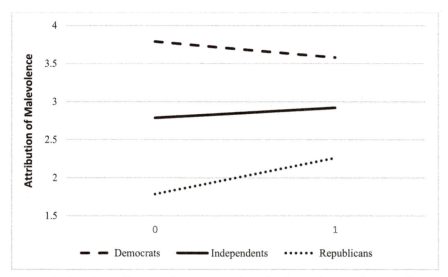

Figure 13.1   The Influence of Negative Political Ads on the Attribution of
Malevolence to the Target Candidate, by Party [*Note:* Graph constructed from
the results of an ordinary least squares (OLS) regression.]

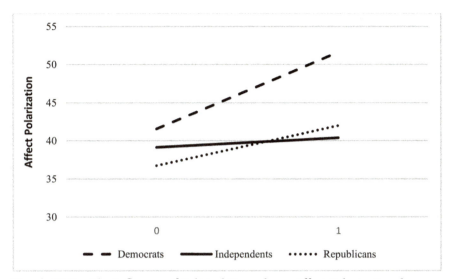

Figure 13.2 The Influence of Political Comedy on Affect Polarization, by Party (*Note:* Graph constructed from the results of an OLS regression.)

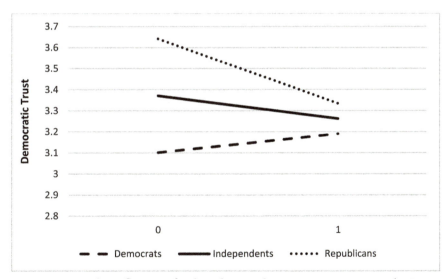

Figure 13.3 The Influence of Political Comedy on Democratic Trust, by Party (*Note:* Graph constructed from the results of an OLS regression.)

The third and final hypothesis projected that the combination of ads and comedy would have a multiplicative effect. The results, however, indicate that this was not the case. The one-sided information flow, featuring both ads and comedy, did not significantly influence any of the three outcome variables.

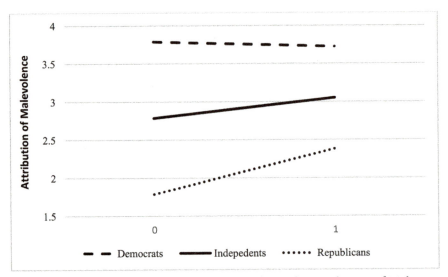

Figure 13.4 The Influence of Political Comedy on the Attribution of Malevolence to the Target Candidate, by Party (*Note:* Graph constructed from the results of an OLS regression.)

The third hypothesis was not supported. Furthermore, there were no conditional effects from party on the combined comedy and ads stimulus. Though separately ads and comedy had marginal, mostly conditional effects, the combination of the two did not influence the normative beliefs of viewers.

Discussion

Our results demonstrate a modest effect of political ads and political comedy on viewers' normative attitudes, and no significant influence was detected when the two forms of political communication were taken together. In what follows, we discuss these results first by contextualizing our observation of minimal effects within the broader conversation about the importance of accounting for nonsignificant findings in published literature (e.g., Levine, 2013). Second we highlight the notable finding that Republican viewers responded to the stimuli with increased skepticism toward Trump. We explain this result as evidence of Muirhead's (2014) theorizing on *ingroup skepticism*. Finally, we conclude with the limitations of our research and future directions for scholarly activity.

As noted in the results section, our experiment yielded marginal effects, some of which reached conventional levels of statistical significance. These results exist contra theoretical and anecdotal expectations regarding both political ads and political comedy. Though arguments like those forwarded by Lau et al. (2007) and Hart and Hartelius (2007) expressing concerns about the undesirable normative consequences of political ads and political comedy have significant purchase in modern scholarship and punditry, our results suggest the need to temper the condemnation of these highly visible forms of political communication. Our results clearly do not (nor can they) disprove the macro-level hypothesis that negative political ads and hyper-critical satire poison our collective political discourse by introducing skepticism, cynicism, and polarization. Our results do point, however, to two meaningful conclusions. First, our results invite the consideration of a "file drawer problem" in political advertising and comedy research wherein researchers have independently produced results that contradict prevailing assumptions, but have not successfully pursued publication as a consequence of long-standing bias in favor of significant results. Second, our explanation performs Levine's (2013) argument regarding the desirability of publishing nonsignificant findings, as the results can be read alongside extant literature to isolate existing knowledge gaps.

The "file drawer problem" manifests when researchers encounter results that fail to reach the appropriate level of significance and are then promptly forgotten. Obviously, many insignificant findings *belong* in the file drawer, in the sense that even a finding that approaches significance does not meet the scientific standards of the political communication community. Not every finding, significant or otherwise, offers a meaningful contribution to political communication scholarship. There is room, however, for a middle ground wherein results that lack significance but invite deeper questions can be published. This middle ground is ignored when reviewers focus exclusively on the publication of significant results. This rejection of insignificant findings is based in a binary thinking that presupposes the total desirability of rejecting the null hypothesis through significance testing (Ferguson & Heene, 2012; Levine, 2013).

In the context of research on political ads research, the literature tells a story of effects primarily focused on vote choice and other persuasive outcomes. Similarly, research on political comedy highlights the effects on knowledge acquisition and persuasion. In the wealth of research on these two vital subjects, however, it is uncommon to find empirical support for our suspicions that these messages result in a host of democratically (un)desirable outcomes such as cynicism and polarization. Despite the dearth of research on normative outcomes of political ads and political comedy, a prevailing narrative persists that casts negative ads and political comedy as controversial and possibly dangerous to democracy. Our results contradict this assessment of these types of messages, as we detect modest effects, if any at all. Furthermore, the more realistic the viewing experience, the less evidence we found of any effects.

Though we do not purport to argue for the null hypothesis that these messages have no effects, we echo Levine's (2013) observation that nonsignificant (ns) results can invite scholars to update unsupported assumptions about large effects:

> Sometimes the lack of a large difference or strong association is interesting. One instance is when an accepted theory or a widely accepted belief suggests big effects. Although an ns finding does not provide evidence of a zero effect, it can provide evidence that an effect is not large. (p. 273)

This study does not eliminate the possibility that political ads or political comedy have normatively undesirable democratic outcomes. However, what our results *do* indicate is that under a controlled condition designed to mimic a naturalistic political information environment, the normative effects of political ads and political comedy on viewers may be minimal, if detectable at all.

Second, though our primary finding is one of minimal effects, we did observe some significant findings with respect to Republicans. Attributing malevolence to the political other could be dangerous for democracy; however, attribution of malevolence to one's own party may be considered reasonable skepticism. It is important to note that it was Republicans (inparty viewers), not Democrats (outparty viewers), that increased in their level of attribution of malevolence to Trump. This result appears consistent with normative theorizing that demands partisanship be coupled with a healthy sense of ingroup skepticism (Muirhead, 2014). A growing body of scholarship rejects the notion of partisanship as inherently negative, pointing to many benefits of parties in their ability to regulate sources of extremism and provide an outlet for political energies that, if improperly applied, could undermine the democratic system (Rosenblum, 2010). Specifically, Muirhead (2014) argues that partisanship may be inevitable, but that the party system offers potential solutions to many of the more virulent ills that plague modern American democracy. However, in order for the system to function, party loyalists must not ignore the faults within their own ranks. Muirhead suggests that

> Party loyalty should not blind people to inconvenient facts and disturbing evidence; it should not generate a "perceptual screen" that filters out all information embarrassing to one's own party, or warrant epistemic closure that makes it impossible to contemplate one's own party's errors and misdeeds. (p. 17)

Republicans' willingness to express greater skepticism about their party's nominee following exposure to political comedy and political ads reveals the capacity for viewers to acknowledge serious errors in judgment. Muirhead (2014) argues that partisanship works when it allows individuals to stand on principle but still demonstrate a willingness to hold their own party account-able. Even if these messages do not change fundamental levels of polariza-tion or evaluation of members of the political outgroup, they may succeed in producing limited desirable democratic outcomes to the extent that they allow for ingroup criticism.

As with all research, our study exhibits limitations to be considered for future research. Though there is evidence to suggest minimal differences between college-age populations and the general public in the context of politi-cal ad effects (Benoit et al., 2007), the use of a student population who is already likely more familiar with political comedy may serve to influence our effect sizes. The use of students in political comedy research is logical, in so far as individuals aged 18 to 25 are the core demographic for political com-edy. Obviously, however, comedic messages exist in a political communica-tion environment consumed by all members of the electorate. As such, future studies should look whether our finding of ingroup skepticism persists in older populations. Our findings here are cautiously optimistic, in the sense that they do not corroborate a broader narrative concerning the democracy-threatening qualities of political ads and political comedy. However, as our findings are set against a backdrop of empirical research corroborating a litany of effects on these different political messages, they imply the need for additional con-sideration of normative democratic outcomes of the most commonplace and inflammatory of political messages.

References

Ansolabehere, S., & Iyengar, S. (1994). Riding the wave and claiming ownership over issues: The joint effects of advertising and news coverage in cam-paigns. *Public Opinion, 58*(3), 335–357. doi: 10.1086/269431

Ansolabehere, S., & Iyengar, S. (1995). *Going negative: How attack ads shrink and polarize the electorate.* New York: Free Press.

Atkin, C. K., & Heald, G. (1976). Effects of political advertising. *Public Opinion Quarterly, 40*(2), 216–228.

Baumgartner, J., & Morris, J. S. (2006). The Daily Show effect: Candidate evalu-ations, efficacy, and American youth. *American Politics Research 34*(3), 341–367. doi: 10.1177/1532673X05280074

Benoit, W. L. (2014). *A functional analysis of political television advertisements.* Lan-ham, MD: Lexington Books.

Benoit, W. L., Leshner, G. M., & Chattopadhyay, S. (2007). A meta-analysis of political advertising. *Human Communication, 10,* 507–522.

Branscombe, N. R., Ellemers, N., Spears, R., & Doosje, B. (1999). The context and content of social identity threat. In N. Ellemers, R. Spears, & B. Doosje (Eds.), *Social identity context, commitment, content* (pp. 35–58). Malden, MA: Blackwell Publishers.

Burke, K. (1984). *Attitudes toward history* (3rd ed.). Berkeley: University of California Press.

Devlin, P. (1993). Contrasts in presidential campaign commercials of 1992. *American Behavioral Scientist, 37*(2), 272–290. doi: 10.1177/0002764293037002015

Ferguson, C. J., & Heene, M. (2012). A vast graveyard of undead theories: Publication bias and psychological sciences aversion to the null. *Perspectives on Psychological Science, 7*, 555–561. doi: 10.1177/1745691612459059

Goldstein, K., & Ridout, T. (2004). Measuring the effects of televised political advertising in the United States. *Annual Review of Political Science, 7*, 205–226. doi: 10.1146/annurev.polisci.7.012003.104820

Haidt, J., & Hetherington, M. J. (2012, September 17). Look how far we've come apart. Campaign Stops Blog - *The New York Times*. Retrieved from https://campaignstops.blogs.nytimes.com/2012/09/17/look-how-far-weve-come-apart/

Hart, R. P. (2013). The rhetoric of political comedy: A tragedy? *International Journal of Communication, 7*, 338–370.

Hart, R. P., & Hartelius, E. J. (2007). The political sins of Jon Stewart. *Critical Studies in Media Communication, 24*(3), 263–272. doi: 10.1080/07393180701520991

Hibbing, J. R., Smith, K. B., & Alford, J. R. (2014). *Predisposed: Liberals, conservatives, and the biology of political difference.* New York: Routledge.

Hollander, B. A. (2005). Late-night learning: Do entertainment programs increase political campaign knowledge for young viewers? *Journal of Broadcast & Electronic Media, 49*(4), 402–415. doi: 10.1207/s15506878jobem4904_3

Iyengar, S., Sood, G., & Lelkes, Y. (2012). Affect, not ideology: A social identity perspective on polarization. *Public Opinion Quarterly, 76*, 405–431. doi: 10.1093/poq/nfs038

Iyengar, S., & Westwood, S. J. (2015). Fear and loathing across party lines: New evidence on group polarization. *American Journal of Political Science, 59*(3), 690–707. doi: 10.1111/ajps.12152

Jones, J. P. (2010). *Entertaining politics: Satiric television and political engagement.* Lanham, MD: Rowman & Littlefield.

Kaid, L. L. (1994). Political advertising in the 1992 campaign. In R. E. Denton, Jr. (Ed.), *The 1992 presidential campaign* (pp. 111–127). Westport, CT: Praeger.

Kaid, L. L., Fernandes, J., & Painter, D. (2011). Effects of political advertising in the 2008 presidential campaign. *American Behavioral Scientist, 55*(4), 437–456. doi: 10.1177/0002764211398071

Kaylor, B. T. (2008). A Burkean poetic frames analysis of the 2004 presidential ads. *Communication Quarterly, 56*(2), 168–183. doi: 10.1080/01463370802026976

Kim, Y. M., & Vishak, J. (2008). Just laugh! You don't need to remember: The effects of entertainment media on political information acquisition and information processing in political judgement. *Journal of Communication, 58*(2), 338–360. doi: 10.1111/j.1460-2466.2008.00388.x

Kissel, R. (2016, March 17). Late-night ratings: Even in repeats, NBC's Fallon and Meyers dominate rivals. *Variety*. Retrieved from http://variety.com/2016/tv/news/late-night-ratings-nbc-fallon-meyers-dominate-even-in-repeats-1201732862/

Late Night with Donald Trump

Lau, R. R., Sigelman, L., & Rovner, I. B. (2007). The effects of negative political campaigns: A meta-analytic reassessment. *The Journal of Politics, 69*(4), 1176–1209. doi: 10.1111/j.11468-2508.2007.00618.x

Levine, T. R. (2013). A defense of publishing nonsignificant (ns) results. *Communication Research Reports, 30*(3), 270–274. doi: 10.1080/08824096.2013.806261

Lodge, M., & Taber, C. S. (2000). Three steps toward a theory of motivated political reasoning. In A. Lupia, M. D. McCubbins, & S. L. Popkin (Eds.), *Elements of reason: Understanding and expanding the limits of political rationality* (pp. 183–213). London: Cambridge University Press.

Lodge, M., & Taber, C. S. (2013). *The rationalizing voter.* New York: Cambridge University Press.

McGinnis, J. (1969). *The selling of the president.* New York: Trident.

Muirhead, R. (2014). *The promise of party in a polarized age.* Cambridge, MA: Harvard University Press.

Murray, M. (2016, June 6). The ad war: Clinton outspends Trump by more than $40 million. *NBC News.* Retrieved from http://www.nbcnews.com/politics/first-read/ad-war-clinton-outspends-trump-more-40-million-n604601

Nakamura, D., & Jaffe, G. (2016, Feb. 10). Frustrated by 2016 tone, Obama warns of "poisonous political climate." *The Washington Post.* Retrieved from https://www.washingtonpost.com/news/post-politics/wp/2016/02/10/frustrated-by-2016-tone-obama-returns-to-political-roots-to-rekindle-hope-of-2008/?utm_term=.2e68a0956f91

Panagopoulos, C., & Green, D. P. (2011). Spanish-language radio advertisements and Latino voter turnout in the 2006 congressional elections: Field experimental evidence. *Political Research Quarterly, 64*(3), 588–599. doi: 10.1177/1065912910367494

Polk, J., Young, D. G., & Holbert, R. L. (2009). Humor complexity and political influence: An elaboration likelihood approach examining The Daily Show with Jon Stewart. *Atlantic Journal of Communication, 17*, 202–219. doi: 10.1080/15456870903210055

Ridout, T., Franz, M. Goldstein, K., & Feltus, W. (2012). Separation by television program: Understanding the targeting of political advertising in presidential elections. *Political Communication, 29*(1), 1–23. doi: 10.1080/10584609.2011.619509

Rosenblum, N. L. (2010). *On the side of the angels: An appreciation of parties and partisanship.* Princeton, NJ: Princeton University Press.

Rosseel, Y. 2012. Lavaan: An R package for structural equation modeling. *Journal of Statistical Software, 48*(2), 1–36. Retrieved from: http://www.jstatsoft.org/v48/i02/

Ryan, P. (2016, March 23). *Speaker Ryan on the state of American politics.* [Transcript]. Retrieved from http://www.speaker.gov/press-release/full-text-speaker-ryan-state-american-politics

Schenck-Hamlin, W., Procter, D., & Rumsey, D. (2000). The influence of negative advertising frames on political cynicism and politician accountability.

Human Communication Research, 26(1), 53–74. doi: 10.1111/j.1468-2958 .2000.tb00749.x

Shook, N. J., & Fazio, R. H. (2009). Political ideology, exploration of novel stimuli, and attitude formation. *Journal of Experimental Social Psychology, 45*(4), 995–998. doi: 10.1016/j.jesp.2009.04.003

Sides, J., & Vavreck, L. (2013). *The gamble: Choice and chance in the 2012 presidential election.* Princeton, NJ: Princeton University Press.

Sims, D. (2016, June 28). Why Seth Meyers can't get enough of Trump. *The Atlantic.* Retrieved from http://www.theatlantic.com/entertainment/archive/2016 /06/how-the-carnival-of-the-2016-election-emboldened-seth-meyers /488981/

Stohr, K. (2017, January 23). Our new age of contempt. *The New York Times.* Retrieved from https://www.nytimes.com/2017/01/23/opinion/our-new -age-of-contempt.html?_r=0

Tajfel, H., & Turner, J. C. (1986). The social identity theory of intergroup behavior. In W. G. Worchel & W. G. Austin (Eds.), *Psychology of intergroup relations* (pp. 7–24). Chicago: Nelson-Hall Publishers.

Warner, B. R., & Banwart, M. C. (2016). A multifactor approach to candidate image. *Communication Studies, 67*(3), 259–279. doi: 10.1080/10510974.2016 .1156005

Welch, A. (2016, May 27). Late-night ratings, May 16–20, 2016: "Late Night with Seth Myers" rises. *TV by the Numbers.* Retrieved from http://tvbythenumbers .zap2it.com/weekly-ratings/late-night-ratings-may-16-20-2016-late-night -with-seth-myers-rises/

Wesleyan Media Project. (2012, October 24). 2012 shatters 2004 and 2008 records for total ads aired. Retrieved from http://mediaproject.wesleyan.edu /releases/2012-shatters-2004-and-2008-records-for-total-ads-aired/

West, D. M. (1997). *Air wars: Television advertising in election campaigns, 1952–1996* (2nd ed.). Washington, D.C.: Congressional Quarterly.

CHAPTER FOURTEEN

Going on Defense: The Unprecedented Use of Defensive Appeals in 2016 U.S. Presidential Debates

Corey B. Davis

Donald Trump: Nobody has more respect for women than I do. Nobody!

[*audience laughter*]

Trump: And frankly, those stories have been largely debunked. And I really want to talk about something different. She mentions this, which is all fiction, all fictionalized, probably or possibly started by her and her sleazy campaign. But I will tell you what isn't fictionalized are her e-mails, where she destroyed 33,000 e-mails criminally, criminally, after getting a subpoena from the United States Congress.

Hillary Clinton: Well, every time Donald is pushed on something which is obviously uncomfortable, like what these women are saying, he immediately goes to denying responsibility. And it's not just about women. He never apologizes or says he's sorry for anything.

Late in the third presidential debate, this exchange represented the climax in a crescendo of vitriol between Hillary Rodham Clinton and Donald J. Trump, spanning three debates in 25 days in the autumn of 2016, in which each sought to convince her or his fellow Americans that she or he should be president. This heated exchange between the two nominees was by no means an isolated skirmish. Rather, the third debate was only the final chapter in a series of presidential debates that will go down, at least to date, as being characterized by unprecedented attacks and defenses, including constant counterattack. Throughout the debates, the two candidates took turns—and sometimes did not wait for their turn, frequently speaking over each other—attacking one another and deflecting the attacks using a variety of defensive strategies.

This chapter focuses on the two candidates' use of such rhetorical defenses. The study begins by providing a review of relevant literature and applied theoretical lenses, followed by a description of the analytical method. Next, applying the Functional Theory of Political Campaign Discourse, the study will examine the extent to which acclaims, attacks, and defenses were used in this series of debates, including historical comparisons to past presidential debates. From there, the study will identify a prominent accusation leveled at each candidate during the debates and provide a rhetorical analysis of the strategies of *apologia* used by Clinton and Trump in response to those attacks. Finally, the discussion will consider the effectiveness of the strategies applied by Clinton and Trump.

Review of Literature

Functional Theory of Political Campaign Discourse

The Functional Theory of Political Campaign Discourse asserts that all campaign discourse serves one of three functions: to attack, acclaim, or defend (Benoit, Pier, & Blaney, 1997). Functional theory has previously been applied to analysis of general and primary TV spots, Web pages, social media posts, convention speeches, talk show appearances, press releases, direct mail advertising, news coverage, and, apropos to the current investigation, political campaign debates (e.g., Benoit, 2000a; Benoit et al., 2007, 2011, 2013, 2014; Benoit & Harthcock, 1999; Benoit, Henson, & Sudbrock, 2011; Benoit, McHale, Hansen, Pier, & McGuire, 2003; Cho & Benoit, 2006). Across all of these message types, in various presidential election years spanning the period of time from 1952–2004, acclaims were most frequent, attacks were less frequent, and use of defenses was a distant third in frequency (Benoit, 2010). The current study reports the frequency of acclaims, attacks, and defenses in the 2016 general presidential debates and provides historical context for interpreting those frequencies.

Political Studies of Image

Regardless of whether they are discussed in the context of acclaims, attacks, or defenses, image and character discourse in political debates are a popular focus of study (e.g., Benoit & Brazeal, 2002; Benoit & Harthcock, 1999; Katz & Feldman, 1962; McKinney & Carlin, 2004; McKinney, Dudash, & Hodgkinson, 2003). Benoit and Harthcock (1999) and Benoit and Brazeal (2002) applied Functional Theory to content analyze the topic of utterances in presidential debates. They found that, in general, debate messages tend to focus more on policy than on character. However, character is certainly not ignored. In the 1960 debates, 22% of utterances concerned character or image (Benoit & Harthcock, 1999). A subsequent study of the 1988 debates found that even more utterances (34%) were character or image focused (Benoit & Brazeal, 2002).

As for the effectiveness of debates in forming image assessments among viewers, there is little dissent. Scholars agree "debate exposure influences viewer perceptions of candidate character or image traits" (McKinney & Carlin, 2004, p. 212) (refer to McKinney and Carlin for a thorough review of image effects of debates). Although this research is important and valuable to understanding the *power* of debates to shape perceptions, this research does not provide analysis of *how* candidates shape perceptions of image, particularly through defensive discourse.

Image Repair Theory

Image repair theory is a subset of the broader study of *apologia*, or speeches of self-defense. Scholars have developed and applied various typologies of strategies for interpreting and better understanding how rhetors use strategies to defend themselves against attacks on their actions or their character (e.g., Benoit, 1995, 2000b; Coombs & Holladay, 2002; Hearit, 1995, 2001; Ware & Linkugel, 1973). Benoit's (1995, 2000b) Theory of Image Restoration/Repair Discourse provides 5 general strategies and 12 substrategies for defending against attacks on one's actions or character. Denial, as a general strategy, offers substrategies of simple denial and shifting the blame. A general strategy of evading responsibility can be employed as provocation, defeasibility, accident, or good intentions. A rhetor can employ the general strategy of reducing offensiveness through substrategies of bolstering, minimization, differentiation, compensation, transcendence, or attack accuser (also referred to as counterattack). Additionally, the general strategy of corrective action can be used to put right what went wrong or to take measures to ensure it will not happen again. Finally, the strategy of mortification can be employed to apologize, accept guilt, and admit wrongdoing (Benoit, 1995). These image repair strategies have been applied to better understand numerous cases of political *apologia* (e.g., Benoit,

2006a, 2006b; Benoit & Henson, 2009; Blaney & Benoit, 2001; Glantz & Davis, 2013; Len-Rios & Benoit, 2004; Liu, 2007).

Debates as Image Repair Discourse

As demonstrated, debates provide an important source of political communication knowledge. Debates also represent a rather unique form of political communication. Recall that in nearly every case, acclaims are most common, followed by attacks, and, in a distant third, defenses (Benoit, 2010). Defenses, in most media, represent a miniscule portion of political discourse. In Benoit's (2010, p. 92) functional analysis of television spots (1952–2004), acceptance addresses (1952–2004), direct mail (1948–2004), and radio spots (1972–1992, 2000), defenses represented, respectively, 1%, 1%, .3%, and 0% of the analyzed message units. Defenses are rarely employed in political campaign communication.

Benoit and Brazeal (2002) suggest three main reasons why defenses are so uncommon in most political discourse:

> First, they can take a candidate off-message to a topic that probably favors the opponent. Defenses may also make a candidate appear weak (on the defensive). Thirdly, if a voter hasn't heard an opponent's attack, defending against that attack will actually inform voters of a candidate's personal weakness. Thus, it is reasonable for acclaims to be most common in campaign rhetoric, followed by attacks, and then, infrequently, by defenses. (p. 228)

Debates, however, represent a significantly different message form when compared to other types of campaign communication. And although defenses are still the least common function of political communication in debates, defenses are significantly more prevalent than in other media. Indeed, across all analyzed primary and general debates from 1948–2004, defenses represented 5% of discourse (Benoit, 2010). In some election cycles, defenses have been even more prominent. Benoit and Brazeal (2002) found that 8% of the message units in the 1988 presidential debates comprised defenses. The 2004 debates saw defenses reach 10%, with defenses accounting for 15% of President George W. Bush's debate discourse. An earlier study by Benoit and Harthcock (1999) found that defenses made up 12% of the discourse in the 1960 presidential debates.

Benoit and Brazeal (2002) speculate that defenses are much more common in debates than in other message forms for two reasons. First, other varieties of political discourse lack the pressure and opportunity to immediately respond to attacks (Benoit & Brazeal, 2002). Second, given that the audience was witness to the attack, a candidate does not risk introducing voters to a negative of which they may be unaware (Benoit & Brazeal, 2002).

When there is no risk of raising the salience of an attack that is already at the forefront, it seems logical that a candidate should respond to an attack on his or her character. In fact, noting the image repair literature's assertion that humans are driven to maintain a positive image, one would expect candidates to repair perceived damage to their images. Indeed, Benoit (2007) analyzed data from 104 different debates, including U.S. general and primary presidential debates, U.S. Senate debates, and debates from non-U.S. campaigns and found that the more often a candidate was attacked in a debate, the more likely that candidate was to employ defensive strategies.

Applying this rationale, Davis (2013) examined Clinton's image repair strategies in a series of 2007 Democratic primary debates, in which she faced attacks for her votes to authorize the war in Iraq. Davis found that Clinton ineffectively used the strategies, employing differentiation to reduce offensiveness, defeasibility to evade responsibility, and qualified mortification in taking responsibility for her vote. Davis and Glantz (2014) performed a similar analysis of the *apologia* employed by then-Senators Joe Biden, Chris Dodd, and John Edwards in attempting to justify or defend those same votes. Although their strategies were also found to be largely ineffectual, Edwards' use of mortification and Biden's use of transcendence were found to be most convincing. Although not examining image repair strategies specifically, McKinney, Davis, and Delbert (2009) examined Clinton's and Obama's use of attack in the 2007–2008 debates, finding that both candidates, but Clinton slightly more so, frequently used counterattack, with both of the Democratic candidates targeting each other and various Republican candidates.

In the case of the 2016 presidential debates, candidates Clinton and Trump both faced image-threatening accusations from moderators, audience questioners, and each other. Having analyzed each candidate's various discursive themes as acclaims, attacks, or defenses across the three debates, the second phase of this study analyzes defenses Clinton and Trump used in response to a prominent attack leveled at each. The next section briefly reviews the method used in both phases (functional analysis and image repair analysis).

Method

Functional Analysis

The sample for this study was the general-election presidential campaign debate discourse of Hillary Clinton and Donald Trump. Over the course of the 2016 U.S. presidential campaign, Clinton and Trump met on the debate stage three times: September 26, 2016, at Hofstra University in Hempstead, New York (a debate that was originally slated for Wright State University in Dayton, Ohio); October 9, 2016, at Washington University in St. Louis, Missouri, and October 19, 2016, at University of Nevada Las Vegas (Commission on Presidential Debates, 2015–2016). Transcripts were obtained for each of the debates. The next step was to break down each transcript into themes, which served as the unit of analysis for the functional analysis portion of this study. A theme is "a single assertion about some subject" (Holsti, 1952, p. 116). If a phrase contained multiple subjects or assertions, it was divided into multiple themes. A code book was then used to code the function of each theme as an acclaim, attack, or defense.

Image Repair Analysis

Ryan (1982) urges rhetorical critics studying *apologia* to always consider both the *kategoria* (attack) and the defense or *apologia* together as a speech set, arguing that one cannot completely understand a defense or its effectiveness without first considering the accusation. Using the data from the functional analysis, the researcher revisited all of the themes coded as defenses, reading for context to determine the attack that prompted each defense. The researcher then determined the accusation/defense speech sets that were at the forefront of the campaign and to which substantial debate time was dedicated.

Findings and Discussion

Results and Historical Discussion of Functional Analysis

Across all three debates and both candidates, acclaims represented 653 (39.4%) out of 1,657 identified themes. Attacks comprised 692 (41.8%) of analyzed themes, and defenses accounted for 312 (18.8%) of the 1,657 analyzed themes. Clinton employed acclaims more frequently than Trump, using 387 (51.3%) of her 754 discursive themes to praise herself, while attacking 260 (34.5%) times and defending herself 107 times (14.2% of her total themes). Trump attacked more often than he acclaimed, employing 432 (47.8%) of his 903 debate appeals to attack Clinton or other targets (Barack Obama, Bill Clinton, congressional Democrats, reporters, etc.), compared to only 266 (29.5%) of themes in which he utilized acclaims. His defenses accounted for 205 (22.7%) of his total appeals. See Table 14.1 for a full summary of the breakdown of acclaims, attacks, and defenses for both candidates across all three debates with historical comparisons, calculated using data from Benoit and Rill's (2013) study of 2008 general election debates.

Although Trump's use of attack was unusually frequent when viewed in comparison to historical trends, he did not eclipse John F. Kennedy's proportion of attacks (48%) in the 1960 debates (Benoit & Harthcock, 1999) or John Kerry's proportion of attacks (54%) in the 2004 debates (Benoit et al., 2007). Trump did, however, use defenses more frequently than any other presidential candidate from 1952–2008. Trump's proportion of defenses, at 22.7%, makes Kennedy's proportion of defenses (14%) (Benoit & Harthcock, 1999)

Table 14.1   Functions of Themes in 2016 General Campaign Debates

	Acclaims	Attacks	Defenses	Total
Clinton				
Debate 1	147 (54.4%)	98 (36.3%)	25 (9.3%)	270
Debate 2	127 (53.1%)	81 (33.9%)	31 (13%)	259
Debate 3	113 (46.1%)	81 (33.1%)	51 (20.8%)	245
Total	387 (51.3%)	260 (34.5%)	107 (14.2%)	754
Trump				
Debate 1	116 (34.1%)	172 (50.6%)	52 (15.3%)	340
Debate 2	82 (28.6%)	142 (49.5%)	63 (21.9%)	287
Debate 3	68 (24.6%)	118 (42.8%)	90 (32.6%)	276
Total	266 (29.5%)	432 (47.8%)	205 (22.7%)	903
Total 2016	653 (39.4%)	692 (41.8%)	312 (18.8%)	1,657
Past Debates (1960–2012)	4,800 (56.7%)	2,958 (35%)	701 (8.3%)	8,459

and George W. Bush's proportion of defenses (15%) (Benoit et al., 2007) look miniscule. Clinton's proportion of defenses (14.2%) in the 2016 debates is more in line with those of Bush and Kennedy, but is still historically high.

Attacks Against the Candidates

Throughout the three debates, Clinton and Trump faced numerous attacks from their counterpart across the stage, from both the moderators and, in the case of the second "town hall–style" debate, citizen questionnaires. These attacks focused on such areas as the candidates' handling of international hot spots like Iran, Iraq, and Syria; international alliances and trade deals; dealings with Russia; domestic issues such as taxation, jobs, and healthcare; rights to abortion and guns; and character-focused accusations that the candidates were unethical or hostile toward each other's supporters (e.g., "basket of deplorables"). But among all of the various *kategoria*, one line of attack directed toward each candidate emerged as the leading form of attack. Trump faced attacks stemming from video that featured him bragging about sexual assault, and Clinton faced accusations that she had illegally stored classified information on a private e-mail server and that, as a result, classified materials had fallen into enemy hands. The subsequent section provides examples of each of these attacks and the image repair strategies the candidates used in their defenses. Table 14.2 summarizes the primary image repair strategies used by both candidates.

Table 14.2   Candidates' Use of Image Repair Strategies

Clinton	Trump
Bolstering	*Bolstering*
Mortification	*Differentiation*
Simple Denial	*Mortification*
	Simple Denial
	Transcendence
	Minimization/Attack Accuser

But Her E-mails: Hillary Clinton's Image Repair

Throughout the debates, and throughout the broader campaign, Clinton repeatedly faced charges regarding her use of a private e-mail server during her service as U.S. secretary of state. For example, during the first debate, moderator Lester Holt referenced an attack Trump had frequently been using on the campaign trail: "He also—he [Trump] also raised the issue of your e-mails. Do you [Clinton] want to respond to that?" In the second debate, moderator Martha Raddatz again brought up the issue:

> And Secretary Clinton, I do want to follow up on e-mails. You've said your handling of your e-mails was a mistake; you've disagreed with FBI Director James Comey calling your handling of classified information "extremely careless." The FBI said there were 110 classified e-mails which were exchanged, eight of which were top secret, and it was possible hostile actors did gain access to those e-mails. You don't call that extremely careless?

And again, in the third debate, Trump announced that Clinton "should never have been allowed to run for the presidency based on what she did with e-mails and so many other things." In replying to these attacks, Clinton used the strategies of mortification, denial, and bolstering.

Mortification

When rhetors employ the strategy of mortification, they apologize, express regret, or admit guilt (Benoit, 1995). Clinton first used mortification in the first debate:

> You know, I made a mistake using private e-mail. And if I had it to do over again, I would, obviously do it differently. But I'm not going to make any excuses. It was a mistake, and I take responsibility for that.

In this response, Clinton uses narrowly focused mortification to admit it was a mistake to use the private e-mail server and regret that she had not handled it differently. She stops short of admitting to any other wrongdoing. In the second debate, Clinton repeated her use of mortification:

> Well, Martha [Raddatz], first let me say, and I said it before but I will repeat it because I want everyone to hear it. That was a mistake, and I take responsibility for using a personal e-mail account. Obviously, if I were to do it over again, I would not. I am not making any excuses; it was a mistake. And I am sorry about that . . .

Clinton again notes that she has previously taken responsibility and continues to take responsibility. She notes once again, as she had in the first debate, that she regrets she did not handle the situation differently, but repeats that she rejects any excuses and admits her mistake.

Simple Denial

Although Clinton admitted to storing e-mails on a private server and that it had been a mistake to do so, she denied other related accusations. Specifically, she denied in the second debate that any of the classified e-mails had ended up in enemy hands:

> After a year-long investigation, there is no evidence that anyone hacked the server I was using, and there is no evidence that anyone can point to at all. Anyone who says otherwise has no basis, that any classified materials ended up in the wrong hands.

Simple denial involves a flat rejection of accusations or evidence to the contrary that implicitly refutes the allegations (Benoit, 1995). Here, Clinton denies that anything bad happened because of how she mishandled the e-mails and flatly rejects the notion that classified information was obtained by the enemy. She provides no evidence that the classified materials are safe, but she denies that anyone has evidence that the secrets are not safe.

In the third debate, Clinton again used simple denial and again invoked the fruitless FBI investigation: "The FBI conducted a year-long investigation into my e-mails. They concluded there was no case." In this version of simple denial, Clinton uses the FBI's dearth of evidence against her to deny that there is a legitimate case against her.

Bolstering

Clinton also used the strategy of bolstering to reduce the offensiveness of the accusations against her. According to Benoit (1995), when a rhetor uses bolstering, she strives to remind the audience of her positive qualities and, by contrast, diminish her negative associations. Clinton only used bolstering in the second debate, but made several such appeals:

> I take classified materials very seriously and always have. When I was on the Senate Armed Services Committee, I was privy to a lot of classified material. Obviously, as Secretary of State I had some of the most important secrets that we possess, such as going after Bin Laden. So I am very committed to taking classified information seriously.

Clinton twice in this excerpt bolsters her serious attitude toward classified files. She further bolsters her credentials and her experience handling classified materials throughout her career in the Senate and in President Obama's Cabinet, even mentioning that she was in on the secret plan to kill Osama Bin Laden. It is her hope that her serious attitude and impressive résumé will overshadow the fact that she improperly stored classified materials and the allegation that those materials were obtained by those hostile to the United States.

Thus, Clinton responded to accusations about her e-mails using the strategies of mortification, simple denial, and bolstering. The analysis now turns to the central accusation leveled against Trump during the debates and the defensive strategies he employed to repair his image.

"Grab Them by the Pussy": Donald Trump's Image Repair

Of all the attacks that Trump faced, at the forefront were allegations of sexism and womanizing, which came to a head three days before the second debate, when *The Washington Post* obtained a 2005 video recording of Trump conversing with Billy Bush, the then-host of the entertainment news television program *Access Hollywood*. In the recording, Trump can be heard making multiple vulgar and demeaning remarks about women. Arguably, the most damning portion of the recording captures Trump seemingly bragging about sexual assault:

> You know I'm automatically attracted to beautiful—I just start kissing them. It's like a magnet. Just kiss. I don't even wait. And when you're a star, they let you do it. You can do anything . . . Grab them by the pussy. You can do anything. (Fahrenthold, 2016)

Although Trump faced attacks about his treatment of women in the first debate, this recorded conversation featured prominently in the second and third debates and brought allegations about Trump's treatment of women to the top of the agenda.

During the first debate, Clinton keyed in on Trump's treatment of women, after Lester Holt had questioned Trump about his September 2016 comment, "I just don't think she [Clinton] has the presidential look." After Trump dodged the question and attempted to change the subject, Clinton directly confronted him:

> This is a man who has called women pigs, slobs and dogs . . . And one of the worst things he said was about a woman in a beauty contest . . . And he called this woman "Miss Piggy." Then he called her "Miss Housekeeping," because she was Latina. Donald, she has a name. Her name is Alicia Machado. And she has become a U.S. citizen, and you can bet she's going to vote this November.

In just the first debate, Clinton's narrative provides a convincing case for Trump's chauvinism. Then came the second debate, three days after the Trump–Billy Bush recording had gone viral. The first question of the second debate came from a voter in the audience and asked if the candidates felt they were acting as positive role models for school children. The initial responses from both candidates were mostly acclaims, describing why they were such good role models. Unsatisfied, moderator Anderson Cooper followed up with Trump:

> We received a lot of questions online, Mr. Trump, about the tape [sic] that was released on Friday, as you can imagine. You called what you said "locker room banter." You described kissing women without consent, grabbing their genitals. That is sexual assault. You bragged that you have sexually assaulted women. Do you understand that?

Ten days later, during the third debate, the controversy was far from over. Moderator Chris Wallace returned to the topic of Trump's treatment of women:

> Mr. Trump, at the last debate, you said your talk about grabbing women was just that, talk, and that you'd never actually done it. And since then, as we all know, nine women have come forward and have said that you either groped them or kissed them without their consent. Why would so many different women from so many different circumstances over so many different years, why would they all in the last couple of weeks make up—you deny this—why would they all make up these stories?

In response to these attacks, Trump employed the image repair strategies of denial, differentiation, mortification, transcendence, minimization/attack accuser, and bolstering.

Denial

Trump frequently used simple denial in response to these attacks. During the first debate, he frequently interrupted Clinton as she was making the case for his sexism: "I never said that . . . I didn't say that . . . Where did you find this? Where did you find this? Where did you find this?" Trump explicitly denies the disparaging quotes about women that Clinton attributed to him. Then, trying to seem incredulous, he repeatedly asks where she got her information, completely questioning its legitimacy, and thus implicitly using simple denial.

Trump again used simple denial in the third debate, responding to Wallace's mention of additional women who had come forward with claims that Trump had groped or kissed them:

> Well, first of all, those stories have been largely debunked. Those people—I don't know those people . . . I would say the only way—because those stories are totally false, I have to say that. And I didn't even apologize to my wife, who's sitting right here, because I didn't do anything. I didn't know any of these—I didn't see these women . . . it was all fiction. It was lies, and it was fiction.

Trump explicitly denies not only that he kissed and groped women without their consent, but denies that he even knows these women. In support of his denial, he makes the argument that the allegations are so bogus, he did not even see the need to apologize to his wife.

Differentiation

Trump employed differentiation as well. In the second debate, Trump sought to redefine the allegations of sexual assault as a lesser offense: "I don't think you understood what was said. This was locker room talk . . . Certainly, I am not proud of it, but it's locker room talk . . . But it's locker room talk, and it's one of those things." Trump repeatedly tries to reframe his comments as boys being boys, or bravado behind the scenes, rather than sexual assault.

Mortification

In the second debate, Trump expressed regret for his choice of words during the recorded conversation:

> I am not proud of it. I apologize to my family; I apologized to the American people. Certainly, I am not proud of it . . . Yes, I am very embarrassed by it . . . I'm not proud of it . . . and certainly I am not proud of it, but that was something that happened . . . I am, absolutely, I apologize for those words.

Trump clearly and repeatedly used mortification in this debate excerpt, expressing regret and shame and apologizing. It should be noted, though, that he is only admitting to the words; he still flatly rejects the accusation that he was bragging about sexual assault.

Transcendence

When a rhetor tries to place accusations against himself in the context of broader, greater concerns, he is attempting to reduce the offensiveness of the allegation through transcendence (Benoit, 1995). Trump attempted transcendence in the second debate:

> But this is locker room talk. You know, when we have a world where you have ISIS chopping off heads, where you have them, frankly, drowning people in steel cages, where you have wars and horrible, horrible sights all over and you have so many bad things happening, this is like medieval times. We haven't seen anything like this . . . We need to get on to much more important and bigger things.

Trump uses transcendence to put the allegations against him in context, arguing that, in comparison to terrorist threats like ISIS, what he said in a private conversation in 2005 should not be the concern of the campaign.

Transcendence also functions as an attempt to change the subject. Trump again used transcendence in the third debate when responding to allegations that he had targeted at least nine other women with unwanted kissing and groping:

> And I really want to talk about something slightly different [Clinton's e-mails] . . . That's really what you should be talking about, not fiction, where somebody wants fame or where they come out of her crooked campaign.

In this excerpt, Trump explicitly asked to change the subject to one that he considered more important, that of Clinton's private e-mail server.

Attack Accuser and Minimization

Attack accuser and minimization are both substrategies of the general image repair strategy of reducing offensiveness. Attack accuser or counterattack represents an attempt to rhetorically turn the tables on one's accuser, questioning their credibility or the choices they make (Benoit, 1995). Minimization seeks to reduce the perceived offensiveness of an allegation by pointing out that it could have been worse (Benoit, 1995). Trump used a combination of counterattack and minimization, arguing that the accusations against him were not nearly as offensive as the transgressions of Hillary Clinton and her husband, former President Bill Clinton. In response to Clinton's attacks on Trump and Clinton's acclaims about her leadership ability, the Republican nominee claimed:

> It's just words folks. It's just words. These words I have been hearing for many years. I heard them when they were running for Senate in New York where Hillary was going to bring back jobs to upstate New York and she failed.

In this segment, Trump minimizes Clinton's claims about herself and about Trump, arguing they are just words and not worthy of attention. He goes on to attack her campaign promises. Minutes later, Trump renews his defense, again applying a combination of minimization and attack accuser:

> If you look at Bill Clinton, far worse. Mine are words, and his was action. His words, what he has done to women. There's never been anybody in the history of politics in this nation that has been so abusive to women. Hillary Clinton attacked those women and attacked them viciously, four of them here tonight . . . So don't tell me about words . . . It is things people say, but what President Clinton did, he was impeached . . . And I tell you that when Hillary brings up a point like that and she talks about words that I said 11 years ago, I think it's disgraceful, and I think she should be ashamed of herself, if you want to know the truth.

Trump vacillates between minimization—arguing his words are not as bad as Bill Clinton's words and actions and Hillary Clinton's defense of Bill Clinton—and attack accuser, admonishing Bill Clinton for his sexual affairs and alleged harassment and Hillary Clinton for standing by him, calling her behavior disgraceful.

Bolstering

Trump also attempted to reduce the perceived offensiveness of his words and alleged action by bolstering his respect for women in both the second and third debates. In the second debate, Trump claimed, "I have great respect for women. Nobody has more respect for women than I do . . . But I have respect for women . . . And they have respect for me." He then broadened his claim of respectfulness, "I am a person who has great respect for people, for my family, for the people of this country." Trump tried the respect line again in the third debate, "Nobody has more respect for women than I do. Nobody . . . Nobody has more respect." Through his use of bolstering, Trump is trying to claim that he is a respectful person, especially of women, counter to the picture that has been painted of him.

In summary, Trump used denial, differentiation, mortification, transcendence, a minimization/attack accuser, and bolstering in responding to charges that he had sexually assaulted women and bragged about it. The following sections will provide an assessment of the effectiveness of the strategies employed by Clinton and Trump in response to the selected accusations.

Evaluation of Image Repair Strategies

Effectiveness of Clinton's Strategies

Recall that Clinton used the strategies of mortification, denial, and bolstering in responding to accusations that she had stored classified materials on a private (unsecure) e-mail server. Mortification was well conceived, as generally, audiences like to hear an apology and admission of guilt. However, for mortification to be effective, the audience must believe the remorse is genuine. Ultimately, the ongoing FBI investigation likely undermined any perception that Clinton was being forthright with voters. Similarly, it is quite likely that the uncertainty caused by the investigation would have made it particularly hard for voters to buy into Clinton's use of denial. Bolstering was also not likely to be a convincing strategy, as it is hard to see the good in someone if you think she is lying to you.

Effectiveness of Trump's Strategies

Trump used simple denial, differentiation, mortification, transcendence, bolstering, and a merging of minimization and attack accuser in response to criticism surrounding his recorded conversation with Billy Bush and in response to the allegations that the comments made in the conversation represented sexual assault. None of these strategies were used very effectively. Of all strategies employed, his adaptation of denial and mortification were perhaps the least bad. Trump's use of denial was limited to the accusations that he was sexist and the accusations that he had kissed and groped additional women without consent. Clearly, he made the right decision in not denying he had made the comments in the recording, as such a claim would have been absurd. He was perhaps also wise to repeatedly dodge the questions of whether or not the behavior he described constituted sexual assault. Obviously, had he admitted that he had engaged in the behavior, he would have put his candidacy in even greater jeopardy. However, had he said that he was just joking around, he would have opened himself up to accusations that he thought sexual assault was something to laugh about. He used mortification somewhat effectively in that he did apologize and said that he was embarrassed. However, his use of differentiation suggests that he may have been unsure what he was apologizing for.

Trump argued, through differentiation, that his remarks were not lewd brags about sexual assault but rather "locker room talk." Immediately refuting this defense were numerous athletes from college to the pros (Blau, 2016), and even shock jock Howard Stern (Taintor, 2016), who rejected Trump's characterization of his comments as locker room talk. To return to mortification, was he then apologizing for using locker room talk in public, rather than apologizing for the actual sentiment?

Attack accuser had the potential to be effective, had he simply attacked accusers on another topic. However, his coupling of that strategy with minimization undercut both strategies. His use of minimization sought to argue that his alleged abuse of women paled in comparison to the alleged abuse by Bill Clinton. In making this argument though, that Bill Clinton was "way worse," there is a suggestion that Trump did do something at least somewhat tawdry himself. It was particularly inappropriate for Trump to attack Hillary Clinton for standing by Bill Clinton when he clearly expected his wife to stand by him through these claims, even though Trump declared that he had not apologized to Melania Trump "because those stories [about himself] are all totally false."

Although bolstering could have potentially been an effective strategy had Trump provided concrete examples of how he is respectful to women, his mere claim that "Nobody has more respect for women than I do," was so absurd that the debate audience in the auditorium erupted in laughter during the third debate. In sum, none of Trump's image repair strategies were very effective in responding to attacks that stemmed from the conversation with Billy Bush.

Post-Debate Opinion Polling

In addition to an examination of the internal logic and consistency of the various strategies, post-debate polling data can offer a glimpse into the effectiveness of the two candidates' respective image repair strategies. Immediately following each of the three 2016 presidential debates, CNN/ORC conducted a poll of voters who watched the debate, and in all three debate polls, Clinton was declared the winner (62%–27%, 57%–34%, and 52%–39%) (Agiesta, 2016a, 2016b, 2016c). The poll results also suggest that during the first debate, Trump failed to discount Clinton's attacks on the whole, whereas Clinton was able to fend off more of Trump's attacks in the aggregate, as "67% of viewers said Clinton's critiques of Trump were fair," but only 51% said Trump's attacks on Clinton were fair (Agiesta, 2016a, p. 2).

In the CNN/ORC poll following the second debate, pollsters specifically asked respondents if they thought Trump's recorded conversation represented his general views about women. Fifty-nine percent said the remarks were representative, and 37% said they were not representative (Agiesta, 2016b). Directly related to Trump's debate defense against this accusation, 58% of respondents said Trump's handling of the video in the debate had no effect on their view of him; 25% said Trump's debate explanation caused them to view him less favorably. Only 16% said his defense improved their view of him, a finding that seems to suggest his debate image repair on this topic was mostly ineffective. In the third CNN/ORC poll neither Clinton (46%) nor Trump (47%) was viewed as sincere or authentic (Agiesta, 2016c) by a majority of respondents. Depending on one's perspective, defenses such as bolstering and mortification were failing with a majority of viewers, or, conversely, the use of attack and counterattack was especially effective.

Implications and Future Directions

None of the strategies really stand out as highly effective. Certainly, a candidate who wins the debates but loses the electoral vote cannot be held up as an image repair success story. Ultimately, although polls of debate viewers can be useful in getting instant results for spin room fodder, they do not predict winners of elections. Conversely, Trump's somewhat effective use of denial and mortification can hardly be heralded as winning strategies when he failed to win the popular vote. Hence, although actual election results merit consideration in determination of effectiveness, Trump's image repair debate performances were hardly worthy of adoration.

Perhaps the clearest takeaway is that debates do not happen in a vacuum. They are but one sampling of campaign discourse, and although illustrative, must be considered in the broader context of other campaign events. Ultimately, although Clinton may have outdueled Trump on the debate stages, allegations about her e-mails were not confined to three autumn evenings in 2016. Clinton not only had to respond to attacks from Trump and his fellow Republicans, but also had to adapt her image repair to shifting rulings from FBI Director James Comey and the fallout from his evolving (and devolving) investigation, which drug on from July 2015 to just three days before the election (Goldman, Lichtblau, & Apuzzo, 2017). Politicians and campaign operatives would be wise to realize that a vindicating debate performance, although potentially catalytic, must be part of a cohesive messaging strategy.

Future studies could dive deeper into this set of debates and examine other prominent rhetorical defenses, such as Clinton's response to the fallout from her "basket of deplorables" comment or Trump's defense against accusations that he was cozy with Russia and Russian President Vladimir Putin. Further, following from the implication earlier, as most attacks and defenses extend beyond the debates, future research might also compare candidates' *apologia* on and off the debate stage.

The results of the functional analysis of these debates also merit a closer look. Although this study merely reported the frequency of acclaims, attacks, and defenses in order to set up the image repair analysis, the historic levels of defense and attack should be considered in the context of topic (policy versus character), and the attacks themselves should be further analyzed to consider target of attack.

Conclusion

In the fall of 2016, Trump sought to bury a recording he never knew about, and Clinton was looking to make people forget about e-mails she had already erased. Results of the functional analysis in this study revealed historically low frequencies of acclaims, higher-than-average proportions of attack, and unprecedented levels of defenses. At the forefront of these defenses were Clinton's unimpressive use of mortification, denial, and bolstering in response to accusations that she had illegally stored sensitive government e-mails. That defensive effort was alongside Trump's equally flawed use of denial, differentiation, mortification, transcendence, minimization/attack accuser, and bolstering to respond to allegations surfacing from his disparaging comments about women and his alleged assault of them. Polls may have shown Clinton to be the debate victor, and election results clearly made Trump the big winner, but the uninspiring nature of the discourse suggests that everyone was a loser.

References

Agiesta, J. (2016a, September 27). Post-debate poll: Hillary Clinton takes round one. *CNN.com*. Retrieved from: http://cnn.com/2016/09/27/politics/hillary -clinton-donald-trump-debate-poll/

Agiesta, J. (2016b, October 10). Clinton wins, Trump exceeds expectations, but few move. *CNN.com*. Retrieved from http://cnn.com/2016/10/10/politics /hillary-clinton-donald-trump-debate-cnn-poll/

Agiesta, J. (2016c, October 20). Hillary Clinton wins third presidential debate, according to CNN/ORC poll. *CNN.com*. Retrieved from http://cnn.com/2016 /19/politics/hillary-clinton-wins-third-presidential—debate-according -to-cnn-orc-poll/

Benoit, W. L. (1995). *Accounts, excuses, apologies: A theory of image restoration strategies.* Albany: State University of New York Press.

Benoit, W. L. (2000a). A functional analysis of political advertising across media, 1998. *Communication Studies, 51*(3), 274–295. doi:10.1080/10510970009 388524

Benoit, W. L. (2000b). Another visit to the theory of image restoration strategies. *Communication Quarterly, 48*(1), 40–44. doi:10.1080/01463370009385578

Benoit, W. L. (2006a). Image repair in President Bush's April 2004 news conference. *Public Relations Review, 32*, 137–143. doi:10.1016/j.pubrev.2006.02.025

Benoit, W. L. (2006b). President Bush's image repair effort on *Meet the Press*: The complexities of defeasibility. *Journal of Applied Communication Research, 34*(3), 285–306. doi: 10.1080/00909880600771635

Benoit, W. L. (2007). Determinants of defense in presidential debates. *Communication Research Reports, 24*(4), 319–325. doi:10.1080/08824090701624221

Benoit, W. L. (2010). *Communication in political campaigns.* New York: Peter Lang.

Benoit, W. L., & Brazeal, L. M. (2002). A functional analysis of the 1988 Bush-Dukakis presidential debates. *Argumentation and Advocacy, 38*, 219–233.

Benoit, W. L., Davis, C., Glantz, M., Goode, J. R., Rill, L., & Phillips, A. (2014). News coverage of the 2008 presidential primaries. *Speaker & Gavel, 51*(1), 1–16.

Benoit, W. L., Glantz, M. J., Phillips, A. J., Rill, L. A., Davis, C. B., Henson, J. R., & Sudbrock, L. A. (2011). Staying "on message": Consistency in content of presidential primary campaign messages across media. *American Behavioral Scientist, 20*(10), 1–12. doi:10.1177/0002764211398072

Benoit, W. L., & Harthcock, A. (1999). Functions of the great debates: Acclaims, attacks, and defenses in the 1960 presidential debates. *Communication Monographs, 66*, 341–357. doi:10.1080/03637759909376484

Benoit, W. L., & Henson, J. R. (2009). President Bush's image repair discourse on Hurricane Katrina. *Public Relations Review, 35*, 40–46. doi:10.1016/j .pubrev.2008.09.022

Benoit, W. L., Henson, J. Davis, C., Glantz, M., Phillips, A., & Rill, L. (2013). Stumping on the Internet: 2008 presidential primary candidate campaign webpages. *Human Communication, 16*, 1–12.

Benoit, W. L., Henson, J. R., & Sudbrock, L. A. (2011). A functional analysis of 2008 U.S. presidential primary debates. *Argumentation & Advocacy, 48*(2), 97–110.

Benoit, W. L., McHale, J. P., Hansen, G. J., Pier, P. M., & McGuire, J. P. (2003). *Campaign 2000: A functional analysis of presidential campaign discourse.* Lanham, MD: Rowman & Littlefield.

Benoit, W. L., Pier, P. M., & Blaney, J. R. (1997). A functional approach to televised political spots: Acclaiming, attacking, and defending. *Communication Quarterly, 45*, 1–20.

Benoit, W. L., & Rill, L. A. (2013). A functional analysis of 2008 general election debates. *Argumentation and Advocacy, 50*, 34–46.

Benoit, W. L., Stein, K. A., McHale, J. P., Chattopadhay, S., Verser, R., & Price, S. (2007). *Bush versus Kerry: A functional analysis of campaign 2004.* New York: Peter Lang.

Blaney, J. R., & Benoit, W. L. (2001). *The Clinton scandals and the politics of image restoration.* Westport, CT: Praeger.

Blau, M. (2016, October 10). Not "locker room" talk: Athletes push back against Trump's remark. *CNN.com.* Retrieved from http://www.cnn.com/2016/10 /10/politics/locker-room-talk-athletes-respond-trnd/

Cho, S., & Benoit, W. L. (2006). 2004 Presidential campaign messages: A functional analysis of press releases from President Bush and Senator Kerry. *Public Relations Review, 32*(1), 47–52. doi:10.1016/j.pubrev.2005.11.001

Commission on Presidential Debates announces sites and dates for 2016 general election debates. (2015, September 23; 2016, July 19). Retrieved from http://www.debates.org/index.php?page=news

Coombs, W. T., & Holladay, S. J. (2002). Helping crisis managers protect reputational assets: Initial tests of the situational crisis communication theory. *Management Communication Quarterly, 16*, 165–186. doi:10.1177/08933 1802237233

Davis, C. B. (2013). An inconvenient vote: Hillary Clinton's Iraq war image repair debate strategies and their implications for representative democracy. *Public Relations Review, 39*, 315–319. doi:10.1016/j.pubrev.2013.07.008

Davis, C. B., & Glantz, M. J. (2014). Resurrecting the also-rans: Image repair debate strategies of Democrats who voted to authorize the war in Iraq. *Iowa Journal of Communication, 46*(2), 159–178.

Fahrenthold, D. A. (2016, October 8). Trump recorded having extremely lewd conversation about women in 2005. *The Washington Post*. Retrieved from https://www.washingtonpost.com/politics/trump-recorded-having-extre mely-lewd-conversation-about-women-in-2005/2016/10/07/3b9ce776 -8cb4-11e6-bf8a-3d26847eeed4_story.html?postshare=24914758705271 01&tid=ss_tw&utm_term=.9fb78378a864

Glantz, M. J., & Davis, C. B. (2013). Kategoria and apologia regarding Nikki Haley's European vacation. *The Carolinas Communication Annual, 29*, 50–64.

Goldman, A., Lichtblau, E., & Apuzzo, M. (2017, January 12). Comey letter on Clinton email is subject of Justice Department Inquiry. *The New York Times*. Retrieved from https://www.nytimes.com/2017/01/12/us/politics/james -comey-fbi-inspector-general-hillary-clinton.html?_r=0

Hearit, K. M. (1995). "Mistakes were made": Organizations, apologia and crises of social legitimacy. *Communication Studies, 46*, 1–17. doi:10.1080/10510 979509368435

Hearit, K. M. (2001). Corporate apologia: When an organization speaks in defense of itself. In R. L. Heath (Ed.), *Handbook of public relations* (pp. 501–511). Thousand Oaks, CA: Sage Publications.

Holsti, O. (1952). *Content analysis in communication research*. New York: Free Press.

Katz, E., & Feldman, J. J. (1962). The debates in the light of research: A survey of surveys. In S. Krause (Ed.), *The great debates: Kennedy vs. Nixon, 1960* (pp. 173–223). Bloomington: Indiana University Press.

Len-Rios, M. E., & Benoit, W. L. (2004). Gary Condit's image repair strategies: Determined denial and differentiation. *Public Relations Review, 30*, 95–106. doi:10.1016/j.pubrev.2003.11.009

Liu, B. F. (2007). President Bush's major post-Katrina speeches: Enhancing image repair discourse theory applied to the public sector. *Public Relations Review, 33*, 40–48. doi:10.1016/j.pubrev.2006.11.003

McKinney, M. S., & Carlin, D. B. (2004). Political campaign debates. In L. L. Kaid (Ed.), *Handbook of political communication research* (pp. 203–234). Mahwah, NJ: Lawrence Erlbaum Associates.

McKinney, M. S., Davis, C. B., & Delbert, J. (2009). The first—and last—woman standing: Hillary Rodham Clinton's presidential primary debate performance. In T. F. Sheckels (Ed.), *Cracked but not shattered: Hillary Rodham Clinton's unsuccessful campaign for the presidency* (pp. 125–147). Lanham, MD: Lexington Books.

McKinney, M. S., Dudash, E. A., & Hodgkinson, G. (2003). Viewer reactions to the 2000 presidential debates: Learning issue and image information. In L. L. Kaid, J. C. Tedesco, D. G. Bystrom, & M. M. (Eds.), *The millennium election: Communication in the 2000 campaign* (pp. 43–58). Lanham, MD: Rowman & Littlefield.

Ryan, H. R. (1982). *Kategoria* and *Apologia*: On their rhetorical criticism as a speech set. *Quarterly Journal of Speech, 68*, 254–261. doi:10.1080/00335638209383611

Taintor, D. (2016, October 18). Howard Stern: I've never heard "locker room talk" like Trump's. *NBC News*. Retrieved from http://www.nbcnews.com/card/howard-stern-ive-never-heard-locker-room-talk-trumps-n668456

Ware, B. L., & Linkugel, W. A. (1973). They spoke in defense of themselves: On the generic criticism of apologia. *Quarterly Journal of Speech, 59*(3), 273–283. doi:10.1080/00335637309383176

Gender and Videostyle in 2016: Advertising in Mixed-Gender Races for the U.S. House

Kelly L. Winfrey and James M. Schnoebelen

"I grew up castrating hogs on an Iowa farm, so when I get to Washington I'll know how to cut the pork."

—Ernst, 2014

Few political campaign commercials are as memorable and exemplary of how to combat gender stereotypes as Joni Ernst's television ad in her 2014 campaign to represent Iowa in the U.S. Senate. The ad gained national media coverage and the attention of late night comedians Steven Colbert and Jimmy Fallon. It put Ernst on the map, and she went on to win the Republican primary and general election, becoming the first woman elected to the U.S. Congress from Iowa. The ad also perfectly demonstrates how female candidates often fight gender stereotypes by showing they are strong and can do anything a man can do.

Republican Claudia Tenney tried a similar approach in her 2016 campaign to represent New York's 22nd District in the U.S. House with a television ad titled "Let's Get Moving." The commercial shows her riding a Harley-Davidson and wearing a motorcycle jacket as a guitar riffed in the background and a gruff male voice talked about her qualifications (Tenney, 2016). As these two examples demonstrate, female (and male) candidates use political advertising to address gender stereotypes and convey that they have the necessary qualities to lead.

This chapter builds on decades of research on political campaign advertising, particularly as it relates to gender, by examining the self-presentation styles of candidates in mixed-gender races for the U.S. House of Representatives in 2016. We examine the issues, image characteristics, persuasive strategies, and production techniques in these ads to determine whether female and male candidates used similar or different approaches to appeal to voters.

Previous Research on Political Campaign Advertising on Television

Political campaign advertising has attracted robust scholarly interest for decades (Benoit, 2016; Bystrom, 2006; Bystrom, Banwart, Kaid, & Robertson, 2004; Kahn, 1993; Kaid, Myers, Pipps, & Hunter, 1984; Miller, 2016; Shames, 2003; Windett, 2014). Benoit (2016) has argued that television ads are crucial for politicians as they provide an efficient means for reaching voters en masse, particularly those individuals who do not actively seek out political information. More specifically, he contends, "political campaign messages are a vital component of the democratic process. Voters need to learn about the candidates to participate in the election; they need to hear what the leading candidates have to say" (p. 134).

Numerous studies have indicated that television ads are one of the leading forms of political communication connecting politicians to voters (Kahn, 1993; Winfrey, Warner, & Banwart, 2014). As Bystrom and her colleagues note, "Televised political ads provide an important resource for documenting the communication styles and strategies of political candidates" (2004, p. 29). Television advertising is a particularly important area of study because it reaches a wider audience than individual speeches and debates, particularly in non-presidential elections, and operates outside the filter of the news media. Thus, television advertising provides a means for candidates to carefully construct and deliver their message directly to a large number of voters.

Research spanning decades has demonstrated that political ads are effective in swaying opinions, increasing voter knowledge, and drawing attention to campaigns (Atkin & Heald, 1976; Bystrom, 2006; Kahn & Greer, 1994; Kaid, Fernandez, & Painter, 2011; Shames, 2003; Tedesco & Kaid, 2003; Valentino, Hutchings, & Williams, 2004; Windett, 2014; Winfrey et al., 2014). Political ads create a sense of intimate "pseudointerpersonal" dialogue between candidates and voters, fostering the potential for persuasion (Kaid & Davidson, 1986, p. 185). Indeed, advertisements can offer more than information; they are often created to sway voters emotionally, either by making them fearful or hopeful (Chang & Hitchon, 2004). Additionally, candidates can use ads to target and persuade specific groups of voters by tapping into various group-identification strategies to more effectively connect with key voting blocs (Winfrey et al., 2014).

Gender has been a significant area of study with regard to political advertising's content and effects (Bystrom, 2016; Bystrom et al., 2004; Dinzes, Cozzens, & Manross, 1994). This makes sense because women are drastically underrepresented in government, and political advertising is still the primary means of communication for candidates competing in statewide and federal races. Advertising is one important way that female candidates can talk to voters, which is especially important as women are more often challengers and, thus, attract less attention than their male incumbent opponents (Chang & Hitchon, 2004) attract. Furthermore, as research has found political leadership to more often be associated with masculinity, political ads can help bolster women's claims to leadership traits and positions.

Television advertising can also serve as a counter to gender-based media bias. For example, Johnston and White (1994) argue that a lack of media attention and being taken less seriously have been significant barriers to women seeking elective office. They contend that female candidates can use television advertising to establish themselves as viable and capable. In one of the first examinations of potential gendered differences in political advertising, Kahn (1993) stressed that the news media sometimes disadvantage women by giving them negative coverage that diminishes their electoral chances and, thus, advertising is often necessary to ensure elective success. Put succinctly, Winfrey and her colleagues (2014) note, "differences that persist in the media coverage of female and male candidates for federal and statewide executive and legislative office may mesh with gender biases in the electorate to put women in untenable positions. By reinforcing some of the traditional gender stereotypes held by the public, the media affect the outcomes of elections and, thus, how the nation is governed" (Winfrey et al., p. 251).

Various analyses of gender and the content of campaign advertising have indicated that male and female candidates are similar in many ways (Bystrom, 2003, 2004; Kaid, 2012; Lee, 2014; Miller, 2016; Shames, 2003). Studies examining diverse candidates and races indicate that men and women discuss many of the same issues, often related to the specific electoral environment, and emphasize similar traits (Banwart, Winfrey, & Schnoebelen, 2009; Benze & Declercq, 1985; Bystrom, 1995; Bystrom et al., 2004; Sapiro, Walsh, Strach, & Hennings, 2011; Windett, 2014). Comprehensive analyses of gender and political advertising also have noted that men and women use their political ads to "underscore stereotypical expectations about the role and behaviors of women and men in today's society" (Bystrom, 2016, p. 73).

At the same time, other studies have revealed some notable differences in how women and men use political advertising. Male and female political candidates differ in how they approach negative ad strategies, how "feminine" issues are addressed in their ads, and in nonverbal aspects of their ads (Bystrom, 2016). For example, Kahn's 1993 study found that male and female candidates will sometimes emphasize different issues—with men focusing more on budget and taxes, whereas women emphasized education and healthcare—and that women are more likely to discuss substantive issues rather than character in their negative ads. Kahn's analysis also revealed that men are less likely to use attacks against female opponents for fear of looking like they are "beating up on a woman" (p. 491).

Robertson and Anderson's (2004) analysis of political ads aired by gubernatorial and U.S. Senate candidates in 1998 also revealed several differences between male and female candidates. Specifically, female candidates used peer endorsement, calls for change, and negative ads more than their male counterparts, whereas men (particularly male incumbents) were more likely to use party affiliation, links to particular groups, appeals to traditional values, and the American flag more often in their ads than women did. Although research has found that male and female candidates use negative campaign ads in similar frequency, women are less likely to attack their opponents on personal characteristics and rarely use statements out of context when compared with their male counterparts (Hernson & Lucas, 2006). Researchers also have found that women use credibility appeals more frequently than their male counterparts, who use logical appeals more often (Robertson, Froemling, Wells, & McCraw, 2009).

A comprehensive analysis of campaign advertising used in races for the U.S. House in 2000 and 2002 revealed that women are more likely to emphasize toughness/strength as a trait they possess in their ads (Sapiro et al., 2011). Robertson et al. (2009) found that male candidates tended to stress past performance and success when compared with their female opponents, who emphasized active participation more often. According to Windett (2014), male candidates will often attempt to "bait" their female opponents into discussing female issues and traits as a way to undercut their credibility in the masculine realm of politics. He found that women gubernatorial and U.S. Senate candidates tend to avoid feminine issue ads, at least early on in their campaigns, whereas men will often use them early on. Still, this may not inherently be a weakness for women, as an analysis of young voters' perceptions of female candidates reveals that they are seen as more effective at balancing both stereotypically male and female traits and more effective than men when addressing stereotypically feminine issues (Winfrey et al., 2014).

Advertising on television is valuable to women politicians as it allows them to navigate stereotypical double binds that can hinder their candidacies. These so-called double binds most often negatively affect female candidates for office as they attempt to demonstrate political leadership (a stereotypical masculine idea) while also trying to satisfy the stereotypical beliefs of voters about how women should behave. Women candidates then must try to balance being seen as masculine enough to lead, but feminine enough to be liked. Advertising provides an important means of communicating this complicated message. Gender stereotypes also affect how voters view candidates as people and their ability to handle issues. For example, male candidates are often assumed to have masculine traits such as being assertive and competent, whereas female candidates are often perceived as having more feminine traits such as being cooperative and honest. Similarly, male candidates are often seen as more capable at handling masculine issues such as national security, whereas women are viewed as better at handling compassion (or feminine) issues such as healthcare and education (Huddy & Terkildsen, 1993).

These gender biases can inform how female and male candidates present themselves in their political advertising. Candidates have the opportunity of capitalizing on the traits and issues they are perceived to have or handle well because of their gender. They also have the challenge of demonstrating those traits and abilities they are perceived to lack. Several studies have indicated that stereotypes are commonly used in political ads (Bystrom et al., 2004; Sapiro et al., 2011; Warner, Winfrey, & Banwart, 2011; Windett, 2014). Lee's (2014) experimental design revealed that positive ads are more likely to employ gender stereotypes, whereas negative ads are more likely to stress opposite-sex stereotypes. Banwart's (2000) qualitative analysis of the advertising aired by former U.S. Representative Anne Northup, a Republican from Kentucky, indicates that political ads can be used to overcome negative stereotypes that hinder one's candidacy. Indeed, political advertising provides a unique opportunity for female candidates to carefully craft and control how their image and ability to handle issues are presented.

How female (and male) political candidates overcome gendered double binds has been analyzed in research guided by a concept known as "videostyle." Originally conceived by Kaid and Davidson (1986) in their content analysis of advertising aired in U.S. Senate races in 1982, the term refers to a candidate's presentation of self via political ads composed of verbal messages, nonverbal messages, and production techniques. Miller's (2016) comprehensive analysis of videostyle research suggests that this approach "is uniquely situated to provide guidance for researchers who wish to understand how these three forms of communication may coalesce, work to inform the voting public, and ultimately affect the election outcomes" (p. 151).

Videostyle explains the manner in which political candidates control their message to create cognitive, affective, and behavioral effects among voters (Nesbit, 1988). Analyses composed of varying methods and focused on diverse levels and types of political campaigns have found that male and female candidates may use specific techniques and messages in their ads to reinforce or defy gendered stereotypes that may hinder their candidacies (Banwart et al., 2009; Bystrom, 1995; Bystrom et al., 2004; Nesbit, 1988; Sapiro et al., 2011).

This is particularly important for women political candidates, as news coverage more closely mirrors the agendas of male candidates as compared to those of female candidates (Kahn, 1993).

Bystrom (1995) was the first to posit a female videostyle distinct from a male videostyle in her dissertation research analyzing the campaign ads used in mixed-gender races for the U.S. Senate in the early 1990s. She concluded that female videostyle was characterized by picturing themselves and their opponents, using more language intensifiers, making more eye contact, smiling more, dressing more formally, speaking more often for themselves, appearing head-on in their ads, and using somewhat different production techniques (e.g., more on-screen text and live audio). Male videostyle, though similar in many ways, differed in that men emphasized their trustworthiness more often, looked more serious and attentive in their ads, dressed more casually, used other people to speak on their behalf, used more testimonials, and used a variety of spot lengths in their ads.

One of the most significant studies to date with regard to gender, videostyle, and political advertising focused on television commercials used in mixed-gender races for governor and U.S. Senate between 1990 and 2002 (Bystrom et al., 2004). Their analysis revealed that ads aired by women and men both spoke about key issues (including taxes, the environment, federal budget, defense, international issues, drugs, immigration, and poverty) in much the same ways, used similar appeals and modes of reasoning, attacked their opponents with negative ads, and utilized similar production techniques. They also found that male and female candidates were both likely to emphasize the traits of toughness and strength. However, they found some important gender differences as well. Although male and female candidates addressed similar issues in their ads, men discussed stereotypical masculine issues (taxes, defense, etc.) more often and women discussed stereotypical feminine, or compassion, issues (education, healthcare, women's rights, etc.) more often. Women were more likely to use so-called challenger strategies (including attacking their opponents' records and taking an offensive, rather than defensive, position on issues); speak for themselves in their ads; avoid featuring members of their families; smile more; and wear more professional attire than their male counterparts. Women also were more likely to make gender an issue in their ads, though this was rarely done.

Bystrom (2016) later noted that, taken together, studies examining the videostyles of female and male candidates running for various levels of political office indicate that women and men are increasingly similar in the self-presentation strategies used in their political advertising. Moreover, research applying videostyle to measure gender differences in political ads suggests that the context of the particular races studied, rather than the sex of the candidates, may have a larger role in determining campaign advertising strategies (Banwart et al., 2009; Bystrom, 2016; Sapiro et al., 2011).

Although studies on the content of political ads have found more similarities than differences, especially in recent years, research has consistently found some gender differences in how male and female candidates present themselves in their political advertising. To investigate the role of gender in political advertising during the 2016 election in female vs. male races for the U.S. House of Representatives, we pose the following research questions:

RQ1: Do female and male congressional candidates present similar issue priorities in their campaign ads?

RQ2: Do female and male congressional candidates present similar character traits in their campaign ads?

RQ3: Do female and male congressional candidates employ similar communication strategies in their campaign ads?

RQ4: Do female and male congressional candidates employ similar persuasive appeals in their campaign ads?

RQ5: Do female and male congressional candidates employ similar visual elements in their campaign ads?

Method

This study examines the videostyle of candidates for the U.S. House of Representatives running in competitive mixed-gender races in 2016. Polling data from Real Clear Politics ("Battle for the House," 2016), The Cook Report ("2016 House Race Rating," 2016), and Roll Call ("Roll Call's 2016 Election Guide," 2016) were used to identify the most competitive races between male and female candidates. In all, 42 races were included for analysis. A total of 187 candidate-sponsored advertisements were collected from YouTube and candidate Web sites after Election Day. Twenty percent of the sample was randomly selected to test intercoder reliability, resulting in a sample of 138 advertisements for analysis; 63% of the ads were from female candidates and 37% were from male candidates.

Four coders received two-and-one-half hours of training over the codebook, coding instrument, and procedures for coding; they then practiced coding ads from a previous election cycle. Coders were then given the set of randomly selected ads to test intercoder reliability. Using Holsti's formula, intercoder reliability across all categories was calculated at a strong .93 (North, Holsti, Zaninovich, & Zinnes, 1963). The remaining ads were then randomly divided among the four coders for coding.

Based on previous research (e.g. Bystrom et al., 2004), advertisements were coded for the issues and candidate traits that were mentioned, as well as their communication strategies, nonverbals, persuasive appeals, and visual elements. Specifically, 29 issues were analyzed. These issues were categorized as economic, compassion, military/security, and neutral based on previous research that has found female candidates to discuss compassion issues more frequently, male candidates to discuss military and security issues more frequently, and both sexes to discuss economic and neutral issues in similar frequency. Similarly, 17 traits were analyzed independently, based on whether they are stereotypically viewed as feminine or masculine.

We also analyzed 24 specific communication strategies, such as mentioning personal experience, calling for change, and promoting traditional values. Communication strategies also were examined based on whether previous research identified them as a feminine, masculine, incumbent, or challenger strategy. The communication strategy of making negative attacks was examined for its frequency; attack type (direct attack against opponent, direct attack against another politician, direct attack against another party, general attack against government, indirect attack without mention of a target); purpose (personal characteristics, issue stands, group affiliations, background/qualifications, past performance in office); who made the attack (candidate, known surrogate, anonymous announcer); and the attack strategy (humor, negative association, guilt by association, name-calling).

The types of persuasive appeals used also were examined as part of the candidates' communication strategy. This category of analysis included whether the emphasis of the ad was on issues or image; the type of appeal (logical, emotional, source credibility); the content of the appeal (emphasis on partisanship, issue concern, vague policy preference, specific policy proposal, personal characteristics, linking the candidate with certain demographic groups); and whether the ad was targeted at a specific group (e.g., young voters, women, veterans, senior citizens).

Ads also were coded for nonverbal elements, including whether or not the candidate appeared in the ad, eye contact with the viewer, facial expressions, use of gestures, body movement, use of touch, dress, and use of language intensifiers. Lastly, ads were coded for their visual content, including the setting of the ad (the specific location and whether it was indoors or outdoors) and who was pictured (the candidate, opponent, and specific types of other people such as children and racial minorities).

Results

To answer our five research questions as to the content of the political ads studied, we used descriptive statistics as well as contingency table analysis to test for significant differences. The results of our findings are summarized as follows.

Issues

The first research question asked whether male and female candidates present similar issue priorities in their campaign advertisements. Table 15.1

Table 15.1   Frequency of Issues in Male and Female Advertisements

	Male Candidates	Female Candidates
Military/Security Issues	15.7%	13.8%
National Security/Defense	5.9%	10.3%
Immigration	7.8%	3.4%
International Issues	2%	5.7%
Compassion Issues	41.2%	39.1%
Senior Citizen Issues	15.7%*	5.7%*
Education/Schools	11.8%	14.9%
Health Care	5.9%	8%
Gun Control/Rights	2%	4.6%
Women's Issues (general)	3.9%	8%
Abortion/Choice	3.9%	1.1%
Equal Pay	2%	4.6%
Drugs/Drug Abuse	3.9%	0%
Support for Disabled	2%	2.3%
Poverty/Hunger/Homelessness	0%	2.3%
Economic Issues	31.4%	43.7%
Economy in General	9.8%	16.1%
Jobs	11.8%	19.5%
Taxes	3.9%	10.3%
Federal Budget/Spending	9.3%	3.4%
Trade Deficit	5.9%	2.3%
Minimum Wage	0%	1.1%
Neutral Issues	56.9%	43.7%
Dissatisfaction with Government	25.5%	21.8%
Veteran Benefits/Support	19.6%	14.9%
Infrastructure/Roads/Bridges	7.8%	3.4%
Environment/pollution	3.9%	5.7%
Agriculture/Farming	2%	2.3%
Energy	0%	2.3%
Ethics/Moral Decline	2%	0%

Note: Items in the same row marked with a * are significantly different at $p < .05$. Issues coded for but not mentioned in any ads: crime/prisons, youth violence, and welfare.

displays the frequency with which each issue and issue category were mentioned. The top five most frequently discussed issues by male candidates were (1) dissatisfaction with government, (2) benefits and support for veterans, (3) jobs, (4) education, and (5) the economy. Though in a different order, the top five issues discussed by female candidates were the same; women most frequently discussed (1) dissatisfaction with government, (2) jobs, (3) the economy, (4) benefits and support for veterans, and (5) education.

Some minor differences did emerge when examining the issue categories. Female candidates most frequently discussed economic issues and neutral issues, followed by compassion issues and military/security issues. However, male candidates most frequently discussed neutral issues, followed by compassion issues, then economic issues, and finally military/security issues. Although these differences are noteworthy, there was not a statistically significant difference in the frequency with which male and female candidates mentioned these categories.

Contingency table analysis was used to test whether there was a statistically significant difference in how frequently male and female candidates discussed the individual issues. Senior citizen issues emerged as the only topic discussed at a statistically significant frequency. Counter to previous research, male candidates discussed senior citizen issues significantly more often than did female candidates, $\chi^2(1, N=138)=3.72, p=.05$. Although not reaching the level of statistical significance, it is also noteworthy that women more frequently mentioned the compassion issues of gun control, equal pay, and women's issues in general. Women also more frequently mentioned the economy in general and taxes, whereas male candidates more frequently mentioned the federal budget and trade deficit. In the area of military and security issues, male candidates more frequently discussed immigration, whereas female candidates more often discussed national security and defense.

Traits

Research question two asked whether male and female candidates emphasized similar character traits in their advertisements. Table 15.2 displays the full list of traits and their frequency. The most frequently discussed traits by male candidates were (1) sensitive/ understanding, (2) action oriented, (3) competency, (4) leadership, and (5) trustworthy/honesty and past performance (tied). Women most frequently discussed traits of (1) sensitive/ understanding, (2) toughness/strength, (3) competency and aggressive/fighter (tied), and (4) past performance.

Women and men both mentioned stereotypically masculine traits most frequently. Women discussed stereotypically feminine traits slightly more often than did men. Contingency table analysis revealed no statistically significant differences in the frequency with which men and women discussed individual

Table 15.2   **Frequency of Character Traits in Male and Female Advertisements**

	Male Candidates	Female Candidates
Masculine Traits	80.40%	87.40%
Toughness/Strength	17.6%	32.2%
Competency	25.5%	29.9%
Aggressive/Fighter	17.6%	29.9%
Past Performance	21.6%	26.4%
Action Oriented	33.3%	25.3%
Knowledge/Intelligent	15.7%	23%
Leadership	23.5%	16.1%
Qualified	17.6%	9.2%
Experience in Politics	2%	8%
Feminine Traits	68.60%	71.30%
Sensitive/Understanding	35.3%	44.8%
Of the People	19.6%	21.8%
Trustworthy/Honesty/Integrity	21.6%	19.5%
Washington Outsider	13.7%	13.8%
Cooperation with Others	13.7%	6.9%
Other Traits		
Parent	5.9%	8%
Spouse	3.9%	4.6%
Religious	0%	1.1%

traits. However, previous research makes it noteworthy that women more often discussed the masculine traits of toughness/strength, being aggressive/fighter, and being knowledgeable/intelligent. Also noteworthy is male candidates' greater emphasis on the feminine trait of cooperation with others and the masculine traits of being action oriented, leadership, and being qualified.

Communication Strategies

Research question three asked if men and women candidates use similar communication strategies in their advertising. Our analysis revealed more similarities than differences. The five most frequently used communication strategies by male candidates were (1) above the trenches (47.1%), (2) use of personal tone (37.3%), (3) use of personal experience, (4) calling for change

(35.3%), and (5) emphasizing own accomplishments (31.4%). The top five traits mentioned by women were the same, but in a different order: (1) calling for change (46%), (2) above the trenches (41.4%), (3) emphasizing own accomplishments (36.8%), (4) use of personal tone (31%), and (5) use of personal experience (31%).

Contingency table analysis revealed women (83.9%) used challenger strategies significantly more often than did men (70%), $\chi^2(1, N=138)=3.68$, $p=.05$. Both sexes most frequently used challenger strategies, followed by feminine strategies, incumbent strategies, and then masculine strategies. No statistically significant differences were found in the frequency with which the individual strategies were used by male and female candidates. However, it is noteworthy that women more frequently attacked the personal qualities of their opponents (25.3% of women's ads and 19.6% of men's) and the record of their opponents (14.9% of women's ads and 7.8% of men's). Women also called for change (46% compared to 35.3% of men's ads) and addressed the viewers as peers (17.2% compared to 7.8% of men's ads) considerably more often than men.

Looking specifically at the use of negative attacks (see Table 15.3), women more frequently made attacks than did men. The most frequently used type of attack by both men and women was a direct attack against the opponent. In fact, this was the only type of attack used by male candidates. Contingency table analysis also revealed some statistically significant differences in how men and women used attacks in their campaign advertisements. Women candidates were significantly more likely than men to make the attack themselves, $\chi^2(1, N=138)=3.98$, $p=.05$. However, both sexes most often used an anonymous announcer to make attacks. Women's negative ads also were significantly more likely to attack their opponents' background and qualifications, $\chi^2(1, N=138)=4.62$, $p=.03$. In addition, the negative ads of female candidates more often attacked their opponents' group affiliations and associations (16.1% of women's ads compared to 5.9% of men's ads), though this difference did not reach the level of statistical significance.

Persuasive Appeals

Research question four asked if male and female congressional candidates employed similar persuasive appeals in their campaign advertising. Women (59.3%) and men (51%) most often emphasized image over issues in their campaign ads. Although we found no statistically significant differences in the types or content of appeals, some interesting results emerged. Women (88.5%) and men (84.3%) both most frequently utilized emotional appeals, but women employed source credibility appeals in 80.5% of their ads compared to men's use in 66.7% of ads. Women (41.4%) also made vague policy preference issue appeals slightly more often than men (35.3%) did, and men (21.6%) made specific policy proposal appeals more often than women (13.8%) did.

Table 15.3   Use of Negative Attacks in Male and Female
             Candidate Advertisements

	Male Candidates	Female Candidates
Negative Attack Made	29.4%	39.1%
Attack Type		
Direct Attack Against the Opponent	29.4%	35.6%
Direct Attack Against Another Politician	0%	2.3%
Direct Attack Against Another Party	0%	1.1%
General, Indirect Attack Against Government and Other Parties	0%	4.6%
Indirect/Implicit Attack Without Mention of Target	0%	0%
Who Makes Attack		
Anonymous Announcer	21.6%	18.4%
Candidate	2%*	11.5%*
Known Surrogate	5.9%	10.3%
Purpose of the Attack		
Attack on Personal Characteristics	19.6%	21.8%
Attack on Opponent's Group Affiliations/Associations	5.9%	16.1%
Attack on Background/Qualifications	2%*	12.6%*
Attack on Past Performance in Office	11.8%	10.3%
Attack on Issue Stands/Consistency	13.7%	9.2%
Attack Strategy		
Negative Association	19.6%	33.3%
Guilt by Association	13.7%	14.9%
Use of Humor/Ridicule	9.8%	12.6%
Name-calling	19.6%	9.2%

Note: Items in the same row marked with a * are significantly different at $p < .05$.

Nonverbal and Visual Elements

In response to research question five, our analysis revealed some differences in the nonverbal communication of male and female candidates. First, gender differences emerged in the dominant facial expression of the candidates in their ads. Women (32.2%) were significantly more likely than men (15.7%)

to be smiling, $\chi^2(1, N=138)=4.54$, $p=.03$. Men (70.6%) were significantly more likely than women (54%) to have an attentive or serious facial expression, $\chi^2(1, N=138)=3.68$, $p=.05$. Women (43.6%) also dressed in formal attire more frequently than men (28.9%). Although not rising to the level of statistical significance, this difference of nearly 15% is consistent with previous research. We found no significant gender differences in the use of eye contact, gestures, touch, body movement, or language intensifiers.

Some important gender differences were found in the visual elements of the ads. Men (33.3%) were significantly more often seen in a general inside setting compared to women (17.2%), $\chi^2(1, N=138)=4.67$, $p=.03$, and women (8%) were significantly more often seen in an outdoor campaign event compared to men (0%), $\chi^2(1, N=138)=4.32$, $p=.04$. Also notable was that men (39.2%) were more frequently seen inside a home or family setting compared to women (29.9%), and women (41.4%) were more often seen inside an office or professional setting compared to men (27.5%) and in an outside family setting (women 17.2%, men 7.8%). Although these differences are important, more similarities than differences were found, as the other eight settings examined were statistically similar in their use.

In terms of who was pictured in the advertisement, 23% of women's ads, compared to 13.8% of men's, pictured the candidate, opponent, and other people. On the other hand, 7.8% of men's ads pictured only the candidate, compared to 2.3% of women's ads. Lastly, women's ads more often pictured children who were not the candidates' (31% of women's ads, 19.6% of men's) and ethnic or racial minorities (40.2% of women's and 25.5% of men's).

Discussion

The results of this study indicate stark similarities in how male and female candidates approached their televised advertisements when campaigning for the U.S. House of Representatives in 2016. Indeed, very few statistically significant differences emerged in the ways that men and women constructed their videostyles in these ads. Although surface analysis might point to a sense of gender equality in this finding, more specific scrutiny reveals that gender stereotypes are still alive and well within campaign advertising. At the same time, it is also clear that both men and women are adapting to stereotypical expectations successfully as they construct their videostyles to reach voters effectively.

First, the ads featured in this study demonstrate that women are adapting to gender stereotypes by discussing more conventionally masculine issues. Specifically, women were more than twice as likely to talk about national security/defense issues, topics that previous research has shown are weaknesses for female candidates in terms of voter perception (Huddy & Terkildsen, 1993). Women also discussed the economy (in general) more often than their male opponents did, which is arguably wise given that economic issues continue to dominate the campaign landscape in the United States. At the same time, women also held fast to discussing stereotypically feminine issues such as women's issues generally, and pay equity specifically, almost twice as much as their male opponents. Although none of these differences reached statistical significance, they arguably confirm prior research that indicates women candidates take a gender-adaptive approach to their campaigns that features elements of both masculine and feminine traits, issues, and production techniques (Banwart et al., 2009; Windett, 2014).

Indeed, in the present study, the only significant finding as to the discussion of issues was that male candidates were more than three times as likely to talk about senior citizen issues, a conventionally feminine topic. For example, Rod Blum, the Republican incumbent running in Iowa's First Congressional District, ran several ads that focused on or mentioned senior issues. In his ad titled "Teamwork," Blum emphasizes his support for issues related to senior citizens. He states, "[T]o keep Social Security and Medicare from going bankrupt, I support a bipartisan solution," and goes on to say, "and I voted for the Cures Act to invest in curing awful diseases like Alzheimer's and cancer" (Blum, 2016a). In another ad titled "Seniors," Blum shares how his mother depended on Social Security survivor benefits after his father's death. He says, "[T]hat's why I am such a supporter for making sure that we fix Social Security and Medicare. Our senior citizens have played by the rules their entire life, now the system ought to be there to help them when they retire" (Blum, 2016b).

As our findings demonstrate, Blum was not the only male candidate who focused on the traditionally feminine topic of senior citizens' issues; male candidates discussed this issue almost three times as often as female candidates. This finding suggests that male candidates are also crafting their message to address their perceived gender weaknesses while targeting an important voting demographic (Banwart et al., 2009; Benze & Declercq, 1985; Bystrom, 2016; Miller, 2016; Sapiro et al., 2011; Windett, 2014).

Adaptation to gender stereotypes was also evident in the candidates' presentation of traits. Women candidates frequently emphasized masculine traits they are often perceived to lack (Bystrom, 1995; Bystrom et al., 2004). Specifically, women emphasized the traits of toughness/strength, aggressive/fighter, and knowledge/intelligent more than their male opponents did. Alabama Republican Martha Roby's ad "Every Day" demonstrates her focus on being tough and a fighter when the announcer explains, "[W]hen Washington special interests attacked a conservative farm bill, Martha Roby stood up for Alabama farmers. When congressional leaders pushed a bill with harmful cuts to the military, Martha pushed back and said no. And when the VA failed Alabama veterans, Martha intervened, saw the director fired and got results" (Roby, 2016). The Democratic candidate for Colorado's Sixth Congressional

District, Morgan Carroll, also demonstrates these stereotypically masculine traits in her ad "Stood Up" when what appear to be average citizens testify that she is a fighter. One woman says, "Morgan stood up to big banks and fought for students like me," and another states, "And it was Morgan Carroll that stood up to lobbyists and fought for my family and for our son, Michael" (Carroll, 2016). In fact, women emphasized traits of being strong in 32% of their ads and a fighter in 30%, a rate nearly twice that of men. This strategy demonstrates a clear effort to communicate that these women have the necessary masculine traits to be political leaders.

Likewise, male candidates, wise to the potential perception that they lack positive feminine traits, exhibited cooperation with others in their ads, while also stressing such positive masculine traits as "leadership," being "qualified," and "action oriented." John Delaney, a Democrat from Maryland, explains how he cooperates in his ad "Collaboration": "In Congress I work across party lines from rebuilding roads to creating jobs and to strengthening Social Security. Roll up your sleeves and work with others. That's what my dad did and it's what I'll keep doing in Congress" (Delaney, 2016). Many of the male candidates who mentioned cooperating with others used similar strategies—focusing on teamwork and bipartisanship. Again, this demonstrates male candidates also are using their advertisements to counter the perception that they lack certain gender-linked traits.

Male and female candidates largely relied on similar communication strategies such as staying above the trenches and calling for change, findings that confirm prior research (Benze & Declercq, 1985; Bystrom et al., 2004; Kahn, 1993; Sapiro et al., 2001). Also consistent with this line of research, women more frequently employed challenger strategies such as attacking their male opponents' record and personal qualities while addressing viewers directly and calling for change (Robertson & Anderson, 2004; Robertson et al., 2009). This finding is particularly noteworthy because of the female ads analyzed: 37.9% were from challengers, 37.9% were from incumbents, and 24.1% were from open seat races. In other words, women were using challenger strategies more often, even when they were not challengers. Recall that women were also significantly more likely to be the person issuing the attack in their ads and to attack their male opponents' background and qualifications. This finding confirms Bystrom's (2016) observation that "female candidates may have more latitude than male candidates to make personal attacks because they enter the race with the stereotypical advantage of being considered kinder" (p. 72). This strategy of female congressional candidates was likely wise, given that Dinzes, Cozzens, and Manross (1994) have indicated that viewers of political ads are more likely to vote for opponents who use negative ads in mixed-gender races.

Women and men focused slightly more on image than issues in their 2016 congressional ads and relied most frequently on emotional appeals. However, women used source credibility appeals nearly 15% more frequently than did male candidates, a finding consistent with previous research (Robertson et al., 2009). Women may rely more heavily on this type of appeal as they attempt to overcome bias that characterizes them as less capable and qualified. For example, Democrat Carol Shea-Porter of New Hampshire explains her credibility by sharing a little about her upbringing in one of her ads: "I loved growing up in a big, middle-class family—three generations under one roof. Mom and Dad had small businesses and we all helped. We learned the value of hard work, responsibility, faith, fairness" (Shea-Porter, 2016). Demonstrating one's own credibility by discussing one's own personal or professional background is a commonly used credibility appeal. Women also used source credibility–based appeals by including endorsements from other well-known and credible political figures or organizations, testimonials from constituents, and attacks on the credibility of their opponents.

Analysis of the nonverbal elements of videostyle revealed two statistically significant findings regarding facial expressions: women smiled more in their ads, whereas men looked "attentive/serious." Additional findings that approached significance also revealed that men and women differ in their attire; women were more likely to dress formally, whereas men were more often depicted in casual clothing. These findings support prior research that has found similar outcomes (Bystrom et al., 2004). They also suggest the persistence of gender stereotypical expectations. A female candidate who is both smiling while dressed professionally visually demonstrates the double bind women face. She looks like a leader through her professional dress while maintaining her femininity with a pleasant, smiling facial expression. However, because male candidates are often perceived as already possessing leadership traits due to their gender, they are able to appear in a wider range of attire, and their more serious facial expression is not seen as a violation of their gender role.

The analysis of the production techniques of the advertisements showed only several noteworthy differences that demonstrate attempts to overcome gender stereotypes held by voters. Men were significantly more likely to be shown inside, particularly in a home or family setting, in their campaign ads, perhaps in an attempt to humanize and soften their masculine image. Women, on the other hand, were significantly more likely to be shown at an outside campaign event (e.g., a rally), probably in an attempt to demonstrate their viability as a candidate through a visual show of support.

Women also were marginally more likely to be shown at an outside family setting, showing women outside the feminine space of the home while assuaging concerns about her potential neglect of feminine family concerns. Women also were more likely than their male opponents to be shown inside in factory or industrial settings as well as in office or professional settings, perhaps in an attempt to associate these female candidates with traditionally masculine spaces. Notably, women also were more likely to feature children who were not their own, which shows they are nurturing without reminding voters they may have their own children at home. Women's ads also more often featured ethnic/racial minorities, implying they are supportive of diversity. Taken together, these findings are supported by myriad past analyses of political advertising (Bystrom et al., 2004; Robertson & Anderson, 2004) and emphasize women's stereotypical strengths.

Limitations and Future Research

This study is not without some limitations. First, it focused only on the most competitive mixed-gender races for the U.S. House of Representatives in 2016. Although this provides important insights on races that are more likely to run advertisements and have the funds to hire consultants, it leaves out those congressional races that run ads not necessarily created by strategists and, hence, handle gender stereotypes in different ways. Our study also does not account for television ads ran in mixed-gender races for the U.S. Senate or governor as well as ads from male and female candidates competing in same-gender races. More studies should examine if male candidates facing male opponents use a similar videostyle to those facing a female opponent, and the same for females running against females. It is likely that the role gender plays in an election between two candidates of the same gender will be different than when between two different genders. Traditionally this line of research has been difficult given the limited number of races between two female candidates, but we hope there will be more opportunity for this line of research in the future.

Another limitation of this study and an area for future research is to examine the role of political party, candidate status (incumbent, challenger, and open seat), and electoral context. The size of this sample did not allow for analysis of these subcategories, but a larger sample, perhaps that includes all U.S. House and Senate races, would allow researchers to better understand what role these variables may have in candidates' videostyle. For example, political party has a large influence on issues and issue positions, so it is possible that female Republicans and female Democrats may talk about very different issues or discuss them in different ways. Furthermore, the candidates' status likely influences communication strategies, and the specific election year will influence what issues are most important to voters.

The changing modes for conveying campaign ads serve as both a limitation and another topic for future research. Citizens are increasingly viewing ads in places other than on television. Social media sites such as Twitter, YouTube, and Facebook are increasingly being used as vehicles for these messages rather than television (Bystrom, 2016). In some cases, candidates run the same ads online as they do on television, but it is possible that the delivery method may alter the perception of such ads by their target audience. In many cases, candidates develop ads that run only online and are developed for the specific platform, and this may also change how candidates use videostyle.

As this study demonstrates, gender is still an important component in political advertisements. Women and men use advertising to combat gender stereotypes that may hurt their electoral chances. Women have the particularly daunting challenge of conveying that they are both masculine enough to lead and feminine enough to be socially acceptable. Our study demonstrates that women do this by communicating their ability to handle masculine issues and their possession of masculine leadership traits and by using certain strategies and production techniques. Similarly, male candidates attempt to overcome the perception that they are cold or uncooperative by displaying more feminine traits and discussing compassion issues. In short, this study indicates that men and women generally have a similar videostyle, but close examination reveals that gender still matters.

References

Atkin, C. K., & Heald, G. R. (1976). Effects of political advertising. *Public Opinion Quarterly, 40*(2), 216–228. doi: 10.1086/268289

Banwart, M. C. (2000). Image building strategies in women's campaign messages: A case study of the 1998 Northup congressional campaign. *The Kentucky Journal of Communication, 19*(1), 39–65.

Banwart, M. C., Winfrey, K., & Schnoebelen, J. M. (2009). "It's 3 a.m.": Strategic communication in Hillary Clinton's 2008 presidential primary televised announcements. In T. F. Sheckels (Ed.), *Cracked but not shattered: Hillary Rodham Clinton's unsuccessful campaign for the presidency* (pp. 149–172). Lanham, MD: Lexington.

Battle for the house 2016. (2016). *Real Clear Politics.* Retrieved from http://www.realclearpolitics.com/epolls/2016/house/2016_elections_house_map_test.html

Benoit, W. L. (2016). American political TV spots. In W. L. Benoit (Ed.), *Praeger handbook of political campaigning in the United States: Foundations and campaign media (Volume 1)* (pp. 123–138). Santa Barbara, CA: Praeger.

Benze, J. G., & Declercq, E. R. (1985). Content of television political spot ads for female candidates. *Journalism Quarterly, 62*(2), 278–288. doi: 10.1177/107769908506200208

Blum, R. (2016a). *Teamwork.* Retrieved from https://www.youtube.com/watch?v=nX2dynjzVQM

Blum, R. (2016b). *Seniors.* Retrieved from https://www.youtube.com/watch?v=fTxCMtEDM-4

Bystrom, D. G. (1995). *Candidate gender and the presentation of self: The videostyles of men and women in U.S. senate campaigns* (Unpublished doctoral dissertation, University of Oklahoma).

Bystrom, D. G. (2003). Advertising, web sites, and media coverage: Gender and communication along the campaign trail. In S. J. Carroll, & R. L. Fox (Eds.),

Gender and Elections: Shaping the Future of American Politics (pp. 169–188). New York: Cambridge University Press.

Bystrom, D. G. (2004). Women as political communication sources and audiences. In L. L. Kaid (Ed.), *Handbook of Political Communication Research* (pp. 435–459). Mahwah, NJ: Lawrence Erlbaum Associates, Inc.

Bystrom, D. (2006). Advertising, websites, and media coverage: Gender and communication along the campaign trail. In S. J. Carroll & R. L. Fox (Eds.), *Gender and elections: Shaping the future of American politics* (241–264). New York: Cambridge University Press.

Bystrom, D. G. (2016). American women and political campaigns: Communication between candidates, voters, and the media. In W. L. Benoit (Ed.), *Praeger handbook of political campaigning in the United States: Messaging, voters, and theories (volume 2)* (67–90). Santa Barbara, CA: Praeger.

Bystrom, D. G., Banwart, M. C., Kaid, L. L., & Robertson, T. A. (2004). *Gender and candidate communication: Videostyle, webstyle, newsstyle.* New York: Routledge.

Carroll, M. (2016). *Stood up.* Retrieved from http://www.womenspeecharchive.org /women/profile/political-ad/index.cfm?ProfileID=458&CommercialID =3533

Chang, C., & Hitchon, J. C. B. (2004). When does gender count? Further insights into gender schematic processing of female candidates' political advertisements. *Sex Roles, 51*(3/4), 197–208. doi: 10.1023/B:SERS.0000037763.479 86.c2

Delaney, J. (2016). *Collaboration.* Retrieved from https://www.youtube.com/watch ?v=jNlPZW8lo08

Dinzes, D., Cozzens, M. D., & Manross, G. G. (1994). The role of gender in "attack ads": Revisiting negative political advertising. *Communication Research Reports, 11*(1), 67–75. doi: 10.1080/08824099409359942

Ernst, J. (2014). *Squeal.* Retrieved from http://www.womenspeecharchive.org /women/profile/political-ad/index.cfm?ProfileID=360&CommercialID =145

Hernson, P. S., & Lucas, J. C. (2006). The fairer sex? Gender and negative campaigning in U.S. elections. *American Politics Research, 34*(1), 69–94. doi: 10.1177/1532673X05278038

Huddy, L., & Terkildsen, N. (1993). Gender stereotypes and the perception of male and female candidates. *American Journal of Political Science, 37*(1), 119–147. doi: 10.2307/2111526

Johnston, A., & White, A. B. (1994). Communication styles and female candidates: A study of the political advertising during the 1986 Senate elections. *Journalism Quarterly, 71*(2), 321–329. doi: 10.1177/107769909 407100206

Kahn, K. F. (1993). Gender differences in campaign messages: The political advertisements of men and women candidates for U.S. Senate. *Political Research Quarterly, 46*(3), 481–502. doi: 10.2307/448944

Kahn, K. F., & Greer, J. G. (1994). Creating impressions: An experimental investigation of political advertising on television. *Political Behavior, 16*, 93–112. doi: 10.1007/BF01541644

Kaid, L. L. (2012). Political advertising as political marketing: A retro-forward perspective. *Journal of Political Marketing, 11*(1/2), 29–53. doi: 10.1080 /15377857.2012.642731

Kaid, L. L., & Davidson, J. (1986). Elements of videostyle: Candidate presentation through television advertising. In L. L. Kaid, D. Nimmo, & K. R. Sanders (Eds.), *New perspectives on political advertising* (pp. 184–209). Carbondale: Southern Illinois Press.

Kaid, L. L., Fernandez, J., & Painter, D. (2011). Effects of political advertising in the 2008 presidential campaign. *American Behavioral Scientist, 55*(4), 437–456. doi: 10.1177/0002764211398071

Kaid, L. L., Myers, S. L., Pipps, V., & Hunter, J. (1984). Sex role perceptions and televised political advertising: Comparing male and female candidates. *Women & Politics, 4*(4), 41–53. doi: 10.1300/J014v04n04_04

Lee, Y. (2014). Gender stereotypes as a double-edged sword in political advertising: Persuasion effects of campaign theme and advertising style. *International Journal of Advertising, 33*(2), 203–234. doi: 10.2501/IJA-33-2-203-234

Miller, J. L. (2016). Videostyle in American campaigns. In W. L. Benoit (Ed.), *Praeger handbook of political campaigning in the United States: Foundations and campaign media (volume 1)* (151–169). Santa Barbara, CA: Praeger.

Nesbit, D. D. (1988). *Videostyle in senate campaigns.* Knoxville: University of Tennessee Press.

North, R. C., Holsti, O., Zaninovich, M. G., & Zinnes, D. A. (1963). *Content analysis: A handbook with applications for the study of international crisis.* Evanston, IL: Northwestern University Press.

Robertson, T., & Anderson, M. (2004). Gender and politics: Messages by female candidates in political ads in 1998 senatorial and gubernatorial. *North Dakota Journal of Speech & Theatre, 17,* 1–18.

Robertson, T., Froemling, K., Wells, S., & McCraw, S. (2009). Sex, lies, and videotape: An analysis of gender in campaign advertisements. *Communication Quarterly, 47*(3), 333–341. doi: 10.1080/01463379909385563

Roby, M. (2016). *Every day.* Retrieved from http://www.womenspeecharchive.org /women/profile/political-ad/index.cfm?ProfileID=252&CommercialID =3051

Roll Call's 2016 election guide. (2016). *Roll Call.* Retrieved from http://data.rollcall .com/electionguide

Sapiro, V., Walsh, K. C., Strach, P., & Hennings, V. (2011). Gender, context, and television advertising: A comprehensive analysis of 2000 and 2002 House races. *Political Research Quarterly, 64*(1), 107–119. doi: 10.1177/1065912 909343583

Shames, S. (2003). The "un-candidates": Gender and outsider signals in women's political advertisements. *Women & Politics, 25*(1/2), 115–147. doi: 10.1300/ J014v25n01_05

Shea-Porter, C. (2016). *Vision.* Retrieved from http://www.womenspeecharchive .org/women/profile/ political-ad/index.cfm?ProfileID=326&Commercia lID=3430

Tedesco, J. C., & Kaid, L. L. (2003). Style and effects of the Bush and Gore spots. In L. L. Kaid, J. C. Tedesco, D. G. Bystrom, & M. S. McKinney (Eds.), *The millennium election: Communication in the 2000 campaign* (pp. 5–16). Lanham, MD: Rowman & Littlefield.

Tenney, C. (2016). *Let's get moving.* Retrieved from http://www.womenspeecharchive .org/women/ profile/political-ad/index.cfm?ProfileID=452&Commercia lID=3418

2016 House Race Ratings. (2016). *The Cook Political Report.* Retrieved from http:// cookpolitical.com/house/charts/race-ratings/10160

Valentino, N. A., Hutchings, V. L., & Williams, D. (2004). The impact of political advertising on knowledge, Internet information seeking, and preference. *Journal of Communication, 54*(2), 337–354. doi: 10.1177/0002764211398071

Warner, B. R., Winfrey, K. L., & Banwart, M. C. (2011). Running down ballot: Reactions to female and male candidate messages. In M. S. McKinney & M. C. Banwart (Eds.), *Campaign communication: The 2008 election* (pp. 197–209). New York: Peter Lang.

Windett, J. H. (2014). Gendered campaign strategies in U.S. elections. *American Politics Research, 42*(4), 628–655. doi: 10.1177/1532673X13507101

Winfrey, K. L., Warner, B. R., & Banwart, M. C. (2014). Gender identification and young voters: Predicting candidate evaluations and message effectiveness. *American Behavioral Scientist, 58*(6), 794–809. doi: 10.1177/0002764214 521769

From Interactivity to Incitement: Ubiquitous Communication and Elite Calls for Participation

Joshua M. Scacco, Kevin Coe, and Delaney Harness

On September 19, 2016, Democratic presidential nominee Hillary Clinton rallied supporters at Temple University in Philadelphia, Pennsylvania. Encouraging those in attendance to engage with the campaign, Clinton repeated what had been a familiar refrain in her stump speeches: "[H]ere's how you can join us. Go to iwillvote.com and register today. Register your friends. Register everyone you know. Text 'join,' j-o-i-n, to 47246 right now, or go to hillary-clinton.com and sign up to volunteer" (Clinton, 2016, para. 37). In the lexicon of American political campaigns, Clinton's exhortation was hardly noteworthy. Like many candidates before her, she urged her audience to take immediate action to improve her prospects of success. That Clinton's remark registers as ordinary is due in no small part to its likely participatory outcomes—increased voter registration and turnout—being understood as normatively desirable.

There is also the possibility that a candidate's discourse might contribute to less desirable forms of political action. Consider campaign 2016's eventual winner, Republican presidential nominee Donald Trump. At a November 21,

2015, rally in Birmingham, Alabama, Trump's speech was interrupted by Mercutio Southall Jr., an activist with Black Lives Matter. Trump responded by encouraging his supporters to "Get him [Southall] the hell out of here, will you, please? Get him out of here. Throw him out!" (Johnson & Jordan, 2015, para. 3). Video captured rally attendees pushing and shoving Southall, with one person apparently attempting to choke him. A similar scene unfolded several months later at a Trump campaign event in Louisville, Kentucky; the candidate responded to protesters by calling on his supporters to "Get them out of here" (Hadley, 2017, para. 1). Trump's actions in the latter case sparked a lawsuit, with a federal judge ultimately concluding that the candidate's "words amounted to incitement" (Nwanguma et al., 2017, p. 13).

In each of these cases, elite communication prompts action—but the potential outcomes are dramatically different. These contrasting examples exist on opposite ends of a political participation continuum. On one end are familiar attempts to generate pro-social engagement and campaign interactivity; on the other are comments that might incite anti-social behavior, even violence. Past research on political participation has focused abundant attention on the positive side of this spectrum, highlighting acts from volunteerism to voting as crucial pro-social outcomes (Bennett, 2012; Dalton, 2008; Verba & Nie, 1972). Comparatively little research in this tradition examines the more deleterious forms of political action. Meanwhile, scholars interested in elite rhetoric have long noted the potential for such communication to harness and even provoke the "darker" side of political engagement. Charting the populist currents that often run through the ocean of political discourse in America (e.g., Kazin, 1995) and abroad (e.g., Jagers & Walgrave, 2007), scholars point out that such communication constructs "the people" in opposition to an expansive and threatening political establishment. In some cases, this rhetoric strays into demagoguery, summoning anti-social participatory outcomes (Mercieca, 2015). Noting the seriousness and complexity of such discourse, Roberts-Miller (2005) called for "a renewed interest on the part of rhetoric teachers, theorists, and critics in the topic of demagoguery" (p. 460).

Our chapter enters this conversation with an eye toward spotlighting elite discourse vis-à-vis political and civic participation in its various forms—including those that might be normatively undesirable. We propose a typology that helps clarify the referents and possible outcomes of elite calls for participation. We then offer three brief case studies from the 2016 campaign and its aftermath that highlight the most normatively concerning forms of discourse present in the typology. Campaign 2016 is a useful context in which to engage these issues for two primary reasons. First, as the "rhetorical presidency" has given way to the "ubiquitous presidency" (Scacco & Coe, 2016), presidential candidates have increasingly engaged in accessible, personalized, and pluralistic forms of communication that might facilitate a broader range of calls for political action. Second, Trump urged political action in both subtle and explicit ways that, given the election's results, have potentially lasting implications for American democracy.

Ubiquitous Communication and Elite Calls for Participation

The communicative role of political elites in shaping the beliefs and behaviors of individuals is a perennial topic in American politics. Bryce (1889), in *The American Commonwealth*, saw elites as central to the formation of mass political attitudes. Elite-based conceptions of public opinion permeate the works of other major communication and public opinion theorists as well (e.g., Katz & Lazarsfeld, 1955; Lane & Sears, 1964; Lippmann, 1922; Zaller, 1992). Our interest is in elite communication as an impetus for political and civic participation. Drawing on past research, we conceive of participatory calls as communication designed to induce behaviors that directly or indirectly influence civic life and/or government selection processes and actions (see Verba & Nie, 1972; Zukin, Keeter, Andolina, Jenkins, & Delli Carpini, 2006). In our thinking, such behaviors might be overtly directed toward an intended political outcome (e.g., casting a vote) or might serve a more immediate need while still ultimately having political importance (e.g., trolling a political candidate online). In cases where elite communication contributes to political participation, the communicative inducement is politically motivated, as is the resulting behavior. For example, during presidential campaigns, candidates give strategically located speeches to encourage volunteerism and voting. In a classic case, when Texas billionaire H. Ross Perot announced his presidential candidacy on *Larry King Live* in 1992, he asked the listening audience to help get him on the ballot: "[I]f you're that serious, you register me in 50 states . . ." ("CNN 20," 2000, para. 11). King later remarked about the strong support that Perot's call to action generated: "[P]eople started calling in saying, where do I help Ross Perot, how do I send money in?" ("CNN 20," 2000, para. 15). In what now seems like a foreshadowing of campaign 2016, Perot's populism—including negativity toward the political establishment—was a strong motivator for individuals who called his campaign hotline (McCann, Rapoport, & Stone, 1999).

Importantly, elite calls for participation need not be explicit to be consequential. Scholars since Aristotle have observed the power of the "enthymeme," an argument in which the premise or conclusion is left unsaid but is nonetheless likely to be grasped by the audience (see Bitzer, 1959). Additionally, political "dog whistles"—messages that speak to a specific audience but are subtle enough to fly under the radar of the broader public—are an important part of modern political communication (Albertson, 2015). In a variant of this strategy, politicians sometimes raise an issue in passing but do not engage it directly, allowing them to downplay it later while still potentially benefiting from the results of their "casual" mention. Mercieca (2016), for instance, explained how

Trump regularly employed this rhetorical device—formally called "paralipsis"—during the campaign, such that he benefitted in various ways from a logic along the lines of "I'm not saying, I'm just saying" (para. 4).

Trump's case is especially instructive because his overt and implicit calls for action often took place on Twitter, underscoring the role that digital technologies now play in generating political participation. These technologies allow presidential candidates, and those who ultimately attain the office, to create a ubiquitous persona in a variety of (non)political settings through communication that leverages heightened accessibility, emphasizes personalization, and embraces or challenges America's growing pluralism (Scacco & Coe, 2016, 2017). In political campaigns, this may mean using digital platforms to induce campaign volunteerism, donations, voting, and online interactivity mainly among campaign supporters (Stromer-Galley, 2014). Presidential candidates are able to mobilize individuals through highly personalized digital communication, which is especially appropriate for messaging efforts that are affect driven (Papacharissi, 2015). Moreover, social and digital technologies have been critical tools in the messaging and engagement surrounding populist-tinged movements in the United States and internationally (see Engesser, Ernst, Esser, & Büchel, 2017; Groshek & Engelbert, 2013). Yet, as we will see, the same digital affordances that facilitate pro-social political participation can be employed to incite darker forms as well.

A Typology of Elite Calls for Participation

As a step toward clarifying the spectrum of elite calls for participation, we propose a four-part typology that positions the referents of elite calls for participation (i.e., those targeted in the call and likely to be most affected by the ensuing participation) along two axes. Specifically, political elites can prompt participation directed at *political* or *nonpolitical entities*, and these entities may be composed of *institutions/organizations* or *individuals/informal groups of individuals*. The referent of the communicative appeal also helps predict what types of participatory outcomes might arise.

Table 16.1 presents this typology, and we elaborate below on each of its four quadrants. Although we present the four quadrants as discrete to aid conceptual clarity, in the practice of politics there is naturally some gray area at the margins. Accordingly, our interest is less in drawing absolute distinctions between the four quadrants and more in illustrating the breadth—and different implications—of such discourse.

I: Political institutions/organizations. Political elites often target their participatory appeals at institutions or organizations with clear political ties, such as government agencies, political parties, or news organizations. Due to their established patterns of interaction and structures for behaviors and practices, political institutions (e.g., news media, U.S. Congress) and organizations

Table 16.1   Referents and Possible Outcomes of Elite Calls for Participation

	Political	Nonpolitical
Institutions/ Organizations	*Referents*: Congress, News Media, Interest Groups, Political Parties/Campaigns	*Referents*: Private Companies, Unions, Non-Political Charities
	Possible Outcomes: Volunteerism, Petitioning, Subscription Renewal/ Cancellation	*Possible Outcomes*: Boycotts, Buycotts, Divesture
Individuals (or informal groups of individuals)	*Referents*: Political Candidates, Elected Officials, Lobbyists	*Referents*: Individual Citizens, CEOs, Celebrities, Guests of the White House
	Possible Outcomes: Voting, Donating	*Possible Outcomes*: Bullying, Violence

(e.g., Republican Party, Brady Campaign) wield power and influence in public affairs (Cook, 2005; Giddens, 1984). This power, whether legal/constitutional, social, symbolic, or cultural, may influence not only how political elites shape participatory appeals aimed at these entities, but also the resulting participatory outcomes. Institutional and organizational resources allow for systemic modes of response and protection, such as public relations teams for image preservation or legal representation. The power afforded by resources applies, with some exceptions for smaller or nonprofit organizations, to nonpolitical institutions and organizations in quadrant two of the typology as well.

Political figures praise and critique political institutions and organizations, potentially influencing participatory outcomes. During political campaigns, for example, candidates regularly invoke political parties as objects of praise or scorn (Jarvis, 2005) and attack or thank interest groups who fund and power campaigns. This communicative behavior continues into the Oval Office. One of the more prominent illustrations of this approach offered in the literature is how the president "goes public" (Kernell, 2007) by encouraging citizens to directly pressure Congress into supporting the presidential agenda. For instance, harnessing digital and social platforms, the president can use the weekly address to encourage individuals to contact Congress to push aspects of the president's agenda (Scacco, 2011). Presidents also confront political parties and interest group politics, the latter often scorned for corruption or slowing the legislative process. In his January 2016 remarks on gun violence, then-President Barack Obama pleaded for individuals to confront gun special interests. "So all of us need to demand a Congress brave enough to stand up to the gun lobby's lies. All of us need to demand Governors and legislatures and businesses do their part to make our communities safer" (Obama, 2016, para. 46). National Rifle Association (NRA) president Wayne LaPierre responded with an eight-minute Web video in which he said the NRA would fight the president's executive actions "more aggressively than we have ever challenged anything," an implicit call for participatory support among his members ("Wayne LaPierre," 2016).

II: Nonpolitical institutions/organizations. Political elites often praise or criticize nonpolitical institutions or organizations (e.g., private companies, unions, charities), potentially resulting in more civic-oriented participatory outcomes. This quadrant of elite communication and participation intersects with consumerism, an increasingly common melding in political life. Bennett (2012) argues that "[Consumerism] has become an increasing focus for the less conventional politics of the age, as activists have mounted numerous campaigns to discipline global corporations that they see slipping the net of national regulations" (p. 27). The intersection of politics and consumerism means the resulting participatory outcomes, such as boycotts and buycotts, align closely with other civic behaviors like raising money for charities or attending nonpolitical community meetings (Gil de Zuniga, Copeland, & Bimber, 2014; see also Atkinson, 2015). We may expect that elite participatory discourse aimed at nonpolitical institutions could encourage these civic-focused outcomes.

Generally, contemporary political elites have been appropriately cautious when invoking consumer-based organizations because of federal restrictions on employee product endorsements. Illustrating this strategy of vague consumer appeals coupled with a call to action in his 2006 year-end press conference, then-President George W. Bush noted, "The recent report on retail sales shows a strong beginning to the holiday shopping season . . . And I encourage you all to go shopping more" (Bush, 2006, para. 17). Yet the emerging practice of elite communicative ubiquity means that political candidates and presidents must speak on a variety of subjects in a range of settings (Scacco & Coe, 2016). Presidents and political candidates often point to specific companies as emblematic of American ingenuity and success. Less commonly, presidents call out specific companies as problematic in some way. As president-elect, for example, Trump issued a tweet critical of the cost of Boeing's plan for a new Air Force One—which caused Boeing's stock to temporarily dip 1% (Kilgore, 2016).

Political candidates perhaps feel a bit more freedom than do presidents to offer praise or critique for specific companies. Before the 2016 New York Democratic primary, U.S. Senator Bernie Sanders released a campaign advertisement attacking Goldman Sachs for its practices that "triggered the financial meltdown" (Geier, 2016). Sanders' campaign also made it a common messaging refrain to refer to the influence of big banks in the political process, including Democratic presidential rival Clinton's paid speeches before

Goldman Sachs. In another instance, the Vermont senator tweeted support for Columbia and New York University students protesting the school's lack of divestment from fossil fuel sources: "Let us stand in solidarity with the students at Columbia and NYU for demanding their schools divest from fossil fuels #KeepItInTheGround" (Long, 2016, para. 5).

III: Political individuals. Individuals make easier targets than do institutions/organizations and often do not have the same resources to respond that a larger entity might. Political individuals are an exception. Candidates and political officials often have the support and apparatus of their associated institution or campaign organization, allowing a formal mechanism of response and in some cases protection. When Democratic Congressman Andre Carson from Indianapolis received death threats in December 2015 in part due to anti-Muslim campaign comments attributed to Trump (Carson is a Muslim), the congressman had law enforcement in Indianapolis and Washington, D.C., investigate as well as media outlets report on the threats (Groppe, 2015).

Elites in the political sphere often praise or attack political opponents to boost enthusiasm among campaign supporters or discourage the opposition. Although political incivility, including campaign name-calling that targets individuals or groups, is not new to the American political process (see Jamieson, 1992), digital technologies afford greater opportunity for the spread and targeting of political and nonpolitical individuals (Coe, Kenski, & Rains, 2014). Notably, after failed Republican presidential candidate U.S. Senator Ted Cruz avoided endorsing Trump in a speech at the Republican National Convention—seen as an explicit attack in primetime—Cruz attempted to fundraise off the speech (Savransky, 2016). Once in office, presidents engage in similar tactics to target political individuals. For instance, presidents "go local" by traveling to congressional districts to target individual members of Congress in an attempt to garner legislative support (Cohen, 2010).

IV: Nonpolitical individuals. Elite calls for participation sometimes target ordinary citizens, famous or not, who do not have any formal ties to the political system. Although some citizen referents in the fourth quadrant may hold significant cultural, symbolic, or economic power and thus have access to particular resources (e.g., Trump's praise of rapper Kanye West), ordinary citizens who lack the capital of celebrities will not have the requisite means to respond to participatory appeals and behaviors. Further, nonpolitical individuals have not necessarily sought the political attention they receive when made the subject of a participatory message.

Criticism of nonpolitical individuals in this quadrant of the typology may encourage anti-social engagement behaviors, such as cyber bullying and harassment (Kowalski, Limber, & Agatston, 2012), digital flaming (the intent to violate interactional norms) (O'Sullivan & Flanagin, 2003), or death threats and violence. Political elites generally refrain from criticizing individuals because the power differential could create a chilling effect on deliberative expression and participation (see Delli Carpini, Cook, & Jacobs, 2004, for a review of deliberation's importance to democratic outcomes).

In a general sense, campaigns often target some informal but identifiable collective of Americans, such as the elderly, women, or ethnic groups, for pro-social participation. On the opposite side of the spectrum, Trump's negative campaign communication toward immigrants and Muslims was linked to 1,094 bias-related events in the month following his election and a 197% increase in anti-Muslim hate groups in 2016 (Potok, 2017). In other cases, a specific individual is the referent. After an 18-year-old college student, Lauren Batchelder, told Trump that he was no "friend to women" at a primary campaign event in New Hampshire, Trump tweeted that she was an "arrogant young woman who questioned me in such a nasty fashion" (Johnson, 2016, paras. 11, 18). As a result, Batchelder faced telephone calls and social media harassment, including threats of sexual violence, as well as photoshopped digital pictures of a sexual nature.

Although normatively undesirable participatory behaviors could be communicatively summoned toward nonpolitical organizations (e.g., vandalism of physical spaces), it is in the third and especially fourth quadrants where the darker side of elite participatory calls most clearly emerges. Because of the power differential between some individuals and elites engaging in communicative appeals, the different resources available to individuals to respond to participatory acts, and the choice made by many to be nonpolitical, participatory appeals directed at citizens should face different scrutiny compared to general appeals directed at institutions and organizations. To better illustrate the normative implications of the discourse common to the third and fourth quadrants, we present three brief case studies of Trump.

The Politics of Incitement: Three Cases

Our chosen cases span the three key contexts of Trump's transition from celebrity businessman to commander-in-chief: the 2016 campaign, the presidential transition, and the first week of his presidency. In each case, we pick events from the third and fourth quadrants of our typology to focus on political and nonpolitical individuals as the referents for participatory appeals that toe the incitement line. In the process, we situate Trump's discourse within relevant historical and political context.

Over the course of the 2016 campaign, the Trump operation developed an ignoble reputation for leaning into incivility, bullying, and even violence. For instance, shortly before voting began in the Iowa caucuses, Trump said to rally-goers: "So if you see somebody getting ready to throw a tomato, knock the crap out of 'em, would you? Seriously. Just knock the hell—I promise you, I will pay for the legal fees" (McCaskill, 2016, para. 3). Given such discourse,

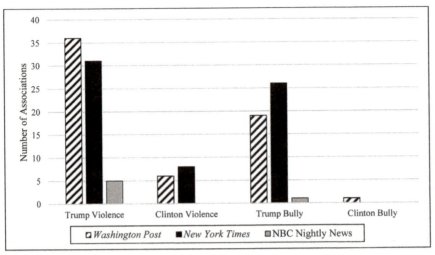

Figure 16.1   Candidate Associations with "Violence" and "Bully" (*Note:* Searches were run in FACTIVA for each candidate's last name within five words of "violence" or "violent" and "bully*" in each of the news media outlets from May 1, 2015, through November 15, 2016.)

it is not surprising that key news outlets were far more likely to connect Trump to the terms "violence" and "bullying" than they were to draw such associations with Clinton (see Figure 16.1). In the aforementioned federal court ruling that found the Trump campaign liable for violence at a campaign rally in Louisville, Kentucky, Judge David Hale devoted 167 words to defining "incitement" in both common and legal parlance (Nwanguma et al., 2017). Put simply, incitement is a communicative act that serves as an inducement for violence. The cases illustrate that the Trump campaign's communication invited responses that encouraged anti-social forms of participation.

"Second Amendment People"

During an August 2016 campaign event in North Carolina, Trump made an aside about Clinton's stance on gun rights: "Hillary wants to abolish, essentially abolish, the Second Amendment. By the way, and if she gets to pick—if she gets to pick her judges, nothing you can do, folks. Although the Second Amendment people, maybe there is, I don't know" (Jacobson, 2016, para. 3). Video of the moment shows at least one audience member reacting as if surprised by the content of Trump's remarks.

What followed was heated debate about the intent of a comment that, as Politifact (2016, para. 11) noted, "certainly left room for interpretation." The NBC Nightly News labeled a lead segment "Dangerous Talk?" In the three-minute segment, anchor Lester Holt discussed whether the statement was a joke or had more sinister implications. The video of Trump's remarks played twice, and there were reported accounts from the Trump campaign and the NRA slamming the "dishonest media" for implying the comment was about violence ("Trump Slammed," 2016). NBC was far from the only outlet to cover the remarks. A FACTIVA news search for "Second Amendment people" during the first two weeks of August 2016 returned 754 articles. Interest also spiked among the public. Analysis of Google trends reveals that searches for "Second Amendment people" and "Trump threat" jumped on August 10, 2016, the day following the event and initial news coverage of it.

Outside the context of a bombastic campaign, Trump's comment may have been interpreted quite differently. Rhetorically, it is possible to interpret Trump's message as an enthymeme. In a campaign marked by Trump's messaging of "Crooked Hillary," support of the rally chant "Lock Her Up," and eventual endorsement of jailing Clinton, the missing components of the argument come into clearer view. Some media outlets argued that Trump engaged in "stochastic terrorism," a dog-whistle technique designed to encourage lone wolf individuals to take violent action (Cohen, 2016).

Notably, the moment echoed events from the presidential campaign eight years prior, when Republican presidential candidate John McCain and vice presidential candidate Sarah Palin faced—and some say incited—moments during campaign rallies when supporters would label Democratic presidential candidate Barack Obama a "traitor" and "terrorist" and shout to "kill him" (Weiner, 2008). A key difference, however, is that McCain and Palin subtly posed a question—"Who is Barack Obama?"—to the crowd and allowed the audience to fill in the answers. McCain also later attempted to soothe the anger this messaging generated.

Fortunately, the darker participatory outcomes that Trump's comment could have encouraged did not come to fruition. Yet the event is nonetheless instructive for understanding elite participatory calls. First, the Clinton campaign used the seemingly dark communicative turn to e-mail supporters and encourage participation and donations to "show that we don't tolerate this kind of politics in America" ("Trump Suggests," 2016, para. 9). Second, Trump's comment did spark social media death threats against Clinton that were reported to the United States Secret Service—in line with what we would expect with the typology.*

Chuck Jones' "Terrible Job"

On December 6, 2016, as President-elect Donald Trump was celebrating his ostensible role in keeping 1,100 jobs from leaving a Carrier plant in Indianapolis, Indiana, *The Washington Post* ran a story that quoted local union

---

*Secret Service documents retrieved from https://www.documentcloud.org/documents/3463903 -Trump-2nd-Amendment-Secret-Service-FOIA.html

leader Chuck Jones saying Trump "lied his ass off" (Paquette, 2016a, para. 5). Jones was upset that Trump had inflated the number of jobs that would remain at the plant during a speech to the affected workers. Trump replied to Jones' remark a day later with this tweet (see Paquette, 2016b): "Chuck Jones, who is President of United Steelworkers 1999, has done a terrible job representing workers. No wonder companies flee country!" Fifteen minutes later Trump followed up with a second tweet: "If United Steelworkers 1999 was any good, they would have kept those jobs in Indiana. Spend more time working-less time talking. Reduce dues."

Two elements of Trump's statements are especially noteworthy. First, they were offered voluntarily. Trump was apparently responding to Jones' comment, but the choice to do so was entirely at his discretion. This was not an interview where a reporter had quoted the remark and asked for a response, as sometimes happens. Second, Trump called out Jones in specific and harsh terms: he provided Jones' full name and title and accused him of ineptitude that cost jobs.

As a useful point of historical contrast to Trump's approach, consider Ronald Reagan's discourse about the Professional Air Traffic Controllers Organization (PATCO) in 1981—one of the most notable presidential engagements with a union in modern history (McCartin, 2011). After months of negotiations between PATCO and the Federal Aviation Administration broke off in early August, Reagan held a press conference to announce that he would fire any striking PATCO members who did not return to work within 48 hours (he eventually did so). Clearly, the stakes were high. If ever a president might have been inclined to disparage a union or its leadership in an attempt to sway public opinion, this would seem to be a likely moment. Reagan did the opposite. He praised "the right of workers in the private sector to strike" (drawing a distinction between private and public employees) and recalled his own labor history: "[A]s president of my own union, I led the first strike ever called by that union" (Reagan, 1981, para. 3). In his most direct statement about the union members themselves, Reagan characterized them as "fine people." He never singled out PATCO's president, Robert Poli, by name and only referenced the "union leaders" in generic and neutral terms.

Reagan's case is not identical to Trump's. Nevertheless, it underscores how a president, in a moment where it might be tempting to call out a private citizen whose interests are at odds with the administration's, can choose a very different path. If Reagan's chosen path seems more obvious than Trump's, that is exactly the point: Trump's discourse stands out because it is so uncommon. Much more common is for presidents and other political leaders to praise people such as Chuck Jones, as presidents do every year during the State of the Union address (Scacco & Coe, 2016). That is precisely what Trump's eventual running mate, then-Governor Mike Pence, had done earlier in the year when Pence posted a picture of him with Jones, tweeting: "Appreciate the chance to meet w/ Chuck Jones & hardworking men of Local 1999 about our efforts to save Carrier jobs" (see Paquette, 2016b).

In much the same way that a positive tweet from the governor might win a union leader praise, a negative tweet from the president-elect might breed incitement. Jones almost immediately received threatening calls, including one that said, "We're coming for you" (Paquette, 2016b, para. 13). As Jones later explained the calls: "Nothing that says they're gonna kill me, but, you know, you better keep your eye on your kids. We know what car you drive. Things along those lines" (Paquette, 2016b, para. 15). In other words, the incitement in this case stopped just short of explicit death threats—a luxury that Chelsea Manning, the subject of our final case, did not enjoy.

The "Traitor" Chelsea Manning

In the early morning hours of January 26, 2017, Trump took to Twitter. On a Thursday that would see the new president issue six tweets, his first was the most striking: "Ungrateful TRAITOR Chelsea Manning, who should never have been released from prison, is now calling President Obama a weak leader. Terrible!" ("100 Days," 2017). Trump's tweet was directed at a former Army private who had released a large volume of classified documents to WikiLeaks and was subsequently sentenced to 35 years in prison—a sentence that Obama commuted shortly before leaving office. This was the first time during Trump's young presidency that he used Twitter to launch an ad hominem attack on a specific individual, and he employed capital letters to make sure his message did not go unnoticed. The president's message appeared 14 minutes after Fox News had shown a picture of Manning underscored with the words "ungrateful traitor" (Kurtzleben, 2017).

The tweet's content is rare when situated in historical context. To call a person a traitor is among the most serious charges one can level at a citizen, and it carries particular weight when the accuser is the president of the United States. Perhaps recognizing this seriousness, modern presidents have rarely used the term "traitor" at all. To understand this history, we searched the entire *Public Papers of the Presidents* via the American Presidency Project's online search feature at www.presidency.ucsb.edu. Focusing on the modern presidency, which is usually understood as beginning with Franklin D. Roosevelt (Coe & Neumann, 2011), our search revealed that across the census of their public communications presidents have used the term "traitor(s)" just 39 times.

A closer look at these instances indicated that virtually all of them were far different from Trump's use of the term. Many of the mentions occurred in the context of partisan bickering, with a president quoting or paraphrasing what those across the aisle had called him (sometimes humorously, other times seriously). Others referenced the Revolutionary War or made abstract references to the risk treason might pose to the nation—with most of the latter type coming during World War II or the early Cold War. Among these various pre-Trump uses, only *twice* did any president come close to calling a specific U.S. citizen a traitor. Both instances came during a March 3, 1949, news conference, during which Harry Truman was asked if he had any comment on "a statement [that] was issued yesterday by the leaders of the American Communist Party on the position that they would take in the event of war between the United States and Russia" (Truman, 1949, para. 58). To this, Truman replied: "I have no comment on a statement made by traitors" (para. 59). He was then asked to repeat himself, and he did. In short, across more than eight decades of public communications, no president prior to 2017 had ever labeled a specific American individual a traitor. Trump did so within a week of taking office.

The rarity of this discourse would seem to suggest that past presidents have carefully weighed the gravity of such specific ad hominem attacks. In Trump's case, he not only dubbed a U.S. citizen a traitor, he did so in an interactive forum that lends itself to immediate, visceral reactions. This context is quite different from, for instance, the news conference in which President Truman called out the leaders of the American Communist Party. In that context, where norms of accuracy and reflection would be more prominent, the journalists seemed surprised by the president's words. One asked, "Mr. President, may we quote that 'no comment' on this statement made by traitors?" and another journalist underscored the seriousness of the charge: "Mr. President, these Communists are already under indictment in New York, but is there any additional prosecution planned on the basis of this thing, in view of the constitutional definition of a traitor?" (Truman, 1949, para. 74).

On Twitter, sober reflections about the implications of the president's label are less likely. Trump's tweet about Manning drew some reactions that underscore the potential for such presidential discourse to tend toward incitement. In one especially telling reply, @politicalbeauty—a Twitter account located in Germany with more than 50,000 followers—posted simply: "Kill him!" (2017). Along with the obvious reference to the most extreme form of violence possible, this tweet also misgenders Manning (she is a transgender woman). Other replies noticed this angle as well. For example, Trump Revolution (2017) tweeted: "Manning, can't even decide which potty to use and now thinks it's [sic] opinion matters." We make no claim about the frequency with which such Twitter reactions surfaced; our method herein is not suited to such analysis. The mere presence of such responses nonetheless indicates the seriousness with which even such seemingly casual presidential discourse must be taken. In making this attack public—and at a tremendous scale, as Trump's account has more than 28 million followers—the new president provided a platform from which those inclined were able to engage in hate speech or threats of violence.

Conclusion

If campaign 2016 and its aftermath illustrated the need to capture the full range of discourse and outcomes associated with elite calls for participation, the time since has only underscored that need. To mark his first 100 days in office, President Trump held a campaign-style rally in Harrisburg, Pennsylvania. After a protester at the rally held up a Russian flag (a reference to the investigation into possible collusion between the Trump campaign and Russian officials to influence the 2016 election), the president yelled "get him out of here." The group "Bikers for Trump" deputized themselves, holding protesters until official law enforcement could escort the protesters from the rally. As a law enforcement official later told *Politico*, "The bikers are a great example of members of the crowd using Trump's words as a call to action. In some instances, they feel like they are instructed to do so, and further feel like their actions to suppress a protest somehow indemnifies their actions" (Vogel & Schreckinger, 2017, para. 13). These are the accounts we should be mindful of when assessing elite targeting of political and nonpolitical individuals (the third and fourth quadrants of the typology).

Participatory communicative appeals—whether digital calls for online interactivity (Stromer-Galley, 2014) or rally exhortations for voting, volunteerism, or immediate physical action—are evolving as political elites continue to adapt to changing audiences and media. An era of ubiquitous communication for presidents and presidential candidates means that not only will elites prioritize accessibility in a variety of media, but also that individuals will come to expect the interactivity and tailoring of messages that come with accessible appeals (Scacco & Coe, 2017). The accessibility of these pro- and anti-social appeals only enhances the possibilities for participatory outcomes. Beginning to capture the evolution of these participatory appeals and outcomes in the typology we have proposed may require political communication scholars to revisit the literature on populism (e.g., Engesser et al., 2017; Kazin, 1995; Roberts, 2006) and demagoguery (e.g., Hogan & Tell, 2006; Mercieca, 2015; Roberts-Miller, 2005).

Seeking a more expansive understanding of elite participatory appeals also will mean fully appreciating how personalization resides at the intersection of contemporary elite communication and political participation. Ubiquitous communication practices hinge on the disclosure and informality necessary for message adaptation in a variety of digital media venues (Scacco & Coe, 2016). These personalized communications can influence feelings of connectedness and parasocial interaction between candidates and individuals (McGregor, in press). Political participation has also transitioned from duty-bound notions of engagement (e.g., voting) to more personal forms (e.g., protest, political consumerism)—tracking alongside social media's emphasis on personal and affective expression (Atkinson, 2015; Bennett, 2012; Dalton, 2008; Gil de Zuniga et al., 2014; Papacharissi, 2015). Scholars should be cognizant of these seemingly personal elite-citizen connections feeding more personalized and anti-social forms of political participation. This development may partially explain why scholars (e.g., Ceaser, Thurow, Tulis, & Bessette, 1981; Edwards, 2003) have been wary of endorsing public communication as a means to bring governors closer to the governed.

Finally, fully understanding participatory appeals and outcomes will require thinking about the nature of democratic citizenship. Much of the foundational work on American political participation, whether scholarly or perspective taking, is replete with mentions of the "good" citizen (Dalton, 2008; Schudson, 1998), as well as the participatory trade-offs between a common and personal "good" (Verba & Nie, 1972). Ironically, notions of political goodness may exist in the mind of the cyber bully inspired to troll an individual or election candidate, or the individual tweeting about "Second Amendment" solutions to an elected official perceived as a threat to democracy. As we have argued, the same discursive army invited by elite communication to engage in participatory activities traditionally considered normatively desirable can be invited to engage in anti-social participatory behavior, including the targeting of and incitement toward election opponents, private organizations, and citizens. Given this, it will take restraint and strength of conscience among political elites to ensure that their calls to action have a better chance of helping democracy than of harming it.

References

Albertson, B. L. (2015). Dog-whistle politics: Multivocal communication and religious appeals. *Political Behavior, 37,* 3–26. doi:10.1007/s11109-013-9265-x

Atkinson, L. (2015). Buying in or tuning out: The role of consumption in politically active young adults. In H. Gil de Zuniga (Ed.), *New agendas in communication: New technologies and civic engagement* (pp. 23–45). New York: Routledge.

Bennett, W. L. (2012). The personalization of politics: Political identity, social media, and changing patterns of participation. *The ANNALS of the American Academy of Political and Social Science, 644,* 20–39. doi:10.1177/0002 716212451428

Bitzer, L. F. (1959). Aristotle's enthymeme revisited. *Quarterly Journal of Speech, 45,* 399–408. doi:10.1080/00335635909382374

Bryce, J. (1889). *The American commonwealth.* New York: Macmillan and Co.

Bush, George W. (2006, December 20). President Bush's news conference. *The New York Times.* Transcript retrieved from http://www.nytimes.com/2006 /12/20/washington/20text-bush.html

Ceaser, J. W., Thurow, G. E., Tulis, J., & Bessette, J. M. (1981). The rise of the rhetorical presidency. *Presidential Studies Quarterly, 11*, 158–171.

Clinton, H. R. (2016, September 19). Remarks in Philadelphia. Retrieved from https://www.hillaryclinton.com/speeches/in-philadelphia-clinton-tells -millennials-she-will-have-their-back-as-president

CNN 20: Ross Perot on "Larry King Live," February 20, 1992. (2000, February 20). *CNN.com*. Retrieved from http://edition.cnn.com/TRANSCRIPTS/0002/20 /sm.12.html

Coe, K., Kenski, K., & Rains, S. A. (2014). Online and uncivil? Patterns and determinants of incivility in newspaper website comments. *Journal of Communication, 64*(4), 658–679. doi:10.1111/jcom.12104

Coe, K., & Neumann, R. (2011). The major addresses of modern presidents: Parameters of a data set. *Presidential Studies Quarterly, 41*, 727–751. doi:10 .1111/j.1741-5705.2011.03912.x

Cohen, D. S. (2016, August 9). Trump's assassination dog whistle was even scarier than you think. *Rolling Stone*. Retrieved from http://www.rollingstone .com/politics/features/trumps-assassination-dog-whistle-was-scarier -than-you-think-w433615

Cohen, J. E. (2010). *Going local: Presidential leadership in the post-broadcast age*. New York: Cambridge University Press.

Cook, T. E. (2005). *Governing with the news: The news media as a political institution*. (2nd ed.). Chicago: University of Chicago Press.

Dalton, R. J. (2008). Citizenship norms and the expansion of political participation. *Political Studies, 56*(1), 76–98. doi:10.1111/j.1467-9248.2007.00718.x

Delli Carpini, M. X., Cook, F. L., & Jacobs, L. R. (2004). Public deliberation, discursive participation, and citizen engagement: A review of the empirical literature. *Annual Review of Political Science, 7*, 315–344. doi:10.1146/an nurev.polisci.7.121003.091630

Edwards, G. C., III. (2003). *On deaf ears: The limits of the bully pulpit*. New Haven, CT: Yale University Press.

Engesser, S., Ernst, N., Esser, F., & Büchel, F. (2017). Populism and social media: How politicians spread a fragmented ideology. *Information, Communication & Society, 20*(8), 1109–1126. doi:10.1080/1369118X.2016.1207697

Geier, B. (2016, April 13). Bernie Sanders rips into $5 billion Goldman Sachs settlement. *Fortune*. Retrieved from http://fortune.com/2016/04/13/bernie -sanders-goldman-ad

Giddens, A. (1984). *The constitution of society: Outline of the theory of structuration*. Berkeley: University of California Press.

Gil de Zúñiga, H., Copeland, L., & Bimber, B. (2014). Political consumerism: Civic engagement and the social media connection. *New Media & Society, 16*(3), 488–506. doi:10.1177/1461444813487960

Groppe, M. (2015, December 8). Muslim congressman reports death threat. *USA Today*. Retrieved from https://www.usatoday.com/story/news/politics/2015 /12/08/muslim-rep-andre-carson-says-he-received-death-threat/76999142

Groshek, J., & Engelbert, J. (2013). Double differentiation in a cross-national comparison of populist political movements and online media uses in the United States and the Netherlands. *New Media & Society, 15*(2), 183–202. doi:10.1177/1461444812450685

Hadley, G. (2017, April 29). Trump is being sued for saying "get 'em out of here" at a rally. He just did it again. *McClatchy*. Retrieved from http://www.mcclatch ydc.com/news/politics-government/article147677504.html

Hogan, J. M., & Tell, D. (2006). Demagoguery and democratic deliberation: The search for rules of discursive engagement. *Rhetoric & Public Affairs, 9*(3), 479–487. doi:10.1353/rap.2006.0077

Jacobson, L. (2016, August 9). In context: Donald Trump's "Second Amendment people" comment. *Politifact*. Retrieved from http://www.politifact.com/truth -o-meter/article/2016/aug/09/context-donald-trumps-second-amendment -people-comm

Jagers, J., & Walgrave, S. (2007). Populism as political communication style: An empirical study of political parties' discourse in Belgium. *European Journal of Political Research, 46*(3), 319–345. doi:10.1111/j.1475-6765.2006 .00690.x

Jamieson, K. H. (1992). *Dirty politics: Deception, distraction, and democracy.* New York: Oxford University Press.

Jarvis, S. E. (2005). *The talk of the party: Political labels, symbolic capital, and American life.* New York: Rowman & Littlefield.

Johnson, J. (2016, December 8). This is what happens when Donald Trump attacks a private citizen on Twitter. *The Washington Post*. Retrieved from https:// www.washingtonpost.com/politics/this-is-what-happens-when-donald -trump-attacks-a-private-citizen-on-twitter/2016/12/08/a1380ece-bd62 -11e6-91ee-1adddfe36cbe_story.html?utm_term=.1dd3b23f6516

Johnson, J., & Jordan, M. (2015, November 22). Trump on rally protester: "Maybe he should have been roughed up." *The Washington Post*. Retrieved from https://www.washingtonpost.com/news/post-politics/wp/2015/11/22 /black-activist-punched-at-donald-trump-rally-in-birmingham/?utm_term =.0e3f0e187ae6

Katz, E., & Lazarsfeld, P. F. (1955). *Personal influence: The part played by people in the flow of mass communications.* Glencoe, IL: Free Press.

Kazin, M. (1995). *The populist persuasion: An American history.* Ithaca, NY: Cornell University Press.

Kernell, S. (2007). *Going public: New strategies of presidential leadership.* (4th ed.). Washington, D.C.: CQ Press.

Kilgore, T. (2016, December 6). Boeing's stock drops after Trump tweet about canceling Air Force One order. *Market Watch*. Retrieved from http://www .marketwatch.com/story/boeings-stock-drops-after-trump-tweet-to -cancel-air-force-one-order-2016-12-06

Kowalski, R. M., Limber, S. P., Limber, S., & Agatston, P. W. (2012). *Cyberbullying: Bullying in the digital age.* West Sussex, UK: John Wiley & Sons.

Kurtzleben, D. (2017, January 26). Trump: Chelsea Manning an "ungrateful traitor" for criticizing Obama. *National Public Radio*. Retrieved from http://www.npr.org/2017/01/26/511781106/trump-chelsea-manning-an-ungrateful-traitor-for-criticizing-obama

Lane, R. E., & Sears, D. O. (1964). *Public opinion*. Englewood Cliffs, NJ: Prentice-Hall.

Lippmann, W. (1922/1997). *Public opinion*. New York: Free Press.

Long, H. (2016, April 19). Bernie Sanders hails fossil fuel divestment at universities. *CNN Money*. Retrieved from http://money.cnn.com/2016/04/19/investing/bernie-sanders-columbia-divestment

McCann, J. A., Rapoport, R. B., & Stone, W. J. (1999). Heeding the call: An assessment of mobilization into H. Ross Perot's 1992 presidential campaign. *American Journal of Political Science, 43*(1), 1–28. doi:10.2307/2991783

McCartin, J. A. (2011). *Collision course: Ronald Reagan, the air traffic controllers, and the strike that changed America*. New York: Oxford University Press.

McCaskill, N. D. (2016, February 1). Trump urges crowd to "knock the crap out of anyone with tomatoes." *Politico*. Retrieved from http://www.politico.com/blogs/iowa-caucus-2016-live-updates/2016/02/donald-trump-iowa-rally-tomatoes-218546

McGregor, S. C. (in press). Personalization, social media, and voting: Effects of candidate self-personalization on vote intention. *New Media & Society*. Online first. doi:1461444816686103

Mercieca, J. (2015, December 11). The rhetorical brilliance of Trump the demagogue. *The Conversation*. Retrieved from https://theconversation.com/the-rhetorical-brilliance-of-trump-the-demagogue-51984

Mercieca, J. (2016, March 9). How Donald Trump gets away with saying things that other candidates can't. *The Washington Post*. Retrieved from https://www.washingtonpost.com/posteverything/wp/2016/03/09/how-donald-trump-gets-away-with-saying-things-other-candidates-cant/?utm_term=.0a439583fef5

Nwanguma et al. v. Trump et al. 3:16-cv-247-DJH. (2017). Retrieved from https://docs.google.com/viewerng/viewer?url=http://wave.images.worldnow.com/library/a049de15-2a71-4579-a390-d18d39535fb2.pdf

Obama, B. (2016, January 5). Remarks on gun violence. *The American Presidency Project*. Retrieved from http://www.presidency.ucsb.edu/ws/index.php?pid=111391&st=NRA&st1

100 days of Twitter: A timeline of President Trump's tweets. (2017, April 29). *ABC News*. Retrieved from http://abcnews.go.com/Politics/99-days-twitter-timeline-president-trumps-tweets/story?id=47042143

O'Sullivan, P. B., & Flanagin, A. J. (2003). Reconceptualizing "flaming" and other problematic messages. *New Media & Society, 5*(1), 69–94. doi:10.1177/1461444803005001908

Papacharissi, Z. (2015). *Affective publics: Sentiment, technology, and politics*. Oxford, UK: Oxford University Press.

Paquette, D. (2016a, December 6). "He lied his a—off": Carrier union leader on Trump's big deal. *The Washington Post*. Retrieved from https://www.washing tonpost.com/news/wonk/wp/2016/12/06/he-got-up-there-and-lied-his-a -off-carrier-union-leader-on-trumps-big-deal/?utm_term=.a3cdb025c069

Paquette, D. (2016b, December 7). Donald Trump insulted a union leader on Twitter. Then the phone started to ring. *The Washington Post*. Retrieved from https://www.washingtonpost.com/news/wonk/wp/2016/12/07/donald -trump-retaliated-against-a-union-leader-on-twitter-then-his-phone-started -to-ring/?utm_term=.07f36ae24e3e

Political Beauty. [politicalbeauty] (2017, January 29). Kill him! [Tweet]. Retrieved from https://twitter.com/politicalbeauty/status/825741540051996673

Potok, M. (2017, February 15). The year in hate and extremism. *Southern Poverty Law Center*. Retrieved from https://www.splcenter.org/fighting-hate/intel ligence-report/2017/year-hate-and-extremism

Reagan, R. (1981, August 3). Remarks and a question-and-answer session with reporters on the air traffic controllers strike. *The American Presidency Project*. Retrieved from http://www.presidency.ucsb.edu/ws/index.php?pid=44138 &st=robert+poli&st1

Roberts, K. M. (2006). Populism, political conflict, and grass-roots organization in Latin America. *Comparative Politics, 38*(2), 127–148. doi:10.2307/20433986

Roberts-Miller, P. (2005). Democracy, demagoguery, and critical rhetoric. *Rhetoric & Public Affairs, 8*, 459–476. doi: 10.1353/rap.2005.0069

Savransky, R. (2016, July 21). Cruz fundraising off GOP convention speech. *The Hill*. Retrieved from http://thehill.com/blogs/blog-briefing-room/news /288636-cruz-fundraising-off-of-gop-convention-speech

Scacco, J. M. (2011). A weekend routine: The functions of the weekly presidential address from Bill Clinton to Barack Obama. *Electronic Media & Politics, 1*(4), 66–88.

Scacco, J. M., & Coe, K. (2016). The ubiquitous presidency: Toward a new para-digm for studying presidential communication. *International Journal of Communication, 10*, 2014–2037.

Scacco, J. M., & Coe, K. (2017). Talk this way: The ubiquitous presidency and expectations of presidential communication. *American Behavioral Scientist, 61*(3), 298–314. doi:10.1177/0002764217704321

Schudson, M. (1998). *The good citizen: A history of American civic life*. Cambridge, MA: Harvard University Press.

Stromer-Galley, J. (2014). *Presidential campaigning in the internet age*. New York: Oxford University Press.

Truman, H. S. (1949, March 3). The president's news conference. *The American Presidency Project*. Retrieved from http://www.presidency.ucsb.edu/ws /index.php?pid=13396&st=traitor&st1

Trump Revolution. [VA4DJT]. (2017, January 28). Manning, can't even decide which potty to use and now thinks it's opinion matters. [Tweet]. Retrieved from https://twitter.com/VA4DJT?lang=en

Trump slammed over Second Amendment comments about Clinton. (2016, August 9). *NBC News*. Retrieved from https://www.youtube.com/watch?v=6VVZNUpIPgg

Trump suggests "Second Amendment people" could stop Clinton. (2016, August 10). *Chicago Tribune*. Retrieved from http://www.chicagotribune.com/news/nationworld/politics/ct-trump-clinton-second-amendment-20160809-story.html

Verba, S., & Nie, N. H. (1972). *Participation in America: Political democracy and social equality*. New York: Harper and Row.

Vogel, K. P., & Schreckinger, B. (2017, May 2). Trump rally altercations could add to legal woes. *Politico*. Retrieved from http://www.politico.com/story/2017/05/02/trump-rally-fights-protesters-237861

Wayne LaPierre: A challenge to the president. (2016, January 13). National Rifle Association. Retrieved from https://www.youtube.com/watch?v=yClzzvWUoG4

Weiner, R. (2008, November 6). Obama hatred at McCain-Palin rallies: "Terrorist!" "Kill him!" *Huffington Post*. Retrieved from http://www.huffingtonpost.com/2008/10/06/mccain-does-nothing-as-cr_n_132366.html

Zaller, J. R. (1992). *The nature and origins of mass opinion*. New York: Cambridge University Press.

Zukin, C., Keeter, S., Andolina, M., Jenkins, K., & Delli Carpini, M. X. (2006). *A new engagement? Political participation, civic life, and the changing American citizen*. New York: Oxford University Press.

PART 3

Communication Attitudes and Behaviors of the Electorate

Corn Belt Controversy: Intraparty Divisions and Political Cynicism at the 2016 Iowa Caucuses

Joel Lansing Reed, Sopheak Hoeun, Josh C. Bramlett, Molly Greenwood, and Grace Hase

The tumultuous 2016 presidential primaries were among the most bitterly contested in the modern era. Even after all the votes were cast and the final delegates were awarded, "Bernie or Bust" Democrats and "Never Trump" Republicans threatened to boycott the general election to protest the primary results. The primary process that exposed deep divisions within both parties began with the first-in-the-nation Iowa Caucus on February 1, 2016. By the time these first voters filtered into their caucus meetings, a clear split had emerged between "insider" and "outsider" candidates in both major political parties. Our study examines intraparty dynamics on the eve of the Iowa caucuses by focusing on one key form of participatory political engagement: attending a political rally. By surveying attendees at rallies of the top-polling candidates leading up to the Iowa caucuses, we hope to shed light on the unique characteristics of rally-goers and the intraparty divisions that came into focus just before the nation's first primary contest. Rally attendees responded to survey items designed to measure their levels of political interest, cynicism, external efficacy, and political information efficacy. Based on these responses, we find significant differences between rally attendees on three of our four variables of interest.

We begin by describing the intraparty dynamics of the 2016 presidential primaries for both Democratic and Republican candidates. We then turn our attention to the extant literature on the Iowa caucuses, political rallies, and our variables of interest. Based on the gaps identified in the scholarly literature, we present two hypotheses and four research questions for analysis. We then outline the method for our field study, which surveyed attendees across four different rallies within 24 hours of the Iowa caucuses. Our results suggest that rally-goers are far from a uniform population and that attendees' levels of cynicism, efficacy, and political information efficacy varied by rally. Finally, implications and limitations of these findings are discussed with an eye toward future research that seeks to better understand political rallies and intraparty politics.

The 2016 Primaries

The 2016 primaries were characterized by similar dynamics on both sides of the aisle. Outsiders Donald Trump and Bernie Sanders challenged party establishment by characterizing the status quo as profoundly corrupt and in need of drastic reform. Trump and Sanders were both well positioned to frame themselves as party outsiders, with Trump having never held elected office and Sanders being one of only two independents in either house of Congress. By contrast, Democrat Hillary Clinton and Republican Ted Cruz had long been active within the party structure and party establishment. Cruz, himself a partisan agitator, might seem to be an ill fit for the category of political "insider." However, as we will demonstrate, there is good reason to treat Cruz as a traditional, albeit radically conservative, politician. The nuances of each race suggest that divisions based on political efficacy and cynicism may help explain what drew early supporters toward the respective candidates.

Dividing Lines in the Democratic Primaries

When Democrats convened in Philadelphia in July 2016 to coronate their presidential nominee, they did so against the backdrop of immense controversy. Former New York Senator and Secretary of State Hillary Clinton had secured enough delegates to be considered the party's presumptive nominee by the start of the convention. Clinton defeated the liberal firebrand, U.S. Senator Bernie Sanders of Vermont, whose supporters had long voiced opposition to the party's system for selecting its nominee. Just days before the convention, the freedom of information activist organization WikiLeaks released thousands of e-mails from Democratic National Committee (DNC) officials. Some of the released e-mails revealed that members of the party's leadership showed a clear preference for Clinton's nomination during the ongoing primary campaign. Some e-mails even suggested that a few DNC officials might have offered direct assistance to the Clinton campaign in defeating Sanders. The WikiLeaks e-mails poured fuel onto an already smoldering fire within the Democratic Party. The significance of the scandal was amplified by the fact that, for Sanders' supporters, it seemed to confirm the dominant message of the Sanders campaign: that government was "rigged" in favor of a wealthy political elite. During the campaign, Sanders often spoke about corruption and the need for a dramatic overhaul of the political system. Sanders positioned himself as an outsider who challenged the status quo by proposing large-scale political and economic reforms.

Well before the DNC e-mails were leaked, Sanders had been highly critical of Clinton for paid speeches she had given to major financial institutions and her initial support of the controversial Trans-Pacific Partnership. Distrust between the two wings of the Democratic Party meant that Clinton would face an unusually hostile crowd in Philadelphia, but these intraparty divisions did not begin at the convention. Sanders' meteoric rise in the polls came in the weeks just before the February 1 Iowa caucuses, and his attacks on the party establishment and political corruption were already in full swing. Sanders rhetorically positioned himself as an outsider by demanding dramatic reform to the system of campaign finance and greater regulation of financial institutions. Sanders often painted a cynical picture of American politics, in which elected officials worked only in the interests of a wealthy elite. During the October 25, 2015, primary debate in Las Vegas, Nevada, Sanders declared:

> As a result of this disastrous Citizens United Supreme Court decision, our campaign finance system is corrupt and is undermining American democracy. Millionaires and billionaires are pouring unbelievable sums of money into the political process in order to fund super PACs and to elect candidates who represent their interests, not the interests of working people.

Sanders' campaign messages claimed that the system was rigged against the poor and middle class. In this way, Sanders was tapping into a sense of cynicism regarding the American system of representation.

Political cynicism offers one potential dividing line between insiders and outsiders in the 2016 primary campaigns. Miller (1974) stresses the affective nature of cynicism as an orientation toward government and the electoral system. Among the broad range of political attitudes and values, political cynicism has been identified by Delli Carpini (2004) as a principal attitude that affects citizens' democratic engagement, such as attending political rallies. Understandings of political cynicism, however, must extend beyond "lack of trust in government" (Lariscy, Tinkham, & Sweetser, 2011). Kaid, McKinney, and Tedesco (2000) posit that political cynicism is a feeling that government in general, and political leaders in particular, do not care about public opinion and do not act in the best interest of the people. During the 1996 presidential election, Kaid and colleagues (2000) discovered a clear link between cynicism and voting, in that nonvoters' political cynicism was significantly higher than voters' cynicism. Although we might imagine that politically cynical citizens would disengage from the political process, they may also believe that outsider candidates can truly effect political change. We hypothesize that as a political outsider, Sanders may have given voice to individuals higher in cynicism and perhaps brought them back into the political fold. Therefore, we propose the following hypothesis:

H1: Sanders rally attendees will report significantly higher levels of political cynicism than Clinton rally attendees.

Pinkleton, Austin, and Fortman (1998) argue that political cynicism is also characterized by a "sense of powerlessness," but Sanders' rhetoric suggested great optimism about the ability of his supporters to fix the problems he identified. The dual features of cynicism about the status quo and efficacy in fixing the dominant social problems are embodied in a declaration from the November 14, 2015, primary debate in Des Moines, Iowa, during which Sanders said, "What my campaign is about is a political revolution—millions of people standing up and saying, enough is enough. Our government belongs to all of us, and not just the handful of billionaires." Such framing was a common feature of Sanders' campaign messages and mirrors the cynicism characteristic of political outsiders, but his inclusion of the rhetoric of revolution also imbues supporters with a sense of political agency.

Political efficacy has been defined as an individual's feeling that he or she has the capacity to influence the political process (Campbell, Gurin, & Miller, 1954). In particular, external political efficacy refers to the responsiveness of the political system to the demands of its citizens (Kaid, Fernandes, & Painter, 2011; Niemi, Craig, & Mattei, 1991). We conceive of efficacy as the power of voting to influence the government. Though citizens may not believe that the current government is responsive to their interests, they may feel that they can hold some sway by voting for a political outsider, such as Sanders, who can transform the form and function of American politics. The prevailing literature suggests a negative relationship between cynicism and political efficacy (Pinkleton & Austin, 2001, 2002), but the unique nature of political outsiders, who give voice to voters' cynicism but also suggest that their election could turn the tide, may complicate this relationship. Although it is difficult to hypothesize about the nature of the relationship, it is possible that rally attendees drawn by insider and outsider candidates may vary in their levels of external political efficacy. Therefore we posit the following question:

RQ1: Do attendees at Sanders' political rally differ in their levels of external efficacy from those who attended the rallies of insider candidates?

Sanders' cynicism about the democratic process was in stark contrast to the rhetoric of his intraparty opponent, Clinton, who spent much of the campaign praising the accomplishments of the Obama administration and lauding her own successes as a former senator and secretary of state. Clinton relied on an image of American politics in which elected officials were already producing positive change, but were increasingly limited by forces beyond their control. For example, in the previously referenced 2015 debate in Iowa, Clinton pointed to the Affordable Care Act (ACA) as a clear example of a Democratic Party accomplishment, but suggested the need for a defensive stance on healthcare. Clinton told the audience with respect to the healthcare law,

> I do think that it's important to defend it. The Republicans have voted to repeal it nearly 60 times. They would like to rip it up and start all over again, throw our nation back into this really contentious debate that we've had about health care for quite some time now. I want to build on and improve the Affordable Care Act.

Unlike Sanders' desire for a "political revolution," Clinton painted a relatively positive picture of the status quo and expressed trepidation about the possibility of making large-scale changes.

In many ways, Clinton was the quintessential insider candidate. Her string of official positions within the party dated back three decades, and she had a considerable lead in endorsements and fundraising before the Iowa caucuses (Cohen, Karol, Noel, & Zaller, 2016). For Republicans, the perceived quintessential insider and clear fundraising leader was Jeb Bush; however, by the start of the Iowa caucuses, Bush had failed to gain a sizeable base of support and finished a disappointing sixth in the caucus voting. In the section that follows, we make the case that an unlikely candidate assumed the mantle of "insider" during the 2016 Republican primaries.

Key Divisions in the Republican Primaries

When Cruz was exploring a run for the presidency, his advisors likely imagined that he would be able to present himself as the challenger to the Republican Party establishment. Cruz was one of the leading voices in the Tea Party movement, which had emerged in response to Barack Obama's election eight years earlier. Although Cruz's rhetoric often put him at odds with leaders in his own party, including 2008 nominee John McCain, his policy positions were those of a traditional conservative Republican. Cruz ran on a platform opposing abortion and same-sex marriage, calling for dramatic tax cuts, and cracking down on illegal immigration. Throughout the campaign he routinely praised President Ronald Reagan and highlighted his own accomplishments as a U.S. senator. Though Cruz often used fiery rhetoric to attack party elites, the emergence of Trump put Cruz in the unfamiliar position of defending a system he often railed against.

As with Sanders, Donald Trump pointed to what he saw as systemic corruption within the process of representative government. On October 13, 2016, in Florida, Trump told a crowd, "The Washington establishment and the financial and media corporations that fund it exist for only one reason: to protect and enrich itself." In Trump's framing, the problem was not just the willingness of Republicans to accept compromises; it was a fundamentally flawed system that needed to be transformed. Although Trump and Sanders disagreed on many of the central issues of the 2016 campaign, they staked out similar ground rhetorically, placing themselves outside of a broken or failing system. Trump's rhetoric painted a similarly cynical image of American politics. Two weeks before the Iowa caucuses, during a CNN (2016) interview, Trump accused his primary opponents of selling their votes to major donors:

> That is the way it is, somebody gives them money, not anything wrong, just psychologically, when they go to that person, they're going to do it . . . They owe them. And by the way, they may therefore vote negatively toward the country. That's not going to happen with me.

Trump grouped all of his political opponents into one category, characterized by corruption and at times opposed to the interests of the American people, but Cruz was the candidate Trump attacked most directly. Later in the same interview, Trump said, "Ted Cruz, he's got a lot of people putting big money in—probably, maybe, Goldman Sachs, we'll have to ask. I mean, they loaned him a million dollars, so they certainly have control over him." Hence, Trump's campaign also deployed a deeply cynical vision of the U.S. political process. As with Sanders, Trump regularly touted his ability to solve even these deep and systemic problems, which may further complicate the relationship between cynicism and efficacy. Therefore, we propose the following hypothesis and research question:

H2: Trump rally attendees will report significantly higher levels of political cynicism than Cruz rally attendees.

RQ2: Do attendees at Trump's political rally differ in their levels of external efficacy from those who attended the rallies of insider candidates?

On both sides of the aisle, the intraparty divisions were on full display in the lead-up to the 2016 Iowa caucuses. As the first contest in the primary process, the Iowa caucuses represent a crucial step on the path to November. Several aspects of the Iowa caucuses make them particularly well suited for the study of intraparty differences. The Iowa caucuses also present ample opportunities to study various forms of political engagement, including attending a political rally. In the following two sections, we survey the extant literature on the Iowa caucuses and political rallies, which provide the sampling frame for our field study.

The Iowa Caucuses

The nation's first primary contest can make or break a presidential campaign. The Iowa caucuses command substantial media attention in the days and weeks leading up to the final tally (Donovan & Hunsaker, 2009; Steger, 2007). The sense of momentum that campaigns generate from the Iowa caucus may be even more significant than the outcome of the caucuses themselves (Steger, 2007). Predicting that momentum before caucus night is uniquely challenging. Meredith Willson's (1962) *Music Man* famously depicted Iowans as stubborn and skeptical of nearly any sales pitch, but to many outside observers of the Iowa caucuses, Iowa voters can appear fickle and indecisive. Public opinion polling in the lead-up to the Iowa caucuses is notoriously unreliable, and late deciders often dramatically sway the election outcome. Erikson and Wlezien (2012) suggest that the early primary season is a period of substantial reshuffling in public opinion. Between January and April of an election year, voters are becoming more familiar with candidates and establishing tentative preferences. Though presidential candidates devote months to eating corn dogs at the Iowa State Fair and traveling the state from Sioux City to Davenport, it is the final days and hours before the caucuses that can be crucial.

In the absence of reliable polling data, popular media often turn to the nebulous factor of enthusiasm, and the crowds at political rallies offer journalists a ready-made approximation for the concept. *The Washington Post* reporter John Wagner (2016) noted "an enthusiastic crowd estimated at 1,700 people" who attended Sanders' final rally just hours before the 2016 caucuses opened. Ted Johnson (2016), a senior editor for *Variety*, similarly characterized Clinton's final event, writing, "Hillary Clinton's closing rally before the Iowa caucuses was primed to counter any perception that her campaign lacked enthusiasm, energy or passion." By contrast, one reporter invoked Macbeth in describing one of Trump's final campaign events in Waterloo, Iowa, noting that "[t]he large room in the Ramada Hotel and Convention Center hung loosely upon the Monday morning rally crowd like giant's robes upon a dwarfish thief" (Petri, 2016, para. 4). Crowds at last-minute campaign events are often presented as an indication of the excitement surrounding a candidate and his or her chances of victory. Our team of researchers distributed surveys at each of these final events so that we could better understand who attends the political rallies that are often seen as a metric for enthusiasm. Even in a highly mediated political environment, these campaign rallies remain at the heart of the caucus process.

Campaign Rallies

Political campaign scholarship has moved away from political rallies toward a greater focus on the role of media in reaching mass audiences and shaping public perceptions. Despite this shift in research, traditional campaign events continue to dominate the schedules of presidential candidates, and events remain a significant focal point for media coverage. Stories of violence at Trump's rallies, protestors interrupting Clinton's and Cruz's speeches, and even a small bird landing on the lectern during a Sanders campaign event in Portland, Oregon, briefly dominated news cycles during the 2016 presidential primaries. Campaign rallies are a significant, but understudied, component of the electoral process; however, researchers have demonstrated that political rallies offer a useful population for measuring normative democratic outcomes (Trent, Short-Thompson, Mongeau, & Metzler, 2017; Warner et. al, 2017). Sanders and Kaid (1981) found a surprising amount of diversity in motivations for attending campaign events, including a desire to learn more about the candidate and to reinforce prior decisions. They also found that rallies increased attendees' evaluations of a candidate's honesty, friendliness, and sincerity. Contrary to popular belief, rally-goers include many nonpartisans, suggesting that individual candidates may motivate persuadable attendees (Sanders & Kaid, 1981). With the surprising diversity in rally attendee motivations, there may even be some differences in the levels of basic political interest reported across the four rallies in our sample.

Researchers who examine political learning and political behavior frequently employ the term "political interest" to signify political motivations (e.g., Delli Carpini & Keeter, 1996; Genova & Greenberg, 1979). Political interest refers to one's willingness to pay attention to politics at the expense of alternative topics (Lupia & Philpot, 2005). People who have a high interest in politics will seek information and therefore consume more political news (Luskin, 1990). Political interest is most commonly measured using self-report items that gauge how closely individuals follow politics, how interested they are in the political process, or how much they care who wins an election (e.g., Delli Carpini & Keeter, 1996; Kwak, 1999).

We expect to find high levels of political interest across the rallies, but Trump's celebrity status and the first female nominee of a major political party may have incentivized attendance from citizens with slightly lower levels of political interest. Because the nature of these differences is not firmly grounded in the extant literature, we do not wish to hypothesize about the nature of the relationship. As such, we pose the following research question:

RQ3: Are there significant differences in political interest between attendees at the four campaign rallies?

Previous studies have uncovered several effects of attending political rallies. Sanders and Kaid (1981) found that candidates who speak at political rallies can effect positive changes in their images, stimulate information seeking, and influence vote choice. Thus, a tangible impact of a nonmediated exchange between a voter and a candidate can make a substantial difference in several political communication variables. Though researchers have attempted to study some of these variables, little is known about the population of rally attendees, including whether or not their participation in a political rally corresponds with a confidence in their levels of political knowledge, or their *political information efficacy*.

Kaid, McKinney, and Tedesco (2007) have established a distinction between political efficacy and political information efficacy (PIE). Researchers of political communication would do well to examine the "attitudinal element of knowledge attainment—specifically, how confident one is in what one knows about politics" (McKinney, Rill, & Thorson, 2014, p. 758). In their explication of the two related constructs, Kaid and colleagues' (2007) concept of PIE is "closely related to internal efficacy, but differs in that it focuses solely on the voter's confidence in his or her own political knowledge and its sufficiency to engage the political process" (p. 1096). The authors find that when citizens have higher PIE, they are more likely to vote. Moreover, PIE can be strengthened when voters believe that their preferred presidential candidate will win the election (Tedesco, 2011), when they view a campaign debate (McKinney et al., 2014; McKinney & Warner, 2013), and when they view televised presidential advertising (Kaid, Fernandes, & Painter, 2011). Because PIE is associated with differences in candidate standing and exposure to campaign messages, there may be significant differences in the level of engagement across the four rallies. We therefore ask:

RQ4: Are there significant differences in political information efficacy between attendees at the four campaign rallies?

This study seeks to better understand the characteristics of rally-goers who were a source of enthusiasm in the early days of the 2016 presidential election. By surveying rally-goers at campaign events in the hours before the Iowa caucuses, we uncovered key similarities and differences between the crowds attracted by each campaign and offer new insights into this population of engaged citizens. Our variables of interest include political interest, cynicism, external efficacy, and political information efficacy. The following section discusses the measures for these four variables of interest and outlines our procedures for data collection.

Method

A team of student researchers from a large Midwestern university distributed surveys at four separate campaign events in the lead-up to the 2016 Iowa caucuses. The campaign events were selected based on their proximity in time to the precinct voting, with each rally occurring in the 24 hours immediately preceding the caucus gatherings. A total of 246 individuals were interviewed. The participants were drawn from the rallies of Ted Cruz ($n=47$), Donald Trump ($n=50$), Hillary Clinton ($n=84$), and Bernie Sanders ($n=65$). Sample sizes from the four rallies varied as a result of differences in access afforded by the four campaigns and limitations imposed by the event setting and level of attendance.

In the overall sample, 50% of respondents were male ($n=123$) and 49.6% were female ($n=122$). Participant ages ranged from 18 to 87 ($M=45.59$, $SD=16.36$). A majority of interviewees were Iowa residents ($n=172$, 69.9%). Approximately 30% of the sample identified as born-again evangelical Christians ($n=75$) with significant differences in religiosity between Republican and Democratic rally attendees. Republican rally attendees were significantly more likely to identify as born-again evangelical Christians, χ^2 (1, $N=246)=28.78$, $p<.01$. At Clinton's rally, 13.4% ($n=11$) identified as born-again Christians, along with 23.1% at Sanders' rally ($n=15$), 65.2% at Cruz's rally ($n=30$), and 38% at Trump's rally ($n=19$).

An overwhelming majority of the sample identified as white, non-Hispanic ($n=192$, 78%), 4.9% as Hispanic or Latino ($n=12$), 4.1% as African American ($n=10$), 2.8% as Asian American or Pacific Islander ($n=7$), and 6.5% as another race or ethnicity ($n=16$). Respondents reported relatively high levels of education, with 34.6% reported having earned a college graduate degree ($n=85$), 30.5% identified a bachelor's degree as their highest level of educational attainment ($n=75$), 26.4% had some college ($n=65$), 6.5% had a high school or equivalent degree ($n=16$), and 2% had some high school ($n=5$).

Measures

Political information efficacy was measured using four items on a 5-point, Likert-type scale ($M=4.25$, $SD=.79$, $\alpha=.887$) designed to test individuals' confidence that they know enough about politics to engage in the political process (Kaid et al., 2007): "I consider myself well qualified to participate in politics," "I feel that I have a pretty good understanding of the important political issues facing our country," "I think that I am better informed about politics and government than most people," and "If a friend asked me about the presidential election, I feel I would have enough information to help my friend figure out who to vote for."

Political cynicism was measured with items adapted from previous research that stressed the significance of trust and honesty in evaluating political cynicism (Craig, Niemi, & Silver, 1990). The three-item scale ($M=3.21$, $SD=.77$, $\alpha=.683$) was designed to measure respondents' cynical attitudes about politics and politicians. Respondents self-rated their levels of cynicism using 5-point, Likert-type scales. These three items were "Politicians can be trusted," (reverse-coded), "Politicians are corrupt," and "Politicians are dishonest." This three-item scale had a reliability score lower than is desirable but within the range reported in previous research assessing cynicism (e.g. De Vreese & Elenbaas, 2008; Lin & Lim, 2002).

External political efficacy was measured using a four-item scale ($M=3.87$, $SD=.94$, $\alpha=.874$) designed to test the extent to which respondents feel that their engagement in the political process will have some effect. The items were selected to test voting and communicative political behaviors, as well as general political participation. Items were adapted from scales proposed by Craig et al. (1990) and Niemi et al. (1991). These items were "I can make a difference if I participate in the election process, "I have a real say in what the government does," "My vote makes a difference," and "Voting gives people an effective way to influence what the government does."

Political interest was measured with three items on a 5-point agreement scale ($M=4.33$, $SD=.85$, $\alpha=.906$): "I am interested in politics," "I follow politics closely," and "Politics are important to me personally." There was some amount of item nonresponse in each of the four measures described earlier. Little's (1988) MCAR test determined that the values were missing completely at random, and the missing data were imputed using maximum likelihood estimation.

Results

The results from multivariate analysis of variance revealed that normative political attitudes differ among rally-goers, Pillai's trace$=.12$, $F(12, 723)=2.56$, $p<.01$, observed power$=.98$. The tests of between-subjects effects further showed that of the four political attitudes, there were significant differences in the level of political information efficacy, political cynicism, and external efficacy, but the differences in political interest were not statistically significant, as shown in Table 17.1.

Hypotheses 1 and 2 predict that participants at Sanders' and Trump's rallies would have higher levels of cynicism than those at Clinton's or Cruz's. Hypothesis 1 was supported. Those who attended Clinton's rally were significantly less cynical than attendees at the Sanders rally ($\Delta M=-.40$, $SE=.12$, $p<.001$). Clinton rally attendees also reported lower levels of cynicism than attendees

Table 17.1   Tests of Between-Subjects Effects of Rallies on
                 Political Attitudes

IV	DVs	SS	M²	F(df)	η²	Observed Power
Rally	Political interest	4.21	1.40	1.98(3)	0.024	.51
	PIE	5.05	1.68	2.73(3)*	0.033	.66
	Cynicism	10.21	3.40	6.14(3)***	0.071	.96
	External efficacy	9.68	3.23	3.75(3)*	0.045	.81

Note: SS=Sum of squares; M²=Mean square; *p<.05, **p<.01, ***p≤.001

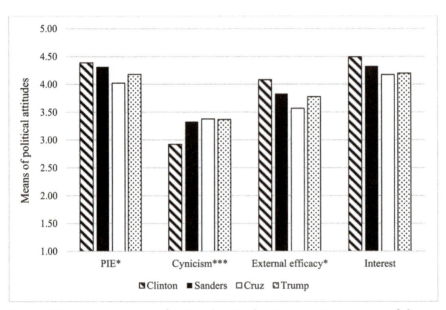

Figure 17.1   Comparisons of Political Attitudes Between Participants of the
Four Rallies (*Note*: *p<.05, **p<.01, ***p<.001)

at Cruz's rally (ΔM=-.45, SE=.14, p<.001) and at Trump's (ΔM=-.47, SE=.13, p<.001), as illustrated in Figure 17.1. Contrary to Hypothesis 2, Cruz rally attendees were not less cynical than Trump rally attendees.

RQ1 and RQ2 asked whether there would be differences between Sanders and Trump rally attendees when compared with insider candidates. Our findings were mixed. Clinton's rally-goers were significantly more externally efficacious than those who attended Cruz's rally (ΔM=.54, SE=.17, p<.001) or Trump's (ΔM=.33, SE=.17, p<.05). When compared to Sanders' rally-goers, Clinton's rally-goers also scored higher (ΔM=.29, SE=.15, p=.059, [LLCI=-.01; ULCI=.59]), but this difference was only approaching statistical significance.

Table 17.2   Means and Standard Deviations of Political Attitudes by Different Rallies

	Hillary Clinton		Bernie Sanders		Ted Cruz		Donald Trump	
	M	SD	M	SD	M	SD	M	SD
PIE	4.39	.67	4.31	.83	4.02	.90	4.18	.83
Cynicism	2.92	.74	3.33	.72	3.38	.78	3.37	.78
External efficacy	4.08	.83	3.83	.98	3.57	1.03	3.77	.95
Political interest	4.49	.66	4.32	.93	4.17	.97	4.20	.90

RQ3 asked about differences in levels of political interest across the four rallies. As shown in Figure 17.1, political interest is high for all rally-goers, but as previously mentioned, there were not significant differences in political interest among participants of the four rallies. Means and standard deviations of each political attitude are presented in Table 17.2.

RQ4 asked whether there would be significant differences in PIE across the four rallies. As illustrated in Figure 17.1, pairwise comparisons showed that Cruz's rally-goers had significantly lower levels of political information efficacy than attendees at Clinton's ($\Delta M = -.38$, $SE = .14$, $p < .01$) and Sanders' ($\Delta M = -.32$, $SE = .15$, $p < .05$) rallies. Although Cruz's rally-goers were lower in PIE when compared to Trump's, the differences were not statistically significant ($\Delta M = -.17$, $SE = .16$, [$LLCI = -.48$; $ULCI = .15$]).

Discussion

Our field survey produced several interesting findings that warrant further discussion about the four leading primary candidates and the broader differences in political attitudes among supporters of insider and outsider candidates. First, results revealed significant differences at the rallies for three of the four political attitudes we examined: political information efficacy, external efficacy, and political cynicism.

Levels of political interest were high across all four rallies, with no significant differences between attendees at the four events. We did not find support for the claim that outsider candidates (Sanders and Trump) attracted audiences with lower levels of interest. Our findings suggest that even in the early days of the campaign, Trump events primarily attracted those with prior interest in politics rather than individuals motivated by his celebrity status. Based on the results of our field survey, political interest could be seen as a fundamental "baseline" attitude to predict political engagement and participation. In their notable monograph on political participation, Verba, Schlozman, and Brady (1995) found that political interest and political knowledge were the most powerful nondemographic predictors of participation. Our results point to similar conclusions, especially because political interest was high for attendees of every rally. Outside of a slightly higher score for PIE among Clinton attendees, means for political interest were the highest of all attitudes measured (see Table 17.2).

Hypotheses 1 and 2 predicted that political cynicism would be higher for the rally attendees for Sanders and Trump compared to attendees of the Clinton and Cruz rallies. Our results were consistent with H1, comparing Sanders and Clinton, but not H2, comparing Trump and Cruz. Consistent with our hypotheses, Sanders supporters reported significantly higher levels of cynicism ($M=3.33$) than Clinton attendees ($M=2.92$). These findings may suggest that early Sanders supporters related to his depiction of the political process as fundamentally corrupt. The differences between the audiences at the two events may speak to some of the key distinctions between the two wings of the Democratic Party and the difficulty Clinton faced in bridging intraparty divisions after the primary campaign.

The second hypothesis predicted that Trump rally attendees would report significantly higher levels of political cynicism than Cruz rally attendees. We did not find statistical support for H2. The absence of significant findings may undercut our argument that Cruz was a political insider. Despite his status as an established Republican politician, Cruz may have attracted supporters with cynicism levels more consistent with Sanders and Trump. In fact, none of the pairwise comparisons between Cruz and Trump supporters illustrated significant differences. An alternative explanation for the absence of significant differences is that Trump appealed to more traditional Republicans than his rhetoric often suggested.

The pairwise differences between Clinton and Sanders supporters, on the other hand, seem to support the insider/outsider dynamics theorized in our description of the 2016 primaries. That Sanders supporters were more cynical than Clinton supporters likely speaks to the rhetorical positioning of the two candidates. It is noteworthy that Clinton supporters reported significantly lower levels of cynicism than attendees of the other three rallies. This finding may lend further support to the framing of Cruz as a political outsider, but the differences may also be indicative of the combined effects of Clinton's insider status and her being closely identified with the incumbent president.

RQ1 and RQ2 asked about the relationship between insiders and outsiders with respect to external efficacy. Results of this study indicate that Clinton supporters had higher external efficacy than Sanders supporters (RQ1), consistent with literature that has found a negative relationship between cynicism and efficacy (Pinkleton & Austin, 2001, 2002). Despite the difference, Sanders supporters still reported moderately high levels of external efficacy ($M=3.83$). There were no significant differences between Trump and Cruz supporters (RQ2).

RQ3 and RQ4 sought to explore the differences in attendees' perceptions of their own political information efficacy and political interest between the rallies. As previously indicated, there were no significant differences in political interest between rallies. PIE (RQ4) was different for attendees at the four rallies; however, the between-rally differences at the pairwise level indicate that Cruz attendees had lower PIE than Sanders and Clinton attendees, but not Trump attendees. This may suggest a partisan difference in Iowa, but, without replication and further theoretical consideration, this finding is speculative.

Limitations

Our field survey encountered some limitations that may have influenced our findings. First, differences in access afforded by the campaigns and attendance at the four events resulted in unequal samples across the rallies. Additionally, our focus on the rallies of the leading candidates in each race limited our ability to draw comparisons between Cruz, who we argue functioned as an insider, and more traditional Republican insiders such as Jeb Bush and Marco Rubio. Furthermore, though our research focuses on an important population at a critical moment in the 2016 presidential campaign, our findings should not be taken as generalizable to the larger population of campaign supporters nationally. Finally, as with any study utilizing a single campaign as a case study, we cannot be sure that inferences about insiders and outsiders drawn from Clinton, Sanders, Cruz, and Trump will be generalizable to future electoral contexts with different candidates and different electoral dynamics.

Conclusion

The Iowa caucuses are a crucial rite of passage for presidential candidates seeking their party's nomination for the country's highest office. During the 2016 campaign, four leading candidates battled over Iowa's delegates and the coveted momentum narrative that a strong showing in Iowa can often generate. Our findings revealed some of the critical dynamics at play in the hours just before the caucus voting began. Specifically, we found that the Sanders rally attracted attendees with significantly higher levels of political cynicism and that individuals across all four rallies expressed high levels of political interest and political information efficacy. In addition to revealing differences between supporters of the four leading candidates, our findings shed light on the important population of rally-goers, who are often used as a proxy for enthusiasm and who dominated media coverage during the 2016 presidential primaries. Future researchers should build on our findings by further testing the role of cynicism and efficacy in intraparty elections. Our study suggests that there is much more to be gleaned from surveying the highly engaged population of rally attendees. The findings lay groundwork for future research on political cynicism and intraparty dynamics in primary elections.

The 2016 election left significant intraparty divisions unresolved. As of the time of our writing, congressional Republicans have struggled to unite around a cohesive policy agenda, and deep intraparty skepticism continues to haunt the leadership of the Democratic National Committee. These struggles suggest that intraparty dynamics, like those discussed here, may continue to define the political landscape for years to come, and the Iowa caucuses will provide the fertile ground in which many of these intraparty dynamics take root.

References

American Presidency Project. (2016). *Presidential debates 1960–2016*. Retrieved from http://www.presidency.ucsb.edu/debates.php

Campbell, A., Gurin, G., & Miller, W. E. (1954). *The voter decides*. Evanston, IL: Row Peterson.

CNN. (2016, January 20). Trump and Sanders using anger against big money to build their movements. *CNN.com*. Retrieved from http://www.cnn.com/2016/01/20/politics/donald-trump-bernie-sanders-money-super-pac/

Cohen, M., Karol, D., Noel, H., & Zaller, J. (2016). Party versus faction in the reformed presidential nominating system. *PS-Political Science & Politics*, 43(4), 1–8. doi:10.1017/S1049096516001682

Craig, S. C., Niemi, R. G., & Silver, G. E. (1990). Political efficacy and trust: A report on the NES pilot study items. *Political Behavior*, 12(3), 289–314. doi:10.1007/BF00992337

Delli Carpini, M. X. (2004). Mediating democratic engagement: The impact of communications on citizens' involvement in political and civic life. In L. L. Kaid (Ed.), *Handbook of political communication research* (pp. 395–434). Mahwah, NJ: Lawrence Erlbaum.

Delli Carpini, M. X., & Keeter, S. (1996). *What Americans know about politics and why it matters*. New Haven, CT: Yale University Press.

De Vreese, C. H., & Elenbaas, M. (2008). Media in the game of politics: Effects of strategic metacoverage on political cynicism. *The International Journal of Press/Politics*, 13(3), 285–309. doi:10.1177/1940161208319650

Donovan, T., & Hunsaker, R. (2009). Beyond expectations: Effects of early elections in US presidential nomination contests. *PS: Political Science and Politics*, 42(1), 45–52. doi:10.1017/S1049096509090040

Erikson, R. S., & Wlezien, C. (2012). *The timeline of presidential elections: How campaigns do (and do not) matter*. Chicago: University of Chicago Press.

Genova, B. K., & Greenberg, B. S. (1979). Interests in news and the knowledge gap. *Public Opinion Quarterly*, 43(1), 79–91. doi:10.1086/268493

Johnson, T. (2016, January 31). Hillary Clinton closes Iowa campaign with contrast to Bernie Sanders. *Variety*. Retrieved from http://variety.com/2016/biz/news/hillary-clinton-iowa-caucus-1201693481/

Kaid, L. L., Fernandes, J., & Painter, D. (2011). Effects of political advertising in the 2008 presidential campaign. *American Behavioral Scientist*, 55(4), 437–456. doi: 10.1177/0002764211398071

Kaid, L. L., McKinney, M. S., & Tedesco, J. C. (2000). *Civic dialogue in the 1996 presidential campaign: Candidate, media, and public voices.* Cresskill, NJ: Hampton.

Kaid, L. L., McKinney, M. S., & Tedesco, J. C. (2007). Political information efficacy and young voters. *American Behavioral Scientist, 50*(9), 1093–1111. doi:10.1177/0002764207300040

Kwak, N. (1999). Revisiting the knowledge gap hypothesis: Education, motivation and media use. *Communication Research, 26,* 385–413. doi:10.1177/009365099026004002

Lariscy, R. W., Tinkham, S. F., & Sweetser, K. D. (2011). Kids these days: Examining differences in political uses and gratifications, Internet political participation, political information efficacy, and cynicism on the basis of age. *American Behavioral Scientist, 55*(6), 749–764. doi:10.1177/0002764211398091

Lin, Y., & Lim, S. (2002). Relationships of media use to political cynicism and efficacy: A preliminary study of young South Korean voters. *Asian Journal of Communication, 12*(1), 25–39. doi:10.1080/01292980209364812

Little, R. J. (1988). A test of missing completely at random for multivariate data with missing values. *Journal of the American Statistical Association, 83*(404), 1198–1202. doi:10.2307/2290157

Lupia, A., & Philpot, T. S. (2005). Views from inside the net: How websites affect young adults' political interest. *Journal of Politics, 67*(4), 1122–1142. doi:10.1111/j.1468-2508.2005.00353.x

Luskin, R. (1990). Explaining political sophistication. *Political Behavior, 12*(4), 331–361. doi:10.1007/BF00992793

McKinney, M. S., Rill, L. A., & Thorson, E. (2014). Civic engagement through presidential debates: Young citizens' political attitudes in the 2012 Election. *American Behavioral Scientist, 58*(6), 755–775. doi:10.1177/0002764213515223

McKinney, M. S., & Warner, B. R. (2013). Do presidential debates matter? Examining a decade of campaign debate effects. *Argumentation & Advocacy, 49*(4), 238–258.

Miller, A. H. (1974). Political issues and trust in government: 1964–1970. *The American Political Science Review, 68,* 951–972. doi:10.2307/1959140

Niemi, R. G., Craig, S. C., & Mattei, F. (1991). Measuring internal political efficacy in the 1988 National Election Study. *American Political Science Review, 85,* 1407–1413. doi: 10.2307/1963953

Petri, A. (2016, February 1). Trump's Waterloo. *The Washington Post.* Retrieved from https://www.washingtonpost.com/blogs/compost/wp/2016/02/01/trumps-waterloo/?utm_term=.5884ffac4ccc

Pinkleton, B., & Austin, E. W. (2001). Individual motivations, perceived media importance, and political disaffection. *Political Communication, 18*(3), 321–334. doi: 10.1080/10584600152400365

Pinkleton, B. E., & Austin, E. W. (2002). Exploring relationships among media use frequency, perceived media importance, and media satisfaction in political disaffection and efficacy. *Mass Communication & Society, 5*(2), 141–163. doi:10.1207/S15327825MCS0502_3

Pinkleton, B. E., Austin, E. W., & Fortman, K. K. (1998). Relationships of media use and political disaffection to political efficacy and voting behavior. *Journal of Broadcasting and Electronic Media, 42,* 34–49. doi:10.1080/08838 159809364433

Sanders, K. R., & Kaid, L. L. (1981). Political rallies: Their uses and effects. *Communication Studies, 32*(1), 1–11. doi:10.1080/10510978109368073

Steger, W. P. (2007). Who wins nominations and why? An updated forecast of the presidential primary vote. *Political Research Quarterly, 60*(1), 91–99. doi:10.1177/1065912906298597

Tedesco, J. C. (2011). Political information efficacy and Internet effects in the 2008 U.S. presidential election. *American Behavioral Scientist, 55*(6), 696–713. doi: 10.1177/0002764211398089

Trent, J. S., Short-Thompson, C., Mongeau, P. A., & Metzler, M. S. (2017). The consistent attributes of the ideal presidential candidate in an increasingly divided electorate. *American Behavioral Scientist, 61*(3), 278–297. doi: 10.1177/0002764217693278

Verba, S., Schlozman, K. L., & Brady, H. E. (1995). *Voice and equality: Civic voluntarism in American politics.* Cambridge, MA: Harvard University Press.

Wagner, J. (2016, January 31). In final rally before Iowa caucuses, Bernie Sanders hits on familiar themes. *The Washington Post.* Retrieved from https://www .washingtonpost.com/news/post-politics/wp/2016/01/31/in-final-iowa-rally -bernie-sanders-hits-on-familiar-themes-in-front-of-crowd-of-1700/?utm _term=.3e91780eca39

Warner, B. R., Galarza, R., Coker, C. R., Tschirhart, P., Hoeun, S., Jennings, F., & McKinney, M. S. (2017). Comic agonism in the 2016 campaign: A study on Iowa caucus rallies. *American Behavioral Scientist.* Advance online publication. doi: 10.1177/0002764217704868

Willson, M. (1957). *The music man.* Milwaukee, WI: Hal Leonard Corporation.

CHAPTER EIGHTEEN

Exploring and Explaining Communication, Knowledge, and Well-Being Sex Differences Related to the 2016 U.S. Presidential Primary Season

R. Lance Holbert, Esul Park, and Nicholas W. Robinson

With the Hillary Clinton candidacy and the election of Donald Trump, it is important to focus attention on potential differences between male and female voters during the 2016 election cycle. Sex differences in the area of media and politics have been the focus of much past research (e.g., Poindexter, Meraz, & Weiss, 2008). Researchers also have looked at gender differences in political attitudes. For example, Inglehart and Norris (2003) produced important work on the shift from the "traditional gender gap" to the "modern gender gap" concerning male-female differences in sociopolitical attitudes. In addition, a tremendous amount of work has examined differences in male versus female voting patterns (see Campbell, 2017, for summary of extant research).

This chapter focuses on three sex differences: a communication gap concerning political media use, a knowledge gap specific to the U.S. presidential primaries, and an experiential well-being gap. Although the first two of these three gaps have been fully explored in past research, it is important for both of these differences to be revisited given the historic nature of the 2016 presidential election (see Bystrom, 2016). The latter of these three gaps is new to the literature and builds off recent work stressing the importance of subjective perceptions of experiential well-being in all facets of a human being's day-to-day activities (see Stone & Mackie, 2013).

The goal of this chapter is twofold. First, we hope to identify potentially important sex differences, both old and new, that could indicate negative normative outcomes for democratic processes that value equality. Second, we hope to explore the effects of a series of third variables that could serve to explain away the influence of biological sex on political media use, political knowledge, and well-being. As argued by Allen (1998), "the biological basis of the answers people provide may or may not reflect the true variable of interest to the researcher" (p. 429).

This chapter will explore the degree to which what at first glance appears to be a sex difference may actually be due to a third variable. Four classifications of third variables are explored: demographics, political individual differences (e.g., ideology), measures of political optimism (e.g., country on right or wrong track), and campaign-specific attitudes and behaviors. It is important to gain a firm understanding of whether differential effects for men versus women persist even with the introduction of additional controls or weaken substantially as soon as a more complicated empirical picture is presented. In addition, if third variables are shown to be the underlying cause for a sex difference, then pinpointing these agents is the first step in attempting to improve our political processes in a manner that will create greater equity.

Political Communication, Knowledge, and Well-Being Sex Differences

There is consistent empirical evidence of sex differences concerning political media use, with men consuming more political media than women (e.g., Knobloch-Westerwick & Alter, 2007; Strömbäck, Djerf-Pierre, & Shehata, 2012). This particular type of gender gap is evident in relation to such varied outlet types as partisan media (e.g., Feldman, Myers, Hmielowski, & Leiserowitz, 2014; Holbert, Hmielowski, & Weeks, 2012); online news (e.g., Best, Chmielewski, & Krueger, 2005; Brundidge, 2010; Chan & Leung, 2005, Chyi & Yang, 2009; Dutta-Bergman, 2004); and satirical news (e.g., Coe et al., 2008; Young & Tisinger, 2006). However, some works have shown that social media outlets like Facebook generate greater news consumption among females than males (e.g., Glynn, Huge, & Hoffman, 2012; Gottfried & Shearer, 2016; Weeks & Holbert, 2013).

Nevertheless, a clear majority of works indicate "women, on average, consume less political news than men" (Benesch, 2012, p. 147). Also a number of studies point to sex differences in relation to various types of political knowledge and the generation of knowledge from news media exposure (e.g., de Vreese & Boomgaarden, 2006; Eveland & Scheufele, 2000; Fraile & Iyengar, 2014; Gil de Zúñiga, Weeks, & Ardèvol-Abreu, 2017; Holbert, 2005; Kenski & Stroud, 2006; Kwak, 1999; Prior, 2005; Shehata, Hopmann, Nord, & Hoijer, 2015). Although many aspects of life point to support for the gender similarities hypothesis (see Hyde, 2014), these respective media and knowledge gaps are well established in the political communication literature. As a result, we posit the following hypotheses:

H1: There is a sex difference in political media use, with men retaining higher consumption levels than women.

H2: There is a sex difference in political primary knowledge, with men retaining higher knowledge levels than women.

The sex differences discussed so far stem from the treatment of citizens as understanding-driven creatures. There is no question individuals seek out information during an election season in order to make informed decisions in the voting booth (Prior, 2010), and an informed citizenry is the basis for a well-functioning democracy (Galston, 2001). Understanding-based approaches of this kind can be contrasted with explorations that derive from the treatment of citizens as consistency-driven creatures (e.g., Levendusky, 2013). Studies of partisan selective exposure to political communication reflect an assumption that people most often gravitate toward communicative acts that serve to reinforce the way in which they already see the world (see Stroud, 2011).

Although the explanatory principles of understanding and consistency are well-reasoned bases for the study of political communication, other approaches may exist that are worthy of investigation (see Pavitt, 2016). In particular, Holbert, Weeks, and Esralew (2013) have argued for the need to explore hedonically grounded lines of research in the study of media and politics. Citizens do not only seek understanding and consistency but pleasure as well within the context of their political activities. Individuals may be driven in part by enjoyment (i.e., hedonic) or meaningful enjoyment (i.e., eudemonic) during the course of an election cycle, and researchers are beginning to explore mechanisms of this kind (e.g., Roth, Weinmann, Schneider, Hopp, & Vorderer, 2014).

It is important to explore whether hedonic-based sex differences exist in relation to our basic democratic processes. One hedonic-based concept that can serve as a foundation for an exploration of this kind is subjective well-being (Stone & Mackie, 2013). Research in this area works from an argument that people seek to maximize their well-being in all aspects of their lives, and it is best to define well-being as a mixture of pleasure and purpose (Dolan,

2014). Much of this work stems from the foundational research of Kahneman, Wakker, and Sarin (1997) showing that experienced utility is distinct from decision utility. Work on decision utility focuses solely on the choices individuals make as rationale actors, but Kahneman and colleagues revealed people are more than the sum of this type of decision making. People will seek to create activities and gravitate toward behaviors that provide them with a balance of pleasure and purpose. A case can be made that it is a normative ideal for our democratic processes to maximize citizens' well-being. If citizens experience high levels of well-being during the course of an election cycle, then a long list of positive outcomes (e.g., sustained engagement, increased trust, and heightened optimism) may derive from this state of being.

Extant research has not explored whether men and women vary in their experiential well-being relative to basic democratic processes. As a result, we present the following:

RQ1: Is there a sex difference in experiential well-being relative to the 2016 U.S. presidential primaries?

The concept of "gender," which is most meaningful theoretically in terms of representing psychological or sociological distinctions (e.g., Bem, 1981; Harnois, 2005), is usually operationalized as a biological sex distinction. As Allen (1998) notes, "social scientists seldom formulate questions or hypotheses on the basis of biological issues" (p. 429). In the context of the sex differences explored in this work, it is difficult to make an argument that having an X versus a Y chromosome is the root cause for differences in political media use. As noted by Delli Carpini and Keeter (1997), "[M]ost theories regarding gender differences in political orientations are rooted in structural and situational explanations: females know less about politics than males because of differences in how the sexes are socialized and because of the different opportunities afforded them to engage the political world" (p. 204). Indeed, "relying on a simple single-item measure that reflects no explicit theoretical premise is doomed to produce useless and meaningless scientific data" (Allen, 1998, p. 442).

Yet empirically validated sex differences do persist in the political communication literature, and it is important to explore what is underlying those differences given that they are most likely not grounded in biology. Thus, the following research question is posed:

RQ2: What third variables may account for communication, knowledge, or well-being sex differences evident during the 2016 U.S. presidential primaries?

Method

Survey Data

A total of 960 U.S. adults completed a 15-minute survey between July 13 and July 15, 2016. This brief window of time falls between the closure of the state-level presidential primary contests and the national political party conventions. All Democratic and Republican primary contests were completed by June 14 (Democratic primary for the District of Columbia) and the Republican National Convention, the first of the two major party conventions, started on July 18, 2016. All respondents were recruited via a Qualtrics online panel. As noted by Qualtrics concerning its recruitment procedures:

> Potential respondents are sent an email invitation informing them that the survey is for research purposes only, how long the survey is expected to take, and what incentives are available. Members may unsubscribe at any time. To avoid self-selection bias, the survey invitation does not include specific details about the contents of the survey . . . Qualtrics respondents will receive an incentive based on the length of the survey, their specific panelist profile, and target acquisition difficulty. The specific type of rewards varies and may include cash, airline miles, gift cards, redeemable points, sweepstakes entrance, and vouchers. (p. 5)

For the purposes of this study, it is important to note that Qualtrics was directed by the researchers to maintain a male-female balance among the respondents.

Dependent Variables

Political Media Use

This is a three-item scale. Respondents were asked the degree to which they use a series of types of media content, with possible responses ranging from 0 (not at all) to 4 (a great deal). The three types of content utilized for this study are as follows: "national news and politics," "the 2016 presidential election," and "international politics and global news." The three items form a reliable scale (Cronbach's α=.85), and the four moments are as follows: M=2.59, SD=0.92, Sk=-0.40, and Ku=-0.43.

Political Primary Knowledge

Respondents were asked seven political primary knowledge questions. The Democratic and Republican primaries were given three items each, and a general question concerning "Super Tuesday" that applied to both parties was included. All questions were multiple choice, and all items were recoded to indicate 1=correct response and 0=all other responses. The descriptive statistics for the 0–7 index are as follows: $M=2.79$, $SD=1.79$, $Sk=0.36$, and $Ku=-0.67$.

Experiential Well-Being

This is a four-item scale (Cronbach's $\alpha=.87$). Respondents were asked the degree to which they experienced "happiness" during the course of the primaries, with responses ranging from 1 (not at all) to 7 (a great deal). In addition, questions were posed concerning whether the 2016 U.S. primaries were perceived by the respondent to be worthwhile and effective at selecting the best people to be the general election candidates. The worthwhile question offered possible responses ranging from 1 (extremely worthwhile) to 5 (not at all worthwhile). This item was recoded to allow greater perceived worth to be coded high. The effectiveness item was measured on a 1–5 scale from 1 (not at all effective) to 5 (extremely effective). Finally, respondents were asked the degree to which they were satisfied with the 2016 U.S. presidential primary process, with possible responses ranging from 1 (extremely satisfied) to 7 (extremely dissatisfied). This item was also recoded to allow greater satisfaction to be coded high. Given different scales were utilized for these items, the standardized versions of the items were employed for scale creation: $M=-0.01$, $SD=3.39$, $Sk=0.33$, and $Ku=-0.83$.

Independent Variable

Biological Sex

The respondents consisted of 485 females and 475 males.

Covariates

Demographics

Four additional demographics are explored in this study: age, income, education, and race. Age is measured on a six-point scale ranging from 1 (18–24) to 6 (65+). The descriptive statistics are as follows: $M=3.75$, $SD=1.59$, $Sk=0.08$, and $Ku=-1.15$. Income is "annual household income" and measured on a 12-point scale from 1 (less than \$10,000) to 12 (more than \$150,000). The descriptive statistics are as follows: $M=6.83$, $SD=3.36$, $Sk=0.08$, and $Ku=-1.30$. Education is a single 9-point item ranging from 1 (grade 8 or lower) to 9 (graduate or professional degree). The descriptive statistics are as follows: $M=6.20$,

$SD=1.98$, $Sk=-0.18$, and $Ku=-0.99$. The race item allowed for six possible responses: white, black/African American, Asian/Asian American, Native American/American Indian, mixed, and other. In addition, respondents were asked a single question of whether they were Hispanic or Latino. From these items, a single dichotomous Caucasian-other variable was created ($N=627$, 65%, Caucasian).

Political Individual Differences

Political interest is measured with responses to a single query: "How interested are you in politics?" with possible responses ranging from 1 (not at all) to 5 (a great deal). Descriptive statistics for this item are $M=3.40$, $SD=0.98$, $Sk=-0.26$, and $Ku=-0.27$. Political ideology is measured on a 5-point scale from 1 (very conservative) to 5 (very liberal), with the following as descriptive statistics: $M=3.05$, $SD=1.15$, $Sk=0.27$, and $Ku=-0.61$. Internal political self-efficacy is a four-item scale consisting of responses to the following statements: "I consider myself well-qualified to participate in politics"; "I feel I have a pretty good understanding of the important political issues facing our country"; "I feel that I could do as good a job in public office as most other people"; and "I feel that I am as well-informed about politics and government as most people." All of these 1–7 Likert-type items were measured with scales ranging from 1 (strongly disagree) to 7 (strongly agree). Two items needed recoding to allow all measures to reflect higher scores indicating greater agreement. The scale is reliable (Cronbach's $\alpha=.87$), and the following are its four moments: $M=4.96$, $SD=1.18$, $Sk=-0.59$, and $Ku=0.16$.

Political Optimism

Respondents were asked a single question of whether they consider the country going in the right or the wrong direction ($N=596$, 62.1%, indicated wrong direction was coded high). In addition, the survey contained the following question: "Compared to 50 years ago, is life for people like you in America worse, better, or the same?" Responses were organized on an ordinal scale from (worse) to (the same) to (better), with the latter coded high. A little less than half of the respondents ($N=446$, 46.5%) indicated "worse," whereas 337 (35.1%) stated "better." The two items were treated as distinct entities, given the former focused on the country and the latter asked participants to think about people like themselves only.

Election

Respondents were asked whether they voted or caucused during the 2016 U.S. presidential primary season ($N=771$, 80.3%, indicated they did vote or caucus). A pair of six-item scales were created to assess citizen-level positivity ratings for Clinton and Trump, respectively. Each of the candidates was rated in accordance with the following traits: trustworthy, qualified, intelligent, and leader. These traits were measured from 1 (low) to 7 (high). In addition, participants were asked to rate each candidate in terms of overall favorability. Once again, these items were measured on 1 (low favorability) to 7 (high favorability). Finally, respective items were offered asking respondents the likelihood they would vote for Clinton or Trump, respectively, in the general election. The initial measures were from 1 (extremely likely) to 7 (extremely unlikely), but were recoded to allow greater likelihood to be coded high. The two 6-item scales were reliable (Clinton, Cronbach's $\alpha = .94$; Trump, Cronbach's $\alpha = .93$). The descriptive statistics for the two items are as follows: Clinton, $M = 6.42$, $SD = 2.97$, $Sk = -0.23$, and $Ku = -1.31$; Trump, $M = 3.30$, $SD = 1.89$, $Sk = 0.45$, and $Ku = -1.06$. The mean difference for Clinton attitudes and Trump attitudes is a statistically significant, paired-sample t-test, $t = 21.66$, $p < .001$.

Missing Data

This study employs a total of 37 individual items for its analyses. Most items retained a very small number of missing values ($N < 5$). The only problematic item in terms of missing values (i.e., missing $N \geq 5\%$) is the "is the country on the right or wrong track" item (missing $N = 73$, 7.6%). Given the nominal and exploratory nature of this item, a decision was made not to seek to replace this variable's missing values. In short, no replacement of missing values was undertaken prior to the study's analyses.

Analyses

First, a single multiple analysis of variance (MANOVA) was constructed with biological sex as a single independent variable and political media use, political primary knowledge, and experiential well-being as three dependent variables. All three dependent variables are correlated with each other at the $p < .001$ level. As a result, it is important to take into account these associations while assessing the influence of the independent variable and any covariates. This MANOVA addresses H1, H2, and RQ1.

Once the initial MANOVA is assessed, a series of multivariate analysis of covariance (MANCOVA) was run with each containing a single covariate. The influence of each covariate and the shift in F-values relative to each dependent variable is judged against those produced in the initial MANOVA in order to assess the degree to which a given covariate sheds light as to the underlying cause(s) for any sex differences indicated in the MANOVA. These analyses are undertaken in relation to RQ2. A reduction in a sex-specific F-value from the MANOVA to the MANCOVA will signal that a portion of the sex difference is explained away by the covariate.

Alpha (Type I Error)-Power (Type II Error) Assessment

A power analysis was conducted in order to establish a proper alpha level for this study's analyses. The goal is to be mindful of the Type II error rate while seeking to introduce a stringent Type I error threshold. G* Power (Faul, Erdfelder, Lang, & Buchner, 2007) was used to assess the ability to detect a small effect ($f=.10$) for a fixed-effects, omnibus one-way ANOVA with two groups and a sample size of 960. The power estimate given these parameters is .87 (i.e., sufficient Type II error rate), given an alpha level of $p<.05$. An alpha level of $p<.01$ was then inserted into the same procedure, but the power level generated given this new parameter was .69 (i.e., insufficient Type II error rate). As a result, the $p<.05$ alpha level was retained for this study.

Results

MANOVA (H1, H2, RQ1)

Biological sex had a main effect at the omnibus level, $F (3, 950)=14.27$, $p<.001$, $\eta^2=.04$. At the univariate level, sex has a statistically significant effect on all three dependent variables: political media, $F (1, 952)=23.49$, $p<.001$, $\eta^2=.02$; political primary knowledge, $F (1, 952)=7.22$, $p<.01$, $\eta^2=.01$; and experiential well-being, $F (1, 952)=17.48$, $p<.001$, $\eta^2=.02$. Women were found to consume less political media (female, $M=2.44$; male, $M=2.73$), retain less knowledge about the 2016 U.S. primaries (female, $M=2.64$; male, $M=2.94$), and experience less well-being (female, $M=-0.46$; male, $M=0.45$). These findings lend support for H1 and H2. In addition, these results indicate RQ1 to be a fruitful query. The two largest sex differences are for political media use and well-being, with the male-female difference for knowledge being less pronounced.

MANCOVA (RQ2)

Demographics

All four demographic variables had an effect at the omnibus level based on the running of four distinct MANCOVAs: age, $F (3, 949)=19.67$, $p<.001$, $\eta^2=.06$; education, $F (3, 949)=8.16$, $p<.001$, $\eta^2=.03$; income, $F (3, 949)=6.91$, $p<.001$, $\eta^2=.02$; and race (Caucasian-other), $F (3, 949)=3.59$, $p<.05$, $\eta^2=.01$. Each demographic had a statistically significant effect on at least one of the three dependent variables at the univariate level: age (knowledge, well-being); education (political media, knowledge); income (political media, knowledge); and race (knowledge). However, all sex differences remain statistically significant for all dependent variables in these MANCOVAs. In short, none of the demographic variables serve to alter the influence of the independent variable in any meaningful way.

Political Individual Differences

The relatively small omnibus effects for the demographic covariates can be contrasted with the large effect produced by political interest, F (3, 949)$=287.71$, $p < .001$, $\eta^2 = .48$. A sizeable portion of this effect can be found in this covariate's influence on political media use, F (1, 951)$=781.59$, $p < .001$, $\eta^2 = .45$. However, its effects on knowledge (F (1, 951)$=39.52$, $p < .001$, $\eta^2 = .04$) and well-being (F (1, 951)$=46.80$, $p < .001$, $\eta^2 = .05$) are also relatively large. The main effect of biological sex for both political media use and primary knowledge becomes statistically insignificant with the introduction of this covariate. The difference between men (adjusted $M=2.63$) and women (adjusted $M=2.54$) for political media use reduces substantially once political interest is accounted for, and this is the case for political knowledge as well (men, adjusted $M=2.89$; women, adjusted $M=2.70$). There is also a reduction in the distance between men (adjusted $M=0.33$) and women (adjusted $M=-0.35$) for the well-being dependent variable. However, a meaningful sex difference remains in well-being even when accounting for this individual-difference covariate. Overall, political interest goes a long way in accounting for the sex differences identified in the initial MANOVA.

Political ideology does not have an effect at the omnibus level, F (3, 949)$=1.36$, $p > .25$, $\eta^2 = .00$. It does not play a meaningful role in predicting any of the three dependent variables, and most certainly is not eating into any of the sex differences. Internal political self-efficacy's influence is much more in line with interest's rather than ideology's effect levels. The following is self-efficacy's effect at the omnibus level: F (3, 947)$=139.54$, $p < .001$, $\eta^2 = .31$. Like interest, efficacy's effects are greatest on political media use ($\eta^2 = .28$), but its ability to affect knowledge is also meaningful ($\eta^2 = .05$). The effect of efficacy on well-being is also statistically significant at the $p < .001$ level ($\eta^2 = .02$). When internal political self-efficacy is introduced as a covariate, the sex differences in political media use (men, adjusted $M=2.61$; women, adjusted $M=2.56$) and primary knowledge (men, adjusted $M=2.86$; women, adjusted $M=2.73$) are reduced to statistical insignificance. There is also a substantial reduction in the distance in well-being between men (adjusted $M=.33$) and women (adjusted $M=-.35$), but this distance is still meaningfully different from zero. Overall, political interest and internal political self-efficacy have proven to be the most effective third variables for reducing the effects of biological sex, and these two political individual-difference variables are functioning in very similar ways.

Optimism

The item concerning whether "people like you" are worse off, the same, or better off (coded high) has an effect at the omnibus level, $F (3, 949) = 18.61$, $p < .001$, $\eta^2 = .06$. Interestingly, this effect is concentrated fully on the well-being variable at the univariate level, $F (1, 951) = 55.55$, $p < .001$, $\eta^2 = .06$. Indeed, the sex difference in this item is reduced as a result of the introduction of this covariate (men, adjusted $M = .39$; women, adjusted $M = -.40$), but not as great as witnessed with the introduction of either political interest or internal political self-efficacy. As for the whether the country is on the right or wrong track covariate, it is also influential at the multivariate level, $F (3, 876) = 85.06$, $p < .001$, $\eta^2 = .23$. Its effect is most sizeable for the well-being dependent variable as well, $F (1, 878) = 239.98$, $p < .001$, $\eta^2 = .22$. It is also statistically significant at the $p < .01$ level for political media use ($\eta^2 = .01$) and political knowledge ($\eta^2 = .03$). Most importantly, the smallest sex difference for the well-being dependent variable is found with the introduction of this covariate, men's adjusted $M = .30$ and women's adjusted $M = -.25$. The right track–wrong track covariate makes the most significant dent in helping explain the sex difference in experiential well-being obtained during the 2016 U.S. presidential primary season.

Election

The effect of voting/caucusing during the primary is statistically significant at the omnibus level, $F (3, 949) = 29.30$, $p < .001$, $\eta^2 = .09$. At the univariate level, its effects are concentrated in political media use ($\eta^2 = .06$) and well-being ($\eta^2 = .04$). None of this covariate's effects eats substantially into the sex differences made known in the MANOVA. The Clinton six-item scale is impactful at the multivariate level, $F (3, 909) = 333.23$, $p < .001$, $\eta^2 = .10$, with its greatest univariate effect on well-being, $F (1, 911) = 96.41$, $p < .001$, $\eta^2 = .10$. It is worth noting its effect on primary knowledge is also statistically significant ($\eta^2 = .01$), but comparatively weak. However, there is no noticeable impact on the sex differences with the introduction of this variable. The Trump scale does not have as large of an impact at the multivariate level, $F (3, 906) = 20.08$, $p < .001$, $\eta^2 = .06$, compared to the Clinton scale. Like Clinton, its greatest impact is on well-being ($F [1, 908] = 54.21$, $p < .001$, $\eta^2 = .06$). However, what is important to note is the reduction in sex differences for well-being when the Trump attitudes scale is accounted for, mean adjusted $M = .23$, women adjusted $M = -.44$. This type of sex difference reduction was not evident with the introduction of the Clinton attitudes scale. Overall, the Trump attitudes covariate does more than the Clinton attitudes measure to help explain the gender difference in experiential well-being derived from the primaries.

Post Hoc Analyses

Once the full list of covariates had been explored, an additional stage of analyses was performed in order to create parsimonious models that serve to account for the gender differences first observed in the MANOVAs. These analyses will serve to identify the least number of covariates needed to explain away the sex differences associated with the respective dependent variables. Three residuals are used as distinct dependent variables. The residuals represent the regressing of one of the dependent variables onto the other two dependent variables from the MANOVA-MANCOVA analyses to account for the relations between the three dependent variables. The unstandardized residuals were saved in each instance and used for the ANCOVA-based analyses.

First, political interest is explored as a covariate, with sex as the independent variable and the political media use-residual as the dependent variable. The inclusion of this single covariate results in a nonsignificant sex difference, $F(1, 951)=0.310$, $p>.55$. This same ANCOVA can also be run with internal political self-efficacy replacing interest as the covariate, and the same nonsignificant sex effect is evident, $F(1, 951)=0.000$, $p>.99$. In fact, self-efficacy covers basically the entire effect space previously associated with biological sex in relation to political media use. In short, the sex difference found for political media use washes away once political interest or internal political self-efficacy is accounted for.

For the primary knowledge-residual dependent variable, internal political self-efficacy was entered as a covariate relative to biological sex as the independent variable. The sex difference effect is nonsignificant in this ANCOVA, $F(1, 949)=2.67$, $p>.10$. Self-efficacy is a variant of perceived knowledge, and perceived knowledge washes away the influence of biological sex on actual 2016 presidential primary knowledge.

As for the experiential well-being-residual dependent variable, the earlier MANCOVA analyses revealed no single covariate serves to render biological sex statistically insignificant. As a result, two covariates were entered into the third and final ANCOVA, country right/wrong (wrong coded high) and Trump attitude. The combination of these two covariates renders biological sex nonsignificant in relation to well-being, $F(1, 836)=0.248$, $p>.60$. Neither covariate on its own explains away the sex difference in full, but the two in combination account for just about all of sex's influence on experiential well-being. It makes sense that these measures of current political perceptions would have the greatest impact on experiential well-being. Once accounted for, men and women retain relatively equal levels of well-being in relation to the 2016 U.S. presidential primaries.

Discussion

An argument is offered in this chapter that an initial set of sex differences can be accounted for by the introduction of third variables that retain even just the slightest bit of face validity. This position does not mean that we believe there are no meaningful differences between men and women. All that is being argued is that any such political differences between men and women are most likely not going to be due to biology (cf., Grabe & Kamhawi, 2006; Soroka, Gidengil, Fournier, & Nir, 2016), and, as a result, a biologically based dichotomous item will not allow us to get at what may be some important normative concerns for our democracy. The effects of the traditional dichotomous measure of male versus female are too weak and easily explained away with the offering of only a slightly more complex empirical landscape. It is important for empirical political communication researchers interested in how men versus women experience and engage in politics to develop measures that best reflect what they are interested in theoretically, and those interests reside more in psychology and sociology than in biology.

In terms of potential differences between men and women, it is important to note that biological sex differences are evident for each of the meaningful covariates identified in this work's analyses. Men retain higher political interest levels (men $M=3.56$, women $M=3.25$), higher self-efficacy (men $M=5.23$, women $M=4.69$), and much more positive perceptions of Trump (men $M=3.62$, women $M=2.99$). All of these mean differences are statistically significant at the $p<.001$ alpha level in a series of one-way ANOVAs. In addition, the women in this sample were more likely to indicate the country was on the wrong track (χ^2 [1] $=14.23$, $p<.001$), with 54% of women indicating the country was on the wrong track versus just 40% of men offering the same response. These differences signal that biological sex could affect levels of political interest, internal political self-efficacy, right/wrong track judgments, and Trump attitudes and that each of these variables affects one or more of the study's dependent variables.

Scenarios of this kind speak to possible mediation-based (i.e., indirect) biological sex effects (see Hayes, 2009). The cross-sectional nature of the data employed for this work does not allow for a proper assessment of mediation, but empirical political communication research may wish to explore the creation of survey designs (i.e., panel data) that would allow for thorough evaluations of these potentially important processes of influence. With this being stated, our primary argument still stands that the use of better measures of gender distinctions would prove valuable for these efforts.

It will be important to analyze the strength of sex differences in other contexts in order to assess whether this study's findings are replicable (Benoit & Holbert, 2008). Primary election seasons represent unique settings within which candidates and parties interact with voters (Kendall, 2016). It will be important for political communication researchers to explore the same line of reasoning presented in this work in the context of general elections and nonelection seasons as well. Only then will the field gain an understanding of whether biology affects how men versus women navigate various democratic processes, gain an understanding of the world around them, and engage in complex forms of political decision making.

References

Allen, M. (1998). Methodological considerations when examining a gendered world. In D. J. Canary & K. Dindia (Eds.), *Sex differences and similarities in communication: Critical essays and empirical investigations of sex and gender in interaction* (pp. 427–444). Mahwah, NJ: Lawrence Erlbaum Associates.

Bem, S. L. (1981). Gender schema theory: A cognitive account of sex typing. *Psychological Review, 88*(4), 354–364. doi:10.1037/0033-295X.88.4.354

Benesch, C. (2012). An empirical analysis of the gender gap in news consumption. *Journal of Media Economics, 25*(3), 147–167. doi:10.1080/08997764.2 012.700976

Benoit, W. L., & Holbert, R. L. (2008). Empirical intersections in communication research: Replication, multiple quantitative methods, and bridging the quantitative–qualitative divide. *Journal of Communication, 58*(4), 615–628. doi:10.1111/j.1460-2466.2008.00404.x

Best, S. J., Chmielewski, B., & Krueger, B. S. (2005). Selective exposure to online foreign news during the conflict with Iraq. *The Harvard International Journal of Press/Politics, 10*(4), 52–70. doi:10.1177/1081180x05281692

Brundidge, J. (2010). Political discussion and news use in the contemporary public sphere: The "accessibility" and "traversability" of the Internet. *Javnost—The Public, 2*, 63–82. doi: 10.1080/13183222.2010.11009031

Bystrom, D. G. (2016). American women and political campaigns: Communication between candidates, voters, and the media. In W. L. Benoit (Ed.), *Praeger handbook of political campaigning in the United States, volume 2: Messaging, voters, and theories* (pp. 67–90). Santa Barbara, CA: Praeger.

Campbell, R. (2017). Gender and voting. In K. Arzheimer, J. Evans, & M. S. Lewis-Beck (Eds.), *The SAGE handbook of political behavior* (pp. 159–176). Los Angeles: SAGE.

Chan, J. K. C., & Leung, L. (2005). Lifestyles, reliance on traditional news media and online news adoption. *New Media & Society, 7*(3), 357–382. doi:10.1177 /1461444805052281

Chyi, H. I., & Yang, M. J. (2009). Is online news an inferior good? Examining the economic nature of online news among users. *Journalism & Mass Communication Quarterly, 86*(3), 594–612. doi:10.1177/107769900908600309

Coe, K., Tewksbury, D., Bond, B. J., Drogos, K. L., Porter, R. W., Yahn, A., & Zhang, Y. (2008). Hostile news: Partisan use and perceptions of cable news programming. *Journal of Communication, 58*(2), 201–219. doi:10.1111/j .1460-2466.2008.00381.x

De Vreese, C. H., & Boomgaarden, H. (2006). News, political knowledge and participation: The differential effects of news media exposure on political knowledge and participation. *Acta Politica, 41*(4), 317–341. doi:10.1057/palgrave.ap.5500164

Della Carpini, M. X. D., & Keeter, S. (1997). *What Americans know about politics and why it matters.* New Haven, CT: Yale University Press.

Dolan, P. (2014). *Happiness by design: Change what you do, not how you think.* New York: Hudson Street Press.

Dutta-Bergman, M. J. (2004). Complementarity in consumption of news types across traditional and new media. *Journal of Broadcasting & Electronic Media, 48*(1), 41–60. doi:10.1207/s15506878jobem4801_3

Eveland, W. P., Jr., & Scheufele, D. A. (2000). Connecting news media use with gaps in knowledge and participation. *Political Communication, 17*(3), 215–237. doi:10.1080/105846000414250

Faul, F., Erdfelder, E., Lang, A. G., & Buchner, A. (2007). G* Power 3: A flexible statistical power analysis program for the social, behavioral, and biomedical sciences. *Behavior Research Methods, 39*(2), 175–191. doi:10.3758/bf03193146

Feldman, L., Myers, T. A., Hmielowski, J. D., & Leiserowitz, A. (2014). The mutual reinforcement of media selectivity and effects: Testing the reinforcing spirals framework in the context of global warming. *Journal of Communication, 64*(4), 590–611. doi:10.1111/jcom.12108

Fraile, M., & Iyengar, S. (2014). Not all news sources are equally informative: A cross-national analysis of political knowledge in Europe. *The International Journal of Press/Politics, 19*(3), 275–294. doi:10.1177/1940161214528993

Galston, W. A. (2001). Political knowledge, political engagement, and civic education. *Annual Review of Political Science, 4*(1), 217–234. doi:10.1146/annurev.polisci.4.1.217

Gil de Zúñiga, H., Weeks, B., & Ardèvol-Abreu, A. (2017). Effects of the news-finds-me perception in communication: Social media use implications for news seeking and learning about politics. *Journal of Computer-Mediated Communication, 22*(3), 105–123. doi:10.1111/jcc4.12185

Glynn, C. J., Huge, M. E., & Hoffman, L. H. (2012). All the news that's fit to post: A profile of news use on social networking sites. *Computers in Human Behavior, 28*(1), 113–119. doi:10.1016/j.chb.2011.08.017

Gottfried, J., & Shearer, E. (2016, May 26). News use across social media platforms 2016. *Pew Research Center.* Retrieved from http://www.journalism.org/2016/05/26/news-use-across-social-media-platforms-2016/

Grabe, M. E., & Kamhawi, R. (2006). Hard wired for negative news? Gender differences in processing broadcast news. *Communication Research, 33*(5), 346–369. doi:10.1177/0093650206291479

Harnois, C. E. (2005). Different paths to different feminisms? Bridging multiracial feminist theory and quantitative sociological gender research. *Gender & Society, 19*(6), 809–828. doi: 10.1177/0891243205280026

Hayes, A. F. (2009). Beyond Baron and Kenny: Statistical mediation analysis in the new millennium. *Communication Monographs, 76*(4), 408–420. doi: 10.1080/03637750903310360

Holbert, R. L. (2005). Intramedia mediation: The cumulative and complementary effects of news media use. *Political Communication, 22*, 447–461. doi:10.1080/10584600500311378

Holbert, R. L., Hmielowski, J. D., & Weeks, B. E. (2012). Clarifying relationships between ideology and ideologically oriented cable TV news use: A case of suppression. *Communication Research, 39*(2), 194–216. doi:10.1177/0093650211405650

Holbert, R. L., Weeks, B. E., & Esralew, S. (2013). Approaching the 2012 US presidential election from a diversity of explanatory principles: Understanding, consistency, and hedonism. *American Behavioral Scientist, 57*(12), 1663–1687. doi:10.1177/0002764213490693

Hyde, J. S. (2014). Gender similarities and differences. *Annual Review of Psychology, 65*, 373–398. doi:10.1146/annurev-psych-010213-115057

Inglehart, R., & Norris, P. (2003). *Rising tide: Gender equality and cultural change around the world.* New York: Cambridge University Press.

Kahneman, D., Wakker, P. P., & Sarin, R. (1997). Back to Bentham? Explorations of experienced utility. *The Quarterly Journal of Economics, 112*(2), 375–406. doi:10.1162/003355397555235

Kendall, K. E. (2016). Presidential primaries and general election campaigns: A comparison. In W. L. Benoit (Ed.), *Praeger handbook of political campaigning in the United States, volume I: Foundations and campaign media* (pp. 31–44). Santa Barbara, CA: Praeger.

Kenski, K., & Stroud, N. J. (2006). Connections between Internet use and political efficacy, knowledge, and participation. *Journal of Broadcasting & Electronic Media, 50*(2), 173–192. doi: 10.1207/s15506878jobem5002_1

Knobloch-Westerwick, S., & Alter, S. (2007). The gender news use divide: Americans' sex-typed selective exposure to online news topics. *Journal of Communication, 57*(4), 739–758. doi: 10.1111/j.1460-2466.2007.00366.x

Kwak, N. (1999). Revisiting the knowledge gap hypothesis education, motivation, and media use. *Communication Research, 26*(4), 385–413. doi: 10.1177/009365099026004002

Levendusky, M. S. (2013). Why do partisan media polarize viewers? *American Journal of Political Science, 57*(3), 611–623. doi: 10.1111/ajps.12008

Pavitt, C. (2016). *Scientific communication theory.* New York: Peter Lang.

Poindexter, P. M., Meraz, S., & Weiss, A. S. (2008). *Women, men, and news: Divided and disconnected in the news media landscape.* New York: Routledge.

Prior, M. (2005). News vs. entertainment: How increasing media choice widens gaps in political knowledge and turnout. *American Journal of Political Science, 49*(3), 577–592. doi:10.1111/j.1540-5907.2005.00143.x

Prior, M. (2010). You've either got it or you don't? The stability of political interest over the life cycle. *The Journal of Politics, 72*(3), 747–766. doi:10.1017/S0022381610000149

Roth, F. S., Weinmann, C., Schneider, F. M., Hopp, F. R., & Vorderer, P. (2014). Seriously entertained: Antecedents and consequences of hedonic and eudaimonic entertainment experiences with political talk shows on TV.

Mass Communication and Society, 17(3), 379–399. doi:10.1080/15205436.2
014.891135

Shehata, A., Hopmann, D. N., Nord, L., & Höijer, J. (2015). Television channel content profiles and differential knowledge growth: A test of the inadvertent learning hypothesis using panel data. *Political Communication, 32*(3), 377–395. doi:10.1080/10584609.2014.955223

Soroka, S., Gidengil, E., Fournier, P., & Nir, L. (2016). Do women and men respond differently to negative news? *Politics & Gender, 12*(02), 344–368. doi:10.1017/s1743923x16000131

Stone, A. A., & Mackie, C. (2013). *Subjective well-being: Measuring happiness, suffering, and other dimensions of experience.* Washington, D.C.: The National Academies Press.

Strömbäck, J., Djerf-Pierre, M., & Shehata, A. (2012). The dynamics of political interest and news media consumption: A longitudinal perspective. *International Journal of Public Opinion Research, 25*(4), 414–435. doi:10.1093/ijpor/eds018

Stroud, N. J. (2011). *Niche news: The politics of news choice.* New York: Oxford University Press. doi:10.1093/acprof:oso/9780199755509.001.0001

Weeks, B. E., & Holbert, R. L. (2013). Predicting dissemination of news content in social media: A focus on reception, friending, and partisanship. *Journalism & Mass Communication Quarterly, 90*(2), 212–232. doi:10.1177/1077699013482906

Young, D. G., & Tisinger, R. M. (2006). Dispelling late-night myths: News consumption among late-night comedy viewers and the predictors of exposure to various late-night shows. *Harvard International Journal of Press/Politics, 11*(3), 113–134. doi:10.1177/1081180X05286042

CHAPTER NINETEEN

Gender and the Vote in the 2016 Presidential Election

Kate Kenski

Following the 2016 presidential election, *Newsweek* national politics corre-spondent Nina Burleigh (2016) wrote an article titled "The Presidential Elec-tion Was a Referendum on Gender and Women Lost," which captured the meaning, magnitude, and consequence of Democrat Hillary Clinton's loss to Republican Donald Trump. The presidential campaign was historic as Clin-ton won the Democratic nomination, making her the first female presidential candidate to have been nominated by a major political party. Throughout the campaign season, Clinton appeared to be the frontrunner over Trump. Clin-ton was one of the most politically experienced candidates in the race, having served as First Lady for eight years, as a U.S. senator for eight years, and as U.S. secretary of state for four years, whereas Trump was among the least experi-enced, having never been elected to political office prior to his 2016 general election victory.

Inexperience, however, did not hold back Republican voters from nomi-nating Trump from a field of experienced party contenders in the primaries, nor did it prove to be a major liability against Clinton in the general election, amid a series of gender-related scandals that would have been nails in the coffin for most other candidates. *USA Today* writer Alia E. Dastagir noted, "Trump's lewd demeanor didn't turn enough white women off. His lecherous behavior did not drive them away. The wave of sexual assault allegations against him was not a death knell" (2016, para. 18). The election was close, with Clinton winning the popular vote 65,853,516 (48.5%) to 62,984,825 (46.4%), but Trump achieving victory with 306 Electoral College votes to Clinton's 232 (CNN, 2016).

This chapter examines the role that gender played in candidate support during the 2016 major party nomination campaigns and general election. Entrance and exit polls collected in 2016 are used to demonstrate how the gender of citizens shaped candidate support. First, a brief overview of gender gaps in politics and candidate gender is presented. Second, significant events involving gender during the 2016 primaries and general elections are described. Third, voter preferences by gender as represented in entrance and exit polls are examined. Among the unexpected findings is the observation that despite overt sexism on display by Trump and his supporters, white women ended up supporting the Republican candidate. Trump's success and Clinton's failure in securing white females tipped the outcome in favor of the Republican political newcomer.

Gender Gaps in Politics

Gender shapes political engagement and electoral outcomes in different ways. At the outset, women have not achieved political equality in terms of elective representation in government. When women run for political office, gender affects how they are covered as candidates by the media. As citizens and voters, women engage in the political process differently from their male counterparts, lagging behind men in most facets of political participation except voter turnout.

Political equality in representation has remained elusive for women. In 2016, women held 19.6% of the seats in the U.S. Congress (Dittmar, 2017). Three women currently serve on the U.S. Supreme Court, bringing the number to four over the history of the institution. No women have served as U.S. president. In spring 2016, 8 in 10 Americans said that the United States is ready for a female president (Neidig, 2016), which was up from a decade previous when 6 in 10 reported that the country was ready. Yet it is notable that even in 2016, one in five Americans did not believe that the United States was ready for its first female president. Democrats and liberals have generally been more likely to report that they would vote for a woman candidate if their party nominated one in comparison to Republicans and conservatives (Falk & Kenski, 2006). This perception, however, is malleable based on the actual candidates running for office. In 2008, the selection of Sarah Palin as the Republican vice presidential candidate changed Republican and conservative perceptions that the United States was ready for a woman president. Prior to Palin's selection, Republicans were significantly less likely to report that the United States was ready for a woman president, but they changed their tune after Palin had been selected (Kenski, 2009). That a candidate's gender matters to a small but notable percentage of the public places a constraint on female candidates running for president, particularly when one side has a female candidate and the other does not.

When it comes to securing major-party presidential and vice presidential nominations, the female numbers are few. In the history of the United States, two women have been selected as vice presidential running mates for the major parties. Democrat Geraldine Ferraro was selected by Walter Mondale in 1984, and Republican Palin was selected by John McCain in 2008. In both instances, the party with a female vice presidential candidate on the ticket did not win the presidency.

Since Victoria Woodhull's 1872 run for the presidency, women have sought the office but have often not been treated by the media as viable candidates in comparison to male candidates (Falk, 2008). Stereotypes about women and their natural proclivities shape how the media frame female candidates. Although a candidate's gender does not appear to influence how much coverage the candidate receives (Bystrom, Robertson, & Banwart, 2001; Devitt, 1999), it shapes how candidates are described qualitatively (Bystrom et al., 2001; Devitt, 1999). Men are less likely to be described by their sex, marital status, and children than are women (Bystrom et al., 2001). Women are more likely to be described by features of their personal life, appearance, and personality (Devitt, 1999). Among the obstacles for women winning elective office are overcoming assumptions about their viability and leadership skills (Bystrom, 2003).

Representation matters because the environment socializes children as to their possibilities in life. When women are absent from political life, girls model that reality. Aside from voting turnout, women do not participate in politics as actively as do men (Burns, Schlozman, & Verba, 2001). Women express less interest in politics (Bennett, 1986; Kenski, 2001) and do not display as much political knowledge as do men (Delli Carpini & Keeter, 1996, 2000; Kenski, 2000; Kenski & Jamieson, 2001).

Clinton's Historic 2016 Run and Trump's Win

Backdrop to the 2016 Primary Season

Clinton had run for the 2008 Democratic nomination for president and been the frontrunner during the preprimary season against then-U.S. Senator Barack Obama, leading by 2 to 1 in several polls. Her campaign had made the cataclysmic mistake of not campaigning aggressively in Iowa, which she lost to Obama. Although Iowa had few delegates seated at the Democratic National Convention, the loss allowed the media to create a narrative that questioned Clinton's viability. The Iowa loss was followed by a moment of emotional openness at a New Hampshire campaign event that the media chose to frame as Clinton being in tears. Clinton's frontrunner status was undone by negative media coverage early in the primary campaign season. Although people claimed in exit polls that neither race nor gender were factors in their vote decisions, Obama won the nomination, in part, because white males were a less stable, more cross-pressured group. Blacks, regardless of gender, overwhelming favored Obama, and white women favored Clinton (Kenski, 2009). Given Clinton's strong lead during the preprimary season, the loss to a relatively inexperienced candidate was unexpected.

Although no prominent female candidates ran for the presidency in 2012, gender was a salient theme, due to the alleged Republican "war on women." This theme arose from two situations, one involving politically insensitive comments about rape from Republican politicians on separate occasions and one stemming from the proposed No Taxpayer Funding for Abortion Act, which was passed in the U.S. House of Representatives but not in the U.S. Senate. Democrats used the phrase "war on women," which was picked up by the news media (Kenski, 2014). The social media environment was ready for Republican missteps when it came to gender. In a presidential debate, Republican presidential candidate Mitt Romney discussed the gender balance of his gubernatorial cabinet with the phrase "binders full of women," resulting in memes on social media. Romney lost the 2012 election with a sizable gender gap in support.

The 2016 Presidential Primary Season

Gender played roles in the 2016 presidential primaries for both parties. In the Democratic nomination race, Clinton was once again poised as the frontrunner who had gained notable foreign policy experience as secretary of state for the Obama administration since her 2008 run. The Democratic preprimary campaign involved challenges, however, from Lincoln Chafee, Lawrence Lessig, Martin O'Malley, Bernie Sanders, and Jim Webb. Sanders, a U.S. senator from Vermont who has been an independent for the bulk of his political career, proved to be a robust challenger to Clinton's nomination, despite only having been a Democrat since 2015. Sanders' viability as a contender for the nomination was enhanced, in part, because of Clinton's gender. It is worth considering that his candidacy might not have had the traction it did had the frontrunner been male.

In the Republican nomination race, several incidents made gender a prominent theme. In *The Week*, Jeva Lange (2016, para. 9) wrote "It's possible that he [Trump] won not in spite of his misogynistic rhetoric, but in part because of it." After the preprimary season's first Republican debate, Trump lashed out at Fox News moderator Megyn Kelly, stating, "She gets out and she starts asking me all sorts of ridiculous questions, and you know, you could see there was blood coming out of her eyes, blood coming out of her wherever" (Hillin,

2016, para. 6). The implication that a female anchor would ask tough questions because of premenstrual syndrome was one of the first obvious signs of sexism present during the campaign. Another incident involved Trump questioning Carly Fiorina's presence in the Republican race by attacking her appearance. "Look at that face! Would anyone vote for that? Can you imagine that, the face of our next president?" Trump asked. "I mean, she's a woman, and I'm not supposed to say bad things, but really, folks, come on. Are we serious?" (Hillin, 2016, para. 9).

In December 2015, Trump commented on Clinton using her Democratic debate break time to go to the restroom stating, "I know where she went—it's disgusting, I don't want to talk about it . . . it's too disgusting. Don't say it, it's disgusting" (Hillin, 2016, para. 14). In April 2016, Trump claimed of Clinton, "I think the only card she has is the woman's card. She's got nothing else going . . . if Hillary Clinton were a man I don't think she'd get 5% of the vote" (Hillin, 2016, para. 24). The Clinton campaign responded by making the "woman card" part of its campaign messaging. According to Wilkie (2016, para. 7), "The flood of donations in response to Trump's 'woman card' comments helped Clinton raise a total of $36 million in April, of which $26.4 million was for use in the presidential primary."

Sexist slogans against Clinton were spread by both Trump and Sanders supporters. Trump supporters used slogans such as "Hillary sucks but not like Monica" and "2 fat thighs, 2 small breasts, 1 left wing" (Hillin, 2016, para. 26). Tweets from a scholar attending a Trump rally described the scene with "Big seller is a shirt that says Trump That Bitch. Everyone wearing one is being asked to pose for pictures. Big thumbs up. Big grins" and "Man posing for pictures wearing t shirt with picture of Clinton in a cage" (see Lange, 2016). Meanwhile, Sanders supporters referred to Clinton as "Killary" and "Shrillary" (Hillin, 2016, para. 26) invoking disparagements about the female voice.

The gendered messaging was not confined to attacks on the female candidates. One vivid exchange underscored the stereotype that penis size is somehow related to strong leadership. Trump referred to U.S. Senator Marco Rubio as "little Marco" (Dicker, 2016). Rubio responded by observing to his supporters, "Have you seen his [Trump's] hands? And you know what they say about men with small hands . . ." (Shapiro, 2016, para. 2). During a debate, Trump said, "I have to say this, he hit my hands. Nobody has ever hit my hands. I've never heard of this one. Look at those hands. Are they small hands? And he referred to my hands if they're small, something else must be small." Trump assured the audience, "I guarantee you there's no problem. I guarantee you" (Gass, 2016, para. 2). In another set of exchanges, attacks were made against Trump's and U.S. Senator Ted Cruz's wives, with Trump tweeting an attractive picture of Melania Trump next to an unflattering picture of Heidi Cruz with the caption "no need to 'spill the beans' the images are worth a thousand words." (see Schleifer & Manchester, 2016).

Trump's appeal as a candidate lay not in convention. His gendered references were not subtle. What was unexpected was that a candidate was able to get away with them unapologetically, especially in light of his lack of political experience. His lack of experience was particularly noteworthy given that one of the major Republican attacks against Obama in 2008 was his inexperience. Kenski, Hardy, and Jamieson (2010) wrote that the "truth on which the GOP assaults relied was that by most, but not all, historical measures, Barack Obama was short on legislative and executive experience" (p. 71) as he had served less than four years as a U.S. senator, and most of that time had been spent running for higher office; he had served only three 2-year terms in the state legislature. Yet, in comparison to Trump, Obama's résumé was substantial as both a candidate and elected official.

Despite experience generally being considered an important trait for candidates to have, lack of experience did not hold back Obama in 2008 against Clinton in the Democratic primary, nor did it hurt Trump in his run against several seasoned Republican opponents in the 2016 nomination process. That Trump received the Republican nomination with little experience and a sexist rhetorical style that is perhaps old-fashioned in sentiment but unprecedented in actual expression is noteworthy. It marks a change in how we understand the boundaries of what candidates can say and do—or at least what male candidates can say and do.

The 2016 General Election

Few people believe that their decisions are guided by gender. Sexism, like racism, occurs while people believe that they are responding to individuals, not the stereotypes about the groups from which they hail. Studies suggest that there is bias against career advancement for women, and this bias is more pronounced for women, particularly conservative women, than it is for men (Bialik, 2017). Such biases may explain why Republican women did not feel cross-pressured to vote for Clinton. One wonders whether a female could ever achieve a major-party nomination with the comparable level of political experience possessed by Trump during the campaign. And would it have been possible for a female candidate to be able to run with multiple marriages in her personal history without being labeled a trollop, hussy, or slut? It seems doubtful.

The downside to experience is having a track record that is not perfect. Two prominent weaknesses in Clinton's background as secretary of state were the deaths of four Americans at U.S. compounds in Benghazi and Clinton's use of a private e-mail server to send government correspondence. Although Clinton maintained that she did not send classified information from the private server, the issue did not go away. In late October 2016, then-FBI director James Comey informed Congress about a renewed investigation into additional e-mails, even though the Department of Justice had warned him that such an announcement violated policies to avoid making announcements right before general elections because they could influence the electoral process. The FBI ended up concluding that Clinton's team erred in the use of the server, but the violations were not substantial enough to bring charges. Comey's announcement, however, appeared to play into the Trump campaign's "Lock Her Up" theme. It was an October surprise that the Clinton team could not afford. Clinton was undoubtedly the most experienced candidate in the race, but perpetual questions about her judgment in using the private e-mail server played into trustworthiness concerns that had long plagued the Clintons. At best, the charges against Clinton dampened enthusiasm about her candidacy, and at worst, they played into the idea that she had violated the law.

The most significant charges about Trump and sexism arrived in October 2016. They were significant because they were based on recorded evidence in Trump's own words. A 2005 *Access Hollywood* taped conversation between Trump and Billy Bush was released on October 7, 2016. In the tape, Trump said: "I moved on her like a bitch, but I couldn't get there, and she was married. Then all of a sudden I see her, she's now got the big phony tits and everything" and "I'm automatically attracted to beautiful [women]—I just start kissing them. It's like a magnet. Just kiss. I don't even wait. And when you're a star they let you do it. You can do anything . . . Grab them by the pussy. You can do anything" (Mathis-Lilley, 2016, para. 1). Those supporting Trump argued that he did not really mean it and was merely engaging in locker room talk. Those opposing Trump took it as further evidence of his failure to respect women or his proclivity toward sexual assault. By the time this evidence was brought forward, the country may have been desensitized to the argument that Trump was sexist. Evidence also suggests that hostility toward women was associated with Trump support (Nelson, 2016). In other words, just as sexist acts repulse some people, they may attract others, and those hostile toward women preferred Trump.

In the third presidential debate, Trump interrupted Clinton's response on how she would raise taxes on the rich to handle debt, calling her "such a nasty woman" (Diaz, 2016). Clinton ignored his attack and continued her response. Ironically, his insult was made after he had maintained earlier in the debate that "Nobody has more respect for women than I do" (Diaz, 2016). Clinton's base responded by embracing the "nasty woman" theme, making up t-shirts to show support for Clinton by using it as an empowering rather than delegitimizing phrase.

Gender of Voters and Candidate Preference

Gender can influence elections even when candidate gender is not an issue, which begs the question: How does the gender of voters affect whom they will support? In this section, gender is examined with entrance and exit poll data from the nomination phase and 2016 general election.

Table 19.1 presents data from the entrance (caucus) polls and exit (primary) polls collected from nine states during the nomination phase. These data allow one to see the role that gender played in the nomination phase. The gender column shows the percentage of voters who were male and female in the respective state contests. The rows show the preference within gender for four Republicans who held out the longest in the primary phase and the top two Democratic candidates. It is believed that females tend to be Democrats and males tend to be Republicans. The data from the primaries/caucuses, however, show that Republicans as a group are only somewhat more male than female. With the exception of the New York primary, which was heavily weighted with male participants (56% male to 44% female), the gender gap in Republican participation ranged from 2% to 6% on average. In eight of the nine states examined (all but Florida), men composed a higher proportion of voters in the Republican races. In Florida, 51% of Republican voters were female.

Overall, Republican men and women shared their top preferences, although gaps could be found in the magnitude of support for the top candidate in each state. For example, in Florida, both males and females supported Trump as the top choice, but a majority of males supported Trump (52%) in comparison to a plurality of females (40%) for a 12% gender gap in Trump support. Only in the Republican Virginia primary did males and females have different top preferences; males preferred Trump, whereas females preferred Rubio by a small percentage.

By contrast, the composition of Democratic primary/caucus voters was heavily skewed in the female direction. In all nine states examined, women made up a greater percentage of Democratic primary/caucus voters than did men. The gender gap in Democratic primary/caucus participation ranged from 6% to 22%. In South Carolina, females made up 61% of Democratic voters in the primary exit polls. In eight of the nine states examined, females preferred Clinton to Sanders; in New Hampshire, females voted for Sanders. In four of nine states, males preferred Clinton; in four states, males preferred Sanders; in one state, males were evenly split in their support for Clinton and Sanders. Even when males and females had the same top choice, the gap in support differed significantly. For example, in South Carolina, males and females preferred Clinton, but there was an 11% difference in the amount of support for her. In Florida, 70% of females preferred Clinton, whereas 57% of males did.

Table 19.2 shows major-party candidate support by gender and the gaps in support between males and females for the presidential candidates from 1972 through 2016. Males and females selected the same top candidate preferences from 1972–1992. In 1996, however, females preferred Democrat Bill Clinton to Republican Bob Dole, whereas males preferred Dole. This female preference for the Democrat and male preference for the Republican appeared again

Table 19.1 Entrance and Exit Poll Candidate Preferences in the 2016 Nomination Phase by Gender

State	Republican Candidates					Democratic Candidates	
	Cruz	Trump	Rubio	Kasich		Clinton	Sanders
IA	**29**	25	25	2	Male (43%)	44	**50**
	27	24	21	2	Female (57%)	**53**	42
NH	12	**38**	9	16	Male (45%)	32	**67**
	11	**33**	12	16	Female (55%)	44	**55**
SC	22	**36**	22	7	Male (39%)	**68**	32
	22	**29**	23	9	Female (61%)	**79**	21
TX	**42**	36	14	3	Male (43%)	**56**	43
	38	29	21	4	Female (57%)	**65**	33
VA	17	**38**	28	11	Male (42%)	**58**	41
	15	31	**36**	9	Female (58%)	**70**	30
FL	17	**52**	21	7	Male (42%)	**57**	40
	18	**40**	33	6	Female (58%)	**70**	28
OH	12	39	2	**46**	Male (44%)	48	**51**
	14	32	4	**48**	Female (56%)	**63**	36
WI	**48**	35	—	14	Male (46%)	36	**63**
	49	34	—	15	Female (54%)	**50**	49
NY	14	**63**	—	23	Male (41%)	50	50
	15	**57**	—	28	Female (59%)	**63**	37

Note: Top candidates listed. States are listed in the order of the date their caucus or primary was held in 2016. Gender column shows column percentages in parentheses. Candidate winning majority or plurality within gender are bolded. Candidate columns show row percentages of support within gender.

Source: https://www.nytimes.com/interactive/2016/us/elections/primary-calendar-and-results.html

Table 19.2 Presidential Candidate Support by Gender, 1972–2016

	Male Support for Democratic Candidate	Female Support for Democratic Candidate	Male Support for Republican Candidate	Female Support for Republican Candidate	(Male-Female) Support for Democratic Candidate	(Male-Female) Support for Republican Candidate	Difference
1972	36	38	**61**	**60**	−2	1	−3
1976	**50**	**50**	48	48	0	0	0
1980	36	45	55	**47**	−9	8	−17
1984	37	44	**62**	**56**	−7	6	−13
1988	41	49	57	50	−8	7	−15
1992	**41**	**45**	38	37	−4	1	−5
1996	43	**54**	**44**	38	−11	6	−17
2000	42	**54**	53	43	−12	10	−22
2004	44	**51**	55	48	−7	7	−14
2008	**49**	**56**	48	43	−7	5	−12
2012	45	55	52	44	−10	8	−18
2016	41	54	53	42	−13	11	−24

Note: Bold numbers indicate preferred candidate of voters by gender.

Source: Data obtained from https://www.nytimes.com/interactive/2016/11/08/us/politics/election-exit-polls.html

in 2000, 2004, 2012, and 2016. Gender differences in intensity of support for candidates first appeared in 1980. Both males and females preferred Republican Ronald Reagan, but males supported him 55% to females 47%. Prior to the 2016 election, the largest recorded gender gap in support took place in 2000 with 54% of females and 42% of males supporting Democrat Al Gore and 53% of males and 43% of females supporting Republican George W. Bush. In 2016, the largest gender gap took place with 54% of females and 41% of males supporting Clinton and 53% of males and 42% of females supporting Trump.

Female support for Clinton practically mirrors male support for Trump in aggregate. Table 19.3 provides a nuanced look at gender, demonstrating that males and females are not monolithic groups of supporters. Kenski and Kenski (2017, p. 303) maintain that "data disaggregation captures a more complex gender reality." Gender interacts with race, marital status, and partisanship

Table 19.3 Candidate Support by Gender Categories in General Election Exit Polls, 2016

Category	% of 2016 Total Vote	Clinton	Trump	Other/No Answer
Men	47	41	**52**	7
Women	53	**54**	41	5
White men	34	31	**62**	7
White women	37	43	**52**	5
Latino men	5	**63**	32	5
Latina women	6	**69**	25	6
Black men	5	**82**	13	5
Black women	7	**94**	4	2
Married men	29	38	**57**	5
Married women	30	**49**	47	4
Unmarried men	18	**46**	44	10
Unmarried women	23	**63**	32	5
Democratic men	14	**87**	9	4
Democratic women	23	**91**	7	2
Republican men	17	7	**89**	4
Republican women	16	9	**88**	3
Independent men	17	38	**50**	12
Independent women	14	**47**	42	11

Source: 2016 exit polls from http://www.cnn.com/election/results/president

in important ways. Race played a role in candidate support in 2016 and interacted with gender. White males (62%) and white females (52%) voted for Trump over Clinton. Based on candidate background characteristics, one would have hypothesized that Clinton should have captured a greater percentage of white women than she did. White women could have swung the election, but they voted in greater numbers for Trump (52% for Trump compared to 43% for Clinton). Latinos and Latinas both voted for Clinton, as did black males and black females. Blacks voted for Clinton in higher percentages than did the other groups, but even here, there was a gender gap—82% of black men voted for Clinton in comparison to 94% of black women. Tyson and Maniam (2016, para. 3) note that "although Trump fared little better among blacks and Hispanics than Romney did four years ago, Hillary Clinton did not run as strongly among these core Democratic groups as Obama did in 2012."

Looking at marital status and gender, married males were more likely to support Trump, whereas married females, unmarried males, and unmarried females supported Clinton. In terms of magnitude of support, married females and unmarried males were fairly close in their support for candidates. Married males and unmarried females, however, looked very different from each other, with 57% of married males supporting Trump and 63% of unmarried females supporting Clinton.

Party identification played a much stronger role in candidate support than did gender. It is worth noting that Clinton needed to get cross-over support from Republican women. That cross-over did not happen. Of Republican women, 88% supported Trump and 9% supported Clinton. Of Republican men, 89% supported Trump and 7% supported Clinton. Among independents, 50% of males and 42% of females supported Trump. Stronger support outside the Democratic base was needed for Clinton to win the presidency.

Conclusion

During the general election, Trump said of Clinton, "I just don't think she has a presidential look. And you need a presidential look. You have to get the job done" (Keith, 2016, para. 30). If by look, Trump meant white male, then indeed Clinton did not have the "look." Clinton managed to win the popular vote, but lost the presidency to a candidate with no elective or military experience who made well-publicized sexist comments toward female members of the media, Republican candidates, and Clinton. Rather than dissuading voter support, Trump's comments gained him media coverage and a solid base of core supporters. It is difficult to imagine any other candidate getting away with comments such as "Grab them by the pussy. You can do anything." And yet, perhaps because of the hostile and polarized media environment or extreme dislike of Clinton, Republican voters stood by their candidate. That included Republican women, from whom one would have expected some modest defection. Clinton, however, did not achieve much cross-over support, nor did she mobilize the Democratic base well beyond what Obama achieved in 2012, which was a necessity for her win.

The 2016 election resulted in one of the largest gender gaps in presidential candidate support in history. Men supported Trump, and women supported Clinton. But women are not a monolithic group. Although Clinton won support of women overall, she lost white women. Through the primary and general election campaigns, Clinton was dogged with the claim that she was untrustworthy and put national security at risk through her use of a private server as secretary of state. Unlike Trump, who managed to have the *Access Hollywood* "grab them" comments bounce off him like Teflon, Clinton's alleged transgressions did not bounce off her. Then-FBI Director Comey's decision to tell Congress that he was renewing an investigation into Clinton's e-mail in late October could not have come at a worse time for Clinton. It may have changed people's vote preferences, but more likely it sent a chill in Clinton's voter mobilization efforts right before the general election. Clinton was the first female major-party presidential nominee who nearly cracked the glass ceiling. Trump, however, prevented her from doing so with a campaign style like no other that basked in male bravado and resulted in a Republican victory.

References

Bennett, S. E. (1986). *Apathy in America, 1960–1984: Causes and consequences of citizen political indifference.* Dobbs Ferry, NY: Transnational Publishers.

Bialik, C. (2017, January 21). How unconscious sexism could help explain Trump's win. *FiveThirtyEight.* Retrieved from https://fivethirtyeight.com/features/how-unconscious-sexism-could-help-explain-trumps-win

Burleigh, N. (2016, November 14). The presidential election was a referendum on gender and women lost. *Newsweek.* Retrieved from http://www.newsweek.com/2016/11/18/hillary-clinton-presidential-election-voter-gender-gap-520579.html

Burns, N., Schlozman, K. L., & Verba, S. (2001). *The private roots of public action: Gender, equality, and political participation.* Cambridge, MA: Harvard University Press.

Bystrom, D. (2003). On the way to the White House: Communication strategies for women candidates. In R. P. Watson & A. Gordon (Eds.), *Anticipating madam president* (pp. 95–105). Boulder, CO: Lynne Rienner Publishers.

Bystrom, D. G., Robertson, T. A., & Banwart, M. C. (2001). Framing the fight: An analysis of media coverage of female and male candidates in primary races for governor and U.S. senate in 2000. *American Behavioral Scientist, 44*(12), 1999–2013. doi: 10.1177/00027640121958456

CNN. (2016). Presidential results. Retrieved from http://www.cnn.com/election/results/president

Dastagir, A. E. (2016, November 10). Voices: What Trump's victory tells us about women. *USA Today*. Retrieved from https://www.usatoday.com/story /opinion/voices/2016/11/10/trump-election-white-women-sexism-racism /93611984

Delli Carpini, M. X., & Keeter, S. (1996). *What Americans know about politics and why it matters.* New Haven, CT: Yale University Press.

Delli Carpini, M. X., & Keeter, S. (2000). Gender and political knowledge. In S. Tolleson-Rinehart & J. J. Josephson (Eds.), *Gender and American politics: Women, men, and the political process* (pp. 21–52). Armonk, NY: M. E. Sharpe.

Devitt, J. (1999). *Framing gender on the campaign trail: Women's executive leadership and the press.* New York: Women's Leadership Fund.

Diaz, D. (2016, October 20). Trump calls Clinton 'a nasty woman.' *CNN*. Retrieved from http://www.cnn.com/2016/10/19/politics/donald-trump-hillary-clin ton-nasty-woman/

Dicker, R. (2016, March 4). Donald Trump's #LittleMarco is the Internet's new favorite thing. *U.S. News*. Retrieved from https://www.usnews.com/news /articles/2016-03-04/donald-trump-called-marco-rubio-little-marco-at-the -gop-debate-and-twitter-went-crazy

Dittmar, K. (2017). Women in the 115th Congress. Center for American Women and Politics, Rutgers University. Retrieved from http://www.cawp.rutgers .edu/sites/default/files/resources/closer_look_115th_congress_1.3.17_0 .pdf

Falk, E. (2008). *Women for president: Media bias in eight campaigns.* Chicago: University of Illinois Press.

Falk, E., & Kenski, K. (2006). Sexism vs. partisanship: A new look at the question of whether America is ready for a woman president. *Sex Roles: A Journal of Research, 54*(7/8), 413–428. doi: 10.1007/s11199-006-9025-z

Gass, N. (2016, March 3). Trump on small hands: 'I guarantee you there's no problem.' *Politico*. Retrieved from http://www.politico.com/blogs/2016 -gop-primary-live-updates-and-results/2016/03/donald-trump-small-hands -220223

Hillin, T. (2016, November 3). Here's every wildly sexist moment from the 2016 presidential race. *Fusion TV*. Retrieved from http://fusion.net/story/363843 /2016-election-sexism

Keith, T. (2016, October 23). Sexism is out in the open in the 2016 campaign. That may have been inevitable. *NPR*. Retrieved from http://www.npr.org/2016 /10/23/498878356/sexism-is-out-in-the-open-in-the-2016-campaign-that -may-have-been-inevitable

Kenski, K. (2000). Women and political knowledge during the 2000 primaries. *Annals of the American Academy of Political and Social Science, 572,* 26–28. doi: 10.1177/000271620057200105

Kenski, K. (2001, November). *Explaining the gender gap in political knowledge: Tests of eighteen hypotheses.* Paper presented at the annual meeting of the National Communication Association, Atlanta, GA.

Kenski, K. (2009). Gender and the election. In N. Anstead and W. Straw (Eds.), *The change we need: What Britain can learn from Obama's victory* (pp. 13–21, 110–111). London: The Fabian Society.

Kenski, K. (2014). The gender gap in presidential vote preference. In D. G. Bystrom, M. C. Banwart, & M. S. McKinney (Eds.), *alieNATION: The divide & conquer election of 2012* (pp. 225–241). New York: Peter Lang Publishing.

Kenski, K., Hardy, B. W., & Jamieson, K. H. (2010). *The Obama victory: How media, money, and message shaped the 2008 election.* New York: Oxford University Press.

Kenski, K., & Jamieson, K. H. (2000). The gender gap in political knowledge: Are women less knowledgeable than men about politics? In K. H. Jamieson (Ed.), *Everything you think you know about politics . . . and why you're wrong* (pp. 83–89, 238–241). New York: Basic Books.

Kenski, H. C., & Kenski, K. M. (2017). Explaining the vote in the election of 2016: The remarkable come from behind victory of Republican candidate Donald Trump. In R. E. Denton, Jr. (Ed.), *The 2016 presidential campaign: Political communication and practice* (pp. 285-309). New York: Palgrave Macmillan.

Lange, J. (2016, July 18). The mounting misogyny of the 2016 election. *The Week.* Retrieved from http://theweek.com/articles/635542/mounting-misogyny -2016-election

Mathis-Lilley, B. (2016, October 7). Trump was recorded in 2005 bragging about grabbing women "by the pussy." *Slate.* Retrieved from http://www.slate .com/blogs/the_slatest/2016/10/07/donald_trump_2005_tape_i_grab _women_by_the_pussy.html

Neidig, H. (2016, March 4). Poll: Most Americans ready for female president. *The Hill.* Retrieved from http://thehill.com/blogs/ballot-box/271866-poll-most -americans-ready-for-female-president

Nelson, L. (2016, November 1). Hostility toward women is one of the strongest predictors of Trump support. *Vox.* Retrieved from https://www.vox.com /2016/11/1/13480416/trump-supporters-sexism

Schleifer, T., & Manchester, J. (2016, March 24). Donald Trump makes wild threat to 'spill the beans' on Ted Cruz's wife. CNN. Retrieved from http://www .cnn.com/2016/03/22/politics/ted-cruz-melania-trump-twitter-donald -trump-heidi/

Shapiro, E. (2016, March 4). The history behind the Donald Trump 'small hands' insult. *ABC News.* Retrieved from http://abcnews.go.com/Politics/history -donald-trump-small-hands-insult/story?id=37395515

Tyson, A., & Maniam, S. (2016, November 9). Behind Trump's victory: Divisions by race, gender, education. *Pew Research Center.* Retrieved from http://www .pewresearch.org/fact-tank/2016/11/09/behind-trumps-victory-divisions -by-race-gender-education

Wilkie, C. (2016, May 2). Trump's 'woman card' remark drives $2.4 million in fundraising—for Hillary Clinton. *Huffington Post.* Retrieved from http://www .huffingtonpost.com/entry/hillary-clinton-donald-trump-woman-card -donors_us_5727b4c5e4b0b49df6ac0b3e

#election#elección: Latino Twitter Users and Reactions to Presidential Political Gaffes

Samantha Hernandez

The 2016 presidential election caught pollsters, scholars, and the general public off guard. The popular belief was that former Secretary of State Hillary Clinton would become the first female president of the United States. In a shocking defeat, New York City businessman Donald Trump secured enough Electoral College votes to capture the presidency. As Democrats and Republicans were processing the Trump victory, pollsters and academics went to work trying to figure out how the models failed. According to Latino Decisions—the lead polling firm of the Latin@ community—there was nothing wrong with the models they used to predict that 79% of Latinos would vote for Clinton ("Lies, Damn Lies, and Exit Polls," 2016). Although the focus of this chapter is not to address polling issues, it is important to note that Trump received 25% of the reported votes of third-generation/U.S.-born Latinos (Latino Decisions, 2016). As this group tends to have younger demographics and has become more acculturated into American society, this percentage suggests that younger, more acculturated Latinos are identifying more with the Republican Party than in the past, and subsequent generations may follow.

This trend becomes more important as we notice how younger generations are paying attention to online campaigns and are more active on social networking sites (SNS). Recent studies by the Pew Research Center (2015a, 2015b) show no notable differences in SNS use among ethnic or racial groups. For example, 65% of Latinos, 65% of whites, and 56% of blacks use at least one SNS (Pew Research Center, 2015b). And 25% of Latinos, 21% of whites, and 27% of blacks use Twitter (Pew Research Center, 2015a). The increasing use of SNS suggests that news of candidate political gaffes, scandals, and campaign happenings will garner more responses or attention on these media. Although these communication modes do not directly correlate to candidate evaluations, they do show attitudes toward specific candidate behavior.

Although political gaffes and scandals are common, they appear to be magnified when involving a specific racial or ethnic group. During the 2016 presidential campaign, both candidates had gaffes involving the Latin@ community. It is important to note that candidates can be unaware of the cultural implications of their campaign outreach efforts. On the other hand, a candidate clumsily discussing an ethnic group may be viewed differently. This chapter will discuss how Latinos reacted to political gaffes involving the stereotypes and identity of the Latin@ community during the 2016 presidential campaign.

Latin@ Identity and Outreach

The creation of the Latin@ identity has roots in the concept of what and who are considered to be white. In his book, *White by Law: The Legal Construction of Race* (2006), Lopez takes a theoretical approach to the creation of race through laws and their effects. He maintains that this creation has caused a social fabrication of race that is still evident in today's society. Lopez's examination of behavior and identification highlights the creation of separate spaces and identities that Latinos and other minorities navigate. In his book, *How Racism Takes Place* (2011), Lipsitz argues that the binary view of American society is defined by the lifestyle that minorities have access to in comparison to whites. He studied the space through which minorities must navigate based on the social and economic opportunities that are present. This established difference calls into question the type of treatment that minorities— in this case, Latinos—are conditioned to expect and receive by politicians. This legal creation and social manifestation of whites and "others" create a binary market for appeals. However, this becomes more complicated through the recognition of various groups, including marketing appeals to Latinos on television (Piñón & Rojas, 2011). By examining case law, we see that minority groups were created by the absence of being white. Segregating and continuously creating smaller groups of minorities highlight the creation of spaces in order to continue a form of racial hierarchy. Yet the cultural implications are still unclear.

Although Latinos have been established as the other, the remaining complexity of how to reach out to the group is convoluted by the many subgroups, variation in language, and division of Latinos by those who target them. Marquez (2007) highlights the difficulties with Latin@ political identity, given the various statuses that are afforded to Latinos. Latinos are not only marked by economic differences, but also by subgroups and generational differences that are highlighted by levels of assimilation. Stokes-Brown (2009) also discusses the types of identification and the importance of self-identification within the Latin@ community. This self-identification of race may differ from the United States' version of classification due to historical and cultural differences. Thus, the space in which Latinos are given to navigate may be alien to their own thoughts on what their status should be or how they are perceived.

If identification varies by group, generation, and other identifiers, the question remains as to how to study political efficacy in such a diverse group and how to appeal to them. Santoro and Segura (2009) examined the likelihood of voting and ethnic political activity among four generations of Mexican Americans. They found that the longer the family had been in the United States, the more likely they were to vote; yet after the second generation, ethnic political activity is significantly decreased. This study demonstrates the issues inherent with attempting to appeal to Latinos based on generational differences. Essentially, the concept of appealing to Latinos as a whole based on generation would yield mix results.

Outreach to Latinos has largely been discussed in both forms of content and how the message is delivered. Piñón and Rojas (2011) examined the increasing inclusion of Latinos and television shows aimed toward Latinos on English-language stations as well as the increase of Spanish-language stations. They concluded that the discussion of appeals on a global and transnational level by these networks demonstrates the complexity that exists within the Latin@ community and, in general, the confusion associated with trying to appeal to one or more specific categories.

Other scholars have further researched the perceived identity of Latinos as well as the created identity founded by the media and its effects on Latinos. For example, Dávila (2012) examined multiples aspects of media targeting of Latinos. She discusses the fact that both political parties are courting Latinos, yet demonstrates the way in which they try not to alienate white or black voters. Dávila finds that Spanish advertisements are aired on Spanish-speaking–only channels. However, although other scholars maintain this is because the majority of Spanish speakers watch only Spanish-language channels, Dávila argues that Spanish speakers watch both English and Spanish channels and that the airing of Spanish ads on Spanish channels is to create an air of inclusion while not isolating other voters who are not fond of Latinos.

In addition, Dávila (2012) examines the notion that Latinos are the "new Republicans," discusses the issues with trying to create advertisements designed for the entire Latin@ community, and addresses the strong geographical differences that exist among subgroups. Dávila's work looks at the differences among subgroups and provides a different explanation for the attempts at indirect communication by politicians to Latinos. This study indicates that there is uncertainty about how to reach out to Latinos and whether or not it is okay to do so.

Through a case study of the 2001 Los Angeles city elections, Abrajano, Alvarez, and Nagler (2005) attempted to examine the role that race played in the races for mayor and city attorney. The two races examined were high profile, with spending reaching 14.6 million dollars in the mayoral race. Like other scholars, Abrajano et al. (2005) noticed the behavioral patterns of whites and Latinos to vote along racial lines as indicated by last name. However, they also noted a movement of voters taking issues into consideration as well. Ultimately, however, the majority of citizens continued to vote based on name identification. This study demonstrates a potential blurring of intersectionality, yet notes that it is not surmountable.

A review of the literature demonstrates the spaces through which Latinos navigate while choosing elected officials. The ways in which political parties and candidates attempt to identify and align themselves with Latinos largely changes the space that they must navigate through elections. When candidates have a political gaffe, they then can quickly create situations that neutralize past outreach efforts.

Political Scandals and Gaffes

Although research on political scandal has been minimal, the importance of its effects can be seen throughout election cycles. Media coverage of scandals can be tied to the ways in which they affect society (Thompson, 2000). Thompson's work on political scandals uses a historical approach to examine the types of scandals that wield the most power and affect society. Neckel (2005) and Thompson (2000) define a political scandal as any action or event involving a politician that is regarded as illegal, corrupt, or unethical and prompts general public outrage. Although Thompson's work is the most comprehensive on political scandal, it is limited by the scope of office—it focuses solely on the presidency prior to 2000 and does not include scandals from lower-level races. Thus, as no cases of scandal involving a female politician are included in his study, it is not informative as to the interaction of gender and political scandal.

Further, Thompson (2000) does not include any public opinion data to determine the effect of scandals. Thus, although Thompson creates categories for scandals, no empirical test exists that examines the effects of scandal on a candidate. Although Thompson's work provides a clear understanding of how to classify scandal, it narrowly defines political scandal and does not account for how political scandals could affect women. In addition, his work is focused on scandals that have occurred while an official is in office and not during an election cycle.

Similar to Thompson (2000), Audt's (2008) work focuses on a historical account of presidential scandal. He argues that political scandals are first reported by smaller newspapers and then picked up by larger newspapers if the scandal is worthwhile. By examining past polling information, Audt determines that the level of trust in government also affects whether the scandal will gain traction. Although an interesting point, his work has limitations that are similar to Thompson's 2000 study. First, Audt's study excludes any cases in which the politician embroiled in a scandal is a woman. Second, like Thompson (2000), Audt (2008) is concerned with a scandal occurring when a president is in office. As he admits, the timing of a scandal is important. However, by focusing solely on scandals while an official is in office, the scope of effects is limited. Furthermore, the effects of political scandal and coverage by the media could be different depending on whether the candidate is an elected official running for higher office, a first-time candidate, an incumbent, or a seasoned challenger.

In another study, Pugilisi and Snyder (2011) focused on newspaper coverage of political scandals from 1997 through 2007. Given the authors' time frame, they analyzed 32 scandals by looking at 200 newspapers. Puglisi and Snyder focused only on financial scandals, excluding sexual scandals and power scandals, both described as important by Thompson (2000) and Audt (2008). The authors found that coverage of financial scandals was linked to the newspaper's political leanings. Thus, if the editorial board was known to endorse Democratic candidates, the coverage of political scandals was more likely to focus on a scandal involving a Republican politician. Further, they found this to be even more significant when dealing with local politicians.

Although Puglisi and Snyder (2011) opened their analysis to focus on offices other than the president, their data make no mention of scandal involving a female candidate. This presents the question of whether women are involved with the types of scandals typically identified by Thompson (2000), Audt (2008), and Puglisi and Snyder (2011) and demonstrates the need to expand the scope of examination of political scandals. In addition, the authors' finding that a newspaper's editorial leaning affects its coverage of scandals highlights the importance of using a neutral tone to determine the effects of gender on scandal. Although the Puglisi and Snyder (2011) study has important findings, it is important to control for tone in order to separate the time frame of when the scandal occurred for someone who was in office versus someone who is running for office and to include the effect of other scandals.

Media Coverage of Female Candidates

Research on female candidates and their media coverage began in the early 1990s with an emphasis on gendered differences (Kahn, 1992, 1994, 1996; Kahn & Goldenberg, 1991). These studies, which focused on stereotypes and gender differences in media coverage, found that male candidates received better treatment and that women running for office were at a disadvantage. In her 1996 work, Kahn explained how women candidates receive different treatment than men in gubernatorial and U.S. Senate races. She found that the media are more likely to focus on the viability of a female candidate and that women receive less coverage than men. Also, Kahn found that the level of political office can make a difference in the media coverage of female and male candidates. In gubernatorial races, the media are more likely to focus on a female candidate's personality traits, whereas in races for the U.S. Senate, the media will focus on the likelihood of a female candidate's electoral success. Overall, Kahn (1996) found that the level of office for which the female candidate is running affects media coverage, with women running for governorships benefiting from less dramatic changes (compared to their male counterparts) than women who run for the U.S. Senate.

Kahn's (1996) findings can be applied to the topic of political scandal as she discusses the traits associated with leaders and compares the type of coverage that female and male candidates receive. When taking into consideration the discussion of political scandal, it becomes clear that the type of scandal—as well as the coverage of the female candidate—is important. In addition, noting the reaction of female candidates involved in scandal becomes important and may vary depending on the gender stereotypes in the media coverage they receive.

Scholars have argued that gender stereotypes do not directly affect women's electability; expectations toward women and men in politics are quite similar (Brooks, 2013; Dolan, 2014); and stereotypes of women (but not men) in politics are different from general gender stereotypes (Schneider & Bos, 2014). Despite this recently described lack of overt prejudice toward women in politics, the question of whether women and men involved in political scandals are assessed in similar ways is still worth investigating. Because women politicians are expected to be more honest than men (Kahn, 1992), they could face more rigid standards in the assessment of their immoral behavior (see Biernat, 2003). When combined, the expectancy violations theory assumes that the same immoral act will be judged differently when committed by a woman as compared to a man. According to the shifting standards theory (Biernat, 2003; Biernat & Manis, 1994), certain groups are evaluated differently, and their members tend to be assessed in reference to the standards prescribed to their particular group. If the moral behavior of women is subjected to higher standards than men, the same immoral act by a female politician will be assessed more negatively than one associated with a man. Integrating both theoretical frameworks, I argue that scandals can result in a disproportionately large loss of support for female politicians who are involved in them as compared to men.

Although research has investigated how a politician's gender may relate to the perceptions of individuals about them, the results are often inconsistent and complex (McGraw, Timpone, & Bruck, 1993; Ogletree, Coffee, & May,

1992; Smith, Smith-Powers, & Suarez, 2005; Stewart et al., 2013). For example, although some older studies (e.g., Ogletree et al., 1992) have revealed that women involved in scandals suffer less negative effects than men, others (e.g., McGraw et al., 1993) have found that female politicians receive harsher treatment. Some studies have even suggested that the sex of a politician plays no obvious role (Bhatti, Hansen, & Olsen, 2013; Smith et al., 2005).

As Biernat and Manis (1994) have suggested, the effects predicted by the shifting standards theory are present mostly among people who believe in gender stereotypes. For this reason, it is possible that female politicians involved in scandals will be treated more harshly than men if voters hold such stereotypes. Therefore, it is important to measure the beliefs regarding the capacity of men versus women in politics. The expectancy violation theory supplements the shifting standards theory by indicating the importance of cultural and political context in which the assessment of behavior is performed.

Gaffes and Scandals in the 2016 Presidential Election

The primary races for the 2016 presidential election had interesting moments for both Democrats and Republicans. Each side had contested races, with Democrats seeming destined to nominating Clinton as their candidate, whereas the Republicans underwent an identity crisis with a full spectrum of choices. With no clear frontrunner for Republicans during the primary stage, media coverage largely focused on the Republican primary debates and the many gaffes of candidate Trump. As it turns out, the Democrats were facing a fractured party as well during the primary stage, with young and more progressive voters flocking to U.S. Senator Bernie Sanders, creating friction within the Democratic Party. While both Democrats and Republicans were having intraparty conflicts, the individual campaigns also were having issues crafting well-received messages.

Abuela Hillary

For Clinton's campaign, outreach toward minority groups was difficult, especially in the month of December 2015. With the news that Clinton would become a grandmother for the second time, a content strategist with her campaign decided to create an article on December 22, 2015, titled "7 Things Hillary Clinton Has in Common with Your Abuela" (Spanish for grandmother). Upon releasing the list comparing Clinton to abuelas, Twitter received thousands of tweets mostly critical or mocking of the comparison. The Clinton campaign responded by saying the list had not been approved, but they thought the comparison was true because Clinton is involved with her grandchildren and does not tolerate disrespect. Twitter responded with the

#NotMyAbuela hashtag and a meme of Clinton's face superimposed onto the Abuelita hot chocolate logo.

The Abuelita tweet reached its height on December 23, 2015, and slowly began to die down on December 24, 2015. A resurgence of #NotMyAbuela happened around the Democratic Candidate Forum on January 17, 2016, in Charlestown, South Carolina, but calmed down until then-FBI Director James Comey sent a letter to the U.S. Congress on October 28, 2016, that the bureau had learned of the existence of e-mails that appeared to be pertinent to its investigation into the private e-mail server that Clinton used as secretary of state.

Bad Hombres

Trump's presidential campaign began in a manner that called into question his feelings and beliefs about Latinos. In the beginning of the campaign, Trump famously labeled all undocumented immigrants as murders and rapists. In an attempt to show he wasn't racist, a Latina supporting Trump shouted out her love and support for the candidate at one of his rallies. On May 5, 2016, the Trump campaign—in an attempt to show how he much he loves Latinos—posted a picture of the candidate eating a taco salad. Although Twitter reacted to this post, the strongest reaction to Trump's portrayal of Latinos was seen after the October 19, 2016, presidential debate.

During the debate, Trump was asked about securing borders. He began talking about deporting drug lords, but the sentiment was lost when he stated "we have some bad hombres here and we're going to get them out" (Diaz & Ahmed, 2016). Almost instantaneously, memes and tweets were sent throughout Twitter. While the "bad hombres" comment was taking over Twitter, another quip by Trump later on the debate, when he called Clinton a "nasty woman," also sparked tweets and memes. It took approximately 14 minutes following Trump's debate comment for a meme to be posted on Twitter.

Analysis of Reactions to Abuela Hillary and Bad Hombres on Twitter

Tweets were gathered for a 24-hour period beginning immediately after the gaffe occurred. Retweets were not counted for this analysis. The focus of the analysis was twofold. First, the goal was to examine whether or not the gaffes involving Latinos and each candidate received the same amount of attention. Second, the way Latinos reacted to the tweets was observed. Although one gaffe occurred during the primary campaign and the other in the general election phase, these were the two most noted gaffes that involved the Latin@ community. Although I cannot say whether those who tweeted actually voted, nor how they voted, I am able to build a consensus of opinion about the gaffes.

Abuela Hillary

Clinton's gaffe saw 2,700 original tweets within a 24-hour period. An examination of these tweets reveals a clear confusion among Twitter users as to why Clinton viewed herself as having the same types of morals, thoughts, or struggles as abuelas. Tweets symbolizing the struggles of abuelas and comparing them to the life Clinton has led were the most popular. "A Wellesley grad, Yale-law 68-year-old millionaire gringa in government since 79 inspired both #NotMyAbuela and #Hispandering? #Priceless LOL," wrote one Twitter user (Belville, 2015). Another Twitter user highlighted her frustration by stating, "You're a white woman in a higher socioeconomic/power position, you are #NotMyAbuela. Minimize our differences & you invalidate our struggles" (la_jeisol, 2015).

Tweeters also brought up Clinton's use of the word "respeto." For example, Tonnet Latino (2015) noted how his abuela helped her community out of respect, not because she wanted votes, but because she knew it was right. "My grandmother would never get involved in politics. She was a very religious person. Hillary is definitely #NotMyAbuela." Another tweeter took note that the Clinton campaign said she read to her grandchildren and responded by saying her grandmother couldn't go to school past second grade.

Such tweets demonstrate how pandering to the Latin@ community by drawing comparisons revealed a misunderstanding about the struggles that generations of Latinos have endured, the amount of respect placed on helping community and working hard, and how struggling can vary by socioeconomic status and ethnicity.

Among the tweets examined, the fewest number associated Clinton with foods characteristically prepared by abuelas, including empanadas, tamales, arroz con frijoles (rice and beans), and pozole (pork and hominy soup). However, these tweets demonstrated frustration about the understanding of what an abuela does and how they can show their love for their grandchildren. "Can you even make empanadas @HillaryClinton? #NotMyAbuela," tweeter Cassie (2015) asked. The discussion of food also highlights an important part of the Latin@ culture that is readily accessible to noncommunity members.

The second least number of tweets with the NotMyAbuela hashtag focused on concerns about Clinton supporting deportations of children and families, as well as her past support of invasions and coups in Latin America. For example, Twitter user Vera Parra posted, "My abuela was exiled from her homeland for resisting a US backed military dictatorship. Clinton supported the coup in Honduras #NotMyAbuela" (Parra, 2015).

One of the most telling tweets wasn't necessarily a condemnation of Clinton herself, but of the Democratic Party and the assumption of who Latinos vote for. "Sorry, @HillaryClinton you are #NotMyAbuela and the Democratic Party doesn't have control over the Latino vote," Samuel LeDoux (2015) tweeted.

Although clear indignation for Clinton's pandering to the Latin@ community was noted in the #NotMyAbuela tweets, it is important to consider the age demographics of those likely to be on Twitter, as well as the fact that many younger voters supported Sanders in the primary stage of the campaign. Thus, although these tweets show anger toward being stereotyped and categorized, the number of supporters Clinton actually lost by comparing herself to an abuela cannot be quantified.

Bad Hombres

Although the Trump campaign had multiple political gaffes and scandals to cover over the course of his primary and general election campaigns, the bad hombres gaffe was one that allowed for a specific time frame that had a clear peak and end. In the 24-hour period examined, 900 tweets used the "badhombres" hashtag. However, #badhombres was used in significantly different ways than #NotMyAbuela. Instead of focusing on candidate Trump, Twitter users took the negative connotation away from the phrase and focused instead on the positive aspects of Latino males. For example, Jorge Solis (2016) tweeted: "I'm a #BadHombre. I take care of my family, paid taxes, vote, and serve my community as much as possible." By embracing the #badhombres campaign, some Latino Twitter users muted the narrative created by Trump. While individual tweets with the "badhombres" hashtag were being sent, one Twitter user created a parody account titled @badhombres. This account sent out tweets focusing on candidate Trump's campaign messages and making them their own, for example: "Don't worry the #BadHombres are here and we only want to make American (sic) Great again" (Bad Hombres, 2016).

In addition to spinning the #badhombres campaign into a positive stereotype for Latinos, the hashtag provided an opportunity for Twitter users to make fun of Trump, his ties to Putin, and his policy stances. Similar to the comparisons made about Clinton with abuelas, Twitter users began to compare Trump to a bad hombre. In turn, they used another phrase coined by the candidate against him. Twitter users also used "bad hombre" to reference Trump's relationship with Russian president Vladimir Putin. Most notably, and in contrast with the Clinton abuela comparison, 20 unique memes were created to make fun of candidate Trump on Twitter. These memes were then retweeted, reaching more people. Examples of memes created included pictures of babies in sombreros, Spider-Man in a sombrero, the Three Amigos, and four Trump/Putin memes picturing their relationship in unflattering ways.

Comparison of the Gaffes

The two gaffes had unique reactions. Of the two, Clinton's abuela gaffe drew more interest and the tweets were more definite in trying to separate the candidate from the Latin@ community as a whole. In contrast, Trump's gaffe allowed for Latinos to define themselves as compared to defending their culture and perceptions of their beloved matriarch. Clinton's gaffe gained 2,700 tweets within the first day alone. Trump's gaffe had 900 tweets within the same length of time. Clinton having three times the amount of tweets as Trump demonstrates expectancy violation theory. The Clinton campaign violated stereotypes and norms that were held for her candidacy, and potential voters reacted. Although Trump's campaign style continued to insult groups of voters, including Latinos, his "bad hombres" comment was met with much fewer reactions because it did not violate expectations.

It is also worth noting that the indignation shown for Clinton was not the same as the attitude toward Trump's gaffe. One possible explanation is that by the time the bad hombre comment was made, voter fatigue had set in. However, as the literature points out, the behavior was less expected from Clinton, creating a stronger reaction in the Twittersphere. We also saw that pandering toward the Latin@ community was ill received, largely because of misconceptions about abuelas.

Conclusion

Do tweets about candidate's gaffes matter? Although this study cannot measure voter effects, we know that 25% of third-generation Latinos voted for Trump (Latino Decisions, 2016). We also know that gender stereotypes for political gaffes appear to have been supported. Although this can all be said, more work needs to be done. Future research should conduct experiments focusing on gaffes when attempting to micro-target groups of voters during campaigns. More work also needs to be done on micro-targeting of the Latin@ community.

This analysis provides an example of what can go wrong when trying to pander to a community, as well as how negative effects can be mitigated. To be fair, by the time the #badhombres gaffe occurred, Latinos may have been simply numb to attacks made toward their community by Trump. It is also possible that because of the wording of his phrase and the fact that Latinos were given actual space to navigate, the community was less offended. It is clear that work remains to be done on how to reach the Latin@ voting bloc without alienating portions of it.

References

Abrajano, M., Alvarez, R. M., & Nagler, J. (2005). Race based vs. issue voting: A natural experiment. *Political Research Quarterly, 58,* 203–218. Retrieved from http://journals.sagepub.com/doi/abs/10.1177/106591290505800202

Audt, A. (2008). *On scandal: Moral disturbances in society, politics and art.* New York: Cambridge University Press.

Bad Hombres (2016, October 19). Don't worry the #BadHombres are here and we only want to make American Great again. [Tweet]. Retrieved from https://twitter.com/TheBadHombres/status/788914485532692480

Belville, Russ. [Radical Russ]. (2015, December 23). A Wellesley grad, Yale-law 68-year-old millionaire gringa in government since 79 inspired both #Not MyAbuela and #Hispandering? #Priceless LOL. [Tweet]. Retrieved from https://twitter.com/RadicalRuss/status/679811322566078466

Bhatti, Y., Hansen, K. M., & Olsen, A. L. (2013). Political hypocrisy: The effect of political scandals on candidate evaluations. *Acta Politica, 48*(4), 404–428. Retrieved from https://doi.org/10.1057/ap.2013.6

Biernat, M. (2003). Toward a broader view of social stereotyping. *American Psychologist, 58*(1), 1019–1027. Retrieved from http://dx.doi.org/10.1037/0003-066X.58.12.1019

Biernat, M., & Manis, M. (1994). Shifting standards and stereotyping-based judgements. *Journal of Personality and Social Psychology, 66,* 5–20. Retrieved from http://dx.doi.org/10.1037/0022-3514.66.1.5

Brooks, D. J. (2013). *He runs, she runs: Why gender stereotypes do not harm women candidates.* Princeton, NJ: Princeton University Press.

Cassie. [Cassandrasfl]. (2015, December 23). Can you even make empanadas @HillaryClinton? #NotMyAbuela. [Tweet]. Retrieved from https://twitter.com/Cassandrasfl/status/679813447773585409

Dávila, A. M. (2012). *Latinos, Inc: The marketing and making of a people.* Oakland: University of California Press.

Diaz, D., & Ahmed, S. (2016, October 20). Who won the presidential debate? #BadHombres. *CNN.com.* Retrieved from http://www.cnn.com/2016/10/19/politics/bad-hombres-donald-trump-hillary-clinton/

Dolan, K. (2014). *When does gender matter? Women candidates and gender stereotypes in American elections.* New York: Oxford University Press.

Kahn, K. F. (1992). Does being male help: An investigation of gender and media effects in U.S. senate races. *Journal of Politics, 54*(2), 497–517. Retrieved from https://doi.org/10.2307/2132036

Kahn, K. F. (1994). Does gender make a difference? An experimental examination of sex stereotypes and press patterns in statewide campaigns. *American Journal of Political Science, 38*(1), 162–195. doi:10.2307/2111340

Kahn, K. F. (1996). *The political consequences of being a woman.* New York: Columbia University Press.

La_Jeisol (2015, December 23). You're a white woman in a higher socioeconomic/power position, you are #NotMyAbuela. Minimize our differences & you invalidate our struggles. [Tweet]. Retrieved from https://twitter.com/la_jeisol/status/679784923402653696

Latino Decisions. (2016, November 2–7). 2016 election eve poll. Retrieved from http://www.latinodecisions.com/files/8614/7866/3919/National_2016_Xtabs.pdf

LeDoux, S. [LeDouxUSA]. (2015, December 23). Sorry, @HillaryClinton you are #NotMyAbuela and the Democratic Party doesn't have control over the Latino vote. [Tweet]. Retrieved from https://twitter.com/LeDouxUSA

Lies, damn lies, and exit polls. (2016, November 10). *Latino Decisions.* Retrieved from http://www.latinodecisions.com/blog/2016/11/10/lies-damn-lies-and -exit-polls

Lipsitz, George. (2011). *How racism takes place.* Philadelphia: Temple University Press.

Lopez, I. H. (2006). *White by law: The legal construction of race* (10th anniversary edition). New York: New York University Press.

Márquez, B. (2007). Latino identity politics research: Problems and opportunities. In R. Espino, D. Leal, & K. Meier (Eds.), *Latino politics: Identity, mobilization, and representation* (pp. 17–26). Charlottesville: University of Virginia Press.

McGraw, K. M., Timpone, R., & Bruck, G. (1993). Justifying controversial political decisions: Home style in the laboratory. *Political Behavior, 15,* 289–308. Retrieved from https://doi.org/10.1007/BF00993439

Neckel, S. (2005). Political scandals: An analytic framework. *Comparative Sociology, 4*(1–2), 101–114. doi:10.1163/1569133054621950

Ogletree, S. M., Coffee, M. C., & May, S. A. (1992). Perceptions of female/male presidential candidates: Familial and personal situations. *Psychology of Women Quarterly, 16,* 201–208.

Parra, V. [VeraParral]. (2015, December 23). My abuela was exiled from her homeland for resisting a US backed military dictatorship. Clinton supported the coup in Honduras #NotMyAbuela. [Tweet]. Retrieved from https:// twitter.com/VeraParral/status/679799536194293760

Pew Research Center. (2015a, February 3). Social media preferences vary by race and ethnicity. Retrieved from http://www.pewresearch.org/fact-tank/2015 /02/03/social-media-preferences-vary-by-race-and-ethnicity/

Pew Research Center. (2015b, October 8). Social media usage: 2005–2015. Retrieved from http://www.pewinternet.org/2015/10/08/social-networking -usage-2005-2015

Piñón, J., & Rojas, V. (2011). Language and cultural identity in the new configuration of the US Latino TV industry. *Global Media and Communication, 7*(2), 129–147. Retrieved from https://doi.org/10.1177/1742766511410220

Pugilisi, R., & Snyder, J. (2011). Newspaper coverage of political scandals. *Journal of Politics, 73*(3), 931–50.

Santoro, W. A., & Segura, G. M. (2009). Generational status and Mexican American political participation: The benefits and limitations of assimilation. *Political Research Quarterly, 64*(1), 172–184. Retrieved from https://doi.org /10.1177/1065912909346738

Schneider, M. C., & Bos, A. L. (2014). Measuring stereotypes of female politicians. *Political Psychology, 35,* 245–266. doi:10.1111/pops.12040

7 things Hillary Clinton has in common with your abuela. (2015, December 22). *hillaryclinton.com.* Retrieved from https://www.hillaryclinton.com/feed /8-ways-hillary-clinton-just-your-abuela

Smith, E. S., Smith-Powers, A., & Suarez, G. A. (2005). If Bill Clinton were a woman: The effectiveness of male and female politicians account strategies following alleged transgressions. *Political Psychology, 26,* 115–134. Retrieved from http://dx.doi.org/10.1080/00224545.2012.744292

Solis, J. [Jorge3763]. (2016, October 20). I'm a #BadHombre. I take care of my family, paid taxes, vote, and serve my community as much as possible. [Tweet]. Retrieved from https://twitter.com/jorge3763/status/789242343979307008

Stewart, D. D., Rose, R. P., Rosales, F. M., Rudney, P. D., Lehner, T. A., Miltich G., Snyder C., & Sadecki, B. (2013). The value of outside support for male and female politicians involved in a political sex scandal. *The Journal of Psychology, 153,* 375–394.

Stokes-Brown, A. K. (2009). The hidden politics of identity: Racial self-identification and Latino political engagement. *Politics & Policy, 37*(6), 1281–1305. doi: 10.1111/j.1747-1346.2009.00220.x

Thompson, J. B. (2000). *Political scandal: Power and visibility in the media age.* Cambridge, UK: Polity Press.

Tonnet Latino. (2015, December 23). My grandmother would never get involved in politics. She was a very religious person. Hillary is definitely #NotMy Abuela. [Tweet]. Retrieved from https://twitter.com/tonnetlatino

CHAPTER TWENTY-ONE

Analyzing Tweets About the 2016 U.S. Presidential "Blunder" Election

Michael W. Kearney

Anyone who watched, listened to, or read coverage of the 2016 U.S. presidential campaigns will likely agree the social media platform called Twitter played a major and high-profile role in the election. Created in 2008, Twitter has become one of the most popular social media platforms in the United States. According to the Pew Research Center, approximately 16% of American adults, or 40 million people residing in the United States, used Twitter as of 2016 (Gottfried & Shearer, 2017). The share of the country that uses Twitter lags behind the roughly two-thirds of all Americans who use Facebook. Nevertheless, among social media platforms, Twitter *seemed* to dominate the headlines in news media accounts of the 2016 election (Kapko, 2016)—especially in the context of the highly contentious presidential election.

The growing role of Twitter in U.S. politics, as demonstrated by the 2016 general election, should not be altogether surprising. The Pew Research Center estimates that as of 2016 nearly 60% of users get their news from Twitter (Gottfried & Shearer, 2017). Research also suggests there is a link between user activity on Twitter and external political events (e.g., Hong, 2012; Jang & Pasek, 2015; Shin, Jian, Driscoll, & Bar, 2016), though the nature of the relationships between traditional media, major events, and Twitter remains largely unknown (Jang & Pasek, 2015). Another report by Pew Research Center, for example, found that although the majority of users were tired of political content and often viewed it as uncivil, a sizable contingent of users still enjoyed political content and maintained high levels of engagement in political conversations on social media (Duggan & Smith, 2016). In short, in the nine years since its launch, researchers have learned a great deal about Twitter in the context of political events, but much remains to be discovered about what Twitter tells us about the general public.

The purpose of this chapter is to explore user activity on Twitter to help make sense of the evolution of public opinion during the 2016 U.S. election—particularly as it relates to the presidential election. Before exploring the data, however, it is important to understand some basic features of Twitter. Thus, this chapter proceeds in three parts. First, Twitter and a number of its features and unique user dynamics are introduced in order to assist in interpreting patterns in user activities on Twitter. Two research questions are then proposed to guide the current study. Second, the research design and data are described—an original study of Twitter users who were randomly sampled from well-known partisan and nonpartisan accounts who were tracked during the 2016 election. Finally, the data are classified as "political" and "nonpolitical" and then explored for trends relating to the frequency and sentiment of content posted by partisan Republican users, partisan Democrat users, and nonpartisan moderate users.

Twitter

Users

Before delving too deeply into what happened on Twitter during the 2016 election, it is first important to understand how Twitter works. Twitter is similar to other social media platforms in that users can form connections, interact, and share content with other users. Though Twitter accounts are often associated with specific people, they are not required to be. In fact, Twitter accounts are often used to represent brands, organizations, gimmicks, or other entities as well. To what degree one can discern information about the operator of a Twitter account depends on decisions made by the user operating the account. At the time of writing, the creation of a new Twitter account required only an active e-mail address or phone number. Whether users share their address, phone number, or other pieces of demographic information with the general public, however, remains up to individual users. Accounts can operate with relative anonymity by withholding identifying information from their user profile pages. By default, posts made by Twitter users are searchable by the general public, but users can also choose to make their accounts "private," which functionally opts them out of default public sharing.

Statuses

Twitter users can engage the social media platform in a number of ways. Perhaps the central feature afforded to users, and the focus of this chapter, is the ability to post statuses on behalf of one's Twitter account. Because statuses posted to Twitter are typically referred to as *tweets*, the action of posting statuses to Twitter is commonly described as *tweeting*. For the remainder of this chapter, the terms *status* and *tweet* will therefore be used interchangeably. Users can post up to 1,000 statuses in a single day (Twitter, 2016), though the average user rarely encounters this limit. Users can post three different types of statuses. The most basic status entails composing and sharing text of up to 140 characters. These statuses can include URLs linking to other content on the Web; clickable keywords, or *hashtags*, denoted via text following the pound sign (e.g., #Election2016); and several types of media entities, for example, images, GIFs, and videos (Twitter, 2016). The other two types of statuses are referred to as *retweeted* statuses (commonly referred to as "retweets") and *quoted statuses*. Retweeted statuses entail the reposting of statuses from other users' timelines. In contrast to retweeted statuses, which simply import and redisplay Twitter statuses originally posted by other users, quoted statuses allow users to prepend original [text] content, which is then displayed above an embedded link to the quoted status. In other words, quoted statuses are retweets plus a bit of commentary provided by the user doing the reposting. Twitter statuses are shared via user timelines, which function like archives for the statuses posted by a single user.

Network Connections

One benefit of studying Twitter is rooted in the way in which users connect on the platform. Unlike many other social media sites, Twitter user networks are composed of a series of asymmetrical connections. In other words, when one user connects with another user on Twitter, they do so unilaterally, so when user A connects with user B, user B does not automatically connect to user A. For contrast, consider Facebook's symmetrical structure to user connections. When a Facebook user successfully connects with another user, both users become "friends." So, when user A friends user B, user B is also friending user A. Similar behaviors occur on Twitter, but not automatically. Continuing with the previous example, Twitter user A is free to decide to connect to, or "follow," user B, assuming user B's account is public.

Users are also exposed to a live feed of statuses posted by accounts followed by a user. Users access the bulk of the content they encounter on Twitter via user timelines, which were described earlier as the collection of statuses posted by a user. When user A follows user B, statuses posted by user B will be included on the timeline of user A. However, because the connections are asymmetrical, the same is not also the case for user B's timeline. Rather, if user A follows user B, then user B's timeline is unchanged. To create a mutual connection through Twitter, user B would have to reciprocate by also deciding to follow user A. The asymmetry in user connections is important on Twitter because it is common for average, everyday users to "follow" public figures—celebrities, athletes, well-known media figures, etc.—and entities—corporations, brands, Web sites, etc. Because the connections are one-way, they reveal more about the preferences of the users who decide to follow another account than they do about the mutual relationship between two users.

The asymmetrical nature of user networks on Twitter often results in a slightly unbalanced friend-to-follower ratio. Specifically, the number of accounts followed by a user (friends) exceeds the number of accounts following a user (followers), creating an average ratio of followers to friends of greater than 1.0 (Liu, Kliman-Silver, & Mislove, 2014). In other words, Twitter users tend to have slightly more connections going out ("friends") than they do coming in ("followers"). This unbalanced distribution of friends to followers is caused by many users following a handful of the same [very popular] users. The verified account of Katy Perry, for instance, followed 200 users (friends) at the time of writing despite being followed by more than 97 million users (followers). Unbalanced user networks on Twitter—with average users often deciding to follow well-known public figures and organizations—provide researchers with unique opportunities to track the media selection behaviors of average users (e.g., Hong, 2012). As such, many users follow one or more political candidates, organizations, or news media sources.

Twitter Data

Application Program Interfaces

Another upside to studying Twitter comes from public-facing account defaults and generous data-sharing policies implemented by Twitter. Unlike Facebook, for example, Twitter makes much of the data documenting the actions of millions of users available to the public. Twitter does this via multiple application program interfaces (APIs). The data analysis that follows was conducted on data collected via Twitter's REST API (e.g., Barberá, 2015; Breen, 2012; Younis, 2015). The REST API allows access to several sources of data, including user metadata, network connections (friends and followers), and user timelines. The rtweet package (Kearney, 2016) in the R environment (R Core, 2017) was used to interact with Twitter's REST API and collect the data.

Twitter data also have several limitations, which restrict the inferences that can be made here. In terms of forecasting the 2016 presidential election, for instance, simple measures of Twitter use appear too crude to capture the complex processes that result in Twitter activity. On the one hand, Twitter activity may have been an early indicator that Donald Trump, who was the vastly more popular candidate on Twitter, would outperform the expectations derived from more traditional polling methods. On the other hand, the same inference would have been wrong had it been applied to the Democratic primary where Hillary Clinton managed to comfortably secure the party's nomination despite a convergence of Twitter activity around her opponent, Bernie Sanders.

Difficulties in drawing inferences from various types of Twitter popularity metrics extend beyond election forecasting as well. Research suggests candidates in closer races do tend to tweet more often; however, the frequency of tweets did not predict the number of followers (Conway, Kenski, & Wang, 2013) or votes (Ammann, 2010) received by candidates. Further, research conducted during the 2012 presidential election suggests there is a strong relationship between media coverage and twitter mentions, but no relationship between candidate activity on Twitter and Twitter mentions (Hong & Nadler, 2012). In light of the emergence of newly available digital sources of "big data," inconsistencies in previous findings highlight the need for more unifying and robust methods for separating the signal from the noise in social media data. Thus, in order to better understand what occurred on Twitter during the 2016 election, this chapter advances a probability-based sampling method using partisan follower networks to analyze the trends and patterns of partisan and nonpartisan Twitter users.

Previous Research

Despite inherent difficulties associated with collecting and analyzing Twitter data, researchers have examined a number of political behaviors on Twitter. For instance, research examining the partisanship of Twitter user networks suggests user connections are largely shaped by partisan orientations (Barberá, 2015; Barberá, Jost, Nagler, Tucker, & Bonneau, 2015), with some research finding the Twitter networks of partisan Republicans, in particular, were more polarized than were the networks of partisan Democrats (Wang, Li, & Luo, 2016). Already there has been research examining the 2016 election as well. To date, research has found high activity from political bots (Kollanyi, Howard, & Woolley, 2016) and the sharing of fake news stories at an alarming rate (Allcott & Gentzkow, 2017). Sentiment analysis of tweets sent from the Republican presidential candidate's Twitter account seemed to suggest the sentiment of the content varied depending whether the status came from one device, which the candidate was known to use, compared to the statuses coming from a device produced by a competing service provider (Robinson, 2016).

This research and the study that follows can tell us much about the nature of media exposure and partisan connections in new media environments, but this research does not describe all user interactions with media. One limitation of research focusing on Twitter is that Twitter may attract certain types of users and user behaviors. For example, experimental research comparing exposure to political content on Twitter with exposure to political content on newspapers found that, compared to those exposed to newspapers, participants exposed to information on Twitter reported higher levels of social presence, stronger agreement among those with favorable attitudes, and more focus on candidates than issues (Lee & Shin, 2012).

Research Questions

RQ1: When and to what degree did users tweet about political compared to nonpolitical topics during the 2016 election?

RQ2: To what extent did the sentiment of tweets vary in relation to major events during the 2016 election?

Method

Sample and Procedures

The sample consisted of users ($N=212$) randomly selected among Twitter followers of partisan Democrat, partisan Republican, and nonpartisan accounts. The sampling frame consisted of three pools of user IDs—the unique identifiers assigned to users by Twitter—constructed using the list of followers of well-known, media-oriented accounts selected to represent each of the three groups. Partisan Democrat users were sampled from well-known media accounts widely perceived to be Democrat partisans, that is, Rachel Maddow (@maddow), Paul Krugman (@paulkrugman), Salon.com (@salon), and Huffington Post Politics (@HuffPoPols). Partisan Republican users were sampled from well-known media accounts widely perceived to be Republican partisans, that is, Sean Hannity (@seanhannity), Sarah Palin (@SarahPalinUSA), Drudge Report (@DRUDGE_REPORT), and Fox News Politics (@FoxNews Politics). Nonpartisan users were sampled from well-known media accounts widely perceived to be oriented toward entertainment, that is, Sports Illustrated (@SInow), CBS Survivor (@cbssurvivor), and AMC TV (@AMC_TV) accounts.

User timelines—the collection of Twitter statuses, or tweets, posted by users—were collected for each of the users in the sample. Because the current investigation is interested in the content expressed by individual users on Twitter, retweets, or reposting statuses from other users' timelines, were filtered out (excluded) during the data collection process. Original content provided alongside embedded links to other statuses was retained for data

Table 21.1   Number of Observed Users and Statuses Summarized by Group and Topic

| Group | Users | Statuses | | Total |
		Political (%)	Nonpolitical (%)	
Democrat	77	3,281 (17.3%)	15,723 (82.7%)	19,004
Nonpartisan	67	615 (03.9%)	15,301 (96.1%)	15,916
Republican	68	3,463 (24.0%)	10,969 (76.0%)	14,432
Total	212	7,459 (15.0%)	41,993 (85.0%)	49,352

analysis. The Twitter statuses ($N = 41,896$) analyzed included original (user-generated) statuses as well as those statuses included when quoting statuses posted by other users. Summary statistics describing the total number of statuses for each group can be seen in Table 21.1.

Results

Combining a probability-based sampling method—that is, randomly selecting followers of highly visible partisan and nonpartisan accounts on Twitter—with textual analysis of statuses posted by the same users over time makes it possible to explore the evolution of public opinion expression of Twitter users during the 2016 election. Before analyzing the tweets posted by users in the sample, however, certain steps were taken to prepare the text for analysis. The process is described in more detail later, but, essentially, Twitter statuses were cleaned and then tokenized, or split, into individual words. More specifically, cleaning the text consisted of removing all user mentions (screen names), symbols, and URLs, leaving the text of hashtags, or hyperlinked keywords denoted by a single pound sign, to be treated like any other word. In addition, all numbers and any of their connecting [nonspace] characters were removed from the statuses. Statuses were then standardized to lowercase, split by space into individual words used in each status, and then analyzed using a number of models described in the sections that follow.

Research Question 1

The first research question asked how often users posted about political compared to nonpolitical topics during the 2016 election. To answer this research question, which not only asked about when users decided to post about politics but also to what degree they did so relative to posts about nonpolitical topics, statuses had to first be classified as "political" or "nonpolitical." Unfortunately, given the nature of communication on Twitter and Twitter's character limit of 140 characters per tweet, discerning the topic of any particular status is no easy task. It makes sense, for example, that whether it is because a user is simply replying to another status, commenting on a trending topic, or avoiding character limits enforced by Twitter, users would forego directly mentioning the topic(s) of a tweet and instead only communicate on an implied subject. It is also likely that new and unexpected conventions, abbreviations, or phrases—many of which may be unique even to Twitter— would emerge.

To tackle challenges related to the classification of Twitter statuses as political versus nonpolitical, a conservative assumption was made regarding an initial set of 64 political keywords. Among others, the keywords included the names of the major-party candidates ("Trump," "Clinton," etc.) and other key political figures ("Obama," "Pence," etc.), the names and nicknames of major political parties and ideologies ("Democrat," "conservative," "GOP," etc.), words associated with major political topics ("warming," "immigration," "terrorism," etc.), and explicit references to words typically reserved with elections ("voting," "caucus," "electoral," etc.). Using these keywords as classifiers of political versus nonpolitical tweets, it was then possible to construct a frequency table and compare the number of times each word appeared in political tweets compared to the number of times it appeared in nonpolitical tweets. Words that appeared more frequently (proportion of occurrences above .50) in political tweets were then added to the list of political keywords, and the process was repeated a second time, yielding a final list of 235 political keywords. The cluster of identified words seemed to comfortably fall within the realm of political. For instance, the five words that had the weakest classification scores but were still considered to be political (because they appeared more than 50% of the time in statuses with political keywords) were "rigged" (a word repeatedly uttered by the Republican presidential candidate), "proven" (an adjective frequently used when describing candidates), "protester," (an intensely political act), "progressive" (another name for values associated with liberal democrats), and "lied" (a verb frequently used when describing candidates). Using the iterative process described earlier, it is possible to expand this list further. However, in the interest of being conservative, analyses proceeded using the aforementioned list of 235 political keywords.

Descriptive statistics in Table 21.1 include the breakdown of the number of statuses classified as political (third column) and nonpolitical (fourth column), as well as their relative proportions by group. Overall, as can be seen in Table 21.1, users in the sample tweeted primarily about nonpolitical topics. About 85% of the observed statuses were classified as nonpolitical. Although nonpolitical statuses were in the clear majority, that still meant users in the sample posted nearly 7,500 political statuses. As one might expect, the partisan groups tended to tweet more about politics (24% of tweets posted by users in the Republican group and 17% of the tweets posted by users in the

Democrat group were classified as political) than did the nonpartisan group (only 3% of statuses posted by nonpartisan users were classified as political).

Following the classification of statuses into political and nonpolitical categories, the number of Twitter statuses was then aggregated by group (Democrat, Republican, moderate) and by topic (political, nonpolitical) using one-day intervals ranging from January 1, 2016, to a week after Election Day, November 14, 2017. Because the research question is about the relative frequency of political tweets compared to other tweets, the daily totals were then used to calculate for each group the daily proportions of statuses that were political, as well as the proportion of statuses that were nonpolitical. These aggregated values can be seen in Figure 21.1 for the Democrat group (blue circles), Republican group (red triangle), and moderate group (purple square). The points in Figure 21.1 were fit using locally weighted regression (LOESS) curves, which are depicted as solid (proportion of nonpolitical statuses) and dashed (proportion of political statuses). The mirrored lines seen in Figure 21.1

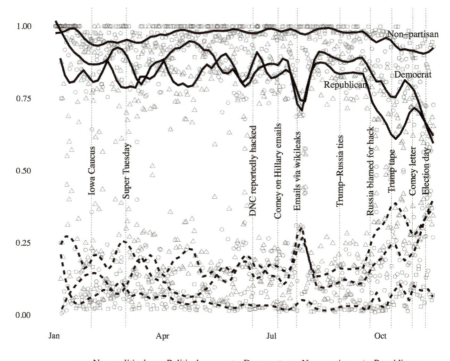

Figure 21.1   Frequency of Political Versus Nonpolitical Statuses Posted by Partisan and Nonpartisan Groups (*Note:* Frequency of political tweets by user group during the 2016 election. LOESS curves fit to aggregated sums of Twitter statuses by day and topic.)

highlight the degree to which the samples mostly posted nonpolitical statuses. Because there were only two categories of tweets, the proportions within groups always sum to 1.0, which explains the mirrored image effect in Figure 21.1—which seems to better highlight the trends.

In addition to aggregated values and smoothed lines, Figure 21.1 flags a number of notable election-related events. Vertical, dashed lines on the dates of these events are labeled with a few key words of vertical-facing text. The events include the Iowa caucuses, Super Tuesday, news of the Democratic National Committee (DNC) getting hacked, findings from the FBI investigation of Clinton's e-mails presented by FBI Director James Comey, the disclosure of stolen (hacked) e-mails by news media outlet WikiLeaks, news of investigations into possible ties between Trump and Russia, news that U.S. intelligence agencies blamed Russia for the hacking of the DNC, the release of the *Access Hollywood* tape of comments by Trump and Billy Bush, Comey's letter to Congress alluding to an investigation including new information that related to Clinton, and, finally, the day of the election. The particular events were chosen based upon the evaluation of the data and consultation of news sources and timeline accounts of the election.

Although it is possible the occurrence of major political events, depicted with dashed vertical lines in Figure 21.1, may have contributed to variations in the frequency of observed tweets, it should be noted that the current study only aims to explore the possibility of a relationship between the two; it does not attempt to provide, nor does it directly provide, any evidence of causality. With that said, a visual inspection of the curved lines suggests (a) the proportion of political versus nonpolitical tweets increases for all groups as the election gets closer, especially in the closing month or so; and, (b) the relative proportion of tweets seems to be particularly sensitive to election-defining scandals for both candidates—e-mails for Clinton and Russia for Trump. To get a sense of how the relative frequencies of political versus nonpolitical statuses posted by users stacks up to mainstream news coverage on social media, the relative frequencies of statuses posted by popular news accounts on Twitter were modeled using the same approach. The blue line in Figure 21.2 depicts the curved fit of the proportion of breaking news statuses about politics, and the green line depicts the curved fit of the proportion of nonpolitical statuses. Though to a seemingly lesser extent compared with what was found in the users' sample, the proportion of political statuses posted by breaking news outlets also seemed to gravitate toward scandalous content. Unlike the statuses posted by the sampled users, there does not appear to be a general, upward trend in the relative frequency of statuses.

Research Question 2

To answer the second research question, which concerned the trajectory of emotion in public opinion expression that occurred via Twitter statuses during

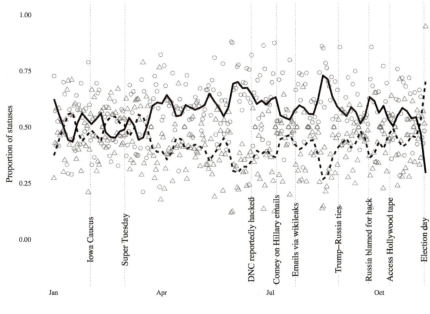

Figure 21.2   Proportion of Political Versus Nonpolitical Statuses Posted by Breaking News Accounts (*Note:* Proportion of political tweets posted by three major news accounts in 2016. Proportions calculated by aggregating number of political and nonpolitical Twitter statuses posted by three major news accounts—@cnnbrk, @breakingnews, and @cnsnews—in two-week intervals.)

the 2016 election, textual analysis was performed only on the tweets that were classified in the previous section as political. Specifically, sentiment analysis was conducted (e.g., Breen, 2012; Younis, 2016) on the cleaned tokens (words) extracted from each political status using the NRC Emotion Lexicon (Moham-med, Kiritchenko, & Zhu, 2013). The NRC Emotion Lexicon is well suited to estimate a range of emotional sentiment scores (e.g., sadness, joy, anger, dis-gust, anticipation, etc.). However, given the exploratory nature of the current study, especially as it relates to the freshly developed classification method for identifying political versus nonpolitical tweets, the analyses reported here only examined the valence—or positive and negative sentiment—of the sta-tuses. Sentiment scores were calculated by matching and then summing posi-tive and negative sentiment values associated with the words used in each status. Time series were then created by aggregating the mean positive and negative sentiment scores using two-week intervals. The time interval of two weeks was selected because it appeared to maximize variability in sentiment scores of user statuses without producing overly volatile estimates otherwise indistinguishable from noise.

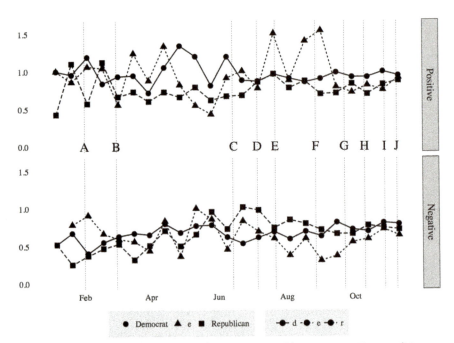

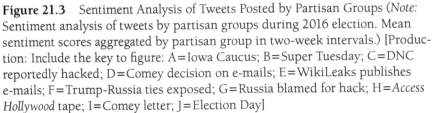

Figure 21.3   Sentiment Analysis of Tweets Posted by Partisan Groups (*Note:* Sentiment analysis of tweets by partisan groups during 2016 election. Mean sentiment scores aggregated by partisan group in two-week intervals.) [Production: Include the key to figure: A=Iowa Caucus; B=Super Tuesday; C=DNC reportedly hacked; D=Comey decision on e-mails; E=WikiLeaks publishes e-mails; F=Trump-Russia ties exposed; G=Russia blamed for hack; H=*Access Hollywood* tape; I=Comey letter; J=Election Day]

A visual depiction of the sentiment analysis via time series can be seen in Figure 21.3, which displays multiple time series for positive (first row/top half) and negative (second row/bottom half) sentiment scores for the three user groups. Dashed vertical lines in Figure 21.3 represent notable events related to the election. The letter associated with each dashed line corresponds to an event listed in the key on the bottom of Figure 21.3. Variations in sentiment appear to roughly reflect at least a few marquee events related to the presidential campaign, such as the Iowa caucuses, WikiLeaks publishing e-mails stolen from a member of the DNC, and major news regarding the exposure of the Republican candidate's alleged ties to Russia along with the possibility of a new federal investigation into past actions involving the Democratic candidate.

Discussion

This chapter aimed to shed light on public opinion as it was expressed on Twitter during the 2016 U.S. general election. Toward this end, a study was conducted that tracked and analyzed the political posts made during the 2016 election (from January until November of 2016) by a random sample of users following well-known partisan and nonpartisan accounts. Specifically, users were selected to represent three groups: partisan Democrats, partisan Republicans, and nonpartisans. Partisans were assumed to follow accounts representing popular media figures commonly associated with one of the two major political parties in the United States. Nonpartisan users were assumed to follow popular accounts that were primarily oriented toward nonpolitical entertainment. Depending on which of the selected media accounts they followed, sampled users were classified as partisan Democrat, partisan Republican, or nonpartisan. Political statuses were then pooled accordingly and analyzed in terms of their frequency, timing, and sentiment.

Before getting to the implications of these results, multiple limitations to the current study are worth noting. For instance, despite having a final sample size of almost 50,000 Twitter statuses, only 212 total users were represented in the data. Such a number makes it difficult to interpret the observed means of sentiment scores or status frequencies as accurate representations of the true means in the population of Twitter users—after all, one or two particularly active users could produce a disproportionate amount of the content. With that said, the probability-based sampling methods used in the selection of this chapter's sample should, at least in theory, limit systematic sources of variation between users. Perhaps a bigger concern regarding the sample relates to the nature of the accounts from which the sampling frame was originally constructed. As described earlier in the chapter, accounts were included in the sampling frame if they followed one or more of the identified well-known partisan and nonpartisan users. Although the accounts selected to represent partisan and nonpartisan sources are frequently used in similar ways in the literature (e.g., Arceneaux, Johnson, & Murphy, 2012; Holbert, Hmielowski, & Weeks, 2012; Wicks, Wicks, & Morimoto, 2014), many of them built their audiences using traditional media. Future research should consider integrating well-known figures that have emerged thanks to exclusively new media.

One notable contribution from this chapter concerns the classification of political versus nonpolitical statuses. Using an initial set of keywords widely known to be used in communication about the 2016 election, a classification system was derived by identifying the words that appeared more often with the political keywords than without them. Use of this technique allowed for the detection of Twitter-specific conventions that may have otherwise been overlooked. By identifying the words correlated with a conservative set of initial keywords, however, this chapter demonstrated a flexible and effective method for classifying the topic of a particular set of Twitter statuses. Political communication scholars should continue leveraging topic modeling and other text-based methods of analysis developed in linguistics and computer science to better understand large amounts of digital data generated during or in reference to important political events.

Following the classification of statuses into political and nonpolitical statuses, time series analysis was then used to analyze the frequency of statuses (by topic) made by users in the sample over the course of the election. The observed time series were then compared with the dates of major election-related news events. Results indicated the frequency of political statuses by partisan Democrat users and partisan Republican users corresponded with notable election-related events—particularly those events related to at least one of the two major presidential campaigns. Though to a lesser extent, a similar trend was observed in the frequency of political statuses made by nonpartisan users. Similar findings emerged when comparing the time series of political versus nonpolitical statuses in the sample with the time series of political versus nonpolitical statuses posted by mainstream breaking news accounts. For the most part, however, the nonpartisan group mostly stuck to nonpolitical topics. Taken together, these results suggest partisan users took to Twitter to comment on major news related to the 2016 election, whereas nonpartisan users mostly continued to tune out—or refrain from—politics altogether.

The observed statuses were then analyzed using sentiment analysis, which consisted of evaluating the emotional tone, simplified into positive and negative dimensions, of the text used in each status. Overall, the dimensions of sentiment—including anger, anticipation, disgust, fear, frustration, joy, sadness, surprise, and trust—were difficult to distinguish from the noise. However, once the index was reduced to positive and negative sentiment, there appeared to be some evidence that variation in the positive and negative sentiment corresponded with major events during the 2016 election. As illustrated in Figure 21.3, variation in positive and negative sentiment arguably coincided with the Iowa caucuses, Super Tuesday, and the conclusion of the FBI investigation into the Democratic presidential candidate. There were also notable spikes in positive sentiment among the nonpartisan group during scandalous events such as the FBI investigation, the hacking of e-mails from the Democratic campaign, and the potential foreign ties of the Republican campaign. Ultimately, scandals and major events from campaign 2016 were important markers for Twitter users. Unfortunately, this may suggest that disengaged nonpartisans interpret election-related scandals as validation of their decision to tune out of politics altogether.

References

Allcott, H., & Gentzkow, M. (2017). Social media and fake news in the 2016 election (No. w23089). *National Bureau of Economic Research.*

Ammann, S. L. (2010, December 10). A political campaign message in 140 characters or less: The use of Twitter by U.S. Senate candidates in 2010. *Social Science Research Network.* Retrieved from http://ssrn.com/abstract=1725477

Arceneaux, K., Johnson, M., & Murphy, C. (2012). Polarized political communication, oppositional media hostility, and selective exposure. *Journal of Politics, 74,* 174–186. doi:10.1017/S002238161100123X

Barberá, P. (2015). Birds of the same feather tweet together: Bayesian ideal point estimation using Twitter data. *Political Analysis, 23*(1), 76–91. doi:10.1093/pan/mpu011

Barberá, P., Jost, J. T., Nagler, J., Tucker, J. A., & Bonneau, R. (2015). Tweeting from left to right: Is online political communication more than an echo chamber? *Psychological Science, 26*(10), 1531–1542. doi:10.1177/0956797615594620

Breen, J. O. (2012). Mining Twitter for airline consumer sentiment. Practical text mining and statistical analysis for non-structured text data applications. In G. Miner (Ed.), *Practical test mining and statistical analysis for non-structured text data* (pp. 134–149). Cambridge, MA: Academic Press.

Conway, B. A., Kenski, K., & Wang, D. (2013). Twitter use by presidential primary candidates during the 2012 campaign. *American Behavioral Scientist, 57*(11), 1596–1610. doi:10.1177/0002764213489014

Duggan, M., & Smith, A. (2016, October 25). The political environment on social media. *Pew Research Center: Internet and Technology.* Retrieved from http://www.pewinternet.org/2016/10/25/the-political-environment-on-social-media/

Gottfried, J., & Shearer, E. (2017). News use across social media platforms. *Pew Research Center.* Retrieved from http://www.journalism.org/2016/05/26/news-use-across-social-media-platforms-2016/

Holbert, R. L., Hmielowski, J. D., & Weeks, B. E. (2012). Clarifying relationships between ideology and ideologically oriented cable TV news use: A case of suppression. *Communication Research, 39*(2), 194–216. doi:10.1177/0093650211405650

Hong, S. (2012). Online news on Twitter: Newspapers' social media adoption and their online readership. *Information Economics and Policy, 24*(1), 69–74.

Hong, S., & Nadler, D. (2012). Which candidates do the public discuss online in an election campaign?: The use of social media by 2012 presidential candidates and its impact on candidate salience. *Government Information Quarterly, 29,* 455–461. doi:10.1016/j.giq.2012.06.004

Jang, S. M., & Pasek, J. (2015). Assessing the carrying capacity of Twitter and online news. *Mass Communication and Society, 18*(5), 577–598. doi:10.1080/15205436.2015.1035397

Kapko, M. (2016, November 3). Twitter's impact on 2016 presidential election is unmistakable. *Chief Information Officers.* Retrieved from http://www.cio.com/article/3137513/social-networking/twitters-impact-on-2016-presidential-election-is-unmistakable.html

Kearney, M. W. (2016). rtweet: Collecting Twitter data. *Comprehensive R Archive Network.* Retrieved from https://cran.r-project.org/web/packages/rtweet/index.html

Kollanyi, B., Howard, P. N., & Woolley, S. C. (2016). Bots and automation over Twitter during the U.S. election. *Data Memo 2016.4.* Oxford, UK: Project on Computational Propaganda. Retrieved from www.politicalbots.org

Lee, E., & Shin, S. Y. (2012). Are they talking to me? Cognitive and affective effects of interactivity in politicians' Twitter communication. *Cyberpsychology, Behavior, and Social Networking, 15*(10), 515–520. doi:10.1089/cyber.2012.0228

Liu, Y., Kliman-Silver, C., & Mislove, A. (2014). The Tweets they are a-changin: Evolution of Twitter users and behavior. *ICWSM, 30,* 305–314.

Mohammed, S. M., Kiritchenko, S., & Zhu, Z. (2013). NRC Canada: Building the state-of-the-art in sentiment analysis of tweets. *Proceedings of the Seventh International Workshop on Semantic Evaluation Exercises*, Atlanta. Retrieved from https://arxiv.org/abs/1308.6242

R Core Team. (2017). *R: A language and environment for statistical computing.* Vienna, Austria: R Foundation for Statistical Computing.

Robinson, D. (2016, August 12). Two people write Trump's tweets: He writes the angrier ones. *The Washington Post.* Retrieved from https://www.washingtonpost.com/posteverything/wp/2016/08/12/two-people-write-trumps-tweets-he-writes-the-angrier-ones/?utm_term=.c0347ec39865

Shin, J., Jian, L., Driscoll, K., & Bar, F. (2016). Political rumoring on Twitter during the 2012 U.S. presidential election: Rumor diffusion and correction. *New Media & Society, 19*(8), 1–22. doi: 0.1177/1461444816634054

Twitter, Inc. (2016). Twitter limits. *Help Center.* Retrieved from https://support.twitter.com/articles/15364

Wang, Y., Li, Y., & Luo, J. (2016). Deciphering the 2016 U.S. presidential campaign in the Twitter sphere: A comparison of the Trumpists and Clintonists. *CoRR, abs/1603.03097.* doi: https://arxiv.org/abs/1603.03097

Wicks, R. H., Wicks, J. L., & Morimoto, S. A. (2014). Partisan media selective exposure during the 2012 presidential election. *American Behavioral Scientist, 58*(9), 1131–1143. doi: 10.1177/0002764213506208

Younis, E. M. (2015). Sentiment analysis and text mining for social media microblogs using open source tools: An empirical study. *International Journal of Computer Applications, 112*(5), 44–48. doi: 10.5120/19665-1366

Understanding the Authoritarian Voter in the 2016 Presidential Election

Sumana Chattopadhyay

The U.S. presidential election of 2016 was a historic contest between Hillary Clinton, the former secretary of state and the first woman candidate to win a major-party nomination, and Donald Trump, the famous reality television show host and property developer who was neither a politician nor a traditional Republican. The campaign was quite the political contest, with Clinton running as the champion of everyday Americans, whereas Trump sought to build a great wall on the U.S.-Mexico border and to "be the greatest jobs president that God ever created" (Stracqualursi, 2016, para. 10).

During the campaign, one concept that was discussed frequently by the media and political experts alike was the notion of authoritarianism, a view that reflects an individual's orientation towards conventional authorities and social conformity (Adorno, Frenkel-Brunswik, Levinson, & Sanford, 1950; Altemeyer, 1996; Hetherington & Weiler, 2009; Stenner, 2005). Discussion of authoritarianism was often triggered by Trump's personality and rhetoric. MacWilliams (2016) notes that starting from his announcement speech, "Trump's message and manner was an unapologetic siren call to American authoritarians. He warned that our 'enemies are getting stronger and stronger . . . and we, as a country are getting weaker." Trump also targeted his attacks on "others" who he claimed were threatening and weakening our country, while he talked down at his opponents, calling them weaklings, all the while donning the mantle of the great leader, one who would make America great again.

Authoritarianism research started with Adorno et al.'s (1950) work on the authoritarian personality, followed by research using Altmeyer's (1996) right-wing authoritarian (RWA) scale and Stenner's (2005) predisposition to authoritarianism scale. Over the years, this line of research has examined the relationship between authoritarianism and ideology (Cohen & Smith, 2016; Mayer, 2011), opinions toward terrorism (Hetherington & Weiler, 2009), prejudice and conservatism (Adorno et al., 1950; Altemeyer, 1981, 1996; Jost, Glaser, Kruglanski, & Sulloway, 2003), and evangelism (Hunsberger, 1995). More recent research has also examined how political expertise conditions the relationship between authoritarian predispositions and conservatism (Federico, Fisher, & Deason, 2011). The current study seeks to expand authoritarianism research by exploring how authoritarian predispositions might have predicted support for Trump in 2016. Building on research by Federico et al. (2011) and Lavine et al. (1999), this study explores how voters' authoritarian predispositions act as a moderator between one's liking for Trump and such variables as political information efficacy, trust, evangelism, political interest, education, and race.

Literature Review

Authoritarianism in Politics

Research on authoritarianism started with the publication of *The Authoritarian Personality* (Adorno et al., 1950) that developed the F-scale of authoritarianism and showed that submissiveness to authority and conventional norms (i.e., characteristics of an authoritarian personality) helped explain prejudice and political conservatism. Adorno et al. (1950) described authoritarianism as being rooted in the repression of hostility toward idealized authorities like parents and the projection of these feelings toward outgroups.

Adorno et al.'s (1950) work was criticized by Brown (1965) on both theoretical and methodological grounds, yet authoritarianism resurfaced with Altemeyer's (1981, 1996) research. This work advanced the RWA scale composed of authoritarian submission to ingroup authorities, authoritarian aggression to outgroups and deviants, and conventionalism. The RWA scale was an improvement to the F-scale, and in keeping with Adorno et al.'s (1950) original authoritarian construct, people with low RWA were shown to be quite different from people with high RWA. High RWAs are more ethnocentric, intolerant, and conservative and exhibit higher levels of traditionalism and a greater resistance to equality. Duckitt (2001), through the development of a dual-process model, showed that RWA is more closely associated with social or cultural forms of conservatism, and Duckitt and Sibley (2009) advanced this work a step further by finding that authoritarian sentiment bears a connection to beliefs in a dangerous world rather than beliefs in a competitive world.

Altemeyer's (1996) approach was also met with criticism because the RWA scale contained some of the political content that it was meant to predict (e.g., attitudes toward minorities and dissidents). Further, items in the scale overlapped with key dependent variables, including political ideology and prejudice. Stenner (2005) called these measurement weaknesses a failure to differentiate between the predisposition to authoritarianism and its political consequences. Instead of being reflective of an authoritarian predisposition, the RWA scale was more "a measure of ideologically infused attitudes about social order" (Federico et al., 2011).

Authoritarian Predisposition and the Child Rearing Scale

Feldman and Stenner (1997) and Feldman (2003) made the case for an authoritarianism measure that represented a generalized motive for maintaining conformity, order, and uniformity that was distinct from specific political preferences. Stenner's (2005) authoritarian predisposition measure is composed of items relating to child rearing preferences, found to be an indicator of an individual's take on authority and conformity and a valid measure across a wide swathe of social contexts (Kohn & Schooler, 1983; Martin, 1964). As Federico et al. (2011, p. 688) concluded, "Preferences for respectful, mannerly, and well behaved children (as opposed to independent, curious, and considerate children) are considered to reflect an authoritarian predisposition." Stenner's (2005) authoritarian predisposition scale thus captures a general psychological predisposition toward authoritarianism, which is an antecedent to the political enactment of authoritarianism.

Other Research on Authoritarianism

Whether authoritarianism is conceptualized as an individual childhood personality trait (Adorno et al., 1950), a socially learned attitude (Altemeyer, 1981, 1996), or a predisposition (Stenner, 2005), authoritarians are immutable thinkers who look at the world in black and white terms (Adorno et al., 1950, Altemeyer, 1981, Duckitt, 1989; Feldman, 2003; Feldman & Stenner, 1997; Hetherington & Weiler, 2009; Stenner, 2005). Uniformity and order are important to authoritarians. They obey, seek order, follow authoritarian leaders, resist diversity, fear the "other," act in an aggressive fashion toward others, and once they have identified friends versus foes, they hold tight in their decision.

MacWilliams (2016) highlighted Trump's authoritarian tendencies by analyzing his actions during the campaign. Trump regularly used us vs. them language to categorize others who posed a threat, including Mexicans and Muslims who he labeled as people who "do not hold our values and are not like us" (MacWilliams, 2016, pg. 717). To Trump and his followers, he alone understood the threat others posed and he alone had the will to defeat the threat. Trump alone rejected the political correctness that allowed others to infiltrate our society, he had the will to deport those enemies among us, and he would stop more of them from entering the United States. Trump's authoritarian messaging and his persona appeared almost like a practical application of authoritarian theory to politics.

The linkage of social and political threat to authoritarianism, however, is not a new phenomenon triggered by Trump. This relationship has been central to understanding authoritarians for many decades as threat and fear play an important role in activating authoritarian behaviors and the expression of authoritarian attitudes (Adorno et al., 1950; Hetherington & Suhay, 2011). As Hetherington and Suhay (2011, p. 547) describe, "Thus it is the non-authoritarians who will become more authoritarian when a physical threat appears, since authoritarians are always activated and have little place to travel in terms of their opinion." This reasoning might also be applied to understanding differences between low and high authoritarianism and help explain the potential role that authoritarianism might play as a moderator between other political attitudes analyzed in the current study.

Authoritarianism was also recently identified as an important determinant of partisan polarization. Hetherington and Weiler (2009) argued, consistent with the issues evolution framework (Carmines & Stimson, 1990), that a coalitional reconfiguration of parties has occurred, with authoritarians increasingly gravitating to the Republican side of the political aisle and nonauthoritarians increasingly attracted to the Democratic side.

Recent research by Federico et al. (2011) has examined how political expertise might affect the relationship between authoritarian predisposition and conservatism. This work is based on other research on ideology that talks about how learning, comprehension, and use of ideological constructs vary in the mass public as a function of expertise (e.g., Campbell, Converse, Miller, & Stokes, 1960; Converse, 1964; Judd & Krosnick, 1989; Zaller, 1992). Other related research views authoritarianism as a *constraint* mechanism for the uninformed due to its strong associations with prejudice (Kemmelmeier, 2009; Stenner, 2005).

Other studies have also shown that people with high expertise can adopt issue attitudes that are more *constrained*, that is, ideologically consistent with one another or with the individual's overall politics (Converse, 1964; Federico & Schneider, 2007; Zaller, 1992). Federico et al.'s (2011) study looked at whether expertise might strengthen the relationship "between ideology and its pre-political antecedents" (pg. 689). This work was based on Jost et al.'s analysis (2009), which found that people who have a better grasp of abstract political concepts and issues that are aligned with different ideological stances are more likely to understand which ideology is a good fit for their psychological needs. Their study also found that the relationship between authoritarian predisposition and conservatism was stronger among experts.

Research has also found that people scoring high on RWA have an increased likelihood of prejudice (Altemeyer, 1998; Pratto, Sidanius, & Levin, 2006), which seems to indicate that authoritarianism might be more prevalent among white versus minority voters (De Koster & Van der Waal, 2007; De Witte & Billiet, 1999). Individuals high on the RWA scale also have a higher likelihood of skewing toward fundamentalist religious beliefs (Hunsberger, 1995), thus suggesting a relationship between evangelism and authoritarian attitudes; and that high RWAs will have less support for democratic values (Canetti-Nisim, 2004). They also score lower in political knowledge and seem to be less interested in learning (Peterson, Duncan, & Pang, 2002). Finally, Lavine et al. (1999) found that authoritarianism moderates the influence of political messages. Individuals with higher authoritarianism responded more readily to threat-laden messages, whereas low authoritarians were found to be more responsive to reward messages (Lavine, Lodge, & Freitas, 2005; Lavine, Lodge, & Polichak, 2002). This suggests that the authoritarian predisposition may moderate the relationship between normative attitudes and favorable attitudes toward Trump during the 2016 presidential election.

Normative Political Attitudes

Delli Carpini (2004) identifies the principal attitudes of democratic engagement as political efficacy, political trust, and the counterpart to political trust, political cynicism.

Cynicism, however, is different from lack of trust in government. Instead, it is a "sense of powerlessness" (Pinkleton, Austin, & Fortman, 1998) and "a feeling that government in general and political leaders do not care about the public's opinions and are not acting in the best interest of the people" (Kaid, McKinney, & Tedesco, 2000). Trust, on the other hand, focuses more on how much a citizen trusts public institutions (Fieschi & Heywood, 2004).

Another political attitude that fits well in an authoritarianism study, given its relationship with political knowledge and expertise, is political information efficacy (PIE). Kaid, Tedesco, and McKinney (2004) advanced the concept of PIE, which is grounded in important theoretical links between political efficacy and one's feelings of confidence in the political knowledge he or she possesses. Whereas traditional political efficacy has been defined as an individual's feeling that he or she has the ability to influence the political process (Campbell, Gurin, & Miller, 1954), the concept of political information efficacy is defined as the level of confidence one has in his or her political knowledge and that one possesses sufficient knowledge to engage the political process through such behaviors as talking with others about politics and voting.

The section that follows posits research questions examining whether authoritarian predisposition moderates the relationship between normative political attitudes, demographic variables, and other political variables (including political interest, conservatism, and evangelism) and one's liking of Trump.

This study decided to examine candidate liking as the dependent variable instead of vote choice because of the "shy-Trumper" phenomenon that may have affected some voters during the 2016 campaign. As Mercer, Deane, and McGinney (2016) explained, "Some have suggested that many of those who were polled simply were not honest about whom they intended to vote for. The idea of so-called 'shy Trumpers' suggests that support for Trump was socially undesirable, and that his supporters were unwilling to admit their support to pollsters." Thus, participants in this study may have been less willing to admit they would vote for Trump than to express their degree of favorability toward Trump.

Research Questions

Research examining authoritarian predisposition as a moderator between attitudes is rare, except for studies like Lavine et al. (1999), which explored the authoritarian construct as a moderator for political messages; and no research to date has analyzed authoritarian predisposition as a moderator in exploring the relationship between this study's independent variables and candidate favorability. Therefore, this study posits exploratory research questions instead of hypotheses.

First, the basic relationships between all the independent variables and favorability for Donald Trump are assessed before moving on to interaction effects:

RQ1: What are the relationships between normative political attitudes, demographic variables, authoritarian predisposition, and the political variables (political interest and evangelism) and favorability for Trump?

The remaining research questions focus on the various tests for moderation in this study:

RQ2: In the general election of 2016, does authoritarian predisposition moderate the relationship between individual normative political attitudes (trust, cynicism, political information efficacy, external efficacy) and favorability for Trump?

RQ3: In the general election of 2016, does authoritarian predisposition moderate the relationship between demographic variables (race, gender, age, party identification, education) and favorability for Trump?

RQ4: In the general election of 2016, does authoritarian predisposition moderate the relationship between political variables (conservatism, political interest, evangelism) and favorability for Trump?

Method

Study Participants

The data for this analysis were collected as part of a larger national election study sponsored by the Political Communication Institute at the University of Missouri, Columbia. A quota-stratified survey was collected through Qualtrics's online panel partners. The sample ($N=2,014$) was proportioned to match the most recent U.S. census on age, gender, and four racial categories. A majority of the sample identified as female ($n=1029$, 51%). More were white ($n=1,392$, 69%) than African American ($n=242$, 12%), Hispanic/Latinx ($n=262$, 13%), or Asian ($n=78$, 4%). A minority ($n=284$, 14%) of the sample identified as born-again evangelical Christian. The survey data were collected between August 26 and August 31, 2016.

Study Variables

Authoritarian predisposition. A four-item scale asked respondents which of the following authoritarian/nonauthoritarian qualities should be emphasized in children: independence versus respect for elders, obedience versus self-reliance, curiosity versus good manners, and being considerate versus being well behaved. The authoritarianism measure is the sum of the four response scores, rescaled so that the measure ranges between 0 and 1. Those who value respect for elders, obedience, good manners, and being well behaved score at the maximum of the scale. Those who value independence, self-reliance, curiosity, and being considerate score at the minimum end of the scale.

Normative political attitudes: The normative political attitudes in this study include political information efficacy, external efficacy, trust, and cynicism. All were measured using a 5-point Likert scale. The political information efficacy (PIE) variable is a four-item scale with items capturing confidence in political knowledge. The cynicism, trust, and external efficacy scales are standard National Election Studies scales that have been used in past research to measure these concepts.

Other political variables of interest: Political interest, evangelism, and conservatism are the other political variables of interest in this study. Though conservatism and evangelism are technically ideological and religious variables, respectively, past research has demonstrated how important these attitudes are in politics. Whereas the political interest scale measures how interested people are in politics, the conservatism scale asks where on a liberal to conservatism spectrum respondents would place themselves. The evangelism scale asks if the respondent is a "Born Again Evangelical Christian."

Demographic variables: Age, sex, race, education, and party identification (ID) represent the study's demographic variables.

Table 22.1   Descriptive Statistics

	N	Minimum	Maximum	Mean	Std. Deviation
Age	2014	18	86	46.61	16.30
Party ID	2014	1	7	3.52	1.86
Conservatism	2014	1	7	3.84	1.75
Favorability for Donald Trump	2014	0	100	30.96	36.72
Political Interest	2014	1.00	5.00	3.58	1.04
External Efficacy	2014	1.00	5.00	3.46	1.01
Trust	2014	1.00	5.00	3.04	0.72
PIE	2014	1.00	5.00	3.68	0.85
Cynicism	2012	1.00	5.00	3.82	0.77
Authoritarian predisposition	1974	.00	1.00	.51	0.35

Dependent variable: The favorability for Trump variable asks study respondents to assign a number between 0 (very much dislike Trump) to 100 (very much like Trump).

Descriptive statistics for all continuous variables are provided in Table 22.1.

Analysis

Hypotheses were tested in ordinary least squares (OLS) regression aided by PROCESS, a conditional and indirect effects analysis tool developed by Hayes (2013). Analysis in PROCESS proceeded with mean-centered variables. The simple moderation model with one moderator in the PROCESS MACRO template was used to calculate the regression coefficients for each characteristic independently. The procedure used by Hayes for moderation analysis examines separate moderation models one by one, testing for the conditional effect of each independent variable on favorability for Trump with authoritarian predisposition as the moderator.

Results

The OLS regression results are reported in Table 22.2. RQ1a analyzes relationships between normative political attitudes, demographic variables, other political variables, and the authoritarian predisposition variable (which will be tested as a moderator in subsequent analysis) and favorability for Trump.

Table 22.2   OLS Regression Results with Favorability for Trump (as DV)

Predictor	Standardized B Coefficient	SE
Age	.075***	(0.04)
Gender	−.053**	(1.24)
White/Caucasian	.055**	(1.43)
Party ID	.540***	(0.48)
Education	−.043*	(0.59)
Income	.011	(0.21)
Conservatism	.115***	(0.53)
Evangelism	.025	(1.42)
Political interest	.076**	(0.87)
External efficacy	.083***	(0.73)
Trust	−.057**	(0.95)
PIE	.036	(1.06)
Cynicism	.006	(0.89)
Authoritarian predisposition	.115***	(0.48)
Constant	−44.207	
F (degrees of freedom)	141.9*** (13, 1953)	
Adjusted R^2	0.482	
N	1966	

Note: Entries are standardized OLS regression coefficients and standard errors.
*$p < .05$; **$p < .01$, ***$p < .001$

Table 22.2 shows that among normative political attitudes, only trust and external efficacy had a significant direct relationship with favorability for Trump. Favorability for Trump was negatively associated with trust in government, and external efficacy positively associated with favorability toward Trump. PIE was not significantly associated with favorability for Trump. All demographic variables were associated with favorability for Trump (except income, which did not have a significant relationship with favorability for Trump). Females and more educated respondents expressed less favorability for Trump, whereas older and white/Caucasian respondents liked him more. Republicans and conservatives were much more favorable toward Trump. People who expressed greater political interest were more favorable toward Trump. Evangelism did not have a direct significant relationship with favorability for Trump. Finally, authoritarian predisposition was positively related to favorability toward Trump.

When testing authoritarian predisposition as a moderator in the relationships between the independent variables and favorability for Trump, five variables showed significant interactions, including trust, PIE, education, political interest, and evangelism, suggesting the presence of potential conditional effects.

The first analysis for conditional effects examined whether authoritarian predisposition moderated the relationship between trust and favorability for Trump. This model was significant, and the interaction term was also significant. Authoritarian predisposition had a significant positive effect on favorability for Trump and the interaction term had a negative effect, whereas trust had no direct relationship to favorability for Trump once the interaction was included ($F(3,1970)=35.61$, $p<.001$, $R^2=.0466$, $N=1974$; for authoritarian predisposition, B=21.24, $t(1970)=9.18$, $p<.001$; for trust, B=1.78, $t(1970)=1.51$ $p=.13$; and for the interaction, B=-6.80, $t(1970)=-2.11$, $p<.05$). According to the PROCESS test results, there was a significant relationship between trust and favorability for Trump in the low authoritarian predisposition level only: B=4.15, $t(1970)=3.07$ $p<.01$ (low authoritarian predisposition), B=1.78, $t(1970)=1.51$, p=.13 (medium/average authoritarian predisposition), B=-.58,

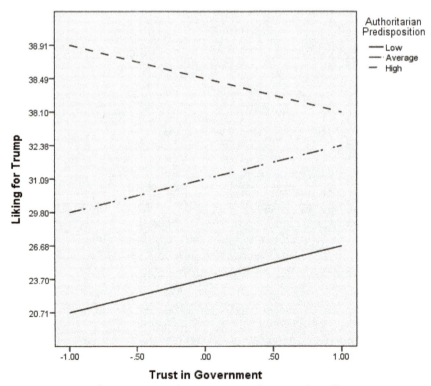

Figure 22.1 Authoritarian Predisposition Moderating the Effect Between Trust and Liking for Trump

$t(1970)=-.31$, $p=.75$ (high authoritarian predisposition). Figure 22.1 shows that at low authoritarian levels, trust in the government was associated with more favorable views of Trump.

The second analysis for conditional effects examined whether authoritarian predisposition moderated the relationship between PIE and favorability for Trump. This model was significant, and the interaction term was significant as well. Authoritarian predisposition, PIE, and the interaction term all had significant positive effects on favorability for Trump ($F(3,1970)=42.44$, $p<.001$, $R^2=.065$, $N=1974$; for authoritarian predisposition, B=22.22, $t(1970)=9.84$, $p<.001$; for PIE, B=5.35, $t(1970)=5.92$, $p<.001$; for the interaction, B=8.49, $t(1970)=3.23$, $p<.01$). The PROCESS results document that there was a significant relationship between PIE and favorability for Trump in the medium and high authoritarian predisposition levels: B=2.39, $t(1970)=1.84$, $p=.06$ (low authoritarian predisposition), B=5.35, $t(1970)=5.92$, $p<.001$ (medium/average authoritarian predisposition), B=8.31, $t(1970)=6.53$, $p<.001$ (high authoritarian predisposition). Figure 22.2 depicts this interaction graphically and offers more clarity on the differences in the relationship between low,

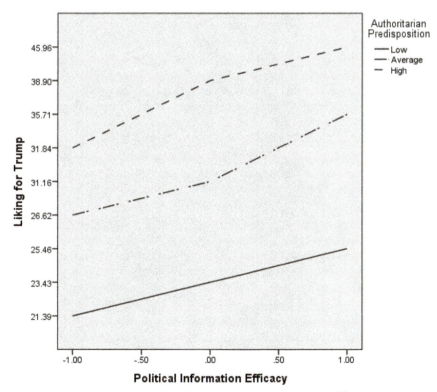

Figure 22.2 Authoritarian Predisposition Moderating the Effect Between PIE and Liking for Trump

medium/average authoritarians, and high authoritarians, with higher slopes at
the medium/average and the high authoritarian conditions. There was a stronger positive effect of PIE on favorability for Trump at the high and medium/
average authoritarian conditions compared to the low condition.

The third analysis for conditional effects examined whether authoritarian
predisposition moderated the relationship between education and favorability for Trump. This model was significant, and the interaction term was also
significant. Authoritarian predisposition and the interaction term both had
significant positive effects on favorability for Trump, but education did not
$(F(3,1970)=34.25, p<.001, R^2=.046, N=1974$; for authoritarian predisposition, $B=21.48, t(1970)=9.26, p<.001$; for education, $B=-.92, t(1970)=-1.18,$
$p=.238$; for the interaction, $B=4.61, t(1970)=2.13, p<.05$). Here, according
to the PROCESS results, there was a significant relationship between education and favorability for Trump at the low authoritarian predisposition levels:
$B=-2.52, t(1970)=-2.44, p<.05$ (low authoritarian predisposition), $B=-.92,$
$t(1970)=-1.18, p=.24$ (medium/average authoritarian predisposition), $B=.69,$
$t(1970)=.61, p=.54$ (high authoritarian predisposition). Figure 22.3 illustrates

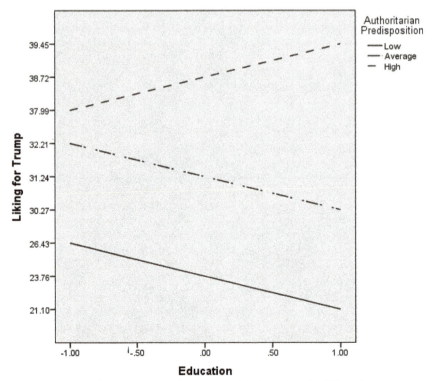

Figure 22.3 Authoritarian Predisposition Moderating the Effect Between
Education and Liking for Trump

that education had a negative effect on favorability for Trump at the low levels of authoritarianism.

The fourth analysis for conditional effects examined whether authoritarian predisposition moderated the relationship between political interest and favorability for Trump. This model was significant, and the interaction term was also significant. Authoritarian predisposition, political interest, and the interaction term all had significant positive effects on favorability for Trump ($F(3,1970)=43.64$, $p<.001$, $R^2=.063$, $N=1974$; for authoritarian predisposition, $B=22.52$, $t(1970)=9.96$, $p<.001$; for political interest, $B=4.59$, $t(1970)=6.24$, $p<.001$; for interaction, $B=4.91$, $t(1970)=2.31$, $p<.05$). The PROCESS results further revealed that there was a significant relationship between political interest and favorability for Trump in all three authoritarian predisposition levels: $B=2.88$, $t(1970)=3.02$, $p<.01$(low authoritarian predisposition), $B=4.59$, $t(1970)=6.24$, $p<.001$ (medium/average authoritarian predisposition), $B=6.30$, $t(1970)=5.58$, $p<.001$ (high authoritarian predisposition). Figure 22.4 depicts the interactions graphically and offers more clarity on the differences in the relationship between low, medium/average

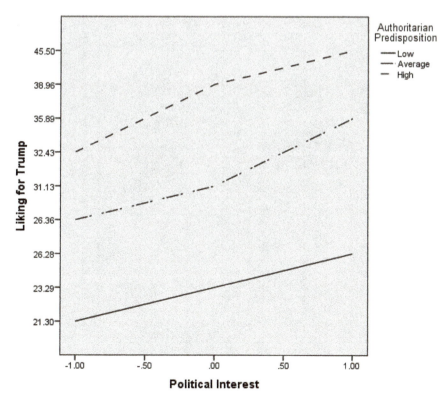

Figure 22.4 Authoritarian Predisposition Moderating the Effect Between Political Interest and Liking for Trump

authoritarians, and high authoritarians. At all three levels there was a significant positive relationship between political interest and favorability for Trump.
However, as authoritarianism increased, the effect of interest on favorability
toward Trump also increased.

The fifth analysis for conditional effects examined whether authoritarian
predisposition moderated the relationship between evangelism and favorability for Trump. This model was significant, and the interaction term was also
significant. Authoritarian predisposition, evangelism, and the interaction term
all had significant positive effects on favorability for Trump ($F(3,1970)=52.73$,
$p<.001$, $R^2=.07$, $N=1974$; for authoritarian predisposition, $B=16.62$, $t(1970)=$
6.85, $p<.001$; for evangelism, $B=14.59$, $t(1970)=7.31$, $p<.001$; for interaction,
$B=-16.73$, $t(1970)=-2.81$, $p<.05$). The PROCESS results further revealed that
there was a significant relationship between evangelism and favorability for
Trump in all three authoritarian predisposition levels: $B=20.41$, $t(1970)=6.40$,
$p<.01$(low authoritarian predisposition), $b=14.59$, $t(1970)=7.31$, $p<.001$
(medium/average authoritarian predisposition), $B=8.77$, $t(1970)=3.47$, $p<.001$
(high authoritarian predisposition). Figure 22.5 presents the interactions

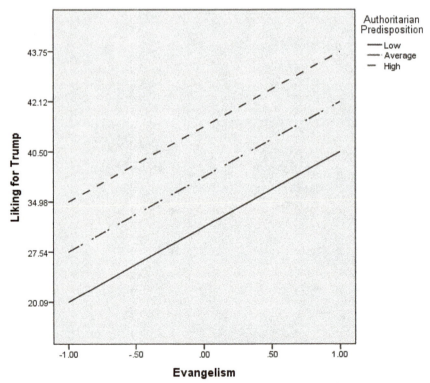

Figure 22.5 Authoritarian Predisposition Moderating the Effect Between
Evangelism and Liking for Trump

graphically. As illustrated, evangelism had stronger effects on favorability at lower levels of authoritarianism.

Discussion

The findings from this study indicate that the authoritarian predisposition of voters played a prominent role in predicting favorability for Trump. Authoritarian predisposition had a positive main effect on favorability for Trump. However, what highlights the importance of the authoritarian predisposition variable is that it not only had a direct influence on attitudes toward Trump; it also moderated other variables' relationships with favorability for Trump, adding to the overall significance of voters' authoritarian predisposition in the 2016 election. PIE was not directly related with favorability for Trump. However, people higher in PIE were more likely to express favorable attitudes toward Trump at higher levels of authoritarianism. The null result was restricted to those low in authoritarianism. This might be explained by past research, as Jost et al. (2009) found that individuals who know more about political concepts and issues have a better understanding of which ideology fits best with their ideological needs. In the high and medium/average authoritarian groups, as people's PIE increases, individuals feel more confident about their political knowledge. This might lead them to believe that Trump is a better fit for them ideologically (because high authoritarians' ideologies are in greater consonance with Trump's worldview than are low authoritarians' ideologies).

The work of Lavine et al. (2005) can help explain the political interest findings of this study, as their research documents high authoritarians respond more readily to threat-laden messages, whereas low authoritarians respond to reward messages (see also Lavine et al., 2002). Because Trump's rhetoric was mostly threat laden, higher authoritarians may have paid more attention to his campaign appeals. Not only did political interest have a positive direct relationship with favorability for Trump; it also had an effect moderated through authoritarian predisposition (Figure 22.4). In fact, in all three levels of authoritarianism, political interest had a positive relationship with favorability for Trump. The more interested in politics a voter was, the more likely it was that he or she would encounter a campaign message from Trump, and because individuals scoring higher in the authoritarian scale tended to respond more to threat messages, favorability for Trump increased.

The findings with relation to the trust variable are also interesting. Once the interaction with authoritarian predisposition was added, trust no longer had a direct relationship with favorability for Trump except for those low in authoritarianism. This could likely be explained by the fact that in the low authoritarian condition people did not always see the world as being under siege or the current government authorities as incapable of doing their job during dangerous times. Also, unlike high authoritarians who have less support for democratic values (Canetti-Nisim, 2004), low authoritarians might have more support for democratic values and might have been drawn to Trump's message for reasons different than the high or medium authoritarians. As Lavine et al. (2005) have found, lower authoritarians respond better to reward messages. As such, these voters might have been paying greater attention to Trump's messages focusing on job creation and building the economy, in which case as their trust in government increased, they might have seen Trump more as the person who could make positive change in those areas. However, the high authoritarianism group might have been paying more attention to the threat appeals found in Trump's rhetoric, with the government seen as either the enemy or an inefficient entity that is not equipped to face the dangers of the current world. For these voters, Trump was the leader who will make America great again.

The education findings relating to authoritarianism are also compelling (see Figure 22.3). The effect of education on favorability toward Trump (higher educated people expressing lower evaluations of Trump) only held for those low in authoritarianism. This finding makes sense based on Trump's campaign rhetoric, as his vocabulary and appeals are often simplistic pleas that might have greater appeal to those with less formal education. However, this does not explain the interaction plot shown in Figure 22.3, which indicates that the high authoritarian group exhibits a positive relationship between education and favorability for Trump (even though this slope is insignificant in PROCESS). This positive relationship could likely be explained again by Jost et al.'s (2009) finding that people with more knowledge about politics are more cognizant of the ideologies that fit them. With higher education, high authoritarians would likely realize that their worldviews fit more with Trump than with other candidates. The lower authoritarian groups with more education, however, might realize that their worldviews do not fit with Trump, which could lead to a decline in their liking for him.

Finally, the evangelism findings are also worth mentioning. Evangelism was not directly associated with favorability for Trump. This might prompt some pundits to suggest that Trump's personal life could explain why evangelicals would prefer other Republicans over Trump. However, the moderation effects tell a different story. As Figure 22.5 clearly shows, all three authoritarian groups show a significant and positive relationship between evangelism and favorability for Trump. However, at the same level of evangelism, the high authoritarian group has a much higher level of favorability for Trump vis-à-vis the medium/average authoritarian and low authoritarian groups; similarly, the medium/average authoritarian group seems to have a higher favorability for Trump than the low authoritarian group at the same level of evangelism. Also, as evangelism increases, the highest favorability for Trump is achieved by members of the high authoritarian group. This is not surprising and supports Grant's (2016) contention that "people who value strong religious authority also tend to be those who show other signs of being authoritarian. Religious authoritarians are often political authoritarians."

As with any study, there are important limitations to this one. First, the current study examined the role of authoritarian predisposition as a moderator influencing relationships between a number of critical variables and favorability toward Trump. However, other moderators might be at play that are not explored by this study. Also, this study, which focuses only on Trump, does not look at whether authoritarian predisposition played any role in explaining one's favorability toward his opponent, Clinton. This study also does not include a measure of political knowledge, instead using PIE, which measures one's confidence in the political knowledge they possess. However, political knowledge has been identified as a key variable in past authoritarianism research, and its exclusion from the current study is particularly felt when making sense of the findings related to PIE and education.

Conclusion and Future Directions for Research

This study explored the relationships between various political normative attitudes (trust, external efficacy, PIE, and cynicism); demographic variables (age, race, gender, party ID, and education); other political variables (political interest, conservatism, and evangelism); authoritarian predisposition; and voters' favorability toward Trump. It also tested whether authoritarian predisposition acted as a moderator of the various independent variables and favorability for Trump. Past research has mostly explored which third variable moderates the relationship between authoritarianism and dependent variables like conservatism and traditionalism; however, authoritarian predisposition itself can act as a moderator. Future research should continue to focus on the influence of authoritarianism and other critical political antecedents and outcomes—as this study illustrates that the political predispositions of authoritarians may be influenced by a different set of attitudes and demographic characteristics.

References

Adorno, T. W., Frenkel-Brunswik, E., Levinson, D. J., & Sanford, R. N. (1950). *The authoritarian personality*. New York: Harper and Row.

Altemeyer, B. (1981). *Right-wing authoritarianism*. Winnipeg: University of Manitoba Press.

Altemeyer, B. (1996). *The authoritarian specter*. Cambridge, MA: Harvard University Press.

Brown, R. (1965). *Social psychology*. London: Collier Macmillan.

Campbell, A., Converse, P., Miller, W., & Stokes, D. (1960). *The American voter*. New York: John Wiley and Sons.

Campbell, A., Gurin, G., & Miller, W. E. (1954). *The voter decides.* Evanston, IL: Row Peterson.

Canetti-Nisim, D. (2004). The effect of religiosity on endorsement of democratic values: The mediating influence of authoritarianism. *Political Behavior, 26,* 377–398. doi: 10.1007/s11109-004-0901-3

Carmines, E., & Stimson, J. (1990). *Issue evolution: Race and the transformation of American politics.* Princeton, NJ: Princeton University Press.

Cohen, M., &, Smith, A. (2016). Do authoritarians vote for authoritarians? Evidence from Latin America. *Research & Politics, 3,* 1-8. doi: 10.1177/20531 68016684066

Converse, P. (1964). The nature of the belief systems in mass publics. In D. Apter (Ed.), *Ideology and discontent* (pp. 206–61). New York: Free Press.

De Koster, W., & Van der Waal, J. (2007). Cultural value orientations and Christian religiosity: On moral traditionalism, authoritarianism, and their implications for voting behavior. *International Political Science Review, 28,* 451–467. doi:10.1177/019251210707963

Delli Carpini, M. X. (2004). Mediating democratic engagement: The impact of communications on citizens' involvement in political and civic life. In L. L. Kaid (Ed.), *Handbook of political communication research* (pp. 395–434). Mahwah, NJ: Lawrence Erlbaum.

De Witte, H., & Billiet, J. (1999). Economic and cultural conservatism in Flanders: In search of concepts, determinants and impact on voting behavior. In H. de Witte, & P. Scheepers (Eds.), *Ideology in the Low Countries: Trends, models, and lacunae.* Assen, Netherlands: Van Gorcum Ltd.

Duckitt, J. (2001). A dual-process cognitive-motivational theory of ideology and prejudice. *Advances in Experimental Social Psychology, 33,* 41–113.

Duckitt, J., & Sibley, C. (2009). A dual process model of ideological attitudes and system justification. In Jost J. T., Kay A. C., &Thorisdottir H. (Eds.), *Social and psychological bases of ideology and system justification* (pp. 292–313). New York: Oxford University Press.

Federico, C., Fisher, E., & Deason, G. (2011). Expertise and the ideological consequences of the authoritarian predisposition. *Public Opinion Quarterly, 75,* 686–708. doi:10.1093/poq/nfr026

Federico, C. M., & Schneider, M. C. (2007). Political expertise and the use of ideology: Moderating effects of evaluative motivation. *Public Opinion Quarterly, 71*(2), 221–252. doi: 10.1093/poq/nfm010

Feldman, S. (2003). Enforcing social conformity: A theory of authoritarianism. *Political Psychology, 24,* 41–74. doi: 10.1111/0162-895X.00316

Feldman, S., & Stenner, K. (1997). Perceived threat and authoritarianism. *Political Psychology, 18,* 741–770. doi: 0162-895X.00077

Fieschi, C., & Heywood, P. (2004). Trust, cynicism and populist anti-politics. *Journal of Political Ideologies, 9,* 289–309. doi: 10.1080/1356931042000263537

Grant, T. (2016). Why is Trump appealing? Religious authoritarians and democracy don't mix. *Corner of Church and State.* Retrieved from http://religionnews .com/2016/03/08/trump-authoritarian-religion/

Hayes, A. F. (2013). *Introduction to mediation, moderation, and conditional process analysis: A regression-based approach*. New York: Guilford Press.

Hetherington, M., & Suhay, E. (2011). Authoritarianism, threat, and Americans' support for the war on terror. *American Journal of Political Science, 55,* 546–560. doi:10.1111/j.1540-5907.2011.00514.x

Hetherington, M., & Weiler, J. (2009). *Authoritarianism and polarization in American politics*. New York: Cambridge University Press.

Hunsberger, B. (1995). Religion and prejudice: The role of religious fundamentalism, quest, and right-wing authoritarianism. *Journal of Social Issues, 51,* 113–129.

Jost, J., Glaser, J., Kruglanski, A., & Sulloway, F. (2003). Political conservatism as motivated social cognition. *Psychological Bulletin, 129,* 339–375. doi: 10.1037/0033-2909.129.3.339

Jost, J. T., Federico, C. M., & Napier, J. (2009). Political Ideology: Its Structure, Function, and Elective Affinities. *Annual Review of Psychology, 60,* 307–38. doi: 10.1146/annurev.psych.60.110707.163600

Judd, C., & Krosnick, J. (1989). The structural bases of consistency among political attitudes: Effects of political expertise and attitude importance. In A. R. Pratkanis, S. J. Beckler, & A. G. Greenwald (Eds.), *Attitude structure and function* (pp. 99–128). Hillsdale, NJ: Earlbaum.

Kaid, L. L., McKinney, M. S., & Tedesco, J. C. (2000). *Civic dialogue in the 1996 presidential campaign: Candidate, media, and public voices*. Cresskill, NJ: Hampton.

Kaid, L. L., Tedesco, J. C., & McKinney, M. S. (2004, November). *Political information efficacy and younger voters*. Paper presented at the annual meeting of the National Communication Association, Chicago.

Kemmelmeier, M. (2009). Authoritarianism and its relationship with intuitive-experiential cognitive style and heuristic processing. *Personality and Individual Differences, 48,* 44–48. doi:10.1016/j.paid.2009.08.012

Kohn, M. L., & Schooler, C. (1983). *Work and personality: An inquiry into the impact of social stratification*. Norwood, NJ: Ablex Publishing Corp.

Lavine, H., Burgess, D., Snyder, M., Transue, J., Sullivan, J. L., Haney, B., & Wagner, S. H. (1999). Threat, authoritarianism, and voting: An investigation of personality and persuasion. *Personality and Social Psychology Bulletin, 25,* 337–347.

Lavine, H., Lodge, M., & Freitas, K. (2005). Threat, authoritarianism, and selective exposure to information. *Political Psychology, 26,* 219–244. doi: 10.1111/j.1467-9221.2005.00416.x

Lavine, H., Lodge, M., & Polichak, J. (2002). Explicating the black box through experimentation: Studies of authoritarianism and threat. *Political Analysis, 10,* 343–361. doi: 10.1093/pan/10.4.343

MacWilliams, M. C. (2016). Who decides when the party doesn't? Authoritarian voters and the rise of Donald Trump. *PS: Political Science & Politics, 49,* 716–721. doi: 10.1017/S104909651600146

Martin, J. (1964). *The tolerant personality*. Detroit, MI: Wayne State University Press.

Mayer, N. (2011). Why extremes don't meet: Le Pen and Besancenot voters in the 2007 French presidential election. *French Politics, Culture & Society, 29,* 101–120. doi:10.3167/fpcs.2011.290307

Mercer, A., Deane, C., & McGinney, K. (2016). Why 2016 election polls missed their mark. Retrieved from http://www.pewresearch.org/fact-tank/2016 /11/09/why-2016-election-polls-missed-their-mark

Peterson, B., Duncan, L., & Pang, J. (2002). Authoritarianism and political impoverishment: Deficits in knowledge and civic disinterest. *Political Psychology, 23,* 97–112. doi:10.1111/0162895X.00272

Pinkleton, B. E., & Austin, E. W. (1998). Media and participation: Breaking the spiral of disaffection. In T. J. Johnson, C. E. Hays, & S. P. Hays (Eds.), *Engaging the public: How government and the media can reinvigorate American democracy* (pp. 75–86). Lanham, MD: Rowman & Littlefield.

Pratto, F., Sidanius, J., & Levin, S. (2006). Social dominance theory and the dynamics of intergroup relations: Taking stock and looking forward. *European Review of Social Psychology, 17*(1), 271–320. doi: 10.1080/10463280 601055772

Stenner, K. (2005). *The authoritarian dynamic.* New York: Cambridge University Press.

Stracqualursi, V. (2016). Key moments of the 2016 election. Retrieved from http:// abcnews.go.com/Politics/key-moments-2016-election/story?id=43289663

Zaller, J. (1992). *The nature and origins of mass opinion.* Cambridge, UK: Cambridge University Press.

CHAPTER TWENTY-THREE

Social Dominance, Sexism, and the Lasting Effects on Political Communication from the 2016 Election

Mary C. Banwart and Michael W. Kearney

Among observers of—and voters in—the 2016 election, sentiment was widespread that sexism played a role in the race for the presidency. Such concerns emerged well before the *Access Hollywood* tape was released by *The Washington Post* on October 7, 2016, in which Donald Trump was recorded "bragg[ing] in vulgar terms about kissing, groping and trying to have sex with women" (Fahrenthold, 2016, para. 1). Concern about (and normalization of) sexism in the 2016 election began during the primary (Bauer, 2016; Lozano-Reich, 2016), continued throughout the general election (e.g., Beinart, 2016; Cole, 2016; Keith, 2016), and remains part of the post-race analysis (e.g., Bialik, 2017; Dastigar, 2016). Outlets such as *Business Insider* even posted an accounting, complete with video snippets, titled, "Here's Every Wildly Sexist Moment from the 2016 Presidential Election" (Hilln, 2016).

Naturally there were naysayers as well, individuals who claimed that it was actually Hillary Clinton who was playing the "sexist card" and that sexism was not behind the offensive messaging typically present at most Trump rallies, in his debate demeanor, and throughout his rallying cries. Looking primarily at voter demographics, Nancy Cohen's *Washington Post* article (2016, November 16) claimed, "Undoubtedly sexism is in the mix for some of the men in Trump's world . . . [b]ut this election was not primarily a referendum on whether America is ready to elect a woman to the presidency" (para. 14). Similarly, an article on the *Real Clear Politics* Web site, using voter demographics, boasted that "the numbers don't bear out the claim that sexism is to blame for Clinton's loss" (Bevan, 2017, para. 6).

In light of these claims, was there enough evidence to suggest sexism influenced the outcome? Just before Election Day University of Michigan political scientists (Wayne, Valentino, & Oceno, 2016) reported results in *The Washington Post* from their June 2016 study—before the *Hollywood Access* video was released—that found significant correlations between support for Trump and participant scores on an index measuring sexism, "even after accounting for party identification, ideology, authoritarianism and ethnocentrism" (para. 4). Perhaps not surprisingly, the authors also found that those scoring high in sexism were less likely to support Clinton. Adding to these findings, a YouGov survey (Schaffner, MacWilliams, & Nteta, 2017) of 2,000 adults conducted in the two weeks prior to Election Day tested for predictability in vote choice with sexism, racism, and economic dissatisfaction. Using items that measure hostile sexism (Glicke & Fiske, 1996), the researchers found a 30-point shift in likelihood to vote for Trump as respondents moved from low to high hostile sexism scores, even when controlling for party affiliation and ideology; the same 30-point shift was found among respondents for racism. However, this level of influence was not found with economic dissatisfaction, and when controlling for racism and sexism, the education gap—the difference in vote preference between college-educated and non–college-educated voters—dropped to that of the equivalent to prior presidential elections.

Though these data demonstrate that sexism did in fact influence vote intentions, *how* did it influence the way in which voters viewed the candidates? This study seeks to answer this question by examining the relationship between sexism and candidate image. We also assess the role of social dominance orientation (SDO) (Pratto, Sidanius, Stallworth, & Malle, 1994) to better understand if and how an overall dominance paradigm functioned to explain voter evaluations of the candidates.

Review of Literature

Candidate Image

To assess the influence of two dominance-related ideologies—sexism and SDO—on voter perceptions of Clinton and Trump in 2016, we turn to the literature on candidate image. In doing so, we argue that a focus on candidate image offers more insights when compared to horse race data or vote choice.

In their 2016 article, Warner and Banwart provide an overview of the literature on candidate image to conclude that three main categories of research findings emerge: that voter perceptions of the candidates influence electoral outcomes, that image is more important than issues in determining for whom to vote, and that election-related communication in varied forms influences the development of candidate images. They also argued that past research lacked both a consistent measure for studying candidate image and one that represented the complexity necessary for a comprehensive image construct.

The authors embarked on the development of a multifactor scale, resulting in a measure that encompassed six categories: character, intelligence, leadership, benevolence, homophily, and charm. By testing the measure in the 2012 presidential election, Warner and Banwart confirmed that "image scores are associated with voting intention above and beyond demographic factors, party identification, and partisan affect" (p. 269). In particular, homophily, character, and benevolence were predictive of vote intention for Barack Obama, and homophily and character were predictive of vote intention for Mitt Romney. Their follow-up study of U.S. Senate races in three states during the 2014 election cycle added further confirmation of the measure's predictive capacity and of the strength of homophily within the measure. The authors concluded that voter perceptions of candidate images are in fact important because image traits are often used "as heuristics to simplify cognitive decision making about representation" (p. 278).

In a media-rich environment such as that of the 2016 election cycle where access to campaign coverage of the candidates is widely available and detailed, voters must process a significant amount of information about the candidates. Image constructs function as shortcuts for voters who seek to match information to their idea of an ideal candidate (Miller, Wattenburg, & Malanchuk, 1986; Popkin, 1991). And with the literature already linking ideology dominance constructs to decision making and behaviors (e.g., Pratto et al., 1994), this study enhances our understanding of decision making in the context of a political election. In particular, it offers clarity as to the importance of such constructs in the outcome of the 2016 election and implications for understanding voter sense-making moving forward.

Sexism

Sexism is intrinsically linked to an ideology of dominance (Dahl, Vescio, & Weaver, 2015) and, as such, is based on a belief system that situates an outgroup (women) as subordinate to the ingroup (men). The ingroup is perceived as holding legitimate power, a perception that serves to justify ingroup control and superior agency. Drawing from ambivalent sexism theory (Glick & Fiske, 1996), sexism is multifaceted and composed of two factors: hostile sexism (HS) and benevolent sexism (BS). Though both factors are normatively undesirable in that they both subordinate women, HS represents a negative attitude toward women who challenge male power, whether directly (e.g., feminists) or through "feminine wiles"; BS represents a patronizing view that considers women fragile and in need of protection, with the protection being idealized as provided by men (Glick et al., 2004). Relatedly, HS and BS are linked to power and security values (Feather & McKee, 2012), negatively correlate with perceptions of gender equality (Glick et al., 2004), and are associated with political ideology (Hodson & MacInnis, 2016).

Politics is still often considered a masculine domain, and women tend to be viewed as violating normative behavior when they run for office. It is worth noting that depending on the context both men and women may be penalized for violating gendered norms; however, in the realm of politics, respondents are more highly sensitive to that violation among women (Paul & Smith, 2008) and particularly when that violation is interpreted as seeking power and influence (Okimoto & Brescoll, 2010). For example, Okimoto and Brescoll (2010) examined responses to male and female political candidates who exhibited power-seeking behaviors. When power-seeking behaviors were linked to the male candidate, he was considered more competent and more assertive, strong, and tough, and respondents were more likely to indicate a positive voting preference for the male candidate. When power-seeking behaviors were linked to the female candidate, she was rated lower on competency and agency (being assertive, strong, and tough) and was the target of backlash through identified emotions such as anger, contempt, and disgust. In addition, perceptions of communality were detrimental to the power-seeking female candidate. It is perhaps not a surprise, then, that those who hold sexist attitudes would respond negatively to both men and women who violate gendered norms. In fact, HS has been identified as a predictor of negative responses to men *and* women who did not fit stereotypical gender-conforming types, and BS has predicted positive responses to women who did fit a stereotypical gender-conforming type (Glick, Wilkerson, & Cuffe, 2015). Further, HS and BS influence perceptions of candidates' abilities to handle specific issues, as well as perceptions of the degree to which candidates possess traits associated with an ideal political candidate (Winfrey, 2012).

Social Dominance Orientation

SDO is the preference that "one's ingroup dominate and be superior to outgroups" (Pratto et al., 1994, p. 792), and has been linked to vote intention (Crowson & Brandes, 2017), as well as political attitudes, particularly that of conservatism, along with aggressive intergroup attitudes (Ho et al., 2012). A number of authors have examined the interaction between SDO and sexism and have found a distinct relationship (e.g., Christopher & Mull, 2006; Dahl et al., 2015; Feather & McKee, 2012; Fraser, Osborne, & Sibley, 2015; Sibley,

Wilson, & Duckitt, 2007). For instance, in addition to their connection of power and security values to sexism, Feather and McKee (2012) examined correlations between sexism and SDO. SDO positively correlated with HS and BS, with SDO mediating some effects of values on HS and BS. Of note, SDO was also related to value dimensions of self-enhancement, in that those with higher levels of SDO also prioritized values reflecting personal benefit vs. communal benefit. In their study linking SDO with HS, BS, and the sexualization of women, Dahl et al. (2015) reported compelling connections with anger and masculinity threats. Specifically, their study found that men were highly likely to experience a masculinity threat when presented with situations in which they perceived themselves to be subordinate to a woman, particularly if the context was within a masculine domain. Men whose masculinity was threatened in turn responded with behaviors that sexualized the women to whom they were perceived as subordinate. Dahl et al. (2015) argue that the response of sexualization functions as ideological dominance and specifically emerges from an anger reaction. In these instances, the dominance response is considered a mechanism of repair to the threat, albeit an aggressive repair function. Though such repair attempts may or may not lead to behavioral attempts at reasserting dominance, such as sexual harassment, engaging ideological dominance has its own debilitating effects in its attempts at subordinating women.

In addition to its connection to sexism, SDO has been strongly linked with political attitudes and orientation. SDO has been linked to left–right political orientation (Grina, Bergh, Akrami, & Sidanius, 2016) and support for military programs, in opposition to social programs and to policies promoting racial equality and women's rights (Pratto et al., 1994). Indeed, with SDO theorized to be an ideology in itself held by those supporting hierarchical ideologies, such connections are reasonable.

A number of studies include analyses of right-wing authoritarianism (RWA) in addition to SDO. Although both RWA and SDO are found to be predictive of prejudice, persons high in RWA typically demonstrate prejudice against outgroups who threaten facets of security and stability, whereas persons high in SDO demonstrate prejudice against outgroups who challenge their dominance, influence, and superiority (Duckitt & Bizumic, 2013). Crowson and Brandes (2017) employed both RWA and SDO in their study of vote intentions in the 2016 presidential election. Seeking to determine if both variables function to form a multifaceted perspective, the authors found evidence that each measure contained multiple factors. An anti-egalitarianism factor within SDO, an authoritarianism factor within RWA, and a traditionalism factor within RWA indicated intentions to vote for Trump over Clinton; a dominance factor within SDO and a conservatism factor within RWA did not function as predictors. Although it is worth noting that both RWA and SDO offered predictive value during the early stages of the general election, and though both constructs function to reveal prejudice, each also serves to answer different questions. Past research has revealed RWA to be more closely linked to a desire for structure (vs. domination of outgroups) and to religious fundamentalism, self-righteous (vs. self-enhancing), and right-wing voting intentions (for a discussion, see Heaven, Ciarrochi, & Leeson, 2011). With these differences in mind and prior work linking SDO and sexism, SDO remains the more suitable measure for exploring potential relationships with sexism and candidate image.

Hypotheses and Research Questions

The purpose of this study is to examine how two dominance-related ideologies—sexism and SDO—influenced how voters perceived Clinton and Trump in 2016. Based on prior research and the contrasting opinions regarding what might have influenced the 2016 election results, we pose the following hypothesis and research question.

Based on prior literature regarding the connections between sexism and SDO, we hypothesize:

H1: SDO will be positively related to ambivalent (e.g., hostile and benevolent) sexism.

We seek to bridge the literature focused on candidate image with a model that can assist in understanding what attitudinal measures may influence voter perceptions of female and male presidential candidates. We posit that if we are to understand the outcome of the election—vote choice—more fully, it is imperative that we understand *how*, or on what basis, many voters made their choice.

RQ1: Can variations in the perceptions of candidate image be explained by the SDO and/or ambivalent sexism?

Method

Respondents and Procedures

An online questionnaire was distributed via Amazon MTurk with workers being compensated 25 cents upon completion of the survey. Respondents ($N=244$) were an average of 37.91 ($SD=12.79$; range $=18$–74) years old and consisted of 130 (53.3%) females and 113 (46.3%) males. The majority of respondents were white (72.1%) followed by African American (11.5%), Asian (8.6%), Hispanic (5.3%), Native American (0.8%), Pacific Islander (0.4%), or another race or ethnicity (0.8%). Ninety-five (38.9%) respondents reported having completed high school, and the highest level of education was "some college" for 66 (27.0%) respondents, "some high school" for 51 (2.9%) respondents, "undergraduate degree" for 27 (11.1%) respondents, and "graduate degree" for 4 (1.6%) respondents.

Measures

Sexism

The ambivalent sexism inventory (ASI) (Glick & Fiske, 1996) was used as the measure of sexism in this study. The ASI consists of 22 items, to which participants indicate their agreement on a 5-point scale (1 = strongly disagree; 5 = strongly agree). The measure is composed of two factors: hostile sexism and benevolent sexism. The HS factor includes items such as "Most women interpret innocent remarks or acts as being sexist"; "Women are too easily offended"; and "Most women fail to appreciate fully all that men do for them." The BS factor includes such items as "Many women have a quality of purity that few men possess"; "Every man ought to have a woman whom he adores"; and "Women should be cherished and protected by men." Higher scores indicate a higher degree of sexism. Descriptive statistics and alpha reliability estimates for all variables can be found in Table 23.1.

Social Dominance Orientation

The eight-item social dominance orientation scale (Ho et al., 2015) was used in this study. Participants responded to questions on a 5-point scale (1 = strongly agree; 5 = strongly disagree). Examples of items from this scale include "An ideal society requires some groups to be on top and others to be on the bottom"; "Some groups of people are simply inferior to other groups"; and "Group equality should not be our primary goal." See Table 23.1 for summary statistics and reliability estimates.

Partisanship

To account for the link between political party preference and perceptions of party-nominated candidates, political partisanship was included as a covariate in all models. Partisanship was measured by asking respondents to locate their political views on an 8-point scale (1 = strong Democrat; 8 = strong Republican) with midpoints used to indicate whether respondents leaned Democrat (4) or Republican (5). To allow for comparisons with the 5-point scales used earlier, partisanship scores were transformed onto a 5-point scale.

Candidate Image

The current study is interested in explaining variations in the perceptions of candidate image along several dimensions—including character, intelligence, leadership, charm, benevolence, and homophily (Warner & Banwart, 2016)—and specifically how these perceptions vary across both of the major party candidates for the 2016 U.S. presidential election. To maximize clarity in results, separate models were estimated for each major-party candidate. Scale reliabilities associated with each candidate are therefore included in the image dimension descriptions provided later. Five-point scales were used for all items, and reverse-coded items are indicated with an "R." All summary statistics and reliability estimates can be found in Table 23.1.

Character. Perceived character of the candidates was measured by asking respondents the degree to which they agreed that each candidate was "trustworthy," "dishonest[R]," and "believable."

Intelligence. Perceived intelligence was measured by asking respondents to what extent they agreed each candidate was "unintelligent[R]," "knowledgeable," and "smart."

Leadership. Perceived leadership was measured by asking respondents to what extent they agreed that each candidate was "strong," "poised," and "a good leader."

Table 23.1 Summary Statistics

Variable	M	SD	Alpha
Benevolent sexism	2.87	.78	.86
Hostile sexism	2.56	.89	.91
Social domination	2.22	1.00	.89
Democrat candidate (Clinton) image			
Character	2.72	1.25	.92
Intelligence	3.88	1.00	.84
Leadership	3.39	1.15	.86
Charm	2.86	1.18	.88
Benevolence	3.53	1.22	.94
Homophily	2.88	1.35	.96
Republican candidate (Trump) image			
Character	2.20	1.20	.89
Intelligence	2.49	1.27	.88
Leadership	2.44	1.23	.87
Charm	2.52	1.16	.77
Benevolence	2.83	1.28	.93
Homophily	2.11	1.32	.95

Charm. Perceived charm was measured by asking respondents to what extent they agreed that each candidate was "charismatic," "likable," and "unpleasant[R]."

Homophily. Perceived homophily was measured by asking respondents to what extent they agreed that each candidate "understands people like me[R]," "understands the problems faced by people like me," and "shares my values."

Benevolence. Perceived benevolence was measured by asking respondents to what extent they agreed with five items: "I believe <candidate> genuinely wants what is best for America," "I trust <candidate> to do what [s]he thinks is best for America," "I worry that <candidate> is deliberately trying to hurt America[R]," "<candidate> is knowingly sabotaging the country[R]," and "<candidate> doesn't care about America[R]."

Results

Hypothesis 1

We hypothesized that SDO would be positively related with ambivalent sexism. Correlation analysis revealed SDO was positively related to HS, $r = .40$, $t(242) = 7.46$, $p < .001$, but it was not related to BS, $r = .10$, $t(242) = 1.52$, $p = .129$. Thus, Hypothesis 1 was only partially supported.

Research Question 1

The research question asked whether variations in the perceptions of candidate image could be explained by social domination orientation and/or ambivalent sexism. To answer this question, ordinary least squares (OLS) models were estimated for each of the six dimensions of candidate image for each major-party candidate. To control for spurious relationships, models also included several covariates, including age, respondent's sex, whether the respondent was white, education level, and strength of partisanship. Regression coefficients and fit indices for the models predicting perceptions of Clinton can be found in Table 23.2 and for Trump in Table 23.3.

Social Domination Orientation

SDO was a significant predictor for one of the candidates in every dimension of candidate image except for leadership. Although no two coefficients were significant within the same dimension of candidate image across both models, one pattern did appear to emerge in the direction of the coefficients. In models predicting perceptions of Clinton, SDO was a negative predictor of candidate image; however, in models predicting perceptions of Trump, SDO was a positive predictor of candidate image. This suggests that SDO was more

Table 23.2 Models Predicting Perceptions of the Democratic Presidential Candidate

	Credible (1)	Intellect (2)	Leadership (3)	Benevolent (4)	Charm (5)	Homophily (6)
Intercept	4.83***	3.11***	4.98***	4.30***	4.80***	5.32***
	(.54)	(.45)	(.48)	(.48)	(.54)	(.58)
Age	-.00	.01***	.00	.00	-.01	-.00
	(.01)	(.00)	(.00)	(.00)	(.01)	(.01)
Sex [male]	-.06	.01	-.11	.29**	-.13	-.13
	(.13)	(.11)	(.11)	(.11)	(.13)	(.14)
Race [white]	-.10	-.08	-.16	.14	-.21	-.23
	(.15)	(.12)	(.13)	(.13)	(.15)	(.16)
HH income	-.01	.03	.01	.03	-.01	-.01
	(.02)	(.02)	(.02)	(.02)	(.02)	(.02)

	(1)	(2)	(3)	(4)	(5)	(6)
Education	.02	.18***	.06	.09	-.02	.03
	(.07)	(.06)	(.06)	(.06)	(.07)	(.07)
Partisanship	-.26***	-.05*	-.19***	-.20***	-.22***	-.28***
	(.03)	(.03)	(.03)	(.03)	(.03)	(.04)
Social dominance	-.00	-.20***	-.05	-.16**	.01	-.05
	(.07)	(.06)	(.06)	(.06)	(.07)	(.08)
Benevolent sexism	-.07	.01	-.08	.01	-.12	-.15
	(.09)	(.07)	(.08)	(.08)	(.09)	(.10)
Hostile sexism	-.44***	-.39***	-.54***	-.53***	-.36***	-.51***
	(.09)	(.07)	(.08)	(.08)	(.09)	(.09)
Observations	241	241	241	241	241	241
R²	.45	.40	.48	.53	.37	.45
Adjusted R²	.42	.37	.46	.51	.34	.43

Note: *p < .05, **p < .01, ***p < .001

Table 23.3 Models Predicting Perceptions of the Republican Presidential Candidate

	Credible (1)	Intellect (2)	Leadership (3)	Benevolent (4)	Charm (5)	Homophily (6)
Intercept	.91*	.05	.45	.16	.89*	.14
	(.49)	(.52)	(.50)	(.51)	(.49)	(.53)
Age	-.00	.01*	.01*	.01**	.00	.00
	(.01)	(.01)	(.01)	(.01)	(.01)	(.01)
Sex [male]	-.29**	-.18	-.14	-.17	-.16	-.22*
	(.12)	(.12)	(.12)	(.12)	(.12)	(.13)
Race [white]	.10	.28**	.18	.30**	.29**	.24*
	(.13)	(.14)	(.14)	(.14)	(.13)	(.15)
HH income	.02	.02	.03	.02	.01	-.004
	(.02)	(.02)	(.02)	(.02)	(.02)	(.02)

Education	-.11*	-.17***	-.21***	-.07	-.12**	-.09
	(.06)	(.06)	(.06)	(.06)	(.06)	(.07)
Partisanship	.22***	.23***	.22***	.29***	.19***	.25***
	(.03)	(.03)	(.03)	(.03)	(.03)	(.03)
Social dominance	**.15****	.02	.06	.04	**.14****	**.13***
	(.06)	(.07)	(.07)	(.07)	(.06)	(.07)
Benevolent sexism	**.18****	**.16***	**.17****	.11	**.23*****	**.24*****
	(.08)	(.09)	(.08)	(.08)	(.08)	(.09)
Hostile sexism	**.36*****	**.50*****	**.44*****	**.38*****	**.34*****	**.40*****
	(.08)	(.08)	(.08)	(.08)	(.08)	(.09)
Observations	241	241	241	241	241	241
R²	.49	.50	.50	.52	.47	.51
Adjusted R²	.47	.48	.48	.50	.45	.49

Note: *p<.05, **p<.01, ***p<.001

likely to explain positive perceptions of Trump and negative perceptions of Clinton.

Ambivalent Sexism

A directional pattern similar to the one observed in the relationship between SDO and perceptions of candidate image also appeared in the coefficients describing the relationship between ambivalent sexism (BS and HS) and perceptions of candidate image. As can be seen in Table 23.2, BS was not a significant predictor of any candidate image dimension with regard to Clinton. However, as seen in Table 23.3, BS was a significant and positive predictor for all dimensions of candidate image in the context of Trump. Although there was some inconsistency in the evidence of a relationship between BS and perceptions of candidate image, evidence of a relationship between HS and perceptions of candidate image appear unequivocal. HS was a significant predictor of all dimensions of candidate image for each of the two major candidates. It was also uniformly negative in the context of Clinton (Table 23.2) and uniformly positive in the context of Trump (Table 23.3).

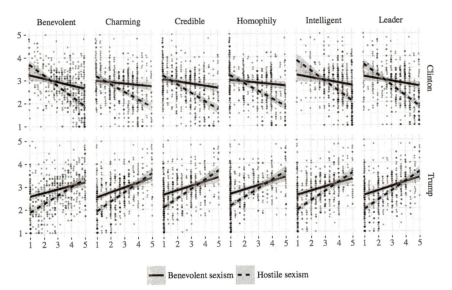

Figure 23.1 Perceptions of Candidate Image with Hostile and Benevolent Sexism (Scatter plots depict associations between perceptions of candidate image [across six dimensions] and hostile and benevolent sexism with respect to the two major-party candidates for president. Points represent mean responses ($n=244$) to related items on 5-point scales. Lines of best fit were estimated using parsimonious [no covariates] linear models.)

Overall, as Figure 23.1 makes clear, the results presented here suggest that benevolent and especially hostile forms of sexism played a prominent role in explaining variations in the perceptions of candidate image during the 2016 presidential election. Furthermore, the relationship between HS and candidate image appeared to even rival the relationship between partisanship and candidate image in terms of both magnitude and direction.

Discussion

The purpose of this study was to provide a better understanding of whether two dominance-related ideologies—sexism and SDO—influenced how voters perceived Clinton and Trump in 2016. Research conducted during the 2016 presidential election provided evidence of the interaction between sexism and vote choice (Schaffner et al., 2017; Wayne et al., 2016) along with SDO and vote choice (Crowson & Brandes, 2017). What remained in question was *how* sexism contributed to vote choice. Therefore, we first tested whether SDO and sexism were positively related (Hypothesis 1), particularly following a contentious public conversation—which was arguably rife with dominance language and ingroup–outgroup language—about who would next lead the country. Our data support previous findings that HS is positively correlated with SDO but not BS (Christopher & Mull, 2006; Sibley et al., 2007). We then tested if variations in perceptions of the presidential candidates' images could be explained by SDO and/or sexism. Though SDO was a positive predictor of evaluations of Trump's candidate image and a negative predictor of Clinton's candidate image, BS and HS offer predictive evidence of the role sexism played in constructing candidate images. In particular, BS influenced evaluations of Trump but not Clinton, whereas HS influenced both candidates at a magnitude that rivaled even party affiliation. We discuss the implications of these findings and the limitations of our study next.

From a dominance perspective, SDO, BS, and HS performed uniquely for both candidates. Though the relationships are varied, the data provide evidence for understanding how those concerned with challenges to their dominance may view women's attempts to claim power and influence on the political stage. A dominance orientation predicted negative views of Clinton's intellect and benevolence but did not significantly predict ratings on any other dimension. Not only did those with high SDO rate Clinton low on whether she was intelligent, knowledgeable, and smart, but they perceived that she was not motivated to help America. The claim from Trump and his supporters that Clinton was "lying," was "crooked," or was "not an intelligent person" was a frequent criticism in many forms during the 2016 election. And the claims—whether or not they were substantiated—spoke specifically to both of these image dimensions. On the other hand, SDO was a positive predictor for Trump on the dimensions of character, charm, and homophily. In other words, high

SDO voters perceived that Trump was trustworthy, honest, and believable, as well as charismatic, likeable, and pleasant. Further, they felt that he held opinions and positions on issues with which they agreed. Considering that those high in SDO are invested in their ingroup being dominant over and superior to members of the outgroup, it would make sense, then, that if they viewed Trump as representative of their ingroup they would also view him highly on traits such as being believable, trustworthy, charismatic, and likeable and as someone with whom they could identify. It is clear, however, that those with a high SDO did not view Clinton in the same light, and in fact were more likely to subordinate her on traits that would specifically justify their diminishment of her credibility—her intellect and the likelihood she had the country's best interests in mind—as a viable president. What these data do seem to clearly suggest, however, is that those with high SDO—those desiring ingroup dominance and superiority—certainly found Trump a like-minded and attractive leader, and one with whom they could identify and find similarity.

The findings presented here also extend the literature on ambivalent sexism to better understand how HS and BS influence evaluations of political candidates, although the role of BS is less clear than that of HS. For both Clinton and Trump, HS predicted perceptions of the candidates across all image dimensions; of note, however, it did so in exactly the opposite direction. HS negatively predicted ratings for Clinton and positively predicted ratings for Trump. Thus, those with high HS were more likely to rate Clinton lower on all dimensions than were those with low HS, whereas those with high HS were likely to rate Trump more positively (higher) on all dimensions. Although national surveys administered during the election found those rating higher in sexism more likely to vote for Trump (Schaffner et al., 2017; Wayne et al., 2016), it is now more clear what they valued in his candidacy over and above those who do not share that same prejudice.

The literature has well documented that sexism functions as an ideology driven by perceptions of ingroup–outgroup differences, whereby the ingroup is perceived as rightfully dominant over the outgroup (Dahl et al., 2015). Ambivalent sexism theory argues that HS represents negative perceptions of women who challenge the status quo and who challenge those who hold male power. Clinton certainly did so in 2016; she ran for the most high-profile, powerful, and influential job in America—a job that has traditionally been held by men—and this job is part of a domain in American society that is still characterized as dealing with issues more suitable for men who possess character traits typically associated with men. Furthermore, the negative backlash against her—on all image dimensions that predict voice choice—was clear. High HS scores, on the other hand, predicted positive perceptions of Trump on all image dimensions. In 2016 those seeking to affirm masculine power and resist being subordinated to a woman viewed Trump positively on all levels—from character to charm, intelligence to leadership, and from their ability to relate to him and his ability to act in the best interest of America.

In terms of the role of HS in 2016, the research on masculinity threat combined with HS provides important opportunities for understanding the characterizations of and comments about Clinton that lacked civility and respect above and beyond what has been witnessed in past election cycles. As has been well documented in the press throughout the election cycle, Trump's rallies were known for men and women advocating against Clinton with graphic messaging. It is not difficult to identify such messaging as laden with dominance language and imagery that subordinated and sexualized Clinton in attempts at restoration from masculine threats: "Trump 2016: Finally someone with balls"; an image of a boy urinating on the word "Hillary"; an image of Trump having knocked Clinton, clad in a clingy tank top, to the floor of a boxing ring; "Hillary couldn't satisfy her husband, can't satisfy us" (for an extended discussion, see Beinart, 2016, para. 4). Anger is known (Dahl et al., 2015) to provide a conduit through which perceived threats to masculinity result in a sexualization of the female target—which is viewed as either having or seeking more power and influence—in order to subordinate her and "put her back in her place." Research illustrates that anger is one of several aggressive emotions—along with contempt and disgust—that yields backlash against female candidates who are perceived as power seeking (Okimoto & Brescoll, 2010). Thus, the energizing of HS is perhaps the more relevant explanation as to why many Trump voters engaged in such lewd communication about Clinton. She represented a threat to the masculine paradigm, and they were unwilling to accept a woman holding a position of power over them.

It is also important to note that HS predicted candidate image ratings at or above that of party affiliation. For those who could not understand how blue-collar union voters did not remain stalwart in their support of a Democrat, this could provide one explanation. In other words, in those states that have traditionally voted Democratic when their presidential candidate was a male, this study may offer insight about what shifted those voters in 2016. The data in this study are insufficient to demonstrate that the "blue wall" (e.g., Michigan, Wisconsin, and Pennsylvania) shifted because of HS, but future research may look more closely at the interaction between party, SDO, and sexism as it relates to various subtypes of female candidates. If negative attitudes toward female candidates are better predicted by HS than even partisanship—particularly when evaluating candidates who violate more traditional female subtypes— do Democratic female candidates stand to lose more of the male voters within their party's base?

It was only through the HS lens—and not the BS lens—that the negative evaluations for Clinton on all candidate image factors was predicted. For those scoring high on BS, this dominance ideology served only as a predictor for

Trump's image construct, albeit for five of the six image factors. BS positively predicted ratings for Trump on character, intellect, leadership, charm, and homophily. BS did not serve as a predictor for the image factor of benevolence for Trump, nor did it predict any image ratings for Clinton. Although those high in HS have a negative attitude toward women, those high in BS are patronizing and idealize the status quo wherein ingroup members are in power. BS still functions to subordinate women, but it does not necessarily correlate with the negative views represented within HS. It is therefore not surprising that BS did not predict a higher degree of negativity toward Clinton among high BS respondents compared to low BS respondents, and ultimately not surprising that high BS voters did not rate Clinton as negatively as did high HS voters. Yet BS did predict image ratings for Trump on all image factors except benevolence. Perhaps those with high BS scores could identify more with Trump and found him to be more "appropriate" for holding office—more charismatic and likeable, more intelligent, and more likely to understand them— although they did not necessarily view him as more likely to have the country's best interests at heart. This offers interesting potential for how we study benevolence as it relates to both candidate image and assignment of goodwill differently—or the same—to female and male candidates.

The current investigation has several limitations. Although we asked respondents about real candidates, data collection took place in the spring following the election. So though the study design may have captured some ecologically valid aspects of the election dynamic, additional post-election feelings could have also developed since the election—this may be further compounded by the number of negative election-related stories published about the new administration in the time after the election but before the conclusion of data collection. It should also be noted that the cross-sectional survey design prevents us from making any causal inferences related to differences in sexism or political candidates, neither of which could feasibly have been re-created via random assignment.

However, the data reported here both expand and generate further opportunities for research development on the role that SDO and sexism play within the context of politics. Though Clinton and Trump are highly recognized public figures, it is difficult to fully generalize any findings of either to candidates more broadly. Moving forward, this study presents a compelling argument for the need to better understand how voters view women at high levels of leadership. Perhaps HS was more energized because of the public's knowledge of Clinton, whereas it could function at a less intense level for a woman whose life and politics have been under a dimmer spotlight. Yet the research on both SDO and sexism suggests that the influence of these two constructs on someone's worldview is pervasive; as such, we argue that the interaction of SDO and sexism on voter likelihood and perceptions of candidate image will remain influential at some level. Thus, we are hopeful that more women will seek to hold public office in 2018 and beyond, and in turn offer more opportunities to better understand the relationship between these variables and candidate image. For 2016, however, the post-mortem seems clear: sexism did play a role in voter preferences for the candidates. Although women have come a long way in this country in terms of equity and opportunity, based on reactions to the candidates in the 2016 election, sadly, our country still has a long way to go.

References

Bauer, N. (2016, February 5). Here's what the research tells us about whether sexism is hurting Hillary Clinton's prospects. *The Washington Post.* Retrieved from https://www.washingtonpost.com/news/monkey-cage/wp/2016/02 /05/heres-what-the-research-tells-us-about-whether-sexism-is-hurting -hillary-clintons-prospects/?utm_term=.08e83a0f0d52

Beinart, P. (2016, October). Fear of a female president: Hillary Clinton's candidacy has provoked a wave of misogyny—one that may roil American life for years to come. *The Atlantic.* Retrieved from https://www.theatlantic .com/magazine/archive/2016/10/fear-of-a-female-president/497564/

Bevan, T. (2017, June 1). Sexism did not cost Hillary the election. *Real Clear Politics.* Retrieved from http://www.realclearpolitics.com/articles/2017/06/01 /sexism_did_not_cost_ hillary_the_election_134063.html

Bialik, C. (2017, January 21). How unconscious sexism could help explain Trump's win. *FiveThirtyEight.* Retrieved from https://fivethirtyeight.com/features /how-unconscious-sexism-could-help-explain-trumps-win/

Christopher, A. N., & Mull, M. S. (2006). Conservative ideology and ambivalent sexism. *Psychology of Women Quarterly, 30*(2), 223–230. doi:10.1111/j .1471-6402.2006.00284.x

Cohen, N. (2016, November 16). Sexism did not cost Hillary Clinton the election: And it probably won't prevent another woman from eventually winning the presidency, either. *The Washington Post.* Retrieved from https://www .washingtonpost.com/posteverything/wp/ 2016/11/16/sexism-did-not -cost-hillary-clinton-the-election/?utm_term=.f3e4da8f289b

Cole, A. (2016, October 19). Why sexism is so central to this presidential race. *Fortune.* Retrieved from http://fortune.com/2016/10/19/trump-clinton -sexism-presidential-debate/

Crowson, H. M., & Brandes, J. A. (2017). Differentiating between Donald Trump and Hillary Clinton voters using facets of right-wing authoritarianism and social-dominance orientation. *Psychological Reports, 120*(3), 364–373. doi:10.1177/0033294117697089

Dahl, J., Vescio, T., & Weaver, K. (2015). How threats to masculinity sequentially cause public discomfort, anger, and ideological dominance over women. *Social Psychology (Göttingen, Germany), 46*(4), 242–254. doi:10.1027/1864 -9335/a000248

Dastigar, A. E. (2016, November 10). Voices: What Trump's victory tells us about women. Retrieved from https://www.usatoday.com/story/opinion /voices/2016/11/10/trump-election-white-women-sexism-racism/9361 1984/

Duckitt, J., & Bizumic, B. (2013). Multidimensionality of right-wing authoritarian attitudes: Authoritarianism-conservatism-traditionalism. *Political Psychology, 34*(6), 841–862. doi:10.1111/pops.12022

Fahrenthold, D. A. (2016, October 8). Trump recorded having extremely lewd conversations about women in 2005. *The Washington Post*. Retrieved from https://www.washingtonpost.com/politics/trump-recorded-having-extre mely-lewd-conversation-about-women-in-2005/2016/10/07/3b9ce776 -8cb4-11e6-bf8a-3d26847eeed4_story.html?utm_term=.e097454b8bf1

Feather, N. T., & McKee, I. R. (2012). Values, right-wing authoritarianism, social dominance orientation, and ambivalent attitudes toward women values and ambivalent sexism. *Journal of Applied Social Psychology, 42*(10), 2479–2504. doi:10.1111/j.1559-1816.2012.00950.x

Fraser, G., Osborne, D., & Sibley, C. G. (2015). "We want you in the workplace, but only in a skirt!" Social dominance orientation, gender-based affirmative action and the moderating role of benevolent sexism. *Sex Roles, 73*(5–6), 231–244. doi:10.1007/s11199-015-0515-8

Glick, P., & Fiske, S. T. (1996). The ambivalent sexism inventory: Differentiating hostile and benevolent sexism. *Journal of Personality and Social Psychology, 70*(3), 491–512.

Glick, P., Lameiras, M., Fiske, S. T., Eckes, T., Masser, B., Volpato, C., . . . Wells, R. (2004). Bad but bold: Ambivalent attitudes toward men predict gender inequality in 16 nations. *Journal of Personality and Social Psychology: Interpersonal Relations and Group Processes, 86*(5), 713–728. doi: http://dx.doi .org/10.1037/0022-3514.86.5.713

Glick, P., Wilkerson, M., & Cuffe, M. (2015). Masculine identity, ambivalent sexism, and attitudes toward gender subtypes: Favoring masculine men and feminine women. *Social Psychology, 46*(4), 210–217. doi:http://dx.doi.org /10.1027/1864-9335/a000228

Grina, J., Bergh, R., Akrami, N., & Sidanius, J. (2016). Political orientation and dominance: Are people on the political right more dominant? *Personality and Individual Differences, 94*, 113–117. doi: https://doi.org/10.1016/j.paid .2016.01.015

Heaven, P. C. L., Ciarrochi, J., & Leeson, P. (2011). Cognitive ability, right-wing authoritarianism, and social dominance orientation: A five-year longitudinal study amongst adolescents. *Intelligence, 39*(1), 15–21. doi: https://doi .org/10.1016/j.intell.2010.12.001

Hilln, T. (2016, November 6). Here's every wildly sexist moment from the 2016 presidential election. *Business Insider*. Retrieved from http://www.business insider.com/heres-every-wildly-sexist-moment-from-the-2016-presidential -election-2016-11

Ho, A. K., Sidanius, J., Kteily, N., Sheehy-Skeffington, J., Pratto, F., Henkel, K. E., . . . Stewart, A. L. (2015). The nature of social dominance orientation: Theorizing and measuring preferences for intergroup inequality using the new SDO$_7$ scale. *Journal of Personality and Social Psychology: Interpersonal Relations and Group Processes, 109*(6), 1003–1028. doi:http://dx.doi.org/10.1037/pspi 0000033

Ho, A. K., Sidanius, J., Pratto, F., Levin, S., Thomsen, L., Nour, K., & Sheehy-Skeffington, J. (2012). Social dominance orientation revisiting the structure and function of a variable predicting social and political attitudes. *Personality & Social Psychology Bulletin, 38*(5), 583–606. doi:10.1177/014616 7211432765

Hodson, G., & MacInnis, C. C. (2016). Can left-right differences in abortion support be explained by sexism? *Personality and Individual Differences, 104*, 118–121. doi:10.1016/j.paid.2016.07.044

Keith, T. (2016, October 23). Sexism is out in the open in the 2016 campaign. That may have been inevitable. *National Public Radio: Morning Edition.* Retrieved from http://www.npr.org/2016/10/23/498878356/sexism-is-out -in-the-open-in-the-2016-campaign-that-may-have-been-inevitable

Lozano-Reich, N. M. (2016, February 8). The blog: Sexism, alive and well in 2016 presidential campaign. *Huffington Post.* Retrieved from http://www .huffingtonpost.com/nina-m-lozanoreich-phd/sexism-alive-and-well-in -2016-presidential-campaign_b_9172186.html

Miller, A. H., Wattenburg, M., & Malanchuk, O. (1986). Schematic assessments of presidential candidates. *The American Political Science Review, 80*, 521–540. doi:10.1017/S0003055400174271

Okimoto, T. G., & Brescoll, V. L. (2010). The price of power: Power seeking and backlash against female politicians. *Personality & Social Psychology Bulletin, 36*(7), 923–936. doi:10.1177/0146167210371949

Paul, D., & Smith, J. L. (2008). Subtle sexism? Examining vote preferences when women run against men for the presidency. *Journal of Women, Politics & Policy, 29*(4), 451–476. doi:10.1080/15544770802092576

Popkin, S. L. (1991). *The reasoning voter: Communication and persuasion in presidential campaigns.* Chicago: The University of Chicago Press.

Pratto, F., Sidanius, J., Stallworth, L. M., & Malle, B. F. (1994). Social dominance orientation: A personality variable predicting social and political attitudes. *Journal of Personality and Social Psychology: Personality Processes and Individual Differences, 67*(4), 741–763. doi:http://dx.doi.org/10.1037/0022 -3514.67.4.741

Schaffner, B. F., MacWilliams, M., & Nteta, T. (2017). *Explaining white polarization in the 2016 vote for president: The sobering role of racism and sexism.* Paper presented at the Conference on The U.S. Elections of 2016: Domestic and International Aspects, IDC Herzliya Campus, Israel.

Sibley, C., Wilson, M. S., & Duckitt, J. (2007). Antecedents of men's hostile and benevolent sexism: The dual roles of social dominance orientation and right-wing authoritarianism. *Personality & Social Psychology Bulletin, 33*(2), 160–172.

Warner, B. R., & Banwart, M. C. (2016). A multifactor approach to candidate image. *Communication Studies, 67*(3), 259–279. doi:10.1080/10510974.2016.1156005

Wayne, C., Valentino, N., & Oceno, M. (2016, October 23). How sexism drives support for Donald Trump. *The Washington Post.* Retrieved from https://www.washingtonpost.com/news/monkey-cage/wp/2016/10/23/how-sexism-drives-support-for-donald-trump/?utm_term=.4890f253855d

Winfrey, K. L. (2012). *The women's vote: Explaining women voters through gender group identification and sex-role ideology* (Unpublished doctoral dissertation). University of Kansas, Lawrence, KS.

About the Editors and Contributors

Editors

Benjamin R. Warner (PhD, University of Kansas) is an associate professor of communication at the University of Missouri. He has published articles and book chapters examining the polarizing effects of partisan media, new media echo-chambers, and presidential debates.

Dianne G. Bystrom (PhD, University of Oklahoma) has served as the director of the Carrie Chapman Catt Center for Women and Politics at Iowa State University since 1996. She has contributed to 21 books—including *alieN-ATION: The Divide and Conquer Election of 2012*; *Gender and Elections*; and *Gender and Campaign Communication*—as a co-author, co-editor, or chapter author. She also has published journal articles on women and politics, youth voters, and the Iowa caucus.

Mitchell S. McKinney (PhD, University of Kansas) is professor of communication at the University of Missouri and currently serves as faculty fellow for academic personnel in the Office of the Provost. Dr. McKinney is one of our nation's leading scholars of presidential debates, having served as an advisor to the U.S. Commission on Presidential Debates where his work was instrumental in developing the presidential town hall debate. He is the author or co-author of nine books and numerous journal articles and book chapters.

Mary C. Banwart (PhD, University of Oklahoma) is an associate professor in the communication studies department at the University of Kansas and director of the Institute for Leadership Studies. She has authored or co-authored book chapters and journal articles on the influence of gender in candidate presentation styles in political campaigns, the evaluation of female and male candidates, the gender gap, and how gender influences one's likelihood to feel competent to talk about politics.

Contributors

Kalyca Becktel (BA, San Diego State University) is a graduate student at San Diego State University. Her primary research focus is on organization–public relationships and brand relationships in public relations.

Joshua P. Bolton (MS, University of Wisconsin-Whitewater) is an assistant professor at Loras College and a PhD candidate in the Department of Communication at the University of Missouri. His research focuses mainly on the messaging and branding of political campaigns using rhetorical methods.

Josh C. Bramlett (MS, Arkansas State University) is a doctoral student in the Department of Communication at the University of Missouri. His research focuses on political campaign communication, political comedy, and the political uses of social media.

Sumana Chattopadhyay (PhD, University of Missouri) is an associate professor in the Department of Digital Media and Performing Arts at Marquette University. Her primary research interests focus on political advertising, public opinion, media use and political participation, and cross-cultural media coverage of crises.

Weiyue Chen (MA with honors, Tsinghua University) is a doctoral student in the Department of Journalism at Michigan State University. Her research interests include audiences' perception of news, financial models of newspapers, and management issues within media organizations.

Heesook Choi (MA, University of Texas at Austin) is a doctoral candidate in the School of Journalism at the University of Missouri. Her research interests include political and civic effects of news media, political entertainment programming, and new communication technologies.

Kevin Coe (PhD, University of Illinois) is an associate professor in the Department of Communication at the University of Utah. His research and teaching focus on the interaction of American political discourse, news media, and public opinion, with a particular interest in the U.S. presidency and religious communication.

Calvin R. Coker (MA, Missouri State University) is a doctoral candidate in the Department of Communication at the University of Missouri. His research focuses on the articulation of marginalized populations in politics.

Jessica R. Collier (MA, University of North Carolina at Chapel Hill) is a PhD student in the Department of Communication Studies at the University of Texas at Austin. Her research focuses on the influence of media effects, digital technologies, and partisan bias on political attitudes and behavior.

Corey B. Davis (PhD, University of Missouri) is an associate professor and the graduate program coordinator in the Department of Communication at University of Wisconsin-Whitewater. His research and teaching interests are in public relations, persuasion, and political communication, focusing on political campaign communication, environmental communication, and corporate and political apologia.

Daniela V. Dimitrova (PhD, University of Florida) is a professor and director of graduate education in the Greenlee School of Journalism and Communication at Iowa State University. Her research focuses on political communication, media framing, and the impact of social media on political and civic engagement.

Molly Greenwood (PhD, University of Missouri) is an instructor in the Department of Communication at the University of Missouri. Her research interests include the effects of political humor within the social media environment and the role of gender in politics.

Delaney Harness (MA, Purdue University) is a doctoral student in the Department of Communication Studies at the University of Texas at Austin. She is interested in political communication in international contexts, including how nongovernmental organizations communicatively negotiate identity within the international system.

Grace Hase (BA, University of Missouri) is a reporter with PolitiFact Missouri. Her research interests include the effects of campaign communication and news media coverage on voter attitudes and behaviors.

Samantha Hernandez (MA, University of Texas at San Antonio) is a PhD candidate in the School of Politics and Global Studies at Arizona State University. Her research interests include political campaigns and news media, identity politics, and race and media.

Sopheak Hoeun (MA, University of Missouri) is a social media manager for BBC Media Action. Her research interests focus on the role of digital media in emerging democracies.

R. Lance Holbert (PhD, University of Wisconsin-Madison) is a professor within and chair of the Department of Communication and Social Influence,

Klein College of Media and Communication, Temple University. His research interests include media, politics, and persuasion.

Will Howell (MA, University of Maryland, College Park) is a rhetoric doctoral candidate in the Department of Communication at the University of Maryland. He researches how entertainment sources affect U.S. citizens' political participation, political identity, and perceptions of political issues and actors.

Freddie J. Jennings (MA, University of Arkansas) is a PhD candidate in the Department of Communication at the University of Missouri. His research interests include information processing and political dialogue in a new media environment.

Vamsi Kanuri (PhD, University of Missouri) is an assistant professor in the Department of Marketing at the University of Miami. His research interests are in the area of empirical marketing strategy, with a specific emphasis on building marketing-mix models that facilitate managerial decision making pertaining to strategic marketing issues.

Brian Kaylor (PhD, University of Missouri) is editor and president of Word&Way and associate director of Churchnet. His research interests center on the intersection of religious and political communication.

Michael W. Kearney (PhD, University of Kansas) is an assistant professor in the School of Journalism and holds a joint appointment with the Informatics Institute at the University of Missouri. His research interests include selective exposure, digital media, data journalism, and data science.

Kate Kenski (PhD, University of Pennsylvania) is an associate professor in the Department of Communication at the University of Arizona. She is co-author of the award-winning book *The Obama Victory: How Media, Money, and Message Shaped the 2008 Election* (2010). Her current research focuses on campaign use of new media, incivility in online forums, and multimedia teaching strategies to mitigate cognitive biases.

Ashley Muddiman (PhD, University of Texas at Austin) is an assistant professor in the Department of Communication Studies at the University of Kansas. Her research interests include the content, perceptions, and effects of political incivility in online settings.

Kimberly Nelson (BA, Buena Vista University) is a graduate student in the Greenlee School of Journalism and Communication at Iowa State University. Her research interests include risk communication and audio communication.

Ryan Neville-Shepard (PhD, University of Kansas) is an assistant professor in the Department of Communication at the University of Arkansas. His research interests generally focus on modern American political rhetoric, rhetorical criticism, and argumentation, with a specific interest in presidential rhetoric.

Meredith Neville-Shepard (PhD, University of Kansas) is a clinical assistant professor in the Department of Communication at the University of Arkansas. Her research centers on rhetorical criticism and public argumentation with a particular emphasis on politics and methods of protest.

Esul Park (MA, Texas Tech University) is a doctoral student in the Klein College of Media and Communication at Temple University. Her research interests include political communication, political and civic engagement, and online political discussion forum.

Trevor Parry-Giles (PhD, Indiana University) is a professor in the Department of Communication at the University of Maryland, College Park, and the director of Academic and Professional Affairs at the National Communication Association. His research and teaching focus on the historical and contemporary relationships between rhetoric, politics, law, and popular culture.

Joel Lansing Reed (MA, Missouri State University) is a doctoral student in the Department of Communication at the University of Missouri. His research focuses on communication ethics and the rhetoric of political compromise.

Nicholas W. Robinson (MA, Texas Tech University) is a doctoral student at the Klein College of Media and Communication at Temple University. His research focuses on the implications of new media platforms and technologies for civic participation and political mobilization.

Robert C. Rowland (PhD, University of Kansas) is a professor of Communication Studies and director of Graduate Studies at the University of Kansas. His research and teaching focus on presidential rhetoric, political communication, public argument, and rhetorical criticism.

Joshua M. Scacco (PhD, University of Texas at Austin) is an assistant professor in the Brian Lamb School of Communication and a courtesy faculty in the Department of Political Science at Purdue University. He also serves as a faculty research associate with the Engaging News Project. His research is focused on how emerging communication technologies influence established agents in American political life, including news organizations and the presidency.

James M. Schnoebelen (PhD, University of Kansas) is an associate professor of communication studies at Washburn University in Topeka, Kansas. His research focuses on gender and political communication, primarily focusing on the U.S. presidency.

Kristina Horn Sheeler (PhD, Indiana University) is a professor in the Department of Communication Studies and associate dean for Academic Programs at Indiana University-Purdue University Indianapolis. Her research interests include gender and political communication, focusing on the ways that candidate identity is constructed and contested in popular media.

Natalie Jomini Stroud (PhD, University of Pennsylvania) is an associate professor in the Department of Communication Studies and director of the Engaging News Project at the University of Texas at Austin. Her research and teaching focus on media effects and politics and public opinion, with a focus on partisanship and exposure decisions.

Kaye D. Sweetser (PhD, University of Florida) is an associate professor of public relations at San Diego State University. She studies political campaigns as a public relations activity through the primary lens of the organization–public relationship theory.

Samuel M. Tham (MA, University of Missouri) is a doctoral student at Michigan State University with research interests in advertising avoidance in digital media, decision making, and media psychology.

Esther Thorson (PhD, University of Minnesota) is a professor in the School of Journalism, College of Communication Arts and Sciences, Michigan State University. She publishes extensively in advertising effects, news media impact, and newspaper financial management.

Kelly L. Winfrey (PhD, University of Kansas) is an assistant professor of journalism and communication at Iowa State University and coordinator of research and outreach at the Carrie Chapman Catt Center for Women and Politics. Her research focuses on gender and political campaign communication, women voters, and news media in elections.

Index